Alexis de Tocqueville and Gustave de Beaumont in America

EDITED BY OLIVIER ZUNZ

TRANSLATED BY ARTHUR GOLDHAMMER

UNIVERSITY OF VIRGINIA PRESS
CHARLOTTESVILLE AND LONDON

Alexis de Tocqueville

and

Gustave de Beaumont

in

America

THEIR FRIENDSHIP AND THEIR TRAVELS

University of Virginia Press
Printed in the United States of America on acid-free paper
First published 2010

9 8 7 6 5 4 3 2 1

LIBRARY OF CONGRESS CATALOGING-IN-PUBLICATION DATA
Tocqueville, Alexis de, 1805–1859.
  [Selections. English. 2010]
  Alexis de Tocqueville and Gustave de Beaumont in America : their friendship and their travels / edited by Olivier Zunz ; translated by Arthur Goldhammer.
       p.   cm.
  Summary: A selection of Tocqueville's writings on America together with letters and sketches from his traveling companion, Gustave de Beaumont.
  Includes bibliographical references and index.
  ISBN 978-0-8139-3062-6 (cloth : alk. paper)
  1. United States—Description and travel—Sources. 2. United States—Social life and customs—1783–1865—Sources. 3. United States—Politics and government—1783–1865—Sources. 4. National characteristics, American—History—19th century—Sources. 5. Tocqueville, Alexis de, 1805–1859—Travel—United States. 6. Beaumont, Gustave de, 1802–1866—Travel—United States. 7. Tocqueville, Alexis de, 1805–1859—Friends and associates. 8. Beaumont, Gustave de, 1802–1866—Friends and associates. 9. Tocqueville, Alexis de, 1805–1859—Archives. 10. Beaumont, Gustave de, 1802–1866—Correspondence. I. Zunz, Olivier. II. Goldhammer, Arthur. III. Beaumont, Gustave de, 1802–1866. IV. Title.
  E165.T53213 2010
  917.30409'034—dc22
                                                                                2010021800

Title page illustrations: Alexis de Tocqueville at 39 (1844) by Théodore Chassériau (*upper left;* The Image Works, Inc.) *and* Gustave de Beaumont at 35 (1837) (*lower right;* Beinecke Library).

CONTENTS

Tocqueville's Travel Notebooks   209

Non-alphabetic Notebooks

Travel Notebooks

PART SEVEN

Tocqueville's and Beaumont's Views of America after 1840   591

Tocqueville's and Beaumont's Letters on America, 1840–58

ILLUSTRATIONS

COLOR ILLUSTRATIONS (FOLLOWING PAGE 208)

ACKNOWLEDGMENTS

Prior to embarking on this volume with Arthur Goldhammer, I had the privilege of being the editor of his translation of Tocqueville's *Democracy in America,* which the Library of America published in 2004. Jointly scrutinizing (and admiring) Tocqueville's classic text led us to this book. We wanted to provide readers with a comprehensive English translation of Tocqueville's little-known American travel notes of 1831–32 and his letters home.

The project grew as we shared the idea with other Tocqueville scholars who met in 2005 to mark the bicentennial of Tocqueville's birth. Frank M. Turner, who hosted a symposium at Yale University's Beinecke Rare Book and Manuscript Library, suggested we include Gustave de Beaumont's American texts, many of which the Beinecke owns. This was an inspired piece of advice. In adding letters from Tocqueville's travel companion and excerpts from Beaumont's American novel, we could provide a much fuller account of the voyage and pinpoint where and why the two friends differed in their assessments of the United States.

Penelope Kaiserlian, director of the University of Virginia Press, immediately expressed interest in publishing our work. The Beinecke Rare Book and Manuscript Library and the Florence J. Gould Foundation generously supported translation and editorial costs as well as the added expense of reproducing Beaumont's magnificent sketchbooks.

Three talented University of Virginia graduate students assisted me in the preparation of the volume. Céline Miani worked with me on text selection, Whitney Martinko on note preparation, and Christopher Loomis on final assembly of the many texts and the introduction.

Among Tocqueville scholars, we owe special thanks to Françoise Mélonio for allowing us to use some still-unpublished letters scheduled to appear in tome XVII of *Œuvres complètes,* which she is editing (see the Note on Sources). Thanks also to Charlie Feigenoff, Laurence Guellec, Maurice Kriegel, James T. Schleifer, and Cheryl Welch for comments on the introduction and specific parts of the manuscript. Allen M. Hale of Buteo Books identified Beaumont's birds.

We express our appreciation to Jean-Guillaume and Stéphanie de Tocqueville d'Hérouville, Augustin de Romanet, Gilles Désiré di Gosset and Alain Talon (Archives de la Manche), and Françoise Cibiel for their assistance in gathering some of the material published here.

In 1856, Tocqueville begged his friend Francis Lieber to read his newly released *L'ancien régime et la révolution* in French: "You know our language well enough that I am very keen to show you my ideas in their national costume. The best translation is never more than a wretched copy." May we prove him wrong!

OLIVIER ZUNZ

Charlottesville, Virginia, Fall 2010

INTRODUCTION

A celebrated voyage from France to America in 1831 helped frame the way we have since thought of democracy in the modern world.

Alexis de Tocqueville believed that only by traveling to America could he understand the future of democracy and equality; Tocqueville was similarly animated by his search for self. As he told Henry Reeve, the young British lawyer who translated *Democracy in America* into English, he was born between the age of aristocracy, "already dead when my life began," and the age of democracy, which "did not yet exist."[1] Tocqueville's family traced its military lineage back to the Battle of Hastings on his father's side and included the highest echelons of the royal administration on his mother's. Though decimated during the French Revolution, the family remained loyal to the Bourbon kings even after they were finally deposed in 1830. Tocqueville himself, however, felt no "natural love" for aristocracy. He had no great affection for democracy either, but he was sure democracy was here to stay. In a draft of a letter Tocqueville wrote to his cousin Camille d'Orglandes, he said he went to America to "clarify" his "thinking on the subject." In the copy he sent, he stressed that he had already given the matter great thought: "I went to America only to remove my remaining doubts."[2]

Tocqueville was twenty-five years old. His travel companion was another young aristocrat, Gustave de Beaumont, three years his senior. Tocqueville had met Beaumont at the Versailles tribunal, where they were both magistrates. Beaumont's family had not endured the same horrifying experiences as Tocqueville's family during the Revolution and its aftermath, and Beaumont's temper was not driven by the same angst that haunted Tocqueville. But the two young men struck up a deep friendship while rooming together and following François Guizot's lectures on the history of civilization with some passion.[3]

In the aftermath of the July Revolution in 1830 and Louis-Philippe's ascen-

---

1. March 22, 1837 (printed in part 6 of this volume).

2. November 29, 1834 (part 6); first draft in a letter initially thought to have been sent to Kergorlay (Tocqueville, *Œuvres complètes* [Paris: Gallimard, 1951–], tome XIII, vol. 1, 374; hereafter cited as O.C.).

3. See Tocqueville's long letter to Beaumont on French and English history, October 5, 1828, O.C., VII, 1, 47–71.

sion to the throne as a constitutional monarch, Tocqueville and Beaumont found their career prospects limited under a regime they could not fully support, despite their considerable ability, resourcefulness, and social connections. Looking to make productive use of their time, they secured an unpaid leave of absence from the justice ministry along with an assignment from the minister of the interior to investigate the American penitentiary system with an eye toward reforming the French one. As Tocqueville wrote his friend Charles Stöffels in November 1830, this was a "pretext, but a very honorable pretext," to extricate themselves from a delicate political situation and at the same time undertake to explore America. The two friends busied themselves collecting letters of recommendation, securing financing from their families (two thousand francs for Beaumont and five thousand for Tocqueville), and packing for the trip. Their baggage included two fowling pieces as well as Beaumont's sketchbooks, watercolors, and flute.[4]

The Evidence Collected during the Journey

In this book, we present most of the surviving letters home, notebooks, and other texts the two friends wrote during the trip, as well as their reflections and correspondence on America following their return to France. The two young men would rely on these texts systematically when writing both their penitentiary report and their individual works on America, Tocqueville's *Democracy in America* and Beaumont's *Marie; or, Slavery in the United States*.[5] Both Tocqueville and Beaumont asked their correspondents to keep their letters, and Tocqueville took copious notes on the spot, which he considered priceless. As he then told his mother, "What is most interesting in what I'm bringing back is two small notebooks in which I have written down word for word the conversations that I have had with the country's most remarkable men. These scraps are invaluable to me, but only to me, given that I was able to sense the value of the questions and answers."[6] Written as tentative drafts, these documents capture Tocqueville in the moment of discovery, with all his enthusiasm and relish for the unexpected. They reveal the encounters between Tocqueville, Beaumont, and their informants, whose identity and precise contribution Tocqueville would later so conscientiously obscure, and their mutual effort to simultaneously discover and interpret America. As the reader will find out, by setting Tocqueville's and Beaumont's texts side by side, we can truly appreciate not only the deep impression that America made on them but also their unique perceptions of the experience.

4. George Wilson Pierson, *Tocqueville in America* (Baltimore: Johns Hopkins University Press, 1996), 39; originally published as *Tocqueville and Beaumont in America* (New York: Oxford University Press, 1938).

5. See the note on sources at the end of this volume for references to the standard editions of Tocqueville's and Beaumont's works.

6. October 24, 1831 (part 1).

They discussed every observation and every idea and yet would make radically different contributions.

It is important to understand that the texts in this volume represent only one component of the two friends' intellectual development. Tocqueville and Beaumont spent only nine months in America, and neither would ever return. Tocqueville elaborated *Democracy* over nine years, beginning with the trip itself in 1831–32 and continuing on through the publication of volume 1 of *Democracy* in 1835 and volume 2 in 1840. He went over his letters and travel notes after he returned to France and complemented them by reading broadly in American sources, including the legal and constitutional commentaries of James Kent and Justice Joseph Story, Thomas Jefferson's *Notes on the State of Virginia,* and *The Federalist,* which he had begun consulting during the trip itself. He was assisted by two Americans living in Paris, Francis Lippitt and Theodore Sedgwick III. In addition to writings on America, Tocqueville read texts in political philosophy.[7]

Tocqueville traveled in 1833 to England, where he sharpened his views on both aristocracy and industrial society. Following the publication of volume 1 of *Democracy,* Tocqueville went to England again, this time with Beaumont. The men continued on to Ireland, where they had a firsthand look at colonization and poverty. All these trips sustained and deepened the comparative reasoning in Tocqueville's writings, and particularly his efforts to triangulate his observations on the United States with England and France.

As for Beaumont, he was the prime author of the prison report, *On the Penitentiary System in the United States and Its Application in France,* which was published at the beginning of 1833.[8] In 1835, he published to significant acclaim the now-forgotten *Marie,* about the love affair of a Frenchman and an American woman with a remote black ancestry. He then left the American field to Tocqueville and began collecting evidence for a work on Ireland (taking another trip to England and Ireland in 1837). He published *Ireland* in 1839, a year before volume 2 of *Democracy* appeared.

Meanwhile, neither Tocqueville nor Beaumont was content to live the life of the mind alone. Both men were elected to the Chamber of Deputies in 1839, with Tocqueville representing Valognes (in the *département* of La Manche) and Beaumont representing Saint-Calais (in the *département* of La Sarthe). They would work on a number of important issues, including the abolition of slavery, the

7. There is considerable speculation over the extent of Tocqueville's reading. R. Pierre Marcel asserted early in the twentieth century that Tocqueville must have read Benjamin Constant; see his *Essai politique sur Alexis de Tocqueville* (Paris, 1910), 180–81. Lucien Jaume claimed recently in *Tocqueville: Les sources aristocratiques de la liberté* (Paris: Fayard, 2008), 180, that Tocqueville was necessarily familiar with Helvétius. Solid evidence for either claim is sorely lacking.

8. Tocqueville wrote the notes and reviewed and commented on Beaumont's draft; Beaumont also sent Tocqueville to look at prisons in Toulon and Switzerland in 1832. André Jardin, *Tocqueville: A Biography,* trans. Lydia Davis with Robert Hemenway (Baltimore: Johns Hopkins University Press, 1998), 181–84.

colonization of Algeria, and the drafting of a new constitution following the 1848 revolution. All of this activity slowed down their literary production. Tocqueville would later briefly rise to become minister of foreign affairs following the establishment of the Second Republic in 1848, but he would retire from political life following Louis-Napoleon's military coup in 1851 and the return of the empire. Although Tocqueville never became a great statesman, he continued to value action above political theorizing even after his exit from politics, and both his and Beaumont's public service enriched their intellectual achievements.

Focusing on American equality, Tocqueville made a lasting contribution to Western political thought by framing modern history as a continuous struggle between political liberty and social equality. He presented the United States as successful in providing the right balance between the two ideals. Beaumont instead chose to center his analysis on inequality and in doing so joined an important but more predictable crusade for social justice. Tocqueville made the American experience an unsuspected guide for modern life. Beaumont concentrated on what shocked him most readily: the brutality of racial prejudice against free blacks, the evil of slavery, and the Indian genocide.

The letters, notes, and other writings included in this book thus offer a starting point for understanding Tocqueville's and Beaumont's intertwined engagement with America. To appreciate Tocqueville's full contribution on America, the reader should turn to the two volumes of *Democracy* as well as the working notes that Tocqueville used as he drafted and redrafted his manuscript.[9] This volume more fully encompasses Beaumont's work on America, providing most surviving letters and significant excerpts of both the penitentiary report and *Marie.*

Gustave de Beaumont himself started to publish excerpts of Tocqueville's papers after his friend's untimely death in 1859, and he completed six volumes between 1861 and his own death in 1866. The Beaumont edition contained some gems but also unjustified cuts, arbitrary selections, and transcription errors. Antoine Redier, a talented writer who wanted to recover Tocqueville for the royalist camp in interwar France, quoted from some unpublished material the family had loaned him in a 1925 biography, but he never returned the original manuscripts entrusted to him.[10]

It was the great Tocqueville scholar George Wilson Pierson who almost single-handedly made the substance of many of Tocqueville's and Beaumont's papers available in English long before they were printed in French. Pierson assumed this task from Paul Lambert White, a young historian at Yale University, who began transcribing the manuscripts immediately following World War I but then died unexpectedly. Then a doctoral student at Yale, Pierson moved in to complete the task. He made frequent visits to the châteaux at Tocqueville

---

9. The working notes are printed in Eduardo Nolla's edition of *Democracy in America,* trans. James T. Schleifer, 4 vols. (Indianapolis: Liberty Fund, 2010).

10. Antoine Redier, *Comme disait Monsieur de Tocqueville . . .* (Paris, 1925).

and Beaumont-la-Chartre in the 1920s and 1930s, was granted wide access to the two family archives, arranged for much material to be hand-copied by a local schoolmaster, and transferred to Yale other available copies. Pierson skillfully wove many of the documents we now present here individually into a seamless narrative of the journey in a book entitled *Tocqueville and Beaumont in America* (1938), which has not lost its sparkle.[11] Tocqueville and Beaumont had at last found a master historian to tell the story of their travels. At the time Pierson published his book, Tocqueville had little following in France and Beaumont had been all but forgotten. Pierson's book signaled a renewed interest in Tocqueville's work that has continued largely unabated until the present day. It also came out at a moment when the enormous growth of the federal government in the New Deal had provoked a renewed debate on the role of civil society in America.

In the 1950s, there was a second wave of Tocqueville enthusiasts in America and France, but for different reasons. American intellectuals made Tocqueville a part of the postwar consensus. They heralded Tocqueville's reliance on the concept of national character to promote American exceptionalism, while in France, Raymond Aron made Tocqueville's method a precursor of the modern social sciences.[12] The first volume of Tocqueville's complete works came out in France in 1951. The project entailed publishing his vast correspondence and political writings, under the sponsorship of a national commission. Twenty-eight books and sixty years later (with the three volumes of tome XVII still to come), the vast editorial project has now absorbed the energies of three generations of editors, who have sorted out the manuscripts, transcribed them, and solved many issues of attribution.[13] Arthur Goldhammer has translated the selected texts from this definitive edition.

Tocqueville's writings might never have been fully published had the Cherbourg fire department not been able to extinguish, after a long battle full of mishaps, a fire that engulfed the family château in 1954 and destroyed most of its interior. Miraculously, the manor's central stone staircase protected Tocqueville's study and the archival *minutier* in the main tower above the study just long enough for it to be saved. Also saved during that fateful night were the papers of

11. Pierson, *Tocqueville in America,* 779–81, 825–33.

12. See James T. Kloppenberg, "Life Everlasting: Tocqueville in America," *La Revue Tocqueville/The Tocqueville Review* 2 (1996): 19–36, reprinted in Kloppenberg, *The Virtues of Liberalism* (New York: Oxford University Press, 1998), 71–81; and Raymond Aron, "Tocqueville retrouvé," *La Revue Tocqueville/The Tocqueville Review* 1 (Fall 1979): 8–23, reprinted in a special Tocqueville bicentennial anthology of the same journal, *Tocqueville et l'esprit de la démocratie,* ed. Laurence Guellec (Paris: Sciences Po Les Presses, 2005), 25–46.

13. Our volume is the first to make most of the included texts available in English. Some were not accessible in French until quite recently; for example, Tocqueville's family correspondence was published only in 1998. We are very grateful to the Commission nationale pour l'édition des œuvres d'Alexis de Tocqueville for allowing us to translate some unpublished letters forthcoming in O.C., XVII.

Tocqueville's maternal great-grandfather, Malesherbes, the director of the book trade under Louis XV and friend of the *philosophes,* who defended Louis XVI during his trial only to pay for it with his own life and the lives of many of his family. There too was correspondence from Louis XIV to Vauban, his master of military fortifications, also a Tocqueville ancestor. No such disaster threatened Beaumont-la-Chartre, but there the rats had silently feasted on Beaumont's American notebooks, of which only a few pages survived. Pierson and André Jardin (who oversaw the French publication of Tocqueville's complete works for many years) published Beaumont's American letters in a French edition only in 1973, thirty-five years after Pierson had first dissected them for his book.

There is a significant advantage in isolating the texts of the trip from the rest of the corpus. What these texts show distinctly in isolation, which may be lost otherwise, are the ways in which the journey turned Tocqueville's strong intuition that democracy was the prominent feature of modern life into a viable theory of democratic practice, based on American ways of preserving individual liberty. He could not have intuited this conclusion without intense firsthand observations, and in retracing them, we also reconstruct which events and encounters led to the theory. We also see how Beaumont, from the same set of observations, went on to a different assessment.

On to America

On April 2, 1831, Tocqueville and Beaumont sailed from Le Havre on an American ship, landing at Newport, Rhode Island, five weeks later. The two commissioners spent much of the summer in New York, including an extended stay in New York City as well as trips throughout the state, where they visited Sing Sing and Auburn prisons. On July 19, they departed from Buffalo for a month-long journey throughout the Great Lakes, traveling to the very edge of the frontier at Green Bay, Wisconsin, before making their way back east to visit Niagara Falls, Montreal, and Quebec City. After departing from Canada on September 2, Tocqueville and Beaumont spent a month traveling through New England, touring prisons in Massachusetts and Connecticut and enjoying the more refined tastes of Boston society. They arrived in Philadelphia on October 12, conducting an extended investigation of Eastern State Penitentiary before traveling on to Baltimore, the nexus of American Catholicism. The pair headed west across Pennsylvania in late November, embarking on a trip that would take them down the Ohio River from Pittsburgh through Cincinnati and all the way to Memphis. The winter journey was the most arduous stage of their travels. Their steamboat from Pittsburgh ran aground, and after another boat was blocked in by ice, they traveled overland through Kentucky and Tennessee—at one point trudging twenty-five miles in the snow to reach Louisville. They then went down the Mississippi River to New Orleans, where they arrived on New Year's Day 1832. Having been recalled to France earlier than they had anticipated, the two Frenchmen made a hasty tour of the South on their way back to the eastern sea-

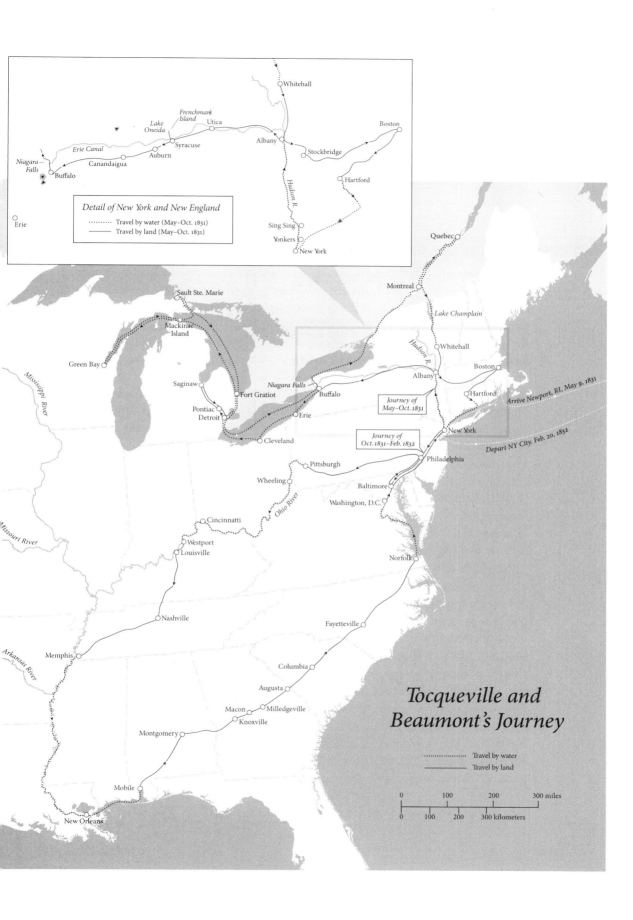

Detail of New York and New England

.... Travel by water (May–Oct. 1831)
——— Travel by land (May–Oct. 1831)

Whitehall

Frenchman's Island

Lake Oneida

Utica

Erie Canal

Syracuse

Auburn

Canandaigua

Niagara Falls

Buffalo

Erie

Albany

Stockbridge

Hudson R.

Hartford

Sing Sing

Yonkers

New York

Quebec

Montreal

Lake Champlain

Sault Ste. Marie

Mackinac Island

Green Bay

Saginaw

Fort Gratiot

Pontiac

Detroit

Niagara Falls

Buffalo

Erie

Cleveland

Hudson R.

Whitehall

Albany

Boston

Hartford

Arrive Newport, RI, May 9, 1831

Journey of May–Oct. 1831

Journey of Oct. 1831–Feb. 1832

New York

Philadelphia

Depart NY City, Feb. 20, 1832

Mississippi River

Pittsburgh

Wheeling

Ohio River

Cincinnatti

Missouri River

Westport

Louisville

Baltimore

Washington, D.C.

Norfolk

Nashville

Fayetteville

Memphis

Columbia

Arkansas River

Augusta

Macon

Milledgeville

Knoxville

Montgomery

Mobile

New Orleans

Tocqueville and Beaumont's Journey

.... Travel by water
——— Travel by land

0		100		200		300 miles
0	100	200	300 kilometers			

board. Following a two-week visit to Washington, D.C., Tocqueville and Beaumont departed New York City on a ship bound for Le Havre on February 20, 1832, carrying home trunks full of documents, sketchbooks, diaries, and records of conversations with more than two hundred known informants.

In reading Tocqueville's and Beaumont's letters home, as well as the extensive notes Tocqueville recorded in his diaries and travelogues, the reader will realize the extent to which the two friends kept interpreting and reinterpreting American society as they probed the nation's political, social, cultural, and religious aspects. They brought a wide range of analytical tools to this task. These included all of the fruits of Tocqueville's education with his tutor, the Jansenist priest Abbé Lesueur. Tocqueville borrowed heavily from Montesquieu's concept of national character. He loved the moralists and quoted frequently from Montaigne and La Fontaine as well as Pascal. Tocqueville and Beaumont also brought their shared interest in Chateaubriand's romantic writings on the American wilderness and its native inhabitants as well as James Fenimore Cooper's works, which were popular in France.

Tocqueville transcribed in minute detail in his notebooks the many conversations they had with the Americans (and Canadians) who became the anonymous informants of *Democracy*. Many of these were among the leading public figures of the day, including President Andrew Jackson, Sam Houston, Albert Gallatin (Jefferson's Treasury secretary), and Charles Carroll (the last surviving signer of the Declaration of Independence). But the most influential of their informants were those they met in Boston, a group that included several former Federalists and others opposed to President Jackson's politics. Jared Sparks, the former editor of the *North American Review* and future president of Harvard, informed Tocqueville matter-of-factly that "the majority of educated people now recognize that General Jackson is not fit to fill the office of president. His lack of experience in matters of civilian government as well as his advanced age make him unsuitable for the position."[14] During their three-week stay in the city, Tocqueville and Beaumont also met Harvard president Josiah Quincy, Senator Daniel Webster, Unitarian minister William Ellery Channing, and former president John Quincy Adams. In their aristocratic instincts and common distrust of the crowd, hosts and guests had much in common, and Tocqueville and Beaumont proved attentive listeners. Indeed, the lessons the pair learned during their tour of New England—most notably the principle of majority rule—later shaped both men's work in profound ways.

Tocqueville consigned to his notes extensive comments on legal, constitutional, and governmental issues, as well as preliminary readings of the founding texts of the American Republic. His notes included comparisons of the Constitution and the Articles of Confederation, and he learned everything he could about the New England town, an institution that served as the point of departure for his analysis in *Democracy*. Through all of this, Tocqueville always

14. Non-alphabetical Notebooks 2–3, September 17, 1831.

kept France clearly in focus, and he wrote back to his father, his cousins Félix Le Peletier d'Aunay and Ernest de Blosseville, and his friend Ernest de Chabrol for details on the French government to aid him in his comparative analysis of the two nations. In addition, Tocqueville engaged law books with analytical precision, especially in Travel Notebook F. He interviewed Supreme Court justice John McLean and future chief justice Salmon P. Chase, as well as a number of judges and lawyers, on the ins and outs of civil and criminal law. Tocqueville dug into the specifics of jurisdictions and procedure, even down to who was responsible for paying trial costs. He was intrigued by the effect of the inheritance laws in equalizing wealth, the ordering force that lawyers and judges exerted on democracy, and the "political utility" (if not legal efficiency) of juries.

Tocqueville's and Beaumont's narratives of their extraordinary excursions in the wilderness are especially interesting as experiments in romantic writing. The influence of the great Chateaubriand and his *Atala* were never far behind; one finds his traces in their correspondence throughout the journey—from the moment their ship entered Long Island Sound up through their trip through the Great Lakes and their visit to Niagara Falls. Tocqueville and Beaumont wanted to see "*wilderness* and *Indians*." But "you have no idea how hard it is to find those two things in America today," Tocqueville wrote to Eugénie de Grancey. "We traveled more than 100 leagues in the state of New York on the trail of savage tribes and never found one. Repeatedly we were told that there were Indians here ten years ago, eight years ago, six years ago, two years ago. But European civilization is spreading like a forest fire and driving them farther inland."[15] Although they eventually found some Indians in upstate New York, these "savages" were a far cry from the fierce specimens they had read about. "In their perfectly natural existence there was something noble and grand. Now they are debased and degraded. They can no longer do without clothing. They need liquor, and it makes them drunk. Beyond that, they take nothing from civilization but its vices and wear nothing but Europe's rags," Beaumont wrote to his sister Eugénie.[16] Both men complained that, in contrast to Atala, Indian women struck them as quite ugly.[17] Shortly thereafter, their yearning to see the very edge of white settlement became the impetus for an extended journey through the Michigan frontier, where they found both the Indians and the virgin forest they had been seeking. Later, they were awestruck by Niagara Falls. Beaumont drew some good sketches but did not venture words—noting merely that Chateaubriand's had been inadequate.[18] Tocqueville did risk two separate accounts.[19] Following their return to France, Tocqueville relied heavily on his notes from

15. October 10, 1831 (part 1).

16. July 14, 1831 (part 1).

17. Beaumont to Chabrol, August 2, 1831 (part 1); Tocqueville to his sister-in-law Émilie, September 7, 1831 (part 1).

18. Beaumont to his father, August 21, 1831 (part 1).

19. Tocqueville to his mother, August 21, 1831 (part 1), and to Dalmassy, late August 1831 (part 1).

the Great Lakes excursion in writing about the tragic fate of American Indians in volume 1 of *Democracy,* while Beaumont made the pair's harrowing trek through the woods between Detroit and Saginaw the backdrop for the final chapters of *Marie.*

While the two men relished describing the grand, inspiring, and sublime scenes they encountered in the wilderness, they also recorded their irritation with some recurring aspects of their social encounters. They were especially harsh on American music, which Beaumont informed Eugénie "is surely the most barbarous in the world."[20] As Tocqueville elaborated to his sister-in-law Alexandrine, "When it comes to harmony, there can be no doubt that no one is less gifted than these Americans. If only they knew the truth, but they are a thousand leagues from suspecting it. We spend our days putting up with yelping the likes of which the Old World has never heard."[21] Although the men initially offered these observations as passing commentary, on their return to France both men would situate their annoyance with Americans' collective tin ear in its broader context, arguing that the people's single-minded focus on commerce—together with the leveling force of democratic public opinion—presented substantial hurdles to the nation's ever achieving cultural distinction.

As befits two traveling bachelors, they observed American women often and speculated on their mores. The men were greeted as celebrities wherever they went, and casual flirtation became an almost routine part of the job. "I talked with her quite a bit, but I don't know if I will ever see her again, so that it was a pure waste of sentiment. It is absolutely the same with all the beauties I meet. Our passions are aroused three or four times a week, and each occasion effaces the last. But there are always new faces, and I believe, God forgive me, that we say the same things to all of them, at the risk of complimenting a brunette on the whiteness of her complexion and a blonde on the rich ebony of her hair," Beaumont wrote his brother Jules after spending an evening with the charming niece of David Sears, a wealthy Bostonian.[22] Tocqueville, who by this time was already in love with Marie Mottley—the Englishwoman he would later marry—tended to be more reserved in his comments, and both men took pains to reassure their friends and family that such encounters were entirely innocent, or at least mostly so. "Our virtue is still holding up, but we are beginning to eye the women with an impudence that ill becomes representatives of the penitentiary system," Tocqueville told Chabrol.[23] As with all of their informants, however, Tocqueville and Beaumont gleaned lessons from the women they met in America, and throughout their notes and correspondence interspersed asides about the charms and defects of particular ladies with commentary about courtship, marriage, and morals in the United States. Tocqueville later incorporated

20. July 14, 1831 (part 1).
21. June 20, 1831 (part 1).
22. September 16, 1831 (part 1).
23. July 16, 1831 (part 1).

INTRODUCTION

many of these insights into volume 2 of *Democracy,* and Beaumont's *Marie* focuses on gender as well as race in both the novel and its lengthy appendices.

Along with their descriptions and analyses of everything and everyone they encountered in America, Tocqueville's and Beaumont's letters and notes give the reader a sense of the two men's investigative process during their journey. They pursued their work together with discipline. Early in their travels, Tocqueville bragged to his father that he and Beaumont were "research machines." They also maintained a busy social calendar that included a seemingly endless series of teas, dinners, parties, and other events in every city they visited.[24] Indeed, their tour of Manhattan society seemed at times a journey unto itself, and at one point Tocqueville noted that he had to send home for extra gloves, ties, and stockings in order to keep their schedule of evening engagements.[25] At the same time, the men enjoyed moments of leisure—as when Tocqueville gave Beaumont swimming lessons in the Hudson River during their stay at Sing Sing—but also experienced fear and hardship, as when the steamboat *Fourth of July* nearly sank in the Ohio or when Tocqueville fell ill, not long after this incident, in the middle of the winter in Tennessee.

The Tocquevillean Moment

A SHARED ANXIETY

The dates of the journey and the encounters with particular groups of Americans are especially important because they influenced Tocqueville's portrayal of American life. First, one has to remember that for Tocqueville the trip was emotionally charged. It came in the aftermath of a revolution in France that replaced an absolute monarchy with a constitutional monarchy. The "legitimate" Bourbons were gone, and even though Tocqueville thought they deserved their fate, France's future under increasingly democratic rule—not to mention Tocqueville's and his legitimist friends' role in that state—was much on his mind.

Tocqueville was concerned about the effect of majority rule. Could equality reduce the sovereign people to a state of powerlessness, just as the monarch had done in the Old Regime? Judging from the Terror, which had sent many of Tocqueville's family to the guillotine, the people could certainly be as autocratic as any king. But would this despotism develop in a democracy like America? Tocqueville posed this question as a very young man and kept working on the answer to the end of his life.

What Tocqueville did not know, and could not have anticipated, is that his American informants had similar anxieties about the United States. A social revolution had followed the political revolution and thrown into question the power and natural place of elites. The Jacksonian era was a period of great leveling, and

---

24. June 3, 1831 (part 1).
25. Tocqueville to Abbé Lesueur, May 28, 1831 (part 1).

by the time Tocqueville arrived in the United States, deference had significantly receded. Nowhere was this shift felt more acutely than in New England.

Consequently, Tocqueville's anxieties as a young French aristocrat coincided remarkably with those of his closest New England informants, many of whom shared similar concerns about the democratization of public life. They developed a sense of kinship with one another, and Tocqueville would correspond with several of them through the years, including Jared Sparks and Edward Everett—a United States congressman who would go on to serve as secretary of state under President Millard Fillmore.

It was Sparks who introduced Tocqueville to the tyranny of the majority. "In this country the political dogma is that the majority is always right," Tocqueville recorded Sparks as telling him. "All things considered, we were right to adopt this principle, but there is no denying that experience has often shown it to be wrong. (He cited any number of examples.) Sometimes the majority has sought to oppress the minority."[26] Tocqueville concurred. He offered his own criticisms of President Jackson in his journals, and he reserved special scorn for Davy Crockett, the backwoodsman turned congressman who, as Tocqueville wrote, was "a man with no education, who can barely read, who owns no property, and who has no permanent address but lives in the woods and spends his life hunting, selling game in order to live."[27] Later on, even Sparks would say that in *Democracy* Tocqueville took the idea of tyranny of the majority—the very idea he had implanted in Tocqueville's mind—too far. But while Tocqueville abandoned the phrase in volume 2, the fear stayed with him.

FRAGMENTATION AS ANTIDOTE TO MAJORITY RULE

The threat of a tyranny of the majority, Tocqueville perceived, was less potent if the majority could effectively be fragmented. Consequently, he was naturally interested in constitutional provisions and other institutional mechanisms through which the popular will could be contained or even countered. He had, after all, heralded his work as a "new political science" for a "world that is totally new."[28] His first serious informant, a New York politician named John C. Spencer, talked with Tocqueville about the benefits of bicameralism. Spencer believed that more experienced statesmen in a second chamber favored "the social order as it currently exists" and helped cool down debates.[29] The power of judges was another potential antidote to the evils of centralized power.

Over time, Tocqueville came more fully to understand the separation of powers and the system of checks and balances.[30] Federalism was especially im-

26. Non-alphabetic Notebooks 2 and 3, September 29, 1831.
27. Notebook E, December 12, 1831.
28. *Democracy in America,* trans. Arthur Goldhammer, ed. Olivier Zunz (New York: Library of America, 2004), 7.
29. Non-alphabetic Notebook 1, July 17–18, 1831.
30. Tocqueville to his father, July 4, 1831 (part 1).

portant in fragmenting the polity. In his letters, Tocqueville at first seems to have been baffled by the almost complete absence of any centralized administration in the United States—he wrote his father from Albany that "the central government here has virtually no existence." But he read up on state constitutions, began studying both Madison and Hamilton during the trip, and all along queried friends and relatives for advice and information to help him with his comparison.

Sparks was again enormously helpful on this issue by introducing Tocqueville to the history of the New England towns. As Sparks explained, in New England the towns preceded the General Court and jealously guarded their power subsequent to its founding, thereby creating a polity of semiautonomous little republics that largely handled their own affairs.

The final result of these efforts was an ambitious account of American government—so thorough that volume 1 was long used as a political science textbook in France. Tocqueville's attention to detail also paid off. He had been terrified of making a mistake and was relieved when American reviews of *Democracy* said that he was "the first European to have grasped the spirit of American institutions and offered an accurate description of them."[31]

CONCEPTUAL BREAKTHROUGH: THE VOLUNTARY ASSOCIATIONS

Tocqueville's disquisition on American government, regardless of its accuracy or the enlightenment it offered French readers, was no revelation to Americans. But upon his arrival in the United Sates in 1831, Tocqueville found himself in the midst of a great associational movement sweeping through the nation. While Americans themselves had long been skeptical of such bodies, Tocqueville either overlooked or disregarded these suspicions and instead formulated his own ideas about their significance. While American critics worried about the potential for associations to factionalize the Republic and threaten majority rule, Tocqueville saw majority rule itself as the overriding threat and conceived of voluntary associations as the crucial antidote to this problem.

If associations led to a certain lack of order, Tocqueville held, so much the better. In associations, citizens exercised their freedom and practiced "self-interest properly understood."

Tocqueville did not capture American associations as completely or accurately as he did Federalism, bicameralism, or other more conventional topics in volume 1. But nonetheless, Tocqueville grasped that America was a "nation of joiners" before Americans themselves fully knew it, and it was through this insight that Tocqueville made his biggest mark.[32]

---

31. Tocqueville to Reeve, November 21, 1836 (part 6); Tocqueville to Beaumont, November 22, 1836 (part 6).

32. To borrow Arthur M. Schlesinger Sr.'s felicitous phrase in "Biography of a Nation of Joiners," *American Historical Review* 50 (October 1944): 1–25.

Associations were a more contentious issue than Tocqueville realized. The Founding Fathers had been worried that associations could detract from the common good and, if they attained sufficient political power, enforce the will of a minority against the majority. George Washington in his 1796 Farewell Address denounced "all combinations and associations, under whatever plausible character," as "destructive" of the "duty of every individual to obey established government."[33] Later, on different occasions, both Federalists and Jeffersonian Republicans argued that civil and political associations outside the state subverted the true voice of the people, fostered divisiveness, and presented a dire threat to the Republic.[34]

The debate about associations was still in full tilt when Tocqueville arrived in America. But Tocqueville effectively bypassed it. From Story's *Commentaries on the Constitution of the United States,* he concluded that associations were constitutionally protected, when, in fact, they were not. With the First Amendment, the Bill of Rights guaranteed the right to assemble; at the time, this was generally understood as a defense against government oppression rather than a broader freedom to associate.[35] In stressing the latter, Tocqueville pointed to the way Dartmouth College had asserted its independence from the state legislature.[36] Conversely, Tocqueville noted the persecution of the Masons but was unsure what to make of it. Tocqueville imagined that great political parties were a thing of the past in America, which, on the eve of renewed party conflict in the 1840s, was not one of his more accurate predictions.[37]

But while Tocqueville did not pay much attention to the founders' arguments about associations, he did not miss their newfound popularity. By 1831 associations had become a generalized phenomenon attracting a broad cross section of America. Nowhere was this more true than in the emergent "benevolent empire," a web of associations dedicated to charity, mutual assistance, and reform, including Bible and missionary societies, Sunday schools, and other educational institutions. Although they were new, Tocqueville took associations for granted as an essential and permanent aspect of American life. He noted the proliferation of temperance societies and the way that Americans seemed to come together to accomplish even the most mundane public purposes, and Tocqueville and Beaumont even marched with voluntary associations in a parade in Albany on July 4, 1831.

Tocqueville came to see associations as an answer to his nagging worries about democracy and despotism. While much different from the kind of check offered by Federalism or other institutional arrangements embedded in the structure of government itself, associations seemed to possess their own guar-

---

33. George Washington, *Writings* (New York: Library of America, 1997), 962.

34. See Johann N. Neem, *Creating a Nation of Joiners: Democracy and Civil Society in Early National Massachusetts* (Cambridge, MA: Harvard University Press, 2008), 56–80.

35. Neem, *Creating a Nation,* 17–18.

36. *Democracy in America* (trans. Goldhammer), 165.

37. Non-alphabetic Notebook 1, July 17–18, 1831.

antee against majority power. As he argued in *Democracy,* voluntary associations represented a vital mechanism for accomplishing public ends of every conceivable type—from building prisons to organizing celebrations.

This was democracy writ small, but with big consequences. Tocqueville wrote in his notebook during his stay in Philadelphia in October 1831, "Liberty fails to execute its projects with the same degree of perfection as does intelligent despotism, but in the long run it produces a greater result. It does not always, in all circumstances, give the people the most skillful and perfect government possible. But it does diffuse throughout the social body an activity, a strength, an energy that would not exist without it, and which works miracles."[38] This energy expressed itself in associations. By fostering local initiative and engaging citizens freely in their own future, voluntary associations epitomized the doctrine of "self-interest properly understood." In contrast to virtue, "self-interest properly understood" called on citizens to set aside only a small portion of their individual resources and invest them in the common good. In so doing, Americans exercised their liberty while also protecting themselves from the tyranny of the majority. For Tocqueville, *democracy* and *equality* were interchangeable words. Association became synonymous with liberty.

The experience of the journey was crucial in helping Tocqueville arrive at these conclusions. He reported associations as blooming everywhere even as America moved toward yet greater equality, and this gave Tocqueville reason for optimism about democracy.[39] This was not a lesson he could have drawn from any existing constitutional or legal text on the subject; rather, it was something Tocqueville had to witness firsthand. As his notebooks and letters illustrate, Tocqueville began formulating his ideas during the trip through observation, conversation, and reflection, then deepened and clarified them when he returned to draft the manuscript. But he never wavered from the central thesis. "Rest assured that the great peril of any democratic age is the destruction or excessive weakening of *the parts* of the social body as compared with the *whole,*" he wrote Reeve in 1840, extolling the benefits of association.[40]

38. Travel Notebook 3, October 25, 1831.

39. "Americans of all ages, all conditions, and all minds are constantly joining together in groups. In addition to commercial and industrial associations in which everyone takes part, there are associations of a thousand other kinds: some religious, some moral, some grave, some trivial, some quite general and others quite particular, some huge and others tiny. Americans associate to give fêtes, to found seminaries, to build inns, to erect churches, to distribute books, and to send missionaries to the antipodes. This is how they create hospitals, prisons, and schools. If, finally, they wish to publicize a truth or foster a sentiment with the help of a great example, they associate. Wherever there is a new undertaking, at the head of which you would expect to see in France the government and in England some great lord, in the United States you are sure to find an association." This is one of the most often quoted passages from *Democracy in America* (trans. Goldhammer), 595.

40. February 3, 1840 (part 6).

The snapshot Tocqueville offered readers in *Democracy* was of American civic life in constant motion. This was by nature an incomplete portrait, and at times Tocqueville struggled to grasp its many details and reconcile inconsistencies. Yet while Tocqueville did not get everything right about associations, he captured just enough of their essential qualities to support his innovative argument about their value to liberty.

Tocqueville was most confused about his most important example: the New England town. Tocqueville questioned Sparks and others on the New England town during his stay in Boston, and later commissioned Sparks to write a longer memorandum on the subject, which Sparks sent to Tocqueville in January 1832.[41] Sparks's detailed report set forth the town as the basic building block of the New England polity, an organization that predated even the state and continued to serve as the primary vehicle through which citizens dealt with public affairs at the local level. Put more simply, the town was the form of government that most citizens encountered and engaged with on a day-to-day basis. Tocqueville jumped on this formulation, which to him offered conclusive proof that Americans had practiced political liberty from the very beginning, a habit that in his view virtually inoculated them against the danger of rising equality. Following Sparks's lead, Tocqueville made the New England town the original voluntary association.

This was true of the New England town's relationship to a distant British Crown. What Tocqueville missed, however, was that the New England town was a covenanted community that included church as well as government. This point was apparently not clear from initial conversations during Tocqueville and Beaumont's stay in Boston. As Tocqueville wrote to Sparks from Cincinnati in December 1831 while reading a book entitled *The Town Officer,* "There is one article in particular in which I confess I am unable to understand anything, the one entitled 'Parish and Parish Officers.' Indeed, it seems to imply that each town is obliged to support a Protestant minister or else pay a fine to the county's court of common pleas. To a certain extent this seems to me to establish a state religion and to mix politics and religion in a way that Americans appear to have taken care to avoid."[42] Sparks thoroughly treated public support for religion in his memorandum, but Tocqueville never fully resolved the question.

In the end, Tocqueville hedged on precise definitions. Although he adopted the New England town as the paradigmatic voluntary association in *Democracy,* he referred to it both in its original sense—as a self-governing, organic whole that included the church and all of the community's other civil institutions—and as a model voluntary society. By happenstance, Massachusetts towns actually were freed from formal ties to religion through disestablishment in 1833

41. Herbert Baxter Adams, "Jared Sparks and Alexis de Tocqueville," *Johns Hopkins University Studies in Historical and Political Science,* 16th ser., 12 (December 1898): 7–49.

42. December 2, 1831 (part 1).

(an event Sparks had told Tocqueville was on the horizon), and this lessened Tocqueville's error in *Democracy*. Still, Tocqueville's treatment of the towns remained muddy. In effect, while Tocqueville articulated a vision of a vibrant civil society set apart from government and established religion—a point that remains his major theoretical legacy—he ended up identifying (in a manner Rousseau would have endorsed) the local government as the embodiment of civil society.

Religion confounded Tocqueville in other respects. Although he witnessed religious sectarianism in the United States, he was preoccupied with the growth of Catholicism in America. He also was concerned by what he viewed as the manifest shortcomings of Protestant doctrine, which he believed fostered a religiosity based more on habit than true faith. He dwelled on the success of Unitarianism and came to see Protestantism receding under the joint assault of Catholicism on one hand and deism on the other. These concerns dominated his interviews with religious figures like William Ellery Channing and found a prominent place in his letters home, most notably to Kergorlay and Chabrol.[43] But in obsessing over doctrine and faith, Tocqueville overlooked questions of ecclesiastical structure. In doing so, he missed perhaps the greatest example of the associational movement he had so cleverly articulated, even as it unfolded right before his eyes. Protestant sectarianism fragmented the majority on a grand scale. Tocqueville understood that such schisms guarded against a tyranny of the majority within the field of religion itself. He wrote at length on how religious practice ensured toleration and enhanced liberty. But he never connected these trends with the associational impulse at work in other areas of civil society.

Beaumont as Social Conscience

Tocqueville knew well that nine months was hardly enough time to learn everything he wanted to understand about America, and he himself remained far from certain about the accuracy or value of his observations. Although Beaumont shared the same body of observations, he focused on different aspects of America. During the initial stages of the journey, both men wrote of the project they would collaborate on once they returned to France. But they soon decided to undertake separate ventures. Tocqueville speculated about pursuing his own project in a letter to his mother from Philadelphia on October 24, 1831, and again in a letter to Chabrol written after the New Year. Beaumont, for his part, first spoke of a work on slavery in a letter to his brother Achille on November 8, 1831. The larger topic was race, inequality, and injustice. Whereas Tocqueville struggled to formulate his project, Beaumont's case was more directly concerned with what he saw of race relations, and at least initially, Beaumont had few doubts about the acclaim his work would bring him. As he wrote Achille in

43. Tocqueville to Kergorlay, June 29, 1831 (part 1), and to Chabrol, October 26, 1831 (part 1).

November of 1831, "I will probably publish all of this in the great work that is to *immortalize me*."

In *Marie,* Beaumont tells the fictional tragic story of a Frenchman, Ludovic, who emigrates to the United States in 1825. Ludovic falls in love with the beautiful and mysterious Marie, the daughter of a wealthy Baltimore merchant named David Nelson, only to discover that she and her brother Georges share a visually imperceptible but nonetheless terrible stigma of black ancestry—a product of their father's marriage to a woman in New Orleans. Their mother died of heartbreak when a former suitor exposed her and her family, and Nelson and his children subsequently fled to Baltimore, where they kept Marie and Georges's lineage a secret. The plot of the novel centers on Ludovic's failed efforts to understand and overcome American racial prejudice in order to pursue his true love. The violent race riot with which white New Yorkers aim to disrupt Ludovic and Marie's wedding represents the extreme consequences of democracy gone awry. Like her mother, Marie dies from a broken heart, while Georges is killed in an abortive uprising by blacks and Indians in the South—a literary treatment of the violent racial clash both Tocqueville and Beaumont saw on the horizon. Together, these tragedies drive Ludovic to become a hermit in the Michigan wilderness, unwilling to return to Europe but unable to live in American society.

Ludovic's wide-ranging travels provided Beaumont with a literary device through which to attempt a broad treatment of America. Although his method is awkward, Beaumont offers up an engaging account of American culture in the middle of the novel, explaining how equality stifles achievement in the arts. Ludovic's courtship of Marie also gave Beaumont a chance to recount American customs of courtship and marriage, and here the author appears to have drawn on both his sociological observations and his own flirtations during the journey. Finally, Ludovic and Marie's retreat into the wilderness gave Beaumont the opportunity to portray the American landscape, and in particular the Michigan forests through which he and Tocqueville had traveled during the summer of 1831.

Beaumont's most important and original contribution, however, was to highlight the pernicious effects of racism, particularly the disenfranchisement and oppression of free African Americans. In tandem with his discussions of free blacks and an elegant essay on slavery he included in the appendix, Beaumont also delved at length into the oppression and degradation of American Indians, whose fate he saw as linked with that of blacks.

Tocqueville also addressed the inequities and injustices that existed in American society—including slavery and the United States government's systematic campaign to remove the Indians—but he nonetheless chose to underscore the one great principle that was going to change the world: that of equality. In deciding to focus on racism, Beaumont highlighted instead the harsh reality of inequality, and consequently, many observations the two friends shared appeared more negative under Beaumont's pen because he made them in condemning rather than praising American society.

Beaumont was animated by an abstract and universal humanitarianism.[44] His most consistent contribution was in exposing the persistence of racial prejudice (and its deleterious impact on civic and political life) long after the emancipation of individual slaves. On this point, his outlook on the future of race relations offered little hope for resolution. Again and again in *Marie,* Beaumont showed how discrimination precipitated and amplified the tyranny of the majority. With the courts and elected officials unwilling to protect free blacks, and with only a handful of white associations advocating on their behalf with varying levels of resolve, they simply could never reap the benefits of Tocqueville's "self-interest properly understood."

Beaumont was well aware that readers of both *Democracy* and *Marie* could not miss the great distance separating the two books even though they were based not only on shared observations but on like-minded interpretations, as reading the letters home makes clear. Beaumont said as much in his introduction to *Marie,* speaking even of the "apparent dissidence" between the books. Yet it seems as though Beaumont's insights had their place in *Democracy,* especially in Tocqueville's chapter on the three races at the end of volume 1, and he may very well have served as Tocqueville's social conscience, something that a close friendship nurtured. At the same time, friendship and separate publications accommodated divergence of views in ways that joint authorship could not.

As Beaumont had predicted, his message of America as a land of injustice was not lost on *Marie*'s readers. The most famous of these, Karl Marx, relied on Beaumont's portrayal of Americans' acquisitiveness in one of his early but most visceral attacks on the evils of money.

Marx learned from both Beaumont and Tocqueville that in America the state and religion can coexist, an important argument in the polemic he had with his former mentor Bruno Bauer on secularization. Beaumont gave Marx ammunition for reducing religion to the cult of "Mammon," although that was certainly not Beaumont's intention. In Marx's essay "On the Jewish Question" (1843), "Jew" stands for money, and New England, without Beaumont's noticing, has been thoroughly "judaized."[45] As Marx quotes Beaumont, "The man you see at the head of a respectable congregation started out as a businessman; his business failed so he became a minister; the other started out as a priest, but as soon as he had saved some money he left the pulpit for business. In many people's eyes the religious ministry is a veritable industrial career."[46] This profile precisely fits the character of Marie's father, David Nelson, a New Englander by birth who is both a wealthy merchant and an ordained minister. Beaumont's rendering was

44. Cheryl Welch, "Les injustices révoltantes: Gustave de Beaumont and the Pre-history of Crimes against Humanity," *The Tocqueville Review/La Revue Tocqueville* 31, no. 1 (2010): 201–19.

45. Karl Marx, *Early Writings,* trans. Rodney Livingstone and Gregor Benton (New York: Vintage Books, 1975), 238–39.

46. Ibid., 238.

sufficiently dark to inspire Marx's image of an American for whom "the world is nothing but a Stock Exchange and he is convinced that his sole vocation here on earth is to get richer than his neighbors."[47]

What if Tocqueville and Beaumont had written their book together, as they had initially intended? The basic disagreement in their separate accounts of America suggests that they could never have reconciled their views, despite their deep friendship and shared journey to America, as well as their subsequent explorations of England, Ireland, and Algeria, their reliance on the same bodies of evidence in their writings, their common political projects, and perhaps above all their determination never to contradict each other in public. In the end, Beaumont and Tocqueville simply drew different conclusions about equality from the same well of observations.

Following the publication of *Marie* and volume 1 of *Democracy* in 1835, the two men did agree on a division of labor that left America to Tocqueville. Beaumont quickly turned to Ireland, although his focus on inequality and oppression remained the same. Beaumont made this clear in the final passages of *Ireland,* when he called the actions of England and the United States "two phenomena of the same nature." He considered as just retribution the difficulty America faced with slaves and England with the Irish, with whom they had dealt as if they were slaves. As Beaumont put it, in America "the leprosy is extending; it is blighting pure institutions, it is poisoning the felicity of the present generation, and already depositing the seeds of death in a body full of life."[48] For his part, Tocqueville, who could never have coauthored these lines, rewrote *Democracy* to reformulate his own findings on a more theoretical plane—nourished by five more years of sustained comparison between aristocratic and democratic societies. Just as Beaumont highlighted the effects of inequality in Ireland, Tocqueville in his second volume continued to focus on the rise of equality and its social and political consequences, and thus the two men's second efforts only underscored the difference of views that began with their American journey.

Common Experiences as Reformers

Although the idea for the prison report began as a "pretext," Tocqueville and Beaumont dove into the project with unexpected zeal once they arrived in America.[49] With the penitentiary notes, the reader will find the two friends heavily invested in the anthropological, sociological, and economic studies their official investigation required—a truly impressive contribution to the rehabilitation of criminals. Following their return from America, Tocqueville and Beaumont could claim to be experts in the field of prison reform.

47. Ibid., 237.
48. Gustave de Beaumont, *Ireland,* trans. W. C. Taylor (Cambridge, MA: Harvard University Press, 2006), 376.
49. On their joint career as reformers, see *Tocqueville and Beaumont on Social Reform,* ed. and trans. Seymour Drescher (New York: Harper Torchbooks, 1968).

INTRODUCTION

In visiting Philadelphia's Eastern State Penitentiary—whose system of enforced solitude Tocqueville later endorsed—as well as Sing Sing, Auburn, and other prisons, the pair made careful observations of each institution's disciplinary regime, management, finances, and mortality rates. They also relentlessly tracked down data on inmate recidivism, and as Beaumont informed his brother Achille, at New York City's juvenile reformatory they even went so far as to construct a longitudinal study on the behavior of inmates who had been released since 1825. They found prison officials to be astonishingly helpful everywhere they visited, and in Philadelphia—by their account, a city that took singular pride in its penal system—the local prison society even appointed a committee to assist them. As with their examination of American society as a whole, the two men studied prisons with an eye to what could be exported back to France, and while their initial visit to Sing Sing left them highly skeptical, by the time they visited Auburn in July 1831, Tocqueville reported to Chabrol that "we have almost made up our minds (after two months of work) that the American system is practicable in France."[50]

The final report, drafted principally by Beaumont, was published to real acclaim at the beginning of 1833. In addition to covering the two major prison models they investigated—the Auburn system, which espoused silent, communal work enforced by the threat of harsh physical punishment, and the Philadelphia system, which centered on the near-total isolation of individual prisoners, who lived and worked in separate cells—the document also included discussions of temperance societies, juvenile reformatories, and the law governing debtors and the poor.

The work was almost immediately translated into English by Francis Lieber. Lieber was a German political exile wounded during the Waterloo campaign while fighting with the Prussian army; he lived in Boston in 1831 and edited the first *Encyclopaedia Americana*. Tocqueville, who remained friendly with Lieber and continued to collaborate with him, was less than thrilled with Lieber's edition, which he felt needlessly loaded down the report with notes and corrections that tended to tilt the document in favor of the Philadelphia system.

Tocqueville and Beaumont had themselves prudently avoided endorsing either the Philadelphia or Auburn model in the report. But from the beginning they had seen the method of incarceration at Eastern State as more humane, if also more costly, and over time they came to advocate more strenuously on its behalf. They ultimately succeeded in pushing through a limited slate of reforms before Louis Napoleon's coup undid much of their work and reoriented the French prison system toward transportation and exile.

50. July 16, 1831 (part 1).

Tocqueville and America after 1840

When Tocqueville and Beaumont returned to France, they pursued parallel lives in letters and politics and also made forays into political journalism. The success of the prison report helped the two men enter political life in the July Monarchy, where they stood for election as "liberals of a new kind," according to Tocqueville's own description. They later rallied to the Second Republic and were sent back to the Chamber of Deputies at the first universal suffrage election in France. Tocqueville served a brief term as foreign minister and used his post to name Beaumont as ambassador to Austria. The two men vigorously opposed Louis Napoleon's coup, a decision that resulted in their brief arrest and precipitated their retirement from public life.

As his interests shifted toward other subjects after 1835, Beaumont gave only occasional thought to the United States—allowing the trip to stand as his main source of knowledge on the subject—but Tocqueville kept up a sustained correspondence with the New England informants he had met during his journey to America, including Jared Sparks and Theodore Sedgwick III. Even as Tocqueville's later writings moved away from explicit treatments of America, these letters suggest how his experiences in the United States continued to inform Tocqueville's thinking until the end of his life.

Much as he had done during the trip to America, Tocqueville relied on this network to inform his perspective on French public life. He kept writing to his American correspondents about prison reform as he reported on the issue to the Chamber of Deputies during the July Monarchy, then sent out queries about matters of universal suffrage, bicameralism, and federalism during the constitutional debates following the formation of the Second Republic.

In addition to political counsel, he also relied on these men's investment advice. In the Yankee spirit of entrepreneurship, Tocqueville and Beaumont had sunk a considerable portion of their personal fortunes into American railroads in New York, Michigan, and Illinois. Having observed firsthand the frequency with which fortunes were made and lost in America, Tocqueville exhibited anxiety whenever the United States economy had a downturn.

Tocqueville kept America in sharp focus when, upon retiring from politics, he exposed French centralization as one of the causes of the French Revolution and the enemy of liberty. In pointing to the loss of communal autonomy at the hands of despots, Tocqueville recalled he had once believed local liberties a trait "peculiar to the New World." But now he had discovered France had known them too. In drawing the contrast between free North American rural towns and French "subjugated communities," Tocqueville concluded their resemblance was as close as that "between a living individual and a corpse can be."[51] Beaumont, seeing the continuity with *Democracy in America,* suggested *Democracy and Liberty*

---

51. *The Ancien Régime and the Revolution,* ed. Jon Elster, trans. Arthur Goldhammer (New York: Cambridge University Press, forthcoming), bk. 2, chap. 3.

in France as a possible title for the second masterpiece Tocqueville published in 1856 as *The Old Regime and the Revolution*.[52]

As for the United States, Tocqueville maintained a certain ambivalence during his later years. He became an especially vocal opponent of slavery and its expansion into the western territories, although the experience of the journey made him sensitive to the historical, social, and political barriers to abolition in states where slavery already existed. Most of the complaints Tocqueville leveled against America during his declining years echoed concerns he had already articulated in *Democracy*. Tocqueville's arguments would have fallen in the mainstream of political debate within the United States at the time.

Tocqueville, however, was less interested in the ebb and flow of American politics than in the ways in which these developments affected the prospects for liberty in Europe. So while Tocqueville expressed genuine moral outrage against slavery itself, he was probably equally concerned about the way that racial injustice detracted from the United States' reputation abroad. As he wrote Sparks in 1840, "Slavery is more deeply and tenaciously rooted in your soil than anywhere else. Neither you nor I will see the end of it. It is for me a very melancholy thought that your nation has so incorporated slavery that you and it have grown up together, so that humanity can only bewail your rapid progress, which without slavery would have been reason for all civilized peoples to rejoice."[53] Even toward the end of Tocqueville's life, when he grew increasingly distressed by the prospect of civil war in the United States, his disapproval sprang mainly from the hope he placed in the American example. "I ardently wish that America's great experiment in self-government will not fail. If it were to fail, that would be the end of political liberty on this earth," he wrote to Childe in 1857. Tocqueville conceded with some pleasure that the trip had transformed him into a "half Yankee."[54] As he wrote Jared Sparks in 1852, when he was already showing signs of the tuberculosis that would eventually take his life, "From my retirement I often turn my attention, with much pleasure mingled at times with a certain anxiety, toward your America, of which I consider myself almost a citizen, so strong is my desire that your country prosper and become a great nation."[55]

52. Gustave de Beaumont to Alexis de Tocqueville, February 7, 1856, in O.C., VIII, 3, 369.

53. October 13, 1840 (part 7).

54. December 12, 1856 (part 7).

55. December 11, 1852 (part 7).

EDITOR'S NOTE

People, places, and events are identified in footnotes at their first appearance in the text. The reader may easily locate these notes by consulting the index. Captions indicate one of two possible sources for Gustave de Beaumont's drawings and watercolors: *GB1* refers to a sketchbook in the holdings of the Beinecke Rare Book and Manuscript Library at Yale University and *GB2* to another sketchbook in a private collection (see the Note on Sources). Beaumont's original sketchbook notations are *italicized* in the illustration captions.

Letters from Tocqueville and Beaumont on Their American Travels

"The only somewhat general ideas that I have thus far expressed about America are contained in letters addressed to my family and a few other people in France," wrote Alexis de Tocqueville to his mother from Philadelphia. "And all of these were written in haste, on steamboats or in some hole where I had to use my lap for a table." Gustave de Beaumont could have penned similar words. The travelers requested family members and such friends as Louis de Kergorlay, the Stöffels brothers, and Ernest de Chabrol to save their correspondence as a unique and detailed chronological record of their trip.

We have translated large excerpts from most of these letters. Mindful of space, we have not included a few repetitive passages, as when either Tocqueville or Beaumont described in comparable terms the same event to several of their individual correspondents or when, in some instances, they duplicated each other. Most of the time, however, they maintained their separate perspectives and their separate voices, which we have rendered as faithfully as possible.

As our intent was to publish a record of the American travels, we have skipped sections on family matters and on exclusively French affairs. For instance, from Beaumont's letters, we have deleted frequent and lengthy pleas to family members for more detailed news from home.

Although we devote a section of this book to Tocqueville's and Beaumont's penitentiary writings, we have not artificially broken up the letters when the writers broached this topic. We have kept their considerations on prisons as part of the larger epistolary narrative of their journey, saving for part 4 only letters primarily devoted to the penitentiary system.

We have included here two letters to Unitarian minister Jared Sparks, who had been a most valuable informant in Boston, as Tocqueville and Beaumont requested from him additional information on American government.

Before the Voyage

From Tocqueville | To Charles Stöffels[1]

Paris, November 4, 1830

... My position in France is bad in every respect, at least to my way of seeing, for either this government will consolidate its position, which is not very likely, or it will be brought down.

In the first case, my situation will remain rather disagreeable for quite some time. I do not wish for advancement, because to do so would be to tie myself to men whose intentions I find suspect. So my role would be that of an obscure assistant judge, confined to a narrow sphere and with no way to make my reputation. If I attempt to oppose the government from within the justice ministry, I will be denied even the honor of dismissal. They'll be pleased to shut me up by preventing me from working in the courts. If I support these people, I will be acting in a manner inconsistent with both my principles and my position. Thus I will have no choice but to remain neutral, the most pitiful role one can possibly play, especially when one occupies a lower rank. What is more, the future remains so murky that it is impossible to decide which party's ultimate victory one ought to favor in the country's interest.

Now suppose that the government is toppled. In the subsequent upheaval there will be no opportunity to make a name for myself, because I will be starting from too low a position. I have as yet done nothing to gain public attention. Try as I might, the revolution would find me too young and too obscure. I would of course warmly embrace the banner of the party that seemed to me most just, but I would serve in its lowest ranks, which would hardly suit me.

Such is my future in France. I have drawn it as I see it, without exaggeration. Now suppose that, without quitting the magistracy or giving up my seniority, I go to America. Fifteen months elapse. Party lines in France sort themselves out. It becomes possible to see clearly which party is incompatible with the grandeur and tranquility of the country. One therefore returns with a clear and forthright opinion, free of any commitment to anyone in the world. The journey itself will have set one apart from the common run of mankind. The acquaintances

---

1. Charles Stöffels (1809–1886) was the brother of Tocqueville's good friend Eugène Stöffels (1805–1852). The brothers came from a middle-class French family, and Tocqueville met them in secondary school in Metz.

one will have acquired in that celebrated nation will bring still further distinction. One will have formed a precise idea of the nature of a vast republic and
of why it is feasible in one place and not feasible in another. Public administration will have been systematically examined in all its aspects. Upon returning to
France one will of course feel stronger than one felt upon leaving. If the moment is ripe, a publication of some sort might alert the public to one's existence
and draw the attention of the parties. If that doesn't happen, the journey will
at least have done no harm, for in America one will have been no more obscure
than one would have been in France, and upon returning one will be as apt for
advancement as if one had stayed.

This, I think, is not an altogether absurd plan. Now, how to carry it out?
Here is our thought: B[eaumont] and I will request a leave of eighteen months
along with a mission to go to America to examine the state of the penitentiary
system. You may not know what the penitentiary system is, and it would take
too long to explain it to you. All you need to know is that the issue is in no
way political and has to do solely with the well-being of society in general. Of
course this is a pretext, but a very honorable pretext, which will make us seem
particularly worthy of the government's interest, whatever the government happens to be, and will ensure that our request is looked upon kindly. We will then
avail ourselves of this mission to explore the Union on behalf of France, which
will give us an undeniable advantage over all other travelers.

In order to obtain this mission we have drafted a memorandum, which I believe is well crafted, in which we set forth our views. We conclude by offering
to undertake the journey at our own expense. The greatest hurdles have already
been surmounted, our application is moving ahead, and unless some unforeseen
obstacle arises, we will achieve our goal within the next few days. . . .

From Tocqueville | To Beaumont

March 14, 1831

[*The beginning of the letter is missing.*]
. . . that I would return this morning. This morning the great man was out.[2] I left
a brief note telling him that I would come tomorrow to receive his orders. These

2. Tocqueville refers to the marquis de Lafayette (1757–1834), who had for a short time
resumed charge of the National Guard during the July Revolution of 1830 and supported
Louis-Philippe's accession to the throne. Lafayette had sailed to America in 1777 at his own
expense. A major general under the command of George Washington, he greatly facilitated
cooperation between French and American forces at Yorktown. During the French Revolution, Lafayette assumed command of the French National Guard at its creation after the
storming of the Bastille and delivered the order to demolish the prison. Though jailed by
the Austrians later during the Revolution, Lafayette returned to France in 1799 and was celebrated as a great friend of liberty both in France and in the United States. Lafayette secured
Napoleon's abdication in 1815. He remained an influential presence in the French Chamber of
Deputies until his death.

various useless errands increased still more the respect I already had for you, if such a thing is possible, for you have done so much with such heroic courage.

Montebello has sent you four or five letters of recommendation along with a very friendly explanation.[3] I think that there is no point in sending it to you. Nothing else has come for you in the past week.

M. de La Luzerne's letters are curious, but there is no reason to regret not having read them together.[4] They contain a large amount of pointless detail that would be very difficult to read out loud.

In regard to M. de La Luzerne, I will tell you that his nephew has offered to recommend us to an American family living in New York who will apparently welcome us as if we were their own children. At least that is what the cousin swears. I believe that this recommendation is one of the most valuable we can hope to receive. What one wants most in a foreign country, especially when first arriving, is people who take a real interest in you.

My sentences all stick together like rabbit droppings, but what of it? I will tell you that I want *to buy* Volney's journey in America and Cooper's letters about America.[5] How does that strike you?

But will we go to America? This is a question I ask myself at least a hundred times a day. Not that I seriously doubt we will go. We have gone too far to turn back now, but will we go with the satisfaction of doing something completely good? I often doubt this, and the thought leaves me strangely perplexed. When I surrender to my imagination and conceive of the future in all its blackness, I think that we're wrong to head off to a faraway place. But when I reason, when I calculate how uncertain are the dangers we fear, our delicate position in France, and the impossibility of playing any role here whatsoever, it seems to me that our decision is only to be applauded and that our only regret should be that we did not act on it sooner. In this way I steel myself against the internal winds that buffet me constantly, but it takes me some time to work up the resolve necessary to escape from this state. . . .

3. Napoléon-Auguste Lannes de Montebello (1801–1874), a peer of France, had traveled to the Caribbean and North and South America in 1828. He held a number of diplomatic positions during the July Monarchy.

4. César-Anne de La Luzerne (1741–91) was the French ambassador to the United States from 1779 to 1783 and played a key role in the peace negotiations to end the American Revolution. Jared Sparks published his letters in volumes 10 and 11 of *The Diplomatic Correspondence of the American Revolution* (Boston, 1830). His nephew, the son of his brother César-Henri de La Luzerne (1737–1814), was a distant cousin of Tocqueville.

5. C. F. Volney (1757–1820) published an account of his American travels entitled *Tableau du climat et du sol des États-Unis d'Amérique* in Paris in 1803. James Fenimore Cooper (1789–1851) published *Notions of the Americans: Picked Up by a Traveling Bachelor* in 1828. A French edition, *Lettres sur les mœurs et les institutions des États-Unis de l'Amérique du Nord*, was published that same year.

Aboard Le Havre

From Beaumont | To his father[6]

Aboard the vessel *Le Havre,* April 25, 1831

... After breakfast, the passengers ordinarily go up on deck. Indeed, the idle remain there all day long, making observations about the weather. Less in need of killing time than they are, we return to our work at 11 o'clock. At the moment, we are translating an English book on the prisons of America, which is so important for the French government to know about that it may find our translation of interest. We will submit it upon our return. Since this kind of work is by nature rather boring, we intersperse it with reading that we find quite interesting and even more useful. We have already read the complete history of the United States. Now we are going all out on political economy with the work of Jean-Baptiste Say.[7] We find the study of this work quite appealing, and we are really quite happy when we shut ourselves up in our little cell to share ideas and pursue the truth in good faith. Tocqueville is a truly distinguished man. There is great loftiness in his ideas and great nobility in his soul. The better I know him, the more I like him. Our lives are now joined together. It is clear that our destinies are and always will be linked. This tie enlivens our friendship and brings us closer together. We are meditating ambitious projects. We will first do our best to accomplish our mission; this is a strict duty, which we must conscientiously fulfill. But as we study the penitentiary system, we will see America. While visiting its prisons, we will visit its inhabitants, its cities, its institutions, and its mores. We will come to know the workings of its republican government. That government is not known in Europe. People talk about it endlessly and make false comparisons with countries that in no way resemble the United States. Wouldn't it be good to have a book that gave an exact idea of the American people, that broadly set forth its history, that boldly portrayed its character, that analyzed its social state and rectified any number of erroneous opinions? What do you think, dear father, about this subject? Tell me, I beg you, how you feel about it.

6. Jules de Beaumont (1777–1851) was the mayor of Beaumont-la-Chartre, a village in the Loire Valley, southwest of Paris in the province of Sarthe. Though he was a conservative from an aristocratic lineage, Beaumont and his family avoided much of the political turmoil in nineteenth-century France by living in this country town, away from centers of discontent.

7. Jean-Baptiste Say (1767–1832) was a French economist whose most noted work was *Traité d'économie politique,* first published in 1803, which argued for the benefits of unrestricted competition and free trade. Say became famous for articulating the principle that supply creates its own demand.

From Tocqueville | To his mother[8]

Aboard the vessel *Le Havre,* May 9, 1831

. . . Last night we heard the cry "Land, ho!" for the first time, but one needed a spyglass to see the shore. Today the rising sun revealed Long Island. We are rapidly approaching the coast, and already we can see grass and leafy trees. It is a delightful sight. I leave you to join the others, who are celebrating on deck. Today no one is bothered by the sea.

During the Journey

FROM THE EAST COAST

From Tocqueville | To his mother

New York, May 14 [1831]

. . . We had sick passengers with us on the ship, and we were nearing the end of our fresh food supplies and even beginning to run short of wood and flour, which was worrisome. All the passengers gathered to insist that the captain avail himself of the west wind and make for the small town of Newport, which lies sixty leagues north of New York.[9] The captain agreed, and at eight o'clock on the evening of the 9th we dropped anchor in Newport's outer harbor. A sailor's dinghy soon came out to greet us. We were so happy to make landfall that all the young people on board and even the captain immediately leapt into the dinghy, and half an hour later we were standing on the dock in Newport, not without having dampened our behinds. I don't think I've ever seen people so happy to be alive. We jumped onto solid ground and pranced about a bit until we felt our legs once again solid beneath us. We then went straightaway to an inn, where the captain stood us to supper. What pleased me most about this meal was something that to you must seem utterly without value: the water. The water on board had not been potable for days (and I must say that the captain, though a fine man and good sailor, did a terrible job of stocking the ship, and a more uncomfortable vessel would be difficult to imagine).

---

8. Tocqueville's mother was Louise Le Peletier de Rosambo de Tocqueville (1771–1836), who married Hervé de Tocqueville in 1793. She came from an aristocratic family, members of the *noblesse de robe,* who derived their status from generations of judicial and administrative service. Her father served as the president of the Parlement of Paris. Her grandfather was Chrétien-Guillaume de Lamoignon de Malesherbes, who protected the *philosophes* while director of the book trade during the reign of Louis XV, served as a reformist minister early in the reign of Louis XVI, and then came out of retirement in 1792 to help defend the king at his trial before the National Convention. Louise's grandfather, parents, sister, and brother-in-law were guillotined in Paris in April 1794.

9. In 1831, just over eight thousand residents lived in Newport, Rhode Island.

To get back to our story, we stuffed ourselves to the gills (or at any rate, my companions did). Later we remembered *la galanterie française,* and after purchasing a substantial quantity of fresh provisions, we returned to the dinghy and were back aboard ship by midnight. Nobody on board was asleep, and, bearing our supplies in triumph, we went below decks to the ladies' salon, and we resumed our supper. I beg you to believe that when I say we supped, I refer in my own case only to the intellectual part of the evening.

The next day we visited the city, which seemed quite lovely. To be sure, we were hardly demanding visitors. The town consists of a cluster of small houses about the size of chicken coops, but agreeably clean, indeed spotless to a degree unimaginable in France. Outwardly the residents do not look very different from Frenchmen. They dress the same, and their features are so varied that it would be hard to say which nationalities they take after. I suppose it must be like this everywhere in the United States.

After savoring the pleasures of land for three hours, we boarded a huge steamship, which had come down from Providence and was on its way to New York. The interior of this enormous machine is difficult to describe. Suffice it to say that it included three large salons, two for men and one for women, large enough for four hundred, five hundred, or even eight hundred people to eat and sleep comfortably. To give you an idea of the ship's speed, I will add that despite the unfavorable wind and sea, we covered the sixty leagues between Newport and New York in eighteen hours.

This part of the American coast is flat and not very picturesque. In a region that was covered with impenetrable forests two centuries ago, there is scarcely a tree to be seen. Yet there was land on both sides of us, since we were navigating between Long Island and the Connecticut shore. At sunrise we approached New York, entering the port from the wrong end. Perhaps we were misled by the relatively unattractive appearance of what we had previously seen of the country as well as by our thirty-five days at sea, but we could not withhold a cry of admiration when we first glimpsed the outskirts of the city. Imagine a coast with the loveliest of silhouettes and slopes covered with grass and trees in blossom descending right down to the water's edge. And on top of all that, an incredible multitude of country houses the size of small cottages but very carefully appointed. Try also to imagine a sea dotted everywhere with sails, and you will have an idea of what it is like to enter New York harbor by way of the Sound.

I was so struck by how comfortable these little houses must be and by the pleasing appearance they lent to the landscape that I will try to get hold of the drawings or plans for a few of the prettiest ones. Émilie might make use of these for Nacqueville.[10] I already know that they don't cost a great deal. We have nothing like them in France.

10. Émilie de Belisle de Tocqueville (1805–1870), Tocqueville's sister-in-law, was married to Hippolyte de Tocqueville (1797–1877). Émilie had inherited Nacqueville, a château in

I am going to try to be brief, for if I start telling you about everything in detail, I'll be sending you a quarto-sized volume.

So here we are in New York: to the French eye the city has a strange and not very pleasant look.[11] There is not a dome, a steeple, or a major building in sight, so that you might easily believe that you were still in the suburbs. The inner city is built of brick, which makes for a very monotonous look. The houses have no cornices, balustrades, or coach entrances. The streets are very poorly paved, but they all have sidewalks for pedestrians.

We had a very hard time finding a place to stay, because at this time of the year the city is full of foreigners and we were looking for a boardinghouse rather than an inn. In the end we found a wonderful place on the most fashionable street, which is called Broadway. By a lucky stroke for which we thank our stars every day, Mr. Palmer, the Englishman I mentioned at the beginning of my letter, had already taken a room in the same house.[12] Because of the friendship we struck up with him during the crossing and, even more, because of his interest in the results of our journey, he is prepared to do whatever he can for us, and he has already been most useful. But the best is yet to come: you have no idea how much help and benefit we will have received here from people eager to assist us in our mission. Americans of every class seem to vie with one another to see who can be most useful and agreeable to us. To be sure, the newspapers, which take an interest in everything, announced our arrival and expressed the hope that eager assistance would be forthcoming wherever we went. As a result, all doors are open to us, and we have received the most flattering welcome everywhere. Having always traveled by stagecoach and stayed in inns, I find this new way of operating most agreeable. A major difficulty that we had to face the moment we left France, and that we are just now beginning to overcome, was that of language. In Paris, we thought we knew English, and in this respect we were like people who, upon graduating from grammar school, think of themselves as learned scholars. It did not take us long to disabuse ourselves of this notion. We knew just enough, however, to be able to learn the language quickly. On the ship we worked incredibly hard. There were times when we sat translating on the bridge in the midst of a storm that made it almost impossible to write. Unfortunately there were too many other passengers aboard who spoke French. Still, we made enormous progress. Once we landed, however, we had to give up our language entirely. Nobody speaks it. We therefore express ourselves entirely in English. It's often pitiful to listen to us, but in the end we manage to make ourselves understood, and we can understand everything. People assure us that we will eventually speak the language remarkably well. This will be a valu-

---

Normandy, in 1822. She and her husband took great interest in improving the grounds and gardens of the estate, and they began their renovations in earnest in 1830.

11. At the time of Tocqueville's visit, over two hundred thousand people resided in New York. Most of the population was concentrated around the southern tip of Manhattan Island.

12. Tocqueville had befriended the Englishman Charles Palmer (1777–1852), a former member of the British Parliament, on board of *Le Havre* on his voyage to America.

able acquisition. The usefulness of what we already know makes me conscious of the folly of people like Monsieur de Belisle, who travel to nations whose language they do not speak.[13] You might as well shutter the windows and take a tour of your bedroom.

You no doubt want to know, *ma chère Maman,* what sort of life we are currently leading. Here is a brief sketch. We rise at five or six and work until eight. At eight, a bell calls us to breakfast. Everyone appears punctually. Afterward, we set out to visit an institution or two or to converse with interesting people. We return for dinner at three. At five we usually go to our rooms to put our notes in order until seven, at which time we call on people for tea. This way of life is quite pleasant and I believe quite healthy, but it is contrary to all our habits. For instance, we were quite astonished the first day to see women coming down for breakfast at eight in the morning fully made up and prepared to remain that way until evening. This, we are told, is the custom in all private houses. It is perfectly proper to call on a lady at nine in the morning.

The absence of wine with our meals was quite disconcerting at first, and we still cannot quite conceive of the multitude of things that people put in their stomachs here. You know that in addition to breakfast, dinner, and tea, with which the Americans eat ham, they also serve a very copious supper and frequently a snack? Thus far this is the only respect in which I am prepared to grant that they are incontestably superior to us. But they believe that there are many others: the people here strike me as stinking with national pride. It shows through all their politeness.

Sunday, [May] 15

I resume my letter, *ma chère Maman,* on returning from high mass at a Catholic church five minutes from where we are staying. I had taken with me the small book that Bébé gave me, and I assure you that I thought of all of you during the mass, of him and you, dear mother.[14] I cannot tell you how moving it is to be so far from home and yet discover all the familiar religious rituals that we have known since childhood. For a moment I was so certain that I was in France that I turned and addressed my neighbors in French, but everyone attending the mass was American. The church, which is large, was as full as could be, and the atmosphere was more reverent than in French churches. The priest delivered a good sermon on grace, in English. We were delighted to discover that we understood perfectly every word he said. After the mass we called on the bishop. Unfortunately he is in Europe at the moment, but we learned that Father Powers, his vicar general, is a kind and friendly man who will surely give us a warm

13. Bon Georges Charles Evrard de Belisle was the father of Tocqueville's sister-in-law Émilie.

14. Abbé Christian Lesueur (1751–1831) was the childhood tutor of the orphaned Hervé de Tocqueville. Lesueur was a Jansenist, and his teachings were inflected by a belief in original sin, divine grace, and predestination. Although Lesueur fled during the Revolution, he returned to France and tutored his former student's three sons. Alexis became particularly close to him and nicknamed him "Bébé."

welcome.[15] We went to see him, but he was not home, so we will call again to-morrow.

Incidentally, the Catholic establishment in New York is quite substantial. They have five churches and more than 20,000 parishioners. I heard from some Americans that the number of proselytes is quite large. It is also growing in the various regions of the Union, and I would not be surprised if the religion, which has come under such sharp attack in Europe, made great progress here. Every year, 15 to 20 thousand European Catholics arrive here and fan out through the western wilderness, where people feel a greater need for religion than anywhere else. They become fervent if they were not already, or at any rate their children do. The need for a religious doctrine is so keenly felt on this side of the Atlantic that I have the impression that even Protestants have little esteem for Catholics who appear to neglect their faith. . . .

You're probably keen to know our plans for the months ahead. We have yet to make any final decisions. We are thinking of staying here for another three weeks or so. After that, we want to go to Boston and then return to New York, from which we will proceed to a small town called Auburn, a hundred leagues northwest of the city. A very famous penitentiary is located there.[16] People here have incredible contempt for distances, since you can travel day and night on the vast rivers whose mouths we have already glimpsed, or on the canals that have been built to connect one to another, making four leagues per hour while resting comfortably in a superb "house" that propels itself through the water without the slightest bump or jolt. You also save the time required to change horses at way stations. So here you don't say that you're a hundred leagues from some place but rather that it takes twenty-five hours to get there. . . .

From Beaumont | To his mother[17]

New York, May 14, 1831

My dear mother,

When I wrote you on May 8 on board *Le Havre,* we all thought we would make landfall the following day. A favorable wind filled our sails. At nine in the

15. The cornerstone for Saint Peter's Catholic Church had been laid in 1785. The bishop of Saint Peter's in New York was Jean Dubois (1764–1842), who had emigrated from France in 1791. He had lived in Virginia and Maryland before going to Saint Peter's in 1826, and he was one of the founders of Saint Mary's University and Seminary in Baltimore. Dubois was on a trip to Rome when Beaumont and Tocqueville visited New York. John Power (1792–1849) was an Irish priest who had arrived at Saint Peter's parish in 1819.

16. New York State built Auburn Prison in 1817. The methods used to manage prisoners—which included maintaining silence, grouping prisoners during the day, making them walk in lockstep, housing them in solitary confinement at night, and instituting harsh punishments for infractions of the rules—were meant to rehabilitate criminals. This system stood in contrast to the Philadelphia system, which sought to reform prisoners by keeping them in solitary confinement throughout the day as well as giving them individual work and instruction.

17. Rose Préau de la Baraudière (1778–1848), the wife of Jules de Beaumont (1777–1851), was from an aristocratic family and was the mother of Gustave and his three siblings.

Newport, 10 May 1831. Church steeple, "a rather remarkable architectural specimen," Beaumont noted on May 14. (GB1 *right;* GB2 *opposite*)

morning we were barely 20 leagues from New York, off Sandy Hook.[18] Suddenly, the wind changed. It turned against us and became quite violent. After being knocked about quite a bit and braving the wind on both tacks, that is, with the wind to both port and starboard, without making any headway, the captain, seeing that our food and other provisions were depleted and that no improvement in the weather could be expected, decided to make for Newport, a city in Rhode Island, one of the United States. We arrived there after passing the coasts of Long Island, Block Island, and Connecticut en route.

The sight of those shores filled our hearts with joy, as you can imagine. Nothing stood out on this part of the mainland, however. The coastal stretches seem almost wild and uninhabited. There were no picturesque sites to be seen. The coastline is low, flat, and unrelieved. But when you glimpse land after forty days at sea, it possesses a beauty and charm having nothing whatsoever to do with accidents of nature. By the time we reached Newport, it was already almost night. Tocqueville and I immediately ordered a dinghy to take us ashore. When we first set foot on land, we felt strangely elated. You become so used to the movement of the ship after a long time on board that when you find yourself back on dry land, it feels as though the ground is moving beneath your feet. Fixed objects seem to be in motion, and you're less steady on your feet than

18. Sandy Hook is a peninsula that juts out from New Jersey, forming the southeastern barrier for Lower New York Bay south of New York City.

you were aboard ship. Some of our fellow passengers joined us in town, and we were all so delighted to be ashore that we exchanged hugs.

Very early the next morning, May 10, we went to ask the customs officer for permission to bring our things ashore, which he granted. He made us swear on the Bible that we had nothing subject to duty, and in exchange for a small payment, one dollar (5.30 francs), we obtained a customs permit. What is more, the inspection of our trunks was highly perfunctory: it seems that the customs inspectors of Newport have nothing at all in common with their French counterparts. Once this formality was completed, we took a stroll around the town. It has a population of 16,000 and a magnificent port, newly fortified, and is full of small houses that might have been modeled on the kitchen at Beaumont-la-Chartre but are so clean that they could be parts of a stage set at the opera. All are painted. There is also a church with a steeple that is a rather remarkable architectural specimen. I did a sketch in Jules's album.[19] We had been told that the women of Newport were remarkable for their beauty, but we found them to be extraordinarily ugly one and all. There is nothing distinctive about the new population we found: it is neither English nor French nor German but a mixture of all nations. This is a mercantile nation. In the small town of Newport, there are four or five banks. The same is true of all the cities of the Union.

I forget to mention one very interesting thing about our stop in Newport.

19. Jules (1797–1877) was Gustave de Beaumont's oldest brother.

How can I express my thoughts about this subject? I am truly embarrassed, but in America there are no chestnut trees like ours. Suffice it to say that Tocqueville, Schérer, and I were in the group, and we laughed a great deal (can such a detail be included with other information that is so much more interesting and serious?).[20]

At 3 o'clock we boarded a steamship, a vast floating house big enough to hold eight hundred to a thousand passengers, all provided with beds. There were only 150 of us on this voyage, however. It took seventeen hours to travel the 60 leagues from Newport to New York.

This brief voyage was quite interesting and had some dangerous moments. To begin with, there is something prodigious about the navigation of such a vessel and the way it is steered. We proceeded along one of the most picturesque American coasts, the left shore of the Sound, which is situated between Long Island and Connecticut and the beginning of the state of New York (I include these details in case you have a map of the United States). Both shores of the Sound are rocky, and among the rocks you see some of the prettiest country houses you can imagine. The Sound is immense but not so wide that you cannot make out everything on both shores. As you approach New York, the channel narrows, and you get a better view of the details of what you initially saw in panorama. The country houses are like gingerbread cottages. They nestle among the trees that grow in profusion along the rocky shores. Numerous bays penetrate inland in the most picturesque manner. The scenery was truly lovely. Of course we have equally beautiful places in France, but not of the same kind. What particularly struck us was the animation imparted to this majestic canvas by the huge number of brigs, schooners, lighters, and barks of all shapes and sizes moving incessantly to and fro. As you know, ships can move in opposite directions by setting their sails in a certain way relative to the wind.

We arrived in New York on the morning of the twelfth. We were quite tired. We entered a kind of a hotel known as a boardinghouse. This is nothing other than a *pension,* and we were introduced to the other guests and immediately felt at home. It is not too expensive. Afterward we went to sleep, even though it was the middle of the day. We were so tired, so beaten down and worn out, that no pleasure seemed greater than that of a comfortable bed. We went to sleep at 4 in the afternoon, and the next morning at 8 we were still in bed.

I won't say anything about the city of New York, because I have not yet had a chance to get to know it. We are living in the prettiest neighborhood, which is not much to look at.[21] I have barely been out except to call on a few people who live quite nearby. Everyone here has been extremely gracious and kind. They vie with one another to welcome us and do us favors. We have a thousand letters of recommendation that we could easily have done without, because people antici-

20. Schérer was the son of General Barthélemy Schérer, commander of the Army of Italy during the Napoleonic campaigns at the end of the eighteenth century.
21. The travelers were staying at a boardinghouse in a fashionable neighborhood on Broadway in Lower Manhattan.

pate our desires. We will soon be forced to bar our door. Our arrival in America *has caused a sensation.* We are in all the American newspapers.

In my next letter I will give you more details about our present situation. I will keep this letter short, because I want to dispatch it by way of England. The packet boat for Liverpool leaves on the 16th of this month, whereas the packet boat for Le Havre will not leave until the 20th. I am going to add these four pages to my brief letter of May 8, which I was unable to send as I had anticipated because we did not meet up as hoped with the Liverpool packet boat. In any case, I will send my other letters via the packet for France on the 20th, and in them you will find details about our crossing that you may find interesting. So tell me which of the two letters arrives first. . . .

From Beaumont | To his father

New York, May 16, 1831

I told Mama in the letter I sent via England about the circumstances of my arrival in New York. I want to bring you up to date, Father, on my position here. Tocqueville and I have been most graciously welcomed by all the Americans to whom we have introduced ourselves. One of our first visits was to the consul of France, the baron de Saint-André, for whom we had a letter from the minister of foreign affairs.[22] He has a wife and children. They are friendly people. He immediately invited us to dinner. There was little to be gained from their conversation, however. They have no knowledge of the country they are living in and are utterly ungifted for observation. We dine with them again today, which is annoying because we have far better things to do. Mr. Palmer, the Englishman I mentioned to you earlier, continues to lavish us with attention and care. He is looking to put us in contact with anyone who might be useful to us. We were introduced to the governor of New York, to the mayor of the city, to the recorder and aldermen and nearly all the magistrates. Several of them even came to us, to offer their services.

We may soon be forced to make ourselves unavailable from time to time, so as to preserve a bit of leisure time to reflect on all the things we have seen.

The new society in which we find ourselves is utterly unlike our European societies. It has no model anywhere. Its basic conditions of existence are also unlike those of any other society, so that it would be dangerous for others to imitate it.

It is a rather remarkable thing to see a great nation that has no army, a vigorous and active country in which the action of the government is almost imperceptible. But what does this signify for the states of Europe? The United States has no ambitious neighbors to fear. It is more powerful than the surrounding nations. What purpose would it serve to have an army?

22. Durant de Saint-André (1767–1860) lived in New York as a French minister to the United States from 1823 to 1831. He began his diplomatic career in 1797 and served as minister to a number of European countries until his retirement in 1847.

In the United States, political parties are almost unknown. Individuals will sometimes vie for offices and public employments, but fundamental arrangements are never questioned. The only interest that is of vital concern to all is *commerce.* This is the *national passion,* and in order for merchants to go about their business there is no need to keep a national guard and infantry regiments under arms. But can the same thing be said of states whose citizens have long been divided by internal strife and in which the government is constantly obliged to use force to disarm factions?

As noted above, the Americans are a *merchant* people: they are devoured by an appetite for riches, which brings in its wake a host of not very honorable passions such as greed, dishonesty, and deception. People here seem to have but one thought and one aim: to get rich. At the same time, bankruptcy, which is common in every city, is considered a trifle, if that.

This is no doubt a serious flaw. Yet it is impossible not to notice that this is a highly moral nation. At first sight, this might seem difficult to reconcile with what I have just said, but let me try to explain.

Morals are extremely pure here. It is said to be very rare for a woman to behave improperly. There are no unhappy marriages to speak of. People gather frequently during the winter, but gatherings are mostly limited to the family. Unmarried men lavish their attention exclusively on single girls. When a woman marries, she is devoted exclusively to her husband. Until she is engaged, however, she will behave quite freely in her relations with men. For instance, girls can be seen strolling about on their own. Young men can approach them or go to the country alone with them, and people find all this quite natural. The parents of a young woman see nothing wrong with her receiving men at home, but this life of liberty ends the day she marries.

On the whole, the apparent happiness of family life is rather appealing. To be sure, I would never want to take a wife in a foreign country, because any number of unwelcome consequences might follow from such a union. But when we see the happiness that is so common here and so rare in other countries, Tocqueville and I cannot help thinking that, should we fall victim to some political eventuality in France, we would bring our wives and children here to live.

What is the source of such impressive morality in the habits of a people who, as we have seen, are not always virtuous? I think that I will be better equipped to answer that question in a little while than I am now. Already, however, I see several possible explanations. First and foremost, society is ruled by the spirit of religion. Nowhere else are religious ideas more respected than they are here. All denominations are free and respected here, but a person who belonged to no denomination would be regarded as *a brute*. This opinion is widely shared, and someday we will explain why this is so. For now I shall merely state it as a fact.

Second, as I was telling you, there is only one class here, the *merchants,* all of whom have the same interest and are competing for only one thing, *wealth*. Hence there is no idle class, and there is no group of men who, if they weren't busy seducing women, would have nothing else to do.

Why are our garrison towns more immoral than other places? Because the presence of a regiment increases the number of idle men in town, men whose only pastime is to corrupt and seduce. Here, commerce and industry absorb everyone's energy. There is no time for mischief. In addition, the American temperament is more cold-blooded than ours. People here therefore find that it is in their interest to be moral. The religion in which they believe commands them to be so, and their blood, rather than stand in their way, encourages this religious disposition or predilection to behave morally.

I intend to study carefully the various religious sects that can be found here and explain how they are able to coexist in such perfect harmony. Catholicism apparently attracts new converts daily. There are several Roman Catholic churches here in addition to a cathedral. We visited them yesterday. The bishop,

Battery and Port of New York, 22 June 1831. "The port is huge" and the rivers filled "with hundreds of ships and boats," Beaumont reported on May 16. (GB1 *opposite top*; GB2)

M. Dubois, is away at the moment. We found this out when we went to see him. We then asked to see the grand vicar, who was also absent. We attended mass, and a Catholic priest delivered a sermon in English, which we understood quite well (we are making good progress in the language, which we speak from morning till night). In the church we found Madame de Saint-André, who invited us to share her pew. Sundays are very strictly observed here. Not a single person works. In contrast to Paris, the shops are closed, and nothing can be read other than the Bible.

I will not describe New York for you, because I am still not sufficiently acquainted with the city. But Saturday night Tocqueville and I were out walking when we saw an open church. It was empty except for a few pious souls at prayer. The door to the stairway leading up to the steeple was open. We climbed the dark, steep staircase from landing to landing and at last, with much difficulty, reached the top, where we enjoyed a lovely view: a city of 240,000 people on an island with the sea straight ahead and, to either side, broad rivers filled with hundreds of ships and boats.[23] The port is huge. Public buildings are rare and on the whole not very distinguished.

The fine arts are in their infancy here. Commerce and industry procure riches but fail to develop good taste. As for the Americans' political ideas about France, you mustn't think that they are as enthusiastic as is sometimes said about our revolutionaries. On the whole, they regard "the hero of two worlds" as a worthy fellow whose judgment left something to be desired and who sought to apply certain political theories to a nation to which those theories were unsuited.[24]

Furthermore, the aristocracy of wealth is as avid for distinctions here as it is elsewhere. A great deal of attention is paid to old families. I was quite surprised to hear these proud champions of equality address one another as "honorable esquire." Their carriages bear their coats of arms.

This eagerness for superiority is ubiquitous. Americans are unusually proud people. This has something to do with the praise that is lavished on their government in Europe. Hence if you want to get on well with them, you must praise them endlessly. I do so wholeheartedly, though it has no effect on the way I see them. Because of this national pride, Americans do everything they can to impress us and show us only the good side of things. I hope that we will nevertheless succeed in discovering the truth.

You cannot imagine how busy we are. We have no time to breathe. There is an endless round of friendly invitations, practical errands, official presentations, etc. *They compete for our attention,* and everyone wants to make our stay in New York as pleasant as possible. The Schermerhorn family, which was with us on the crossing, is one of the wealthiest and most respectable in the city.[25] They

23. The 1830 census counted the population of New York to be 202,589 persons.
24. Beaumont is referring to the marquis de Lafayette.
25. Peter Schermerhorn (1781–1852) and his wife and three sons were returning to New York after living in Europe for two years. Schermerhorn had made a fortune in the family's shipping business and was a prominent member of New York society.

have been most kind to us. Mr. Prime, our banker, who is the wealthiest man in the area, has also been extremely attentive.[26]

So there you have it, and we have as yet made use of only two of our letters of recommendation. We have seventy more to go, and we see now that we could have done without any at all. I will not try to persuade you that Tocqueville and I have adhered strictly to our good intentions over the past two months. Nor will I say that we are so delighted with our good behavior that we hope never to stray from the straight and narrow. To say such things would be presumptuous rather than a mark of fortitude.

Although we are obliged to spend substantial sums for a certain number of things, we do not find life here very expensive. We anticipate that we will have all the money we need for our trip and perhaps more. We aim to be as economical as we can, and we are spending only what is absolutely necessary to live and to maintain our position appropriately.

A packet boat left Liverpool (on April 8) and arrived here last night. It brought English newspapers, and thus I was able this morning to read the very interesting news from France. It seems that we are more than ever at peace. The coffers have begun to fill again, and the government seems to be consolidating its position.

However much I might wish to continue this letter forever, I absolutely must bring it to an end. I will enclose it with the letter I'm sending to Achille.[27] If I continue to fill volumes this way, I will certainly ruin you with postage fees. But please remember that you haven't received a word from me for six weeks, and had I written once a week you would have had to bear the cost of six deliveries, which together would surely have cost as much as this one. I promise to be less garrulous in the future, however. Still, although I beg your pardon for writing at such length, I want you to know that my most ardent desire is to receive interminable missives from you.

When you answer, Father, please tell me what you think of the ideas I have ventured to put down on paper about what I have seen thus far, and above all let me know what you think of the country in which I find myself. Do you believe that this country is destined to a great place among the civilized nations of the world? Do you think that its institutions rest on solid foundations? Do you believe that it will remain united for long?

If the states of the Union were to separate, do you think that their republican institutions would survive? Wouldn't war between brothers require placing all social forces in the hands of one man? Wouldn't this lead to dictatorial and soon monarchical authority? What is your opinion of the American character? What do you think is responsible for the purity of their morals? Do you consider them to be a great and virtuous people?

26. Nathaniel Prime (1786–1840), a self-made man of fortune, was the first president of the New York Stock and Exchange Board.

27. Beaumont's brother Achille (1799–1871) was at Beaumont-la-Chartre.

There are a thousand other questions that might be asked. But I see that I am starting yet another sheet of paper though I had sworn not to add further to the weight of this essay.

The letters I send you contain my first impressions, and I may someday enjoy rereading them even if my opinions have changed completely, so I ask you to hold on to them.

Since some blank paper still remains and there is no longer any chance of sparing you this page, I will use the space to ask for your private opinion about *American government* in general, apart from the observations that I have sent you. I ask you this because it is very important to know what the general view is in France. If we publish a book someday, we will have to write it in a way that can be clearly understood, and we will need to know what readers think before they open the book. Two months ago, I saw things the same way as everybody else does. But what I've seen since then has inevitably altered my opinion, and I am not sure that I will be able to recover my previous state of mind. . . .

From Tocqueville | To Louis de Kergorlay[28]

[New York] May 18, 1831

. . . Until now, nothing I've seen has aroused my enthusiasm, because it's all more a product of nature than of man's will. So much for my impressions so far. Still, it's a vast spectacle to behold. No nation has ever enjoyed such a promising and hopeful situation. Here human freedom acts in all the plenitude of its power, and its energy feeds on anything that is useful to someone without doing harm to anyone. To be sure, there is something *feverish* about the energy that drives industry and the human spirit here. Thus far, however, this fever seems only to have increased man's strength without denaturing his reason. Whatever people do, physical nature always dominates all efforts to make use of the resources it provides. What remains to be done seems to expand in proportion to what has already been done. New York, whose population was 20,000 at the time of the American war, now boasts 200,000, and its annual growth is prodigious, adding considerably to the country's grandeur with each passing year. People assure us that the population of the Mississippi wilderness is growing even more rapidly. Everyone agrees that the most fertile soil in America is to be found there in virtually endless supply. Amid all the incredible material bustle, the political agitation strikes me as quite secondary. It is on the surface and doesn't stir the masses

28. Louis de Kergorlay (1804–1880) was a cousin and childhood friend of Tocqueville. After Kergorlay refused to swear an oath to Louis-Philippe, his military career stalled, and he led an inactive life in the decades when Tocqueville's fame was growing. In 1833, Kergorlay was imprisoned for supporting a legitimist attempt to overthrow Louis-Philippe and to instate as monarch the duchesse de Berry, the widowed daughter-in-law of Charles X, who created a scandal when she secretly married an Italian commoner. Tocqueville argued his only case in a court of law when he defended Kergorlay at trial in 1833. Despite their divergent political leanings, the two remained close friends throughout their lives.

deeply. We are told that it is difficult to persuade men to accept public office that would take time away from private affairs. The fact is that society steers itself and is fortunate to encounter no obstacle in its path. Government here seems to me in the infancy of the art. . . .

From Tocqueville | To Ernest de Chabrol[29]

New York, May 18, 1831

My dear friend,

Here I am, arrived in this country. It wasn't easy, I assure you. First, heavy winds kept us on the Newfoundland bank for nearly ten days. When at last we finally drew within sight of the American coast, bad weather combined with a shortage of fresh food to force us to land in Newport, a town some 60 leagues from New York.

We dropped anchor there on May 9, 35 days after departing Le Havre. Beaumont and I were so tired of the ocean and of the uncertain winds that instead of remaining aboard and continuing under sail to New York, we boarded a steamboat that brought us here in 18 hours and in the utmost comfort. Rest assured that I am properly pleased to be back on land. Nevertheless, of those on board, we tolerated the crossing far better than anyone else. I was sick only two days, and Beaumont not at all.

The time passed more quickly than you might think thanks to translations from English into French, reading books about America, conversations in English, and rather pleasant company. And in the end we would have gotten used to this life if we had been able to see something other than sky and water. But ultimately the solitude and monotony of the Atlantic weigh on the mind and sap the soul.

There were some extraordinary and sublime sights along the way, but I will keep all that for a time when we are together again in front of the fireplace in that fine, close intimacy that I constantly miss. For now, I have many other things to tell you, and the ship that is to carry this letter sails on the next tide, which, as you know, waits for no man.

We have not yet received any news from France. You cannot believe, dear friend, how trying this is. We left our country and all whom we hold most dear in a position so critical that we cannot enjoy a moment's peace.[30]

What has become of you—you in particular? When I left you, you were close to a major decision. Did you in fact make up your mind? Will you introduce us to Madame de Chabrol on our return? All of this interests me greatly. I

29. Ernest de Chabrol-Chaméane was a childhood friend of Tocqueville. Chabrol had replaced Beaumont as deputy public prosecutor at Versailles in 1829 and had lived with Tocqueville before his departure for America.

30. In July of 1830, the French Bourbon king Charles X had issued a series of ordinances that restricted political rights, dissolved the Chamber of Deputies, and called for new elec-

am enclosing a thick letter for Marie.[31] I cannot tell you how often I've thought of her since leaving France. Call it a mystery of the human heart, if you like, but I assure you that I have never loved her as much as since she has been out of my sight. Until now, absence has had the opposite effect on me. The fact is that I didn't think I was so attached to her. When you reply, I beg you to tell me everything you know about her. Tell me what has become of her and what she is doing. Does she ever think of me? Send me details. I thank you in advance.

That is not the only favor I have to ask of you. For Beaumont's sake as well as mine, I ask that you write as much as you possibly can about—you may laugh—what people in France think about this country. Since leaving France, we have lived with Americans, both aboard ship and since our arrival here, with the result that we slowly and gradually became accustomed to the new order of things in the midst of which we find ourselves. We have already shed most of our national prejudices about Americans. Yet I'm sure that you can sense how much we need to know the prevailing opinions at home if we hope to change them, and even just to decide what we need to study more closely here in order to provide useful instruction back home.

So do what you can to gather your thoughts and the thoughts of others on this subject and send them to us. For instance, what idea of American political institutions exists in France? And what ideas of the national character, the various classes of society, the commercial state, the future of this country, and its religious situation?

---

tions. Riots erupted in the Paris streets in protest of these ordinances on July 27, 1830, and lasted for three days. Two factions developed among the insurrectionists: the republicans and the constitutional monarchists. The constitutional monarchists triumphed when Lafayette proclaimed from the Hôtel de Ville in Paris that Louis-Philippe, duc d'Orléans and a member of the younger branch of the Bourbon family, would become king of France. Charles X abdicated on August 2, and Louis-Philippe was installed as king one week later.

Tocqueville witnessed the first street riots in Paris and was shocked and dismayed at the violence. He volunteered his service to the resurrected National Guard at Versailles in an attempt to help keep peace at the seat of the Bourbon monarchy, even though he thought the Bourbons had acted cowardly in the face of the revolts. There he helped to prevent a massacre when a mob of protesters seized arms stored in the palace's barracks. Although Tocqueville pledged allegiance to Louis-Philippe, the new regime sensed his ambivalence as a legitimist who had supported the previous, elder line of Bourbon rulers. The new government's distrust of Tocqueville, paired with his increasing discomfort in France, prompted his trip to America with Beaumont.

31. Tocqueville is referring to his sweetheart, Mary "Marie" Mottley (1799–1864). An orphaned Englishwoman, Marie was raised by an aunt in France. She and Tocqueville met in 1828, and by 1830 they had established a close relationship. Tocqueville sent his letters to her via Ernest de Chabrol. Alexis de Tocqueville and Marie Mottley married in 1835, but Tocqueville's family never completely welcomed her into the fold because she came from a middle-class British family.

While I'm on this subject, I would like to ask you a series of questions, to which you may respond if you choose.

What is your idea of the power of Congress over the Union in general and each state in particular? To what cause do you ascribe this nation's prosperity? What degree of civilization do you think the American people have achieved, and precisely what forms does this civilization take? How do things here stand, in your opinion, with respect to the spirit of society, the literary spirit, the pleasures of the imagination, and the fine arts?

Do you think that there are political parties in the United States? How far do you think they have taken the spirit of equality? Is it in mores or in laws? What form do you imagine it takes?

How do you understand freedom of the press in the United States, freedom of commerce, the right to vote, and the right to run for office?

Chat, gossip, and expand on all these questions in your reply. And that is not all. You need to share with us your ideas about what it would be most useful for us to examine in this country and what issues would be most likely to attract public attention and be most useful to society as it is in France today.

If I weren't so certain of your friendship, my dear Chabrol, I wouldn't impose such a thankless task on you. You may find this letter tiresome, because I have deliberately avoided talking about America lest I have on you the same effect that my traveling companions had on me. But I promise you that I will make up for this abundantly in my next letter, which should arrive shortly after this one. . . .

I have another favor to ask of you. We cannot find here a book that we badly need to help us make sense of American society: Guizot's lectures and essays of the past three years on Roman society and the Middle Ages.[32] I have copies of all the printed lectures, which I placed in one of the compartments of my small hanging bookshelf. Would you do me the favor of packing them up and sending them to me here, care of Mr. Prime? I'm not sure what the best way to pack them is, but I trust you to figure it out and dispatch the parcel as soon as possible. . . .

I do not think I will violate my own resolution if I tell you that we are leading a very pleasant life here. Our letters, along with the publicity that has been given to the purpose of our trip, have opened all doors to us. We are the objects of much attention and consideration. Our travels are therefore much more pleasant than they might have been otherwise, and our observations are greatly facilitated. The language is still a problem, but we are beginning to understand everything, and before long I hope we will be able to express ourselves freely. We absolutely must master English, because French is little spoken here.

---

32. François Guizot (1787–1874) held the chair in modern history at the Sorbonne, where Tocqueville and Beaumont followed his famous lectures on the history of civilization. A major conservative political figure of the July Monarchy, serving as minister of the interior, minister of public instruction, minister of foreign affairs, and prime minister, he was the effective head of the cabinet after 1840.

This is how we are living: we get up at five and breakfast at eight. After breakfast, we do our business and visit public institutions. At three, we dine. After dinner, we either take a walk or go back to work, and in the evening we take tea in homes to which we are invited. Our good behavior thus far is a terrifying thing to behold: we haven't yet . . . not once. Believe it if you can. What is more, we have made the heroic resolution to persist in this course. As to whether or not we shall succeed, I hesitate to be quite so categorical.

We do not yet know exactly how we shall proceed henceforth. We intend to remain here for at least another three weeks, however. After that, we will probably go to Boston and then up the Hudson and to Niagara Falls. Our plans are still vague. In the meantime, remember that you should always write to us here, no matter where we may be in America. . . .

Whatever happens, do not forget that I am the one who sent you the girl next door.[33] Any favors you do for her will mean more to me than if you did them for me personally.

Farewell, my good friend, I embrace you with all my heart.

From Tocqueville | To his brother Édouard[34]

New York, May 28, 1831

. . . We are really and truly in another world. Political passions here are merely on the surface. The deep passion, the only one that deeply moves the human heart, the passion that is always present, is for the acquisition of wealth, and there are a thousand ways to get rich without involving the government. In my opinion, you'd have to be really blind to want to compare this country with Europe and adapt what works in one place for use in the other. I believed this before I left France. I believe it more and more as I study the society in which I am living at the moment. This is a nation of merchants, which takes up public affairs when its work leaves it the leisure to do so. I hope that when we return to Europe, we will be in a position to say some pertinent things on this subject. Perhaps no one has ever been better situated than we are to study a people. Our mission and our letters give us access everywhere. We have regular contact with all classes of society. We are supplied with all the documents anyone could wish for. Finally, our purpose in coming here was purely serious. Our mind has been focused steadily on the acquisition of useful knowledge. The labor is immense but not arduous because in a way we are soaking up ideas through every pore, and we learn as much in a drawing room or on a walk as we do when closeted in our studies.

But will we have the time to complete our undertaking? Will events that I

33. Marie Mottley.
34. Tocqueville's brother Édouard de Tocqueville (1800–1874) was the second child of Hervé and Louise de Tocqueville. Édouard served in the army until 1822, and after his marriage to a wealthy woman in 1829, he became the proprietor of a country estate at Baugy.

hope will not occur yet that without being a wizard one can foresee bring us back to Europe? . . .

From Tocqueville | To Abbé Lesueur

New York, May 28, 1831

. . . In my last letter, I think I told you that we had had a good voyage and had found a very comfortable and pleasant place to stay in New York. Our satisfaction has not diminished, and if we were not so preoccupied by thoughts of what might be happening in Europe, we would consider ourselves quite happy.

You cannot imagine how warmly we have been received here. As I told *Maman,* the newspapers have on several occasions mentioned the purpose of our mission (and let it be said in passing that the national pride of our hosts finds it quite flattering), and the result has been a degree of attentiveness that astonishes us daily. Not only do we have free access to all public places and documents, but the people in charge of institutions seek us out in order to show them off.

Yesterday, the mayor and aldermen of New York, . . . twenty-five or thirty in all, took us on a ceremonial visit to all the city's prisons and poorhouses.[35] Afterward, we were invited to a lavish dinner, the first such we have attended. I want to describe it for you, but the task is not an easy one. Imagine a long table, such as you might see in a refectory, at the head of which sat the mayor, flanked by your humble servants. The rest of the guests were arrayed around the table, all of them personages so serious that the sight of them would be enough to make you weep: laughter is rare on this side of the Atlantic.

As for the dinner itself, the culinary arts here are still in their infancy: vegetables and fish were served before the meat, oysters for dessert—in a word, utter barbarity. My first glance at the table took a great weight off me. I saw no wine but only, as usual, water and spirits. Accordingly, I sat myself down with appropriate gravity to the mayor's right and awaited what was to follow. Unfortunately, after the soup was taken away, wine was served. The mayor toasted our health in the English manner, which consists in filling a small glass, raising it while fixing an eye on one's guest, and drinking it down, all with the utmost solemnity. The person toasted in this manner is expected to respond in exactly the same way. So we each drank our glass of wine, still with appropriate dignity. Thus far all was going well.

We began to tremble, however, when we saw that each of the guests saw it as his duty to honor us in the same way. We resembled hares closely pursued by a pack of hounds, and the fact is that they would soon have had us at their mercy if we had allowed them to go on. With the third glass, however, I decided to swallow no more than a mouthful, and in that way I managed quite felicitously to make it to what we in France call the end of the dinner, which here is but the first act. By this point most of the dishes had been removed, and the

35. Walter Browne (1770–1846) served as the mayor of New York during Tocqueville's visit.

waiters came in with lighted candles and dishes on which were arrayed several cigars. Each guest took a cigar, a cloud of smoke enveloped the company, another round of toasts began, the guests' muscles relaxed ever so slightly, and the world's most lugubrious exercise in gaiety began.

Now you have a clear idea of what a ceremonial dinner in America is like. I confess that during this august ceremony I could not help laughing up my sleeve at the thought of the difference that 1500 leagues of ocean makes in a man's position. I was reminded of the less than insignificant role that was mine in France two months ago and of the comparatively high place in which we find ourselves here, as well as of the little notice our mission has attracted at home compared to the attention it has drawn here—and all of this is due to that short stretch of ocean I mentioned earlier.

I assure you, though, that we're not playing the *grand seigneur*. On the contrary, we're the best princes in the world and are a long way from accepting the attentions we receive as our due. But these people, who have no important political interests to argue about and who see nothing more worthy of a government's attention than the state of prisons and penal legislation, insist on treating us as supremely worthy young men entrusted with an extremely important mission. Even French officials treat us as very distinguished visitors and, since they know our families, supply us with useful details—because you know that in this republican country, people are a thousand times more impressed with nobility, titles, medals, and all such European trinkets than we are in France. The greatest equality prevails here in the law and apparently even in mores, but I tell you, the Devil is none the worse off for it. And the pride that cannot be shown outwardly has no trouble finding a good hiding place in the depths of the soul. Occasionally we share a good laugh at the eagerness of people we know to show off their connections with the leading families of Europe, and at the effort they make to cling for dear life to whatever social distinction they are permitted to attain, no matter how trivial.

Tomorrow we go to Sing Sing, a village on the North River ten leagues from New York.[36] We will spend a week there studying the discipline in the vast penitentiary that was built there recently.[37] Thus far we have seen enough to persuade us that prisons here arouse general interest and that in several respects they are much better than prisons in France.

But that's still only a superficial impression. We're really pleased to be going to Sing Sing. You can't imagine anything more beautiful than the North or Hudson River. The immense width of the river, the admirable richness of the north bank and the steep mountains along the east bank make this one of the world's

36. Sing Sing, now known as Ossining, New York, is thirty miles north of New York City. It is located on the southern part of the Hudson River, which was commonly called the North River.

37. Mount Pleasant Penitentiary, now known as Sing Sing Prison, opened in 1828. Wardens used the same management system as at Auburn.

loveliest sites. But this is still not the America I would like to see. Every day we envy the first Europeans who, two hundred years ago, discovered the mouth of the Hudson for the first time and who sailed upstream when both banks were blanketed with vast forests and one saw only the smoke from the campfires of savages above the place now filled with the bustle of New York's 200,000 inhabitants—which goes to show that man is never satisfied with anything.

To get back to more positive thoughts, the country we find ourselves in is most unusual: the cost of living—eating and sleeping—is no higher than in Paris, but everything man-made costs a fortune. A suit of clothes costs 200 francs, a pair of trousers, 50, boots, 40 francs, and so on. It's all the same to me, because I think I have enough clothes for the entire trip, and I will have some shoes made.

But here is something that may turn out to be a considerable expense for us: a pair of kid gloves costs six francs here. As you know, gloves of this sort can only be worn once, you can't go out in the evening without them, and we are out on the town every night. It occurred to us that we could save a great deal by having gloves sent to us from Europe, for even with the cost of shipping and customs the price would be only about two-thirds of what it is here. I am therefore asking Édouard to buy some gloves for us, pack them up, and ship them to New York by whatever means people in Paris say is best. I am asking him also to include a pair of silk stockings for the evening and one or two black silk ties. Silk costs a fortune here. Papa will reimburse him.

Thus far we are fairly pleased with the state of our finances, or at any rate we are quite certain that it would be impossible to live more economically. Tell Papa for me that to date we haven't spent one *sou* that wasn't absolutely *necessary* in every sense of the word. At the end of our first month here, I will send him a rough accounting of our expenses in America. I assure you that I am very keen to weigh on his budget as little as possible, and I will do my utmost to achieve that end. . . .

From Tocqueville | To his father[38]

Sing Sing, June 3, 1831

You will never guess, my dear father, where I'm writing you from. I want to begin my letter by describing the place. I am at the top of a fairly substantial hill on a bank of the Hudson. A hundred paces from where I sit, the country house we are staying in occupies the foreground of the landscape. At the foot of

38. Hervé de Tocqueville (1772–1856), from an old family of the *noblesse d'épée* (the French aristocracy distinguished by their military service), was orphaned at the age of thirteen and educated by Abbé Lesueur. After narrowly escaping the guillotine during the Terror of the French Revolution, he became the patriarch of his extended family. He held minor political offices under the rule of Napoleon, of whom he disapproved from his legitimist view that the Bourbons were the rightful rulers of France. During the Bourbon Restoration from 1814 to 1830, Hervé de Tocqueville served as a prefect for a number of departments. He was appointed to the Chamber of Peers in 1827, but he lost his seat under the July Monarchy.

Mount Pleasant, 3 June 1831. House, river, and boats; "the river's banks are as lovely to look at as anything in the world," Tocqueville wrote on that day. (GB2)

the hill lies the river, which is a league and a quarter wide and filled with sails. It flows down from the north, where it vanishes into a background of tall blue mountains. The river's banks are as lovely to look at as anything in the world. There is an air of prosperity, activity, and industry about them that is a joy to behold. The whole scene basks in lovely sunshine, which penetrates the humid atmosphere and bathes everything in a soothing, transparent glow. As you can judge from the length of the description, the writer is seated in a comfortable place from which to observe the landscape. Indeed, there is atop the highest hill in the area an enormous plane tree, and I am perched in its branches to avoid the heat. It is from there that I write. Beaumont has gone down to the foot of the hill to draw what I am describing to you in words. As you see, we complement each other. Now I must tell you where we are, why we are here, and how we got here. Sing Sing, named for an Indian chief who lived here sixty years ago but whose tribe has since moved farther inland, is located on the Hudson eleven leagues north of New York. It is a town of 1,000 to 1,200 people, which is famous because of its prison. This institution, the largest in the United States, holds 900 inmates under the penitentiary system. We have come here to study this system in depth. We have been here a week and are enjoying ourselves more than you can possibly imagine. We had begun to tire of the extreme bustle of life in New York, of the number of visits that we were obliged to make and receive every day. Here, life is both as full and as tranquil as can be. We are staying with a respectable family of Americans, who are most solicitous of our welfare. In the village we have made the acquaintance of a few people, whom we will call on when we are at liberty to do so. The rest of our time is spent visiting the prison, taking and revising notes, and collecting as much practical information about the penitentiary system as we can. Our work is made easier by the eagerness of government officials to provide us with whatever documents we may need. Unfortunately, some of what we need doesn't exist. Generally speaking, in regard to administration, this country seems to suffer from precisely the opposite excess as France. With us, the government is involved in everything. Here, there is no government, or at any rate there appears to be none. They seem to know as little about the good points of centralization as about the bad. No central motor regulates the operation of the machine. Thus it is impossible to form general conclusions about many things. To apply this point to the penitentiary system, it is impossible to obtain any fully satisfactory figures about the number of recidivists. Yet as you know, it is absolutely essential that we determine this number.

It would take a very long letter to describe the impression that the prisons we have visited have made on us. I don't want to embark on such a description now. You would come to the conclusion that the penitentiary system is the only thing we have been concerned with in America. That is far from the case, I assure you. On the contrary, we are using our time here in a myriad of different ways. Maybe that is why it seems to be slipping through our fingers with frightening speed. I think that even if we don't manage to produce anything passable about the United States, we won't have wasted our time if we devote ourselves fully to our work, of which there is enough to occupy all our time. The truth is that we have had only one idea since we arrived: to get to know the country in which we are traveling. To do this, we first have to analyze society and ask ourselves what elements compose it at home in order to ask useful questions here and not leave anything out. This research, which is very difficult but also very absorbing, has revealed a wealth of details that can be easily lost if not incorporated into an analysis; it has also led us to make innumerable observations and discover many practical ideas that would never have occurred to us otherwise. Already our work has given rise to a series of questions that we endeavor constantly to answer. Since we know precisely what questions we want to ask, even the most trivial conversation is instructive, and we can say with confidence that there is no man, no matter what his station in society, who has nothing to teach us. We would be perfectly content with this life, which is a mixture of intellectual and physical activity, were it not for the gulf that separates us from France. But the thought of being so far away from you spoils everything. I've no doubt said this before, my dear father, but I feel the need to repeat it: to live so far away from everyone one loves is to be only half alive. It is life lived in the head, in which the heart plays no part. The consequent aridity of our impressions is dispiriting. Now that we have become *research machines,* my dear father, you may want to ask what about this country has struck me most. It would take a volume to tell you everything, and tomorrow I may change my mind, because we are not, I assure you, wedded to any system. Yet there are two or three vivid impressions that I would indeed like to share with you. At this point two ideas loom large: the first is that these people are among the happiest in the world; the second is that they owe their immense prosperity not to their own virtues and still less to a form of gov-

A mill, a cow, and a bull, New York, 18 June 1831. (GBI)

ernment that in itself is superior to others but rather to the special conditions in which they find themselves, unique conditions that establish a perfect relationship between their political constitution and their needs and social state. This may be a bit metaphysical, but you will understand what I mean quite well when I tell, for example, that nature here has so much to offer human industry that the class of theoretical speculators simply does not exist. Everyone works, and the mine is still so richly endowed that everyone who works quickly acquires what he needs to live a happy life. The most active minds as well as the most tranquil characters find here everything they need to fill their lives and need not look for reasons to trouble the government. The restlessness of spirit that is gnawing away at our European society seems to contribute to the prosperity of society here. It is channeled entirely into the acquisition of wealth, which here can be had in a thousand ways. Hence politics occupies but a tiny corner of the canvas. I have no doubt that even the most apparently peaceful states in Europe are more troubled by political activity than is the entire American confederation. Among the newspapers we read every day there is not one in which the price of cotton does not take up more space than general questions concerning the government. The rest of the space is taken up with discussions of local interests, which feed the curiosity of the public without disrupting society in any way whatsoever.

In sum, the more I see of this country, the more convinced I am of the following truth: that there is virtually no political institution that is radically good or radically bad in itself, and everything depends on the physical conditions and the social state of the people to which it is applied. The institutions that I see succeeding here would inevitably bring upheaval to France. Others, which suit us, would clearly be destructive in America. Yet either I am seriously mistaken, or man here is not different or better than at home. He is merely situated differently. On another occasion I will tell you what strikes me about the American character. Don't you find that just now I bear a close resemblance to *"Maître corbeau sur un arbre perché"*?[39] I shall finish my orison with that. I am so pleased to be on my branch, so *comfortably* situated in every way, that I am actually afraid of falling asleep. In which case I might suffer the same fate as my friend Robinson Crusoe and cry out "My dear parents!" as I wake up on the ground. I have therefore made up my mind to climb down from my perch. I will finish my letter tomorrow. . . .

From Beaumont | To his mother

New York, June 7, 1831

. . . I must tell what I've been doing for the past ten or twelve days. I think that Jules will have forwarded my letter to him, so I will resume the narrative where I left off.

Tocqueville and I went up to Sing Sing ten days ago, as planned. We returned last night. All the time in between we devoted to the penitentiary system. No sooner did we arrive in Sing Sing, in the company of a very distinguished lawyer from New York, than we were offered every kind of assistance you might imagine. The prison warden and guards—everyone who works there—couldn't do enough to help us. They let us examine their books and opened all the doors we needed. We moved into a room that is normally reserved for prison inspectors and worked there *as if we were at home.* We observed the prison for an extended period of time and did important research. There is no doubt that the disciplinary system at Sing Sing is quite remarkable. The prison holds nine hundred prisoners serving sentences of varying length. They are made to work either in the prison yard, which is not enclosed, or in the quarries a short distance away. Although they wear no manacles or leg irons, they diligently perform the most arduous tasks. Escapes are extremely rare. This seems so incredible that you can stare at the fact for a very long time without coming up with any explanation for it.

We have succeeded, however, in discovering the secret of this marvelous discipline. It is based on a few key principles:

The first is the *absolute silence* to which the prisoners are condemned: they are not allowed to exchange a single word, and the truth is that in all the time I spent among them, I did not hear a single one allow so much as a word to escape from his mouth.

The second major rule is extreme severity in the punishment of disciplinary infractions. Maximal rigor is strictly enforced, because prison discipline is left

39. "Master crow perched on a tree." Tocqueville refers to Aesop's fable "The Fox and the Crow." In this tale La Fontaine told again, a fox sees a crow perched on a tree, clutching a piece of food in its mouth. The fox calls to the crow, asking whether its voice is as beautiful as its appearance. In opening its mouth to sing and prove the beauty of its voice, the crow drops the food to the fox below.

to the discretion of the warden, who bears full responsibility for the institution.

In addition, the guards are well aware that they are outnumbered by the prisoners nine hundred to thirty, so the threat of rebellion is a source of constant fear. Hence they are generally quite fair in inflicting punishment. They understand that any injustice or cruelty on their part could lead to rebellion. Despite these various methods of maintaining order, it is still hard to understand how such impressive results have been achieved.

One general reason stands out above the rest, however, to supply an answer to the question.

There is no denying the fact that nine hundred criminals, nine hundred bandits, outnumber and could easily overpower the thirty men assigned to guard them. Clearly, it would be absurdly easy for them to overcome any resistance. Yet although they are physically stronger, are they the equal in moral force to the small number of people who watch over them? No, because they are isolated from one another. All force stems from association, and thirty individuals *united* by constant communication, by common ideas and projects, and by joint plans have more real power than nine hundred prisoners enfeebled by isolation.

But I have dwelled too long on the penitentiary system. I'm very afraid that I've bored you. Still, how could I possibly avoid speaking of something that has occupied me for the past two weeks? To finish off this discussion, I should say that despite our admiration for what we have seen, we still have many doubts about the solidity and efficacy of the system. The discipline that is maintained here seems to us a slippery slope. Intelligent men of firm resolve may successfully stand on such a slope, but they may just as easily fall. It would be dangerous, moreover, for a nation with a passionate and capricious character to imitate one whose character is serious and grave. Finally, the system would be costly to apply, and the benefit (at least thus far) is not sufficiently clear to permit such a step without extensive further reflection. I have just begun a long report about Sing Sing that we will forward to the Ministry of the Interior. There will be an extensive description of the prison, but I will refrain from giving my own opinion. The purpose of the report is to let the government know that we are performing the mission that has been entrusted to us. The government needs to delve into the subject and ponder our findings in an unbiased way. We want to draw the government's attention to what we have done while withholding definitive opinion for the time being.

As much as I would like to drop the subject of prisons and discuss other things, I absolutely must say a word about a related matter that struck me as odd: the fact that moral and religious instruction is one of the methods used to reform the inmates. Every Sunday the prisoners attend a religious service, and there is always a sermon. So far, so good. But the strange thing is that the service is led one week by a Presbyterian minister, the next week by an Anabaptist, etc. In short, ministers of various Christian denominations officiate by turns at Sunday services, and all the prisoners attend, many of them likely unaware of the differences between the denominations of the various preachers. If they are unaware, so much the better. But if they know the differences, they must find it quite difficult to choose the best and only true denomination among the variety offered to them. Indeed, even though indifference as to the *nature of the various denominations* is perfectly common in the United States, it does not prevent people from fervently preferring whichever sect they happen to have chosen. The fact that this extreme tolerance for different denominations in general coexists with rather intense zeal for one's own brand of religion is a fact that I cannot yet explain. I would like to know how such lively and sincere faith can coexist with such perfect tolerance. How can people exhibit equal respect for religions whose dogmas differ? And finally, given the fact that the outward manifestations of the religious spirit in America cannot be denied, what is the actual influence of religion on the moral behavior of Americans? Might the outward manifestations of religion be superficial rather than signs of deep belief? Might the variety of denominations in the United States explain why each tries to outdo the others in religious observance and the inculcation of moral principles? If so, some of their virtues might be attributable to pride and emulation rather than to conviction and a sentiment of truth.

I hereby end the grave and philosophical portion of my epistle and turn now to less austere subjects. I told you that we regularly worked during the day at Sing Sing, but you still do not know where we were housed.

Two or three hundred yards from the small town of Sing Sing there is a charming country house, which stands atop a hill on a bank of the Hudson. It is occupied by a lady who takes in boarders by the week or month. This is where we stayed. Several other guests preceded us, including an Englishwoman, Mrs. Mac Heidge, and her daughter, whose company we found quite pleasant. At five in the morning we regularly took a short walk. At 8:30, after breakfast, we took a second walk; and at 7 in the evening we went for a swim in the Hudson. I am beginning to swim reasonably well. Tocqueville is giving me lessons with all the zeal of a friend who senses what a difficult position I would be in if I were accidentally to fall into one of America's broad rivers. In the place where we were staying, the width of the Hudson is a league and a quarter. In the evening, after leaving the prison, we called on various people in town or thereabout. Everyone lavished kindness and invitations upon us. The chief profit I derived from these social calls was to speak a lot of English. We are making progress. Still, we frequently commit some rather strange errors. We are never quite sure what people are telling us. In ordinary conversation, a mistake has no consequence, but it's different when someone invites us and we don't understand. Sometimes we get the date wrong when we're invited for tea. Just the other day, *un gros seigneur* in the area, a member of the Livingston family, went to a lot of trouble to receive us.[40]

40. Members of this powerful New York family descended from Robert Livingston, who immigrated to America in 1673 and became a substantial landowner in the colony. During the time of Tocqueville's visit, a number of Livingstons held prominent posts in the United States government, including Edward Livingston, who served as secretary of state.

Mrs. Smith's house, near Sing Sing, 25 June 1831. "A charming country house, which stands atop a hill on a bank of the Hudson," possibly the house Beaumont described to his mother on June 7 and where the two travelers boarded. (GB2)

He had laid on a splendid dinner and invited a lot of people in our honor. His dinner was set for 3 o'clock. He waited until 5 for us, but we didn't show up. Alas! At that moment we were sitting quietly at home, completely unaware that people were waiting for us!

From this you may conclude that our English is not yet very good. I readily concede the point. In France, however, we would enjoy a reputation for speaking the language as Londoners do, and even if we say things in the most maladroit way imaginable, we say them with confidence.

In Sing Sing we enjoyed the company of a number of friendly people. American women suffer from one fault that we cannot forgive: they are terrible musicians and yet are always making music. They have no taste for it; it is simply a matter of fashion. They sing in a hilarious manner, with a certain cooing in the throat that I cannot describe but which has nothing in common with the laws of harmony. If you say to them, "You sing wonderfully," they reply with rare candor, "Yes, that's quite true." They study the piano for three months and then play on the slightest pretext while letting you know that they are crazy about music and truly gifted for it. There are of course a few exceptions to the rule. But in general they are as I have described them. In any case, all Americans love to be praised and can never get enough of it. We regularly observe the truth of the adage that every flatterer lives at the expense of the person he flatters. We

do not stint on praise, and they spoil us in return. We are held in such high esteem that they see it as an honor to do us favors. Do we need documents? They
give us books; they send us handwritten notes. The other day, I submitted to
Mr. Cartwright, an engineer of many talents, two pages of questions on various
subjects and asked him to answer in writing.[41] He eagerly complied. We needed
certain plans he had drawn up, and he gave them to us. We have put literally all
our friends to good use, even Miss Mac Heidge, who, after much pleading, rewarded me with a brief description of the American character.

She jotted her sketch down on pretty pink notepaper. Although it contained
accurate observations, on the whole it didn't amount to much. (Miss Mac Heidge
is educated and quite friendly but very ugly.) Nevertheless, I was obliged to tell
her more than once how charming she was. My calculated adulation ended with
this fib, however.

When I return to Beaumont-la-Chartre I will bring two sketches, one of the
house in which we stayed, the other of the town harbor. Jules and Achille will
find these useful: they can serve as the basis for two charming landscapes. I will
try to draw the prettiest views wherever we go, but I worry about the time that
must be devoted to this work.

All in all, the ten days we spent in Sing Sing were most useful to us. We
made a lot of progress in our work on the penitentiary system. We also made
many observations of a more general kind. Now that we're back in New York
City, we plan to remain here ten more days, during which time we will contact
some of the leading men. We will again visit institutions that we still know only
superficially, and then we will go to Wethersfield (Connecticut), where there is a
penitentiary of note.[42] From there we will go to Massachusetts. We still have not
decided what route to take after that. Time is passing rapidly. We are caught up
in the work. Yet we still keep an eye on France. The political situation seems to
have taken a turn for the better. I can't say that I am glad to see the new order
taking hold, but I can say without fear of upsetting you that I am happy at the
thought that your tranquility will not be disturbed and that France will remain
calm. Still, there are so many things to fear! The country we find ourselves in at
the moment has not experienced civil or political upheaval for quite some time.
The truth is that there is only one party in America. The disputes about which
one reads in the papers or hears in society have much more to do with personalities than with issues. Few people covet the highest public offices. Only one
thing arouses real ambition, and that is wealth. Credibility, prestige, and power
all stem from fortune alone. Public offices are poorly paid and do not bring

41. George W. Cartwright was an engineer responsible for the construction of Mount
Pleasant Penitentiary at Sing Sing.

42. Wethersfield Prison, which opened in 1827, was run by the Auburn system of daily
communal work and overnight isolation. However, in the place of physical punishment, wardens punished bad behavior with solitary confinement, additions to the length of a prisoner's
term, and smaller food portions.

prestige, power, or credibility. They are sought only by those who have nothing better to do. This indifference is an important source of social peace and order. Since with us the passion for public positions, honors, and employment is a source of disorder and unrest, the more we contemplate American society, the more we see it as made up of distinctive elements that make it quite dangerous if not impossible to imitate.

We spend half of our time taking notes. I forgot to tell you about an incident that took place on the way back from Sing Sing. Since I have half a page left, I'll tell you about it now.

Upset at having been impolite to Mr. Livingston without intending to, we decided to pay him a courtesy call. His country house is located between Sing Sing and New York, so it was on our way back.[43] Thinking that he dined at 2 o'clock, we arrived at his house at 3. Unfortunately, we were wrong and arrived just as the family was sitting down to dinner. So we were invited to join the company at the dining table but decided not to eat, because then our visit would no longer have been a courtesy call. Think of the position in which we found ourselves: we were dying of hunger, and the dishes were passing beneath our noses. We were urged to eat some excellent ice cream, which had been hastily prepared expressly for us. We could hardly refuse. We devoured what was put in front of us. But the steamboat was scheduled to arrive at 4, and we were supposed to board. It was the only way for us to leave. When the clock struck four, however, there was no boat. Someone said that it had already passed, leaving us in a state of mortal embarrassment. Because if we stayed in the house, how could we dine after having said that we had dined already? We saw ourselves going to bed with nothing but ice cream for dinner. We couldn't help laughing at our comical predicament. Fortunately, the steamboat, which was late, arrived and delivered us.

We saw enough of the Livingston household to hope that we might find an opportunity to return.

From Tocqueville | To his sister-in-law Émilie

New York, June 9, 1831

... Our life is like a series of images from a magic lantern: a new world. You know the person who has the honor of writing to you well enough to know that such a life suits his character. On top of that, the weather is magnificent (though a little hot) and the country is lovely. As for the countryside, I don't know if anyone has told you that the country houses around New York remind me of your *baronnie* at Nacqueville. There are no castles in this country. Wealth is too limited. The division of the estate on the death of the father is too extensive for anyone to think of amassing a very vast or durable fortune. Instead, Ameri-

---

43. A number of Livingston properties were located on the Hudson River north of Yonkers.

cans spend relatively little to build houses that are quite picturesque and elegant in outline and placement. They situate these houses in the best possible spot on their property, if possible with a view of the sea. It is hard to imagine anything more gracious or imaginative. To my taste, a house of this sort in Nacqueville would make it a charming place for you to live. The problem is how to convey to you exactly what I have in mind. Beaumont is not a bad artist, and I'll ask him to sketch the prettiest country houses in the environs of New York. All the wealthy families here maintain summer homes. Since several people have already invited us, it shouldn't be very difficult to do.

We are living, dear sister, in the most unusual country in the world. You have of course heard that in England women lead sedentary lives, whereas young people enjoy the greatest freedom. Can you imagine that here they are about as far from England in this respect as England is from us? When a woman marries, it is as though she entered a convent, except of course that no one sees any problem with her having children, indeed many children. Otherwise, she leads the life of a nun: no balls and virtually no society, a husband as respectable as he is chilly to all guests, and so it remains until she goes to her eternal reward. I ventured the other day to ask one of these recluses how a woman in America might spend her days. With the utmost aplomb she responded, "In looking up to her husband." I am very sorry, but "to look up to" is a literal translation of the English *to admire*. I tell you this so that if you find yourself bored at home, you will know what you must do.

So much for married women. You would find it even more difficult to imagine the lives of young men and women. Imagine the daughters of the leading families, nimble and dressed to the nines at one in the afternoon, strolling daintily along the streets of New York, exploring the shops, mounting horses, with nary a father nor mother, uncle or aunt, or even a servant in sight. And that is not all: imagine a young man who crosses the path of one of these ladies about town—this has happened to us more than once. If they know each other, they stop, lean upon a roadside marker while chatting amiably for fifteen minutes or so, and when the conversation is finished, the young lady will invite the young man to call on her and mention a time when he is likely to find her at home. At the appointed hour you go and ask for Miss So-and-so, and often you find her alone in her father's drawing room, where she receives you in style. Everyone assures us that these manners have none of the drawbacks that one might imagine, so long as the intimate conversation remains confined to subjects such as the price of wool or cotton, as we are similarly assured it does. In society we frequently run into what they call "engaged" couples, that is, a young man and a young woman who are to marry within a few months and who in the meantime are always together, courting each other in the chilliest way imaginable. There is no fluttering around young women here. Pox! You would quickly burn yourself in the candle flame. These people are most righteous. They take every word literally. If you don't follow the wise man's advice to bite your tongue seven times before speaking, you can easily embarrass yourself....

From Tocqueville | To Ernest de Chabrol

New York, June 9, 1831

... I don't mean to imply that I'm overwhelmed by an embarrassment of riches. I'm just giddy with everything that I've seen and heard and don't know what would be most interesting to write about. But I have to say something. Otherwise it wouldn't be worth the trouble to have come so far.

Imagine if you can, my dear friend, a society comprising all the nations of the world: English, French, Germans. . . . All people having different languages, beliefs, and opinions. In short, a society without roots, without memories, without prejudices, without routines, without common ideas, without national character, a hundred times happier than ours. More virtuous? I doubt it. That is the point of departure. What ties these very diverse elements together? What makes a people of all this? Self-interest. That is the secret. Private interest rears its head here constantly, reveals itself openly, and proclaims itself to be a social theory.

We are a long way from the ancient republics, of that there can be no doubt, yet this nation is republican and I am certain will remain so for a long time to come.[44] It believes, moreover, that the republic is the best form of government. The only way I can account for this is to believe that America at the moment finds itself in such a fortunate situation, both physically and politically, that private interest never comes into conflict with the general interest, which is certainly not the case in Europe.

Broadly speaking, why do people feel compelled to make trouble in a state? Either because they desire power or because they cannot achieve happiness by any ordinary means.

Here, there are no public authorities and, to tell the truth, no need of any. The territory is divided into quite small districts. The states have no enemies and therefore no armies, no taxes, no central government. The executive power is merely the designated executor of the will of elective bodies: it brings neither money nor power. As long as things remain this way, who would want to trouble himself to attain a high office?

Consider now the other part of the proposition and you will come to the same conclusion, for if political careers are all but out of reach, thousands of others are open to energetic individuals. Here, the whole world seems malleable, and man can turn and fashion it any way he chooses. A vast domain is open to industry, only the smallest part of which has yet been explored. There is not a single person who cannot reasonably hope to achieve a comfortable existence, not a single person who does not believe that love of labor is the key to success.

Thus in this fortunate country, nothing attracts the restless human spirit to political passions. On the contrary, everything drives it toward activities that pose no danger to the state. I wish that all those who invoke America as the

---

44. Montesquieu, whom Tocqueville had read closely, argued that ancient republics encouraged the virtuous sacrifice of individual interest for the common good. Tocqueville eventually argued that for Americans, personal interest and public good were compatible.

38   LETTERS FROM TOCQUEVILLE AND BEAUMONT ON AMERICAN TRAVELS

basis of their republican dreams for France could come here and see for themselves what it is really like.

The explanation I have just proposed, which I believe is of the utmost importance, also accounts for the two salient traits that set the American people apart: their industrial spirit and their instability of character.[45]

Nothing is easier than to strike it rich in America. Because the human spirit needs a dominant passion, all thought naturally turns to gain, so that at first glance Americans seem like a company formed for some mercantile venture. And the deeper one delves into the national character, the more clearly one sees that Americans measure the value of all things solely in terms of the answer to the following question: How much money will it bring in? As for the instability of character, it is visible in a thousand places. An American will take up, abandon, and resume ten different situations in the course of a lifetime. He will change his place of residence repeatedly and regularly embark on new enterprises. He is less afraid than people elsewhere of risking an acquired fortune, because he knows how easily he can acquire another. Change, moreover, strikes him as man's natural condition, and how could it be otherwise? Everything around him is constantly in flux: laws, opinions, public officials, fortunes. The very face of the earth changes here daily. In the midst of such universal movement, the American cannot stand still.

Here, therefore, one must not look for the notable qualities that distinguish the old societies of Europe, such as family spirit and ancient traditions of honor and virtue. A people that seems to live only to enrich itself cannot be a virtuous people in the strict sense of the word, but it can be *well-behaved*. It has none of the vices associated with idle riches and little if any time to waste on women, who are valued, it seems, solely as mothers and household managers. Morals are certainly pure: the European *roué* is completely unknown in America. The passion to amass wealth stimulates and overshadows all others.

As you will have guessed, my dear friend, everything I am telling you is but a *rough approximation* to the truth. I have been in this country for only a short time. Yet I have already had abundant opportunity to learn. My father has no doubt told you that we have been received with extraordinary kindness. Not only have public officials favored us with substantial assistance, but we have also been invited to private homes, and the only thing we have to complain about is the large number of social obligations we owe to the kindness of our hosts.

Living from morning till night with men of all classes of society, speaking the language poorly but understanding it well enough that few things escape us, and possessed as well of an immoderate desire to learn, we are in a rather good

45. Tocqueville copied out portions of his June 9 letter to Chabrol into his Non-alphabetic Notebook 1 for June 10. In the notebook version (not printed here), Tocqueville modified his wording. He underscored "two most prominent characteristics of the people here, namely, the industrial spirit and the restless spirit."

position to do so quickly. Nevertheless, I beg you to take what I have just said merely as my first impressions, which may well change in the days to come.

I hope not to make a habit of writing only about general ideas of the sort I set forth above, but I do not know which details to include. I hope you will ask me questions. I will try to respond as best I can. . . .

From Beaumont | To his brother Achille

New York, June 18, 1831

In two days, a packet boat will leave for France, and although you're annoyed with me, my dear Achille, I want to chat with you a bit. I might be tempted to feel angry at your silence, but you have no idea how precious letters are to one who is separated from his friends by an ocean. So I forgive you. In any case, I hope that the first packet boat from Le Havre will bring me a letter from you. I am impatient for its arrival. It was supposed to leave Le Havre on the 15th, so it should be here soon.

Despite the oppressive heat, we continue to work diligently. Our health is still good. I've never felt better. I have adopted all the habits of the "native-born" and drink tea like an American. This change in my ways was essential; wine here is worth its weight in gold. Although we are leading very respectable lives, we are not spending much, and all signs are that our expenses will not increase when we change our residence.

Upon our return from Sing Sing we found our friends in New York warmer than ever. They continue to be most attentive to us. We are currently studying an institution that interests us greatly: a reform school for young delinquents.[46] It is perhaps the only prison whose disadvantages do not outweigh its advantages. Little is to be expected, I think, of a hardened criminal, inured to corruption. It is different with a child, whose bad habits can be corrected if caught early. We are spending entire days in the reform school. We have been examining all the records, and right now we are looking at the behavior of all the former inmates who have returned to society since 1825. This is no small job, as you can imagine. But our research will give us a very clear idea of the actual influence of the institution on those who are sent there.

We always return home by 3 o'clock, which is the dinner hour. The people with whom we dine make for pleasant company. In the evening we visit friends, and every day we make new acquaintances. We have made contact with the most distinguished people in New York. We have just been introduced to Mr. Galatin [Gallatin], the former United States ambassador to France, England, and Russia.[47] He is quite a remarkable man. Although I speak English like a *real lion,* it

---

46. This was the house of refuge run by Nathaniel C. Hart. It was founded in 1825 by private subscribers. It inspired similar reform schools in Boston (1826), Philadelphia (1828), and Melun in France.

47. Albert Gallatin (1761–1849) emigrated from Switzerland to the United States at the age of nineteen. He aligned himself with the Democratic-Republicans and served in the Penn-

does not upset me to run into people with whom I can speak French, because in that language I can express myself *even more* clearly. Mr. Gallatin speaks marvelous French. We have had some very interesting conversations with him, which have shed a lot of light on any number of things that we had previously found obscure. We have also recently made the acquaintance of Chancellor Kent, the author of a celebrated commentary on the laws of the United States.[48] He is the American Blackstone. He presented us with a copy of his book, along with a very friendly letter.

We went the other day to a sort of ball at Colonel Fish's house.[49] The next day, we went dancing in the evening at Mr. King's.[50] There we met two Frenchmen who had just arrived, the baron de Courcy and the vicomte de Neverley (Neverlée).[51] These gentlemen are traveling for pleasure, they tell us, but the society horrifies them and they deliberated all day before deciding whether or not to come to Mr. King's. I would like to know what good their trip can do them. They plan to visit all the states one after another. I expect that they will acquire a thorough knowledge of the roads and inns. We tried to engage them in conversation, but I doubt that there are two more stupid fellows anywhere in the world. The day before yesterday we went to dinner at Mr. Schermerhorn's country house, which is only a league outside of town. His home, which is quite charming, is situated close to the Sound, on the banks of the East River. Mr. Schermerhorn invited all of our erstwhile traveling companions (from *Le Havre*). Miss Edwards was there. We leapt, danced, and frolicked. The only thing missing was music, but we had a little music box that we used in lieu of an orchestra. Yesterday evening was far more pleasant. One of Mr. Prime's daughters got married, and he gave a lovely party at his country house.[52] He is a neighbor of Mr. Schermerhorn's, but his house is incomparably more beautiful and more pleasant. There was an enormous crowd: all the elegant ladies of New York were there. It was the first time we saw a large number of women gathered in one place. Several of them seemed quite pretty to me. Miss Fulton is rightly consid-

---

sylvania legislature and the United States Congress before acting as Thomas Jefferson's secretary of state and of the treasury from 1801 to 1814. He served as an ambassador to France from 1816 to 1823 and to England from 1826 to 1827. In 1831, he became president of the Bank of New York and turned to intellectual pursuits, such as studying ethnology and founding New York University.

48. James Kent (1763–1847), a native of New York State, published *Commentaries on American Law* in four volumes between 1826 and 1830.

49. Colonel Nicholas Fish (1758–1833) was a lawyer and celebrated Revolutionary War veteran. He had married into the powerful Stuyvesant family and was a friend of Alexander Hamilton and the Livingston family.

50. James Gore King (1791–1853) was the son of the American politician Rufus King. Although he had studied law, he became a businessman and banker in New York. He was an associate of Nathaniel Prime and would later become president of the Erie Railroad.

51. It is possible that these Frenchmen were Philippe de Neverlée (1807–1879) and either Léon (1798–1874) or Adalbert (1805–1839) Roussel d'Epourlon de Courcy.

52. Matilda Prime (1810–1849) married Gerard Coster on June 9, 1831.

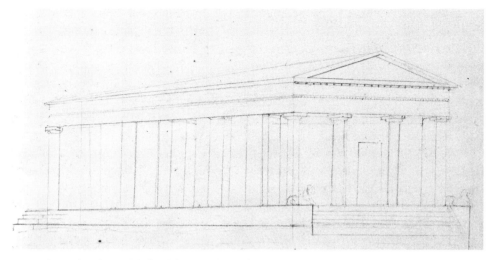

Peter Schermerhorn's Greek billiard house, Belmont farm on the East River, New York, June 1831. "Situated close to the Sound," Mr. Schermerhorn's home "is quite charming," Beaumont told his brother on June 18. (GBI)

ered the most beautiful woman in New York.[53] I paid her the tribute of my unremitting admiration. We went for a delightful moonlight stroll. Unfortunately, the odds are a hundred to one that I will never see her again. She is the daughter of the famous Fulton, the inventor of the steamboat. Apparently the great man did not apply his method to the creation of children, because she in no way resembles a woman with the vapors.

Tonight we will attend a banquet at the home of Mr. Emmet, the son of the celebrated lawyer in whose memory the Americans have erected a monument.[54] This is an obligation that I would have preferred to avoid. What we fear most are the political toasts: if they drink "to the health of republics," we are determined to remain silent. But I have a minor worry: it is likely that people in France who know us have spread the word here about our *political line.* They seldom if ever speak to us about La Fayette. What is more, the "hero of two worlds" seems to have forfeited much of his reputation here. Those who do speak about him praise his honesty and unselfishness but look upon him as a misguided man whose opinions represent a danger to his country. We are continuing to collect material for our major work. We question everyone we meet. We hound anyone who comes our way. And every evening we write down what we heard during the day. We have already collected a respectable pile of docu-

53. This is a reference to Julia Fulton (1810–1848), daughter of steamboat inventor Robert Fulton and his wife Harriet Livingston.

54. Robert Emmet (1792–1873) was a prominent New York lawyer who secured a number of political appointments thanks to his friendship with Martin Van Buren. He was the son of Thomas Addis Emmet (1764–1827), an Irish revolutionary who came to the United States in exile. In New York, the elder Emmet had served as the state's attorney general.

ments. When our day is done, we are so tired the mere thought of a restful night brings genuine pleasure. So we sleep the sleep of the dead on beds that are as hard as rock (good beds are unknown in America).

The other day, while reading the paper, we came across an article about us that treated us very kindly. You will find it easy to translate it for your friends and acquaintances: "It will be recollected that a few years ago, we noticed the fact of a commission having been appointed by the King of France, to visit our country with the View of acquiring an intimate Knowledge of the system of the prison discipline practiced in the United States. M. de Beaumont and M. de Tocqueville, the distinguished gentlemen composing the Commission, have spent the last two weeks in this place and after a most laborious and careful inspection of the prison here, its construction, its order, cleanliness, discipline and regularity, together with a strict investigation into all the minutiae of its government and its operation, we are gratified with the opportunity of stating that they are highly pleased with the institution, and do not hesitate to pronounce it superior, in many of its branches, to any which they have ever visited in Europe. They are gentlemen of engaging manners, of first-rate talents and acquirements; and have been repeatedly honored with distinguished offices by their country. We trust that the attention and kindness of the American people, who cannot but feel flattered with the object of their mission, will render their visit throughout the Union both pleasant and profitable."[55]

This article appeared in one newspaper and was then repeated the next day by all the others. It is true that we are examining the penitentiary system very carefully. There are moments when we've had it up to our eyes. But we are determined to do a conscientious job. As soon as we've exhausted the reform school, which I think should be within a week, we will leave for Auburn, where the most famous prison is located. We initially intended to visit Wethersfield in Connecticut, but we began our work with the prisons of New York and want to do them thoroughly. Auburn is in the state of New York.

From Tocqueville | To his mother

New York, June 19, 1831

. . . We are received everywhere in fine style and are leading a very agreeable life here. Still, as all good things must come to an end, we plan to leave New York at the end of the month. Our intention was to go first to Boston, but we have changed our plan entirely. Instead of beginning in the north, we are going to head west to a small town named Auburn, which can be found on the map just below Lake Ontario. The most remarkable prison in the United States is there. We will stay there for about ten days, as at Sing Sing, and then go to see Niagara Falls, which is nearby. We will then board the Lake Ontario steamboat, which will take us to Quebec in two days' time. From there we can make our way to Boston quite easily and then return to New York. This trip, which looks quite

55. *Westchester Herald,* June 7, 1831.

ambitious on the map, *is all the rage here;* it takes less time than you can imagine but we will travel at our own pace because we plan to stop in Albany, Auburn, Montreal, and Quebec. Canada piques our curiosity greatly. The French nation has been preserved there intact: the people there have the mores and speak the language of the century of Louis XIV.[56] We were advised to go there primarily by Mr. Powers, the vicar-in-chief of New York, whom I've mentioned to you. He lived in Canada for many years and has given us letters of recommendation to use there.

Mr. Powers is a very friendly man, who was raised in France and speaks French almost as well as his own language. He has told us some very interesting things about Catholicism in this part of the world, and I will write about them in another letter when I have more time. It's partly because of him that we changed our original plan, which was to head west this autumn. People often come down with tertiary fever in the fall because of the abundance of water there and the way the summer sun partially dries it up. By contrast, the coastal regions and Pennsylvania are the healthiest places in the world all year round. My only complaint is that they are too hot. The summer heat has been overwhelming, yet it is not unusual for this climate. Seasons in America are on the whole more marked than in Europe. In New York, for example, the summer is like Italy and the winter like Holland. It seems that the human body is wonderfully adapted to these transitions. At any rate, doctors attribute the longevity of the people here largely to this cause. . . .

From Tocqueville | To his sister-in-law Alexandrine[57]

New York, June 20, 1831

. . . We are leading the same life as always: *study and society.* Our days are full and our nights long. As you can see, there is no need to worry about us. The other day we went for the first time to something that resembled a ball. There is a nice custom here: a few days after a young woman marries, she invites all her acquaintances to call on her at her own or her parents' home at such-and-such a time. As word gets around, everyone who has any connection with the family calls on the bride, and all the wedding visits are thus gotten out of the way at once. It was to a gathering of this nature that we were invited.[58] The place was two leagues from New York in a charming country house on the seacoast. It was a splendid evening, and the sea breeze cooled the air. The lawn on which the house was located stretched right down to the shore. Tall trees rose on both sides. In this part of the country there are flies that give off as much light as glow worms. The woods were full of these small insects, so that the air seemed

56. The Bourbon king Louis XIV ruled from 1643 until 1715.
57. Alexandrine Ollivier de Tocqueville (1803–1883) had married Édouard de Tocqueville in 1829.
58. Tocqueville attended the reception of Mathilda Prime.

illuminated by a million flying sparks. And the scene was truly extraordinary. Nothing was excessive except the music. Don't think I'm a barbarian: it was too much because it was like the music you hear at the fair in Loges. When it comes to harmony, there can be no doubt that no one is less gifted than these Americans. If only they knew the truth, but they are a thousand leagues from suspecting it. We spend our days putting up with yelping the likes of which the Old World has never heard. What the young ladies who regale us with this caterwauling admire most is the difficulty of the music. And I assure you that if their goal is to produce broken, discordant sounds, they could not do better, and it would be difficult to outdo them. Not to mention the fact that you're never sure when the song is over. The end always reminds me of a book from which the last page has been torn out. At first I thought that the singer was merely pausing, so I was still listening when everyone else had begun to applaud. It may seem to you that I speak of this subject with a kind of *indignation,* but I beg you to notice that, quite apart from the displeasure you feel at having to listen to such execrable performances when you're familiar with good music, there is also the feeling that you've been subjected to moral violence, because you're forced to listen whether you like it or not and, what is more, obliged to seem pleased.

À propos, I experienced a pleasant distraction the other day. A lady we were visiting began to sing a national song with very funny words and tune. After the first stanza, everyone laughed, and I laughed along with them. This was a way of applauding. During the second stanza my thoughts turned to something else, and I became so lost in thought that I had absolutely no idea what was going on around me. In the midst of my flight of fancy, I realized that the song was ending and remembered that laughter was expected, so I laughed, actually rather loudly. With that explosion of gaiety everyone turned and looked at me, and I was chagrined to discover that the humorous song of which I had heard the beginning had ended five minutes earlier and that the one that had filled me with such hilarity was the most plaintive and tearful of romantic melodies, the most *chromatic* in the entire American repertoire. . . .

From Tocqueville | To Ernest de Chabrol

New York, June 20, 1831

. . . The life we are leading here still suits us well, except for the penitentiary system, by which we are beginning to feel snowed under. We are doing an enormous amount of work on the prisons. Will it be useful? I have no idea, but I do flatter myself that it will be complete. We have had great difficulty obtaining documents that offer a comprehensive view. This is because this country is fortunate enough to have no real government. It has not occurred to anyone, nor does anyone have the power, to collect from the several states or even from the several parts of any one state the information that would be necessary to paint a picture that would be even moderately satisfactory. We are therefore obliged to do much of this work ourselves, and I swear to you that it is by the sweat of our brows.

We do allow ourselves the occasional distraction, however. Yesterday, we went to superior court to observe the trial of a notorious thief. The district attorney (equivalent to the *procureur du roi*) had invited us and reserved seats for us. It was the most important case of the session. Unfortunately, it turned out that the accused had not had sufficient time to subpoena an important witness, much to the disappointment of the district attorney and the court, who had wanted to show us a fine specimen of a criminal trial. They tried to put a thousand obstacles in the poor devil's way in the hope of forcing him to proceed with the case forthwith. I was afraid they might condemn him without a trial just to show how much they loved us. After an hour and a quarter of wrangling, however, the case had to be postponed until the next session. As you can see, people on this side of the Atlantic are not very different from people on our side.

Once the major case fell apart, they dispatched three or four minor ones in our presence. The basic procedure is the same as in France, but the formalities are much simpler. Jurors for all the cases are drawn the same day, but the accused is allowed to reject a certain number. There is no bill of indictment or examination; the whole procedure is quite similar to that of our lower criminal courts. The defense attorney and prosecutor have absolutely the same instincts as in France: they are the champions of two distinct *causes,* and the word "impartiality" is not so much as mentioned. The judge gives a brief summary of the case, expresses his opinion, and offers advice to the jury. The jurors deliberate without withdrawing into a jury room, and in two minutes the man is found guilty. His sentence is not pronounced until the end of the session.

There is good and bad in these procedures. I think that ours are better for major cases, but I am convinced that if we ever decide to have trial by jury in minor cases, as sooner or later we surely will, we will be forced to do as the Americans do.

I hope in any case that we never acquire the informal manners that are so prevalent here. The prosecutor speaks with his hands in his pockets, the judge chews tobacco, and the defense attorney picks his teeth while examining witnesses. I doubt that such manners are absolutely necessary to the proper administration of justice. Furthermore, it is obvious that judges and attorneys here are all cut from the same cloth. Strictly speaking, there is no magistracy, only lawyers who have become magistrates. As far as I can see, this does not have the negative consequences that we would naturally expect in France. In general, the position of lawyers here is quite different from what you might imagine. I don't have the time to explain why. Suffice it to say for now that they constitute the *resistance,* or in other words, the *stationary* class. I will explain this another time. . . .

From Tocqueville | To Eugène Stöffels

New York, July [June] 28, 1831[59]

My good friend,

Here we are, separated by quite some distance, yet in spite of that distance our hearts are linked. I, for one, feel as keenly as in France, if not more so, that we are bound to each other for life and that, no matter what fortune may bring, we can always count on each other for friendship and assistance.

When we were at school, and later when we were studying law, and still later when I had a permanent post and you a tranquil and secure position, who could have predicted that a political tempest would force us to put a quarter of the earth's diameter between us, and who knows even now what the future may hold? Here we are, or at any rate here I am, at sea with no land in sight: God only knows where and when I shall make landfall. In any event, I would be loath to complain if I were alone. But what frightens me and makes me look with apprehension to the future is the thought of parents, friends, and family, some of whom are elderly or ill.

As you know, we set sail on April 2, past midnight. At first the weather was favorable. It seemed as though we were gliding across the sea. I cannot tell you how impressive the solitude of the mid-Atlantic is. For the first few days thick flocks of birds followed the ship. The sea was alive with fish swimming near the surface. Not an hour went by without someone spotting a sail on the horizon. Before long, however, these sights became increasingly rare, until finally the birds, the fish, and the ships disappeared. Above us, below us, and all around, deep solitude and complete silence reigned. The ship then became our universe. Experiences of this sort make an impression on me, as you know, but when the emptiness continues without end, unchanged day after day, it begins to weigh on the soul and become oppressive.

As we drew near the Newfoundland bank, the sea began to sparkle. I believe that this effect is produced by millions of small phosphorescent animals that are tossed about in the waters. In any case, I have never seen anything more extraordinary. I remember one evening in particular when the weather was quite stormy. Our ship, propelled by a violent wind, split the sea in two, throwing up an enormous foamy wake on either side. The foam seemed made of fire. It was as if the vessel were sailing through one of the big smelting furnaces I saw at Hayange,[60] where the different ores run together. It left a long fiery trace behind. The night was perfectly black. You could barely see the rigging of the ship against the sky. It was a scene of ineffable beauty.

Several days after that, there was a strong but not dangerous blow. Our vessel was large enough to withstand the wind, so there was no need to be afraid. We had been out of sight of land for thirty-five days when the first shouts

59. The date is incorrect; it should be June 28. The error is Tocqueville's, copied by Beaumont.

60. In Lorraine, near Metz.

of "Land, ho!" were heard. The American coastline before us was flat and barren. I imagine that the Europeans who first visited here three centuries ago found it unappetizing.

We had nearly reached port, or so we thought, when a storm blew up in the southwest and forced us to sail rapidly away from New York. Since we were running low on wood and sugar and were about to exhaust our supply of bread, and there were a number of sick people on board, the captain decided to abandon the plan to land in New York. Instead we made for a small port sixty leagues farther north called New Port. Believe me, it feels good to walk on land again after you've crossed the huge gulf that separates Europe from America.

The next day we boarded a steamboat, which brought us here in eighteen hours. It was an immense machine, bigger than a house and capable of carrying five or six hundred to a thousand people in vast cabins. There were beds available, good food was served, and all the while we made our way at three or four leagues per hour, unaware that we were moving at all.

New York is situated in one of the loveliest settings I know. It has a huge harbor, at the mouth of a river, and warships can navigate as many as thirty leagues upstream.[61] This is the key to North America. Through this port thousands of foreigners arrive every year. These are the people who will populate the wilderness to the west. The port also receives manufactured goods from Europe, which are then rapidly shipped inland. Accordingly, the population of the city, which was just 20,000 fifty years ago, is today 230,000.

It is a clean city, built of brick and marble, but entirely devoid of noteworthy public monuments. In short, it bears no resemblance to a European capital.

We have been received warmly. The French are generally well liked. In addition, our mission has given us a special claim on the kindness of our hosts. We have accordingly received a most flattering welcome from public authorities and private individuals alike. All the public records we want have been placed at our disposal, and all the information we have asked for has been supplied at once.

As you might imagine, it is too early for me to form an opinion about the American people. At first sight, they seem, like all other peoples, to combine vices and virtues in a way that is rather difficult to characterize and does not define a single identity. Morals here seem to be quite pure. The marital bond is more sacred than anywhere else in the world. Respect for religion is taken to an extreme. For example, no one would allow himself to hunt, dance, or even play an instrument on Sunday. Even foreigners are not free in this regard. I have seen streets in front of churches blocked off during the hours of religious services. Here you have republicans who are not at all like our French liberals. There are millions of other differences in regard to ideas, the country's physical situation, and mores, but I haven't time to go into them.

That is the good side. The bad is an unrestrained desire to make a fortune

61. The Hudson River separates the island of Manhattan from the mainland on its west side.

and to make it quickly. It is perpetual instability in people's desires, a constant need for change, an absolute absence of ancient traditions and ancient mores, a commercial and mercantile spirit that is applied to everything, even where it is least appropriate. That is New York, at least to judge by outward appearances.

Tomorrow we will head farther inland. We will take the North River as far as Albany. From there we will go to see Niagara Falls. After visiting the Indian tribes that live along Lake Erie, we will return by way of Canada to Boston and then to New York, before embarking on a new journey. . . .

From Tocqueville | To Louis de Kergorlay

Yonkers, June 29, 1831
20 miles from New York

. . . In your last letter you asked me if anyone here held any *beliefs*. I do not know what precise meaning you attach to the word. What strikes me is that the vast majority of people share certain *common opinions*. To date, this is what I envy most in America. For instance: (1) I have yet to find anyone of any rank who entertained the idea that a republic was not the best possible form of government or that the people might not have the right to choose whatever government they want. The vast majority understand republican principles in the most democratic sense. In a few cases, it is possible to detect certain aristocratic tendencies, which I shall try to describe below. But no one—not magistrates, merchants, or artisans—seems to doubt that republican government is good or natural. This opinion is so widespread and so little discussed, even in a country where the freedom of speech is unlimited, that one might almost call it a belief. A second idea strikes me as similar in character: the vast majority of people have *faith* in human wisdom and common sense, and faith in the doctrine of human perfectibility. Few if any are willing to contradict this belief. No one denies that the majority might be mistaken, yet everyone believes that in the long run it is necessarily right, and that it is not only the sole legal judge of its own interests but also the most reliable and infallible judge. It follows from this idea that enlightenment must be spread widely among the people, who cannot be too well educated. You know how often we (and thousands of others) in France struggled with the question of whether it was desirable to educate all ranks of society or alarming. This question, which was so difficult to answer for France, seems not even to have occurred to anyone here. I have already put it to a hundred of the most thoughtful people I've met, and from the way in which they answered it was clear that they had never considered the matter and that the mere statement of the question struck them as somehow shocking and absurd. Education, they said, is the only protection we have against the aberrations of the multitude.

So much for what I would call the country's *beliefs*, my dear friend. They sincerely believe in the excellence of their government; they believe in the wisdom of the masses, provided they are educated; and they do not appear to suspect that there may be kinds of education that are necessary to govern a state yet the masses can never share. As for what we generally understand by *beliefs*—

ancient mores, ancient traditions, powerful memories—I have thus far discovered no trace. Indeed, I doubt that even religious opinions are as influential as one is inclined to think initially. The religious state of the American people may be the most interesting thing to study here. I shall try to tell you what I know about it when I resume this letter, which I must interrupt, perhaps for several days.

Calwell [*Colwells*] *45 miles from New York.* My mind has been turning over so fast since I began this letter this morning that I feel the need to resume writing without knowing exactly what I want to say. I was speaking last about religion. One is struck on arriving here by the strictness of religious practice. Sunday is observed Judaically. I have seen streets in front of churches blocked off during religious services. The law insists on these things, and opinion, which is more powerful than law, demands that everyone attend church and abstain from all amusement. And yet either I am seriously mistaken or there is a vast reservoir of doubt and indifference hidden beneath these external forms. In contrast to France, irreligion here contains no admixture of political passion, but religion is not in consequence more influential politically. Religion was once a very potent force but has lately been in steady decline. Faith has clearly become passive. Enter any church (any Protestant church) and you will hear talk of morality but not a word about dogma. There is nothing that might in any way shock one's neighbor, nothing to arouse thoughts of dissidence. Yet when a belief grips the mind strongly, people want to explore the abstractions of dogma; they want to engage in the kind of debate appropriate to religious doctrine. Americans used to be like this. This so-called tolerance, which in my opinion is nothing but crass indifference, is carried so far that in public institutions such as prisons and reform schools for young delinquents, ministers of seven or eight different sects preach one after another to the same congregation. I asked how the men and boys who belong to one sect receive the minister of another. Inevitably, the answer was that since the various preachers deal only in moral commonplaces, they do one another no harm. Furthermore, it is clear that, generally speaking, religion here has no profound effect on the soul, whereas in France those who believe demonstrate their belief by sacrificing time, energy, and fortune. One senses that they act in the grip of a dominant passion, whose agent they have become. To be sure, there are also brutes who are horrified by the very word "religion" and who have difficulty distinguishing between good and evil. Neither of these classes seems to me to exist here among the masses of Protestants. People adhere to a religion as our fathers took medicine in the month of May: if it does no good, they seem to say, at least it can do no harm, and in any case it is appropriate to conform to the general rule. When all is said and done, why would you expect anything else? The reformers of the 16th century made the same compromise in religion that people nowadays try to make in politics. They said: such-and-such a principle is bad until this or that consequence flows from it; then it becomes good, as surely you must agree. Or the other way around. But some people—people with ardent and logical minds—would not put up with halfway compromises. This created a vast new realm for the human mind to explore, and, I assure you, the opportunity was seized. The sects in America have proliferated and subdivided *ad infinitum,* in a way that is a wonder to behold. It's as though a series of circles had been drawn around a common center. Each new circle stands a little farther from the center than the previous one. The Catholic faith is the fixed point from which each new sect recedes in the direction of pure deism. You might imagine that this spectacle would inevitably raise inexpugnable doubts in the mind of any thinking Protestant, and I think I perceive such doubts in the recesses of nearly every soul. It seems clear to me that the reformed religion is a kind of compromise, a sort of *representative monarchy* in religious matters that may well satisfy an epoch and serve as transition from one state to another but cannot be a final state; and it is in fact drawing to a close. What will replace it? Here my doubts begin: for the answer to this question, which is of course a *human* question, this country can provide very valuable data, since all the religious and irreligious instincts that can exist in man develop here in perfect freedom. If I were to describe this strange spectacle for you, you would see in it the two conflicting principles that elsewhere divide the world of politics. Protestants of every congregation—Anglicans, Lutherans, Calvinists, Presbyterians, Anabaptists, Quakers, and a hundred other Christian sects—make up the population. It is both a practicing and an indifferent population, which lives from one day to the next and has become accustomed to a *middle of the road* that calms even if it does not satisfy, a middle of the road in which all *proprieties* are respected. These people live and die by vague general precepts and have no wish to delve into things more deeply. They no longer proselytize. Then there is a handful of Catholics, who rely on the tolerance of their old adversaries but who remain essentially as intolerant as ever—intolerant, to put it bluntly, because they *believe.* For them, truth lies in but a single point, apart from which there is only eternal damnation. These Catholics live in civil society but preclude any relation between themselves and the religious societies around them. I have a feeling that their dogma on freedom of conscience is almost the same as in Europe, and I am not sure that they would not persecute the others if they became the more powerful group. Though generally poor, these Catholics are full of zeal. Their priests make a cult of sacrifice, which they have embraced. If Protestant ministers are the industrial working men of religion, these Catholic priests are something else. The Catholics are growing in number at a prodigious rate. Many new arrivals from Europe swell their ranks, but conversions are also numerous.[62] New England and the Mississippi valley have begun to fill with them. Some Protestants have naturally religious minds. They are sound, serious people who find the vagueness of Protestant doctrine tiresome and who feel an urgent need of religion. Such Protestants are giving up in despair on the search for

---

62. By 1830, Catholics made up about 2.5 percent of the American population, compared to about one-half of 1 percent fifty-five years earlier. Irish immigration and French missionary activity, as described by Tocqueville during his travels in the Northwest, contributed to this growth of Catholic Americans.

truth and abjectly surrendering to the empire of *authority*. Reason is a heavy burden for them to bear, and they are glad to sacrifice it. They are becoming Catholics. Catholicism exerts a powerful hold on the senses and the soul. It is better suited to the people than the reformed religion is. The majority of converts belong to the working classes of society. So much for the one end of the chain; now consider the other. On the fringes of Protestantism there is a sect that is Christian in name only: the *Unitarians*.[63] Among the Unitarians, that is, among those who deny the Trinity and know but one God, there are those who see J.C. as nothing more than an angel, others who see him as a prophet, and still others as a philosopher like Socrates. They are pure deists. They speak of the Bible because they don't wish to offend public opinion, which is still entirely *Christian*. They have a Sunday service, which I have attended. There they read verses of Dryden and other English poets about the existence of God and the immortality of the soul.[64] There is a speech on some point of morality, and that is the end of it. This sect is winning proselytes at almost the same rate as Catholicism, but it draws its recruits from the upper rungs of society. Like Catholicism, it has profited from Protestant losses. It is obvious that Protestants have cold and logical minds, and the *argumentative* classes, the people whose habits are intellectual and scholarly, seize the opportunity to join an entirely philosophical sect, which enables them to make an almost public profession of pure deism. In any case, this sect is nothing like the Saint-Simonians in France.[65] In addition to having a quite different point of departure, the Unitarians eschew anything pompous or *ridiculous* when it comes to doctrine or ritual. On the contrary, they seek to resemble the Christian sects outwardly as much as possible, so that they cannot be derided in any way. No partisan spirit drives them or holds them back. Their appearance is naturally grave, and their rituals are simple. As you can see, Protestantism, a mixture of authority and reason, is thus being shattered by the two absolute principles of *reason* and *authority*. Much the same spectacle can be seen everywhere by those who have eyes. Here, though, it is striking, it is obvious. Because in America no power, whether of fact or opinion, impedes the progress of human intelligence and passion in this regard, they follow their natural penchant. I feel sure that it won't be long before the two extremes confront each

63. Unitarianism emphasized the importance of reason in spiritual life and enjoyed great popularity in New England in the second quarter of the nineteenth century. William Ellery Channing (1780–1842) took the lead in defining the central tenets of the Unitarian faith in America, which included the anti-Trinitarian belief in a single God, the innate goodness of humans, the humanity of Jesus, and the importance of reason. The speech he gave in Baltimore at the ordination of Jared Sparks in 1819 was one of the most important moments in the definition of these beliefs.

64. John Dryden (1631–1700) was a popular English poet.

65. The Saint-Simonians were a group of French social activists in the second quarter of the nineteenth century who hoped to shift power from aristocrats to the working and middle classes by increasing industrial organization. Led by Claude Henri de Rouvroy de Saint-Simon, these men turned to the arts—music, ceremonies, and plays—to advance their ideas.

other. What will the final outcome be? At this point I lapse entirely into vagueness and lose my way. Can deism ever suit all the classes of a people? Above all, can it suit those most in need of the brake of religion? I cannot persuade myself that this is the case. I confess that what I have seen here leaves me more disposed than I was before to believe that so-called natural religion can suffice for the upper classes of society, provided that faith in the two or three important truths that it teaches is real and that some sort of outward ritual is adopted that can visibly unite people in the public profession of those truths. But either the people must become something different from what they have been and still are the world over, or they will find nothing in natural religion other than the absence of all belief in the afterlife and succumb straightaway to the pure doctrine of self-interest.

But to return to the current situation in the United States, what I've just said should not be taken as a hard and fast judgment. I have described a clear *tendency* in American thinking, not a *fait accompli.* To my knowledge, clearly, this country still has a deeper reservoir of Christian religion than any other country in the world, and I have no doubt that this mentality continues to influence the political regime. It gives a moral and disciplined coloration to ideas. It prevents the spirit of innovation from getting too far out of line. Above all, it makes people less likely to be rigid in their thinking than in France, where it is common to choose a goal and pursue it stubbornly no matter what. Here, no matter how much a party wants to achieve a certain result, there is no doubt that it would nevertheless feel obliged to respect at least the appearance of *morality* and avoid openly offending religious beliefs, which, even when they are false, are always more or less moralistic.

But don't you admire the wretchedness of human nature? One religion has power over the will, it dominates the imagination, it gives rise to real and profound beliefs, but it divides the human race into the blessed and the damned, creates divisions on earth that are supposed to exist only in the afterlife, and leads to intolerance and fanaticism. The other preaches tolerance and subscribes to reason, which it takes as its symbol. It acquires no power. It is a passive thing, impotent and almost lifeless. Enough about this subject, which consumes my imagination and would ultimately drive me mad if I dwelt on it too much. In any case, there are still many other things that I feel I must tell you about.

Do you know what strikes me most vividly about politics in this country? The effects of the inheritance laws. At the time of the American Revolution, the colonists enjoyed political equality but not equality of wealth. The English had brought with them their laws of primogeniture, under which the eldest son inherits three-quarters of his father's estate. As a result, the country was filled with vast estates passed on from father to son, thus perpetuating wealth within families, so that, by the Americans' own telling, there was a class not of nobles but of large landowners, who lived simple but rather intellectual lives, exemplified a certain tone and polite manners, respected the family spirit, and upheld a code of honor. A certain number of these families took England's side and thereby helped spark the Revolution. All this took place less than 60 years ago. The laws of inheritance were changed. Equal division replaced primogeniture.[66] The result was an almost magical transformation. Estates were divided up and passed on to new owners; the family spirit dwindled; the aristocratic tendency that had distinguished the early years of the republic gave way to an irresistible democratic tendency, against which all thought of struggle became hopeless. Now the division of fortunes is immense; the rapidity with which property changes hands surpasses anything I might have imagined. I have met quite a few descendants of the old families in question. In their heart of hearts they are clearly quite uneasy about the new order. They regret the loss of patronage, of the family spirit, and of refined manners—in short, of aristocracy. Yet they submit to what has now become an irreparable transformation. They admit that, within the states, they are now but one group among others, but they bow gracefully to necessity, because even if they are no longer more favored than others, at least their former position has not become a symbol of exclusion. Because their forebears took part in the Revolution and they themselves never fought against the extension of democracy other than indirectly, public opinion never turned systematically against them. I have heard people in Europe say that there is an aristocratic tendency in America. Those who talk this way are mistaken. This is one conclusion I am prepared to state categorically. On the contrary, democracy is proceeding apace in some states and easy to imagine in its fully mature form in others. It affects mores, laws, and the opinion of the majority. Those who oppose it hide their true opinions and are reduced to flying democracy's colors in order to make headway. In New York, only vagabonds are deprived of the right to vote. The effects of democratic government are everywhere visible. There is perpetual instability in people and laws, outward equality is carried to an extreme, and the tone of society is uniformly common, as is the pattern of ideas. There can be no doubt that the law of inheritance is one of the main reasons for this total triumph of democratic principles. Americans recognize this themselves, whether to complain about it or rejoice in it. It is the law of inheritance that has made us what we are, it is the cornerstone of our republic: one hears this sort of thing every day. It has led me to ponder the matter seriously. If it is true that equal division of property leads more or less rapidly but infallibly to the destruction of families and the family spirit and the complete negation of aristocratic principles (as now seems clear to me), does it not follow that all countries that have established similar civil laws will rapidly proceed either to absolute government or to republican government, and that any attempt that one makes to *permanently* block either of these two routes will prove chimerical? Applying these ideas to France, I cannot help thinking that the charter of Louis XVIII was inevitably

66. The state of New York first passed a law to establish the principle of equality among heirs in February of 1786. Many states followed suit. Tocqueville discussed this change in inheritance rules with members of the Livingston family of New York, who had had extensive landholdings in the state since the seventeenth century.

doomed to fail.[67] He created aristocratic political institutions but left in civil law a democratic principle so potent that it was destined in short order to destroy the foundations of the structure that rested on it. The blunders of Charles X no doubt hastened these developments, but we were headed in that direction anyway.[68] We are proceeding toward unlimited democracy. I do not say that this is a good thing. On the contrary, what I am seeing in this country persuades me that France will adapt to it badly. But we are driven in this direction by an irresistible force. Any efforts to halt this change will only slow it down, since there is no human force that can change the law of inheritance, and with the law of inheritance our families will disappear, property will pass into other hands, wealth will tend to be distributed more and more equally, the upper class will dissolve into the middle, and the middle class will grow vast and impose its equality on all. To refuse to accept these consequences strikes me as a form of weakness. I am therefore led to the inevitable conclusion that the Bourbons, rather than seek openly to reinforce the moribund aristocratic principle in France, should have endeavored with all their might to foster among democrats an interest in order and stability. In my opinion, the communal and departmental system should have been the focus of all their attention from the beginning. Instead of making do with Bonaparte's communal institutions, they should have been eager to modify them, to involve local people gradually in communal affairs, to develop interests in them over time, to create local interests, and above all to establish if possible those *legal habits and ideas* that are in my opinion the sole possible counterweight to democracy. That way they might have diminished the danger to themselves and the state of the change that was already under way. In short, it seems to me that democracy is now something that a government can seek to *regulate* but not to halt—no. It was not easy, I assure you, for me to come to this conclusion. What I have seen in this country has not persuaded me that even in the most favorable circumstances—which existed here—government by the multitude is an excellent thing. People here all but agree that in the early days of the republic, statesmen and members of Congress were far more distinguished than they are today. Nearly all of them belonged to the class of landowners I described above. Now the people no longer have *so sure a touch*. Generally speaking, they choose those who flatter their passions and stand on their own level. This effect of democracy, combined with the extreme instability of all things and the total absence of persistence and continuity that one finds here, persuades me more and more that the most rational government is not one in which *all* interested parties take part but one that is led by the most enlightened and ethical classes of society. Yet it cannot be denied that, on the whole, this country

67. Louis XVIII (1755–1824) passed the Charter of 1814 soon after his restoration to the throne. This charter declared freedom of religious worship and equality before the law as rights of all Frenchmen, regardless of their rank.

68. Charles X (1757–1836) had been deposed by the July Revolution of 1830 after coming to the throne six years before.

is admirable to behold. I will tell you frankly that it persuades me that a free government is superior to any other. I am more convinced than ever that not all nations are capable of enjoying it to the same degree, but I am also more inclined than ever to regret that this should be the case. The universal satisfaction with the existing government here is unimaginable. There is no denying that the people here rank higher on the scale of morality than the people in France. Because everyone has a sense of his independent position and individual dignity, they are not always very pleasant to approach, but ultimately this independence and dignity encourage them to respect themselves and others. I especially admire two things: the first is the extreme respect that people here have for the law: it rules irresistibly on its own, without any apparatus or public force. Indeed, I think the principal reason for this is that the people make the law themselves and can change it. It is a commonplace that thieves who break all the laws of their country will scrupulously obey the laws they impose on themselves. I believe that something similar takes place in the spirit of a nation. The second thing I envy about the Americans is the ease with which they do without government. Each individual here sees himself as having an interest in public security and in the enforcement of the law. Instead of relying on the police, they rely on themselves. As a result, public force is everywhere, even though it remains invisible. It is, I assure you, truly incredible to see how these people maintain order solely by virtue of the notion that the only safeguard against themselves lies within themselves.

As you see, I am reporting all my impressions as best I can. All in all, they are more favorable to America than they were during the first days after my arrival. The canvas reveals an abundance of minor flaws, but taken as a whole it grips the imagination. I am quite prepared to believe that its effect on logical but superficial minds is irresistible, and the combination of logic with superficiality is not uncommon. The principles of government are so simple, and the consequences follow with such perfect predictability, that unless one is careful the mind is won over and swept away. You have to examine your own reactions and struggle against the current to see that these simple and logical institutions are unsuited to a great nation that needs a strong domestic government and a stable foreign policy, that the government is not durable by nature, and that it requires of any people that adopts it a long familiarity with liberty and a substantial amount of *true* enlightenment, which is seldom achieved, and, even then, only over a long period of time. And after you have told yourself all that, you nevertheless still feel that it is a beautiful thing, and sad that man's moral and physical constitution precludes his achieving it always and everywhere.

I earnestly hope that you will respond to me about all of this if you have the time and are inclined to busy yourself with theoretical matters. Thus far we have not had a real exchange, even though we have communicated. I still haven't received an answer to the first letter I wrote you. While I divert myself here with any number of theories, the memory of France gnaws at me like a worm. It catches me unawares when I am at work during the day or when I lie awake at night. The most recent news worried me a good deal. It seemed to me that there were signs of serious unrest in the west. As you know, I have never believed that an insurrection could succeed. I would therefore die of worry if I learned that one had taken place. We have been in New York for two months. Now we're moving on a bit, but no more than a week's travel away. Every five or six days, a ship leaves for Europe, so I am able to do what suits me best. I am still of the opinion that I shared with you before leaving. As long as Louis-Philippe remains, my hands are tied.[69] But if anyone takes his place, no matter who it is, I shall resign my public functions and resume responsibility for my conduct and my actions.

Farewell, my dear friend. My uncertainty as to your fate is one of the things I find most difficult to bear. The sadness of tone and distaste for mankind that dominated your last letter distressed me. Not a day goes by that I do not wish I were with you to share your fortune, good or bad. Farewell once more. I embrace you with all my heart. Keep this letter. It will be interesting for me to read it later.

From Beaumont | To his father

New York, June 29, 1831

. . . We will spend two or three weeks in Boston. We have a lot to look at there. Apparently, it is the most intellectually vibrant city in the United States. People say that it even outdoes Philadelphia in this respect. But it is especially noteworthy for its pervasive religious spirit. In this respect it exhibits a rather strange phenomenon: it is the home of the most austere Presbyterians, yet right next door the University of Cambridge is the seat of a sect of philosophers known as Unitarians, who, while wearing the mask of religion, attack all dogma and principle and attempt to reduce all religious beliefs to natural religion.[70] This philosophical sect is growing rapidly, we are told. It has already reached New York, but it is most powerful in Boston, and that is where we must go to study its influence and doctrines. You can imagine what the consequences of this might be: Unitarianism tends to dissolve all religious bonds, which are the most substantial underpinning of American society. Clearly, there is a tendency in all Protestant denominations to move to one extent or another toward the position of the Unitarians. If they were to reach that point, they would in fact cease to be religions, leaving the Catholic religion alone in the field. If the Catholics, who are attracting many new converts daily, were to find themselves the sole oppo-

---

69. Louis-Philippe (1773–1850) had ascended the throne during the July Revolution of 1830. Because Tocqueville's parents were supporters of the Bourbon Restoration and Charles X, Tocqueville helped them go into hiding during the three days of street fighting (*"les trois glorieuses"*) from July 27 to July 29. Even though he took an oath of allegiance to the July Monarchy, Tocqueville felt his hands were tied because of his family's allegiance to the previous Bourbon regime.

70. Here Beaumont refers to Harvard College as the University of Cambridge.

nent of one large philosophical sect, they would become enemies of that sect and eventually enter into open battle with it, no doubt at the instigation of the latter.

There is probably no single issue that comes closer to the central questions of whether American society will endure, what its character will be, and how it will progress. So we will do our best to ascertain what is happening in order to divine, if possible, what will happen in the future. As I discover new things and identify problems that seem difficult to resolve, I will let you know and ask the advice of the family council. For now, what do you think of this philosophical movement, which is currently agitating Boston and the surrounding area?

The Unitarians, it should be noted, are the first Protestants who deny the divinity of Jesus Christ and yet still call themselves Christians. They do so because they consider Jesus Christ to be God's agent. They acknowledge the divinity of his mission while maintaining that he is only a man. Bossuet predicted that the Reformation would end only when it became natural religion.[71] Bossuet had a fairly good head and was a good judge of the implications of certain facts. But to what extent will this religious revolution influence the peace and prosperity of American society? What moral consequences will it have? What influence will it have on the nation's political character? I have no clear ideas about these things and would like to figure them out.

From Tocqueville | To Abbé Lesueur

New York, June 30, 1831

... We are planning to leave this city tomorrow, my dear Bébé. We have now seen all the interesting things and people. We have been here for six weeks, and we shall be leaving with very pleasant memories.

Our intention is to proceed up the North River to *Albany.* From there we will go to *Auburn,* a town situated above [sic] Lake Ontario. We will probably stay ten to twelve days to study the well-known prison there. From there, we will go to Niagara Falls and make our way to Boston via Montreal and Quebec. Here they call this "the fashionable tour." Many people take this route during the summer. It's a journey of a month to five weeks. We will take a little longer, because we will be stopping in several places.

To give you an idea of how rapid travel is here, I will tell you that at Fort Niagara you board a steamboat, which takes you to Montreal in thirty-six hours. You can see from the map that this is quite some distance. The vicinity of Lake Ontario, which twenty years ago was wilderness, is now covered with towns and villages. You have to travel a hundred leagues inland to reach the real wilderness now. The short journey we are about to take would please us no end if we were not worried about having to go too long without mail and about not

71. Beaumont is most likely referring to the conclusion of the book *Histoire des variations des églises protestantes* (1688), by Jacques-Bénigne Bossuet (1627–1704), a French theologian with close ties to the court of Louis XIV.

being able to write to you exactly as we have done thus far. As you can imagine, being so far from New York, it will be impossible for us to time our mailings so as to be sure that our letters reach the city before the departure of the packet boats, which now sail every ten days. Inevitably, some letters will suffer a ten-day delay, and some ships will bring you nothing. I am telling you this because I know that you worry about me and know how easy it is for you to imagine that some misfortune has befallen us. . . .

The Americans, or at any rate the educated ones, have more reasonable opinions than I had thought about the state of France. I assure you that, although they are republicans at home, they do not believe that republican government can take hold in a great nation any more than we do.

Nevertheless, opinion is much more divided than I had thought about La Fayette. Generally speaking, the educated classes judge him as we do.[72] Few people in France suspect this. . . .

From Beaumont | To his brother Jules

Albany, July 4, 1831

My dear Jules,

I don't want to delay my reply to you any longer, and even though there is no ship leaving for Le Havre before the 10th of this month, I am going to begin my letter today and continue it over the next few days if I don't finish it right away. If you meant to make me happy by writing a good long letter, I assure you that you have fully achieved your purpose. I read your letter with a joy I cannot put into words. It was of the utmost interest, not only for the feelings it contained but also for your observations concerning the country in which I am traveling.

I am deeply grateful that you have taken an interest in America while I am here, and I'm sure that brotherly affection has lent charm and interest to your reading.

If postage weren't so expensive, I would send you a map of North America more detailed than the one you have already and similar to the one we are forced to use for our travels. I am afraid that you may find it difficult at times to follow our progress. Thus far, it wasn't very hard, because we didn't leave New York except to go to Sing Sing. But now we are on our way, and if you really want to follow our route, you may need to wear out your eyes reading the map.

We left New York on June 30. We had one visit to make, to a Mr. Livingston, who lives on the banks of the Hudson seven or eight leagues from New York. Our intention was to travel by steamship, but that day the boat service was suspended. We were therefore forced to resort to another means of transportation. In the port we stumbled upon a sloop (a small, single-masted vessel)

72. Tocqueville, Beaumont, and their families regarded Lafayette's republicanism as extreme and dangerous. Beaumont was a distant cousin of Lafayette and later married one of his granddaughters.

View of the Hudson at "Younker." Twenty miles from New York, 30 June 1831. At left Tocqueville is returning from his hunt, where he "waged a war to the death on the birds of America," wrote Beaumont four days later. (GB2)

headed where we wanted to go. We embarked at once, and after a pleasant sail of two or three hours we arrived in Yonkers, a village not far from Mr. Livingston's home.[73] The Livingstons were absent, however, so we had to return to Yonkers. But what were we to do next? Where were we to go?

We would have liked to continue up the Hudson, heading for Albany and stopping at various places that warranted a closer look, such as West Point, where the United States military school is located, and Catskill, where the heights offer a much-renowned view. But we had no means of transportation, so we were stuck in Yonkers with no way to continue.

We spent the evening as best we could. After consuming a small meal, Tocqueville took his rifle and I my portfolio and album, and, sitting on top of a hill, I drew a view of the Hudson, next to which I carefully placed Yonkers and the sloop that brought us there, while Tocqueville waged a war to the death on the birds of America.

The birds are on the whole delightful. Many are all blue, while others have black bodies and a very pretty yellow band around the neck. These are very common. We haven't yet had many occasions for shooting. We forgot to bring

73. Founded in the mid-seventeenth century by the Dutch, Yonkers is located on the Hudson River about twenty miles north of New York City.

our rifles with us to Sing Sing. In any case, given our position, hunting is a decidedly minor occupation.

Meanwhile, back in Yonkers, evening's shadows had begun to blot out the light of day, so I had to close my album. We made our way down the hill and, upon reaching the bank of the river, jumped into the Hudson for a pleasant swim. I swim rather well now thanks to my friend Tocqueville's lessons. He has been very persistent in helping me acquire this talent, which is most useful to sailors.

That night, we found waiting for us at our lodging two wretched beds located in a sort of attic, which the last rays of the setting sun had left so warm that I thought we might suffocate during the night. The next morning, the New York–Preskill [Peekskill] steamboat came to our rescue. We planned to take this to Callwell [Colwells], a very picturesque village on the left bank of the Hudson and then, after spending the necessary time there, to take another steamboat to West Point. We did in fact make it to Callwell. There we took a delightful hike through the woods and over the rocks and sweat blood and tears to reach the summit of a very tall mountain, at the top of which we enjoyed one of the most beautiful sights and impressive panoramas that the North [Hudson] River has to offer.

Mountain chains were visible in every direction. Closer to us was a bay called Antoine's Nose, which is the most picturesque sight you can imagine.[74] We waited until nightfall for a steamboat to arrive. With its customary haste it appeared at nine o'clock. It did not pull up to the place where we were waiting, because that would have taken too much time, but instead launched a dinghy into which we were hurled like cargo along with our baggage. Then we were towed over to the steamboat. It all happened so fast and in such darkness over such a vast expanse of water that there was something almost magical about our abduction. Shortly thereafter we were in for another surprise: as we arrived in Newburgh, which is a few leagues from Callwell, fireworks were launched from the steamboat. Rockets were fired into the sky, and the ship was illuminated with some sort of combustible material, probably sulfur and resin, which cast so bright a light in all directions that it seemed like midday.

Imagine the state of mind of the passengers who were treated to this unexpected spectacle while floating in the middle of a river a league wide and flanked by steep walls 1,000 or 1,500 feet high. Add to that the effect produced by the small town of Newburgh on the shore in front of us, which our fireworks illuminated so clearly that we could make out the houses and the crowds gathered on the bank to watch us pass. The town answered with rockets and fireworks of its own.

We had no idea of the reason for these celebrations. It was the first of July. At first we thought that they might be celebrating the Declaration of Indepen-

74. Hiking around the foothill terrain of Colwells provided an excellent view of West Point and of Anthony's Nose, a peak overhanging the Hudson River that looks like the profile of a man with a large nose. This feature had been named and was well-known in the Hudson Valley region by the late seventeenth century.

dence of the United States, which took place on the fourth of July. But then why not await the fourth instead of celebrating four days ahead of time?

Eventually we found out that our steamboat, the *North America,* had left New York at the same time as another boat and that the two were engaged in a race. The *North America* was in the lead and was celebrating its victory in every port. And since this race had been publicized, the bank was lined with people who wanted to see the outcome.

In any event, this race, which rewarded us with several interesting experiences, was also the cause of one genuine disappointment. Shortly after coming aboard, we told the captain that we wanted to go to West Point. He replied that he couldn't stop there, so we had to continue on. As a result, we reached Albany, which is about 50 leagues (144 miles) from New York, on the morning of July 2.

You can find Albany on the map if you start at New York and follow the Hudson from south to north. Albany is a town of 25,000 inhabitants.[75] It is a fairly pretty place, nicely situated. It looks a lot like Amiens. The Hudson, which by this point has lost all its grandeur and majesty, reminded me quite a bit of the Somme.[76]

Albany is the capital of the state of New York. It owes this advantage to its central position. Its population has doubled over the past ten years, and all signs are that its growth will not slow at anytime soon. The Hudson allows for convenient communication with New York, which is the intermediary between Albany and Europe, and there is a canal which joins the waters of the Hudson to those of Lake Erie,[77] so that Albany is the marketplace for all the settlements in this part of the west. Trade will soon become even easier thanks to a railroad that is now under construction and will eventually run from Albany to Schenectady.[78]

Upon arriving here we searched out a gentleman to whom we had letters of introduction: Mr. Cambreling [Cambreleng], a member of Congress.[79] He is a resolute and practical man. He received us most handsomely and immediately introduced us to the secretary of state (that is, the minister of the interior of the state of New York). The secretary of state is a small man of very abstracted appearance. He looks like a clerk and wears blue stockings; the rest of his attire is equally negligent. He always sleeps at the inn, and his official salary is no more

75. Albany, built on the site of the seventeenth-century Dutch Fort Orange, became the state capital in 1777. The 1830 census recorded over twenty-four thousand inhabitants of the city.

76. The Somme River is located in northern France.

77. The Erie Canal was completed in 1825.

78. Completed in the fall of 1831, the Mohawk and Hudson Railroad was one of the earliest railways in the United States. It later became known as the Albany and Schenectady Railroad and was incorporated into the New York Central Railroad.

79. Churchill C. Cambreleng (1786–1862), a wealthy merchant who had moved to New York around 1800, served in the U.S. House of Representatives from 1821 to 1839. He was a political ally of Andrew Jackson and of New Yorker Martin Van Buren.

than seven or eight thousand francs. One would fare almost as well as a deputy in Paris as a minister in America.

Mr. Flagg (for that is his name) gave us a multitude of invaluable documents: brochures, reports, books, plans.[80] He sends us these at all hours of the day and regards them as gifts to the commissioners of the French government (as he calls us).

We will leave here tonight, but we wanted to see the Fourth of July ceremony first. Since it is only 7 in the morning and I have not yet seen anything of the celebration, I cannot tell you about it. After leaving Albany we intend to spend two days in Saratoga, whose waters attract a multitude of foreigners as well as Americans.[81]

You asked me a number of questions about American mores that I think I more or less fully answered in my previous letters. Nevertheless, at the risk of repeating myself, I am going to take each of your questions and place an answer next to it. If I repeat what I said before word for word, you may infer that I maintain the opinions I expressed previously. If I contradict myself, it will be because fresh observations have altered my feelings.

How, you ask, do wealthy people live? What are their occupations, and how do they dress? How are the hours of the day regulated?

First, mark one thing well: in the state of New York there are no "rich people" in the sense we ordinarily ascribe to the word. Broadly speaking, we use the word "rich" to describe those whose only occupation is to spend their wealth, people who live on their rents, who have either retired to their country estates or consume their income in the cities.

In the state of New York, everyone is engaged in commerce and industry. So vast and fertile are the resources in land and so easy the access to markets owing to the region's broad rivers and excellent harbor, that all of its inhabitants can engage in commerce and acquire wealth.

In most countries there are those who work and those who consume. Here everyone works, as far as I can see. The consumers are in the countries to which the state of New York sends what it grows and manufactures. New York's great advantage is to be the port for all of Europe, which supplies the needs of all the regions of North America. You can imagine the habits that such a state of affairs inculcates in a people: everyone one meets is engaged in business. Money is the deity that everyone worships, and it is so easy to make a fortune in this country that one cannot help but forgive the Americans for having such an avidity for wealth.

80. Azariah Flagg (1790–1873) was a newspaper editor who served as secretary of state for New York from 1826 to 1833. He was also a political ally of Andrew Jackson and Martin Van Buren.

81. Saratoga Springs, fifty miles west of Albany, was a popular tourist site throughout the nineteenth century. Travelers spent time at the natural springs in the town for pleasure and for health.

You may be thinking that since it is so easy to get rich, there must be *rich people* and therefore people living on their rents. But no, at least not in the state of New York. The fortunes that are amassed with such prodigious speed through industry are destroyed just as promptly by the inheritance laws, which mandate equal division of estates. In addition, it is rare for a man who has been in business his whole life to quit before reaching a quite advanced age. Finally, even a man who has amassed a large fortune through work will nevertheless insist that his children go into business, as if they had to in order to live. Thus you see the most distinguished "American gentlemen" leave their countinghouses to attend a ball. In the morning you'll find them in their shops ready to sell you a yard of cloth, and in the evening you're dancing opposite them in a contradance.

This industrial state, which is the basis of society, influences all the manners and all the habits of men and women alike. The men are obliged to be on their feet early in the morning, hence they are hungry early. Breakfast is therefore served at 7:30 or 8 at the latest. The women are used to diligence and *forced to shun idleness*. It's therefore quite common to find them in the streets at 7 in the morning. By 10 or noon at the latest they're dressed in their finest clothing. Since they are not as busy as their husbands, they walk a great deal, unless they are kept at home by the need to care for the family. What is more, it is the unmarried young women who are the most relentless strollers. In New York there is a place called Broadway, which means "big street," where you are sure to find all the elegant women of New York between noon and 3. The young ladies walk alone. And if a young man of their acquaintance should meet some of these young ladies? He will approach them straightaway, chat with them, and stroll about with them as long as he pleases. He may not, however, offer his arm to one of them unless they happen to be "engaged," that is, pledged to marry. Yet there is no such thing as "betrothal" here. They merely court for an appropriate length of time before *agreeing* to wed. If you see a young man and a young woman *arm in arm,* it is as if the marriage banns had been published. It follows that to offer one's arm to a young lady is truly tantamount to asking for her heart and her hand.

The fair sex spends its time strolling, reading, making music, etc. I had thought that the young ladies here had rather little taste for needlework, yet I've seen some who do marvelous embroidery. They seem to have more talent for work of the head than for work of the imagination. Nearly all know or have learned French; a few speak it well. It is a widely held opinion that knowledge of our language is an essential element of their upbringing. Their music is barbarous, and when making music ceases to be fashionable, nothing will be lost and everyone will be better off. Dinner is served at 2 or 3, tea at 7, and supper at 10.

In the evening one visits or receives. Generally speaking, when you visit a home in the evening, it is to remain there, and if you rise to leave after an hour you are confronted with faces astonished by your exit.

On the whole American women dress quite expensively but lack taste. They imitate French fashions in everything. All their accoutrements come from Paris, and France does quite a brisk business as a result. But the Americans often take what is least good in our fashions, and they frequently exaggerate. They decorate themselves with ornaments but distribute them badly about their persons. They overdo their jewelry and drape themselves with clashing colors. The whiteness of their complexion is remarkable, but I have yet to find a perfect beauty exhibiting every aspect of *le beau idéal.*

They are very eager to please and most gracious and attentive to strangers. If one wished to engage in intrigues, it would be enough to let oneself go. But I do not think it would go very far without some indication of an intention to wed, in which case *it would end in farce.* You will agree, I'm sure, that the game isn't worth the candle, and I'd rather go after Mademoiselle B. at Château-du-Loir and live as her spouse in my château de Vaux or in my still-untouched land at La Moussardière than settle in America far from my family and friends.[82] So you can rest assured that I will return from the land of liberty still a free man. Nothing less than love of the fatherland is needed to turn me so strongly against any idea of settling in this country, because the women here are so faithful to their husbands, which is tempting to those who are not accustomed to the sight of such a phenomenon.

But after all, as La Fontaine says, "Does this mean your hat sits less comfortably on your head than usual?"[83] I don't know what gossip I've got myself into. Instead of describing the mores of the Americans, I am telling you about mine. I return to your letter and your questions.

How, you ask, do they amuse themselves?

They have few diversions. It seems that during the winter there are many balls, but because the temperature has been 25 degrees since my arrival, there have been few gatherings of this kind. At the moment, the most fashionable and common diversion seems to be horseback riding. No one owns horses. You rent them. You can find very handsome and very good horses for 7 or 8 francs for half a day. Every evening, you find a host of amazons and their mounted escorts in the city and the surrounding countryside.

In the house in New York where I was staying were two very pretty ladies, daughters of the owner. They were therefore obliged to wait on us from morning till night, providing linen, laying the table, etc. At night, however, they would undergo a complete metamorphosis and change of appearance: they put on very fine riding costumes, donned fine plumed hats, and rode across town

82. Beaumont is referring to a cousin who lived at an estate owned by another branch of his family, saying that he would rather marry her and live near the family home in Beaumont-la-Chartre than marry an American woman and stay abroad.

83. Beaumont refers to a line from Jean de La Fontaine's poem "The Magic Cup" (1671):

I'd like to state the arguments thanks to which I find
That to be a cuckold is entirely in one's mind.
Does it make your hat no longer fit?
Not the teeny tiniest little bit.

with a triumphal air. And when they returned home, they would prepare us a glass of sugared water.

The stage is of little use to society. It is not the fashion to attend plays. The theaters are poor, and there is no decent music to be heard in any of them.

Thus you see, more or less, how Americans live. They have little need for amusement, because their lives are very busy and active. The women, moreover, are far more distinguished specimens of their kind than the men. The men exhibit little in the way of polite manners. They are either rude and coarse or else carry politeness to the point of indiscretion. Their helpfulness is at times extremely oppressive, and when they have taken it in mind to be of service to you, there is no escape.

The fine arts are in their infancy here. Nature has not made them fit for music. I do not believe that they are any better suited to painting. You ask me if there is a museum in New York. Indeed, there are several. But what do you think is in them? A magic lantern and a few stuffed birds. Tocqueville and I laughed like madmen when we entered a building marked "American Museum" and saw such things instead of the paintings we expected to find.[84]

There are a few public libraries, but they hold no more than 20,000 volumes, and no one uses them. In any case, literature is scarcely cultivated. Everyone learns to read, write, and calculate. In short, they want to know enough to do business, but they don't care much about *belles lettres*. We are told that it is different in Boston and Philadelphia. We shall see.

There is one form of literature that one finds on the streets and in the home of the cobbler as well as the wealthiest banker: newspapers. Even the servants read them. Generally speaking, no one has a private library. Newspapers are the reading matter for the whole household. The newspapers are almost entirely devoted to business matters. They are enormous, and three-quarters of the columns are filled with advertisements similar to M. Williaume's notices. To all intents and purposes, the commercial and mercantile spirit predominates. Political discussions have no other subject. In this respect, the major dispute at the moment is the one that pits the North against the South over the tariff. In the North there are newly established manufacturers who would find it difficult to survive without the help of the tariff, which imposes import duties on foreign manufactured products. The inhabitants of the South, who have no manufacturing, suffer from the tariff, the effect of which is to force them to pay more for the manufactured goods they need.

Utica, July 6

My political discussion was interrupted, my dear Jules, and since then I have traveled a good way. I am writing now in great haste from an inn in Utica,

84. P. T. Barnum purchased this museum in 1841 and turned it into a showplace of human curiosities, performances, and artifact displays that gained notoriety in the quarter century that followed. In his autobiography, Barnum describes the American Museum that Beaumont visited; also known as Scudder's Museum, it was founded in 1810 and displayed taxidermied animals and curious specimens from the natural world.

where I have half an hour to wait for a carriage.[85] I just want to close my letter and post it in time to reach New York before the 10th of this month, when the boat leaves for Le Havre.

In my next letter, which I am planning to send to Eugénie, I will have several things to tell you about, including a visit we made to the Quakers, a religious community three leagues from Albany, as well as the details of the ceremony marking the anniversary of the Declaration of Independence on July 4. It was that damned ceremony that first distracted me from my correspondence. I had to join Tocqueville to watch the *procession*. We were honored on that occasion as we have been on others, and we crossed the city in great pomp at the head of the column, between the governor and the chancellor, who vied with each other to lavish us with their attentions. It was impossible to be less than civil toward such people.

In any case, this ceremony impressed us in various ways about which I am eager to tell you.

I have no idea, dear friend, how I could have written you such a long letter without saying anything interesting. When I glance at the preceding pages, I see only more or less insignificant details. When it comes to writing you long letters, however, I remain incorrigible. Now I am headed west. You can probably find Utica on the map if you follow the Mohawk River almost to Schenectady. From here I go to Syracuse. It was on the banks of the Mohawk that Cooper set *The Last of the Mohicans*.[86] The countryside is very beautiful. From Schenectady to here is one vast forest dotted with a few clearings containing homes. The banks of the Mohawk could hardly be more picturesque. The river often flows between vertical stone walls of prodigious height. You often encounter waterfalls spilling from the mountaintops. The wealth of nature is everywhere, and many sites are completely wild. The land seems fertile wherever it has been cultivated. There are parts of the valleys we have explored that remind us strongly of Normandy in regard to the fertility of the soil and the lushness of the vegetation. I add this reservation because the French province of which I speak has nothing as picturesque as this region. We have departed, as you will have noticed, from our original travel plan. We intended to go first to Saratoga after leaving Albany, but we have postponed that errand.

I have no time to tell you of the emotions we have experienced in exploring this half-wild, half-civilized country, which fifty years ago harbored numerous and powerful nations that have since vanished from the land or been driven into still more remote forests, and in which new people have rapidly settled, building splendid towns and ruthlessly supplanting the hapless Indians, who were too weak to resist them. Half a century ago the names "Iroquois" and "Mohawk"

85. The Erie Canal made Utica a significant city in upstate New York; in 1830, the city had over eight thousand residents.

86. James Fenimore Cooper published *The Last of the Mohicans* in 1826. It quickly became one of the most widely read books of the era in America and Europe.

filled this region, but now little remains of these once-powerful tribes but the memory. Their majestic forests are daily cut down. Civilized nations have settled on the ruins until other peoples subject them to the same fate.

But I almost forgot that the carriage is to arrive any minute. There are frequent announcements. I have another letter to seal and ought to be doing many other things as well: for instance, I intended to write my sister a note to thank her for the kind words in her last letter. I see that I must postpone that pleasure, and that I must also put off to another day my compliments on your new posterity, which will probably have hatched by the time this letter arrives. Last but not least, I want to give a warm hug to my nephews François and Léonce, whom I love with all my heart. Hugs as well to their father and mother.

Farewell . . .

From Tocqueville | To his father

Albany, July 4, 1831

. . . The city named in the dateline of this letter is located on the Hudson, about fifty leagues from New York. The steamboat takes you there in twelve hours. It is a city of at least twenty-five thousand people and the seat of the central government of the state. The latter is its only claim on our attention, and there are a good many documents here that we would not be able to obtain anywhere else. So we have been here for four or five days. We leave tomorrow for the waters of Saratoga, which are located some fifteen leagues to the west. Here as elsewhere the authorities have shown us every kindness. They have *given* us everything that exists in the way of printed documents, and we'll be bringing a *trunk* full of them back to France.

For the rest, the central government here has virtually no existence. It is responsible only for matters pertaining to the state as a whole; otherwise, localities manage their own affairs. With this system they have made republican government practical. Each limited ambition finds a small center of action within its reach, around which its activity can be deployed without danger to the state. I imagine that if the Bourbons, instead of fearing the organization of the towns, had sought gradually from the beginning of the Restoration to ascribe a certain importance to each locality, they would have found it less difficult to contend with the massive passions that various people had stirred up against them.

We will stay only two days in Saratoga, which no doubt resembles every other spa in the world and can therefore offer us more pleasure than real utility. From there we go to Auburn. We have already done a huge amount of research on the penitentiary system. I believe that the bulk of the work is done, and I'm quite delighted by the thought. The results of our work are less satisfactory than we had hoped, however. We will return to France with some new facts and very fresh ideas but not much that can be put into practice. For the rest, I assure you that we will be well-versed in our subject. . . .

FROM THE OLD NORTHWEST
(AND BACK TO ALBANY BY WAY OF CANADA)

From Beaumont | To his sister, Eugénie[87]

Auburn, July 14, 1831

... Four leagues from this town there is a settlement of Quakers (called Shakers).[88] This religious sect is much discussed in Europe and America, but few people are really familiar with it. My ideas are still far from clear. But I will tell you what I saw, and since I will tell you everything I know, you can easily judge what I don't know.

We found the Quaker settlement in a perfectly isolated spot in the middle of the woods. The buildings they live in are very clean and built of wood, as are all American houses outside the cities. Some of the residences are set aside for men, others for women. The latter are separated from the former in such a way that communication between them is impossible. It is a strange new sight for us, to find a community of religious men adjacent to a congregation of religious women and in a sense living under the same roof, albeit separately. Both men and women are pledged to remain celibate forever. In so doing they claim to be acting in conformity with the will of God, and they hold that everyone in this world should do as they do. I do not understand how, with such a system, the human race is not supposed to end after a single generation. As in all countries, there are people here with sharp tongues, and they say that even if everyone became a Quaker and lived as virtuously as the Quakers do now, the world still would not end all that soon ... but, frankly, I do not believe this slander. The Shaker Quakers have based their community on the sharing of all property. Though founded on the most antisocial principle that one can imagine, this little society has survived until now. I hope the Saint-Simonians do as well.

All Quakers work ardently for the common good. They own land, which they farm themselves, and live on what they grow. At the moment there are about a hundred of them, men and women alike. According to several people with whom I discussed the matter, the members of the community were not highly respected individuals before joining the group, which supposedly recruits only men and women whose social position has declined and who find more actual advantages in the Quaker society than in the communities in which they lived previously. I have not yet verified this, however.

In any case, at ten thirty we entered the room in which we knew they were to hold their service. Several benches had been arrayed around the room for observers who came from Albany and the surrounding region to see the Shakers.

87. Eugénie de Beaumont (1796–1855) was Gustave's only sister. She had married Pierre-Henry de Sarcé in 1820.

88. Sometimes called the Shaking Quakers, the American sect of Shakers was founded by Ann Lee (1736–1784). Lee and a small number of followers emigrated from England to the United States in 1780 and settled just outside of Albany, New York.

You should know that in English the word "shake" means to move about. You will see in a moment whether the Quakers we had gone to observe deserved to be called Shakers.

In the portion of the room opposite the area reserved for spectators, five or six benches had been arranged on the right and an equal number on the left. The women entered first and took their places on the benches to the right. Some were quite old, others very young. The latter were ugly, some of the others pretty. Two or three were mere children. They dress differently from other American women. Their clothing was all white, and they wore slender gray hats. Upon entering the room, they removed these to reveal a very plain cap underneath. All were dressed the same way. Once seated, they laid a white handkerchief across their laps and placed their hands on it very carefully as if performing some sort of exercise. Once their hands were placed in this way, they did not move them again until the next phase of the ritual. The men entered a moment later and seated themselves opposite the women, on the left. They, too, were of all ages. Some struck me as men of dubious character, while others seemed respectable enough, but I am reluctant to judge by appearances. All were very well dressed. Their linen was very clean, and all wore purple suits and large hats with long, broad brims. This is the only aspect of their attire that distinguishes them from other American men. Once the men had taken up their position facing the women, everyone stood. They remained standing for at least five minutes without saying a word. Then one of them stepped forward to speak and explained on behalf of the community that the only purpose of their meeting was to glorify God and sing His praises. No sooner did he finish speaking than all the Shakers, male and female, began singing a hymn that I cannot recall even though they went on singing it over and over again for twenty minutes without interruption. I simply have no memory for American music, which is surely the most barbarous in the world. All the men and women swayed back and forth as they sang, so that they resembled a dancing bear swaying to the sound of fife and drum. I noticed that the older women sang much more loudly than the younger ones and also moved a good deal more. By contrast, the young novices took a much more lively interest in their surroundings and gazed at the audience with eyes that were not dead to this world.

A second orator then stepped forward, and when he had finished, the singing and dancing resumed. This time, when they stopped, they knelt down, but they remained on their knees only momentarily and thereafter never knelt again.

At this point the really burlesque part of the ceremony began. They had previously sung "praise the Lord" and danced about in ways that could perhaps be explained by exaltation and enthusiasm. But now, suddenly, they began dancing in earnest. Together they moved forward and backward and sang, or rather shouted, in unison. A dozen men formed a line and seemed to move their hands in such a way as to direct the dancing of the others. On the opposite side, a similar number of women did exactly the same thing. As they danced, they all waved their hands, which they held chest-high.

I cannot describe the distress I felt at the sight of such folly and absurdity in a religious ceremony. There was something hideous in the spectacle of white-haired elders dancing, something monstrous in the way they coupled these grotesque dances with an observance that claimed to be Christian. The grave mien of the dancers only confirmed my impression. I would have been tempted to laugh had I not been moved to a profound feeling of pity by what I had observed. By the way, every speaker had been at pains to say that the Quaker doctrine was the one true religion. One of them deplored the fact that it was so hard for many people to recognize this and that there exist so many contrary religious beliefs. They seem to be aware, however, that there is something funny about at least the outward form of their practice, because one of them admonished the audience not to laugh. Everyone had been very sober to that point, however, so this was a recommendation, not a reproach.

The ceremony ended with a special dance. Men and women alike began to leap about the room one after another, while fifteen or twenty Quakers stood still in the middle of the circle. In this final exercise, they waved their arms wildly, jerked their bodies around, and sang more stridently than before. I almost forgot to mention that from time to time they stopped and clapped their hands, rather like dancers doing what we call *La Boulangère* or *Le Carillon de Dunkerque*.[89]

What would one think of our poor species if one saw such scenes often? These men and women who struck me as so pitifully demented are human beings. They have sound ideas about everything except religion. A great many of them seem to me perfectly sincere in their extravagance. What is the cause of such aberrant behavior?

There is no denying the fact that the human mind, left to its own devices, easily goes astray. The Catholic religion established the principle of authority. The Reformation came. Once begun, it did not end. The Reformation was the work of *reason,* and reason, once liberated from the yoke of authority, gave rise to a thousand Christian sects, some of which are as absurd and senseless as one can imagine.

All this idle talk aside, you will have gathered that I have not yet made up my mind about the Quakers and Shakers. They are religious hermits who nevertheless do frequent the towns from time to time and do maintain relations with the rest of society. I can understand the Trappist who flees the world to lose himself in solitude and who in his austere surroundings digs his own grave.[90] I see this as a consequence of a deep faith and of an exaltation that can be ex-

89. Both dances were rhythmic French country dances whose quadrille forms had become popular at bourgeois balls. The former took its name from a popular song, "La boulangère a des écus," and the name of the latter refers to the bells of the town of Dunkirk.

90. The Trappists are a monastic order of the Roman Catholic Church called the Order of the Cistercians of the Strict Observance. This order, which was founded in the twelfth century (and revived in the seventeenth), follows the Rule of Saint Benedict to maintain a lifestyle devoted to contemplation.

plained by the human passions. What I cannot understand at all is the life of a monk who withdraws from the world but continues to frequent others who remain in it. Even less do I understand a religious community that takes vows of chastity yet keeps a community of women constantly before its eyes, apparently to claim still greater merit for itself.

But I have already written too much on this subject and beg your pardon, my dear friend, for my prolix narrative and overabundance of detail. I am so pressed that I have no time to be brief.

The day after our visit to the Quakers was the Fourth of July. On that day Albany, along with every other city in the United States, celebrated the anniversary of the Declaration of Independence (which was issued in 1776). Some early-morning artillery salvoes heralded the holiday, and flags hung from every window. At ten o'clock, the militia, civilian authorities, and representatives of every association that exists in the city gathered and marched in a procession to a church, where the Declaration of Independence was read and a speech was delivered.

The order in which the authorities were ranked was not the same as in France. Militia officers led the parade, followed by high officials of the civilian government such as the governor, the chancellor, the secretary of state, the treasurer, etc., and then members of various departments and deputations. What is more, priorities here are not fixed by any law. On the eve of the holiday, citizens or their representatives meet to decide on the order of march, and next year they may change their minds. You should also know that in the parade at Albany last July 4th were two very distinguished men who just happened by chance to be there at the time. You would have been very surprised to find them in the front ranks, between the governor and the chancellor. Those two great men were Tocqueville and myself. The governor and the secretary of state called for us at our hotel, and we were obliged to participate in the ceremony from beginning to end.

There was nothing brilliant about the occasion. In terms of impressiveness, it could not compare with the most insignificant of our political or religious ceremonies. Yet there was something great in the very simplicity of the celebration. No fine uniforms or embroidered robes are to be found here. One must think instead about the great event that the occasion is meant to commemorate and ponder the emblems by which the idea of that event is engraved in the nation's memory. Some marchers carried, in great pomp, an old bullet-riddled American flag that had survived the War for Independence. Others rode in a wagon at the head of the procession: three or four old soldiers who had fought with Washington. The city cherishes them as though they were precious relics, honored by all its citizens. Later in the parade came a richly decorated wagon, which carried the printing press that was used to print the first copies of the Declaration of Independence. Representatives of all the industrial and commercial trades carried banners bearing the names of their organizations. It would be easy to ridicule banners with inscriptions such as "Butchers' Association," "Apprentices' Association," etc. But when you think about it, you realize that it is only natural that a nation that owes its prosperity to trade and industry should honor such symbols. The Declaration of Independence was read in the Methodist church (a Protestant denomination) by an official whose functions are similar to those of the royal prosecutor in France. He read with a good deal of warmth and dignity. It is truly an admirable piece, and the emotions that it aroused in the audience were not feigned.

The reading was preceded by a prayer offered by a Protestant minister. I mention this because it is typical of this country, where nothing is ever done without the aid of religion. I do not think that they are any the worse for it.

A young lawyer then delivered a political speech, a rhetorical exercise in which he took pains to mention every country in the world.[91] The main idea of the speech was that all nations are finding their path to freedom or will do so eventually. To prove to you that the speaker really did omit nothing from his oration, suffice it to say that he found a way to mention our mission to America.

Finally, the ceremony ended with a hymn to liberty sung to the tune of *La Marseillaise*. Each verse was sung more or less badly by various amateur singers, who raised their voices one after the other, while everyone repeated the chorus. This part of the ceremony was rather bizarre. The song's message was exactly the same as that of the speech I just described. I nearly laughed once or twice as the orchestra, which consisted of a single flute, played the same refrain verse after verse. You cannot imagine a more meager sound than that of this lonely instrument all by itself in a large auditorium, suddenly piping up as the tumultuous sound of the chorus subsided at the end of every verse. Once again, however, good taste and refinement are not the things to look for in these popular celebrations. All in all, this ceremony, with its parade of people dressed for business, with its commercial signs and its one flute repeating the same tune, made more of an impression on me than our great celebrations in France, such as military review, the mass of the Holy Spirit, procession, birth of a prince, anniversary, etc. Our celebrations are more impressive, but in the United States there is something more genuine.

Do not interpret these words to mean that I feel a great deal of enthusiasm for the government of the United States. I think it is very good for the Americans, yet every day I become increasingly aware of the impossibility of establishing their political institutions in France. I am making many observations about this, and someday you will read about them in our great work. For now, however, there can be no doubt that the government that has been established in North America is quite conducive to the country's prosperity and to the well-being of its inhabitants. When this same territory is home to forty million more people; when the various resources that now enable people to make their fortunes have been depleted; when the moral energy which exists in all men and which in America is now expended in commerce and industry is no

91. John B. Van Schaik gave this speech, which was never published.

longer fueled by circumstances to the same degree (which will inevitably occur as status differences narrow); and finally, when that energy, ceasing to be industrial, turns intellectual and focuses on political interests—when all these things have come to pass, I wonder if political disputes won't then erupt along with parties and their divisions, etc., and I have no idea what this would mean for a government in which the central power is so feeble.

During the evening of July 4, we left Albany for Auburn by stage coach.[92]

If you are ever seized by a desire to travel, I advise you not to choose the part of America where I find myself now. The roads are terrible, horrible, and the carriages are so crude that even the toughest bones are at risk of breaking. In my last letter to Jules I described the places we had passed through on the way to Utica, where I ended my letter. At the risk of repeating what I said then, I must try to give you an idea of the area I've been traveling in. As I told Jules, I had the sense that I was traveling in a forest in which there was only one road. I can't think of any way to describe my impression more clearly. There is no doubt that the natural state of the land here is to be blanketed with forest. This is the untamed state of nature, and untamed nature remains sovereign in these parts, which civilization first touched only forty or fifty years ago. The woods symbolize the *wildness* of the place (we have no word to capture this idea, which English expresses so well with the word "wilderness"). Accordingly, all of civilized man's energy seems to be directed against the forest. At home, people cut wood to use it; here, they cut wood to destroy it. They invest prodigious energy in demolishing the forest, yet frequently their efforts are not enough. The vegetation grows so rapidly that it thwarts man's initiatives. Americans who live in the country spend half their lives cutting trees, and their children learn very early to wield ax and saw against their enemies, the trees. In America there is a widespread feeling of hatred for trees. That is why some of the prettiest houses in the country lack shade. They think that the absence of forest is a sign of civilization. Nothing seems uglier than a forest, whereas they find charm in a field of wheat. Indeed, such fields are strange to behold. They are filled with tree trunks that have been crudely chopped at waist height, whose presence serves as a reminder of the forests that have been laid waste and that they would rather forget.

I said that the whole country is nothing but forest. I might add that wherever you find a clearing, which you seldom do, that clearing is a village. They name these villages for the most celebrated ancient and modern cities: Troy, Rome, Liverpool, etc. What is more, it takes no more than eight or ten years for a town to become a city wherever people gather and a certain number of buildings go up. The houses, which are generally made of wood, do not lack for elegance. Their style often borrows from the Greek. The inns are especially noteworthy in this regard. As for the small, isolated dwellings that one finds in the woods, they build them out of logs piled one on top of the other. They call them log cabins.

92. This is a journey of 175 miles.

There is nothing extraordinary about the landscape. It is a lot like France. You don't see any high mountains. On the road from Albany to Utica, the only really picturesque views were on the banks of the Mohawk, where you find some quite remarkable cliffs and waterfalls.

The foliage is not the same as in France, where it is uniform and monotonous. Here, the leaves of the trees are much more varied, and in all the forests the pines form a somber backdrop that brings out the remainder of the foliage. Since I don't share the American enthusiasm for fields of wheat, I am sad that so many fine trees have been chopped down. How beautiful these forests must have been before the hand of man dishonored them! Now one might compare them to a beautiful woman who has been partly shorn of her hair.

From Utica we went to Syracuse, where we hoped to see Mr. Elam Lynds, the founder of the penitentiary system.[93] It was on the way from Utica to Syracuse that I saw my first Indians. There is a small village called Oneida Castle, which is entirely populated by a tribe that remains almost savage though surrounded by civilization. These Indians are allowed to live in peace, moreover. The tribe abides by American laws, and if an Indian breaks those laws, he or she is tried in an American court.

I didn't stop in Oneida Castle, but I saw two Indian women walking barefoot on the road. Their hair was black and dirty, their complexion coppery, and their faces quite ugly. They were wrapped in woolen blankets, even though it is July. They reminded me of the poor in France, those living in the most wretched misery. For all their barbarity, these savages nevertheless possessed a certain dignity. In their perfectly natural existence there was something noble and grand. Now they are debased and degraded. They can no longer do without clothing. They need liquor, and it makes them drunk. Beyond that, they take nothing from civilization but its vices and wear nothing but Europe's rags. Their mores; their transitional state between a barbarity that has ended and a civilization that does not yet exist; their relations with the Americans, who drive them deeper and deeper into the wilderness—all of these things will be the focus of my attention as I travel further west, closer to the place to which most of their tribes have retreated. I can't think of anything of greater interest to study.

After reaching Syracuse, we spent a day talking about penitentiaries with Mr. Elam Lynds, who seemed quite flattered by our visit.

Four leagues from Syracuse is Oneida Lake. It is a charming lake with an island in the middle called Frenchman's Island.[94] Local tradition has it that at the time of the French Revolution, an émigré came and settled there with his

93. Elam Lynds (1784–1855) was an administrator at Auburn Prison when it was founded in 1817, and he became its warden in 1821. New York charged him with building a new penitentiary in 1825; he chose Sing Sing, New York, as the new site and used prisoner labor to build the prison. He continued to work at Sing Sing and Auburn prisons intermittently throughout his life.

94. See Tocqueville's essay "The Journey to Oneida Lake" in part 3 for a full account of the legend Beaumont mentions here and of the travelers' visit to the island.

wife. In those days, there were still Indians living all around the lake, and this Frenchman was careful to conceal his arrival. We were curious to see our compatriot's solitary retreat. Who knows if we might not someday be happy to find asylum there ourselves? So we set out in search of the house. Alas, no trace of the dwelling remains. But we did find a large apple tree and a huge vine that indicated roughly where the house must have stood. The whole island is covered with enormous trees. It would be hard to imagine a prettier site or one that speaks more eloquently to the imagination. We spent two hours there in true ecstasy. Afterward, we returned to Syracuse without once leaving the forest.

While traveling in these eternal forests, I think how happy M. de Sarcé would be to see them. He would be a worthy admirer. I don't know if he would find much game. I saw only a few squirrels. I have heard, though, that there are several varieties of deer.

From Syracuse we proceeded on to Auburn. We passed two lakes: Onondaga, near Salina, just after leaving Syracuse, and Skaneatheles [sic], halfway to Auburn. We have been working for the past five or six days nearly all day long on the penitentiary system. Auburn is undoubtedly the finest institution of this type in America, and we are determined to obtain as much useful information about it as we can.

A few days ago, we went to visit Mr. Throop, the governor of New York, who is living at the moment in a small country house one league from Auburn.[95] He is a man of very plain manners and not particularly wealthy. The state pays him a salary of only 20,000 francs, which is very little for a man in his position. He therefore spends only five or six months a year in Albany (the political capital of the state), while the legislature is in session. The rest of the year he spends in the country. His country seat is nothing more than a small farm, which he farms himself. The house he lives in with his wife seems barely large enough for the two of them. It is charmingly situated, however. The yard touches Lake Owasco, and a forest of tall trees lies just beyond on the other side. The governor took us for a walk in these woods. While admiring the beauty of the trees, we spotted a squirrel, whereupon the governor took off running toward the house in search of his rifle. He soon returned, out of breath and armed with this lethal weapon. The little varmint had been patient enough to wait, but the great man proved to be a clumsy shot and missed four times in a row.

The governor is a very good fellow but hardly a distinguished man. Mr. Elam Lynds, who came to see us at Auburn and to whom I confided my opinion of Mr. Throop, said that he agreed with me. "Why, then," I asked, "did the

95. Enos T. Throop (1784–1874) was governor of New York from 1829 to 1832. Throop had practiced law and served in the U.S. Congress before his election as lieutenant governor of New York in 1828. When his friend Martin Van Buren was appointed secretary of state in 1829, Throop succeeded him as governor of New York. Beaumont met him at his estate, Willowbrook. After a long political career, Throop moved to Michigan for several years but returned to Willowbrook at the end of his life.

people of New York elect him governor?" Mr. Lynds replied that it was because "men of great talent would not accept such a job. They would rather be in business and commerce, where you can make *more money.*" There, in a nutshell, is the American character.

I will now be obliged to tell you just as concisely that I love you with all my heart. Farewell, then, my good Genius, and my affectionate regards to M. de Sarcé and Clémence.[96] If you have the chance, remember me to your friends, especially Madame d'Argence and the Maillys.[97]

I forgot to mention that from now on you mustn't count on my letters to arrive with any regularity. The wind at sea often dies down in this season, besides which the postal service will get worse as we move farther west.

From Tocqueville | To Ernest de Chabrol

Auburn, July 16, 1831

Here I am at last in Auburn, my dear friend, the famous Auburn of which we have so often spoken and about which those who live off the penitentiary system in France have said such beautiful and erroneous things. Not that the institution is not very fine indeed, but it is not as our esteemed friends, the philanthropists of France, imagine it.

For instance, it is quite true, as they say, that the health of the inmates of Auburn is incredibly good, that discipline is admirable, and, finally, that the labor of the inmates covers the costs of the establishment and then some. All that is true, but they forget to say that it is obtained not by conviction but with the aid of an instrument that the Americans call "the cat" and we, if I'm not mistaken, call the whip. The whip: that is what M. Lucas has been advocating for the past ten years and tenderly urging in the name of philanthropy.[98] Doesn't it make you think of M. Jourdain: "Terrific! What great fun!"[99] All joking aside, and forgetting our theoreticians for a moment, I should say that what we have here is an admirable penitentiary. It would take too long to give you the reasons on which my opinion is based, but I will say that, on the whole, what we have seen has rather exceeded our expectations than fallen short. We have almost made up

---

96. This was Beaumont's niece, Eléonore-Clémence de Sarcé (1821–1904).

97. Madame d'Argence was possibly the marquise Joumard d'Argence, a distant cousin of Beaumont. Beaumont also sent his regards to Adrien-Auguste-Amalric de Mailly (1792–1878), former aide-de-camp of the duc de Berry, and his wife.

98. Charles Lucas (1803–1889), a French lawyer, became the most notable authority on prison reform in the nineteenth century. Between 1828 and 1830, he published *On the Penitentiary System of Europe and the United States* in two volumes, and in 1830, he was appointed inspector of prisons in France. In 1831, Lucas cautioned Tocqueville and Beaumont against observing American penitentiaries too closely, and Tocqueville came to view Lucas as a rival.

99. Tocqueville refers to Molière's play *Le bourgeois gentilhomme,* first performed in 1670, by alluding to the main character, Monsieur Jourdain. Jourdain, who spoke in "prose" without knowing it was so called, aspired to become knowledgeable but was always fooled, much as Charles Lucas, in Tocqueville's judgment.

our minds (after two months of work) that the American system is practicable in France. Keep this to yourself. We do not want to appear to have an opinion.

I was not able to write you with the last post because time was short, as Marie may have explained to you. Today I am more at leisure, and I want to make up for my lapse by describing for you a public ceremony I recently witnessed in Albany. The details will interest you.

The ceremony in question was the Fourth of July celebration. The famous Declaration of Independence was signed, as you may know, on July 4, 1776. Every year a parade is held on that day to commemorate the event. This year marked the fifty-fifth anniversary. They invited us to take part, and we gladly accepted.

I want you to have a clear picture of this spectacle, which, though vulgar and even burlesque in some of its details, also conveyed a lofty idea that touched the heart.

Leading the march was the militia, or national guard, although this is a country utterly devoid of martial spirit. What sort of *pigeons* these honest citizens must have been I leave it to you to judge: their military get-up was really quite amusing to behold. Behind the militia came several wagonloads of elderly men who had served in the War of Independence and witnessed the triumph of the American cause. It was truly a very good idea to include these eyewitnesses of the great events that the ceremony was intended to commemorate.

Behind the wagons marched long lines of artisans of various sorts. Each trade marched beneath its own banner, as in feudal times, with the difference that here everyone was free to choose his own association, whose only power over its members is that which they chose to grant it. All the marchers were strikingly peaceful and quiet. I detected no sense of joy in the people around me. The procession might as well have been a convoy as a public celebration. But there is seriousness in everything here. Indeed, the people seemed to be marching without having been commanded by anyone but themselves and to be engaging in a kind of business: no one wore ceremonial dress, officials mingled with the crowd, and although there were no armed guards and only a few constables with white clubs, perfect order was maintained.

We came to a church, where a podium had been set up. Thinking like a Frenchman, I imagined that the governor of the state and city officials would be seated here. But instead the banners of the trades were arrayed alongside the podium, along with the county flag, which had been carried into battle in the Revolutionary War, and then the old soldiers I mentioned were seated among the flags.

People distributed themselves throughout the church, facing the officials. A minister appeared, climbed up to the podium, and offered a prayer calling upon Heaven to bestow its blessing on the United States. The congregation responded, "Amen," and a young man then went to the podium and began the customary reading of the *déclaration des droits*.[100] This was truly a beautiful sight.

100. The Declaration of Independence.

The congregation sat and listened in reverent silence. When Congress in its eloquent indictment listed the injustices and tyrannical acts that England had committed, a murmur of indignation and wrath rumbled through the audience. When it invoked the justice of the American cause and expressed its generous resolve to free America or die trying, it seemed that a momentary electric current caused all hearts to vibrate as one.

This was not, I assure you, a theatrical performance. In this reading of the promises of independence, which have been so well kept; in this remembrance by an entire people of their nation's inception; in this union of the present generation with a generation that has passed away but whose generous passions everyone briefly shared—in all this there was something deeply felt and truly grand.

It should have ended there. But after the reading of the *déclaration des droits,* a lawyer regaled us with a lengthy rhetorical amplification, bombastically reviewing the entire globe before culminating with the United States, which he described as being in every respect the center of the world. This performance exhibited all the features of slapstick comedy. We see this sort of thing in France when one of our *great men* is buried.

I left cursing the speechifier, whose voluble and idiotic national pride partly ruined the deep impression that the rest of the occasion had made on me.

We had planned to spend several days in Albany, because the city is the capital of the state of New York. The state bureaucracy is located here, and the legislature convenes here as well. We hoped to gather valuable information about what characteristics of central government might exist in this country. All the bureaus and records were open to us, but as for *government,* we are still searching. There really is none. The legislature regulates all matters of general interest; the municipalities do the rest.

The advantage of setting things up this way is that each locality is encouraged to take a very active interest in its own affairs, and political activity is much encouraged. But the drawback, even in America, is that there is absolutely no uniformity in the administration of affairs, general measures become impossible, and potentially useful projects must put up with a degree of uncertainty that you could not possibly imagine.

We are in an unusually good position to observe the effects of this absence of centralization on the prisons. There is nothing fixed or certain in their discipline; personnel come and go and, with them, so do systems; modes of administration change with each administrator, because there is no central authority capable of imposing a common procedure on all. The United States should thank Heaven that it thus far finds itself in a situation where it does not need a permanent army or police force or a shrewd and persistent foreign policy. If any of these three necessities should ever arise, one need not be a prophet to predict that the country will either lose its freedom or move toward a greater concentration of power.

We have thus far traveled through very strange country, which I will describe for you when I have the time. We've just passed through the region inhabited by the notorious Iroquois Confederation, which was much discussed at one time.[101] Today the territory is home to a handful of savages in rags, who inspire more pity than fear. The rest are dead, or else they have moved west beyond Lake Ontario and vanished into the wilderness.

Farewell, my dear friend, I embrace you with all my heart.

Our virtue is still holding up, but we are beginning to eye the women with an impudence that ill becomes representatives of the penitentiary system.

Farewell, a thousand regards to our colleagues.

P.S. Do not forget to keep my letters.

From Tocqueville | To his mother

Auburn, July 17, 1831

... We left New York on June 28. The beginning of our trip was marred by an annoying incident. That evening we boarded a steamboat, which was supposed to take us to West Point on the North River. West Point is a famous place from the American war.[102] It is also one of the most picturesque sites in the country. We had planned to arrive that night and spend the day there, but after getting under way we learned that our boat would not be stopping at West Point but would continue directly on to Albany. We were in the position of a man who takes the wrong stagecoach and ends up in Rouen rather than Compiègne, except that you can get off a stagecoach but not a steamboat. We therefore had to resign ourselves to our fate. Not only did we not visit West Point, but we traveled the entire length of the North River, one of the most picturesque in the world, in the middle of the night and arrived in Albany at five in the morning.

There our misfortunes came to an end, and a very pleasant journey began. We spent three or four days in Albany, just gathering statistical documents we need from the central government of the state of New York. I believe that we'll need a trunk to transport all the notes, books, and brochures that we collected back to France. While in Albany we attended the Fourth of July ceremonies. July 4 is the anniversary of the Declaration of Independence, and on that day the Americans commemorate the event with a procession and a religious ceremony. Shall I recount the procession for you? We spent two hours watching it

101. The Cayuga, Mohawk, Oneida, Onondaga, Seneca, and Tuscarora peoples made up the Iroquois Confederacy. The confederacy had garnered power in the eighteenth century by negotiating British and French colonial rivalries to its advantage. The removal of the French from North America, following their loss of the Seven Years' War, deprived the confederacy of this strategy. Already enervated, the Iroquois Confederacy split during the American Revolution, with the majority of its members supporting the British, and never re-formed a strong alliance.

102. The United States government built the military post at West Point in 1778, making it the first American-built post. Benedict Arnold, the notorious American general convicted of treason, was the first to command West Point. The government founded the United States Military Academy at the site in 1802.

beneath the most beautiful sun in the world. But I would rather tell you about our visit to the Quaker Shakers.

The Shakers are a religious community of men and women who share responsibility for farming a certain piece of land, take vows of chastity, and own all their property in common. One of their settlements is located in the woods three leagues from Albany. We went there on Sunday at ten in the morning and immediately went to the temple, which is nothing but a large room, very spare, with nothing resembling an altar or a house of worship. Half an hour later, two groups of Shakers, male and female, entered the room by different doorways. The men assembled at one end, the women at the other. The men were dressed almost like peasants in our theaters: white shirts with big sleeves, gray felt hats with wide brims, ample jackets with pockets. Except for the shirt, everything was purple and like new. The women were all in white. Some were quite old and others very young, some ugly and some pretty. But the old women sat in front, with the young close together in back. The same order was observed among the men. The two groups sat facing each other for about five minutes, awaiting an inspiration. One of the men, feeling inspiration coming on, stood up and made a long, rambling speech about the religious and moral duties of Shakers. Then both groups began to sing the loudest song I've ever heard in my life. The most fervent members of the congregation marked the beat with their heads, which made them look a little like those China dolls with which our grandmothers used to decorate their fireplaces. To this point, however, the ceremony was no stranger than a Jewish Sabbath. When the song was finished, however, both groups lined up single file: five men and five women stood with their backs to the wall and began singing in spirited and rapid tempo. At that signal, men and women, young and old, began to prance about until they were breathless. The sight was not so much funny as pitiful, with white-haired elderly people exhausted by the heat and activity nevertheless cavorting as gleefully as the rest. From time to time, the dancers clapped their hands. To imagine what this dance was like, you have to compare it to the *Carillon de Dunkerque.* During a pause, a member of the congregation improvised a short religious speech, and then the dancers started up again, in preparation for still more preaching. As in other Quaker congregations, there is no minister. Anyone can say whatever seems appropriate. After nearly two hours of this terrifying exercise, men and women arranged themselves in pairs around a circle. They brought their elbows in close to their bodies, reached forward with their forearms, and allowed their hands to hang down, which gave them the look of trained dogs forced to march on their hind legs. Thus prepared, they belted out another song still more awful than the rest and began revolving around the room, which they continued to do for a full quarter of an hour. After that, one of them gave a little speech, assuring us that the Shaker way was the only path to salvation and urging us to convert. Then the congregation withdrew in perfect order and total silence. I suppose the poor devils needed a rest. But do you see, my dear Maman, what extremes the human spirit is capable of when left to its own devices? We had with us a young American Protestant, who said to us on leaving, "A couple of more displays like that one and I'll be ready to turn Catholic."

We left Albany in what they call a "stagecoach." These are carriages with suspensions made entirely of leather, which proceed at a good clip along roads as dreadful as those of Lower Brittany. Within a few miles your bones are shattered, but we didn't think to complain as we were entirely absorbed by the amazing sights that greeted our eyes. It was our first trip inland. Until then we had seen only the seacoast and the banks of the Hudson. Inland everything was different. In one of my letters I think I lamented that there was virtually no more wood to be found in America. Here I must confess that I was wrong. Not only is there wood, and woods, in America, but the entire country is still nothing but one vast forest in which a few small areas have been cleared. When you climb to the top of a steeple, you see nothing but treetops undulating in the wind like ocean waves, as far as the eye can see. All signs are that this is a new country. What they refer to here as "clearing land" means cutting a tree three feet from the ground. With the trunk cut down, they plow around the stump and plant their seeds. The result is that in the midst of the most abundant harvests you find stumps by the hundreds, all that is left of the ancient trees that once blanketed the earth. And that is not all. As you can imagine, land cleared in this way still contains the seeds of a thousand wild plants, so that in the same field you find young shoots, tall grasses, climbing plants, and wheat. It all grows pell-mell. It's a kind of jumble, in which everything grows rapidly, a sort of battle between man and forest from which the former does not always emerge victorious. Yet although the country is new, what you recognize wherever you go is that it is inhabited by an old people. When you reach a dwelling after traveling through the wilderness on some awful road, you are astonished to discover a civilization more advanced than that which exists in any of our villages. The farmer is carefully dressed. His house is perfectly clean. Usually you find him with a newspaper at his side, and his first concern is to talk politics. I could not possibly tell you which obscure and forgotten corner of the world we were in when we were asked how we had left France. What was the relative strength of the parties, etc.? And who knows what? A thousand questions that I found it difficult to answer without laughing when I thought about who was asking them and where they were being asked. The whole territory that we just crossed was once occupied by the famous Iroquois Confederation, which caused such a stir in the world. We encountered the last of them on our route. They begged for handouts and were as inoffensive as their fathers had been fearsome.

Here we are in Auburn, in a splendid hotel right in the middle of a small town of two thousand people, all of whose homes are well-stocked shops. Auburn is today a major commercial center. Twenty years ago, people hunted here for deer and bear. I am beginning to get used to the rapid spread of society. Much to my surprise, I already find it all quite routine, and I find myself saying, as the Americans do, that a settlement is very old if it has been in existence for thirty years. . . .

From Beaumont | To Ernest de Chabrol

Aboard the *Ohio* on Lake Erie, July 24, 1831

We remained in Auburn until the 19th of this month, my dear Chabrol. We studied the prison in that town extensively, and I believe it to be the fullest implementation to date of the penitentiary system. It is truly an admirable institution, and it would be good if people in France were to have an accurate idea of it, for then they would be sure to imitate it. You will tell me that it is up to us to enlighten the government on this point, and I will answer that we will do everything we can. I would add, however, that it will do little good to show the government what good can be done if we cannot persuade the public at the same time. That is the rub, and I still don't know what we should do to overcome this obstacle.

We then left Auburn and set out for Buffalo.[103] Buffalo is situated on the shore of Lake Erie, not far from Niagara. We passed Lakes Seneca, Geneva, and Canandaigua. On a hill overlooking Lake Geneva is a charming little town of the same name. To get there you have to cross the lake via a bridge that is nearly half a league in length. It is crudely built, however, and remarkable only for its length. Lake Canandaigua is perhaps the prettiest of all the lakes I've seen. It is less picturesque than Lake Oneida, which is more unspoiled, but on its shores there are quite a few country houses, which give it an air of civilization without robbing it of its natural splendor. We spent two days in Canandaigua, because that is the home of Mr. Spencer, a very distinguished member of the legislature, whom we met in Auburn and who invited us to spend some time with him in the country.[104] I have not met anyone else as knowledgeable about his country's institutions, and we found his conversation invaluable. I left Canandaigua on the 22nd and arrived in Buffalo the same day. Our original intention was to stop in Buffalo only on the way to Niagara. But when we arrived, we learned that a steamboat would be leaving the next day, the 23rd, for Detroit by way of Lake Erie, a journey of less than two days. Detroit is in Michigan, on the spit of land that stands between Lake Erie and Lake Huron. This is a region we very much want to visit: it is still wilderness; the Europeans who have settled there number only in the hundreds; and the surrounding countryside is full of Indians who are far from civilized.

103. Located on Lake Erie, Buffalo was a town of about fifteen hundred inhabitants in 1831. It was on the verge of a large population growth that accompanied the arrival of the Erie Canal, which connected Lake Erie to the Hudson River and New York City.

104. John C. Spencer (1788–1855) was a lawyer active in New York politics. He was one of three individuals who revised the statutes of the state of New York between 1827 and 1829. Tocqueville considered Spencer the first significant informant of his trip to America in 1831 and spoke to him about the American judiciary, bicameralism, freedom of speech and of the press, and the relationship between religion and government. Spencer's thoughts helped form Tocqueville's conclusions in *Democracy in America,* and Spencer arranged for the publication of the American edition of that work, for which he wrote the introduction and notes, in 1838 and 1840. He continued to correspond with Tocqueville throughout his life.

Many immigrants from England and Ireland are headed there in search of cheap land. It would be quite interesting to see how these new arrivals go about establishing themselves and finding ways to survive on virgin land still covered with forest. Unable to resist such an opportunity, we immediately bought tickets for the next day's voyage.

On the night of our arrival in Buffalo, we witnessed a strange spectacle that elicited all our pity.

The government of the United States purchased land belonging to the Indians of North America. At regular intervals the government pays the Indians sums of money it owes on this purchase. Living near Buffalo is a tribe of Indians, some of whom came to the city on the day we arrived to receive one of these payments. No sooner do the Indians receive their money than they spend it, apparently. They buy clothing and farm implements. If that was all they bought, it would be a fair exchange, value for value. Unfortunately, they also hand over their cash in exchange for brandy and whisky, which kills them. When we arrived, the streets of Buffalo were full of drunken Indians. I saw one who was dead drunk. We stopped nearby. He lay perfectly still. A female Indian, said to be his wife, approached, shook his head roughly and banged it against the ground, and, when the poor wretch gave no sign of life, gave a shout and began to laugh in a stupid manner. A little further on, we saw an Indian woman, completely drunk, being carried out of town by two or three Indian men returning home to the forest. Generally speaking, the Indians are quite ugly. The women are hideous. Their complexion is dark copper, their mouths wide, their hair long and dirty. There is something savage in their features, and nothing noble or dignified in their bearing. Their taste for strong liquor has reduced them to brutes. Their relations with Europeans have utterly destroyed their character. In the past there was something beautiful in their complete nudity and something noble in their savage existence. But once they quit the forest, they took nothing from civilization but its vices and nothing from Europe but its rags. They go barefoot, wear tattered garments, and generally wrap themselves in woolen blankets even in the summer.

The government of the United States is moving rapidly toward the destruction of this race, which once dominated the land that is now America. It would be difficult to wipe them out by waging war: that would exact a toll in men and money. A more reliable and economical way of achieving the same end is to wait a little longer and resort freely to more perfidious means. Although Americans supposedly live on good terms with the Indians, they repeatedly find pretexts to drive them farther and farther west. They sign treaties with the tribes, but it is the stronger of the two groups that interprets the terms of these agreements.[105] The Indians have entered into commercial relations with the Ameri-

105. The most recent of these initiatives was the Indian Removal Act of 1830, supported most vigorously by President Andrew Jackson. Enforcement of this legislation involved a great deal of coercion and corrupt treaties that forced American Indians to move west of the Mississippi River with inadequate compensation and provisions.

cans: they give them animal hides, in exchange for which the Americans give the Indians brandy, which destroys them. They abuse liquor to such an extent that more of them die from drink than in battle. In any event, I will know more about both their customs and their character in a few days, and if I learn anything interesting about this subject, I will not fail to let you know.

Farewell . . .

From Tocqueville | To his sister-in-law Émilie

Batavia, July 25, 1831

I am in such an excessively sentimental mood today, dear sister, that it would not take much for me to write you an idyll. Rest assured, however, that I shall do nothing of the kind. I will nevertheless tell you about the visit we made the other day to Oneida Lake. If you don't dream about it for the next week, and I mean "dream wide awake," then I no longer know who you are.

First I must tell you (because one must always begin at the beginning) that around forty years ago, a Frenchman whose name no one has been able to tell me, but who apparently belonged to a noble and wealthy family, landed in America after being forced to leave his country during the Revolution. Our émigré was young and in good health. He never suffered from stomach troubles (note this point well). He also had a wife, whom he loved dearly. Still, he had not a cent to his name. A friend to whom he appealed for help offered to lend him some money to buy the necessities of life and establish himself in some corner of the earth where land might not be so expensive.

At that time, the western part of the state of New York was still uncultivated. The woods that blanketed the region were inhabited by the Indian tribes of the Iroquois Confederation. The émigré thought that this might be the place for him. He shared his plan with his young bride, who was courageous enough to follow him into the wilderness.

So the two young people set out and courageously made their way to the shores of Oneida Lake. In exchange for some powder and lead, they bought from the Indians the island in the middle of the lake. No European and perhaps no human being had ever imagined making this place his home. Hundred-year-old trees had to be cut down, land thick with roots and brambles had to be cleared, and then a cabin had to be built, and all of life's needs had somehow to be supplied. The first months were difficult, especially for people like this Frenchman and his wife, who were used to all the finer things of civilized society. By the second year the work had become easier. Little by little the couple became so completely accustomed to their lot that, to believe the story, neither had ever been happier or more pleased with the other.

The book from which I learned these details said nothing more about their fate,[106] and no doubt that would have been the end of it had our route not taken

---

106. This book, originally published in German as *Erscheinungen am See Oneida* in 1798, was written by Sophie von La Roche (1731–1807). It presents an embellished account of the

us within four leagues of Oneida Lake. If I'm not mistaken, we arrived in the vicinity on July 9. We mounted horses and rode out in search of our Frenchman and his wife. For several hours we rode through one of those dense American forests that I hope to describe to you someday, and at last, without quite realizing where we were, we found ourselves at the door of a fisherman's cabin right on the shore of the lake.

Imagine a body of water several leagues in length, transparent and still, surrounded on all sides by thick woods, with water lapping at the roots of the trees closest to it. Not a sail on the lake; not a house on its shores; no smoke above the trees; a perfect calm, a tranquility as complete as it must have been at the beginning of the world. We could see our island a mile from shore. It was nothing but a leafy grove in which no trace of a clearing could be seen. I had begun to fear that the traveler who preceded us to this spot has amused himself by inventing a romance, but just then we met the wife of the fisherman at whose home we had arrived. We asked her what the island in front of us was called. She replied that people in the vicinity referred to it as Frenchman's Island. We asked why, and she told us that many years ago a Frenchman and his wife had come and made their home there. "A poor investment," she added, "because at the time they were too far from any market to sell their produce. In any case, they settled there, and they were still there when we came to live here some twenty-two years ago.[107] That year, it so happens, the Frenchman's wife died. After that, her husband disappeared, and no one knows how he made his way across the lake or where he went. Around that time I decided to go out to see the island. I still remember their little cabin. It stood on one end of the island under a big apple tree. The French couple had a grape vine growing right next to the cabin and had planted flowers all around as well, for what purpose I do not know. It was sad to see how the fields had already been overgrown and filled with weeds. I haven't been back since."

I'm sure you'll have no difficulty imagining, my dear sister, that in spite of the good woman's story, we wanted to visit the island, but it was more difficult to persuade her that this was what we wanted. She opened her bleary eyes as wide as she could and once again assured us that we would be making a poor decision if we decided to settle on the island, given how far it was from the

life of Louis des Watines, a French nobleman who lived with his family on a western island in Oneida Lake from 1792 to 1793. Watines moved his wife and three children to the northern shore of the lake in 1793 and, after financial failure, returned to France in 1799. La Roche heard this story from her son and daughter-in-law, who had lived in the United States and had befriended a number of French émigrés displaced by the French Revolution.

In 1803, Joachim-Heinrich Campe (1746–1818) published a French edition of this story as a children's book entitled *Voyage d'un Allemand au Lac Onéida*. Tocqueville read the book as a young boy and, as evinced by his account of his journey to the island, adopted its romantic account of Watines as truth.

107. In his travel notes, Tocqueville recorded that the woman said that she arrived after the Frenchman had already left the island.

market. When she realized that we were determined to go anyway, she pointed to her husband's boat (he was ill) and gave us permission to use it. We rowed like the devil, and before we had raised half a dozen blisters on each hand, our little canoe reached the island.

Making our way ashore was not easy, because our Frenchman, in order to make the approach more difficult and hide himself more completely from the world, had been careful not to clear any passage to the water's edge. We therefore had to make our way through a barrier that would have been difficult for even a wild boar to penetrate. What we found then was wonderful but sad to behold: the whole center of the island showed clear signs of human labor. We saw at once that trees had been carefully cleared, but time had already erased the vestiges of this unfinished work of civilization. The surrounding forest had rapidly spread its offshoots into the Frenchman's fields. Vines and weeds had colonized the land and begun to weave together the new trees that were springing up everywhere.

For two hours we searched this chaotic landscape in vain for signs of our man's house. We found none, nor did we find vestiges of his lawn or flower beds. We were about to leave, when Beaumont spotted the apple tree that our elderly hostess had mentioned. Nearby was an enormous vine stock, which at first we took for ivy and which wound its way up to the treetops. At that moment we realized that we were standing on the site where the house had stood, and after clearing back the growth that covered that little patch of earth, we in fact found vestiges of the dwelling.

You and others imagine, dear sister, that because a man wears a square hat on his head and sends other men to the galleys he is nothing but a reasoning machine, a sort of syllogism incarnate. I am glad to tell you that you are wrong and that when a magistrate starts to think about things other than law, you never know how far his thoughts will take him.

In any case, we left Frenchman's Island with a pang in our hearts, each more moved than the other by the fate of this man whom we had never met and whose name we did not know. Is there a destiny to compare to his? Men drove him from their society as if he were a leper. He accepted his fate and created a world of his own. There he lived peacefully and happily. He remained just long enough to be completely forgotten by his friends in Europe. Then his wife died, leaving him alone in the midst of wilderness, as incapable of leading the life of a savage as that of a civilized man. And despite it all, I ask you, *entre nous* and *sotto voce* so that our grandparents, who are such excessively reasonable people, won't take us for lunatics, is there not something that appeals to the imagination in the hidden life away from the world that these two poor people led for so many years? Unfortunately, there are no doctors in the wilderness, and unless you're as robust as a peasant it's best not to think of living there.

After Oneida Lake, we went to the prison at Auburn. I would call this a precipitous drop, but contrasts, they say, are the charm of travel. After immersing ourselves in the penitentiary system, we moved on to Canandaigua, to the country house of a member of the legislature named Spencer. I confess, dear sister, that our week there was as pleasant as can be. Canandaigua sits beside a charming lake (yet another lake! I can hear you saying), but there's nothing wild about this one. Indeed, everything around it calls to mind the pleasures of civilized life. Our host is a man of intelligence, and our mornings with him are most interesting. Not only is there a very fine library, but there are also two charming daughters, with whom we "get on" very well, as common people in France would say. Although they don't know the first word of French, they have, among other charms, four blue eyes (that is, two apiece) such as I'm quite sure you've never seen over there across the water. I would describe them for you if I weren't afraid of becoming tedious. Suffice it to say that we examined them even more enthusiastically than we examined their father's books. Beaumont and I discussed the discovery between ourselves and with characteristic sagacity made up our minds to resume our journey as quickly as possible. The very next day we put our resolution into practice by crossing the lake, not by swimming, as Mentor and Telemachus might have done, but by steamboat, which was safer and more practical. So here we are today in Batavia, somewhat disappointed no longer to be in Canandaigua and yet happy to have left. . . .

From Beaumont | To Ernest de Chabrol

August 2, 1831, aboard the *Superior* on Lake Huron[108]
Before explaining my reasons for embarking on yet another voyage, my dear Chabrol, I must tell you what has happened since my arrival in Detroit. On landing, we went to see an old Catholic priest, Monsieur Richard, who we had been told was a very worthy fellow who would be able to supply us with much precious information about Michigan.[109] We found him in his presbytery teaching a class of a dozen children. He speaks French very well. He was born in Saintonge and left France when the Revolution began persecuting the Catholic clergy. He made up his mind at that time to go to Detroit. He has remained here ever since, steadfastly devoting himself to the *conversion of infidels*. Here as in France, the Catholic clergy are out to convert as many people as they can. The gentleman in question sees this goal as more important than anything else and spoke to us at length about his successes, which left us bored at times, because he left our questions unanswered. His activities pleased us, however. What is rather remarkable about his position is that he was sent to Congress by Protestants despite his position as a Catholic minister. At first this surprised us greatly, but the people

108. For another account and more detailed notes regarding this segment of the journey, see Tocqueville's essay "Two Weeks in the Wilderness" in part 3.
109. Gabriel Richard (1767–1832) was educated by the Sulpicians and ordained in 1791. He immigrated to North America in 1792, and after teaching at Saint Mary's in Baltimore and working in the Illinois Territory, he arrived in Detroit in 1798. He founded a school for both white and native settlers, established the first newspaper in the Michigan Territory, and served in the U.S. House of Representatives from 1822 to 1824.

here do not judge of religious matters as we do. Hostility between different denominations is not the same, and no one asks what religion a person belongs to in order to judge his character. What surprises me is that the Protestants chose him even though he attacks them freely. He is zealous in his crusade: "They have an endless number of denominations," he says. "There are now 450 of them. They do not believe in *anything*. They are neither Episcopalians nor Methodists nor Presbyterians but *nothingists*." What is more, he agrees with me that this variety of denominations will one day lead either to natural religion, meaning the absence of any exterior form of religious practice, or to Catholicism.

After gathering information from two or three other people, we decided to set out for Saginaw.[110] Saginaw is located a few leagues from the bay of the same name, which is part of Lake Huron. Having made up our minds, we rented two saddle horses, and on July 26 (if I remember correctly) we mounted two rather undernourished old nags, with rifles and game sacks slung over our shoulders, straw hats on our heads, and jackets covering our torsos. The rest of our affairs were stuffed into saddlebags. I forgot to mention that, because we were told that Saginaw and its environs were infested with mosquitoes, we had gone to a merchant in Detroit and purchased mosquito nets. While the woman in the shop was searching for the merchandise, my eyes happened to fall on a small engraving that hung on the wall. It depicted a very well-dressed woman above the following caption: *"Mode de Longchamp 1831."* What do you think of the fact that the residents of Michigan follow the Paris fashions? In the smallest villages in America, people are aware of French fashion and believe that Paris sets the tone in all such matters.

This anecdote might lead you to believe that Detroit is quite civilized. In fact, it is not very far removed from the wilderness and its denizens. Half a league beyond the city limits, the woods begin, and, once begun, there is no end to them. For proof I can do no better than relate the true story of something that happened here last year: some dogs chased a bear out of the woods and down the main street of Detroit, much to the delight of the Americans, who no doubt maintained their customary gravity throughout.

Enough digression: I must get back to the Saginaw road, where our poor steeds await.

Our first day was fairly rough. We had 18 leagues to ride. Our goal was to reach the Flint River by way of Pontiac. We found a well-blazed trail through the woods and at intervals encountered isolated dwellings. Despite what I just said about the bear, you should know that in a number of places people use them as watchdogs. I saw several tied up alongside cabin doors.

In the inn where we dined, we were told that a rattlesnake had been killed the night before. Until we reached Pontiac the path that had been cut through

110. Saginaw, Michigan, is located about seventy-five miles northwest of Pontiac, near the southwestern tip of Saginaw Bay, which extends from Lake Huron. The American Fur Company had founded a trading post there in 1815, but it failed to flourish.

the forest was monotonous, the terrain uniform. After Pontiac, however, the aspect of the landscape changed completely. We encountered a wide variety of sites, including many small valleys containing any number of lovely small lakes. No longer was the forest thick and impenetrable. There were many clearings, and it looked like a plantation of trees that had been designed as a place to stroll in the woods.

A league outside of Pontiac we stopped to visit Mr. Williams, who is said to be the man in these parts with the best knowledge of the Indians, the trade in hides, and the best ways of contacting the tribes.[111] He urged us to engage a guide to show us the way to Saginaw and told us that we could trust an Indian guide and run no risk whatsoever. But we didn't need a guide yet, so we continued on our way.

Barely half a league farther on, we saw an Indian walking in the woods like a wild animal and eating wild fruit. A moment later, another Indian appeared in front of us. He was armed with a rifle. His body was half naked. His gaze was fierce and forbidding, like that of most Indians. Had Mr. Williams not just sung the praises of the Indians, we would certainly have taken him for a robber. He stared straight at us without a hint of tenderness in his eyes. We smiled back amiably. At that point his expression changed and became quite gracious. But it was only a momentary respite, and his severe countenance returned, as though he regretted his smile. We had made up our minds to continue on our way. We were not a little surprised to find our Indian running after us, dogging our steps. If our horses slowed, he stopped. If we trotted, he galloped just behind our rear horse's tail. Despite Mr. Williams's assurances, this behavior struck us as odd. We stopped, he stopped. I again smiled at him in a very kindly way, and he smiled back even more warmly. What did he want? I offered him brandy. He drank some and seemed to find it quite good. But he kept on following us just the same. I stopped again. Two birds that he had killed hung about his neck. I suppose he may have wanted to sell them. I conveyed my wish to buy them by means of sign language and offered him two shillings (25 *sous*). He readily accepted the bargain but continued to follow us. He kept this up for two more leagues, running all the while. Eventually we came upon a band of Indians, men, women, and children, scattered in the woods near the road. Our man now left us and rejoined his companions without looking at us or saying a word. I still don't know why he followed us.

The group of Indians that he joined numbered about twenty-five or thirty. They were lying on the ground and eating roast meat. Quartered deer hung beside the fires around which they had gathered, while the still-palpitating heads of these animals lay on the ground nearby.

These Indians were on their way home from Canada, where they had gone to receive the gifts that the English give them every year. These gifts include

111. Major Oliver Williams (1774–1834) and his family were some of the earliest American settlers of the area. They arrived from Massachusetts around 1819.

blankets, rifles, ammunition, and the like. It is easy to see the motive for this English generosity: they want to maintain friendly relations with the natural enemies of the Americans. It is also a way of arming the Indians, which would be of
great help to the English in case of war with the United States.

I am greatly interested in everything to do with these savage tribes. I don't
know what to think about the conditions under which they live. Are they living
as one should in accordance with the simple laws of nature? Or have they succumbed to a state of degradation incompatible with man's fate? Or have they
begun to become civilized? If the latter, it must be granted that their childhood
lasted a long time, because their origins are shrouded in the night of time.

It seems clear to me that they do not constitute a race distinct from the
European race: there is no marked difference between the shape of their body,
the outline of their face, or the nature of their countenance and ours. The same
cannot be said of the Negroes, who appear on close examination to have been
organized differently.

How did these Indians find their way into the forests of America? Did they
come from Europe by land? Or was there a special creation for the hemisphere
in which I find myself at present? These latter questions are somewhat theoretical, but I would be pleased to know the answers. I am currently reading a
well-written book on the subject by MacCulloch and a rather interesting traveler's account by MacKennery [MacKenney].[112] I am more interested in practical
questions than in purely speculative ones, and I believe it is better to know what
is than to search arduously for what was.

The study of these savage peoples is not idle or frivolous. There is no better way to learn about civilized societies than to study those that are not. Sound
judgment is impossible without comparison. I sometimes wonder if these Indians, whom the Europeans hold in contempt, deserve to be called savages. The
ones I saw en route to Saginaw live peacefully in their forests. Everyone who
has relations with them praises their honesty, sincerity, and generosity. Of course
Europeans who do business with them enjoy one great advantage, that of cheat-
ing them repeatedly.

The territory that is America once was theirs, but every day they are driven
out of another piece of it. On the road to Flint River, I saw a group of poor
Indians in a field that was theirs a few years ago. To be sure, they drink too
much spirits, but who is more barbarous: the person who accepts liquor without
knowing its dangers, or the one who sells it knowing that it can kill? Rattlesnakes are common in the area around Saginaw. The Indians have an infallible remedy for snakebites. When I asked if they demanded payment for their
remedy, I was told that nothing pleases them more than to save a life and they

112. J. H. MacCulloch, *Researches, Philosophical and Antiquarian, Concerning the Aboriginal
History of America* (Baltimore, 1829), and Thomas MacKenney, *Sketches of a Tour to the Lakes, of
the Character and Customs of the Chippewa Indians, and of Incidents Connected with the Treaty of Fond
du Lac* (Baltimore, 1827).

never ask for any reward. Are these people more barbarous than Monsieur Dupuytren and others of his ilk?[113] In any case, Indians are as contemptuous of Europeans as Europeans are of them. They consider themselves superior to all other peoples. To them, nothing is more vile than to work for *money,* and they regard their idle lives as the only truly independent way to live and the only kind of life worthy of a man.

Their society is not burdened with all of our political and civil institutions. Nearly all of our laws are made for the defense of individual property, the basis of European societies, which does not exist among the Indians. They think that nature as a whole belongs to all men, and they do not divide up the forests, which are big enough to accommodate everyone. They commit so few crimes that they don't need courts. They must be very just indeed if they can do without a system of justice. Homicide is virtually the only crime they commit, sometimes in vengeance, other times because of drunkenness. In case of murder, friends and relatives of the victim have the right to kill the murderer, although he usually redeems his life for a sum of money equivalent to about 150 francs. Their religion is quite simple: they worship the great Manitou, creator of all things. They believe that there is another life after this one. To the good are given superb forests in which to hunt deer for all eternity, while the wicked are banished to barren lands devoid of game and condemned to forgo the pleasures of the hunt.

The Indians, for all their crudeness and ignorance, are happy. Those who know them best say that they are free of care and exempt from suffering. When they kill enough game, they eat like wolves. If the hunt goes badly, they do not eat and await better luck without complaint.

So much for this lengthy digression on the Indians, which has not advanced my narrative at all. I'm not sure how to get back to the Saginaw road at the place where I left it. To save myself the trouble, I will go straightaway to Pontiac, which is halfway between Detroit and Flint River. Shortly before reaching Pontiac, I killed a small blue bird, and I painted it at the inn while the horses were resting. My paintings aren't very pretty, but they amuse me no end.

Nothing really noteworthy occurred the rest of the way to Flint River. We were nevertheless surprised to find a highway that was both very broad and quite straight in a region with neither homes nor residents (you can travel up to 10 leagues without seeing a house). It's really quite a clever system, however, to build roads before there is anyone to use them: that is why Michigan and the other states of America have been settled so quickly. The major roads do not increase the population, but they provide a means of access for prospective settlers. Since April of this year, the state of Michigan alone has attracted three or four thousand new settlers.

America will not be populated in any other way. I have yet to meet a single person who was born in the place where he now resides. This society, which is made up entirely of emigrants, is unlike any other. These are all people who

113. Guillaume Dupuytren (1777–1835) was a successful French surgeon.

have no homeland and who came here for purely self-interested reasons. They come in search of cheap land: an acre sells for 6 francs. Since settling in a new country is a form of speculation, it attracts industrious people, who remain true to their character. Thus there is not a single farmer who does not also engage in trade or pursue some industrial activity. One such activity is a natural consequence of the circumstances: settlers serve as innkeepers for new arrivals, and they do not offer their services for free. The current residents of Michigan will continue to ply this trade for some time to come. You mustn't think of these American homes that take in travelers "on foot or on horseback" as being anything like our inns and taverns. The people who live in them have some education. Their language is not that of the dregs of the populace. There is not a single log cabin in which newspapers are not read and tea is not served twice a day. And while there is no lower class here, neither is there an upper class. There is just one uniform society, without top or bottom, up or down. It is not miserable, but it is not in any sense distinguished either. It is the happiest of societies, I believe, but, to my way of thinking, not the most agreeable.

With these thoughts and many others in mind we were approaching Flint River when night overtook us, still in the middle of the woods. The moon did its utmost to light our way, but the path remained uncertain. We came to a river, thinking it was the Flint. A hundred yards ahead we glimpsed some houses. Leaving his horse with me, Tocqueville ran off through the woods to find out what he could. He soon realized that the houses we had seen were still unfinished. There was nobody in them. He informed me of his discovery by shouting at the top of his lungs. I responded in kind and told him to continue on his way. Our voices echoed endlessly in woods whose silence was seldom broken, and after some arduous hiking we finally managed to find each other again, although we still had no idea how far we were from our destination.

Setting aside our anxiety, the night was gorgeous! I stopped more than once to contemplate the sky. The moonlight that filtered through the thick foliage described a scene so stunning that it is impossible to convey in words.

After proceeding for about an hour through patches of open wood that we thought might be the trail, I saw a light. I climbed down from my horse and walked straight toward it. Five minutes later, I was close enough to make out a wooden house with no door and only half a roof. Someone was walking about inside but not showing himself, and he seemed to be trying to cover the light that illuminated the interior of the house. At length, speaking in the mildest, humblest voice I could manage so as to reassure anyone inside who might have taken me for a robber, I asked if anyone could show me the way to Mr. Todds' house (this was the name of the person with whom we hoped to stay in Flint River).[114] With that, a half-clad woman appeared with a torch and told me in the kindest way that Mr. Todds' house was nearby (the poor woman was alone in that abandoned house, at the mercy of the elements). I didn't have time

114. This was likely Major John Joseph Todd, an early resident of Flint and Pontiac.

to pity her misfortune, however, and made my way back to Tocqueville—not without difficulty, however, because I had stumbled into a swamp and for a moment thought I would never escape. At last we found shelter with Mr. Todds, and by 11 o'clock we were asleep, one in a bed, the other on the floor.

The next morning at 5, we were on our way again. Mr. Todds found us an Indian guide, who crossed the Flint River running and leaping like a deer, and we followed as best we could, though even at a brisk trot our horses had a hard time keeping up.

At this point the look of the countryside changed. Previously we had been traveling through woods, but woods that bore the imprint of the European's axe. The forest had been cut back ten to fifteen feet on either side of the road. At intervals we came upon a field or a small wooden cabin. The presence of civilized man was apparent everywhere, and even where the forest remained untamed, trunks strewn about the forest floor and half-burned stumps attested to the effort to destroy it. After Flint River we saw no more of this: the virgin forest stood forth in all its primitive beauty. We saw trees immense in both height and circumference. I measured a pine that was twenty feet around and an oak that was eighteen. Not a single tree had been chopped down. We saw any number that had been toppled by the wind or had fallen on their own from old age. To get to Saginaw on horseback one must pass beneath these majestic trees and over the remains of fallen trunks. There is one narrow path, which those who make this journey customarily follow. Thousands of fallen trees block the way, and the horses must pass over them or else detour through the underbrush. On the 27th we traveled this way all day long. From time to time we saw a few Indians scavenging the forest for fruit. In one quite deserted place I saw a woman sitting alone at the foot of an oak tree. She was very ugly and wore little clothing. I have no idea where M. de Chateaubriand found the model for Atala.[115]

115. François René de Chateaubriand (1769–1848), a leading French Romantic writer, traveled through America in 1791 and 1792. Atala was a beautiful, pious Christian Indian woman in his book *Atala,* published in 1801. The novel opens with a prologue that describes the flora and fauna of the French territories in North America in great, exotic detail. The main narrative is set in the late seventeenth century and follows the story of Chactas, a Natchez Indian who lives with the Spanish at Saint Augustine for a short time and then is captured by the Muscogule Indians in the Louisiana Territory while trying to return to his home farther west. While in captivity, he falls in love with a beautiful Muscogule Indian woman, Atala, who has converted to Christianity. Atala frees Chactas and runs away with him north to the Ohio River valley, though she refuses to marry him because he is not a Christian. Atala's mother made her daughter take a Christian vow never to marry, and just as Atala poisons herself because she loves Chactas, a solitary Catholic missionary tells her that she can reverse the vow and marry Chactas. As Atala dies, Chactas promises her that he will become a Christian.

This novel was influential in creating an image of America and American Indians in the popular French culture.

Chateaubriand's brother, Jean Baptiste de Chateaubriand, guillotined during the Terror, was Tocqueville's uncle.

I've seen a few male Indians who are handsome enough, but the women are awful and repulsive.

After five or six hours on the road, we were hungry, but we wanted to find a spot near a river or stream from which we could drink. How were we to know when we might find one? Our guide knew not a word of English, and we not a word of Indian. I signaled that we needed to stop at the first stream with such enthusiasm that eventually he understood what I was saying. A short while later, he stopped and led me to a spring a few yards from the path. I also asked him by means of signs how far we were from Saginaw, having been on the road for four or five hours already. He answered by drawing a line on the ground. He put Flint River at one end and Saginaw at the other and then marked our position, about a third of the way to our destination.

When he realized that I wanted to shoot birds, he pointed them out when I didn't see them. As a result, I shot a very fine bird of prey. We hunted without getting down from our horses, which did not flinch when we fired. We saw lots of game: stags, pheasants, partridge. But we didn't kill much.

Because we were very tired, we slowed our horses now and then, but each time the Indian would turn back toward us and shout, Saginaw! Saginaw! while pointing at the sun, which had already begun to set. Then he would set off again running at top speed.

The distractions of the hunt had delayed us a bit. I also stopped occasionally to collect wildflowers whenever I spotted a pretty one.

We had left the trail we had been on about an hour before. We were now proceeding through the thick of the forest. I was surprised by this change and mentioned it to Tocqueville. We came to a place that we later found out was a small Indian village on the elevated and picturesque banks of a river (Cash River). Our guide suddenly stopped, pointed to the sun, which was now only a few hours from setting, and signaled to us that Saginaw was still very far away, so that we would have to make camp at this spot by the river, at the risk of being devoured by the thousands of mosquitoes that mass wherever there is moisture in clouds so thick you can't see through them. The situation was critical. With gestures I indicated to the Indian that we were most displeased. He tried in turn to make me understand that if we continued on, we risked being caught in the forest at night. We had with us a small wicker-wrapped bottle of brandy. We had noticed that of all our equipment, it was this small bottle that the savage admired most. I signaled to him that if he could get us to Saginaw that night, I would give him the bottle. After a moment's hesitation, he leapt to his feet and resumed running with shouts of "Saginaw!"

Night soon overtook us, but faithful Phoebus[116] again came to our rescue and at 9:30 in the evening we found ourselves standing on the bank of the Saginaw River. But we were not yet at the end of our journey: we still had to cross the river, which is as wide as the Seine, and there is no bridge. Our Indian gave

116. Or Apollo, Greek god of light.

out with a few sharp yelps, and a short while later we saw a small canoe arrive, steered by a person whom we might have taken for a savage had we not heard him utter several words of French. He invited us aboard his small bark, which like all Indian canoes was made from the hollowed-out trunk of a single tree. I did not find this system of navigation at all reassuring, and I confess that I was almost certain that we would eventually find ourselves swimming. The hardest part of the crossing was to get our horses to the other side, but our Indian took them by the bridle and led them across. The boatman began to paddle, and we found ourselves on the river in a nutshell, escorted by our poor horses, which, though extremely tired, were forced to swim behind the canoe. Fortunately the night was very beautiful, and the moon was so bright that anyone standing on the river bank could have witnessed our crossing, which was indeed something quite extraordinary.

We found a good stopping place in Saginaw. I had expected to find a kind of city and was rather surprised to discover that the entire settlement consisted of only five or six houses. We spent a day there. The Americans who live in the town settled there solely in order to do business with the Indians. We spent our time persuading them to tell us about their relations with the savages. They didn't know what to make of us: some thought we had come to buy land and settle down; others saw me painting birds and imagined that we had come to do research in natural history. Among the settlers were some Canadians, who seemed delighted to see us: "You've come from old France," they said. That is what they call France, because Canada used to be "New France." In the evening we went out on the Saginaw in a canoe. I have never seen a prettier river: the water is almost white, and the banks are covered with woods or meadowland.

View of Fort at Sault St Marie from the steamboat Superior, *7 August 1831.* (GB1 *opposite bottom;* GB2)

Tocqueville and I were alone in our little bark. The weather was as beautiful as could be, the sky was cloudless, the sun was going down, and all of nature was shrouded in silence. Some distance from Saginaw there is a place called Green Point, where the river widens out into a kind of bay enclosed in a forest of very tall trees. That is where we steered our canoe. Nature was so calm that the surface of the water shone like a mirror. The thick forest all around gave echo to the slightest sound. When we fired a shot from a rifle, the reverberations were incredible. During our short stay in Saginaw, I saw two hummingbirds. I would have liked to kill them but wasn't able to. Another strange thing is the vast number of rattlesnakes. "They kill their man every time," a Canadian told us as we were walking with him through the weeds. Last but not least, Saginaw is quite famous for the number of mosquitoes that infest the place. It was impossible to sleep, and I thought they would drive me mad. I had time to paint a bluebird.

We returned from Saginaw as we had come. Only we did it without a guide and did not once go astray. We ate a meal in the middle of the forest, as we had the first time. Nothing particularly interesting happened on our way back to Detroit. We did stay a while in Pontiac, however, long enough to collect some detailed documents concerning the way in which newcomers establish themselves in the region, the quantity of provisions they need to bring, the way in which they clear trees and cultivate the land, the price of labor, and the cost of various supplies, among other things.

We have precise information about all these things. These are not mere objects of curiosity. I am convinced that there are thousands of people in France who might be interested in coming to America and acquiring excellent land at a good price, but most of them have no idea about what things are like here. It might be a service to our country to provide information about what there is. When people emigrate to a new country, the difficulty they usually face is the difference of language, but that obstacle does not exist in Michigan, where a quarter of the population speaks French.

I was back in Detroit on August 1. Tocqueville and I went to reserve our places on the voyage to Buffalo when someone came and announced that a large steamboat, the *Superior*, with 200 passengers on board, had just arrived in Detroit from Buffalo and would be going to Green Bay at the far end of Lake Michigan, after stopping at Saut-Sainte-Marie [*sic*], which separates Lake Huron from Lake Superior, and at Michilimackinac, which is situated between Lake Michigan and Lake Huron.[117] Nothing can compare with the beauty of the Great Lakes. The places I've just mentioned are virtually unknown, and for the first time a steamboat filled with fashionable passengers would be heading into these unsettled regions where no vessel of any size had yet ventured. At first we said, "We won't go," but the temptation was unbearable, and we finally gave in.

Adieu . . .

From Tocqueville | To Abbé Lesueur

Detroit (Michigan), August 3, 1831

You may be surprised, my good friend, to be receiving a letter sent from Detroit. We decided to come here for several reasons. We were extremely eager to see territory that man had only recently won from nature. When we reached Buffalo, we were told that we might find what we were after in Michigan. Eventually we found a steamboat that sails every day from Buffalo to Detroit and generally completes the journey in two days and one night, although the two cities are separated by about 100 leagues (in French measure). We therefore set out for Detroit instead of going directly to Niagara, as we had intended to do. We crossed all of Lake Erie, which is exactly like the Atlantic Ocean, so much so that I suffered a bit from seasickness during the first day. The day after we arrived in Detroit, we rented two horses and set out for a place called Pontiac, which is located 25 miles north of Detroit in the Northwest Territory. . . .

From Beaumont | To his brother Achille

Aboard the *Superior*, Lake Michigan, August 11, 1831

Yet another unplanned voyage. Instead of returning to Buffalo on August 1, we left for Green Bay. We have been en route for ten days now, and when we return to Buffalo we will have traveled 1,810 miles, or 608 leagues, in two weeks. As you can see, it's more than Hippolyte de Montulé.[118] I want to describe this voy-

---

117. The *Superior* was a lavish steamship built in 1822, and its tour of the Great Lakes was popular among American and European tourists.

118. Beaumont most likely meant Édouard de Montulé, author of *Voyage en Amérique, en Sicile et en Égypte en 1816, 1817, 1818 et 1819* (Paris, 1821) and *Voyage en Angleterre et en Russie en 1821, 1822 et 1823* (Paris, 1825).

View of Lake Superior from the Pointe aux Pins. "Nothing can compare with the beauty of the Great Lakes," Beaumont wrote Chabrol on August 2, 1831. (GB2)

age to you, my dear Achille, as well as our reasons for undertaking it. The day we had planned to leave Detroit for the state of New York, we learned that a superb steamboat, the *Superior,* would be departing on a voyage that would cover the full extent of the Great Lakes. The newspapers had been speaking about this excursion for some time as a voyage likely to stir the interest of avid explorers. We went to inspect the vessel. It was already full of travelers, English as well as Americans, and most of them had no other purpose for traveling than to enjoy themselves for a few days. The captain assured me that the voyage would take no more than eight or ten days. The opportunity was tempting. It was the first time that such a large ship would venture into such remote regions, and for anyone hoping to study the country closely, this would be no mere pleasure cruise. To make a long story short, we decided to book passage. We were assigned two rather uncomfortable beds in the gentlemen's cabin, and in less than an hour we were on our way. We settled in and soon found ourselves steaming down the Saint Clair River, which leads to the lake of the same name and then into Lake Huron. But before retracing our itinerary, I want to describe the people who traveled with us.

There were about two hundred passengers. Each one has his or her own bed. From that you can imagine the size of the ship. It is an enormous moving or, rather, floating house, which is more surprising than the buildings in the city of Venice *with its residents,* for those buildings are as you know *built on pilings.* Of the two hundred individuals among whom I find myself, I have nothing at all to say about three-quarters and a half of them. Nor do I have much to say about the second half of the last quarter. But among our traveling companions is an Englishman, Mr. Vigne, quite a good fellow and an intrepid traveler, who was in Russia last year and who told me yesterday that he hopes to be in Egypt next spring.[119] There is also Mr. Mullon, a Catholic priest from Cincinnati (Ohio).[120] He is going to Michilimackinac expressly to engage in public debate with a Presbyterian minister on a controversial point of religion. Mr. Mullon is a tall, thin man whose Catholic zeal borders on intolerance. The religious spirit in this part of the country is nothing like it is in the state of New York, especially in the big cities. In New York and Albany different denominations live in peace with one another and help each other out. No such unity exists here among the different communities: "These Presbyterians," Mr. Mullon told me, "are as nasty as snakes. Smash their skulls and they'll stand up on their tails." It seems that Catholicism is making a good deal of progress in the western United States. There are already twelve bishops in the major cities such as New York, Philadelphia, Boston, New Orleans, Cincinnati, etc.[121] These bishops are chosen by the Catholic clergy of the United States and approved by the Pope. Papal authority is as great here as in Rome itself, and, as in France, Catholic ministers here are entirely subject to the Roman Church. As you will have gathered, the government has absolutely nothing to do with the selection of bishops. Of course you would infer from the nature of the government that this would have to be the case. It is no more concerned with religious affairs or with the ministers of the various denominations than they are with it. All the Catholic priests that I have met in this country take the view that this complete separation of church and state is a great advantage to Catholicism. I am sorely tempted to share this belief: the alliance of the state and religion in France has been deleterious to the latter. As long as the government with which the church was allied had the upper hand, the church was also strong. But when the government was all-powerful, the political parties that attacked it and worked to overthrow it could not help but attack the clergy as well, its most faithful supporters. And one cannot attack the ministers of a religion without harming the religion itself. Because innovators opposed Catholic priests as champions of an order they no longer wanted, they convinced themselves and the public that the religion of which those priests were the ministers was also an adversary. I find it difficult to explain in any other way why certain parties in France were so passionate in their attacks on a religion that here is exempt from political passions of any kind. In addition to Mr. Mullon, we have two other men of the cloth, a Presbyterian and an Episcopalian.

The majority of the steamboat passengers are Presbyterian, hence it was the Presbyterian who officiated the other day (Sunday). The service was held in the gentlemen's cabin. The Episcopalians, who aren't terribly demanding, were

119. Godfrey Thomas Vigne (1801–1863) was a lawyer and cultivated English gentleman.

120. James Ignatius Mullon had founded a mission in Michilimackinac in 1829. By the next year, he was a church leader in Cincinnati, and in 1834, he was transferred to New Orleans.

121. There were eleven, not twelve, bishoprics in the United States. The one in Detroit was not established until 1833.

Steamboat on Lake Huron at Michilimackinac, 7 August 1831. (GB2)

quite comfortable with the service run by their Protestant colleague, and the adherents of one denomination are generally no less satisfied with the ministers
of another. This may be tolerance, but I would sooner die than call it faith. As
for Mr. Mullon, he is not quite so indifferent on the subject. He stuck his nose
in while the service was going on and when he saw what was happening fled
as though from the fires of hell. I was sitting close to my bed when the service
began, and I did not get up. Instead, I alternately listened and fell asleep, depending on whether the preacher raised or lowered his voice.

Among the people with whom we associate regularly, there are three or four
young Americans, good fellows but with very little to recommend them. They
look as though they're dying of boredom, and it is easy to imagine why: every
American is a businessman. They spend their lives in commerce and industry.
They don't know how to do anything else. They are incapable of intellectual
work of any kind. One of them told me that all he had seen on our voyage
were some "big expanses of water." To be sure, water forms the background of
the canvas, since other than a few hours on land we have been out on the lakes,
which are like small seas. For anyone with an observant cast of mind, however,
there is plenty to see besides the liquid surface.

The women aboard are not worth much more than the men. Their only advantage is that of numbers, and few exhibit any kind of distinction. Miss Clemens is a well-educated Englishwoman with an ardent and very romantic imagination, an enthusiastic personality, and, I think, a very tender heart. She would
be charming if she were ten years younger. She told me stories, some of which
were probably fairy tales. Although quite friendly, she is boring, because, having
made her acquaintance, it is hard to get rid of her. These damned women who

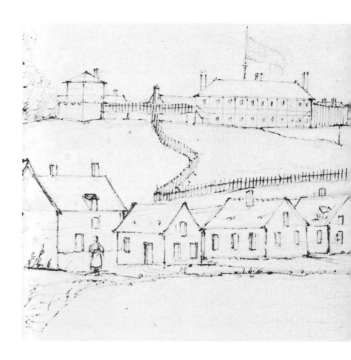

Michilimackinac, Lake Huron, August 1831. (GBI)

once were pretty can never get it through their heads that they no longer are. Among the young ladies are the daughters of Mr. Mac Comb, a major general in the American army. One of them, Mathilda, is friendly and rather pretty.[122] Traveling with them is an uncle, who was extremely polite to us at first but who since the day before yesterday has been snubbing us, I don't know why. Miss Thomson is a small woman with a wasp waist, as light as a butterfly, lovely to look at, and stupid as a goose, etc. As you can see, the company is not very appealing, and we have been living with it since August 1. The first day we didn't know anyone. Now we are on good terms with everyone. On August 2 we arrived in Fort Gratiot, which is at the mouth of the Saint Clair River where it flows into Lake Huron.[123] Our arrival was rather picturesque. It was evening. The sun had just gone down. Storm clouds filled the sky. Lightning flashed all around. We were dancing on deck to the sound of a violin and English horn. The vast waters of Lake Huron rolled ahead of us like the waters of the Atlantic. When the ball ended, the orchestra played *La Marseillaise.* This evoked in me memories that overwhelmed possible beauty in the music: it was exactly a year ago that I heard that tune for the first time in Paris, on the place Vendôme and

122. Alexander Macomb Jr. (1782–1841) was born in Detroit and became a member of the Army Corps of Engineers at age twenty. He earned distinction in the War of 1812 and was commanding general of the U.S. Army when Beaumont encountered him. Matilda Macomb (1812–1834) was his sixth child.

123. During the War of 1812, the United States government charged Captain Charles Gratiot with building a fort (later called Fort Gratiot) at this spot.

in the courtyard of the Palais-Royal.[124] Played in such circumstances, it was like an echo of the cannon of July, still reverberating. But who would have predicted that I would be listening to it a year later on Lake Huron?

We were scheduled for only a brief stop at Fort Gratiot, but the weather was so bad and the wind so contrary that we dropped anchor. Two days passed with no improvement in the weather, so we were stuck all that time in a place where there was nothing at all to see.

On August 4 we left Fort Gratiot, and the next day at 5 we arrived in Saut-Sainte-Marie.

Saut-Sainte-Marie is situated between Lake Huron and Lake Superior. To get there you must travel the whole length of Lake Huron. In good weather the voyage is lovely: the water of the Great Lakes is clearer than you can possibly imagine without having seen it. You can almost always see the bottom, no matter how deep. As you approach Sainte-Marie, the lake narrows and you have to thread your way through a multitude of islands of various sizes. The scenery is quite pretty. The landscape is always changing, and in addition to being picturesque it holds your attention and interest because of the danger it poses to navigation. But when I say "danger," I am exaggerating: the only risk is that of running aground and getting stuck for a week while you wait for another ship to come rescue you. We nearly suffered this unenviable fate: a few inches more and we would have dug ourselves in.

124. The singing of the "Marseillaise" had been forbidden during the Bourbon Restoration (1814–30), but the revolutionaries of July 1830 revived it.

My impressions of the moment tend to evaporate quickly. I am sorry that I cannot describe for you the feelings aroused in me by the contrast between the sight of such vast solitudes and the civilized society with which we traveled in our floating house. We traveled a hundred leagues on Lake Huron and in the bay adjacent to Saut-Sainte-Marie without seeing anything but canoes of quite savage Indians. The sound of our boat and our music brought them out of their forests to catch a glimpse of our steamboat. I have no difficulty imagining their stupefaction, because even for a European these large steam-driven vessels are undeniably one of the wonders of modern industry. While some of the Indians admired our means of transport, we tossed them two or three bottles of brandy, which they received with abundant joy and gratitude. They reserved a similar welcome for some loaves of bread that we dropped into their canoe.

The farther north we travel, the more Indians we find. Perhaps it would be better to say that the savages are more numerous wherever Europeans have yet to set foot. Around Saut-Sainte-Marie there are areas in which the Indians will remain for some time to come. The land in these places is almost barren. There is only rock, which stands in the way of farming. In any case, it is enough for Europeans to appear for the Indians to flee. They do so not because of their *feelings* but because the game they live on has already gone.

Many people believe that the Indian races are nearly destroyed and all that remains is a few tribes roaming the forests of the North. This is wrong. There are still three or four million savages in the northern United States alone. It is rather difficult to judge the mores and character of these savages by observing the Indians one meets in the environs of cities. The latter have already acquired a patina of civilization, which deprives them of their primitive characteristics. It seems that the savages who live at a distance from Europeans have quite a remarkable character.

It was late when we reached the vicinity of Saut-Sainte-Marie. We therefore remained aboard ship until the following morning. The place where we stopped was lovely, and that evening we had a concert and ball. The forest echoed back everything that was played by the English horn. I was curious to try the harmony of the virgin forests of America myself, so at midnight I played variations of *Di tanti palpiti* on deck.[125] Nothing could compare with the beauty of such a night. The sky was sparkling with stars, which were reflected in the water, and at intervals along the bank we saw the campfires of Indians whose ears had detected an unusual sound as they listened, no doubt for the first time, to airs of Rossini and Auber.[126]

Early in the morning on August 6 we entered the village known as Saut-Sainte-Marie. It was given this name because the river that passes nearby and

125. "Di tanti palpiti" was a well-known song from the opera *Tancredi* (1813), by Gioachino Rossini (1792–1868).
126. Daniel François Esprit Auber (1782–1871) was a French composer of operas.

joins Lake Superior to Lake Huron descends rather steeply at this point between rocky banks and thus seems to "jump" [*sauter*] from one place to another. Sainte-Marie, like all the other European settlements in these parts, was founded by the French.[127] Note that Sainte-Marie is on the left bank of the river, and the right [left] bank is on the Canadian side, which once belonged to France. Everyone in Sainte-Marie speaks French. There are as many Indians as there are Canadians. The two populations mingle constantly. This half-European, half-Indian population is not unpleasant. There is something fierce in the features of the Indians that this mixture softens. The eyes of the savages have a natural gleam that I have never encountered in a white man. They suffer from being both hard and severe, but the fire that burns in their gaze is quite beautiful when it loses something of its primitive awkwardness without losing its ardor. That is what happens when the Indian and the European marry. The Canadians refer to the issue of such marriages as *métiches* [half-breeds]. I have seen some young female *métiches* who struck me as remarkably beautiful.

No sooner had we arrived in Sainte-Marie than we took a canoe and set out to see Lake Superior. Miss Clemens, Miss Thomson, Mathilda, and several other ladies came with us. We paddled two leagues upstream to a place called Pointe-aux-Pins, where Lake Superior begins.

This lake is quite like all the others, although I believe that its water is the purest of all. In addition to its vast size, it shares another characteristic with the sea: a tide that ebbs and flows. I found this outing delightful. The boatmen who served as our guides were Canadians of charmingly gay temperament. As they paddled, they sang any number of old French songs, certain verses of which were quite droll. The short time I spent with them demonstrated how difficult it is to shed one's national character, particularly the French character. The French gaiety that the boatmen have preserved intact makes a stark contrast with the glacial sangfroid of the Americans. Note, too, that the French of Canada are gayer than we are now in France. The reason for this is simple: their circumstances have changed less than ours. They did not live through the Revolution, which had such a powerful influence on the new direction our national character has taken. Their attention, unlike ours, is not riveted exclusively on political interests. It is therefore true to say that, with respect to the *ancient character* of the nation, they are more French than we are.

We explored Pointe-aux-Pins for an hour or two. I was introduced to an Indian chief who was smitten with my lever-action rifle. I fired a shot for him. He was so pleased that, as a token of his gratitude, he gave me a small tortoise shell.

I drew a view of Lake Superior. Afterward, we returned by way of the

127. Although this site had already become a settling place for natives and European trappers and traders, French missionaries named Sault Sainte Marie in 1668. After that, cities grew up on both sides of the river, in present-day Ontario and Michigan.

"Giant's Arch," *Michilimackinac, Lake Huron, August 1831.* (GB2) "To get a better angle, I went out in a small boat," wrote Beaumont.

Sainte-Marie River. We had bravely descended the Saut by canoe. There is no danger, because you are led by skillful boatmen with a marvelous knowledge of the river and its shoals. But the boat goes so quickly, and there are so many rocks capable of smashing the canoe into a thousand pieces, that it is hard not to feel afraid. We were in any case obliged not to fear for our own lives because we had ladies with us. They set an example of courage, and not one of them uttered the slightest cry. We stayed only a short time in Sainte-Marie, and at 3 o'clock the same day, August 6, we set out again for Michilimackinac. The name belongs to an island located between Lake Huron and Lake Michigan. We saw nothing noteworthy on this leg of the journey. To give you an accurate idea of the region, suffice it to say that the forest is dotted with countless lakes and ponds. One seldom sees the color of the earth; the forest so dominates the landscape as to keep it virtually always hidden. The view eventually becomes monotonous. You have to find a pastime to keep yourself amused. I am reading a little and writing a lot. The point of writing letters is pleasure, but I doubt that mine will be a pleasure for those obliged to read them. As you can see, they suffer from being long and badly written. They are probably also confused. It is devilishly difficult to find privacy in the midst of such company, and disturbances are constant. When I see a pretty bird, I paint it, but that, too, is difficult on a boat that is always moving.

The other day, I was sitting with my box of colors at my side. A little lady came up to me and said, "Oh, sir, paint my portrait."

"I couldn't," I answered.

"I will pay you well," she added.

"But I don't want your money!"

"Well, then, I will give you something else." I had all the trouble in the world to make her understand that I paint for my own pleasure and that I would be incapable of doing a miniature.

No sooner had I finished with her than another woman came to me with a similar request. "If you paint the steamboat," a third woman said to me, "include me in the picture. Now, I'm wearing a very ugly dress at the moment, but come, I have a very pretty one in my room, that's the one you must paint."

When I told these stories to the people with whom I associate, they had a good laugh.

As for painting, the Englishman I mentioned, Mr. Vigne, paints quite well. He deserves special praise for his lovely colors. I took advantage of his kindness to paint a bluebird with his colors. It bears no resemblance to the one I tried to paint earlier.

We arrived in Michilimackinac on August 7. This little island is the most picturesque thing I have seen in this part of the country yet. On the whole, the terrain is quite flat, and there is seldom any relief (I am speaking only of the area adjacent to the Great Lakes). By contrast, Michilimackinac is bordered almost entirely by rocks. It is protected by a fort that benefits greatly from its natural position and needs little additional help from the hand of man.[128] It is occupied by a hundred American troops. The population of the island is composed of the same elements as that of Sainte-Marie but is larger, numbering around four hundred. It, too, is an entirely industrial and commercial population. Everyone speaks French, and several residents of the island are wealthy and distinguished, including Mr. and Mrs. Abbot, who gave us a warm welcome, although Tocqueville and I appeared at their home without any introduction.[129] The only things that seem to stir the passions of the people on this small island are the desire for wealth and religion. Their ardor for wealth, like that of all Americans, is incredible, but they also have what other Americans do not, namely, religious enthusiasm of a sort that turns the members of different denominations into enemies. The Catholics are the most numerous. Michilimackinac was the destination of our steamboat priest, Mr. Mullon. We spent the entire day of August 7 on the island. I saw few Indians there. A few days earlier, there had been a lot of them,

128. Originally built by the French on the tip of Michigan's Lower Peninsula, this fort was rebuilt by the British at Michilimackinac on the adjacent island in 1781. It remained an important military and trading post in the Great Lakes region.

129. Samuel Abbot, originally from Detroit, was an agent for the American Fur Company.

but they were already far away. They travel enormous distances in small canoes, quite similar in size to the little boat you built twenty years ago, and on which you sailed as a latter-day Columbus across the Ocean of Beaumont-la-Chartre, to wit, the fountain in the lower garden. We spent the day visiting two of the island's natural curiosities: the first is a natural arch in a very high cliff. Some call it Pierced Rock, others Giant's Arch. The sculpting of the rock is in fact quite extraordinary. I studied it from every angle and climbed to the top with Tocqueville and two of our companions. The climb is quite easy, and the only thing to worry about is getting dizzy. We had a guide who suffered a spell of vertigo, and the poor fellow immediately began shaking all over. He saved himself by sliding very slowly all the way to the bottom. To get a better angle, I went out in a small boat with the Englishman, and the two of us sketched Giant's Arch from a small distance out.

The other, no less curious sight is found in the middle of the island: it is a pyramid that seems to rise with geometrical regularity to a height of fifty feet. It is in fact a rock never touched by the hand of man. In this rock there are crevices and slits in which the Indians have deposited the bones of the dead. I found a small deposit of such relics, and this is *one of the riches* that I will take back to my homeland.

We left Michilimackinac on the night of the 7th. On the morning of the 9th we arrived in Green Bay.[130] You will find this place on the map in one of the corners of Lake Michigan. We departed again on the 10th. I spent my time there in a rather unusual way. There were quite a few Indian huts along the river. I went from one to the other, by myself. I chatted as best I could with the savages I found. Some of them speak a little French. There isn't one who doesn't know how to say *bonjour*. That's one way to break the ice. In any case, they like the French quite well. With those who didn't understand a word of French, I spoke by signs. When I wanted to please them, all I had to do was show my album. There was one rather pretty young Indian girl who gave me a necklace of pearls and shells in exchange for a painting of an American woodpecker: tell me I don't know how to drive a hard bargain! As you see, having frequented so many Americans of late, I have begun to adopt their industrial spirit. Fortunately, I still have the anecdote of the ladies who asked me to paint their portraits to prove that I am still a man of honor and generosity and by no means *mercantile.*

In the hut of one of my savages I amused myself by painting the face of a little Indian boy: I painted a bird on one cheek, a galloping horse on the other, and a cat on his chin. His comrades admired my masterpieces. As you know, the Indians are in the habit of painting their faces. They do it very crudely, without taste or art, so they were charmed by a few colors applied with a certain amount of method. I learned more about Indian customs in a half a day with them than

130. Green Bay is a western arm of Lake Michigan, between present-day Michigan and Wisconsin.

I would have learned by reading thousands of volumes. I will not try to describe what I learned. They seem like excellent people, all things considered. But they are like a diamond in the rough, crude and unpolished, so they seem, and are in fact, inferior to other gems far less precious but embellished by art. While I made my expedition among the savages, Tocqueville went hunting and came close to drowning. He is very nearsighted, so when he came to what he thought was quite a narrow river, he did not hesitate to swim across. But he was wrong: in fact, the river was so wide that he was dead tired by the time he made it to the other bank. People who don't swim very well never encounter such dangers.

The area around Green Bay is so flat that there are no good vistas, except perhaps Fort Howard, which is occupied by several American companies. All the military posts in this remote territory have but one purpose, which is to inspire respect in the Indians and drive them ever farther west. Thus the American army has very little to do. The Indians are on the whole resigned to their fate; they recognize the superiority of their enemies, the Europeans. To be sure, there was recently a minor Indian uprising against the United States on the banks of the Mississippi, but it went nowhere.

The United States has only 6,000 regular troops, but that number is more than sufficient for what they are asked to do. All army officers are chosen from among the graduates of the military school at West Point. Noncommissioned officers are never promoted to the rank of officer. This is because the army is all volunteers, hence the ranks are full of not very respectable men who join the army because they have no other prospects. What a fate for an officer to be sent to Green Bay or to Prairie du Chien, which is even farther! Incidentally, they are much better paid than in France.

We left Green Bay on August 10 and returned to Michilimackinac on our way back to Detroit. As luck would have it, we arrived in Michilimackinac just as Mr. Mullon was to deliver his polemic against the Presbyterians. Tocqueville and I went to hear him in the Catholic church. We found a good many people assembled there. This particular religious dispute aroused quite a bit of emotion in the people. Mr. Mullon spoke with a good deal of warmth and considerable talent, but he seemed to me to treat his adversaries with a vehemence and severity that were by no means evangelical. If his moderation left something to be desired, his zeal did not, for there is no denying that he traveled two hundred leagues to make his case and would travel two hundred more on the trip home.

On the 12th we left Michilimackinac and now find ourselves on Lake Huron, where I have resumed the letter I began the day before yesterday. Tomorrow, the 14th, we will be in Detroit, and when we arrive I shall make haste to post my letter so that it arrives in New York before the departure of the packet boat on the 20th. We will be stopping only briefly in Detroit before continuing on to Buffalo. We have to see Niagara, etc. I will keep you informed of our progress. You must have received a precise account of my doings thus far. I wish I could say the same about yours. On August 20 it will be two months since I have received a letter from France. I hope to find some mail waiting in Buffalo, where I asked to have my correspondence forwarded.

Adieu, my dear Achille, write me often. I will not rail against your laziness, because there may right now be two or three letters from you en route across the ocean or along the roads of America. But bear in mind this very important truth: for a poor exile, a few lines written by a friendly hand are of inestimable value.

I warmly embrace Father and Mother, to whom I send my love.

Gustave.

From Tocqueville | To his father

On Lakes Erie, Huron, and Michigan
August 14, 1831

In my last letter home, my dear father, I told you that I was leaving for Buffalo and that from there I would head for Boston by way of Canada. That was indeed our intention. Apparently, however, it was written that our plan should not be carried out. On our way to the post office to post our letters, we learned that a large steam vessel had just arrived and that it would be making a quick tour of all the Great Lakes before returning to Buffalo, all quite comfortably and within twelve days. We succumbed to temptation. So instead of leaving the next morning for Buffalo, as we had planned, we set out for Lake Superior. In other words, we added nearly 1500 miles, or 500 French leagues, to our original plan. . . .

We quickly crossed Lake Saint Clair and proceeded up the Saint Clair River, and after being stopped for a day at the entrance to Lake Huron owing to contrary winds and a shortage of wood, we finally resumed our course into that vast lake, which resembles the ocean in every way except that its waters are marvelously clear, clear enough to see objects thirty feet below the surface. We made our way across Lake Huron for two days and one night, making three leagues per hour, and still we could not see the end. On the morning of the third day we spotted for the first time a place inhabited by whites. This was Sault Sainte-Marie, located on the river of the same name, which joins Lake Superior to Lake Huron. There we dropped anchor and made our way to dry land. There were no really good vistas along the vast stretch of coastline we had traversed in the course of our voyage, nothing but plains covered with forests. Yet the landscape left us with a deep and lasting impression. A vast lake with not a sail in sight and a coastline bearing not a trace of human presence and bordered by an ageless forest—I assure you this is more than just great poetry. It is the most extraordinary sight I have ever seen. This land, which is still nothing but an immense forest, will someday be one of the richest and most powerful in the world. You don't have to be a prophet to see this. Nature has laid the groundwork with fertile land and shipping routes unlike any other in the world. Nothing is lacking but civilized men, and they are knocking at the door.

August 15

Back to Sault Sainte-Marie. The river here is no longer navigable. Our boat stopped, but we didn't. The Indians have taught Europeans how to make canoes from bark, which two men can carry on their shoulders. I will bring home a sample of the bark from which these boats are made. You will agree with me that the first man to step into such a boat must have been a hardy soul. The savages can build a canoe of this sort in five days. It is terrifying to see such a nutshell darting among the reefs of the Sainte-Marie River and shooting the rapids with the speed of an arrow. Yet the fact is that there is no danger. I have more than once found myself in one of these canoes in the company of ladies, and no one displayed the slightest apprehension. On our journey the boatmen carried the canoes on their backs to a point upstream of the rapids, then put them in the water, and we lay in the bottom. The entire population of Sainte-Marie is French. These are happy, lively Frenchmen, much as their forefathers were but we are no longer. As they paddled our canoes, they sang old tunes that are all but forgotten at home. What we have found here is the France of a century ago, preserved like a mummy for the edification of the present generation.

After proceeding nearly three leagues up the Sainte-Marie River, we landed on a promontory known as the Cape of Oaks. From there we could at last see the extent of Lake Superior, stretching off to the horizon. There are still no settlements along its shores, and the rapids still prevent any ship from entering. Then . . . But if I tell you everything in detail, I'll never get to the end of the story. I am forced to abridge, because we are approaching Detroit, and time is short. After conversing for some time with the Indians who live near the cape, we returned to our boat. From Sainte-Marie we descended to Michilimackinac, an island at the entrance to Lake Michigan. From there we went to Green Bay, which is sixty leagues south on Lake Michigan. After several excursions along the Fox River (or *rivière du Renard*), where we shot some game, we resumed our voyage, and here we are. I don't think that there is a single person in France who has made the same journey. The Canadians assured us that they had never seen a Frenchman. If I were able to convey what I saw and felt in the course of this brief journey, the portrait might have some interest. I have tried to do it and am discouraged. The impressions have come too quickly. I would like to recount what I have seen, but only while seated beside the fire. . . .

From Tocqueville | To Ernest de Chabrol

Buffalo, August 17, 1831

Human life is very odd, my dear friend. We were on our way to Buffalo to see Niagara Falls. A departing ship offered us the opportunity to spend two days sailing across Lake Erie en route to Detroit. It was hardly possible to turn down this chance to see one of the frontier provinces that stands between the United States and the vast solitudes of the West. We asked for just ten days: it was La Fontaine's story of the pigeon.[131]

131. Tocqueville is referring to Jean de La Fontaine's story "The Two Pigeons." In the poem, one of the pigeons says, "Three days at most will satisfy my curious soul."

So we embarked. We explored the Michigan district, and when our ten days were up, we returned to Detroit with the intention of sailing the next day for Buffalo.[132] But as we approached the shore, we spotted a large steamboat about to depart and found out that it was headed for Lake Superior and then on to Green Bay, which is on Lake Michigan. This ship sails only once a year and traverses regions that are almost totally unknown. The passage was supposed to take just twelve days. We hastily returned to our inn, paid our bill, and packed our things. We boarded the ship, and . . . guess how many leagues the voyage was? Five hundred, neither more nor less—that is, the distance from Paris to Cadiz.

And now we are back where we started and, God willing, safe from new complications. Furthermore, although the excursion cost us a good deal of time, it stimulated our curiosity and even yielded a few precious documents. Twenty years ago, the Michigan Territory was almost entirely unpopulated. Since then, however, the flow of immigrants has reached this region.[133] The influx has now attained unprecedented proportions, and we could not have chosen a better place to study the way in which an American province is populated and the character of those who take upon themselves this arduous and fruitful labor. I want to discuss this with you in this letter: I have seen so much, and my time is so limited, that I have to choose my subjects carefully.

The United States does not allow private individuals to purchase lands that belong to Indian nations. The federal government purchases these lands itself and then resells them at low prices. I went to the Land Office in Detroit, which is in charge of the sale of Indian land, and there I learned the following:

Since the last thaw, from May when the lake became navigable until July 1, approximately 5,000 "new settlers" arrived in Michigan (I am using the English phrase because we have no equivalent). The magnitude of the figure surprised me, as you might imagine, particularly since I believed, as people in Europe generally do, that all these new settlers were Europeans.

The land agent told me that of these 5,000 individuals, not even 200 were immigrants from Europe, and even that proportion was higher than normal. So I asked the agent what might impel such a large number of Americans to leave the place where they were born to settle in the wilderness? "The answer is simple," he replied. "The law stipulates that upon the death of the father, the children divide his property equally. Hence each generation finds itself poorer than the preceding one. When a small landowner in one of our populous states finds it difficult to scrape by, he sells his land, moves his whole family out to the frontier, uses the small sum of capital that he has amassed from the sale of his land to buy a very substantial piece of land, and within a few years makes his fortune. Upon his death, if that fortune is not sufficient to satisfy his children, they will

132. For a full account, see Tocqueville's essay "Two Weeks in the Wilderness" in part 3.
133. In 1830, the Michigan Territory had over 31,000 inhabitants. Michigan achieved statehood in 1837, and by 1840, over 212,000 people lived there.

do as he did and amass another fortune in some new wilderness. Thank God, we have enough to reach all the way to the Pacific Ocean."

There is enough in this one answer to fill a large book, don't you agree? How can one even imagine a revolution in a land where man has such opportunities to satisfy his needs and passions, and how can the political institutions of such a people be compared to those of any other?

Continuing my investigation, I learned that the vast Michigan peninsula is divided into acres (an acre is almost as large as a French *arpent*). You choose on a map which acres you want and pay ten American shillings per acre, or about seven and a half francs.[134]

We have since explored a substantial number of these new settlements, and we took special care to find out how people go about establishing themselves.

Here is a summary: the initial expense (and this is what I would like people in Europe to know) is still fairly high. You need five to six hundred francs to clear the necessary land. Part of this amount goes to buying enough salt pork and flour to last six months, and with that the pioneer sets off into the wilderness. He usually takes a few animals with him and lets them forage in the woods, so they cost nothing to feed.

His first order of business is to cut down some trees and build a crude dwelling known as a log cabin. He then begins clearing a small field near the house, then another, and another. He attacks the forest in a thousand different ways and does battle with it on many fronts, though he doesn't always come out on top. I will try in my [next] letter to describe exactly what one of these new settlements looks like and paint a portrait of the family that occupies it, but today I haven't enough time or paper.

I have been reading the newspapers. The latest news from France frightens me and worries me greatly. Either I am seriously mistaken, or else our country has recently experienced or may even be in the throes of a violent crisis. This is the conclusion I draw from a host of observations and items of news that have come to our attention. I am consumed by anxiety. In Buffalo I found your package of May 27. Those of June 1, 10, and 30 await me in Albany, where I will arrive in a few days. God willing, I will find good news. . . .

From Beaumont | To his father

Lake Ontario, aboard *The Great Britain,* August 21, 1831
. . . No sooner did we arrive in Buffalo than we set out again for Niagara. For traveling companions we had Mr. Vigne, an Englishman, and an Englishwoman, Miss Clemens. I think I mentioned these two people to Achille, because they

134. The Land Ordinance of 1785 and the Northwest Ordinance of 1787 established the process of claiming and buying land in the Northwest, including the Michigan Territory. Surveyors divided the territory with a grid consisting of numbered ranges, townships, and sections. Settlers could inquire about purchases at a number of government land offices throughout the territories and could easily identify a tract by using the grid system.

were among the group that traveled to Green Bay. The former is a quite likable fellow, who travels for both education and pleasure. The latter is the best person on earth, but it would be impossible to be more boring. She has quite a romantic imagination and thrives exclusively on fiction, emotion, and moonlight. When she sees something she likes, she can respond only with cries of joy, and admiration without ecstasy is utterly foreign to her. At 20 she would be charming, but she is at least 40, which makes her merely ridiculous. She conceived quite a passion for us. I made the mistake of being polite, and she mistook politeness for flirtation. Aboard the steamboat, I had to resort to numerous stratagems to escape the charms of her conversation. First I had to listen to her declaim certain verses, and then there was some delightful sight that she wished me to join her in admiring. On the whole I was able to avoid her with one pretext or another, but there was no way to escape as we were leaving Buffalo. "I am going to show you my favorite place to stay and make a fuss over you when we arrive," she told us. She must spend half her life at the falls. She might be called "the madwoman of Niagara." Why doesn't she stand under the falling water? The showers might cure her. In any case, we embarked with our old traveling companion, and three hours later we reached the spot nearest the falls. This place is called Niagara Falls. You should know that Niagara is an Indian word that means "thundering water." It would be impossible to find a better name. We could hear its muffled growl and roar from a league and a half away, and it sounded a lot like distant thunder. I will not describe Niagara for you. I don't really know what I would say after M. de Chateaubriand, although his portrait seems quite inadequate.[135] Not that I think one could do better: I believe that the thing is beyond description. It is surely one of the most marvelous and gigantic of all the works of creation. Nowhere is nature more sublime or impressive. M. de Chateaubriand said that Niagara Falls was "a column from the water of the Flood." This is a great image, and I see nothing else in his description that captures the immensity of the thing. I saw Niagara in all its beauty. The weather was lovely. During the day, the falls, which are shrouded in billows of clouds that emanate from the falling water, are crowned by a perpetual rainbow. At night, a different kind of rainbow could be seen above the falling water: it was an effect of the stunning moonlight. . . .

From Tocqueville | To his mother

August 21, 1831
On Lake Ontario

. . . We stayed only an hour in Buffalo before setting out for Niagara. Two leagues from the falls, the noise was already as loud as a thunderstorm. Niagara in Indian means "thunder of waters." A more splendid or accurate description would be impossible to find. The Indian tongues are full of images of this sort,

135. In the epilogue of his book *Atala,* Chateaubriand published a description of Niagara Falls written from the perspective of the fictional French traveler who narrates the story.

Niagara Falls, 16 August 1831, from Canadian side. (GB2)

and far more poetic than ours. But to get back to Niagara, we pushed on toward the sound, unable to imagine how close we were to the falls.

Indeed, no visible sign warns you that you are drawing near. A great river (which is in fact the outflow from Lake Erie) flows slowly through a plain. No cliff or mountain is visible on the horizon. And so it remains until you reach the very edge of the cataract. It was a moonless night by the time we arrived, so we put off our first visit until the next day.

The next morning, August 18, we went to the falls in perfect weather.

I would inevitably indulge in *pathos,* my dear *maman,* if I were to attempt to describe the spectacle that lay before us. Niagara Falls in my opinion surpasses all that has been said and written about it in Europe, as well as any idea that the imagination can conceive in advance.[136] The river divides in two just before reaching the chasm that opens up before it, and it forms two falls separated by a small island. The larger of these falls is horseshoe-shaped and about a quarter of a league in size, or about twice the width of the Seine. When the water reaches the edge, it drops 149 feet straight down. The steam that rises from the bed below resembles a cloud, above which hovers a vast rainbow. It is quite easy to make your way onto a spit of rock that is almost entirely surrounded by water and that protrudes out over the chasm. The sublimity of the view from this spot

136. By the time of Tocqueville's visit, Niagara Falls had become an international tourist destination. Like Beaumont, Tocqueville probably had in mind the description that Chateaubriand had published in his book *Atala* (1801).

Niagara Falls 19 August 1831, with travel companions from the trip to Green Bay, including "the madwoman of Niagara." (GB2)

is without equal, especially at night (as we discovered), when you can no longer see the bottom of the abyss and the moon creates a rainbow above the cloud. I had never seen a nocturnal rainbow. It has the same form as the daytime one but is perfectly white. I saw it as I made my way from one bank to the other above the chasm. At first it seems difficult to advance a hundred paces or so under the sheet of falling water, but in fact it is rather easy. At that point a protruding rock prevents you from going any further. The darkness here is deep and terrifying, occasionally relieved by a fleeting light, which allows you to see the entire river as it seems to pass right above your head. It is hard to describe the impression produced by this ray of light when, after it has allowed you a momentary glimpse of the vast chaos that surrounds you, it once again abandons you to the darkness and the din of the falls. We spent a whole day at Niagara. Yesterday we proceeded across Lake Ontario. . . .

From Tocqueville | To Dalmassy[137]

[late August 1831]

. . . It's quite easy to gain access to this watery hell, as someone has called it, I no longer remember who. From below you then have to crawl out onto a ledge, below which opens the most immense *vade in pace* you can imagine. I have seen more difficult trails in the Alps, but here there are aggravating circumstances peculiar to this particular case (bear in mind that the traveler is a royal prosecutor). Through this narrow passage blows a wind so violent that you have to double over to hold your place against it. A blinding torrent of water hits you smack in the face. It feels as if three fire pumps were aimed directly at you. The farther you proceed, moreover, the thinner the air becomes, until it becomes difficult to breathe. You continue this way for perhaps a hundred paces to a point where the path is blocked by a projecting rock. I almost became sick at that point for want of air. Only after pressing my face to the rock for quite some time did I feel strong enough to lift my head. I seem to recall M. de Chateaubriand saying that the water you see falling from that spot resembles the torrent from the Flood. That comparison, which you probably find exaggerated, would seem [*illegible word*]. I assure you that there was nothing at all amusing about the spectacle before us at that moment. Behind us a cliff, against which you periodically had to press your mouth in order to breathe, before us the entire river, which formed a crystal vault almost impenetrable by the rays of the sun, enveloping everything in a suspect white light. Around us a humid obscurity and an air of destruction and chaos, which was truly impressive. I took two or three small stones from that very spot. You can find stones exactly like them on the avenue de Paris. Yet I am sure that you will not refuse the gift of one as a souvenir when I return. Make no mistake: these are no rubies, just ordinary stones. At least you can be sure that I didn't buy them at the Palais-Royal.

Why aren't you with me, my dear friend, or even here in my stead? To tell

137. Another young magistrate from the Versailles tribunal.

the truth, I am not worthy to enjoy such sights. They lodge themselves in my memory and remain of no use to anyone else. You would allow all your friends to share in your admiration. But if you want to see this place in all its grandeur, hurry. If you tarry, your Niagara will soon have been spoiled. Already the surrounding forest is growing thin.

The Romans added steeples to the Pantheon. I give the Americans ten years before they build a sawmill or a flour mill at the base of the cataract.

I beg your pardon, my dear friend, for this lengthy description, but as you know, travelers are long-winded. They babble before their time. Perhaps, by the time this letter reaches you, your mind will be on things other than the waterfalls of America. Perhaps, even as I write, political events in France are taking a sinister turn. Something tells me that we will not avoid civil war. These ideas torment me, my dear Dalmassy. They will not go away and stand as a screen between me and the world. Believe me when I say that more than once I've felt as if I would give up America and all its wonders just to be with those whose fate is most precious to me.

I shall end where I should have begun. Chabrol tells me that Madame de Dalmassy has given birth to a daughter. You wanted a boy, but you will get over it. I'll bet that the new arrival looks like her older sister, so I can't bring myself to feel sorry for you.

I beg you to give my regards to Madame de Dalmassy. Farewell, I embrace you.

From Beaumont | To his father

Albany
September 5, 1831.

... In two days we will be in Boston. But before speaking of cities where I am to go in the future, I must say a few words about those I have already visited. My last letter was dispatched from Montreal the moment I arrived. We did not stay in that city very long. It is large and sits on an island in the middle of the Saint Lawrence River. Its population is 25 or 30,000.[138] It is the largest city in Canada but not the capital.

We had a letter for the superior of the Montreal seminary.[139] We found a very amiable and quite distinguished Frenchman. He is a priest who came to Canada from Saint-Sulpice four years ago. He received us warmly and gave us a great deal of invaluable information about Canada. We were quite interested

138. By 1831, the population had expanded beyond the city walls, and the entire number of inhabitants was closer to forty thousand.

139. Joseph-Vincent Quiblier (1796–1852) had immigrated to Canada from Paris in 1825, and he directed a seminary in Montreal from 1831 to 1846. Tocqueville and Beaumont met with Quiblier on the recommendation of Father John Power, whom they had met in New York City.

in the country. Of its 900,000 inhabitants, more than 800,000 are French.[140] Under English dominion since the shameful treaty of 1763 ceded the country to England, Canadians still remain a population apart, entirely distinct from the English who have tried to settle among them.[141] They retain their language, customs, and nationality. The English government is very mild and not at all tyrannical, but it is the victor and therefore resented by the vanquished. The latter cannot forget their defeat, even if the former may no longer remember their victory.

Seeds of discontent, malaise, and hostility toward England exist in Canada. The people in the narrow sense of the word cannot explain why they feel as they do, but the educated class, which is still quite small, has been at pains to lead them and supply their passions with reasoned arguments.

It is impossible to imagine a population happier than the rural population of Canada. The purity of morals that prevails in all the villages would be impossible to believe in a European city. In Canada moral crimes and misdemeanors do not exist. The only public official in the parishes is the priest. His moral authority is enough. There is uniformity of religion: everyone is Catholic. Traces of feudalism remain: the land is divided into *seigneuries,* or estates, and each tenant is required to pay dues to the lord. The dues are minimal: for example, 5 or 6 francs for 90 acres. The lord has a special pew in the church. Apart from that, he is "lord" in name only and enjoys no privilege of any kind. The priest takes a tithe on the harvest, a share of 1/26th of the total. This system is quite favorable to the inhabitants, who have no taxes to pay. We visited a few of them. Their homes and their surroundings exhibit an air of comfort and well-being that attests to a contented state. Yet their happiness may not last for long. Every year a new crop of adventurers arrives from England, Ireland, and Scotland in search of cheap land. The English government, which has an interest in increasing the English population of Canada, does its best to direct them toward French areas, so that soon the poor Canadians, if they are not careful, may find themselves surrounded by a *foreign majority,* which will quickly absorb them. The danger is increased by the fact that the wealthy class in Canada is entirely English. The English control large-scale commerce and industry. They fill the two big cities, Quebec and Montreal. They do everything they can to crush the Canadian population, whose poverty they despise and whose happiness they do not understand.

The immigration from Great Britain will continue unless European peace is threatened. Canadians are already alarmed by this. Efforts are already being made to bring enlightenment to them through education so that they can bet-

140. In 1831, the Canadian population included fewer than 600,000 people, around 450,000 of whom were of French descent.

141. In 1763, the Treaty of Paris ended the Seven Years' War and transferred all French North American colonies to Great Britain.

ter understand their political interests. The entire clergy opposes the government. It is strange to see good country priests rather like the curé of Marçon or Beaumont-la-Chartre preaching liberalism and speaking like demagogues.[142] It is likely that it will all end in a violent uprising, but it is difficult to predict which of the two populations (English or Canadian) would prevail.

On August 24 we left Montreal aboard the *John Molson,* a very beautiful steamboat, which took us to Quebec in less than twenty-four hours (a distance of about 60 leagues).[143]

It is impossible to imagine a river more beautiful than the Saint Lawrence. In fact, it is the biggest river I know: 10 leagues from Quebec, it broadens out to a width of 7 leagues and remains that wide for the next 50 leagues, after which it broadens out still more until it merges completely with the sea. Quebec is very picturesquely situated. It is built on Cap Diamant. The French, who founded the city, fortified it. The English government is having additional work done on the citadel, which looked quite strong to us. Quebec is the capital of Canada and the seat of the English administration.[144] A large garrison is stationed there. England pays the cost. Maintaining Canada costs it more than 6 million a year, but it holds on to the colony because it is of great political utility, especially for the timber that it supplies for the construction of British ships.

The parts of Canada that I saw seemed to me to have a distinctive character. Fertile regions where farming is most productive are usually not very pretty to look at, whereas the most picturesque regions are generally the least profitable by way of compensation. The banks of the Saint Lawrence are both unusually fertile and as impressive and splendid to look at as any place you can imagine. Wherever you look, you find plains covered with wheat through which the broad river wends its way between tall mountains on either side.

We made a point of contacting all the most distinguished men in Quebec. They welcomed us with open arms. All were delighted to see Frenchmen from old France. One of them, Mr. Neilson, seemed especially interested.[145] He took us to many places and was kind enough to show us everything that was interesting to see. With him and my friend Tocqueville I visited a substantial parish that goes by the name Beaumont. It is located three leagues from Quebec and is the center of an estate that was established in the age of Louis XIV by a Monsieur de Beaumont, who came from France, although no one knows from which

142. Marçon was the village next to Beaumont-la-Chartre.

143. The boat was named for the man who introduced steam navigation to the Saint Lawrence River in 1809.

144. Quebec City is about 150 miles north of Montreal on the Saint Lawrence River. It was founded in 1608 by French explorer Samuel de Champlain and was ceded to the British in 1763.

145. John Neilson (1776–1848) printed *La Gazette de Québec* from 1797 to 1848. He served in the legislative assembly from 1818 to 1834. Although he supported the nationalist cause, he withdrew his support for the Patriote party of Papineau in 1830 in favor of a more moderate stance.

Montmorency Falls, two leagues from Quebec, 240 feet high. "Although it is quite beautiful, it cannot be compared to Niagara," Beaumont told his father on September 5, 1831. (GB2)

province. The story of this Beaumont would have interested me a great deal had I not remembered that in those days the Beaumont family to which I am privileged to belong was still called Bonnin or at most Bonninière. Nevertheless, I was still treated as the lord of this place.

Another no less interesting errand took us to the place where the Montmorency River falls a distance of 240 feet into the Saint Lawrence. Although it is quite beautiful, it cannot be compared to Niagara. It is the difference between a river and a stream: Montmorency Falls is pretty, whereas Niagara Falls is splendid and magnificent. I also saw many other things in Quebec, such as a convent with many distinguished women, all of whom have relatives in France. I saw a judge, Monsieur Taschereau, whose family is from Touraine.[146] From what he told me, I gather that he is related to our Taschereau de La Chartre. He is the only Canadian in Quebec whom the English government has entrusted with an official post—a lucrative one for him, since his salary is 25,000 francs. I dined with him at the home of one of his relatives. The latter I found to be a model of French gaiety and of our old ancestral customs. Since I have been in America, I

146. The Taschereau family, which had French origins in the Loire Valley of France, was prominent in Quebec. Beaumont spoke to Jean-Thomas Taschereau (1778–1832), who was a journalist and lawyer before he became a judge in 1827.

View of the St. Lawrence from Quebec. (GB2)

have seen laughter only in Canada. At dessert, everyone had to sing a song. One is sure to find good cheer and cordiality whenever one is with Canadians.

Religion is a very powerful influence on society. The Catholic clergy is universally respected. There is not one philosopher who is not also a religious man or at any rate who dares to appear otherwise. I went for a walk one day with one of Quebec's *democrats.* Whenever we passed a church, he made the sign of the cross.

Speaking of churches, the rural ones are remarkably pretty. They are built with extraordinary taste. I saw quite a few, and I did not encounter one that would not have fit quite well in a big city.

We left Quebec on August 31. We headed back up the Saint Lawrence as far as Montreal in the steamboat *Richelieu.* We arrived in Montreal on September 2 and left immediately for Albany. A steamboat (the *Voyageur*) took us to La Prairie. There we took a carriage to Saint John, where we embarked on another steamboat (the *Phoenix*) to cross Lake Champlain. On September 4 we arrived in Whitehall, and there we took a carriage, which brought us today to Albany. The only noteworthy site in the course of this journey was the region around Lake Champlain. The mountains of Vermont, which loom in the distance, are quite high.

Today in Albany I saw several people. We are still received with the same kindness as always. We leave tonight for Boston, where we will get back to work on the penitentiary system, which we have neglected somewhat for the past month. We will stay there two or three weeks, after which we will return to Philadelphia.

Adieu . . .

From Tocqueville | To Abbé Lesueur

Albany, September 7, 1831

. . . We've just completed a long journey through the West and North of America. The past two weeks have been devoted to visiting Canada. The last time I wrote you, I didn't think I'd be making this trip. The lack of political news had become so unbearable that we planned to head straight for Albany. Fortunately we had news from France en route, and we felt we could afford an extra week to travel along the Saint Lawrence. We are very glad now that we took this trip. The part of the country that we've just explored is quite picturesque. The Saint Lawrence is the widest river in the world. At Quebec it is already quite wide. A little further downstream, it is seven leagues from one bank to the other and remains that wide for fifty more leagues. Then it widens out to fifteen, twenty, and even thirty leagues before finally mingling its waters with those of the Atlantic Ocean. You might compare it to an inland English Channel. This immense volume of water is hardly surprising when you remember that the Saint Lawrence is the sole outflow for all the Great Lakes from Lake Superior to Lake Ontario. They're all connected like grapes in a bunch and ultimately end up in the Saint Lawrence Valley in Canada.

Monument to Montcalm and Wolfe, Quebec, 25 August 31. (GB2)

But what interested us most about Canada was the inhabitants. I am astonished that so little is known about this country in France. Not six months ago, I believed along with everyone else that Canada had become completely English. I had never gone beyond the 1763 report, which put the French population at only sixty thousand.[147] Since then, however, growth has been as rapid as in the United States, and today, in the province of Lower Canada alone, there are 600 thousand people of French descent. I vouch for the fact that their origin cannot be challenged. They are as French as you and I. Indeed, they are more like us than the Americans of the United States are like the English. I cannot tell you what a pleasure it was for us to find ourselves amongst this population. We felt that we were at home, and everywhere people welcomed us as compatriots, children of old France, as they call it. In my opinion, however, the epithet is ill chosen: the old France is in Canada; the new France is where we live. In Canada, and especially in small villages far from the big cities, we found the old habits and mores of France. Around a church topped by a cock and a cross with *fleurs-de-lys,* the houses of the village cluster close together, because Canadian landowners do not like to live in isolation on their farms as the English and the Americans of the United States do. These houses are well built, solid outside, clean and well tended inside. The peasant is wealthy and pays not a cent of tax. Four times a day, the family, consisting of vigorous parents and plump, joyful children, gathers around a round table. After supper they sing old French songs or tell the story of some great feat by one of the early French settlers in Canada, perhaps involving a mighty blow of the sword in the days of Montcalm and the wars with the English. On Sundays they play and sing after services. The priest himself shares in the communal gaiety so long as it does not degenerate into licentiousness. He is the oracle, the friend, and the advisor of the population. Rather than accuse him of being a lackey of government, the English attack him as a demagogue. Indeed, he is the first to resist oppression, and the people look upon him as their regular mainstay. Hence Canadians are religious on principle and by dint of political passion. The clergy constitute the upper class, not because laws place them at the head of society but because public opinion and mores do. I have seen any number of these ecclesiastics, and I am convinced that they are in fact the most distinguished men in the country. They are very much like the old French priests. They are generally happy, amiable, and well-bred.

Along with religious ideas, mores have been kept up. Public opinion has incredible power in these villages. The people would never turn a thief over to the authorities, but the minute suspicions are raised against a man, he is forced to leave town. Nothing is rarer than a girl who has been seduced. In one respect they are like our peasants, however: they dearly love equality and independence and cordially detest anything reminiscent of feudal lords and dues.

Isn't it tempting to think that the national character of a people depends more on the blood in its veins than on the political institutions or nature of the

147. In 1831, Canada was home to approximately 450,000 francophone inhabitants.

country? Here you have Frenchmen who have mingled with the English population for eighty years, who have been subject to the laws of England and more separate from the mother country than if they lived at the antipodes. And yet they are still French trait for trait, not only the old people, but all of them, right down to the youngster spinning his top. Like us, they are active, alert, intelligent, sarcastic, hot tempered, big talkers, and quite difficult to manage when their passions are inflamed. They make fine warriors and are fonder of action than of money. They live alongside Englishmen who were also born in Canada, just as they were, but who are as phlegmatic and argumentative as if they lived on the banks of the Thames. They are enamored of precedents and want you to prove the major premise before even thinking of passing on to the minor. They are respectable citizens who believe that war is the greatest scourge of the human race and yet who make war as well as any other people, because they have calculated that there are any number of things more difficult to bear than death [*illegible passage scratched out*]. . . . positive and reflective, who imagine nothing beyond physical well-being and who, when it comes to the rest, are tempted to say, like the mathematician, "What does that prove?" . . .

From Tocqueville | To his sister-in-law Émilie

Albany, September 7, 1831

. . . I have just completed a vast inland journey. One step at a time, following up opportunities whenever we found them, we came at last to Lake Superior, which is almost 400 leagues from New York. We saw millions of acres of woods to which no one has ever taken an axe and countless Indian tribes. À propos, do you know anything about Atala and her ilk? I shall have to describe her for you, so that you can judge how closely she resembles the Atala of M. de Ch[ateaubriand]. Atala is an Indian woman the color of dark *café au lait,* whose stiff, shiny hair hangs like drumsticks all the way down her back. She usually has a big fat hooked nose, a broad mouth armed with sparkling teeth, and two black eyes that look in broad daylight the way a cat's eyes look at night. Make no mistake: for all her natural beauty, she does not neglect to make herself up. Not at all. To begin with, she draws a black ring around her eyes, then a nice red stripe underneath, then a blue one, and then a green one, until her face looks like a rainbow. From her ears she hangs what looks like a set of Chinese gongs that must weigh half a pound. The most fashionable of these ladies also wear a large tin ring in their nostrils, a ring that hangs down over the mouth to produce a most pleasing effect. They also wear necklaces made of large disks on which images of wild animals are engraved. Their clothing consists of a sort of canvas tunic, which comes down to just below the knees, and they usually wrap themselves in a blanket, which at night they lie down on. The portrait is not yet complete: the fashion in the forests is to go pigeon-toed. I don't know if this is more unnatural than having the toes turned outward, but our European eyes have a hard time adjusting to this type of beauty. Can you believe that in order to achieve it, the feet of young Indian girls are bound? By the time they're twenty, the toes of their two feet touch when they walk. This garners a great deal of praise and is reputed to be quite fashionable. All that I know is that I would not want to play the role of Chactas[148] with one of these women for all the gold in the world. In any case, the Indian men are better than their women. They're strong and tall, built like deer, with all that animal's agility. When they smile, their faces take on a certain charm, but when they're angry, they look like the devil incarnate. We have seen fewer of them than we would have liked, but the forests are emptying out at an unbelievable rate.

We returned by way of Canada. If you ever go to America, dear sister, that is where you must live. You will find your beloved Lower Normans, trait for trait. Monsieur Gisles, Madame Noël—I saw all those people in the streets of Quebec.[149] The handsome men in those parts resemble your cousins *de la* . . .—I've forgotten their name, but they're spitting images, and the peasants assured us that they never felt any need to go to town because *creatures* took it upon themselves to knit and make clothes for them. . . .

FROM BOSTON, NEW YORK, PHILADELPHIA, AND BALTIMORE

From Beaumont | To his brother Jules

Boston, September 16, 1831

. . . We left Albany for Boston on September 6. In a few hours we traveled approximately 10 leagues and reached Stockbridge, where we went to visit Miss Sedgwick, renowned as the author of several American novels.[150] She had invited us to come see her in the country, but owing to an unfortunate mix-up we did not find her at home. She had left the morning of our arrival and was not expected to return until the following day. Her brothers and sisters gave us a warm welcome, but this reception did not satisfy our objective, which was to see a person whose work had made her famous. We could of course have seen

148. Atala's lover in Chateaubriand's novel.

149. Lower Normandy is a part of western France on the English Channel. Madame Noël, most likely a resident of Cherbourg, and Madame Gisles, the wife of the mayor of Valognes, north of Cherbourg, were both friends of the Tocqueville family who lived in Lower Normandy.

150. Stockbridge is located in the Berkshire Mountains in western Massachusetts. Catharine Maria Sedgwick (1789–1867) was the author of popular fiction throughout the second quarter of the nineteenth century. Her early novels included *A New England Tale* (1822), *Redwood* (1824), and *The Traveler* (1825). In his travel notes, Tocqueville described his conversation with her brother Theodore Sedgwick Jr. (1780–1839), who had served in the Massachusetts legislature and was a proponent of the abolition of slavery. Tocqueville would later work with Sedgwick's son, Theodore Sedgwick III (1811–1859), a lawyer who helped to prepare *Democracy in America* for publication while serving as an assistant to the American minister Edward Livingston in Paris in the 1830s. This younger Sedgwick and Tocqueville renewed their acquaintance in Europe in the early 1850s and corresponded regularly about American politics and the economy.

her by staying a day longer in Stockbridge, but we were very impatient to get to Boston, where we knew that letters awaited us. We therefore continued on our way, and in a day and a half we had crossed Massachusetts and reached Boston.

The country we traveled through was remarkably picturesque. The many mountains make for scenic vistas that stand in striking contrast to the western part of New York State through which we traveled from Albany to Buffalo. As you know, that part of the country is flat, and you seldom see a hill or valley. We were struck by the appearance of wealth and prosperity that prevails in Massachusetts. All signs point to a happy population. There is no more of the untamed nature that one finds everywhere in the western states. The virgin forest vanished long ago, and no trace of it remains. Massachusetts, which as you know once bore the name New England, is obviously an old region: by "old" I mean a country that has been in existence for two hundred years. Two centuries amount to veritable antiquity in this country, where most cities are scarcely ten or twenty years old. In Massachusetts you don't find tree stumps in the fields or log cabin dwellings. Fields are meticulously fenced. Various crops are grown, and all signs indicate that the farmers exploit the land to maximum advantage, because the region is already crowded. The increase in the population of Massachusetts is no cause for alarm in American society, however. Every year, a substantial number of people leave the region for western New York in search of cheap land and new settlements. They have to travel no more than 50 leagues to find as many acres as they want at 10 shillings apiece (roughly 6 to 7 francs). Hence there is no reason to fear a superabundant population. There is no real misery, and the people, who are, if not happy, at least free to become so, feel no disposition whatsoever to be discontent with their government. No one cares about how the country is administered because everyone is preoccupied with his own affairs. Thus the whole art of government here is not to make the government's influence felt, and the less the government does, the happier people are. This is a society that runs on its own. The only thing that could prevent it from running smoothly would be to meddle in its affairs. Nearly all Americans of any distinction with whom I have talked about this situation understand perfectly well how exceptional their country is, and they feel pity for European theorists who would like to apply American institutions to nations whose position bears no resemblance to that of the United States.

My father, who wrote recently and whose letter I received at the same time as yours, says some very accurate things about the exceptional situation of the United States. He seems to have seen what is happening here with his own eyes, and I entirely share his view that the progress and prosperity of American society prove nothing and offer nothing for the old nations of Europe to imitate. I am nevertheless pleased to be acquiring an intimate knowledge of this republic, which is so much talked about and so often used as a basis for arguments in favor of democratic innovations. There are many people who sincerely regard the United States as a powerful argument in favor of republican government. I am pleased to be in a position to respond to them. The study of contemporary peoples is no different from the study of history: it should be undertaken not so much to find examples to follow as to learn to be wary of suggestions to imitate them.

I do not know why the American people, who seem so happy, are so often fragile and delicate when it comes to health. The women especially are extremely thin and all seem to suffer from maladies of the lungs. I do not know if this is a result of the climate, which is variable and constantly veering from one extreme to the other, or if it should be attributed to the way women live. It is utterly unthinkable here for a woman to work the land or take part in farm chores in any way. All women's work is therefore indoors and limited to household chores. Perhaps this indoor existence is unhealthy. Since coming to America (and except for Canada), I have not seen a single woman who can bear comparison in any way with our peasant women.

Boston is a city of 60,000.[151] Its harbor is magnificent. It is in the middle of an island and accessible from all directions via roadways that cross the water. There is much less commercial bustle than in New York, but the general appearance of the city is far more pleasant than that of New York. The latter city sits on flat ground, and the eye inevitably sees only a single row of houses from any angle. By contrast, Boston is built on uneven, hilly terrain, so that when you look at the city from a certain distance, certain features please the eye. The city contains many private homes designed with taste and elegance. As for public buildings, only the statehouse strikes me as worthy of note.[152]

We are staying in the city's best inn (Hemont [Tremont] Hotel).[153] Everything here is impressive. There are approximately 150 foreigners in residence at the present time. The service is magnificent, and it is scarcely more expensive than other places. From the moment we arrived, we have been trying to make contact with the best people in the city. On the first day our efforts proved unavailing: we were unable to contact anyone. We found ourselves in an embarrassing position, because we had no letters of recommendation for Boston. When Tocqueville and I conversed after these unfruitful attempts, we gave in to some rather morose reflections: "Have we been received so warmly until now," we wondered, "only because of the pieces of paper we bore? Judged by our own merits, are we not worthy of the slightest consideration? So much for our self-esteem. Here we had begun to think of ourselves as distinguished men, but

151. Boston, which had a population slightly larger than sixty thousand residents, was located on a peninsula connected to the mainland by a small neck of land. City engineers continued to widen this neck with fill land throughout the nineteenth century. In 1831, four main bridges linked the peninsular city to the mainland suburbs that surrounded it.

152. Charles Bulfinch (1763–1844) built the statehouse in 1798. Its dome was one of the most recognizable features when viewing the city, as Beaumont describes. One of the first American architects by profession, Bulfinch redefined Boston's cityscape in the early nineteenth century with his neoclassical, "federal" style.

153. Opened in 1829, the Tremont was a celebrated luxury hotel with ornate architecture and valets, yet its lodging prices remained quite moderate.

when we have nothing but our personal qualities to recommend us, no one will even look at us." And other complaints of similar ilk.

Our fears were exaggerated, and our imaginations too dark. Because we arrived without recommendations, people were not as quick to receive us. But when they found out who we were and what our social position was, they treated us very well. As for our merits, there is no doubt that ultimately they were recognized.

It was our impression that people here are less quick to throw themselves at foreigners than in New York, but there is more true politeness. Society does not consist solely of businessmen. People here take an interest in art and literature. There is a class of people who do not engage in commerce or industry and who spend all their time enjoying the fruits of an advanced civilization. This class, which consists of those who inherited enough from their parents to live without participating in business, is not very large, but it is quite agreeable.[154] It is by nature somewhat variable, because the equal division of inheritances means that no family can maintain its fortune for long, but new fortunes are created every day. In any case, the law of inheritance is a long way from being as democratic as ours. In France equal inheritance is obligatory for all; here, when a father dies intestate, the law divides his estate equally. But he has the right to leave all his real and movable property to any one of his children, and if he so chooses, his will is respected. This right, which makes paternal authority much more effective than it is in France, exerts a very great moral influence throughout the society, while at the same time preventing extreme division of properties.

We dined the other day at the home of Mr. Sears.[155] He has a fortune of five or six million. His home is a kind of palace. The level of luxury is very high indeed. He treated us splendidly. Nowhere have I seen *a more sumptuous dinner.* Among the ornaments of the table was a very pretty young woman who I believe is his niece. I talked with her quite a bit, but I don't know if I will ever see her again, so that it was a pure waste of sentiment. It is absolutely the same with all the beauties I meet. We see quite a few in society. Our passions are aroused three or four times a week, and each occasion effaces the last. But there are always new faces, and I believe, God forgive me, that we say the same things to all of them, at the risk of complimenting a brunette on the whiteness of her complexion and a blonde on the rich ebony of her hair. But all that is a mere bagatelle, which occupies a very small place indeed in the lives of two political men fully engaged in the loftiest speculations.

We have already been to two balls and will attend another this evening.

154. This combination of wealth and intellectualism distinguished a segment of the city's elite known as the Boston Brahmins.

155. David Sears (1787–1871), one of Boston's wealthiest citizens, had built an enormous house on fashionable Beacon Hill in 1819, designed by the architect Alexander Parris. Sears doubled the size of the house in 1832. The granite structure is located at 42 and 43 Beacon Street, across from the Boston Common and Public Gardens, and is now home to the Somerset Club.

The ladies' toilette is exactly the same as in France. French fashion rules in the United States, and they are perfectly up-to-date concerning the latest fashion revolutions. Many ladies have questioned me about this. I answered as confidently as if they had consulted me about the penitentiary system and discussed hair ribbons with them as knowledgeably as Michalon or Alcibiades.[156] Music is cultivated here somewhat more successfully than in New York, but the masses have no innate feeling for it. There is a museum in which paintings are shown, but since I have not yet seen it, I beg your permission to say nothing more about them.

On the 12th of this month (September) I attended a rather curious ceremony. The Bostonians celebrated the consecration of two flags that they are sending to Poland. Both the militia and regular troops assembled for the occasion. The authorities, learned societies, and others gathered and marched in procession to a place called Faneuil House, where political bodies often meet to deliberate.[157] We were of course included in the procession as distinguished foreigners. Upon entering the hall we were greeted with an immense gallery entirely filled with well-dressed ladies but not a single man. This separation of men and women is a feature of nearly all public gatherings in the United States. The ceremony began with a prayer for the Poles led by a Congregationalist preacher. The holy man launched a scathing tirade against despotism and oppression and lavished pompous praise on insurrection and liberty. Then the two flags were displayed to the public. They bore any number of inscriptions, including the last words of Poniatowski: "Better to die with glory than surrender."[158] The audience frequently broke out in applause, especially when La Fayette's name was uttered. The flags are to be sent to him, and he will then ensure that they reach their ultimate destination. The ceremony ended with the recital of odes, singing of hymns, etc.

Many of those in attendance found this pretentious patriotic display ridiculous. What good will these flags from Boston do for the Poles? This display of enthusiasm for the cause of the brave Poles might have some real substance if they sent money along with their fine words, but they raised barely enough to cover the costs of the ceremony. I saw quite a few intelligent people who seriously regretted this foolishness. But it was organized by young people, who set

156. These were famous Parisian hairdressers.

157. Faneuil Hall, a large brick market and meetinghouse, was built in 1742 with funds given by Boston merchant Peter Faneuil. It was called the Cradle of Liberty and became a Boston landmark after the American Revolution, when Boston patriots frequently met there. Bostonians continued to use it as a civic meeting place thereafter.

158. Stanislas Augustus Poniatowski (1732–1798) was the last king of the Polish Commonwealth. He was forced to abdicate in 1795. By then, Poland had been partitioned three times and had come under the control of Russia, Prussia, and Austria. The Polish people struggled to create an independent nation throughout the nineteenth century. The ceremony that Beaumont describes supported a militant Polish uprising against Russia that had begun in Warsaw the previous year.

the wheels in motion before anyone could stop them. Fortunately for the United States, such things can be done here with impunity. But I think that we carry on in France exactly as though we were in the United States.

The news that we receive seems so implausible that I hesitate to respond to it in any way. In any case, Europe seems to me a volcano ready to erupt. While European politics gives rise to revolutions, here it is physical nature that is experiencing severe convulsions. People talk of nothing but terrible hurricanes and horrible devastation. New Orleans and the Antilles are the places beset by these misfortunes.

I'm coming to the end of my paper. I don't want to end this letter without a word about the penitentiary system. That is why we are in America, but really you'd never guess. Yet we have done serious work for the past three days, and our research is not yet finished. We have identified the most knowledgeable people here: Messrs. Dwight, Clay, Gray, etc.[159] We visited two well-run prisons based on the new model, that is, the principle of solitary confinement.[160] People everywhere recognize the incontestable advantages of this system, which is now generally adopted in all the states of the Union. I haven't the slightest doubt about its superiority. The only question in France will be the cost of introducing it. Building institutions of this sort is easy for a country that has nothing else to do but deal with matters of internal administration and no great expenditures weighing on its budget. But we are in quite the opposite situation. I believe that in France we should aim rather at a series of modest improvements. And when we build a prison, it will not cost more to build it one way or another.

In any case, we will return home with a rich trove of documents and observations. We will surely be the *leading penitentiary experts* in the world. If only we are fortunate enough to find some semblance of government to which we can report on our mission when we return!

I intended to write to Félicie today, but the thought that I had nothing very interesting to say to her stopped me.[161] As soon as I have something less insignificant than my life in Boston to talk about, I will seize the opportunity. I beg you to tell her so and ask her not to hold it against me that I haven't written sooner. . . .

159. Louis Dwight (1793–1854) was the secretary of the Prison Discipline Society in Boston and drafted the annual reports of the society. He was an avid opponent of the Philadelphia system of solitary confinement.

Mr. Clay was a Georgia planter whom Tocqueville had met in Boston.

Francis Calley Gray (1790–1856) was a Massachusetts senator who was in charge of inspecting prisons. He pursued many civic and literary interests, and he later wrote a treatise entitled "Prison Discipline in America."

160. The travelers visited the prison at Charlestown, Massachusetts, and a house of refuge for juvenile delinquents.

161. Félicie de Bonnet de Bellou Beaumont (1805–1870) was the wife of Achille de Beaumont. They had married in 1826 and had three children.

Beaumont | Diary fragments

[September 1831]

Tariff. In Boston there is a large party that naturally favors the tariff, consisting of manufacturers and their supporters. Large factories in Lowell.[162]

"Mr. Webster was against the tariff on principle, and several years ago he spoke in Congress against it. But he now holds the opposite opinion, since a large number of fortunes are invested in firms that would fail without the support of the tariff" (analogy with our iron manufacturers) (18 September 1831, Boston).[163]

Mr. Sears said: "Free trade can exist only if it is reciprocal. If you sell your products to America without taking what it produces, it is obvious that eventually America will have given you all its money and will have nothing left with which to buy anything."

Put another way, does this not mean that a nation must take in as much money as it pays out in order to do business? This is the system of balance of trade, which is acknowledged to be false (Boston, 19 December [September] 1831).

Mr. Sparks, former editor of the *North American Review,* author of a still-unpublished history of the United States, Boston, 29 September 1831.[164]

New England is the cradle of American democracy. It was there that the men who organized the principle of universal representation of the people met. Whenever an issue of any kind arose, the entire population assembled. This was the origin of the "town meetings." Citizens of Massachusetts took their ways with them to Connecticut, and, having experience with the practical workings of their principles of liberty, they founded a pure democracy in Connecticut,

162. Throughout the early nineteenth century, Americans fervently debated protective tariffs, which placed heavy taxes on imported foreign goods. Daniel Webster had argued against tariffs in 1816 and 1824, but he supported the 1828 tariff increase because of the growing prominence of factories in New England. Southerners, because of their agricultural economic basis, deplored the tariffs as unfair American favoritism toward New England. The debate over tariffs came to a head in a South Carolina convention in 1832, during which representatives declared the protective tariffs of 1828 and 1832 null and void. After a tense conflict over the rights of states to nullify federal laws, South Carolina repealed these measures in exchange for a lower tariff.

163. Daniel Webster (1782–1852), a famous orator and politician who began his political career in New Hampshire, was a great spokesperson for New England interests and was an avid opponent of Andrew Jackson. Webster became a lawyer in Boston and was elected to Congress first as a Massachusetts representative in 1822 and then as a senator in 1827. He became a leader of the Whig Party upon its formation in the 1830s.

164. After a short career as a Unitarian minister in Baltimore, Jared Sparks (1789–1866) returned to the Boston area in 1823 to begin a literary career. He edited the *North American Review* from 1823 to 1826, and in 1827, he began long-term efforts to collect and publish historic manuscripts, including the papers of George Washington, Benjamin Franklin, and the American Revolution. He became a professor at Harvard University in 1838 and later served as the institution's president.

which was better organized and more rational than anywhere else. Massachusetts as point of departure recurs constantly, and town meetings are nothing but the application of the democratic principle. There is no drawback in this for us. There are no *political parties* as such. There is scarcely anything but local interests and questions of personality. The great division at present is between the friends of General Jackson and those of Mr. Clay.[165] This is a question of *general policy* and does not agitate *the state in particular*. *Everyone* without exception can attend town meetings. The principle is that the *majority* is always right. It is a pure majoritarian system. Sometimes this is only a fiction, and we see this even in our legislative assemblies. On the whole, however, we are comfortable with this. I do not believe, however, that similar principles would suit the nations of Europe. I believe quite the opposite.

Freedom of the press, which is unlimited here, has a purely local influence. There are almost a thousand newspapers in the states. The newspaper of a big city has very little influence on the other cities of the state. Each city has its newspaper and prefers it to the others. This newspaper is dedicated to defending local interests. There is nothing here like your Paris newspapers with their influence. Freedom of the press here is not without abuses. Newspapers are sometimes guilty of slander. If individuals are slandered, they complain, and the journalists are prosecuted, but if public officials are slandered, they never complain. They have the right to do so, but they do not exercise it.

In this climate of extensive freedom and unlimited democracy, there is scarcely any evidence of *power* or of the *government* of society. The leading state official is the governor. He appoints a large number of other officials. He is in constant contact with the legislature and senate. He has the right to pardon and the right to veto laws passed by the legislature. His veto suspends execution of the law, and he can extend it as long as he wants. The governor serves for only one year, as do the members of the senate and legislature. There are benefits from making these functions temporary and of short duration. They are less important in consequence, less desired, and less likely to arouse passionate ambitions and therefore intrigues. Governors are frequently reelected. The present one, Mr. Lincoln, has been governor for seven years.[166] If all the members of the legislature and senate were replaced, there would be a problem with inexperienced legislators ignorant of the traditions of the past. But even though

165. Andrew Jackson (1767–1845), who served as president from 1829 to 1837, led the Democratic Party in an agenda that valued westward expansion, minimal federal regulation in favor of local law, the expansion of suffrage, and Indian removal.

Henry Clay (1777–1852), the famous congressman from Kentucky, was the chief opponent of Jackson in the presidential election of 1832. He was a leader of the emergent Whig Party, which sought to promote economic development rather than territorial expansion, a strong federal government, and a number of social reforms, such as increased public education, improved penitentiaries, and new Sabbath laws.

166. Levi Lincoln (1782–1868), descendant of an old Massachusetts family, was governor from 1825 to 1834.

all terms expire every year, it is understood that three-quarters of the legislators will be reelected. As you can imagine, there are many base intrigues associated with these elections, as is the case everywhere.

The governor and two chambers constitute the legislative power and promulgate laws applicable to the entire state. Otherwise, the action of the central government is difficult to make out and remains to be defined. There is no book that spells out the general principles that govern this action and shows how separate localities are joined together by a common bond without sacrificing any part of their independence.

For all local interests, the smallest group of citizens is sovereign and settles its own issues without the slightest interference from the central government.

Public opinion recognizes a certain priority of *senators* over ordinary members of the legislature, but the difference is almost imperceptible.

A moment ago I was speaking of the democratic spirit of New England. In fact, this is the point of departure for all republican institutions in the United States. New York borrowed our principles. Originally, New York was not the city it is today, and New York State was not the state it is. It was a royal colony. They imported New England's mores. Later, the state of New York copied our institutions, or, rather, our institutions made their way into New York. Traces of this still remain: for example, several estates belong to one or more families with vast holdings in real estate (such as the Van Rauslaer [Rensselaer] and Livingston fortunes).[167]

New York has recently done an excellent thing: its revised statutes are a code, and the state now enjoys the benefit of finding documents pertaining to a particular subject grouped together, whereas in Massachusetts they are scattered throughout a multitude of laws (29 September 1831).

From Tocqueville and Beaumont | To Jared Sparks

(Questions left with me by MM. Beaumont & de Tocqueville—Oct. 1st. 1831)[168]

MM. de Tocqueville and de Beaumont will be in Philadelphia until the end of November and in Washington until March 20. Answers to these questions can therefore be sent to the consul or the ambassador of France.

Are there any general principles that might regulate the relation between towns and their citizens, between one town and another, and between towns and the state?

167. The progenitors of each of these families had obtained large land grants when New York was a Dutch colony. They and their descendants became patroons, or landlords who collected rents from many tenants on their large plots of land in the Hudson River valley and upstate New York.

168. In this questionnaire, the travelers sought to probe Sparks about the community life and local characteristics of New England. Sparks responded in an essay entitled "Observations on the Town Governments of Massachusetts" that Herbert Baxter Adams published in 1898.

Is there any work in which these principles can be found, together with the reasoning behind them and the way in which they are applied?

Entering into detail with respect to these general ideas, I would in fact like to know the answer to the following questions:

Is there a permanent executive power in every town comparable to the mayors of large cities? If so, who chooses the executive? What are the nature and extent of his functions?

When a town wishes to embark on some enterprise, is it completely free to do as it pleases, or does it need to seek authorization from some higher authority? For instance, if a town wishes to sell or buy, can it do so without authorization? If a town wants to plead a case or enter into a bargain, can it do so without authorization? Are towns free to borrow money?

In all the above cases, how is the public will of the town expressed, and who represents it? What elements compose the town's representative body?

Can towns exercise police powers? Who wields these powers? Who judges infractions of police ordinances?

When a town incurs an expense, how are taxes apportioned to pay for it?

Who is responsible for spending the money raised?

When a town is sentenced to pay a fine or damages, how is the judgment enforced?

Can several towns join together to work toward a common goal? Can towns confederate and enter into relations with one another?

Can they deliberate on political issues? File collective petitions?

To what degree is the legislature permitted to intervene in the internal administration of towns? What precisely is the "charter of incorporation" that is granted to a city?

Purely political questions, in the answers to which I am particularly interested:

Have you ever noticed that towns left to administer themselves internally have made errors or blunders as a result of their lack of [*illegible word*] brought ill-conceived lawsuits, mismanaged their revenues, or contracted burdensome debts?

If this has not occurred, do you see a general cause at work or causes that pertain solely to you?

Have you ever felt the need or utility of a central administration—what we call centralization—in town affairs? Have you seen any indication that the independence of the *parts* has harmed the nation as a whole, impeded uniformity within the state, or stood in the way of national projects? In other words, what are the negative aspects of your system, since even the best systems have them?

Have any towns attempted to impede the work of the central administration?

Do your poor classes secretly envy the rich, so that the latter often find themselves humiliated or oppressed by the former (who are always in the majority) and passed over for public office? If this attitude exists, what do the wealthy classes do?

Have schemers often wielded great influence over towns? Broadly speaking, by what means do they obtain such influence? To what class of society do they belong? What is done to remedy this ill?

Do you find that the people generally make good choices? Do you think that their choices would be better if the suffrage were not so broad?[169]

Road System

What sort of road system does Massachusetts have? Are certain roads, bridges, and canals built by the state?

If roads are built by the towns, are they good? How are they maintained? Are there coercive means that can be used against the towns? Does the state inspect the roads?

Can the state lay out the overall route of a road or canal and force one or more towns to contribute to its construction?[170]

Public Schools

What is the general system of public schooling in Massachusetts?

What subjects are taught to children in the primary schools?

Are there schools intermediate between the primary schools and advanced university instruction.

From what class are schoolmasters generally chosen? Are they ecclesiastics?

What is the place of religion in the schools? Are children in the primary schools given some ideas about the history and laws of their country?

Do many people receive instruction above the primary level?

Do you think that the effects of education are uniformly good? Have you not found that a person educated above his social station becomes a restless and troublesome citizen?[171]

Are schools subject to any inspection or oversight? How is oversight exercised, and what does it cover?

I believe that the district and county stand above the town. I am very eager to know:

What constitutes a district? Is it represented by an assembly? How is this assembly chosen? What issues does it deal with? What is the extent of the assembly's power? Is this power precisely defined by certain laws? Do the district assemblies ever attempt to control the legislature and set themselves up as a political power?

169. All of these questions pointed to Tocqueville's interest in the lack of centralization in America. Sparks responded that this situation worked well: Americans decided elections according to the merit of candidates and issues because everyone had a vested interest in his own town.

170. Tocqueville was interested in the American economy, and he sought to understand how means of transportation constructed by public funds (including town, state, and national projects) and private funds compared to one another.

171. Many American leaders would have agreed with Sparks's response to questions about education. He professed that an elementary education was necessary for all Americans in order to make them good republican citizens.

I ask the same questions in regard to the counties.

Do you find that public offices in the towns, districts, and counties are coveted by citizens, satisfy their ambitions, create a political life that satisfies them, and appeal to their interests sufficiently that they are content to confine themselves to local politics?

Do you know approximately how large the districts and counties are and what their minimum and maximum populations are?

From Tocqueville | To his father

Hartford, October 7, 1831

We left Boston three days ago, my dear Papa, and we are now settled in Hartford. Although it is a very small town, it is the capital of the state of Connecticut and sits on the bank of the river of that name.[172] For us, its greatest virtue is that it is located one league from one of the famous prisons in America, the Wethersfield Prison. Since the weather is superb, we go back and forth to the prison every day on foot, which is quite healthy as well as quite economical.

The financial accounts of the Wethersfield institution are the strongest argument that can be made in favor of American prison discipline. Before the reform, it cost the state thirty thousand francs a year. Today it brings in forty thousand. These are not theories but hard numbers, supported by written records. Yet in spite of all this, you will very likely find us less *peremptory* on the penitentiary system than when we left France. As you know, the general rule is that people are never so certain or assured as when they are speaking about subjects of which their knowledge is less than perfect. Now that we have begun to acquire a tolerable familiarity with our subject, we remain sure of only two things: first, that the American system is more economical than ours, and second, that the men who are subject to it never leave prison worse than when they went in. But are they really reformed? I am no more certain of this here than you are sitting by your fire. What is certain is that I would not trust any of these honest folks with my wallet.

You could do me a great favor, my dear Papa, and with the leisure that you enjoy now, I don't think it would cost you much. Here is what I want to say: one of the things that interests me most about the United States is the internal administration of each state as well as of the Union as a whole. I am trying to understand as clearly as I can what share of responsibility for government is assigned to the towns, to the provincial bodies, and finally to the central government, insofar as the administration of the country is concerned. A major obstacle impedes my progress in this regard. Individual facts lack all character and are of limited scope because I cannot make comparisons. In order to judge America, nothing would be more useful to me than to know France. It is the latter knowledge that is lacking. I know that in general our government is mixed up in almost everything. The word "centralization" has been dinned into my ears in-

172. In 1830, just over seven thousand people lived in Hartford, Connecticut.

cessantly, but the thing has never been explained. I have never had the time or opportunity to examine any of the various administrative mechanisms that operate throughout France. You have acquainted yourself with all of this, my dear Papa, through reflection and necessity. You have seen the administration act in ways both great and petty, and I think that you are familiar enough with the subject to be able without much trouble to provide me with the documents I need.

I would like to know what exists in France in the way of internal administration. First, what principles are generally accepted? Second, how are these principles applied, that is, what degree of independence are *communes* allowed, what can they do and not do? What are the powers of the *conseils d'arrondissement* and *conseils de département*?[173] Finally, precisely when do the prefect and central government become involved? If you could break down the word "centralization" for me, my dear Papa, you would be doing me an enormous favor, not just for now but for the future as well.

As you can see, all of this work is merely a matter of providing factual evidence. If you could include a few political observations in a second part, the whole would be that much more useful. For instance, I would like to know where in your opinion the action of the central government ought to stop, and what sort of independence ought the towns to be allowed. What is the use of administrative tribunals? How much power can departmental assemblies be allowed without courting danger? The trouble is that if you are willing to do this little job, my dear Papa, you'll need to send it soon, because time is passing quickly and our stay here is limited. . . .

From Tocqueville | To Ernest de Chabrol

Hartford, October 7, 1831

. . . Our stay in Boston was most useful. We met quite a number of distinguished men and found many invaluable documents. But as we repeatedly discover, not knowing is the greatest obstacle to learning.

On countless points, we do not know what questions to ask, because we do not know what exists at home, and without comparisons to make we are at a loss as to how to proceed. It is therefore absolutely essential for our friends in France to make up in part for what we lack if we hope to discover any useful ideas here.

What is most striking to anyone who travels in this country, whether or not he reflects on what he sees, is the spectacle of a society that proceeds on its own, without any guide or support, merely through the cooperation of individual wills. Try as you might to locate the government, you won't find it anywhere, and the truth is that, in a manner of speaking, it does not exist.

As you can imagine, in order to understand how such a state of affairs can come to pass, one has to dissect the social body with great care, examine each of

---

173. For administrative purposes, France is divided into departments, and each department is divided into arrondissements. Communes are similar to municipalities or cities.

its organs separately, and then determine to what sphere of action each must be confined if the whole is to constitute a nation. To conduct such a study fruitfully, you would need to have devoted a lot more thought than I have to the general principles of government. I have never had time to delve into such things.

I would at least like to know what *in fact* exists in France. As I just said, government here is such an insignificant thing that I cannot imagine why it is so important in France. The 1200 employees of the Ministry of the Interior strike me as something inexplicable. I know that you have paid no more attention to administrative matters than I have, so I will not ask you for general principles, but perhaps you could obtain some practical information that I would find invaluable.

I would like to know about the division of labor within the Ministry of the Interior, or, rather, the Ministries, because today there are two of them, and insofar as possible what all these people do. Perhaps there is something in print about all this. In that case, please send it to me, not by the post but posthaste. Maybe there is a regulation covering the various assignments. I would like to decipher the word "centralization," which is so vast and vague that it tires the mind without leading it anywhere.

I admit, my dear friend, that if someone were to make a similar demand of me, I would not know how to respond. Perhaps you, too, will find it impossible. Still, you know so many people, and you have lived so long with the powers of this earth, that I cling to the hope (*adjuvante amicitia*)[174] that you may succeed. Try to send me factual material; do not be afraid to go into detail. If you can obtain this information, you will be doing me a great service.

If I have the time, I will attach to this letter another for Blosseville.[175] I intend to send him some questions about administrative courts, an institution absolutely unknown in the United States. I hope he will reply.

The difficulty of our position here is that we are forced to become involved in too many things at the same time. If we have an idea and don't write it down at once, we're almost certain never to see it again.

If we see a special man and fail to ask him the most useful questions right away, it's a missed opportunity. We never have enough time to approach ideas in a roundabout way. We have to catch many things on the fly without pausing for details and move from one subject to another faster than I ever imagined. So I'm not entirely sure that I won't go crazy before returning to France. The brain is in constant ferment here.

Nevertheless, this style of life has its charms. There is nothing else that takes you so completely outside yourself, and as you know, the real purpose of this life is as much as possible to forget that you exist. To my mind, it's slander to

174. "With the help of friendship."
175. Ernest Poret, vicomte de Blosseville (1799–1886), was a distant cousin of Tocqueville. He was counselor and then secretary general of the Versailles prefecture from 1827 to 1832. In 1831, he published a history of the English penal system in Australia.

say that former ministers who dream of returning to office are dying of ambition. I think they are dying mainly of idleness. A minister becomes completely alienated from himself while he is minister. Afterward, he can no longer get used to living in his own company. He's like a confirmed bachelor for whom one tries to find a wife. . . .

From Tocqueville | To Eugénie de Grancey[176]

New York, October 10, 1831

I cannot tell you how touched I was by your letter and your mother's. Words of friendship do the most good when the heart aches. In any other circumstance, I would have been almost ashamed that you had written first, but I confess that my guilt was completely overwhelmed by my pleasure at the sight of your handwriting and my gratitude for all your kind words.

I thank you, my dear cousin, for the way in which you have shared our misfortune. You know our feelings well enough to appreciate the extent of our suffering. Many people believe that the loss we have experienced was routine, but you know that the man we mourn was almost a father to us.[177] He was as attentive as a father and cared for us as one. It was on his lap that we learned to distinguish between good and evil. It was he who began our early education, the lessons that stay with a child throughout his later life and that made us, if not distinguished men, then at least honest men. I confess that this loss has seriously affected my daily pleasure in my travels. The things around me remain the same, but they look different to me. I often feel that I would rather be back in Europe, yet I confess that the idea of returning leaves me with a certain bitterness.

You are no doubt already more or less familiar, my dear cousin, with the details of our trip. We have been warmly received in this country, so warmly that we had trouble at first believing that all this politeness was intended for us. We found ourselves at times in the position of the duchess (created by Bonaparte) who, upon hearing herself announced at the door of a salon, thought that it must be someone else and stepped aside to allow *herself* to pass.[178] The fact is that in France you would need nothing less than a magnifying glass to make us out, but people here see us through a telescope. The illusion persists, although we continue to be as polite as can be and have not yet been able to accustom ourselves to the bluntness and impertinent manners of *people of consequence.* To explain this, I must also tell you that we have benefited from a mistake to which all Americans are quite naturally prone. In the United States there are

176. Eugénie de Cordoue, comtesse de Grancey, was a first cousin to the mother of Alexis de Tocqueville.

177. Tocqueville is writing of the death of Abbé Christian Lesueur (1751–1831), his childhood tutor.

178. Tocqueville refers to Catherine Hubscher, the wife of French general François Joseph Lefebvre. Called Madame Sans-Gêne, she was an illiterate woman of low-class birth who shocked the court of Napoleon with her bad manners, poor language, and lack of refinement.

no wars, plagues, literature, eloquence, revolutions, or fine arts, and there are few great crimes, hence none of the things that attract attention in Europe exist here. Americans enjoy the most insipid happiness that can be imagined. Political life is spent in discussing whether a road needs to be repaired or a bridge built. Hence in the United States they look upon the construction of a fine prison as though it were the pyramid of Cheops, neither more nor less.[179] And therefore, we, who pass in a sense for the penitentiary system made flesh, look like giants when placed beside the pyramid. You have the clear sense that because the French government has charged us with the mission of visiting the prisons of the United States, we must be men of extreme importance, for what could possibly be greater than a prison? If we were to tell these poor folks that there are not a hundred people in France who have any precise idea of what the penitentiary system is, and that the French government is so innocent of grand ideas that it probably is unaware that it even has agents on a mission to America, they would no doubt be quite astonished. But as you know, veracity consists not in telling the whole truth but rather in refraining from uttering falsehoods. In any case, I confess that *glory* has its unfortunate aspects. Since the penitentiary system is our industry, we must exploit it every day, whether we like it or not. In vain do we try to shirk our obligation. Everyone nevertheless finds a way to slip into the conversation a helpful sentence or two about prisons. Wherever we go in the evening, either the mistress of the house or her daughter, beside whom one of us has been carefully seated, feels absolutely obliged to break the ice by discussing hangings or cell bolts. Not until they have exhausted a subject which they know pleases us and about which they presume we will have something to say do they even try to turn the conversation to more vulgar matters. You cannot imagine, my dear cousin, what a whirlwind of activity we have found ourselves involved in from the moment of our arrival. We have barely had time to take our bearings. Ideas, impressions, and faces have followed one another at an incredible rate. We have been swept up in a current that makes it impossible to figure out where we are. For a man as distracted as I am, the effort to observe on the run is often futile. Usually I remember what I wanted to ask a person a moment after bidding him farewell for good. Yet I confess that this febrile state is not without its charms. The monotony of Versailles was killing me. In any case, isn't the principal point of this life to forget as much as possible that one exists? Well, I defy you to imagine a life (other than that of a government minister) that draws a man more completely out of himself than the one we are leading. Speaking of ministers, I imagine that the oft-heard allegation that they die from ambition after leaving office is in many cases pure slander: for example, our cousin Molé, whom they say turned quite green with envy after losing the ministry of justice.[180] I am more charitable: I believe that what kills them after

179. The Great Pyramid of Cheops (or Khufu) is the largest in Egypt.
180. Louis Matthieu Molé (1781–1855), a cousin of Tocqueville, was one of the few among his relatives who supported Napoleon and later Louis-Philippe. Molé was minister of

having been strangers to themselves for so long is that they can no longer get used to living constantly in their own company.

Well, I seem to have wandered quite a long way from the subject of America. I believe I was discussing our arrival in New York. After six weeks in that city, we felt the need to talk about something other than prisons, and we decided to make our getaway and take a tour of the West. We wanted to see *wilderness* and *Indians*. But you have no idea how hard it is to find those two things in America today. We traveled more than 100 leagues in the state of New York on the trail of savage tribes and never found one. Repeatedly we were told that there were Indians here ten years ago, eight years ago, six years ago, two years ago. But European civilization is spreading like a forest fire and driving them farther inland. At last we arrived in Buffalo on the shore of one of the Great Lakes, and still we had not seen a single Indian. How could we return to France without an image in our heads of a savage or a virgin forest? It was out of the question. As luck would have it, a steamship was leaving Buffalo at precisely that moment to explore the entrance to Lake Superior and the shores of Lake Michigan. We decided to seize the opportunity, and in so doing we added a new leg of 500 leagues to our journey. This time, at least, we were completely satisfied. We passed miles of shoreline where no white man had yet felled a single tree, and we visited countless Indian nations. Someday I hope to tell you about many episodes of this long journey, but today I must restrain myself.

What unusual people these Indians are! They believe that when a man has a blanket to put over him, weapons to hunt game, and clear skies above, he has nothing more to ask of fate. For the refinements of our civilization he has nothing but contempt. It is absolutely impossible to get an Indian to submit to any of our customs. They are the proudest creatures under the sun. They smile with pity at the trouble we take to avoid fatigue and protect ourselves from the elements, and there isn't a single one of them who, when rolled up in his blanket at the foot of a tree, doesn't feel superior to the president of the United States or the governor of Canada. Of all my European paraphernalia, the only thing they coveted was my double-barreled rifle, a weapon that had the same effect on them as the penitentiary system on the Americans. I recall among others an elderly chief whom we met on the shore of Lake Superior, where he sat impassively beside his fire, as befits a man of his rank. I sat myself down alongside him, and we chatted quite amiably with the help of a French Canadian, who served as interpreter. He examined my rifle and noticed that it was not made like his. I told him that my rifle was unaffected by rain and could be fired when wet.

---

justice under Napoleon, served as a minister during the Bourbon Restoration, and was named a peer of France in 1840. He mentored Tocqueville during the July Monarchy, while most other family members remained steadfast legitimists, loyal only to the elder line of Bourbon rulers. In the late 1830s, Tocqueville styled a new group of political associates as the "young Left" to distance himself from Molé, who for his part unsuccessfully opposed Adolphe Thiers, Odilon Barrot, and François Guizot in advising the king.

He refused to believe me. But I dipped it in a nearby stream and then fired it in his presence. When he saw that, the Indian showed signs of the deepest admiration. He again examined the rifle and then gave it back to me with the sententious observation that "the fathers of the Canadians are great warriors!" As we were leaving, I noticed that he wore a headdress of two hawk feathers. I asked him what it signified. He smiled at the question in quite a friendly way, revealing two rows of teeth that would have done honor to a wolf, and replied that he had killed two Sioux (the name of an enemy tribe) and wore the feathers as a sign of his double victory. Would you be willing to give me one? I asked. I will wear it in my country and say that I got it from a great chief. It seems that I had plucked his heartstring, because my man then stood up, removed one of the feathers from his head with a majestic gesture that was not without its comic side, and gave it to me. Then he pulled his bare arm out from beneath his blanket and offered me a large, bony hand, from which I had a hard time extricating mine after he had shaken it.

As for the Indian women, I will tell you only that you must read *Atala* before coming to America. No Indian woman can be considered perfect unless she is the color of chocolate and has small eyes like those of a wildcat and a mouth that stretches more or less from ear to ear. So much for nature, but art too comes to her aid. An Indian woman who indulges in the slightest coquetry, and I assure you that they are not without it, will take care not to put rouge on her cheeks as in Europe but rather to draw lines in blue, black, and white, which is far more complicated. Those are the commonplace devices of fashion, however. Here as in France I have seen women who are great innovative geniuses. For instance, I remember meeting one young Indian girl whose face was painted black to the eye line, with the other half red. But that, I think, may have been an unfortunate experiment. As you know, no matter how much influence certain women have on fashion, they do not always succeed in persuading others to adopt their more unusual inventions. What is more general, one might almost say more classical, in the adornment of Indian women is a large ring in the nostrils. I find this abominable, yet I ask you quite humbly to explain to me why it is more natural to pierce the ears than the nose. There is one final respect in which the beauties of Lake Superior are essentially different from ours. You know that among us women torture their feet to force them to turn outward. Would you believe that Indian women have the bad taste to go to just as much trouble to turn them inward? Truly, they are miserable savages!

In any case, I took advantage of the opportunity to buy from one of them a type of slipper that they wear on important occasions, what is called a moccasin. If you are at all curious about these objects, it would be a real pleasure for me to offer them to you as a gift. If memory serves, each of these moccasins is big enough to hold two feet the size of yours, so it is not my intention that you should reserve them for personal use. . . .

From Tocqueville | To M. le vicomte Ernest de Blosseville

New York, October 10, 1831

I must count on your kindness, sir, to ask of you a favor which, though easy for you, will inevitably distract you from your many occupations. Here is the gist of it. As you know, we are particularly interested not only in the prisons here but also in everything to do with judicial institutions. After studying the regular courts, we turned our attention to special tribunals. Thus far we have found no trace of administrative judges, nothing at all resembling our prefectural councils or Council of State.[181] Yet there are administrative cases. Who judges them? How do they manage to do without administrative tribunals as such? What are the political consequences of this system? The answers to these questions are not clear to us.

I confess that my greatest difficulty in discovering what is done in America in this regard is that I am almost completely ignorant of what exists in France. As you know, with us, administrative law and civil law constitute two separate worlds, which do not always live in peace but which are neither sufficiently friendly nor sufficiently hostile to know each other very well. I have always lived in one of these worlds and am quite ignorant of what goes on in the other. Now that I feel the need to acquire the overview of administrative law that I lack, it occurred to me that I could do no better than turn to you for assistance.

Would it therefore be presumptuous of me to ask you to describe briefly how administrative tribunals are constituted in France and to outline the limits of their jurisdiction? I confess that this is not yet the whole of my request. What I am particularly interested in is your thoughts about the usefulness of these tribunals and the political influence they may exert. In other words, I am asking you for the kind of information that can't be found in books, information that is valuable precisely because it comes from someone whose judgment and broadmindedness one knows one can count on.

I hardly need add that if you are curious to see any *positive* documentation about America, I would be happy to try to provide it. In any case, I will do my best. For now, allow me to say nothing about the United States. Since we have been in this country, we have seen so many people and things that when we feel the urge to talk about America, our minds fill with such a confused mass of ideas and memories that it is often difficult to choose among them. . . .

---

181. Napoleon founded the Council of State in 1799. Along with legislative duties, the council was responsible for settling disputes within the French governmental administration and also between citizens and the administration. The Napoleonic Codes emerged from this body.

The prefectural councils were subordinate to the Council of State. They had the ability to hold trials that ruled on disputes between citizens and the governmental administration of the departments. These trials were independent of the regular court system and usually offered a quicker and cheaper alternative to the regular judiciary. Appeals of the decisions of the prefectural councils could be made to the Council of State.

From Beaumont | To his father

Philadelphia, October 16, 1831

In one of your last letters, my dear father, you mentioned that you attached some value to the exactness with which I wrote you in each of my letters. Are you aware that I am no less concerned to hear your news with equal precision? The *Henri-IV,* which left Le Havre on August 20, has just arrived in New York after a crossing of 56 days. I was extremely impatient for it to arrive. I went to the post office twice a day without fail, yet the packet boat, when it did arrive, did not have a single letter for me, not a word from you or *all the others,* namely, Eugénie, Jules, and Achille. I do not address my reproaches to you or Mother. When I add things up, you are still the one who writes to me most often, yet I would find it perfectly comprehensible if you were to avoid an activity that you find tiring. But my anger and indignation are directed to my elder siblings, who I grant write me very friendly letters but whose fault is that they don't write often enough. Would it be so difficult for them to send me a page or half a page with each dispatch? That wouldn't tire them unduly, yet it would be extremely precious to me. I submit this thought to their good judgment, and I would remind them that the sadness I feel when I receive no news is matched only by the happiness I experience when a letter arrives. I truly believe that they are afraid of ruining me with postage charges. Jules writes in the smallest possible hand. Achille continues to decorate his letters with lines diagonal, horizontal, and vertical. I am of course charmed by the systems adopted by each of them. . . .

We arrived in Philadelphia on the 12th. This city, with a population of about 200,000, is unlike any that I have seen previously.[182] It is laid out with such regularity that it is tempting to see it as too perfect. There is not a single street that does not run the whole length of the city in one direction or another. All the streets are aligned with geometric precision. The buildings are clean, extremely well maintained, and have all the freshness of new construction. It is a charming city and quite practical for people without carriages in that every street is bordered by broad sidewalks. Its only flaw, I repeat, is that its beauty is somewhat monotonous. As for its residents, I do not yet know them very well. We had a good many letters for Philadelphia. We have already delivered quite a few of them. But we have thus far had little of the pleasure of society because from the moment of our arrival we were taken up by people connected with the penitentiary system. There is no other city in which prisons, the method of running them, and the theories that concern them—in short, everything associated with the prison system—play a greater role or occupy a greater place than in Philadelphia. The prison society was quick to appoint a commission to supply us with any documents we may need.

The day after our arrival, we were obliged to digest a large dinner to which we

182. The city plan of Philadelphia, in which William Penn laid out a street grid and city squares between the Schuykill and Delaware rivers in 1682, made it the city most admired by Americans in the early nineteenth century.

were invited along with all the philanthropists of the region. I believe that Philadelphia exhibits the abuse of philanthropic theories that we have seen wisely applied in other states. The prison is truly a palace. Each inmate enjoys all the conveniences of life. To build such a prison costs an insane amount of money: each cell is two to three thousand francs! I wonder what we would do in France if we had to build such prisons for 32,000 prisoners (the number of inmates in France's various institutions). Although we were immediately struck by the flaws in a system of this sort, we must carry on our study with as much interest and attention as if we hoped to derive real benefit from it. We are dealing with well-meaning people who attach tremendous importance to their experiments and who would be wounded as much by a superficial study as by a severe critique. We therefore spend entire days in the penitentiary. The work is not entirely useless, because it is interesting to learn how one can stray from what is basically a good path.

As for our evenings, this is how we have spent them thus far. The first day we went to the theater. *Napoléon à Schönbrunn et à Sainte-Hélène* was on the program.[183] This French play was performed by actors from New Orleans. It was interesting for us to see a play that we had seen at the Porte-Saint-Martin in Paris performed here. Once our curiosity was satisfied, however, our pleasure was at an end. The theater is awful, and the actors were horrible. The next day, we were invited to an evening of music at the home of Mr. Walsh, a very distinguished Philadelphian.[184] The singing was *decent*, which is to say that no American performed. An Italian and several Frenchwomen bore the burden. The Americans, who are by nature as cold as ice, must have taken the Italian singer for a madman, since he gesticulated a great deal as he sang and repeatedly struck dramatic poses. The concert ended with waltzes and contredanses. We spent the following evening at the Philadelphia Philosophical Society, where we were introduced by M. Duponceau, the president of the society, who is a former French citizen and a highly educated man.[185] I found the evening boring and met no one I wished to see again. Finally, yesterday, we dined with M. de Choiseul, the former prefect of Corsica, successor there to Lantivy, and today the French consul in Charleston, who happens to be in Philadelphia at the moment.[186] He has

183. *Napoléon à Schönbrunn et à Sainte-Hélène,* a historical drama about the emperor, opened at Porte-Saint-Martin Theatre in Paris on October 20, 1830.

184. Robert Walsh (1784–1859), born to an Irish Catholic father and a Pennsylvania Quaker mother, was a wealthy, well-respected writer. He wrote a number of political pamphlets, founded the *American Review of History and Politics* in 1811, and ten years later began the *National Gazette,* which he edited until 1836. He moved to Paris in 1836 and later accepted a diplomatic post there.

185. Pierre-Étienne Duponceau (1760–1844) traveled from France to America in 1777 as an aide to Baron von Steuben during the American Revolution. He was extremely interested in the study of language, and he served as president of the American Philosophical Society in Philadelphia from 1828 to 1844.

186. Xavier de Choiseul (b. 1787), a diplomat under the July Monarchy, served as consul in Charleston, South Carolina, from 1831 to 1856. In 1830 Choiseul had served as prefect of Corsica, a position held by Beaumont's cousin the Count of Lantivy from 1824 to 1827.

a very nice wife and two friendly and pretty daughters. He seems like a friendly enough chap but is incredibly uninteresting, and it was difficult to overlook his stupidity given that he was once in charge of administering a *département*. We were introduced to him by the French consul in Philadelphia, M. d'Hannery [Dannery].[187] The latter gentleman does not lack for wit, but he is curt and quite cutting and so full of pretensions that in the end he is unbearable. You can scarcely imagine how mediocre most of France's representatives abroad are. They are either oafs or imbeciles. M. d'Hannery is still the best we have seen. He is either a relative or a very close friend of M. Benoist, the former director general of indirect taxation and a country neighbor of my uncle Eugène.[188] When he was in France, he often visited Monsieur Benoist, and he occasionally visited La Roche, where he says he saw some very pretty young ladies.[189] He asked me if that was an accurate description. We were in perfect agreement on that score.

When I have thought a bit more about deeper things, I will stop writing about such superficial matters. We are going to spend at least another month in Philadelphia. There are many people here from whom we can gather invaluable documents concerning a host of matters into which we need to delve further. While all that is going on, we are managing things as best we can. We have taken care that our expenses have not exceeded our projections. Not only will what you have given me to carry me through to January 1 suffice, but I am sure that I won't be needing more until April or May, which is probably about when we will return. I might add that among the expenditures we have made, there is not a single one (without exception) that we would hesitate to lay before you or Tocqueville's father. . . .

From Tocqueville | To his sister-in-law Alexandrine

Philadelphia, October 18, 1831

. . . We left New York a week ago to take up residence here. Philadelphia is an enormous city. You can convince yourself of this, because it occupies all the space between the Delaware and the Schuykill [*sic*].[190] All the houses are made of brick and have no coach entrances, following the English custom, and the streets are laid out in straight lines. The regularity is vexing but very convenient. Philadelphia is, I think, the only city in the world where people have thought

187. Jean Germain Samuel Adam Dannery (1795–1837) was born in Boston, where his father was serving as a French foreign minister. Dannery had held a number of diplomatic posts throughout North and South America before his assignment to Philadelphia in 1829.

188. Pierre-Vincent Benoist (1758–1834), descended from a leading family of magistrates, held several political appointments throughout his life. He served as a minister of state under Charles X but retired from politics upon the July Revolution in 1830.

189. La Roche is a town in the Loire Valley.

190. The Delaware and Schuylkill rivers are about two miles apart in the city, and over eighty thousand people lived in Philadelphia when Tocqueville visited.

to identify streets by number rather than name. The street system is so regular that if you start at the Delaware, where street no. 1 is located, you proceed one by one all the way to the Schuykill. I live on street no. 3. Don't you think that a people must have quite a frigid imagination to invent such a system? Europeans never fail to link some idea to every external object: a saint, a famous man, an event. But these people know nothing but arithmetic.

In any case, I mustn't say nasty things about them, because they continue to treat us wonderfully. Philadelphia is especially enamored of the penitentiary system, and since the penitentiary system is our *industry,* they vie with one another to spoil us. There are two kinds of people here who take an enormous interest in prisons, even though they have very different points of view on the subject: the theoreticians and the practitioners, those who write and those who act. The two groups are battling to see who will monopolize us completely. A week before we arrived, the head warden of the institution left his card with the French consul and insisted on being notified the moment we set foot in the city, while at the same time a society devoted to the study of theories of the penitentiary met and appointed a committee to help us with our research. One day we received an invitation to dine with the warden and a letter from a Quaker (a consummate theoretician) who did not bother to begin with "Monsieur" and addressed us familiarly as *"tu"* while inviting us to supper with him and some friends. Since our role is to listen to everyone without necessarily believing any of them, we enjoy an excellent reputation with both sides and gladly accept all the books and dinners they lavish upon us.

Basically, these are all good people, but political rivalries and, even more, small-town rivalries preoccupy them almost as much as if they were French. Someone said to me the other day: "The result of the last elections was to take control of the prisons out of the hands of some very capable men."

"But what do elections and prisons have in common?" I asked.

"Not much," was the answer, "but in the prisons, as in other departments, the jobs go to the winning party." As you know, there is no need to travel two thousand leagues to see such things. . . .

From Tocqueville | To Eugène Stöffels

Philadelphia, October 18, 1831

. . . We set out by ship from Buffalo, a small town at the lower end of Lake Erie. After traveling 600 leagues, we came to the entrance to Lake Superior and continued on almost to the end of Lake Michigan. A glance at the map will help you follow our route. After returning to Buffalo, we visited Niagara Falls. Then we went down the Saint Lawrence River and visited the two Canadas,[191] from which we returned via Lake Champlain to explore the states of New England, especially the one of which Boston is the capital, and from there on to New

191. The colony was divided into Upper Canada and Lower Canada until the Act of Union in 1840.

York. Here we are at last in Philadelphia, after doing what no one from our nation has done in many years. Not that the journey is difficult, but the opportunity is rare. The shores of Lakes Huron and Michigan, which within a century will be lined with cities, are today totally deserted. Even the pioneers have yet to take an axe to forests that have been growing there undisturbed since the world began. So no one travels to these places on business, and it was totally by chance that we stumbled on a ship about to sail this route.

It was in the midst of one of these forests, through which Beaumont and I were traveling alone with Indian guides, that I suddenly remembered that it was July 28!!![192] I cannot convey to you, my dear friend, the effect that the memory of that day had on me: I covered my face with both hands. For a brief moment my mind took me back to those scenes of civil war that we witnessed together. Perhaps no past event has ever impressed itself so vividly on my imagination. All the feelings and passions that agitated my soul back then, from my mother's drawing room to the little house in Saint-Cloud—all of it gripped my memory with unimaginable violence. Afterward, as I looked around and contemplated the strange scene before my eyes, the darkness of the forest, the litter of fallen trees, and the savage faces of our guides, I felt a moment's doubt that I was still the same man who had experienced the events that my memory had just dredged up. What seemed certain, though, was that more than a year had passed, though to tell the truth, I still can't believe it. The alarm bells in the night, the shooting in the streets, our escape from Paris, our armed patrols in Versailles, the nights spent in the guard room—all of it still seems a dream to me, the memory of someone else's life and not my own. . . .

I will stay here for just a month. In November we'll head for the Mississippi and then downriver to New Orleans. We will then return to New York by way of Savannah, Charleston, and Washington. This is a very long trip: more than 1500 leagues by the French measure.

You may be peeved that I haven't told you more about this country, but I don't know what to tell you. It would take a whole volume, and I haven't the time.

From Tocqueville | To Ernest de Chabrol

Philadelphia, October 18, 1831

My dear friend,

I've just this moment received your letter of August 15. It was on the high seas for 56 days. I was beginning to despair of receiving it.

You ask for details of the two levels of jurisdiction in criminal as well as civil matters. I have some thoughts about this, but they're not yet clear enough to discuss them with you. In two weeks I'll have a better grasp of things and will hasten to let you know what I have learned. Send me as many questions as

192. The three days of street fighting (*"les trois glorieuses"*) during the July Revolution lasted from July 27 to July 29, 1830.

you wish. Remember, and this is not just a manner of speaking, I am delighted when I am able to do you a favor, and, what is more, quite frankly, questions like yours are useful to me. They force me to clarify what I have seen in a confused and imprecise manner. So do not hesitate to ask.

Speaking of service, I hear from time to time about your *underhanded ways.* The other day I learned indirectly that you were the author of a certain article that was published in *Le Moniteur* and word of which reached us here. That is what I call committing a crime in the dark. I thank you profusely for this brief article, my dear friend. It said everything we would have wanted said and not a word more. But Lucas must have turned yellow. He probably thought that the piece came from the ministry and figured that he was done for.

For us the penitentiary system is merely an hors d'oeuvre, but for him it's his "industry." He lives on philanthropy as if it were his estate, from which he draws a large income every year, and he cannot stand the thought of others planting in his field. In one respect, at least, he is wrong to panic. We do not want to become specialists on penitentiaries. On the contrary, our intention is to be of absolutely independent mind on all issues pertaining to the penitentiary, so that we can coolly and clearly discuss the advantages and disadvantages and ascribe exactly as much importance to it as reason suggests it ought to have. . . .

From Tocqueville | To his mother

Philadelphia, October 24, 1831

I have no news to send about myself, my dear Maman. Alexandrine will no doubt have read you my last letter. Nothing about my situation has changed since then: prisons, learned societies, and gatherings in salons for the evening—such is our life. I continue to fare quite well—that is a point on which you will be glad to be reassured. The fall here is lovely, with clear skies and sparkling stars as on the finest summer days. The foliage in the woods is much more varied than in Europe at this time of year. Every shade of red and green blends together. This is truly the time when the full glory of America is on display.

Don't believe half of the critical things that S. has told you about this country.[193] He does not really know it, and what he does know he has learned from a certain class of French with whom he associates here exclusively and who, in America as elsewhere, seem to typify all the defects of the French spirit. Along with England, this is the strangest and most instructive country that one can possibly visit, and, more than England, it enjoys the singular privilege of exemplifying childhood as well as virile maturity—which lends quite an extraordinary appearance to the place.

I concede that not all the inhabitants of the country make for the most pleasant company. A great many of them smoke, chew tobacco, and spit right in front of you. Yet they constitute a remarkable race. What is more, though their manners are uninhibited, they gladly put up with the same in reverse. There is

193. The identity of the person to whom Tocqueville refers is unclear.

nothing in the world more difficult than to make an American angry. Unless you plant your fist in the middle of his face, he will have no idea that you wish to offend him. He attributes everything to chance and nothing to your intention. Yet these are the things that S. finds so deeply outrageous. He would gladly allow Americans to be liars, dissolute, scoffers at religion, and even thieves, but let them step on your toe without begging your pardon or spit without taking [*two illegible words in manuscript*], these are intolerable abominations that dishonor a nation. I concede that, broadly speaking, they lack refinement, grace, and elegance. In America one is constantly aware of an upper class still in its childhood, which, if only it existed, could set the tone for all the rest. But this, after all, is but a superficial impression, and it is unreasonable to leave it at that. [*Several illegible lines in manuscript.*]

As you can see, this comes down to very little. If I ever write a book about America, I will undertake to do so in France and with the documents that I will bring back with me. I will leave America in a position to understand documents that I have not yet been able to study. This is the clearest result of the journey. In any case, what I have regarding this country is a jumble of notes, any number of disconnected ideas to which I alone possess the key, and some isolated facts that call to mind a host of others. What is most interesting in what I'm bringing back are two small notebooks in which I have written down word for word the conversations that I have had with the country's most remarkable men. These scraps are invaluable to me, but only to me, given that I was able to sense the value of the questions and answers. The only somewhat general ideas that I have thus far expressed about America are contained in letters addressed to my family and a few other people in France. And all of these were written in haste, on steamboats or in some hole where I had to use my lap for a table. Will I ever publish anything about this country? I truly do not know. It seems to me that I have some good ideas, but I still don't know how to frame them, and publicity frightens me. . . .

Farewell, my dear mother. An east wind is blowing, and I hope to receive news of you in two days' time. I would never have believed that I would come to like the rain, yet that is what has happened since my arrival here: rain here means an east wind, and an east wind means the packet boat from France.

From Beaumont | To his sister-in-law Félicie

Philadelphia, October 26, 1831

. . . The society here is quite interesting to examine. Pennsylvania, of which Philadelphia is the capital, is only 150 years old and already has a population of 1,300,000.[194] It is the center of the civilization of the United States and exhibits several distinctive features that make it easy to tell it apart from the other

194. In 1681, William Penn (1644–1718) received a charter for the colony of Pennsylvania from King Charles II of England. Penn was a Quaker and established religious freedom throughout his colony, so Pennsylvania became a haven not only for the persecuted Quak-

states. Penn, the founder of Pennsylvania (which took his name), was a Quaker, and for a very long time Quakers were the only inhabitants of the region. The Quakers I am speaking of are nothing like the Shaker Quakers I saw near Albany, about whom I remember having written in a letter to Eugénie. The ones in Pennsylvania were remarkable only for the austere simplicity of their mores and the unusual character of some of their customs. They preached the principle of total equality of human conditions, with no difference between a shoemaker and a legal expert. Luxury and superfluity were entirely banned from their society, and they allowed themselves none of the usual social diversions such as dance, theater, gambling, etc. For many years these beginnings exerted a considerable influence on Pennsylvania society, and that influence is still felt today. The number of Quakers is now not very large. The severity of their doctrine is ill matched to an advanced civilization, which cannot exist without indulging many vices incompatible with their principles. They lose adherents daily. Clearly this sect is headed for utter ruin. Nevertheless, it did a great deal of good. It enjoyed a full career. Its reign is past, but it was quite beneficial to humanity. The Quakers created a free, moral, and hard-working society. It is to be hoped that this society will work as well without them as it did with their assistance.

I am in touch with two very distinguished Quakers, Messrs. Roberts [*sic*] Vaux and Wood.[195] The first is very well-known in America. He is the great philanthropist of the United States. He gave me quite a number of books and pamphlets, all of which were very interesting. He heads all the charitable institutions, including schools for the poor, institutions for the deaf and mute, hospitals, etc. The second, though much less famous, has I think more genuine knowledge. Mr. Vaux speaks volubly and well. Mr. Wood expresses himself rather poorly, but acts.

I am trying to collect as many documents as I can about many subjects here. Pennsylvania has a large German population about which I would like to know more. These Germans emigrated from various parts of Germany, and for the past twenty years they have been coming to the United States, where they tend to settle in rather homogeneous communities. There are some 140,000 of them. Among them there is not one person from any other country. They speak only German; they have their own newspapers, published in their language; and they retain their Germanic customs. It is difficult to predict when this population, so separate from other Americans by virtue of its language and customs,

---

ers but also for the Mennonites, French Huguenots, Lutherans, and Jews. In 1830, the census counted 1,348,233 inhabitants in Pennsylvania.

195. Robert Vaux (1786–1836) was a wealthy merchant known for his philanthropy and interest in reform. He drew the plans for Cherry Hill Prison in Philadelphia and wrote a number of essays about prison reform.

Samuel R. Wood was warden of Cherry Hill Prison from 1829 to 1835. A Quaker, he was a proponent of solitary confinement.

will assimilate.[196] Yet sooner or later it will inevitably occur. There is also another population in Philadelphia whose fate is quite interesting to consider: the people of color. They are no longer slaves. According to the Constitution, they are the equal of whites and have the same political rights.[197] But laws do not change mores: people are accustomed to seeing Negroes as *slaves* and continue to treat them accordingly. It is strange to see how much aristocratic pride there is in *these free men,* whose government rests on the principle of absolute equality. Here, the color white is a mark of nobility and the color black a symbol of slavery. The fact is not difficult to observe, but it is the consequences that one needs to predict. The ignorance of the blacks is diminishing daily, and when they are fully educated, there is reason to fear that they will avenge themselves violently for the contempt in which they are held.

A myriad of other things attract our attention in this country. Every night I write down my observations of the day, and I already have many notes on Pennsylvania. There is also something else about Philadelphia, a subject quite as interesting as the Germans and the Negroes, namely, the pretty women. I have seen several remarkable beauties. They dress exactly like Frenchwomen, with the only difference being that they have less taste. Since no one here has a carriage, they walk, and one meets them constantly in the streets, where they are quite sumptuously attired, so that they look rather like those *princesses de boulevards* that one finds in such abundance in Paris.

Young ladies here are brought up to enjoy a considerable degree of freedom. I hope that this circumstance will not deprive me of my own. I can even say that I'm quite sure of it, for I would rather be hanged than marry in a foreign country. They are nevertheless quite friendly and have a perfect ear for banter. Nothing is more common than to spend an entire evening in conversation with the same person, and no one else will join in.

The day after tomorrow we intend to go to Baltimore (Maryland), where we will stay for only a few days before returning here. We will probably remain in Philadelphia for about a month. Then we will head for the Mississippi by way of the Ohio en route to New Orleans by water. I am going to send Jules a map of the state that I intend to explore. I will not enclose it with this letter for two reasons: the first is that the postage from Le Havre to Mortagne would be enormous (this consideration is of no importance on my end, because the post for

196. A number of German American communities continue to exist in the state today, mostly among Americans of the Amish and Mennonite faiths. These people and their German dialect are known as Pennsylvania Dutch.

197. In 1830, Pennsylvania was home to nearly thirty-eight thousand free persons of color. This population was based primarily in Philadelphia. The Pennsylvania government had passed a law in 1780 instituting gradual emancipation. However, individuals born into slavery remained in bondage until the age of twenty-eight, and slaveowners often wielded control over families who had just a few enslaved members. In 1830, the census counted four hundred slaves in Pennsylvania, and slavery was not abolished outright in the state until 1847.

the crossing from New York to Le Havre is no more for a fat letter than for a thin one). Second, my other reason is that I have an opportunity to send him the map via another route.

This requires a somewhat lengthy explanation.

As you may know, someone has just written us from Paris to say that everyone there is terrified of cholera morbus; that a reliable remedy for this illness has just been discovered; that this remedy is an oil produced in the Molluca [Molucca] Islands known as oil of cajeput; that only a small quantity of this oil is to be found in France; and that, since it has been recognized as a sovereign remedy, it is impossible to get any from the usual dealers without worrying about its quality.[198] Finally, we have been asked to send some from America if we can find any.

No sooner did we receive this news than we set out in search of this oil, which all the pharmacists and druggists of Philadelphia carry. The first shop we visited had only one ounce. We eagerly purchased it and would have paid a hundred *louis* had we been asked. In other shops we eventually found as much as we wanted. We have packed a case with two full bottles of this oil, and we are sending it to Chabrol, our common friend in Versailles. He will divide the case between the Tocqueville and Beaumont families. He will send the *Beaumont bottle* to Achille, who will divide it among the denizens of Beaumont-la-Chartre, Gallerande, and Le Guillet. We have been told that oil of cajeput is to be taken in very small doses, not to exceed five drops, and not to be repeated more than once every few hours.

I will tell you that in our heart of hearts we believe that our errand was utterly futile. It seems as clear as day to us that there is as much cajeput as one might want in Paris and other French cities. If this is true, you will have a good laugh at our gullibility when you receive our shipment from America, but we were told that it does not exist in France, that lives were at stake, and therefore that we must not hesitate, and we would rather risk doing something absurd or even ridiculous than fail to do something useful. In any case, I will put Jules's map in the case with the bottles and ask Chabrol to deliver it along with the bottle to Achille, who will send it on to you.

Please tell Jules that I will write immediately to Monsieur de Saint-Pater in answer to the letter I received from him at the moment of my departure. I haven't yet seen the people about whom he spoke to me, but I have heard talk of them. I still hope to meet them.

I leave you, my dear sister, for a musical evening. We are told that we are to hear a wonderful English singer this evening. I find this hard to believe, because

198. Cholera originated in India and was a highly contagious and fatal disease in the nineteenth century. Humans contracted it after consuming contaminated food or water, and the disease spread to Europe for the first time in 1832.

Cajeput oil is produced from a tree native to Southeast Asia. It has mild antiseptic and antimicrobial properties and produces heavy sweating in those who ingest it.

English males, like American females, are an antimusical breed. Please give my regards to Monsieur and Madame Descorches.[199] If they are afraid of cholera morbus and cajeput turns out to be a rare and useful medicine, I hope they will look upon the portion destined for Les Guillets as belonging first to them. I also hope that there is at Les Guillets a new boy or girl, whose existence is of great interest to me even before I receive the news. Please hug all your little children on behalf of their Uncle Gustave. . . .

From Tocqueville | To Ernest de Chabrol

Philadelphia, October 26, 1831

My dear friend,

I've just received a letter from you that I wasn't expecting. It should have reached me three weeks ago, but by mistake it was forwarded to Albany, which I had already left. It was only when I wrote to acquaintances there that I was able to have it forwarded to me here.

In this letter I found the article that you placed in *Le Moniteur* regarding our trip, along with the questions that Bouchitté sent me.[200] I will do my best to respond to them today, in the first place because they are already quite old and in the second place because they deal with issues that do not require a rigorous treatment.

As for your questions about the two levels of jurisdiction, I ask your permission to postpone them once again until the next mail.

In this same letter, which has seen so much of the world in its travels, you ask me to obtain Mr. Livingston's codes for you.[201] You have to be clear on this point.

You ask for:

1. Mr. Livingston's first report on the projected penal code. I am sending it to you, as I explain below.
2. You want to know how Congress has acted with respect to this code. This matter does not pertain to Congress. The code was prepared by the state of Louisiana, and it was up to Louisiana alone to adopt it, but the state refused to do so. I don't yet know the reason why, but I believe that

199. Marie-Louise-Gabrielle Bonnet de Bellou (1771–1849) was the aunt of Félicie. She had inherited an estate known as Les Guillets (or Le Guillet) during her first marriage. She married her second husband, Marie-François Descorches (1769–1836), in 1814.

200. Louis Firmin Hervé Bouchitté (1795–1861) was a Catholic scholar and professor. He was a childhood friend of Tocqueville, and the two corresponded regularly.

201. Edward Livingston (1764–1836) was directed to revise the Louisiana penal code in 1821. He finished the project in 1825 and drafted reports that encouraged the prevention, rather than simply the punishment, of crime. Although it was never implemented, the plan earned Livingston a reputation as a legal and penal reformer. He served as secretary of state from 1831 to 1833. Livingston was exceptionally helpful to Tocqueville and Beaumont's study of American prisons and was the only person Tocqueville thanked by name in the preface to his first volume of *Democracy in America*.

Mr. Livingston's code was designed for a social state more advanced than that of the region for which he drafted it.

You also asked me for the codes of criminal procedure and police, if they exist. If by that you mean codes drafted by Mr. Livingston, I am not aware of his having done anything of the kind. If you mean existing codes, what you are asking for is impossible. Strictly speaking, there are no codes of criminal procedure or police in the United States but rather *customs* that vary widely among the 24 states of the Union. I doubt that there are even general principles, and I am not sure that I will ever discover them with my books and *questions*. I am therefore forced to limit my dispatch to the single small volume that I mentioned earlier. But how will this small volume reach you? That's another long story. The last mail brought a letter from the mother of our friend Louis de K.[202] with the news that:

1. There is great fear of cholera in Paris.
2. An effective medicine has recently been discovered: a certain cajeput oil, which comes straight from China. But it is almost impossible to find this oil in Paris, or at any rate to find the genuine article, and I was asked to send some from America (an unusual route by which to order medicine from China). In fact, I have found some here. As you might imagine, I have little faith in the remedy, but the mere suggestion that it might be indicated is enough that I do not dare forgo the opportunity to acquire some. Fortunately, it is taken in very small doses. Beaumont and I therefore bought two bottles of cajeput, and we have decided to send it to you so that you can distribute it. If you see this request as somewhat comical, blame Madame de K . . .[203]

After you receive the package, you will need to obtain some vials. You can then divide the cajeput in two parts. I do not know what Beaumont wants you to do with his share, but mine should be divided in three parts: one for Madame de K., another for my father, and the third for your neighbor. I hardly need add that you should first take your own share from the two bottles.

You will of course decide on the best way to ensure that the three vials reach their destinations. I hope you don't mind if I prevail on our friendship in this way. The truth is that I am ashamed that I am doing so little myself, but sending the package to you was the only way to share its contents with your neighbor. I do not believe in this remedy, but in love as in religion there are superstitions that must be forgiven, and this is one.

But I am not done yet. No one here could tell me whether or not the cajeput would be prohibited by customs. The merchant advised me to label the bottles "oil of cubebs," which I have done. Later, however, I remembered that cubebs is celebrated as a cure for venereal disease, no less, and I feel badly about openly sending you such a drug. I thought that the name "Carné" was less well-known

202. Louis de Kergorlay.
203. Blanche de la Luzerne de Kergorlay (1770–1859) was the mother of Louis de Kergorlay.

than yours, so I addressed the package to him.[204] Please take care to warn him so that he will give it to you without opening it.

Whew! At last I am done with these apothecary matters and free to take up Bouchitté's questions.

Bouchitté asks me if Catholicism is on the rise in the United States. My answer is yes, remarkably so. Forty years ago, there were thirty Catholics in New York, and all of them could fit in the chapel of the Spanish consulate. Today there are 30,000 Catholics, who have paid for the building of six churches. The same is true in all the other big cities. Even Boston, the center of English Puritanism, has two Catholic churches and a convent. The religion is said to be spreading rapidly in the West. We found it to be almost universal in Canada. There are now 700,000 to 800,000 Catholics in the United States, twelve seminaries, and a large number of other institutions of one sort or another.

So much for the facts. Now what are the causes? The most important of all is immigration. Every year, thousands of Irish, French, and German Catholics pour into the United States.

In addition, it is said that many conversions are taking place in the new settlements in the West. I have no way to be certain of this, but I confess that I find it easy to believe. Protestantism has always seemed to stand in the same relation to Christianity as constitutional monarchy to politics: it is a kind of compromise among contrary principles, a halfway point between two opposite states—in short, a system incapable of tolerating its own consequences or fully satisfying the human spirit. As you know, I have always believed that constitutional monarchies would end up as republics, and I am similarly convinced that Protestantism will soon end up in natural religion. Many religious people here feel this strongly. They recoil from this consequence of their doctrines, and the reaction impels them toward Catholicism, the principle of which is highly debatable but in which everything is at least logically related.

Note that in the United States, no one would ever think of treating religion lightly. People here talk and argue more about this subject than anywhere else in the world. They are a long way from the indifference that with us excludes the danger of infidelity. Consequently, intelligence in America is more taken up with religion than anything else except politics. It is obvious that people here with cold and calculating characters or argumentative and logical minds are more than likely to move by degrees toward deism, whereas people of ardent soul and passionate imagination are drawn to Catholicism. The latter will someday find itself pitted against natural religion; I have no doubt that this will happen, though I have no idea when.

That, I think, sums up the Catholic movement in the United States. Next we must consider the political situation of Catholics in relation to civil and religious government.

204. Louis de Carné (1804–1876) was a Catholic legitimist journalist who joined the July Monarchy.

A fair number of religious prejudices are still held against them, yet it is fair to say that these prejudices have no influence on their political situation. They stand on exactly the same footing as everyone else, not only in law but also in practice. In society, it is impossible to distinguish them from the Protestants, alongside whom they occupy the posts made available by the choice of government or popular favor. The attorney general of the United States is Catholic, as are some members of Congress.[205]

So much for the state of political opinion in regard to the Catholic population. But what attitude do they take themselves? I will surprise you by saying that the demagogues and levelers are Catholics. Nevertheless, I am more than ever convinced that in itself the Catholic religion has a strong tendency toward absolute monarchy or at least an aristocratic republic. I have spoken with a good many priests: their democracy is purely skin-deep. One senses in the depths of their souls a great contempt for the rule of the multitude and a great desire to rule and direct society. To speak frankly, I even believe that they are tolerant only because they have given up hope of dominating. But why then are Catholics democrats? Because they are poor and the Protestants are rich, and because in the country from which most of them come, the aristocracy is Protestant. I concede that religions have political inclinations; this cannot be denied. But I think that in the world of theory these inclinations are exaggerated. Religion is surely one basis of political opinion, but social position and interest are the most important of all grounds for political judgment.

Finally, I should say a word about the situation of Catholics as a religious society. A rather odd complication is apparent here: American Catholicism is at once more rational and more dependent on the pope than European Catholicism. What I mean is that, owing to the extreme division of the Protestant sects, Catholic society is now the largest denomination. It is thoroughly united and marches in lockstep. As is the case everywhere, it has adopted a proud and disdainful pose. Firm in its beliefs, it remains aloof from all other religious groups. All the Protestant sects help one another to some degree, while Catholicism stands apart, eternally unchanging. Yet it has changed: it has quietly renounced whatever it could without altering its essence. There are no monasteries in America, no ridiculous external rites, no obvious superstition. Catholicism consistently appeals to reason, and it has to some extent given up the bombastic style that one nearly always finds in the language of the pulpit in Europe. It *professes* religious freedom and openly states that it has *no* need of the state and wishes to do *without it.*

Despite this, American Catholics are more dependent on the pope than Catholics anywhere else in the world. There are several reasons for this singular state of affairs. American Catholics are generally poor. Despite their zealous

205. Roger Taney (1777–1864) was the first Catholic attorney general of the United States. He served in the post from 1831 to 1833 and went on to serve as secretary of the treasury and as a Supreme Court justice.

ardor to create seminaries, they have for a very long time not been in a position to do so, so that most of their priests are foreigners without ties to their flock and without authorization from the civil authorities, which stay out of religion. These priests, who come from outside, naturally feel that they represent pontifical authority alone. What is more, Catholics are scattered throughout the vast American continent and therefore have no common bond, no social organization, and no collective power to resist. Hence in a practice that might seem bizarre in a democratic republic, the pope alone appoints all bishops and enforces church discipline—in short, he can do here what he is not allowed to do in states whose political principle is more compatible with the principle of papal power.

One final observation, which may be more convincing than the foregoing: American Catholicism was established at a time when the people of Europe had lost their rights in church government and when the civil authorities were the only counterweight to the power of the pope. Transplanted to a country where the civil authorities do not interfere with religion, Catholicism naturally surrendered unconditionally to the court of Rome. I do not believe that this situation will last. The new generation of priests will be national. Indeed, the court of Rome has already been obliged to use its power with the greatest care, and I suspect that it will not be long before the limits of that power are codified and currently absent guarantees are put in place.

Bouchitté, in a letter he wrote me on the eve of my departure from France, asked me to find out what I could about the Quakers.[206] He seems to have formed an idea of their influence here that I find exaggerated. Quaker doctrine has certainly had some influence on the religious direction of America. The Quakers emphasized all the *emotive* aspects of the Christian religion. They were the first to set an example of pragmatic tolerance and familiarized people with its principles.

Yet I doubt that their influence would have been sufficient had it not been aided by the advance of civilization and, it must be said, by the progress of indifference as well. What is certain, however, is that Quaker influence is virtually nonexistent today. Nearly all the Quakers sided with the English at the time of the American Revolution, at which time they ceased to be popular, and since then they have become progressively less so. But the greatest misfortune of the Quakers is to have been possessed by the obsession with rules and inquisitorial mania of the Roman church without the support of the dogma of infallibility. If a Quaker has dubious morals, if his behavior is not sufficiently exemplary, or if he marries a woman of another faith, they excommunicate him. To be a Quaker it is not enough to adhere to a certain doctrine; one must also address others familiarly, avoid certain company, and wear clothes cut and buttoned in a certain way. They squander their power over souls in minute regulations, and the sect

206. In the nineteenth century, American Quakers espoused pacifism, abolition of slavery, social reforms to improve the lives of the poor and imprisoned, and simplicity of dress.

grows steadily purer as its numbers diminish. I believe that it will be one of the first Protestant sects to disappear.

A new sect in America that is worthy of the most serious attention is the Unitarian. Bouchitté may be familiar with it, but I had never heard of it before coming here. The Unitarians are the outermost ring of all the sects that stand between the Catholic religion and pure *deism*. They claim to have freed themselves not only from the church but also from all the sectarians of reform and to accept only that much of the Bible which is compatible with reason. Based on this principle, they reject all the mysteries, even that of the Trinity, and they do not accept the doctrine of expiation, which as you know is the basis of Christianity. I spoke at length with their ministers and have acquired most of their books. Ask Bouchitté if he knows the works of Mr. Channing, the leader of the American Unitarians. He is a very eloquent man, whose works expound the doctrine. He gave us copies. If Bouchitté does not know them and does know English, I can think of nothing more likely to arouse his curiosity and interest. Standing at the outer limits of Christianity, the Unitarians insist that having gone so far, they will stray no farther, but their own momentum carries them along, and the final limits will soon be breached. In any case, one could write volumes about this subject, and I want to end this letter. Show all this scribbling to Bouchitté and hug him for me.

Farewell, my dear friend, and take care of my vials. I embrace you with all my heart. I copy verbatim the following sentence from Marie's last letter, which was written on the day you left for vacation. "I was quite sad all Monday, the day of M. de Chabrol's departure." You see your standing in the house.

A. de T.

P.S. Via an indirect route, I have just received news of France from Sept. 16. I see that the cholera is beginning to arouse universal concern and that cajeput is said to be a good remedy. This means that my shipment is to be taken seriously. You will find a small vial in the crate (the smallest). I have more confidence in that one than in the others, because I have confidence in the source from which I obtained it. My dear friend, I beg you to take the share of this that belongs to me and give it *personally* to my mother. I confess to you that I am beginning to be consumed by worry for all the people I hold dearest in this world.

If cholera comes to France, Marie must leave our country. I confess that it is terribly sad for me to think that she might leave forever, because I love her more than I can say. But her life is more precious to me than anything. Her health is delicate. Like me, she suffered for quite some time from internal pains. She would be more vulnerable than most, and that thought makes me desperate. Do what you think best: give the advice and take the steps that you deem most appropriate. Please bear in mind that what is at stake for me is not pleasure or personal benefit; my interest is real and immense, a deep feeling that fills my heart. I confess that my soul feels enormously burdened as I write this letter. I have no more time today to write to Marie, but tell her that she is with me even more than usual, that words prove nothing, and yet I cannot help but say that what I most desire in the world would be for her to be in my place and me to be in hers. If that were out of the question, I would at least feel happier to be with her where there is danger and share all the risks.

Beaumont tells me that he has just written to you that you should send a *part* of each vial to his family. What I have said about my mother therefore applies only to my share.

From Beaumont | To his brother Achille

Philadelphia, November 8, 1831

... I have just received from the minister of justice a letter in which His Excellency urges me to return as soon as possible without specifying a precise date. With that in mind, we will interpret our instructions broadly and continue our journey in such a way as to maximize its benefits, but I do not think that we will stay beyond next March. With this new arrangement, we will be forced to cancel our trip to New Orleans, which would take too long, and limit ourselves to Cincinnati (in Ohio), Charleston (in South Carolina), and finally Washington.[207] Meanwhile, we made a brief excursion to Baltimore, the capital of Maryland, which I will now describe.

We arrived there on October 28. On the day we arrived, there was a huge subscription ball for which tickets were being sold at 25 francs apiece. If we had had to pay that much, we would not have gone, as you might imagine. But being "distinguished foreigners," we were admitted free. Thus on our very first day we had an opportunity to see the best of Baltimore society gathered in one place. The women of this city enjoy quite a reputation, and truly they deserve it. I saw any number of very pretty ones. They dress well and are very friendly and excessively flirtatious. I am convinced, however, that their flirtatiousness holds little danger for them, because they know very well when to call a stop. Nevertheless, I did meet a petite Miss Mary Randolph, as pert as can be and completely scatterbrained, who will I think do some *foolish things,* if only out of naughtiness, whenever she sets her heart on a young man as prone to mischief as she is.[208] The next day, we enjoyed a different sort of scene: a very fine horse race. Every year Baltimore hosts a series of races that lasts three or four days. On this occasion, all the finest horses of Virginia and New York took part. The race is held at a track two leagues from the city. The organization of the races is exactly the same as ours on the Champ de Mars. On the day I was there, I saw five horses run in one race. They had to run a distance of four miles, or a league and a third. The two horses that stood out were *Black Maria,* a mare from New York, and *Trifle,* a small Virginia mare. The latter's name suited her well: she truly looked like *une bagatelle,* a trifle. She was so thin, weak, and seemingly frail

207. In the end, Beaumont and Tocqueville canceled their trip to Charleston in favor of a visit to New Orleans.

208. The identity of this woman is uncertain.

that we assumed she would stumble at the first gallop. She was almost transparent, with muscles visible beneath her skin. I thought she would break as easily as glass. Nevertheless, she twice took the stakes of 4,000 francs. *Black Maria,* whose name reminded me of the mare at Beaumont-la-Chartre, lost, but with honor. *Trifle* ran the four miles in seven and a half minutes the first time and a few seconds under eight minutes the second time. Between the two races there was an interval of only half an hour. The horses in this country are not of any peculiarly American breed. There were no horses here before the Europeans arrived. This was one of the things that most astonished the Indians. The horses that I saw race were Arabians. There is a type of race here that we never see at home: a trotting race, which always comes after the main race. There is a truly extraordinary breed of trotters in this country, and English horses are truly at a disadvantage when racing against them.

But enough about horses. Let's talk about people. We were delighted with the people of Baltimore. The week we spent there was a *real carnival.* We went from banquet to banquet. We didn't dine at our inn a single night. There was always another gala to attend. The sumptuousness of these grand dinners is unbelievable. If these people host dinners like this frequently, they must be ruining themselves. In any case, some of them are quite wealthy. For example, Mr. Charles Carroll has an income of 400,000 pounds.[209] This Charles Carroll is an elderly man of 95, very well preserved, who was a member of the great American Congress of 1776. He is the only signer of the Declaration of Independence still alive. He is a very amiable fellow and remembers all the events of his youth quite well. He told me that he was raised in France by Jesuits, who he says were very worthy men. He is Catholic and rather aristocratic, though quite devoted to his country. He spoke to me about his excellent friend La Fayette, who he says understands nothing about politics. In Baltimore I also saw a Frenchman whom I was quite pleased to meet: Monsieur de Menou (Count Jules), who is related to the Tocqueville family and knows my uncles André, Charles, and Armand.[210] He also told me that he once met my father in Touraine. We prized his company because he spoke to us about France and our friends. He is quite an eccentric, moreover, and we're not really sure why he stays in America. The day we left Baltimore, we were beginning to flag beneath the weight of all the celebrations. The last was given in our honor by the governor of Maryland, Mr. Howard,

209. Charles Carroll (1737–1832), a native of Baltimore, gained notoriety after 1826 as the last surviving signer of the Declaration of Independence. He was also the only Catholic signer of the document, and he had been schooled by Jesuits in France.

210. As a young boy, Jules de Menou came to the United States with his mother after his father was guillotined during the French Revolution. He returned to France during Napoleon's reign. He served in the government of the Bourbon Restoration, became an ambassador to Washington, D.C., in 1819, and served as secretary of the legation of France in the United States from 1822 to 1830.

Beaumont's uncles were André (1761–1838), Charles (1768–1836), and Armand (1782–1859) Bonnin de La Bonninière de Beaumont.

who invited quite a few guests.[211] We had to down many toasts, which, however well-intentioned, did us no favor by forcing us to drink too much, something to which we are not accustomed.

When we returned to Philadelphia, we found a very flattering article about us in a Baltimore newspaper, which lavished praise *on our merits and virtues.* It is true that we are becoming more and more poised, and when we are invited out now, we say appropriate things in the friendliest possible way.

I would never end this letter if I told you everything we did in Baltimore. There was one thing of particular interest, namely, *slavery,* which is still legal there. On this point I made any number of observations, which in my mind do not reflect very favorably on the people to whom they apply. But I will probably publish all of this in the great work that is to *immortalize me,* and it is to that book that I refer you if you wish to know the rest.

In any case, here are four well-filled and tolerably well-scrawled pages of little squares to cure you forever of this system of writing. I chose this method solely to *vex* you: you need to discover all its drawbacks for yourself.

Take care of yourself, old man, and write often, even in *little squares* if you must. No matter what the form, your letters will always bring pleasure to your brother and friend for life.

From Tocqueville | To an unknown recipient

Philadelphia, November 8, 1831

Monsieur,

When I received your letter two weeks ago, I was upset that I had waited so long to write you myself, an obligation that I have been putting off for the past three months. Nevertheless, I hope that since you have taken it upon yourself to write first, you will accept this proof of friendship and forgive my long silence. The life I am leading here, if you can imagine such a thing, is that of a minister of government, minus the glory and the insults. Business, visits, dinners—nothing is left out. Amid all this bustle one finds time to think of one's friends but not always time to tell them so.

I know, moreover, that rather than make excuses for myself, I would do better first to discuss your letter. I will not tell you that it is full of kindness and wit: that is no way peculiar to this recipient. But I will thank you for your repeated assurances of friendship and your abundant good advice. As to the latter, I confess, however, that I am afraid I may not profit from your counsel.

You bring up the subject of what one might write about America, but I have absolutely no idea whether I will ever have the opportunity to publish the slightest piece on the subject. A comprehensive portrait of English America would be an immense work and totally beyond my capabilities. It would be dif-

211. George Howard (1789–1846), a staunch anti-Jacksonian, was governor of Maryland at the time.

ficult in any case to take that path without succumbing to the style of a geographical dictionary. And if one gives up the idea of a comprehensive portrait, it is no longer clear which details are particularly worthy of attention.

I have therefore limited myself thus far to assembling a substantial number of documents of various sorts along with numerous fragmentary observations. This work amuses me and interests me greatly, but will it ever amount to anything more? To be frank, the more I go on, the greater my doubts.

Nevertheless, as you say, there may be room to present a few observations about this country, which, even if they lack flavor, might at least be new, for, with the exception of a dozen or so people in Paris who, like you, sir, are not wholly absorbed in the politics of the moment, America is as unknown as Japan, or, rather, people talk about it precisely as Montesquieu spoke of Japan. In pursuit of genuine principles, people attribute to Americans a multitude of words and deeds of which the humble citizens of this country are, I assure you, quite innocent.

I must admit, though, that there are at times extraordinary points of similarity between America and France, but those go unnoticed.

In that connection I must tell you at once, while it is on my mind, about a conversation that I had only yesterday with Charles Carroll. Charles Carroll is a small, elderly man of 95, as erect as an I, still keen of hearing and even better at speaking. That alone is deserving of notice. What is more, Charles Carroll is the last surviving signatory of the Declaration of Independence. In 1773 [*sic*] he was a conspirator who risked not only his head but a good deal more in the way of material possessions than his colleagues: 20,000 acres of land and five or six hundred slaves, which he owned in Maryland and which could easily have been confiscated. Having avoided the scaffold, he became a great man, something one sees commonly in politics. He also kept his 20,000 acres and six hundred slaves. But since not everyone lives to be 95, his friends and relatives are dead, and for sixty years he has seen their descendants grow poor, noble families disappear as a consequence of the new law of inheritance, and democracy seize the power that in his day belonged to the great landowners.

In the course of the conversation, I ventured to ask him if those who led the way to the American Revolution thought that things would go as far as they did. "Oh, my God, surely not," Charles Carroll answered, "we all loved England, but both sides dug in their heels, the movement grew, we found ourselves being pushed, no one could stop, and the Revolution indeed had to be made."

But, I responded, once the Revolution had taken place, what forced you to destroy English institutions and establish democracy? "We were divided after the victory," he replied. "Each party sought to use the people and in order to secure their loyalty granted them new privileges, until ultimately they became our masters and threw us all out."

How do you like that little bit of history? Might something like it not have been said in Paris toward the end of 1830 or at any rate in 1831? Yet I am very faithfully reporting his exact words.

You say that American society has nothing which speaks to the imagination. That is true of Americans individually but not of America in general. Each detail of the edifice is paltry, but the whole exhibits new and colossal shapes that stun the mind. Although man here is no less petty than he is everywhere, I assure you that humanity is impressive. More than anywhere else in the world, one feels here that the universe is made for us to use and that we can fashion it as we will.

Do you know that I traveled three hundred leagues in the West before encountering the first Indian station. I was told everywhere that Indians were here as recently as ten, six, or even two years ago, but civilization is driving them out with unbelievable speed. A forest fire whipped by the wind does not move through woods more rapidly than the white race in America. In many places along my way I came upon cities that had been planted only yesterday in the heart of the wilderness. I found roads in the middle of forests and railroads in places that were still wild.

We traveled a hundred leagues via a canal that links the Mississippi to the North River, so that the traveler coming from New York can today disembark in New Orleans without having set foot on soil in between, after traveling as great a distance inland as he traveled in crossing the Atlantic to get to America.

No one has ever fully rendered the foreign visitor's first impression of American society, and I believe that it is impossible to do so.

There is initially something bewildering about the impetuous movement that America imparts to everything, about society's febrile agitation. Americans themselves share that impression, and I have no doubt that it exerts a great influence on the national character. Everything around them is changing, everything is in motion, everything seems to be moving rapidly toward unknown and unlimited prosperity. The idea of stability is nowhere to be found. Men, fortunes, laws, and political institutions are changing constantly. Not far away, Indian nations that were powerful forty years ago have disappeared without a trace. In their place, new states appear every year and take their place in the confederation.

Nature, elsewhere so static, here seems subject to even more revolutions than man. The aspect of the land changes, rivers diminish, even the temperature of the seasons is no longer what it was before the Revolution.

As the author of all these changes, himself caught up in the movement that he set in motion, the American ultimately feels impelled by an irresistible need for action. For him, the possible has virtually no limits. In Europe there are philosophers who say that humanity is steadily improving. That idea has become commonplace in America. It seems to emerge from the facts themselves: for an American, to change is to improve. This ever-present image of unlimited improvement makes his heart extraordinarily restless and fills him with disgust for the present.

Here, the pleasures of the soul do not count for much, the pleasures of the imagination do not exist, but an enormous portal is opened onto material happiness, and everyone rushes through it. To achieve prosperity, everyone is prepared to abandon parents, family, and country. All bonds become matters of indifference, all states equally good. In the course of a single lifetime, a man will try ten paths to achieve his fortune. At one time or another he may have been a priest, a doctor, a merchant, or a farmer.

I do not know whether people are happier here than they are elsewhere, but existence certainly weighs less heavily on them, and they come to the end of the road without having had the time to measure the distance traveled.

These people call themselves virtuous, but I find them merely disciplined. They respect their neighbor's wife, yet they rob him. I can explain this only by thinking that they love money and have no time for wooing.

But I see that I am lapsing into philosophical nonsense, which, as you know, is the essence of all nonsense. So as not to leave you with this terrible impression, I must close with a short anecdote that was good enough to wrest a smile from even the gravest of Americans.

As you may know, in Philadelphia all the streets are laid out as straight lines, and each is so like the next that he who has seen one has seen them all. Recently, a watchman patrolling one of these streets at midnight encountered a short gentleman whose extreme agitation and unusual behavior drew his attention to the point where he felt obliged to arrest him. When called upon to explain his actions, the young gentleman told the following tale:

He had arrived in Philadelphia for the first time that very day. At the time he was accompanied by a pretty young woman from New York, whom he had spirited away from her parents and whom he hoped to marry that evening, before their elopement could be discovered.

On reaching Philadelphia, the two fugitives went first to the home of one of the gentleman's relatives, but she had just left for the country. Fortunately, the eloping beauty remembered the name of one of her friends, who agreed to take her in, but she insisted that her lover find an inn until the wedding ceremony, because in America, as in England, sin is tolerated but not the appearance of sin, and one may not enter a woman's bedroom except to sleep with her.

As the hour set for the wedding arrived, our man spruced himself up with pomade and perfume. At the first street corner, however, he hesitated, looked around, and realized that he had forgotten the way to the house where his intended was staying. But surely he could come up with the name of the friend who had taken her in? No, in his amorous ecstasy he had thought about the charms of his intended, about his father-in-law's fortune, about past, present, and future—in short, about everything except writing down the essential name, which his murky memory absolutely refused to disclose.

A Frenchman would surely have hanged himself from the nearest lamppost. The American decided to run from door to door, looking at every nameplate, for the owner's name is inscribed on every home. While he exhausted himself in this manner, the appointed time came and went. His despair grew with each passing minute. What would people say about such strange behavior? How could he explain it? How could he get anyone to believe him?

Who knows what vexation is capable of when aided by reason? The poor man saw himself losing both his love and her dowry. But what could he do other than keep on running and keep on looking? It was while he was engaged in this frantic search, bathed in sweat and filth and about to collapse in a heap next to a street sign, that the watchman nabbed him. He took the man back to his inn, where he learned that an unknown servant had come twice earlier in the evening to ask after him with a worried air.

He had to sleep alone that night, as he had the night before. What happened next I do not know, but this much of the story is enough, I think, to teach a valuable lesson to anyone who, even if he doesn't wish to marry, occasionally needs not to forget an address.

Farewell, sir, and please accept the friendship that I have promised you for life. Think of me, I beg you, when you have nothing better to do.

From Tocqueville | To Ernest de Chabrol

Philadelphia, November 19, 1831

My dear friend,

As you know, we have completely changed our plans. Instead of leaving on April 1, we will depart on February 16 (I told my family the 10th so as not to frighten them with the equinox). And if we are not eaten by the fish, as we well could be, we will reach England on March 8 and France at the beginning of April.

I confess that *cholera morbus* has played a considerable part in hastening our return. But this is between us. I am telling my parents the opposite. It is unbearable to be so far away from loved ones in times of danger. In any case, we actually have very sound reasons to do what we are doing. The minister's last letter made it clear that we would be ill-advised to ignore its contents. We would risk creating ill will that could deprive us of the fruits of our journey: that is one reason for our return that we can admit openly. The second reason, which is no less significant than the first, is that even if we return in February, we will have seen almost everything we needed to see to form a complete idea of the United States.

On nearly every important point we are bringing back a terrifying mass of documents. We have filled a large crate with them.

As for the penitentiary system, which is the heart of our "industry," as Lucas would say, we can say without boasting that we have learned all there is to know about the subject. We have the wherewithal to prove that the penitentiary system both reforms and does not reform; that it is both expensive and economical; that it is both easy to establish and completely impractical; and, in short, that it is either suited to France or not suited, depending on the interlocutor. And we promise to back up each of these assertions with very cogent examples.

I am joking of course. The truth is that our journey has taught us two or three profound truths about penitentiaries that may be quite useful. But when it comes to the system's applicability in France, we are left with substantial doubts, which we shall set forth quite frankly when we return.

We have already submitted four reports to the government from America. You will see the notes. They are two inches thick and must be worth something, if only by the pound.

But the more closely I examine this country and everything else, and the longer I live, the more frightened I become by what little certainty man is in a position to acquire in this world. The deeper one goes into any subject, the vaster it becomes, and behind every fact and observation lurks a doubt. Everything we possess in this life is like the backdrop at the opera, which prevents you from making out the precise contours of what lies behind it.

There are people who are content to live in such perpetual semiobscurity. I find it tiresome and dispiriting. I would like to hold political and moral truths as I hold my pen, but doubt assails me.

Yesterday, an American asked me how I classified human misery. Without hesitation I answered that I ranked chronic illness first, death second, and doubt third. He stopped and gave a cry. I have thought about it since and stand by my classification. But enough philosophy.

To you, my dear friend, I confess that I am not in good spirits at the moment. You have probably already noticed. Sometimes I dance, and often I laugh, but in the depths of my heart there is an unbearable malaise. I am cheerful in society and downcast when alone. I am tormented by a thousand worries about the future. What has become of my loved ones in France, and what will have become of them five months from now? What will I do when I return? What career can I embark on or honorably pursue? Should I aim to continue in public service? Should I resign? My position seems false in every respect.

Think about this. Think about it with just your head and leave your heart out of it. In the midst of this inner turmoil, the thought of Marie occupies a place in my heart that often surprises me. This is between us. I think about her constantly. Her image is mixed up in everything I do, and I never feel so attached to her as when I am sad and unhappy. Right now she is one of the stoutest bonds holding me fast to life, and all things considered, I think what I would most regret in the world would be never to see her again.

This, too, is between us and must not be repeated. I would find it difficult to speak to you about this if I thought my words were repeated.

She will no doubt let you know the new instructions I have given her in my letter concerning how she should address her letters to me. I will not repeat them here, because time is pressing, but they concern you as well.

Farewell, I love you and embrace you with all my heart.

From Tocqueville | To his brother Édouard

Aboard the *Fourth of July*
November 26, 1831

I am beginning this letter, my dear brother, in the steamboat that is taking us from Pittsburgh to Cincinnati. I will not finish or date it for several days, when I reach the latter city. We are right now making our way down the Ohio, which at this spot is as broad as the Seine in Paris yet, as you can see on your map, still quite far from its junction with the Mississippi.

Just now the river is flowing through the most beautiful mountains in the world. Unfortunately, they are covered with snow. Winter has finally hit us. We encountered it in the middle of the Alleghenies, and it has been with us ever since. But we are fleeing, and in a week we will have nothing more to fear. Pittsburgh is what the French used to call Fort Duquesne, one of the causes of the war of 1754.[212] In America the French displayed extraordinary genius in the deployment of military posts. At a time when the interior of North America was still entirely unknown to Europeans, the French established posts in the middle of the wilderness from Canada to Louisiana—a series of small forts in places that have been recognized, now that the country has been thoroughly explored, as the best for building flourishing towns and attracting commerce and controlling navigation on the rivers. Here as in so many other situations we did the work of the English for them, while they reaped the benefits of an ambitious plan that they did not conceive. If we had succeeded, the English colonies would have been encircled along a broad arc with Quebec and New Orleans at the two extremes. Pressed in the rear by the French and their Indian allies, the Americans of the United States would not have rebelled against the mother country. They all acknowledge this. There would not have been an American Revolution, and perhaps not a French Revolution either, at least not under the conditions in which it took place.

The French in America had everything it takes to make a great nation. They are still the finest offspring of the European family in the New World. But overwhelmed by numbers, they inevitably succumbed. Their surrender was one of the most ignominious moments of the shameful reign of Louis XV.[213]

In Canada I have just seen a million stalwart, intelligent Frenchmen, perfect for the constitution one day of a great French nation in America, who live more or less as foreigners in their own country. The conquering people control commerce, employment, wealth, and power. They constitute the upper classes and

212. To defend their claims to the land against British challenges, French troops built Fort Duquesne in 1754 as one of a number of forts in the Ohio Valley and Great Lakes region. The fort was destroyed in 1758, during the Seven Years' War, and the British built Fort Pitt on a nearby site. The town of Pittsburgh grew up around this fort and had a population of approximately thirteen thousand people in 1831.

213. Louis XV (1710–1774) sat on the throne of France from the age of five until his death.

dominate the entire society. The vanquished people, wherever they lack vast numerical superiority, gradually lose their mores, their language, and their national character. There you have the effects of conquest, or, rather, of surrender.

The die has now been cast: all of North America will speak English. But are you not struck by how impossible it is for people to sense the future implications of current events, and how likely they are to grieve or rejoice without discernment? When the Battle of the Plains of Abraham, the death of Montcalm, and the shameful treaty of 1763 put England in possession of Canada and of a country larger than all of Europe that had formerly belonged to France, the English experienced a joy that was almost extravagant.[214] Neither the nation nor its greatest men suspected at the time that, because of this conquest, the colonies would no longer need the support of the mother country and would begin to aspire to independence, which twenty years later they would have, or that England would be dragged into a disastrous war that would leave her with a vastly increased debt. Or that, in this way, an immense nation would be created on the continent, a nation which, though speaking the English language, would become Britain's natural enemy and which is certainly destined to deprive it of its empire of the seas. . . .

From Tocqueville | To Ernest de Chabrol

Aboard the "Fourth of July" on the Ohio, November 26, 1831

My dear friend,

Today I want to say a word about civil justice in America, as I have been promising I would do for some time. But I warn you that my treatment of the subject will be very superficial, first because it is too vast to squeeze into a letter and second because my ideas are still very incomplete and I haven't had time to organize them.

Today I will confine myself to the "order of jurisdictions," which is what you seem most interested in. In doing so, I will inevitably touch on a number of other important points.

I will limit my remarks to the state of Pennsylvania, with whose laws I am most familiar, and it has the simplest of the various state codes. Listen carefully, because we are about to enter a world that will be totally new to you. Give up any notion of similarity between us and these people.

In the United States there two entirely distinct systems of civil courts: the federal courts and the state courts. Each state is an independent sovereign entity:

---

214. The Battle of Québec, also known as the Battle of the Plains of Abraham, was fought on September 12, 1759. When the forces commanded by General James Wolfe resisted French troops led by the marquis de Montcalm, French troops within the city decided to retreat from the spot that they had held against British siege for three months. General Montcalm, as well as General Wolfe, was killed in this short but important battle.

In 1763, the Treaty of Paris ended the Seven Years' War and ceded all French North American colonies to Great Britain.

that is the principle. The states have ceded certain of their rights to the Union: that is the exception.

Thus, certain cases, which have to do with international law, suits between states, and suits between citizens of one state and citizens of another or between Americans and foreigners, are judged by special tribunals known as courts of the United States.

For present purposes I have no need to discuss how these courts are organized. Suffice it to say that their jurisdiction is defined clearly enough that conflicts are said to be rare. That brings me to the civil courts that each state has established to deal with cases involving the interests of its own citizens, and I will use Pennsylvania as my example.

The permanent judiciary of Pennsylvania consists of two courts: the inferior court, or court of common pleas, comprises twelve judges; the superior court has five.

This simple description has probably led you to assume that the one of these courts hears appeals from the other, so that the inferior stands to the superior as our courts of first instance stand to the royal court. But in fact this happens only in certain special cases, which need not detain us here because they are exceptional.

Broadly speaking, it is fair to say that what we understand by "appeal" does not exist in Pennsylvania's civil procedure. The simplest way to explain how things work is to look at the progress of a case before the inferior court.

Pennsylvania is divided into twelve judicial districts, each of which contains a certain number of counties. These counties are much like our subprefectures. To each of the twelve judicial districts is assigned one of the twelve judges of the inferior court.

Every three months, this judge appears at least once in the county seat of each county, where he presides over a jury trial of civil suits on the county docket.

I must digress for a moment, my dear Chabrol, to tell you that you should be grateful to me for all this information, because the task of explaining all this is one of the most thankless imaginable. The subject is vast. To cut it down to size, I must cut to the quick, slashing right and left with no regard for logic, merely to provide you, after much arduous effort, with a wholly inadequate idea of the subject. But never mind: it's the intention that counts, not the result.

The court is composed, as you can see, of two parts: the judge and the jury. Different guarantees were required against errors of judgment by each.

The guarantees that American law provides against the errors of juries are quite unusual, and I suspect that you have no idea of what they are. This subject deserves a letter of its own. Guess what power the judge has in theory: the power to overturn a jury verdict *straightaway,* not only on grounds of *law* but also on grounds of *fact.*

That is the principle, but how is it actually applied in practice? In practice, the judge never overturns a verdict *on factual grounds* unless there is a gross error or it is clear that the jurors have been swayed by passion. By contrast, dismissals *on legal grounds* are common. Thus as you see, regardless of appearances and regardless of what people say, you may rest assured that, under English legislation, the power of juries to decide matters of law is a farce. No matter what the jury says, it is merely the judge's mouthpiece.

But, you may ask, since that is the way things are, why not divide the labor clearly between judge and jury? I think I could give you excellent reasons to justify the English method, but in the interest of sticking to the main subject at hand, I will leave that chore for another occasion.

So, there you have a first guarantee for the unfortunate plaintiff or defendant. But suppose that the judge does not use his power to dismiss the verdict summarily and allows it to stand. The losing party may then file a kind of appeal, which is called a writ of error. This is filed not with the higher court but with the very court of which his judge is a member, which meets in full panel every three months to hear such appeals. There, the appellant explains the case once again, files new motions, and produces new witnesses. He tries to prove either that the jurors were mistaken or that the judge misled them as to the law.

The court, on which the original trial judge himself sits, examines the record and either dismisses the appeal (which ends the case) or overturns the verdict, but without offering a new verdict of its own. It sends the case back for retrial before the same judge who previously heard it and who must now hear it again but with a new jury. If a new verdict is reached, it, too, can be appealed, and so on until the end of time, *theoretically speaking.*

In practice, however, when the full court has twice overturned a verdict, the judge who rendered it gives in to his colleagues, and the jury follows his recommendation.

Now you are more or less familiar with the English system as it is applied in Pennsylvania. As you see, I was right to say that, strictly speaking, there is no such thing here as an appeal. The case is in a sense submitted to the same judge who has already delivered his verdict. The full court that considers the writ of error does not deliver its own judgment, as our Cour d'Appel do. Rather, it proceeds in the manner of the Cour de Cassation, except that it judges the case as to the facts as well as the law and then refers it back to the same judge rather than appointing a new one.

At this point you are probably wondering what the superior court is for. Normally, the superior court has no connection with the inferior court. It acts in a higher sphere, but entirely independently. It is legally responsible for hearing cases of a certain gravity. It is a more enlightened tribunal, ranked higher by public opinion but not *hierarchically* superior to the court of common pleas. Within its sphere of action, it renders judgment just like the lower court and follows absolutely the same rules.

You now have a general though incomplete idea of the judicial system of Pennsylvania. What distinguishes this state from other states of the Union is the fact that it has eliminated certain special tribunals found in English law and allowed by most of the other states. For example, in Pennsylvania there is strictly speaking no court of Doctors' Commons, the purpose of which is to decide all cases pertaining to marriages and wills.

There is also no Court of Chancery, which is such an important part of the English judicial system. The Pennsylvanians have folded the jurisdiction of both of these courts into that of the court of common pleas. The result is a simpler but less comprehensive set of laws, for there are things that these two special courts could do but the court of common pleas cannot, such as enforcing contracts. Under the customs of England, which still have force of law here, the court of common pleas can only impose damages in case of failure to carry out a contract. The Court of Chancery has the power to compel execution of the contract to the letter.

That is all I can tell you today about civil law. As I said earlier, it's pitiful to abridge such a subject so drastically. I have made numerous notes and observations. For better or for worse, I think I could write a book about the subject, especially in regard to the jury: how it is constituted, what rules it must follow, and how useful it is.

I hope we someday have a chance to discuss all these things to our hearts' content. For now I must leave you. I haven't told you anything about justices of the peace, because I already discussed them with Elie, who must have shown you my letter. What I said is accurate. About everything else, it contains bold opinions that it would be dangerous to take literally.

In the next letter, I will try to say something about criminal law. That will be simpler and easier.

Farewell, my good friend, I embrace you with all my heart. Regards to all my colleagues.

November 28

My dear friend,

Marie will tell you that these lines came close to being the last ones I ever sent you. Two nights ago, our ship, driven by the current and all the force of steam, was cracked open like a nut on a rock in the middle of the Ohio. The sound of the collision, we later learned, could be heard a quarter of a league away. Shouts of "We sink!"[215] were heard at once. The ship, crew, and passengers all seemed headed for kingdom come.

I have never heard a more sickening sound that that of the water rushing into the ship. But that is not what I wanted to discuss in continuing this letter, other than to tell you not to mention this accident to my family.

My intention was to let you know that I've just given an American a letter of recommendation addressed to you. He is a young man whom I do not know, but he is a friend of the famous Robert . . . ,[216] the great American penitentiary

215. In English in the original.
216. Robert Vaux.

expert, with whom we became intimately acquainted, as you might imagine. He is also the nephew of the wealthiest man in Philadelphia, who welcomed us with open arms. You will therefore be doing me a favor to welcome this man warmly, should he turn up. I think he is looking for information about our judicial system. If you think it worthwhile, you might introduce him to legal scholars such as Elie, Carné, and others you may know. In any case, do your best.

I am in a hurry and have only enough time to embrace you.

From Tocqueville | To his sister-in-law Émilie

On the Ohio, November 28, 1831

. . . I've already *roamed* this world quite a bit. I have seen people in positions different from ours but no proof that anyone is fundamentally better off. Here, for example, I see reduced versions of all the ugly political passions that our revolutions have made so glaring in France. But I will stop there for fear of *lapsing* into considerations of high politics, philosophy, metaphysics, economics, and ethics from which I would be unable to extricate myself without putting you to sleep. In any case, I was saying that America is no better than France. Let me take for example what is called, in the style of madrigal, the fair sex. I confess that from a certain point of view, this country is the El Dorado of married men, and that one can almost certainly find perfect happiness here if one has no romantic imagination and asks nothing of one's wife other than to make tea and raise one's children, which, as everyone knows, is the most fundamental of the duties of marriage. In these two respects, American women excel. They are reasonable people who stick to the basics, as people say, who confine themselves to their teapots and never leave their homes once they have uttered the famous "yes." Yet despite this incontestable advantage, which I freely grant, I often find myself asking whether ultimately—note that I say ultimately—they do not bear a prodigious resemblance to European women. I beg you, do not look at me as a woebegone philosopher, but hear my reasons. I am going to lay them before you in four points. My first and greatest reason is that before marrying, they all have a flirtation that surpasses our best efforts in this regard. To be sure, there is no question here of love in the strict sense, and that is a great boon for the tranquility of the society. I have not heard of a single person hanged or drowned anywhere in the Union since the Declaration of Independence. There are no fights, and there is no talk of impetuous actions. Young women are perfectly free to choose, and yet their choice always falls on the man whom the family notary would have chosen had he been consulted. As you can see, I am impartial. Yet it remains true that they are outrageously flirtatious. I confess that their flirtatiousness is *reasonable* and that their advances almost never fail to be addressed to men who, apart from their qualities (advantages to which too much attention is often paid in Europe), also have the benefit of a respectable income. This fact does honor to their uprightness of spirit. What remains to be understood is how such accomplished women achieve so little until (but only until) they marry, having been flirtatious up to the very day, and how suddenly they cease to be so from that day on. How can one explain so sudden a change at so convenient a moment? I could accept a miracle once by chance, but if the miracle recurs day after day, I can no longer understand what is going on. Might one not assume, might it not be possible to imagine, would we not have certain reasons to believe—you see how circumspect I am, and sufficiently skeptical—that the recovery is merely apparent and that the flirtatiousness remains, though it cannot show itself? As travelers invariably remark, the fact is that married women in America are nearly all languid and feeble. I am not far from thinking that they are all ill, afflicted with repressed flirtatiousness. Why not? Don't we daily see men turned green as meadows from repressed ambition? In any event, this is pure speculation, to which I do not personally attach much value. But I've said enough to prove that, all things considered, it's still better to live in France than in America. . . .

Beaumont | Diary fragments

[December 1831]

December 1 [1831], departure from Wheeling, ten miles from Pittsburg[h], on the steamboat [*New Jersey*]. The Ohio covered with ice. Its banks covered with snow. Navigation said to be dangerous at night, especially when the night is dark. Yet we continue on . . . around midnight, cry of alarm: "All lost!" It was the voice of the captain, we had hit a reef (Burlington Bar). Our boat was smashed. It was visibly sinking. Stunning sight: two hundred passengers on board and only two lifeboats, each capable of holding ten or twelve people. The water kept rising. It was already filling the cabins. Admirable calm of the American women. There were fifty of them. Not a single cry at the prospect of imminent death. Tocqueville and I took one look at the Ohio, which was more than a mile wide at this point and filled with enormous floating chunks of ice. We shook hands in a mark of farewell. . . . Suddenly, the ship stopped sinking. Its hull was hung up on the very reef that had smashed it. What saved it was the depth of the gash and the rapidity with which the inrushing water caused it to settle onto the rock. . . .

Out of danger. . . . But what would become of us now, stuck in the middle of the river like prisoners on pontoons?

Another steamboat, the *William Parsons,* passes and takes us on board. . . . We continue our route. . . . December 2, arrive in Cincinnati, hasten to depart again; the cold urges us on. . . . The 3rd, departure from Cincinnati. . . . Severe cold. On the 4th our boat stops, caught in the ice. Twenty-four hours spent in a little creek, where we had taken refuge while awaiting a thaw. The thaw never comes. The cold grows worse.

The captain decides to deposit us on the riverbank, which we approach by gradually breaking the ice and thus opening a passage for our boat.

Debark in West Port, a small Kentucky village about 25 miles from Louisville.

Burlington Bar on the Ohio between Pittsburgh and Wheeling, three miles from the place where the steam-boat Fourth of July *broke up on November 25, 1831, at 7 in the evening. House where we spent the night. This is the most picturesque spot one could find to have a shipwreck and drown.* (GB2)

Impossible to locate a wagon or horses to take us to Louisville. We must walk. Our baggage loaded onto a cart, which we escort. We walk all day through the woods in half a foot of snow. America is still nothing but forest.

Evening of December 7, arrive in Louisville. Same problem there. The Ohio is no more navigable here than in West Port. What to do? Retrace our steps? Revisit places already seen? Unacceptable. But how to go on?—Means of salvation: we are told to head overland to a more southern location, where Mississippi navigation is never hindered by ice. Someone directs us to Memphis, a small town in Tennessee on the left bank of the Mississippi . . . roughly four hundred miles (nearly 150 leagues).

On the 9th, leave Louisville on the Nashville stagecoach, two days and two nights on the road. Upon reaching Nashville, we are pained to learn that the Cumberland (a tributary of the Ohio) is frozen.

December 11, departure from Nashville. As we travel southward, we encounter more biting cold. Never in living memory can anyone recall such a thing, we are told. This is what people always say to those who come but once. . . . Cold ten degrees below freezing. The cold is getting steadily worse. Our stagecoach turns into a wagon with open benches. Horrible roads. Steep descents. Restricted view. The road is nothing but a passage cut through the forest. The stumps of badly cut trees mark the trail, and we're constantly running into them. Only ten leagues per day.—An American says to me, "You have some very bad roads in France, don't you?" "Yes, sir, and you have some fine ones in America?" He doesn't understand me. American pride.

After Nashville, not a city on our route. There are just a few scattered villages all the way to Memphis.

On December 11, a piece of the suspension and a wheel broke, and then an axle. Half the distance on foot. We curse our fate. Others ask why we are complaining. The day before yesterday one traveler broke an arm on the road, another broke a leg.

On the 12th the cold gets even worse. We take a ferry across the Tennessee, on which float huge cakes of ice. Tocqueville is frozen through and shivering. He has lost his appetite. His head is affected. Impossible to go on, we must stop. . . . Where? How? No inn on the road. Extreme anxiety. The stage continues on. . . . At last, a house: Sandy Bridge (place name), log house! Never mind. We get off there.

December 13: What a day! What a night! The bed Tocqueville slept in is in a room whose walls are made of rough-hewn oak logs piled one on top of another. It's cold enough to split rock. I light a huge fire. The fire crackles on the hearth, stirred by the wind that blows right through all four walls. Moonlight seeps in through the gaps between the logs as well. Tocqueville cannot get warm unless he smothers himself beneath his sheet and all the blankets I pile on top of him. No help to be had from our hosts. Depths of our isolation and abandonment. What to do? What will happen if the illness gets worse. What is this illness? Where to find a doctor? The nearest one is more than 30 miles

View from Wheeling, Ohio, 29 November 1831. (GB2)

away. Need more than two days to get him and return. Upon my return what will I find?

Mr. and Mrs. Harris (our hosts), small Tennessee landowners. They have slaves. As slave owners, they do nothing. The husband hunts, hikes, rides horseback. Certain airs of a gentleman. Petty aristocrats with feudal habits, offering hospitality to travelers in exchange for a hundred *sous* a day.

The 14th, Tocqueville better. It may not be an illness. Too weak to start out again, however. Hard to find food that suits him. Prodigious diplomatic effort to obtain from Mrs. Harris a rabbit that Mr. Harris has killed, which I feed to my patient instead of the eternal *beacon* [*sic*] (hog meat).

December 15th, major progress; the 16th, Tocqueville completely well; appetite returns. Very eager to escape this inhospitable place as soon as possible. The Nashville–Memphis stagecoach passes. What a stagecoach! Tocqueville climbs aboard, not without difficulty. The cold is still intense. Two days and two nights on the road. Further accidents, not serious but not without suffering.

December 17, arrive in Memphis. Alas! The Mississippi is also covered with ice, and navigation has come to a halt.

Memphis!! As grand as Beaumont-la-Chartre. What a place to land! Nothing to see, neither people nor things.[217] Our walks in the forests of Tennessee. Tocqueville pleased after killing two parrots with the most charming plumage. We find Shakespeare and Milton in a log cabin.

December 24. The cold recedes suddenly.—In the evening, a steamboat (the *Louisville*) arrives. It is headed downstream. In a few days, it takes us to New Orleans, where we are now: January 1, 1832.

From Beaumont | To his brother Jules

On the Ohio, December 4, 1831

I have just left Cincinnati, my dear Jules. I find myself aboard a boat steaming westward down the Ohio, which eventually will join the Mississippi. We decided to travel to Charleston by way of New Orleans. This is certainly not the shortest route on the map, but there is no doubt that we will get to Charleston faster this way than by any other route. Tomorrow morning we will be in Louisville (a city on the banks of the Ohio in the state of Kentucky). Once we board another ship in that city, we will make nearly a hundred leagues per day and by our calculations should reach New Orleans in seven or eight days at most. The steamboats that travel the Ohio and Mississippi are on the whole quite handsome and comfortable vessels. Each passenger has a bed. Three good meals are served every day. To be sure, there is the men's side and the women's side, as in the public baths. *The two sexes* come together only to eat. Since Americans are not very talkative, it is rare for a man to speak to a woman at dinner, even when they know each other. Otherwise, we spend the time reading, writing, looking

217. About fifty-five hundred people lived in Shelby County, Tennessee, which includes the town of Memphis.

at scenery, and composing questions. At times the boat vibrates so badly because of the steam engine that it is impossible to write legibly. Today it so happens that the boat I'm on is enjoying an unusually smooth ride, so I decided to write you a short note whose length will be determined by how long it takes us to reach Louisville. I want to post my letter from there, because as I travel farther from where you are, letters take longer to reach New York. Although I wrote to Eugénie three days ago for the packet boat of December 10, I don't think that my letter from today will arrive soon enough for any boat but the one scheduled for the 20th. I want you to receive news from me with each packet boat, but I can see that it will very soon become almost impossible to stick to this resolution. Nevertheless, I will remain punctual as long as I can. I do not know which among the inhabitants of Beaumont-la-Chartre, Le Guillet, and Gallerande was guilty most recently of being less scrupulously prompt than I am, but what is certain is that someone is *to blame.*

Your letter of September 25 reached me via the October 1 packet boat from Le Havre. This is the letter that contains a sketch of the political situation in France and some very interesting clippings from several newspapers regarding recent sessions of the Chamber of Deputies.[218] This letter interested me greatly, and I want to thank you profusely for all the details you provided. But my joy in receiving it was somewhat diminished by a really unfortunate thing that occurred at the same time: the packet boat that left Le Havre on October 10 arrived in New York on the same day as the packet boat of the 1st, and it brought me no letter. My father told me in one of his last letters that you had all agreed to write me in turn. I have told you what I think of this arrangement, which seems seriously flawed to me, in that it destroys all hope of receiving more than one letter at a time. Yet as bad as this procedure is, now that you have adopted it, you must at least stick to it. Otherwise I will suffer in any case: if the person who is supposed to write because it is his turn does not write, I won't receive a letter from anyone, because the others will have respected the agreement and not written. So anyone who fails this way in his *duty* bears a twofold responsibility: he is guilty not only of having failed to write but also of having prevented others from writing. I confess that I have no philosophy to help me bear disappointments of this kind, and I think that I would be quite *angry* if I did not recall a time when I received more letters than I wrote. What is happening right now is an abject expiation of sins in this regard. I am not sure that the punishment does not exceed the crime, because in the period when I incurred this guilt only fifty leagues separated me from those from whom I am now separated by an ocean. I mention these *reproaches* all the more readily in this letter to you, my dear Jules, because I have fewer of them to make to you personally. The good, long letters that do reach me most promptly are the best consolation for all that

218. Casimir Pierre Périer (1777–1832) was president of the Chamber of Deputies. The chamber was debating the appropriateness of the force that Périer had used to put down riots in Paris that year.

I still await. So note well that my complaints are in no way directed at you. I alert you to them as one tells a friend about what one has suffered. I nevertheless confess that I would be pleased to know that *the guilty parties* are made aware of them.

I won't respond to all the things you tell me about politics in France. The answer arrives so long after the question that it is quite difficult for the interlocutors to understand each other. In any case, the events you've described for me are already old, and they will be older still when my letter reaches you. Others, perhaps more serious, will already have replaced them, so the discussion would be both pointless and uninteresting. So I think it would be better to continue as we have done thus far, with each of us playing the role that appears to have been assigned to us by our respective positions: you will speak to me of France, and I will speak to you of America.

I have just spent four days in Cincinnati, the principal city of Ohio. It is perhaps the strangest city I have seen. I do not believe that there is another city in the world that has grown so prodigiously. Thirty years ago, the banks of the Ohio were empty. Cincinnati is now a city of 30,000.[219] Its population has doubled in the last five years. The entire state of Ohio is no less extraordinary to behold. Its population is now one million, all of whom arrived over the past thirty years. An air of universal well-being and prosperity is evident everywhere. The soil is extremely fertile, and no region could be better situated for commercial ventures. These traits are easy to see, but when it comes to examining the society more closely, it becomes rather difficult to gauge its true character and complexion. The population of Ohio is composed of many disparate elements. The first people to settle in the region came from New England, from which a large number of immigrants still come every year. At the same time, others came and are still coming from Virginia and the other southern states, whose mores are very different from those of the North. Finally, there are in Ohio Germans and Irish who have come from Europe and who are still arriving with different ideas and different mores.[220] All these various peoples find themselves blended into one, and this alloy constitutes a moral person whose character would be rather difficult to draw. The character of this society is not to have a character.

The state of Ohio is remarkable in other respects as well. Of all the United States it is perhaps the one in which democracy has been pushed to its most rigorous consequences. It reigns there in all *its purity,* and a European who had not had a foretaste of republican government before coming to Ohio would be unable to conceive how the unrestricted republican principles that prevail there

219. In 1820, just over 9,600 people lived in Cincinnati, but by 1830, the population had nearly tripled to just under 25,000. The city continued to grow rapidly.

220. Both ethnic groups remained a fairly small percentage of the population, but they represented the largest groups of immigrants. Most Germans farmed or worked at skilled trades in cities, and the majority of Ohio Irish worked in manual labor, particularly in canal and railroad construction.

can serve as the basis of a society. Equality of political rights is total, and no one is denied the right to vote. Since everyone in Ohio is a new arrival, they do not know one another well. In such an instant society, no one is subjected to the influence of long-established mores. Memories have no hold on a people born yesterday. Unknown to one another, they are not subject to the influence that domestic virtues normally exert. Enjoying the same political rights, each person proceeds in total freedom, with nothing to restrain his interests or passions.

Such a state of affairs would be ideal if the people were never wrong, but their judgment is less sure than their passions, and they are in the habit of yielding to whoever flatters them the most. They are grossly deceived again and again by the most cunning intriguers, who court them shamelessly and whose true nature it is impossible to discover in a place where everything—people as well as things—is new. In the last elections in Ohio, the people elected to the legislature an unknown attorney who only three years earlier had distinguished himself selling cookies on the streets of Cincinnati. The people had confidence in him because he was one of them. To succeed in an election, candidates must enter into very intimate relations with citizens (and everybody is a citizen). They have to drink with them in their taverns, ask for their votes, etc. Any man who enjoys a modicum of distinction by dint of his education and social position would never want to do this. So everyone whom the people of Ohio choose to govern them is more or less mediocre. Yet this society is full of life and prosperity. The source of its vitality is not its extreme democracy, however, as European demagogues maintain. To anyone willing to see things as they are, it is obvious that its prosperity stems from material causes quite independent of this democratic excess, *despite which* it prospers. One of the most important reasons for its rapid progress can be found in its political constitution, which prohibits slavery. Two of the states that share borders with Ohio—Virginia and Kentucky—are home to large numbers of slaves, and there can be no doubt that the existence of slavery in a state is harmful.[221] Without this constitutional ban, slavery would have insinuated itself into Ohio, and that would have been a great evil. During my stay in Cincinnati I saw an example of the influence of slavery and freedom on the prosperity of states. Cincinnati, which is part of the free state of Ohio, is just across the river from Kentucky, where there are slaves. The soil of Kentucky is as fertile as that of Ohio. The two states enjoy absolutely identical material advantages. Yet Ohio enjoys a prosperity to which Kentucky does not even come close. The latter state was founded twenty years earlier than the former, yet its population is only 500,000, whereas Ohio's is a million.[222] The reason for this difference is that immigration flows by and large to the free state and flees

221. Article 6 of the Northwest Ordinance of 1787 had prohibited slavery in all states created from the Northwest Territory. Ohio affirmed this principle in its state constitution. In 1830, Kentucky had just over 165,000 slaves and Virginians owned nearly 470,000 slaves.
222. Kentucky's free population was over 500,000; its total population was 687,917 in 1830.

the slave state. Second—and this is the main reason—wherever there are slaves, labor, which is their exclusive attribute, is considered to be dishonorable and unworthy of free men. So in every slave state a part of the population does not work. Another point to consider is that in free states everyone works for himself, whereas in slave states the slaves *do not work for themselves.* It is easy to see why their labor is therefore less productive than free labor.

I must now end my description of Ohio, my dear friend. Although I began my letter on December 4, I am finishing on the 5th. It is only 8 in the morning, and we are approaching Louisville. . . .

From Tocqueville | To Jared Sparks

Cincinnati, December 2, 1831

. . . The farther I travel from Massachusetts, sir, the more seriously I regret not having remained there longer. Nowhere in the parts of the Union that I have explored since leaving Boston have I found town institutions that seem to me to come anywhere near those established in New England. Of course I may not yet be a very competent judge of the truth of this assertion, but the educated men in the states I have visited all agree. It would therefore have been immensely important for me to have studied on the spot the principles, forms, and means of action of *local government,* of which we in France have long felt the need and searched for a model. There is nothing more difficult than trying to understand how such machinery works by reading descriptions in books, especially books that contain no general ideas and adopt no methodical order. The only work from which I have thus far been able to derive any enlightenment about the *practical* workings of your town system is entitled *Town Officer.*[223] It was pointed out to me by Mr. Quincy, the president of the University of Cambridge.[224] This is a book without literary or philosophical merit, and its purely practical value still presupposes a reader familiar with local customs and laws, so that I fear I may often have gone astray in reading it.

The first thing that struck me about this work was the large number of different officials included in your municipal magistracy. For instance, in addition to the principal officials, the work in question considers various other public officials, such as fence viewers, field driver, fire ward, hog reeve, measurer of wood, parish officers, sealer of weights and measures, surveyor of highways, surveyor of lumber, town clerk, tithingmen. . . . Do these officials exist *in fact* or only in law? Do they exist everywhere, or only in large *townships*? I cannot make out the answers to these questions.

If these officials are in fact appointed every year, do they fill the exact roles ascribed to them by the author of *The Town Officer*? I am still in the dark on this

223. Isaac Goodwin, *The Town Officer; or, Laws of Massachusetts Relative to the Duties of Municipal Officers* (Worcester, MA, 1825).
224. Josiah Quincy III (1772–1864), a former Federalist politician, served as president of Harvard University from 1829 to 1845.

point. I know only that in all countries there is a wide gap between the letter of the law and its execution. I see in the article "Selectman" that when the selectmen see that a resident of the town is squandering his health or wealth on habitual drinking, they are supposed to post that individual's name in the taverns, and tavern keepers then may not serve them wine or spirits. The selectmen are also supposed to submit to a probate judge the name of anyone whose misconduct is serious enough to result in proscription. Do selectmen in fact have these powers, and, more important, do they use them?

Another example: the constable and tithingmen are supposed to see to it that Sunday is observed as a day of rest. They are supposed to prosecute blasphemers and gamblers. They are supposed to stop people traveling on Sunday, inquire about their reasons for traveling, and prevent them from continuing on their way if the reasons offered are deemed inadequate. Haven't such laws fallen into disuse?[225]

There is one article in particular in which I confess I am unable to understand anything, the one entitled "Parish and Parish Officers." Indeed, it seems to imply that each town is obliged to support a Protestant minister or else pay a fine to the county's court of common pleas. To a certain extent this seems to me to establish a state religion and to mix politics and religion in a way that Americans appear to have taken care to avoid.[226]

Somewhat farther on I read that any town resident may quit a parish, but only on condition of joining another. From this I conclude that the law requires everyone to have a religion, even though it takes no position regarding the various Protestant communions.

I thought that each congregation here had the exclusive right to hire or fire its own pastor, but I see from reading *The Town Officer* that the religious congregation designated by the name "parish" can dismiss a pastor only in specific instances and according to certain prescribed procedures, which would seem to make the minister a sort of civil official. On all these points there are obviously certain general principles of which I am ignorant and which would supply me with the key I need to understand all the rest.

Broadly speaking, I am beginning to be fairly familiar with the *structural* features of your municipal organization. I see the letter of the law, but its spirit escapes me. I know the statutes but lack the facts. It seems that, theoretically speaking, you did not choose for the unincorporated towns the same representative system that you established everywhere else. Your towns seem to me to *gov-*

225. In his letter of February 2, 1832, Sparks replied that public officials fulfilled the duties of their appointments quite strictly. Though Tocqueville worried that the execution of these duties might lead to oppression, he came to agree with Sparks that the election of public officials guaranteed liberty to the American people.

226. In 1780, Massachusetts passed a law that required every person to belong to a church, which could tax its members. Though this law allowed individuals to choose the church to which they belonged, it in fact supported Congregationalism as the state religion. Massachusetts was the last state to disestablish a state church in 1833.

ern themselves in the natural sense of the word, like the towns of antiquity. The management of town affairs is not entrusted to a corps of administrators elected annually. The people are *directly* in charge, and the selectmen must consult them in regard to all important measures; the selectmen are purely and simply the executors of the people's will.

These, I believe, are the principles of the law. Am I mistaken? How are these principles put into practice, and what are their effects? This is no less important to know, and no book can teach me. Is the entire town actually consulted very often? What is the nature of these assemblies? How are delicate matters dealt with, and is it possible to adopt any systematic form of administration? Don't centers of intrigue develop, and aren't these assemblies, like all large popular assemblies, likely to be swayed by passion far more than argument? . . .

From Tocqueville | To his mother

Louisville, December 6, 1831

We arrived here this morning, my dear Maman, and we will attempt to depart again this very day for New Orleans. We are eager to reach more temperate latitudes. The difference between this continent and Europe with respect to cold is incredible. Right now I believe that we are at the latitude of Sicily, yet it's several degrees below freezing. The ground is covered with snow and the rivers with floating ice. The winter here is like winter in the north of France. Travel becomes difficult and depressing in such weather. Fortunately, in another week we will be in a tropical climate. I don't know if we had already decided to go to Louisiana when I wrote my last letter. What persuaded us to take this route was what we learned in Cincinnati: the route through Kentucky is considered impracticable in this season, so it turned out to be shorter to travel down the Mississippi with all its twists and turns rather than take the shortcut by land. We will barely touch down in New Orleans in order to reserve as much time as possible for Charleston and Washington.

We were quite pleased with our stay in Cincinnati, which we found extremely interesting. We had no idea about the western states. One can judge them rapidly when one has seen the others, but one wouldn't be able to imagine them without seeing them. Everything that is good and bad about American society stands out here with such relief that it's like reading a book with large letters intended to teach children how to read. Things here are inconsistent and extreme. Nothing has yet found its final place: the society is growing more rapidly than its people. Thirty years ago, the place where Cincinnati now stands was still blanketed with forest. The sight of this city today is unlike anything I've ever seen. Signs of its rapid growth are everywhere: beautiful houses and humble cottages, barely paved streets, imperfectly aligned and clogged with construction materials; places without names, houses without numbers—it's more like a blueprint for a city than a city. Amid these crude structures, however, one hears the sounds of life, of a population whose activity has something feverish about it. That is Cincinnati today. It may not be like this tomorrow. Each day leaves it unrecognizable even to the people who live there. When Europeans came to America, they left much of their past tradition behind them, along with their institutions and the mores of their homeland. They built a society that is in some ways analogous to that of Europe but which in fundamental ways is radically different. Over the past forty years, another swarm of emigrants has arisen from the bosom of this new society and headed west, as their forefathers once headed for the coasts of New England, South Carolina, Virginia, and Maryland. Like their forefathers, they relinquished the ideas of their homeland along with the soil to which they were born, and in the Mississippi Valley they founded a new society that no longer bears any analogy to the past and that remains attached to Europe solely by language. One must really come here to judge what is surely the most singular state of affairs that has ever existed under the sun. A people absolutely devoid of precedents, traditions, habits, or even ruling ideas has unhesitatingly charted a new course in civil, political, and criminal legislation. It has done so without casting so much as a glance at the wisdom of other peoples or the memory of the past. Rather, it has built its institutions, like its roads, in the midst of the forests in which it has chosen to live and where it is certain of encountering neither waypoints nor obstacles. It is a society still without political or hierarchical bonds, without social or religious ties, in which each individual is a power unto himself because it pleases him to be so and not to look out for his neighbor, a democracy without limit or measure. In the other states of the Union there is virtually no patronage based on wealth or birth, but there are personal influences. In the West, no one has been able to make a name for himself or had the time to establish a reputation. With this final barrier gone, democracy has here been able to reveal itself with all of its distinctive attributes: its fecklessness, its violent passions, its instability, and its restless character. These people inhabit the most fertile land in the world. There are only a million of them in a state that could accommodate ten million. And do you think they have settled down? Not at all: they are once again on the march. Thousands of them cross every year to the right bank of the Mississippi, where they will claim still newer tracts of wilderness. Indeed, there is in America a race of men known as pioneers, whose taste for the adventurous life rises to the level of passion. The pioneers lead the white race on its march into the American wilderness, serving as a sort of advance guard whose mission it is to drive out the Indians by destroying their game and to explore the forests and map out a path for the civilization that will follow.

The nomadic families of the pioneers settle in the loneliest of places. There they live for a few years in almost savage freedom. When the sedentary population begins to overtake them, they pick up stakes and plunge still further west with their women and children. One might say that the perils and miseries of existence have for them taken on an ineffable charm. Solitude has become as necessary to them as society is to other men. They need to work new soil, to pluck out old roots, to cut down trees, to do battle with wild animals and Indians. They take pleasure in these things, just as other men take pleasure in tapping a large income and living within four walls. . . .

From Tocqueville | To Ernest de Chabrol

Louisville, December 6, 1831

My dear friend,

You must forgive me for writing such a brief letter today, because we've been dragged from place to place without a moment's respite.

I've dated this letter from Louisville, but I am writing you from the Ohio River, before landing at Louisville. This river travel definitely does not suit us. Although we are at the latitude of Palermo and it is only December 6, the cold this morning was so intense that the Ohio has frozen. Nobody was prepared for this.

At the moment, we are forced to cut our way slowly through the ice. With the help of the current and steam, we are still managing to make headway, but so much is being demanded of the boat that we are afraid it may not hold together. On top of that, your ears freeze if you so much as stick your head outside: it's as cold as a Russian winter. Nobody here recalls having seen anything like it.

The new western states through which we have been traveling have provided us with the opportunity to make hundreds of unexpected observations. You have no idea of a social state like this. It beggars the imagination. You have heard that when Europeans came to the New World, they left behind all the national prejudices and habits of their ancestors in order to build society on a new foundation. This is true.

Well! The new settlers of the western states are to the old what the earlier settlers were to Europe. A second emigration has rid them of the last vestiges of the earlier settlers' influence for good or ill.

The result is a society in which everything is new: laws, institutions, mores, and ideas. The experience and wisdom of the past count for nothing. Man has boldly and forthrightly set out on the path of endless innovation, accepting no rules other than those of his reason and his fancy. It is a society in which the individual stands forth everywhere, where each man is himself because there is as yet no public opinion to which he must pay homage and no conventional ideas to create a family resemblance among different minds.

In this country, where democracy is free not only of the obstacles that rank may elsewhere put in its way but also of the personal influences that some men might exert if they had had the time to establish their reputations, laws change as rapidly as fortunes and as the face of the earth itself.

Amidst the chaotic tumult of growth, everything seems to thrust and collide, yet the public prosperity is immense. Society is visibly growing. Industry and wealth stand out everywhere. Yet will this immense prosperity come as a result of democracy or in spite of it, because of its laws or in spite of them?

That is a question that your servant finds quite difficult and has no time to discuss.

Farewell, I hope to be able to write you a long letter from New Orleans, in which I will answer your questions about public education.

I embrace you with all my heart.

Right now the boat is creaking from stem to stern.

From Beaumont | To his mother

Sandy Bridge, December 15, 1831.

Before giving you any details of my travels, dear mother, I must tell you about the place in which I find myself at this moment. Sandy Bridge is nothing more than a small inn built of logs piled one atop the other.[227] It stands on the road from Nashville (the capital of Tennessee)[228] to Memphis, a small town on the banks of the Mississippi between the 34th and 35th degrees of latitude, almost on the border between Tennessee and the state of Mississippi. In the room in which I am writing there are three beds, upon which visiting travelers hurl themselves regardless of number or sex. A huge fire is burning in a fireplace similar to what one might find in an ancient castle. It is large enough to hold ten logs, each with a circumference of three feet. Despite a fire hot enough to roast an ox, the room is freezing. A short time ago, someone brought me a glass of water, but I was imprudent enough to let it stand for five minutes before trying to drink it, and when I went to take it, I found that it had frozen solid. There were two reasons for this: first, it is eight or ten degrees outside, and second, between the logs that make up the wall of the inn there are gaps large enough for air to circulate freely. The harsh cold and the half a foot of snow that has come with it are rather unusual for this degree of latitude, which is that of Egypt. But the climate in America is like this: in the southern states, where the summer heat is excessive, people die of cold during the winter.

To get back to my lodging, you know that it is located on the road from Nashville to Memphis, but I haven't yet described its actual geographical situation. I can't give you a very clear indication, because on the road in question there is not a single town or place that is marked on any map. But imagine a straight line from Nashville to the place where you can use my previous explanations to locate Memphis. This line represents a distance of about a hundred leagues. I am 35 leagues from Nashville and 60 leagues from Memphis. Now you can see fairly clearly where I am. My hosts are very upstanding people, quite proud though innkeepers and quite lazy though poor. They are proud because they live in a land of slaves. There is not a single small landowner, no matter how down-at-heels, who does not own two or three Negroes. In the home of any white family, Negroes are as much an obligatory part of the furniture as an armchair or a table. As a result, anyone who is not black and who is therefore free looks upon himself as a privileged person, so that in this region color is a veritable title of nobility. The convenience of being served by slaves makes

227. Tocqueville and Beaumont had set out from Louisville for Memphis, Tennessee, in a carriage. When Tocqueville became ill, they stopped in Sandy Bridge, Tennessee, for several days.

228. Nashville had a population of approximately fifty-five hundred people.

whites indolent and lazy, and the fertility of the soil, which yields a good crop without much labor, favors this disposition. Last but not least, the climate, which is extremely hot during the summer, encourages this penchant. In any case, I believe that the influence of the climate is less important than the influence of slavery, because if men were indolent or laborious depending on the degree of heat or cold registered by the thermometer, the people of this region, who are so idle during the summer, ought to become quite active during the winter. But this does not happen. My small landowner considers labor to be a degrading thing, which is rightfully left to slaves. He has feudal habits: he spends his time hunting, riding, or doing nothing. He has a superb carbine, which he uses skillfully to hunt deer and other game. He has no trouble at all killing birds with bullets. His carbine is so heavy that I can barely carry it. This morning I wanted to do a little hunting. I scoured the woods for an hour or two. There I saw a good many delightful birds, including red and yellow parrots of matchless beauty. But armed as I was, I wasn't able to kill a single one. While hiking together, my little republican lord asked me who owned the woods in France. He saw no benefit in private ownership of the forests because he is surrounded by woods that no one owns and no one bothers to claim. When we need fuel, someone goes to the forest and cuts down a big oak tree, and our lord's slaves have soon cut it up into logs.

You are no doubt wondering what I am doing in this Sandy Bridge inn, where I seem to have settled in without any idea of when I may leave. To help you out, let me say that on the way here from Nashville I rode in an uncovered carriage that looked for all the world like a farm wagon with benches. Tocqueville and I found ourselves in the company of several other travelers, traveling by night and day and each more frozen than the next. Fortune decided that we needed to warm up, however, and sent three minor accidents our way, nearly ending our journey on the open road in the middle of the forest: first, the undercarriage broke, then a wheel, and finally an axle. With the help of some oak trees that we cut down in the forest that surrounded us from the beginning to the end of our journey, we managed to fix up our poor dogcart, which was coming apart at the seams and *limping on all fours* by the time we arrived in Sandy Bridge. Now you can understand why we were unable to continue on. Until the legs of our mount have been repaired, we must resign ourselves to remain here. But you may be wondering now why the devil we went to Nashville? And for what purpose are we going to Memphis?

I will answer your questions at once. You may recall that in my last letter to Jules, I told him that I had arrived in Louisville aboard a steamboat making its way down the Ohio. It is a fact that as I was finishing my letter, everyone aboard was saying, "We are no more than seven or eight leagues from Louisville." It should have taken no more than two hours to get there at the boat's usual pace. But all at once our progress was halted by an invincible and totally unexpected obstacle. For two or three days the weather had been very cold. The freeze was so severe that the Ohio was clogged with ice. Nevertheless, boats continued to operate. Imagine our dismay when we discovered, just as we were to arrive in Louisville, that the river had frozen solid and our boat had been forced to a halt. The distance of seven or eight leagues, which would have been nothing for our boat, became an immense obstacle for us. We were cast out on the bank of the river with all our belongings in a small village called Westport. There it proved impossible to find any means of transportation to take us to the city. After many inquiries, however, we managed to find a cart, in which we placed our trunks and knapsacks. This wagon then set out for Louisville, escorted by a driver and the two of us. In this way we traveled eight leagues through the snow along a narrow path that quite pleasantly wound its way through the woods and amidst an endless series of mountains and valleys. For the aficionado of landscape nothing could have been more picturesque, but when you are tired, the beautiful undulations of the terrain lose much of their charm. When we finally arrived in Louisville, we were thrust from the frying pan into the fire. We were no doubt lucky to find lodging and rest our truly weary bones, but unless we planned to establish our winter headquarters in Louisville, what were we to do, what was to become of us, and where were we to go?

We had intended to travel down the Ohio and then the Mississippi in order to proceed on to Charleston by way of New Orleans. Since the Ohio was blocked by ice, all our plans were upset. To retrace our steps and revisit all the places we had already been was an *odious* idea, the mere thought of which revolted us. To wait for the Ohio to thaw would have been a very risky option, although everyone assured us that the freeze would surely not last more than two days. We chose a middle course, which we thought and still think the wisest option. Since steamboats travel up and down the Mississippi all the time, we thought it would be enough to reach that river, which never freezes, to be sure of finding transportation by water, the only means of travel that is not deadly slow.

Memphis, December 18

My narrative was interrupted by a very happy event: someone came and told us that we could continue on our way. I have just arrived in Memphis, the only place where there is any chance of finding a steamboat to New Orleans. But now we are faced with another disappointment: the Mississippi is half frozen, and no boats are moving on the river. Never in living memory can anyone recall such a calamity. All the people of the South are totally dumbfounded. But the weather has turned milder today, and we hope that navigation will soon resume in the wake of the thaw. We have decided to wait a week. If things do not improve in the meantime, we will retrace our steps and head for Washington.

I am hastening to finish my letter so that I can send it off immediately. I know that it will take more than twenty days to reach New York, and since you will not receive any letter from me on the January 1 packet boat, I want to be sure at least of not missing the January 10th boat.

View through cedars "amidst an endless series of mountains and valleys," Beaumont wrote his mother on December 15, 1831. (GB2)

From Tocqueville | To his father

Memphis, December 20, 1831

The place from which I write you, my dear father, may not exist on the map. Memphis is a very small town located on the banks of the Mississippi at the extreme southwestern border of the state of Tennessee. What chance finds us in Memphis rather than in New Orleans, where we expected to arrive a few days ago? The story is a long and unhappy one, which I shall try to recount as briefly as I can. In my last letter, I was traveling down the Ohio and about to arrive in Louisville. There, on the night of December 4, I was counting on finding a steamboat about to leave for New Orleans, a voyage of six or seven days. The weather, which was already cold, all at once turned icy with such fury that the Ohio, despite its current and width, suddenly froze up, and we found ourselves stuck in the ice. You have to understand that Louisville is at the latitude of Sicily. It doesn't often freeze there, and in living memory no one could recall a freeze beginning before the end of January. That's what I call a *stroke of luck!* In any event, we managed to reach the shore, where we learned that we were nine leagues from Louisville. A big, strapping pioneer from the area offered to take our trunks to Louisville in his wagon. Our ten traveling companions decided to follow suit, so there we all were, on foot in the middle of the Kentucky woods and hills in places where no cargo-laden wagon had passed since the beginning of time. It got through, however, thanks to some stalwart shoulders and an adventurous driver. But we were walking in snow up to our knees. This method of travel ultimately became so tiring that our companions began to abandon us, one after another. But we trudged on and at last reached Louisville at around nine in the evening. The next day we learned that the Ohio was frozen downstream as well as upstream of the point we had reached and that it would be necessary to establish our winter headquarters in Louisville unless we wanted to retrace our steps. But there was also a third option. On the banks of the Mississippi, in the state of Tennessee, we were told that there was a small town called Memphis, where all the steamboats making their way up or down the river stopped to take on wood. If we could get there, we could be certain of resuming our journey, since the Mississippi never freezes. Since this information came from eminently trustworthy sources, we left Louisville for Memphis without hesitation. The two cities are roughly 150 leagues apart. To cover this distance we had to travel by the most abominable trails, in the most wretched wagons and, worst of all, in the most incredible cold you can imagine: the natural order seemed to have been stood on its head expressly for us. Tennessee is situated at almost the same latitude as the Sahara desert in Africa. Farmers there grow cotton and a whole range of exotic plants, yet when we passed through it was freezing at fifteen degrees. No one had ever seen anything like it. Yesterday we reached Memphis at last and learned that, a few miles upstream, the Mississippi itself had frozen and that several steamboats were caught in the ice. You could see them, sitting there as still as if they were rocks. We now have to decide what to do next. Our intention is to stay here a few days to see if this unnatural cold is going to end. If our hopes are disappointed, we will give up the journey to the South and go straight to Washington by the shortest possible route. Were it not for the vexing fact that our plans have been all but scuttled (through no fault of our own), we would not regret the journey we just took through the forests of Kentucky and Tennessee. There we encountered a type of person and way of life of which we had no idea. This part of the United States is populated by only one kind of people: Virginians. They have preserved a physical and moral constitution that is all their own. They are a people apart, with their own national prejudices and distinctive character. This was our first opportunity to examine the effects of slavery on society. On the right bank of the Ohio, activity and industry are everywhere; work is honored; there are no slaves. Cross to the left bank, and the scene changes so suddenly that you would think you were at the other end of the world. The spirit of enterprise ends abruptly; work is not only a hardship, it is shameful, and the man who submits to it degrades himself. To mount a horse, hunt, and smoke like a Turk in the bright sun—that is the destiny of the white man. To use one's hands is to toil like a slave. Whites south of the Ohio constitute a veritable aristocracy, which, like every other aristocracy, combines any number of prejudices with its nobler sentiments and instincts. People say, and I am quite inclined to believe, that these men are sensitive to questions of honor to a degree absolutely unknown in the North. They are open, hospitable, and value many things more than money. Yet ultimately they will be dominated by the North. The North is daily growing richer and more populous, while the South is standing still or growing poorer. The population of Kentucky and Tennessee is scattered across vast forests and deep valleys.[229] After a long day in those woods, we came upon a cabin made of wood, with the joints not well sealed, so that through the cracks we could see a big fire crackling inside. We knocked: two mischievous dogs, as big as donkeys, were the first to answer the door. Their master followed immediately, gave us a bluff handshake, and invited us in. To complete the picture there was a fireplace that filled half of one side of the dwelling, in which an entire tree was burning, a bed, a few chairs, a carbine six feet long, and, hanging on the wall and swinging in the wind, several powder horns. The mistress of the house sat next to the fire, with the quiet, modest look typical of American wives, while four or five plump children clad as lightly as if it were July rolled about on the floor. Under the mantle of the fireplace, two or three squatting Negroes seemed to find it less hot than in Africa. In this impoverished setting our host nevertheless did the honors of his house easily and courteously. Not that he lifted a finger of himself, but the poor blacks saw that strangers had entered the house, and one of them, acting on the orders of his master, served us whiskey, while another served corn cakes and venison, while a third was sent to fetch more wood. The first time I saw the order for wood given, I thought that it was a matter of going down into the cellar or out to the woodshed, but soon I heard the sound of hatchet blows and realized that the man was chopping down the tree whose wood was needed. That is the way things are done here. While the slaves were occupied in this way, the master, quietly seated in front of a fire hot enough to roast an ox to the very marrow, soon enveloped himself in a cloud of smoke, while between puffs he beguiled the time for his guests by recounting all the great hunting exploits he could remember.

I must tell you another brief anecdote to give you an idea of the value that people here ascribe to a man's life if he has the misfortune to have black skin. Nearly a week ago we had to cross the Tennessee River. To get to the other side we had only a paddlewheel steamer maneuvered by a horse and two slaves. We had no trouble making it across, but since the river was churned up a good deal, the boat master was afraid of taking on the wagon. "Don't worry," said one of our traveling companions. "We'll be responsible for the price of the horse and the slaves." This argument carried the day. The wagon was loaded onto the boat and taken across.

229. Kentucky and Tennessee each had a population of just under 690,000 people.

From Tocqueville | To his mother

December 25 [1831]
On the Mississippi

At last, at last, my dear Maman, the signal was given, and here we are sailing down the Mississippi with all the speed that steam and current can impart to a vessel. We were beginning to despair of ever leaving the wilderness to which we found ourselves confined. If you take the trouble to study a map, you will see that our position was not a happy one. Before us lay the half-frozen Mississippi and not a single boat to take us downriver. Above our heads, a Russian sky, pure and frigid. You may be thinking that we might simply have turned around and gone back to where we had come from, but that option, too, was unavailable to us. During our stay in Memphis, the Tennessee had frozen, so that wagons could no longer be ferried across. So we found ourselves in the middle of a triangle formed by the Mississippi, the Tennessee, and impenetrable wasteland to the south, as isolated as if we were sitting on a rock in the middle of the ocean, living in a small world precisely tailored to our tastes, without newspapers, without news of the rest of mankind, and with the prospect of a long winter ahead of us. And so we remained for a week. Except for our anxiety, however, the days passed rather agreeably. We were staying with good people, who did what they could to be kind to us. The most admirable forest in the world began a few yards from our house, and the place was most sublime and picturesque, even when covered with snow. We had all the rifles, powder, and lead we could want. A few miles from the village lived an Indian tribe (the Chickasaws). On their land we could always find a few who asked for nothing more than to hunt with us. Hunting and warfare are the Indians' only occupations and only pleasures. We would have had to go too far to find real game in any quantity, but we did manage to kill quite a few handsome birds that are unknown in France, a feat that did little to increase our allies' esteem for us but did manage to keep us perfectly amused. And so it was that I killed red birds, blue birds, and yellow birds, to say nothing of the most brilliant parrots I've ever seen. That is how we passed the time, without difficulty as to the present, although the future continued to preoccupy us. Finally, one fine day, we spotted a faint puff of smoke above the Mississippi, almost at the horizon. The cloud slowly drew closer, and out of it emerged not a giant or a dwarf as in some fairy tale but a huge steamboat headed upstream from New Orleans. After parading in front of us for a quarter of an hour, as if to leave us in doubt as to whether it would stop or continue on its way, it gave off a snort like a whale and at last headed toward us, breaking the ice with its stout hull and tying up along the bank. The entire population of our small world turned out on the riverbank, which, as you know, used to constitute one of the extremes of our empire. The whole city of Memphis was in turmoil. No bells were rung, because there are no bells, but people shouted Hurrah! and the newly arrived passengers disembarked on the flat as if they were Christopher Columbus. But our salvation had yet to be determined. The destination of the boat was Louisville, farther upstream, while we wanted to head downstream to New Orleans. Fortunately, we had fifteen companions in misfortune who were no more eager than we were to make Memphis their winter headquarters. So we all besieged the captain: What was he going to encounter upstream? Inevitably he would find himself stuck in the ice. The Tennessee, the Missouri, and the Ohio were all frozen solid. Every one of us swore to have witnessed this with our own eyes. His boat would surely become stuck and be damaged if not smashed to pieces by the ice. If we told him all this, it was only in his own interest. It goes without saying—his interest properly understood. . . . The love of one's neighbor lent such warmth to our representations that ultimately we began to sway our man. Yet I am convinced that he would not have turned around were it not for a certain happy event, to which we are indebted for the fact that we did not become citizens of Memphis. As we were negotiating on the riverbank, we could hear an infernal music resounding in the forest. There was the sound of a drum, the neighing of horses, and the barking of dogs. At last we saw a sizable band of Indians emerge from the forest: old men, women, children, baggage, and all, the whole troop led by a European and heading straight for the capital of our triangle. The Indians were Choctaws, as they pronounce it. On that subject, I must tell you that Monsieur de Chateaubriand was a bit like La Fontaine's ape: he did not mistake the name of a port for that of a man, but he bestowed upon a man the name of a powerful tribe of the American South.[230] In any case, you are no doubt wondering why these Indians had come to this place and what good their arrival did us. Patience, please, for today I have time and paper and do not want to hasten my tale.

You shall therefore learn that the Americans of the United States, who are rational and unprejudiced people as well as great philanthropists, believe, as do the Spanish, that God gave them the New World and all its inhabitants as their own.

They also discovered that, since it has been proven—hear this well—that a square mile can feed ten times as many civilized men as savages, reason indicates that wherever civilized men are able to establish themselves, the savages must give up their territory. As you can see, logic is a beautiful thing. Consequently, whenever the Indians begin to discover that they are a little too close to their white brothers, the president of the United States sends them an emissary, who points out to them that, in their own interest properly understood, it would be good for them to retreat ever so little farther west.[231] The land they had been living on for centuries of course belonged to them. No one denied them this in-

230. Tocqueville compares Chateaubriand to the ape in La Fontaine's fable "The Ape and the Dolphin." Lines 33–34 read, "Our ape had taken, getting it wrong, / The name of a seaport for that of a man." In *Atala,* Chateaubriand had named his Indian character Chactas, similar to the Indian tribe of the Choctaws. He identified Chactas as a member of the Natchez tribe; Natchez, Mississippi, was a wealthy port city on the Mississippi River.

231. The Five Civilized Tribes of the Southeast bore the brunt of these removals at the insistence of President Andrew Jackson.

contestable right. But that land was after all uncultivated wilderness, forest, and swamp—really poor property. Across the Mississippi, by contrast, lay magnificent expanses where the game had never been disturbed by the sound of the pioneer's axe, where Europeans would never tread. They were still more than a hundred leagues away. Add to that gifts of inestimable worth, calculated to buy the Indians' indulgence: kegs of brandy, necklaces of glass beads, earrings, and mirrors. And all of this backed by the insinuation that if they refused, the Americans might feel compelled to force them out anyway.

What to do? The poor Indians took their elderly parents in their arms. The women hoisted their children onto their shoulders. At length the nation began to move, carrying its most precious riches with it. It abandoned forever the ground on which its fathers had lived for perhaps a thousand years to settle in a wasteland where the whites will not leave it in peace for ten. Do you see what high civilization brings? The Spaniards, true brutes, loosed their dogs on the Indians as they would on wild animals. They killed, burned, massacred, and pillaged the New World as if it were a city seized in war, pitilessly and indiscriminately. But one cannot destroy everything; fury has its limits. The remnants of the Indian populations ultimately mingled with their conquerors and adopted their mores and religion. In any number of provinces they reign over those who previously conquered them. The Americans of the United States, more humane, more moderate, more respectful of rights and legality, and never bloodthirsty, have been more profoundly destructive of the Indian race, and there is no doubt that within a hundred years not a single tribe will remain in North America nor even a single man belonging to the most remarkable of Indian races.

But I've lost the thread of my story. I was speaking, I think, about the Choctaws. The Choctaws were a powerful tribe that inhabited the border region between the states of Alabama and Georgia. After lengthy negotiations, they were finally persuaded this year to leave their land and emigrate to the right bank of the Mississippi.[232] Six or seven thousand Indians have already crossed the great river. The ones we saw arriving in Memphis had come with the purpose of following in the footsteps of their compatriots. The American government agent who accompanied them and who was supposed to pay for their crossing hastened to the riverbank after learning that a steamboat had arrived. The price that he offered to transport the Indians sixty leagues downriver finally made up the wavering captain's mind. The signal for departure was given. The bow of the ship was turned southward, and we gleefully climbed up the same ladder that other, disappointed passengers had to climb down after learning that instead of continuing on to Louisville, they would be forced to wait in Memphis for a thaw. So goes the world.

232. The Choctaws, whose population numbered about twenty thousand individuals, signed a treaty in September of 1830. The U.S. government did not provide the compensation agreed to in the treaty, and over a third of the Choctaws died from the hardship of inadequate food and resources in the following years.

Memphis, departure of the Indians, Choctaw tribe crossing the Mississipi [sic] *under escort from the government of the United States on their way to Arcansas* [sic] *where a new reservation has been set aside for them. 24 December 1831.* (GB1 *top* and GB2 *bottom*)

But we had yet to begin our voyage. The exiled tribe still had to embark, along with its horses and dogs. At this point began a scene that was in many ways truly lamentable. The Indians moved gloomily toward the riverbank. The horses had been sent ahead, and several of them, unaccustomed to the ways of civilized life, were gripped by fear and plunged into the Mississippi, from which they were retrieved only with great difficulty. Then came the men, who, in accordance with their usual custom, carried nothing but their arms. Then the women, carrying children fastened to their backs or wrapped in blankets. They also bore bundles that contained all their earthly belongings. Finally, the elderly were led aboard. Among them was a woman aged 110. I have never seen a more terrifying figure. She was naked except for a blanket through which one could glimpse the most emaciated body one can imagine. She was escorted by two or three generations of offspring. What a wretched fate, to leave her homeland at that age to seek her fortune in a foreign land! Among the elderly there was one young woman who had broken her arm the week before. For want of treatment, her arm had frozen in position below the fracture. Yet she too was obliged to travel with the rest. When all the Indians had passed, the dogs proceeded toward the bank, but they refused to board the boat and began to howl in the most frightful way. Their masters had to force them onto the vessel.

Overall, there was about this spectacle an air of ruin and destruction, something that felt like a final farewell, with no return. It was impossible to witness the scene without feeling a pang in the heart. The Indians were calm but somber and taciturn. I asked one who spoke English why the Choctaws were leaving their homeland. "To be free," he answered. I couldn't get anything else out of him. Tomorrow we will deposit them in the solitudes of Arkansas. It must be said that it was a stroke of fortune that brought us to Memphis in time to witness this expulsion, or one might say this liquidation, of one of the last remnants of one of the most celebrated and ancient American tribes.

But enough about savages. It is high time to rejoin the world of civilized people. One more word about the Mississippi, which, to tell the truth, scarcely deserves the attention. It is a broad yellow river which flows rather slowly through the most profound solitudes, through forests that it floods in springtime and fertilizes with its silt. On the horizon no hills are visible, but one sees woods, and more woods, and then still more woods. There are reeds and vines and a profound silence, with no sign of man, not even the smoke of an Indian camp.

From Tocqueville | To Ernest de Chabrol

On the Mississippi, December 27, 1831
. . . Have you heard that we literally came close to spending the winter in a small town called Memphis, which is located on the banks of the Mississippi at the far eastern [*sic*] end of the state of Tennessee? In front of us flowed the Mississippi, so laden with floating ice that no vessel could move an inch upstream or down.

Aground in Mississippi, "so laden with floating ice that no vessel could move an inch upstream or down," Tocqueville noted on December 27. (GB2)

To our left stretched vast woodlands, still populated solely by Indian tribes, and at our backs a broad, deep river known as the Tennessee, which froze after we got here so that we could not go back the way we came. If you look at the map with Marie, you will see that we were stuck at the center of a triangle whose sides marked the outer limits of our world. We spent a week without newspapers or news in total isolation from the rest of humanity and spent our time sleeping, eating, and hunting—in a miserable state, I might add, and quite anxious about the future. It was only the luckiest of breaks that finally rescued us from our unfortunate predicament. But as you well know, bygone woes have no more reality than dreams, so let me speak no more of them.

In your last letter you asked if I could give you information about public education in the United States. Before answering, let me remind you again that when I speak of America, you should only half believe me. There are 24 states in the Union, and their laws differ markedly, partly because of their different situations but partly because of vanity as well. I speak only of those I have seen, but they are the most powerful and most enlightened.

The general principle in public education is that anyone is free to establish a school and run it as he pleases. Education is an industry like any other, in which the *consumers* are the judges and the state does not interfere in any way. You ask whether this unlimited freedom has negative consequences: I believe that its effects are all good. Note, however, that none of the antireligious passions that torment us are prevalent here. Hence the greatest danger to freedom of education that we see in France does not exist. Left to themselves and their natural inclinations, men always prefer moral and religious schools to all others. It is striking that in America, where there is no state religion, education is almost exclusively the responsibility of the clergy, or, rather, of *clergies.* They absolutely dominate and control the instruction of children.

As I said, the general principle is total freedom of education. But there is one exception to this principle: schools founded by the state. Or perhaps it would be more accurate to say that in this case, the state is subject to the same law as any private individual, which is that it may run schools that it establishes as it pleases. This has important implications, as you will see. In all New England, and in the state of New York, for example, the law requires each town (of twenty to thirty thousand people) to maintain a free (or nearly free) school. In addition, the state maintains a fund (the school fund) for the purpose of helping towns fulfill this requirement. If they refuse to establish a school, they must pay a fine.

There are many observations one might make about this system. I will confine myself to one: the state must oversee its schools either directly or indirectly. In the state of New York, there is a central official responsible for inspecting all the schools annually as well as for examining teachers, students, and books and making a report to the legislature. To the states of New England this procedure seemed too *governmental,* so they bestowed this power instead on annually elected local school committees. These committees publish their reports, but no standards are imposed on public education.

That is the long and the short of the American system, to the extent that I have been able to study it. In actuality, the state plays a leading role in supervising the public schools, but these are its own institutions; it has no power over schools in general.

The efforts to expand education in this country are truly prodigious. The universal faith in the efficacy of education strikes me as one of the most remarkable things about America, particularly since I confess that, to my mind, the issue is not yet entirely settled. But it certainly is settled in the minds of Americans, regardless of their political or religious opinions. On this point, Catholics are one with Unitarians and deists. The result is peaceful but irresistible progress of the sort that sometimes occurs when a country pursues a goal with a common and universal purpose. Never has a people been as enlightened as the inhabitants of the northern United States. As a result the nation is stronger, cleverer, and more capable of governing itself and of enduring freedom than any other country in the world—that much is undeniable. But are the people improved morally? I seriously doubt it, no matter what anyone says. But if I start on this question I will never end, and time is pressing. . . .

Gulf of Mexico near the Bay of Mobile, 4 January 1832. (GB2)

From Tocqueville | To Ernest de Chabrol

From Chesapeake Bay, January 16, 1832

My dear friend,

I am writing you only briefly today, because tomorrow I arrive in Washington, where I expect to find four letters from you and to answer them at leisure. This is but a short, friendly note to go with the mail of January 20.

I learned yesterday, upon arriving in Norfolk, that the cholera had spread to England last November. This was only a rumor, but it seemed quite likely. If it is confirmed, we will give up the idea of returning through England and will proceed directly to France, where in all probability we will arrive in the first two weeks of March.

God willing, we will find no disease at home! This is my hope more than my expectation. As for the certitude that it will soon arrive, I have always thought so, and today more than ever. Cholera will spread throughout the world. It is the most dreadful scourge that God has ever visited upon the world, because neither climate nor season can stop it, and it never leaves a place for good.

I see from your neighbor's letters that she is very frightened. Do what you can to settle her down, my friend. In epidemics, extreme terror can sometimes predispose a person to the illness. In any case, no matter how rapidly the disease spreads, I hope to be in France before it arrives. If it does come and Marie is still there, I can almost promise to restore her customary calm.

I am nearing the end of a strange and very tiring journey, marked by a thousand vexations, which have pursued us for the past two months: broken and overturned wagons, washed-out bridges, swollen rivers, shortage of rooms: these have been our everyday experiences. The fact is that to cross this vast expanse of country, as we have just done, and to do it in such a short time and in the middle of winter, was not a very practical venture. But we succeeded, and therefore we were right: that is the moral of the story.

Our stay in New Orleans, though short, was quite interesting and most agreeable. When you meet people who say that climate has nothing to do with the constitution of nations, tell them they are wrong. We have seen the French in Canada: they are a tranquil, moral, religious people. In Louisiana we found other Frenchmen, anxious, dissolute, and loose in all respects. Fifteen degrees of latitude separate these two groups, and that is the best explanation I can give for the difference.

What mores one finds in a southern region where slavery is allowed! You cannot imagine it.

Farewell, time is running short. I embrace you with all my heart.

BACK TO WASHINGTON

From Beaumont | To his mother

Washington, January 20, 1832.
. . . I must say a word about my stay in Washington. Immediately upon arriving we went to see the French ambassador, Monsieur Sérurier, with whom we have been in correspondence for several months and who received us with particular kindness.[233] The dear man is somewhat unhappy at the moment with the government of Louis-Philippe, which has made up its mind to economize on ambassadorial honoraria: he now gets only 40,000 francs. The most insignificant *chargé d'affaires* is paid more, and it is upsetting that the French ambassador finds himself in such an inferior position, especially when compared with the English ambassador, who gets 150,000.

Last night Monsieur Sérurier introduced us to the president of the United States. General Jackson, who is an elderly man of 66, is well preserved and seems to have retained all his vigor of mind and body. He is not a man of genius. He once enjoyed a reputation as a duelist and hothead. His great achievement was to have won the Battle of New Orleans against the English in 1814. The victory made him popular and got him elected president, owing to the indisputable fact that in all countries military glory confers a prestige that people find irresistible, even in nations composed of merchants and businessmen.

The president of the United States lives in a palace that in Paris would qualify as a handsome private home. The interior is tastefully but simply decorated. The salon in which he receives guests is far less impressive than the salons of our

233. Louis B. C. Sérurier (1775–1860) was French minister to the United States from 1811 to 1816 and again from 1831 to 1836.

ministers. No guards stand watch at his door, and if he has courtiers, they are not very assiduous in their attentions, because he was alone when we entered his salon, even though it was a day of public reception. During the whole time we were there, no more than two or three people entered the room. We spoke about rather insignificant things. He served us a glass of Madeira, and we thanked him and called him "sir" just as any other visitor would. People in France have entirely the wrong idea about the presidency of the United States: people look upon it as a sort of political sovereignty and are always comparing it to our constitutional monarchies. The power of the king in France would surely be reduced to nothing if it were modeled on the power of the American president. But the authority of this president would be a thousand times too broad if it resembled that of the king of France.

Today I visited the Senate and the House of Representatives of the Union. These two political bodies meet in the Capitol, a very handsome palace that truly deserves to be mentioned as a splendid monument. Yet the Americans greatly exaggerate its value. They will often inquire naively of foreigners whether anything comparable to their Capitol exists in Europe. The debate in the chambers is somber and impressive. Seldom do political passions intrude in such a way as to disrupt these discussions. One of the great advantages that the government of the United States enjoys is that its seat is a small town: the population of Washington is barely 20,000.[234] The authors of the Constitution deliberately chose it to be the home of the supreme authority. In a big city with a large population including many of the lower orders, the deliberations of important political bodies are never free. The men I saw assembled today debated and deliberated with all the more decorum because the atmosphere in which they worked was calm. We were introduced to the Senate and House by Mr. Poinsett, a very distinguished man whom we met in Philadelphia and were delighted to meet again in Washington.[235] He has played a very important political role in this country. He was the one who sparked a revolution in Mexico a few years ago. I do not know anyone who has *been around* as much as he: he has made the crossing from America to Europe and back twenty-two times. He is a very interesting man to listen to, and his conversation is quite absorbing. We have run into many people here whom we had met previously in the course of our travels, so that here in Washington we have not had to face the usual difficulty of making new acquaintances when first arriving in a city. We plan to make the best possible use of our time during our two weeks here. On February 3 or 4 we will head for

234. The 1830 census counted fewer than nineteen thousand residents. Although the city had been designed specifically to become the nation's capital in the 1790s, it grew slowly and was known for its underdeveloped cityscape.

235. Joel Roberts Poinsett (1779–1851), a doctor and statesman, served as the first American minister to Mexico from 1825 to 1830. He was active in South Carolina state politics when Tocqueville met him. Later in the decade, Poinsett would serve as the secretary of war for President Martin Van Buren.

New York by way of Philadelphia, where we will spend a day saying good-bye to a number of people. Then we will go directly to New York, where we will have two days to prepare for our departure.

This is already a long letter, dear mother. Yet I won't end it today, and before sending it to New York, from which it will not depart until February 1, I will add a little more to let you know how I'm spending my time in Washington.

January 22.

We are well launched in Washington society. We spent part of yesterday making visits, escorted by the first secretary of the legation, who made the introductions.

Accordingly, we traveled all over the city. Although the population is not very large, the city is immense in size. The distances are almost as great as in Paris. The houses are therefore sparse, scattered here and there, with no relationship, order, or symmetry. Besides being ugly to look at, this is most annoying for people with errands to do. I spent the evening at the home of the secretary of the interior, Mr. Edward Livingston, the most famous writer in America. He is a man in his sixties, quite friendly, who speaks marvelous French. He is almost French in his manners, because he was born in Louisiana and spent nearly all his life there. His soirée was charming. The music was *bad,* because that is the only kind of music they make in America, but the concert did not last long, and soon there was dancing. Between contredanses and waltzes I had some very interesting conversations with Mr. Livingston about the penitentiary system and especially the death penalty, thus passing from the grave to the pleasant, from rigadoon to syllogism. There is nothing unusual about society here. It is absolutely the same as a European salon, for one very simple reason: the members of the diplomatic corps set the tone. French is the common language, and it is easy to imagine that you are in a Paris salon.

January 23.

Yesterday we dined with the French ambassador, who served us an excellent dinner despite the reduction of his honoraria. His wife is pretty and quite friendly.[236] We spoke a good deal about France. In a few days they are going to give a great ball in our honor, with three or four hundred guests. Our entire week should be very pleasantly busy. Tomorrow evening we will spend with Mr. Livingston. Wednesday we have a ball at the home of Mr. Patterson, who is a commodore in the American navy.[237] Thursday, a state dinner at Mr. Livingston's. Friday, a ball at the home of Mr. MacLane, who is secretary of the trea-

236. Sérurier was married to Estelle Pageot, a woman who had fled violent slave uprisings in the French colony of Saint-Domingue and had settled in Philadelphia.

237. Daniel Todd Patterson (1786–1839), connected to the New York Livingston family by marriage, had distinguished himself in military service during the War of 1812, particularly the Battle of New Orleans in 1814. He commanded the Mediterranean Squadron from 1832 to 1836.

sury.[238] Saturday we dine with Mr. Adams, the former president of the United States.[239] I am afraid that they may end up giving us indigestion. All our evenings are taken, as you can see. As for our days, we spend them almost entirely in the Senate and House. We are as welcome there as the members of these bodies themselves.

Nevertheless, I do not think that my stay in Washington is as profitable as it might have been. Despite all my effort to focus on the interesting things around me, I am perpetually preoccupied with the idea of my return. As long as I had only the prospect of several months of absence to look forward to, I did not lack for courage and bore up rather well, but now that I have only two more weeks to spend away from you, I feel my strength flagging.

I am more impatient than you can possibly imagine, unless you are subject to much the same feeling, which would not surprise me greatly. Try as I might to think of other things, I return constantly to one subject: my ship. It is the *Charlemagne,* one of the best packet boats of the line. I should point out that there isn't the slightest danger in crossing the Atlantic on a ship of this kind. We will arrive before the windy period associated with the equinox. In any case, even in less favorable seasons, there is really nothing to worry about.

We will leave Washington on February 3 or 4. We will arrive a day later in Philadelphia and need to stay there for twenty-four hours. Then we will return to New York, where we will have two or three days to do our final packing and say our farewells to a number of people who were particularly kind to us.

Since I want this letter to arrive in New York in time for the February 1 packet boat, I am going to end it today and post it immediately. So this will be my last word, Mother, and henceforth, rather than send you letters, I will come and hug you in person.

Farewell . . .

From Tocqueville | To his brother Édouard

Washington, January 20, 1832

For you alone

. . . I am leaving America, having used my time here in a useful and agreeable way. I have only a superficial idea of the South of the Union, but to know it as well as the North, I would need to spend six months there. Broadly speaking, two years are necessary to form a complete and accurate picture of the United States. Nevertheless, I hope that I haven't wasted my time. I'm bringing back a good many documents. I have talked and dreamed a good deal about what I

238. Louis McLane (1786–1857) served Delaware in the U.S. Congress for over a dozen years. He was a foreign minister to England for two years before he became secretary of the treasury in 1831. He would replace Edward Livingston as secretary of state in 1833.

239. John Quincy Adams (1767–1848) served as the sixth president of the United States from 1825 to 1829. After Andrew Jackson defeated Adams in the election of 1828, Adams represented Massachusetts in the U.S. Congress from 1831 until his death in 1848.

have seen. I think that, when I return, if I have some free time, I might be able to write something passable about the United States. To embrace the whole thing would be madness. I cannot aspire to universal precision: I haven't seen enough for that. But I think I already know more about this country than we are ever taught in France, and certain aspects of the picture may hold great interest, perhaps even topical interest. . . .

From Tocqueville | To his father

Washington, January 24, 1832

. . . Just now I am mulling over many ideas about America. Many of these I am still turning over in my mind. A fair number have been set down in embryo and in no particular order on paper or remain scattered throughout the notes I made of my conversations after returning home in the evening. You will see all of these preparatory exercises. In them you won't find anything interesting in itself, but you will be the judge of whether anything can be made of them. During the past six weeks of travel, with my body more tired and my mind calmer than it has been for some time, I have thought a great deal about what could be written about America. To attempt a full portrait of the Union would be quite impossible for a man who has spent only a year in this vast country. I believe, moreover, that such a work would be as tedious as it was instructive. By being selective, on the other hand, one might present only topics more or less directly related to our social and political state. In this way the work might have permanent as well as topical interest. That is the general framework. But will I have the time and will I find the ability needed to accomplish the task? That is the question. There is also another consideration that weighs on my mind constantly: I shall either write nothing or write what I think, and not all truths are good to tell. In two months, I hope, at the latest, we will be able to discuss all of this at our leisure.

We have been here for a week. We will stay until February 6. Our time here has been useful and pleasant. At the moment the most prominent men in the Union are in Washington. We are no longer casting about for ideas about things of which we are ignorant, but in our conversations with them we go over nearly everything we have learned. We clarify some doubtful points. This sort of cross-checking is quite useful. We are always treated with great respect and consideration. Yesterday, the minister of France presented us to the president, whom we readily addressed as "Sir" and who shook our hands as he would shake the hand of a colleague. He treats everyone exactly the same. . . .[240]

If you want an idea of man's power to reckon future events, you must visit Washington. Forty years ago, when the issue was where to build a capital for the Union, there was naturally debate regarding the most favorable location, as was only reasonable. The place chosen was a vast plain on the banks of the Potomac. The broad, deep river at one end of this plain was supposed to bring the

240. The cut is in Beaumont's copy of this letter, the original of which has been lost.

12 March 1832. On return trip dead calm after six days of storm. Aboard Le Havre, *entering the English Channel. View of the English coast.* (GBI)

products of Europe into the new city. The fertile regions of the hinterland were to keep the market supplied and ensure that the capital would be surrounded by a substantial population. Within twenty years Washington was supposed to become the leading domestic and foreign trading city of the Union. It was expected to have a million residents within short order. Public buildings suitable to such a large population were therefore begun. Very broad streets were laid out. And above all, trees were hastily felled as far as the eye could see, so that nothing would stand in the way of building homes. All of this was nothing other than the story of the milk pitcher writ large:

When I had it, it was of reasonable size.

I shall have . . .

The milkmaid and Congress reasoned in exactly the same way. The population did not come. Vessels did not navigate up the Potomac. Today, Washington is an arid, sun-parched plain across which are scattered two or three sumptuous buildings and the five or six villages that make up the city. Unless one is Alexander or Peter the Great, one had best not try to create the capital of an empire. . . .

From Tocqueville | To Ernest de Chabrol

Washington, January 24, 1832

My dear friend,

I have received four new letters from you. I cannot thank you enough for your diligence in writing. I wish that I had been able to reciprocate in every instance. But I am sure that you appreciate the reasons that have forced me to remain silent. In any case, you will have no further grounds for complaint:

the packet boat of February 10 will bring you not a letter from me but myself in person. With the help of God, because the season is quite bad for an ocean crossing.

Don't worry, though (I say the same thing to your neighbor). Over the past eight or ten years, there have been only two accidents: one packet boat vanished without a trace, while another broke apart on the French coast. The probability of disaster is therefore quite small, since a ship departs every ten days. It is true that the two disasters occurred in March, but I will arrive before the equinox.

We can no longer remain in America. Our feet are burning. Everything that moors us to life is in France, and under the current circumstances it is too painful to be so far away. It is not just the approach of the cholera that is hastening our return. So it's very difficult to keep our impatience in check and calmly profit from the last few days we'll have to accomplish anything useful here. . . .

My uncertainty about how things currently stand in France makes it impossible for me to know exactly what I'll do after my return. I am filled with doubt on this score. I don't know whether I should withdraw completely, as I have often been tempted to do, or try to advance. What I see clearly, though, is that I will not return to my post as deputy judge. Versailles will see no more of me, unless it is in some other capacity. On this point my mind is made up (but please keep this to yourself). I believe that to act otherwise would be to make a fool of myself.

When I say that Versailles will see no more of me, I am of course exaggerating. Indeed, I will probably be there within two days of my arrival. But my visit will be *incognito,* and it will not be to deal with either political or judicial affairs. I hope that you will be able to spare me a bed in your apartment for one night. I may not make much use of it, but this is how things must be done. You are well aware of my most important reason for visiting you so promptly, and it would hardly become me to deny it. But I want you to know that my pleasure in returning to Versailles will be twice as great because you are there.

Our friendship, my dear Chabrol, has been fast from the beginning, and the bond between us is still tighter today. I hope it will help us find our way out of the maze in which we are currently lost.

Thanks to you and Blosseville for the information you sent on the administration. It has already proved useful. I imagine that the additional material you have promised will arrive in America after my departure. But I have already left instructions that it should all be forwarded immediately to France. I already know enough, I think, about the very simple and frequently very incomplete administration of this country to be able to make use of your observations without being here.

I have not dropped the idea of publishing something about the United States. Indeed, I have a work in mind, which, though far less comprehensive than the one you sketched in one of your letters, may nevertheless be more feasible, since I was not able in one year to amass the huge number of documents that your idea would require. In any case, all of this is still very confused in my mind. I have nothing clearly worked out. I do not know if I will have the resolve or the leisure or above all the means to begin anything.

I leave this question (along with so many others) for another day.

We had hoped to present some very interesting findings on the theory of penal laws, but we have had incredible difficulty obtaining detailed documents. What we will bring back is merely a set of observations, nothing complete.

I will leave you for now, dear friend, and will say nothing today about America. Frankly, I am already living more in France than in the United States. But whether here or there, you may always count, I hope, on my unshakable devotion. . . .

American goldfinch (*Carduelis tristis*). *Bird killed near Cicero on way back from Oneida Lake, July 8, 1831. Painted the same day in Syracuse.* (GBI)

Blue jay (*Cyanocitta cristata*) *painted in Pontiac, July 29, 1831.* (GBI)

Butterfly *painted at Fort Gratiot, August 3.* (GBI)

American kestrel (*Falco spar-verius*). *Bird killed at Fort Gratiot by Tocqueville and painted on August 3, 1831. Bird of Prey.* (GBI)

Northern flicker (yellow-shafted group), a species of woodpecker (*Colaptes auratus*). *Green magpie, August 13 and 14, 1831. Steamboat Superior. Lake Huron and St Clair.* (GBI)

Montmorency Falls, 2½ leagues from Quebec City. 240 feet high. August 25, 1831. (GBI)

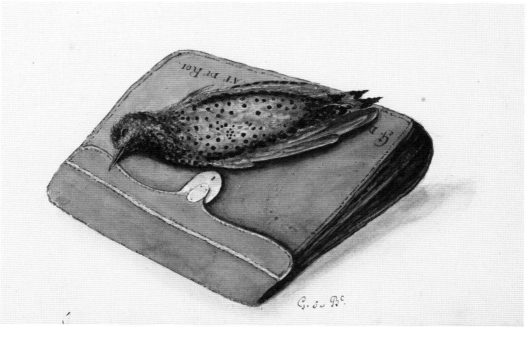

Parrot and other birds painted from nature in Memphis on the banks of the Mississippi, 22 and 23 November 1831. One green woodpecker with gray head. (GBI) *Left to right:* Carolina parakeet (*Conuropsis carlinensis*; this species is now extinct); eastern bluebird (*Sialia sialis*); northern cardinal (*Cardinalis cardinalis*);

Stockbridge. Miss Sedgwick, September 7, 1831. (GBI)

red-headed woodpecker (*Melanerpes erythrocephalus*); northern flicker (yellow-shafted group), a species of woodpecker (*Colaptes auratus*).

Bird *sketched at Sandy Bridge, I couldn't paint it because the good brush was frozen.* (GBI)

Niagara Falls, American side, August 18, 1831. (GBI)

OPPOSITE PAGE

Mallard (*Anas platyrhynchos*). (GBI)

Northern cardinal (*Cardinalis car-dinalis*). *Red bird killed by Tocque-ville in Memphis on the banks of the Mississippi, 19 December 1831, and painted by me from nature the same day.* (GBI)

Alexis de Tocqueville. Indians, drawn on the back of a manuscript page of *Two Weeks in the Wilderness.*

part 2

Tocqueville's Travel Notebooks

"What I have regarding this country is a jumble of notes, any number of disconnected ideas to which I alone possess the key, and some isolated facts that call to mind a host of others," Tocqueville told his mother, while noting that these "scraps" were "invaluable" to him.

Throughout his trip, Tocqueville confided in his diaries his thoughts on politics, law, society, and mores and carefully transcribed the conversations he had with his many American and Canadian informants. Tocqueville liberally used excerpts from these conversations in volume 1 of *Democracy in America* but without revealing his informants' identity for fear of causing them "chagrin and embarrassment." Particularly telling in this regard are his conversations with John Quincy Adams, Jared Sparks, John Spencer, and Sam Houston.

We present the notebooks in the order in which Tocqueville kept them. He labeled them alphabetically and numerically. We have skipped only short passages that were repetitive or that, while descriptive, did not convey a clear point. We did not include a small fascicle of notes on James Kent's *Commentaries on American Law,* as Tocqueville added little to this work but was quite explicit on legal and constitutional issues in other parts of his travel notebooks.

Save for a few pages (two of which are translated in part 1), Beaumont's diaries have not survived, but his beautiful sketchbooks have, and we present his sketches throughout this volume.

Non-alphabetic Notebook 1[1]

Conversation with Mr. Livingston,[2] at Greenburgh on the Hudson, 7 June 1831[3]

Me: One of the shortcomings of American society, in my opinion, is the lack of intellectual spirit here.

Him: I agree with you. And in that respect we are not making progress but losing ground every day.

Me: To what do you attribute that?

Him: Primarily the laws of inheritance. I can still recall from my youth seeing this region populated by wealthy landowners, who lived on their land in the manner of the English gentry, men who kept their minds occupied and even maintained certain traditions in ideas and manners. At that time there was a class of people with elegant manners and lofty minds. The law that imposed equal division of estates whittled away great fortunes, and those manners and ideas began to vanish, until now they are nearly gone. Land changes hands with unbelievable rapidity. No one has time to form attachments to a place. Everyone is obliged to work to maintain the same position as his father. By the second or third generation nearly every family has disappeared.

Me: Is there anything that resembles the influence of landed proprietors or patronage?

Him: No. Here each man counts as one individual.

Me: How do the rich tolerate such conditions?

Him: They tolerate it as a necessary condition, which they must accept because there is no way to prevent it.

Me: But is there any animosity between the rich and the common people?

Him: Not at all. All classes participated in the Revolution. Since then, the power of democracy has proved to be so insurmountable that no one dares resist it. Generally speaking, the people are by no means unwilling to vote for the wealthiest and best educated among them.

---

1. Tocqueville copied parts of his June 9 letter to Chabrol (printed in part 1) at the beginning of this notebook.

2. It is unclear exactly which member of the Livingston family Tocqueville engaged in this conversation.

3. Tocqueville and Beaumont had just visited the prison at Sing Sing and stopped at the Livingston properties north of Yonkers on the Hudson River.

Me: What strikes me on the surface in American society is the extreme equality that exists in social relations. The wealthiest man and the humblest artisan will shake hands in the street.

Him: There is a great deal of equality, but less than a foreigner might suppose. The manners that you find so striking are frequently a mere formality, with no greater significance than the words "your humble servant" at the bottom of a letter. Here one has to be polite to everyone, because everyone has political rights. In New York the newly rich are quite proud of their wealth. We have an aristocracy of wealth just like everywhere else, if the word "aristocracy" can be applied to something that changes constantly and has pretensions rather than power.

Me: Broadly speaking, what sorts of men hold public office?

Him: In general, posts are filled by men who are second-rate in ability and character. These positions don't pay enough or confer sufficient prestige or power to attract truly distinguished men. This was not the case in the early days of the Republic. Nowadays you find no great men in politics. People put their energy and resources into other sorts of career.

Mr. Livingston has been to Europe. He belongs to a very old family and seems to be a man of intelligence.

* * *

Conversation with Mr. Gallatin (who served for some years as a minister in France and England). New York, 10 June 1831.

Him: We have no villages in America, if by village one means places inhabited by people who cultivate the land. The owners of property live on their land, and their houses are scattered across the countryside. What you take to be villages should rather be called towns, because their population consists of merchants, artisans, and *lawyers*.

Me: Let me stop you at that last word. Are there that many lawyers among you?

Him: Many more, I believe, than anywhere in Europe.

Me: What are their social position and character?

Him: The one thing explains the other: lawyers are the most prominent members of society, and their influence is great. Hence they are men of rather stable character, rather than restless and agitated as in Europe. Were it not for the lawyers, we would have reformed our civil laws by now, but there are certain abuses and obscurities of the law from which they profit and which they therefore support.

Me: Do they play an important role in public assemblies?

Him: Yes, they constitute a majority of such assemblies. But it has been observed that our most distinguished orators, much less our greatest statesmen, have not been lawyers.

Me: Describe the background, standing, and character of your magistrates.

Him: All magistrates are recruited from the ranks of lawyers, and outside the courtroom, where certain formalities obtain, their status is equal to that of lawyers. Our magistrates are extremely well respected. Since their power ultimately derives solely from public opinion, they must strive constantly to keep the public on their side. Their integrity is beyond doubt. I regard the judiciary, *which of course enjoys the consistent support of the members of the bar,* as the mechanism that keeps our democracy on an even keel and running smoothly. Note that because the judiciary can refuse to enforce an unconstitutional law, it is in a sense a political body.

Me: Is it true, as I am told, that morals are pure?

Him: Marital fidelity is admirably preserved. The same cannot always be said of virtue before marriage. In rural areas (as opposed to towns), young people of both sexes enjoy a considerable degree of freedom, and this quite often leads to trouble. The savage tribes that surround us further exacerbate the tendency to neglect chastity prior to marriage. They do not regard it as a moral obligation.

That same day, I visited a club, where someone said that as Americans moved inland, their fleet would shrink. Mr. Gallatin estimated the number of seamen currently sailing under the American flag at (roughly) sixty thousand.[4] He added that "since we employ neither the English practice of impressment nor the French practice of *inscription maritime,* I predict that if war comes, we will find it impossible to enlist enough sailors to man a dozen of our ships."

* * *

Conversation with Mr. Maxwell, 27 June 1831.

Mr. Maxwell served as a district attorney for ten years.[5] He is one of the founders of the reform school (for delinquents and foundlings) and has the reputation of being a "broad but very able man."[6]

Me: What do you think of the prison system?

Him: You have to distinguish between prisons properly speaking and reform schools. I believe that discipline in the penitentiaries is excellent: an admirable order is maintained, and the convicts are employed in productive labor. I do not believe, however, that they are effective in altering the inclinations or habits of prisoners. In general, I *do not believe that it is possible to reform a mature criminal,* no matter how one goes about it. My opinion is that they come out of prison as hardened criminals. My thinking about the reform schools is different. I believe that juvenile delinquents can be reformed, and I think that the only way

4. Far fewer men were enlisted in the navy and coast guard. Official records suggest that no more than fifty-five hundred men served in these combined forces in 1831.

5. Hugh Maxwell (1787–1873) served as district attorney for New York from 1819 to 1829.

6. This school was founded in 1825 by private subscribers, and it was directed by N. C. Hart. It inspired similar reform schools in Boston (1826); Philadelphia (1828); and Melun, France.

to reduce the number of crimes in a country is to build more and better institutions of this sort. When I was district attorney, the number of juvenile delinquents was quite alarming and growing rapidly. Several people had the idea of establishing a reform school to deal with this problem. It took a good deal of effort to persuade the public that this was a good idea, but now the success of the project has made it popular. The number of juvenile delinquents is now only a fifth or a sixth of what it was five years ago.

Me: Can you document that assertion?

Him: No, but based on my own personal knowledge, I can assure you that it is true. I believe that reform schools will spread not only to other states but to other districts within each state. Sending a child to a distant reform school can be quite expensive, and the child is often further corrupted in the course of travel.

Note: The belief that the penitentiary system is useless for the purpose of moral reform seems to be widely shared by many of the very able men we have met thus far, including men of practical experience.

See the article "Penitentiaries."[7]

* * *

Conversation with Mr. Elam Lynds, in Syracuse, 7 July 1831.

We were most curious to see Mr. Elam Lynds, whose practical talents are universally acknowledged, even by his enemies, and who is regarded as the father of the present penitentiary system, whose successful establishment owed much to his perseverance and energy.

We therefore arrived early for our visit. We found him in a hardware store, of which he is the owner. He was dressed as a shop clerk and performed a clerk's functions. Mr. Lynds is a man of utterly common appearance, and I believe that his speech is similarly vulgar. A note he handed to us revealed that his spelling is also quite poor. Yet he seems quite intelligent and unusually energetic. We could not speak with him immediately, because there was no one to watch the store, but he called at our inn a half an hour later, and we had the following conversation:

He: I spent ten years of my life as a prison administrator. I had long been a witness to the abuses that were common in the old system. They were terrible; the prisons cost the state a great deal of money. The prisoners lost whatever morals they had left, and disorder was ubiquitous. Had this state of affairs persisted, I think we would have reverted to the barbarous laws of an earlier time. At any rate, the majority had begun to turn against philanthropic ideas of every sort, which in practice yielded little benefit and did a great deal of harm. I tried to reform Auburn but ran into serious obstacles in the legislature and even met with opposition from the public at large. I was accused of high-handedness. Yet I ac-

7. See Alphabetic Notebook A, "Penitentiaries," "Sing Sing, 29 May 1831," pp. 329–30.

complished what I wanted to do.[8] When it came to building Sing Sing, and I suggested putting prisoners to work in open fields, people refused to believe that this could be done. I did it, yet many people remain opposed to the idea or jealous of my success. I retired a year ago, feeling that I had done enough public service and that it was time to look to my own fortune.

Q: Do you think that the disciplinary system you established can work outside of America?

A: I am convinced that it will succeed if my approach is followed. In fact, I think it is more likely to succeed in France than here. In France, the prisons are under the direct control of the government, which can offer prison officials substantial and permanent assistance. Here we are slaves to public opinion, which changes constantly. In my opinion, a prison warden needs absolute, unimpeachable authority, especially if he wants to change the way things are done. In a democratic republic like ours, he cannot count on this. He has both to win the support of the public and to follow through on his reforms, and it is frequently impossible to reconcile these two goals. In France his position is less complicated.

Q: We have heard Americans say that the success of the penitentiary system must be attributed in part to the fact that people here are in the habit of scrupulously obeying the law, and we are quite prepared to believe this.

A: I think just the opposite. At Sing Sing, a quarter of the prisoners were foreigners. I subjected them to the same discipline as the Americans. The ones that gave me the most trouble were the Spaniards from South America, a race of men closer to wild animals and savages than to civilized human beings. The easiest to deal with were the French, who were quick to accept their fate. If I had a choice, I'd rather be warden of a French prison than an American one.[9]

Q: So what is the secret of the potent disciplinary system you've been describing, the effects of which we were able to see for ourselves at Sing Sing?

A: It would be quite difficult for me to say. It is the result of persistent daily effort, which has to be seen to be believed. There are no general rules. You have to keep the prisoners working and maintain continuous silence, and to do that you have to be vigilant at all times and keep an eye on your guards as well as your prisoners; you have to be pitiless and just. Once the machine is in operation, it runs quite smoothly. If I were in government and wanted to improve the condition of the prisons, I would look for an able and intelligent man. He ought to have seen a prison like ours with his own eyes or at least ought to have as accurate as possible an idea of what such a prison is like. After selecting such a person, I would give him the power to make changes. My principle has always

8. When Auburn was founded in 1816, prisoners were kept in constant solitary confinement. In the early 1820s, Elam Lynds began to experiment with a system of directing group work among the convicts at Auburn. He enforced silence, directed the convicts to walk in lockstep, and returned them to individual cells at night. This type of prison management became known as the Auburn system and was also instituted by Lynds at Sing Sing Prison.

9. Tocqueville and Beaumont did not agree with this opinion.

been that in order to do this kind of work, all power and responsibility should be vested in one person. That way, the government increases its likelihood of success and virtually guarantees it. Whenever inspectors tried to give me a hard time about my management of the prison, I said, "You're perfectly free to fire me. I serve at your pleasure. But as long as you choose to keep me on the job, I shall follow the plan I have set forth. The decision is yours."

Q: Do you think that it is possible to dispense with corporal punishment?

A: I am absolutely convinced of the opposite. I regard whipping as both the most effective and the most humane punishment, because it does not damage the prisoners' health and forces them to lead basically healthy lives. By contrast, solitary confinement is often ineffective and almost always dangerous. I have seen many prisoners who could not be subdued in this way and who left solitary confinement only to enter the hospital. I do not believe that it is possible to run a large prison without resorting to the whip, no matter what people whose only knowledge of human nature is gleaned from books may think.

Q: Don't you think it's risky to let prisoners at Sing Sing work in open fields?

A: I would rather be warden of a prison run that way than of any other. In a closed prison, you don't get the same level of surveillance or care from the guards. Once the prisoners have submitted completely to the disciplinary system, they can be put to work wherever you see fit. Once discipline has been improved, the state can use criminals in many different ways.

Q: Do you think it is completely impossible to establish sound discipline in a prison without cells?

A: I think that order could be maintained in such a prison and that work could be made productive, but you could not prevent a host of abuses of a very serious kind.

Q: Do you think that cells can be installed in older prisons?

A: That depends on the location. I have no doubt that the change can be made in most old prisons. It is quite easy and not very expensive to build wooden cells. The drawback is that such cells retain foul odors and sometimes become unhealthy.

Q: Do you truly believe that it is possible to *reform* large numbers of prisoners?

A: Let's be clear about what we mean. I do not believe in complete reform (except for juvenile delinquents). In other words, I do not believe that there are many examples of adult criminals turning into pious and virtuous people. I do not believe that the men coming out of prisons are saints, and I do not believe that the chaplain's sermons or the prisoner's private meditations ever make good Christians. It is my view, however, that many former prisoners do not lapse back into crime, and some even become useful citizens, having learned a trade in prison and acquired the habit of constant work. That is the only reform I ever hoped to achieve, and I believe that it is the only reform that society can expect.

Q: What do you think of prison labor for outside firms?

A: I think that it is very helpful to hire prisoners out, *provided* the warden retains full control over them and the use that is made of their time.

Q: In France, the price of prison labor is set very low.

A: It will increase as discipline improves. That is what we have seen here. Prisons used to cost the state a lot of money; now they bring in money. The well-disciplined prisoner works longer and harder and never spoils his raw materials, as prisoners in poorly run institutions sometimes will.

Q: What in your opinion is the most important quality to be looked for in a prison warden?

A: Practical know-how in the management of men. He must above all be deeply convinced, as I was, that a dishonest man is always a coward. He will quickly communicate this belief to the men in his charge, and it will give him irresistible power over them and make many things that might at first sight appear difficult seem easy.

Throughout this conversation, which with frequent interruptions went on for several hours, Mr. Elam Lynds repeatedly returned to the idea that the prisoner must above all be reduced to a state of *passive obedience.* Once this was achieved, everything became easy, no matter how the prison was organized or what the nature or the place of work.

* * *

Second conversation with Elam Lynds.[10]

Q: What do you think the prisoner's behavior while in prison says about his prospects for ultimate reform?

A: Nothing. If I had to give a general prognosis, I would go so far as to say that the prisoner who behaves impeccably in prison will probably revert to his old habits upon release. I have always felt that the worst criminals made excellent prisoners. They are generally more self-possessed and intelligent than the rest. They are quick to see that the only way to alleviate their fate is to avoid the painful and repeated punishments that disruptive behavior inevitably brings. Hence their behavior improves, but they do not. It follows from this that a prisoner should never be granted a pardon for good behavior in prison. This is a risky business, and its effect is merely to make the inmates hypocrites.

Q: Yet nearly all the *theorists* recommend this method, do they not?

A: On this point as on so many others, they are mistaken because they know nothing of the actual prison population. For example, if Mr. Livingston were to apply his system of imprisonment to men born as he was born, namely, into a social position that fosters intelligence and moral responsibility, I believe that it would yield excellent results. But in fact the prisons are full of coarse men with no education whatsoever and who have a very hard time grasping ideas or even

10. Tocqueville and Beaumont encountered Lynds again when they visited Auburn Prison during July 9–11.

responding to intellectual stimuli. By offering such men instruction that is of use only to men of a different sort, Mr. Livingston for all his talent has nevertheless committed the error to which I just alluded.

* * *

Conversation with Mr. Spencer, Canandaigua, 17 and 18 July 1831.

Mr. Spencer is a distinguished lawyer. He has been an attorney at law, district attorney, and member of Congress and is currently a member of the legislature of the state of New York. He was one of the drafters of the *Revised Statutes*. His mind appears to be clear and perspicacious.

Q: Are the members of the two houses of the various legislatures elected in the same way and under the same conditions of eligibility?

A: Yes. In the state of New York in particular, both houses are indeed filled with the same kind of men.

Q: In that case, what is the point of having two houses?

A: The importance of having two houses is immense, and everyone in America feels this so keenly that it is taken as axiomatic that a unicameral legislature is a detestable institution. Pennsylvania, which made the mistake of adopting one, has been obliged to give it up.[11] The main advantages of a bicameral legislature are the following. First and foremost, every bill must surmount two hurdles. Between the two debates, time passes, during which common sense and moderation come into play. Very frequently the Senate, though composed of the same elements and dominated by the same spirit as the House, looks at an issue in a different light and corrects what the House cannot correct because it has already passed the bill. The second benefit of our Senate, as I see it, is that members remain in office for a longer period of time than representatives and are not all replaced at once, so that there is always a body of men in the legislature who are familiar with past legislation and well versed in the ways of politics. They bring to the legislature practical skills and consistency that might otherwise be lacking.

Q: Broadly speaking, how would you characterize the attitude of lawyers as a body?

A: One hears the complaint that they are resistant to change. In France, I know, the opposite complaint is heard. In my opinion, the reasons for the difference are these: first, lawyers in America have no interest in change. They favor the social order as it currently exists. Furthermore, I believe that there is a general principle in our civil laws that is different from yours, on account of which our lawyers have developed different attitudes and customs. Our civil law is based entirely on *precedents*. A magistrate is absolutely bound by what another judge has previously decided. As a result, there is practically no debate about

11. In 1776, under the leadership of Benjamin Franklin, Pennsylvania adopted a constitution that created a single legislative body with executive veto. In 1790, the state adopted a new constitution that created a bicameral state legislature.

the law here. Everything comes down to ascertaining the facts of the case. The point is to be familiar with previous decisions in similar cases and to be able to discuss the degree to which the precedent applies to the particular facts of the case at hand. As you may imagine, this sort of study is not likely to develop a taste for theory. Indeed, it often narrows the mind. By contrast, your lawyers, as far as I can judge from reports, at any rate, feel obliged to plumb the very foundations of society to resolve a case about a compost pit.

Q: Do judges exercise disciplinary power?

A: Yes. They can reprimand lawyers, fine them, expel them from the bar, or even, in extreme cases, send them to prison. Judges do not occupy a superior position, however. Outside the courtroom they stand equal to lawyers.

Q: What criticisms are leveled at your magistrates?

A: The only criticism I would make is that they are a little too fond of flattering the people and lack the courage to stand against an opinion when they believe it is held by the masses. We've seen some examples of this in trials with a political interest. In ordinary cases they usually err on the side of leniency for this reason and not so much because they really believe in it.

Q: What is the influence of the press on public opinion?

A: It has great influence, but it isn't exerted in the same way as in France. For instance, we don't ascribe much value to the opinions of journalists. Journalists gain influence only through the facts they reveal and the manner in which they express them. Sometimes they lead the public astray in regard to an individual or measure. Basically, the press will always be a powerful instrument, no matter what the country or the nature of the government.

Q: What limits are imposed on the freedom of the press?

A: On that score we adhere to a very simple principle. When it comes to the expression of opinion, there is total freedom. No one will stop you from printing that monarchy is the best form of government whenever you choose. But if a newspaper publishes slander or alleges guilt without proof, it is liable to prosecution and a heavy fine. I can cite a recent example of this. In a trial having to do with the disappearance of Morgan (the Masonic case), a newspaper said that the jurors had reached their guilty verdict because they were under the influence of a *party*. I prosecuted the author of the article and won the case.[12]

Q: What do you think is the best way to reduce the power of periodicals?

A: I am completely convinced that the most effective method is to encourage as many newspapers as possible and to prosecute them only in extreme cases. Experience has taught us that the more numerous they are, the less powerful they become. I have heard that in France there are only two or three respected

12. In 1826, William Morgan, who had undertaken to reveal the secret rituals of Freemasonry, disappeared from a Canandaigua prison and was either murdered or forced to leave the country. Three Masons were charged with Morgan's kidnapping, and their trial prompted the rise of anti-Masonic sentiment throughout the country. John Spencer was appointed a prosecutor in the case, sided against the Masons, and later wrote a tract on Masonic practices.

major newspapers. Under such conditions I imagine that the press might become a destructive influence. Furthermore, I believe that the influence of the press will always be of greater concern in your country because of your social situation. Paris will always exert an immense influence on the rest of the country. Here, interests are divided in a thousand ways. There is no primary center of action, and it is almost impossible to stir up public opinion over a vast region. The New York City papers have no more influence over us than the papers of the next town. Another reason why journalists who express their personal opinions don't exert much influence is that they didn't use this power well during the early years of the Republic. It was demonstrated at the time that most of them were in the pay of England, and they forfeited the confidence of the public.

Q: Do influential people write for your papers?

A: Party leaders often do, but without signing their names.

Q: What do you think is responsible for the religious tolerance that prevails in the United States?

A: Primarily the fact that there are so many denominations (the number is virtually unlimited). If two religions were to square off, we'd cut each other's throats. But since no denomination has a majority, tolerance is essential for all. What is more, many people, including myself, are of the opinion that some kind of religion is essential if man is to live in society, and the freer men are, the more necessary religion becomes. I've heard that in France people have toyed with the idea of giving up positive religion altogether. If that is true, even with your love of liberty you are nowhere close to establishing free institutions on a firm footing, and you will have to await the next generation.

Q: What in your opinion is the best way of restoring the natural empire of religion?

A: I think that the Catholic religion is less well suited to the idea of liberty than the Protestant religion. Nevertheless, if the clergy were completely deprived of all temporal influence, I cannot help thinking that in time it would regain its natural influence. I think that the best and only way to help the clergy is to pretend to ignore it without becoming hostile. If you do that, you will find that public education will slowly fall into its hands, and over time the younger generation will change its way of thinking.

Q: Is the clergy in charge of your public schools?

A: Absolutely. I know of only two counterexamples in the entire state of New York. This seems only natural to me.

Q: What are your poor laws?

A: In this and many other areas, we followed the English example for many years. In the end, though, we gave up the English system, because we found it too costly. A new system was introduced in the state of New York a few years ago: each county has an almshouse, to which vagrants can be sentenced and to which an official known as the overseer of the poor has the power to refer individuals who cannot support themselves. The almshouse maintains fields that its inmates must work. The intent of the law is to cover the costs of the establishment through the revenue earned by farming. We have high hopes that this will work. The house to which paupers are sent is determined by their place of residence rather than their place of birth.

Q: How are the public schools paid for here?

A: The state has a special fund for the purpose. Portions of this fund are allocated to towns that need assistance, in proportion to the effort they are willing to make on their own. As a general rule, we hold that the state should always *aid* rather than *assume full responsibility*. We believe that people who give their own money and are present locally will have an interest in controlling costs and managing the schools better than a large bureaucracy would be able to do. We also want to foster as many local interests as possible. The combination of state and local money serves both purposes admirably. Everyone here is interested in education. Since the people are indeed kings, everyone feels the need to educate everybody.

Q: Do you find that the recent law abolishing property qualifications for voting had negative results?

A: No, on the contrary. Because the demands of the people were fully satisfied, they are no longer subject to the influence of agitators.

* * *

Conversation with Mr. Mullon.[13]

Mr. Mullon is a Catholic priest who seems quite ardent in his faith. When I met him, he was on his way to Michilimackinac to give religious instruction to a colony of Catholic Indians newly settled at Arbre-Croche.[14]

Q: Do you think that government support is helpful to religion?

A: I am deeply convinced that it is harmful. I know that most Catholic priests in Europe think the opposite. I understand why they see things as they do. They are wary of freedom, which initially was turned against the church. Because they had long enjoyed the protection of monarchical institutions, it was only natural that they should regret the loss of that protection. Thus they fell victim to an inevitable error. If they lived here, they would soon change their minds. All religious beliefs here are on the same footing. The government doesn't support or persecute any of them. Yet surely there is no other country in the world where Catholicism has more fervent supporters or more numerous converts. I will say it again: the less religion and its ministers are mixed up with

---

13. Bound for Michilimackinac, Tocqueville and Beaumont met James Ignatius Mullon on the boat *Superior* on the Saint Clair River. Mullon had founded a mission in Michilimackinac in 1829. By the next year, he was a church leader in Cincinnati, and in 1834, he was transferred to New Orleans.

14. Michilimackinac, now known as Mackinaw City, sits at the northern tip of the lower Michigan peninsula. Arbre-Croche, now Cross Village, was a settlement twenty miles southwest of Michilimackinac on the shores of Lake Michigan.

government, the less they are involved in political debate, the more influential religious ideas will become.

Q: Which denominations are most hostile to Catholicism in the United States?

A: All of the Protestant denominations join in their hatred of Catholicism, but only the Presbyterians are violent. They are also the most zealous.

Q: Do you see signs of the Jesuits' work with the Indians?

A: Yes. Some tribes retain confused ideas of religion that they learned from the Jesuits and if they can be reached are quick to return to Christianity. Some of the families at Arbre-Croche were taught the basic principles of Christianity one hundred and fifty years ago, and traces of that education remain.[15] Generally speaking, the tribes respect the memory of the "Black Robes." In the wilderness you occasionally see a cross erected years ago by the Jesuits.

Q: Is it true that the Indians display a natural gift for eloquence?

A: Yes, indeed. I have often admired the profundity and brevity of their speech. Their style is rather laconic.

Q: Do they still wage war with ferocity?

A: Yes, indeed. They burn their prisoners and torture them in a thousand ways. They scalp the dead and wounded. Yet they are gentle, honest people when their passions are not aroused by war. I've witnessed their war dances, and never did I see a more terrifying spectacle. The dancing braves make themselves up to look as frightening as possible, daubing themselves with a variety of colors. In the dance they mimic the kinds of barbarous acts to which Indian wars always give rise. They pretend to smash their enemy's skull or torture him or scalp him. Some years ago, the bishop of Cincinnati suggested that one of the tribes (I have forgotten which Mr. Mullon said it was) send him a certain number of children for instruction. I witnessed the deliberations that this offer initiated, and I can assure you that, even though the assembly consisted of savages, it was nevertheless quite impressive. They sat in a circle, and each man spoke in turn with a great deal of gravity and natural eloquence. An Indian will never interrupt a speaker in the middle of a speech.

Q: What form of government exists among the savages?

A: They have chiefs. Some are hereditary, and a chief's family retains its rights unless some shameful crime has been committed. Over near the Saint Joseph River there is an Indian chief who can trace his ancestry all the way back to the one who welcomed the first French explorers in his region.

Q: Are the Indians at Arbre-Croche fervent believers?

A: (With this question Mr. Mullon became extraordinarily animated.) I know of no other Christians as fervent as they. Their faith is pure, and their obedience

15. Beginning in the late seventeenth century, Jesuit missionaries established missions among Native American communities throughout the Great Lakes. In 1741, a number of Jesuits followed a group of Christian Ottawa Indians who moved from Michilimackinac to Arbre-Croche.

to the laws of religion is complete. An Indian convert would rather be killed than fail to observe the rules of abstinence. They lead very moral lives. You saw how warmly the Indians of Sault-Sainte-Marie greeted me when they found out that there was a priest on board. I have baptized many children.

Q: How is the American clergy recruited?

A: To date most priests have come over from Europe. We are only beginning to see priests who were born here (which is much better). We now have twelve or thirteen seminaries in the United States. Catholicism has made unbelievable progress here over the past forty years.

Q: How are the expenses of the church paid for?

A. Voluntary gifts. Family pews are the principal source of revenue.

Q: How are bishops selected?

A: The pope appoints them directly, but in practice he consults the bishops already in place. On occasion he has not done this, and in those cases his choices were seldom happy ones.[16]

* * *

Conversation with some Canadians (doing business with Indians).

On the evening of August 7, while walking along the bank of the Mackinac, I came upon a Canadian camp. I sat by the fire and had the following conversation with the leader of the Canadians (I took from this conversation only those observations that accord with my earlier impressions):

Q: What became of the Hurons and Iroquois who played such an important role in the history of the colonies?

A: The Hurons have virtually disappeared.[17] The Iroquois, half destroyed as well, have nearly all joined the Chippewa. Many have settled in or around Green Bay. The Iroquois were a clever tribe, always ready to fall in with us or the English depending on which fortune seemed to favor.[18]

Q: When you trade with the Indians, do you have anything to fear from them?

A: Virtually nothing. Indians are not thieves, and in any case we're useful to them.

Q: Do you think that Indians become better or worse from contact with Europeans?

A: I think that they're much better when they don't have contact with us, and they're certainly happier. You'll find better order and government among

16. The United States had eleven bishops at the time. About 2.5 percent of Americans were Catholic.

17. The Hurons frequently allied with the French and were enemies of the Iroquois.

18. A western arm of Lake Michigan forms Green Bay, between present-day Michigan and Wisconsin. The Iroquois were able to manage advantageous alliances among European and American forces until the American Revolution.

them as you move further into the wilderness. I make an exception, though, for Christian Indians and especially for Catholics. They're the best of all.

Q: Do the Indians you mention who live in the wilderness have leaders?

A: Yes, sir, they have chiefs, whose authority they respect in times of peace. The position of chief is hereditary, and its origins go back to time immemorial. In wartime Indians choose the bravest among them to be their leader. They have nothing quite comparable to our idea of justice, but when a murder is committed, they will turn the murderer over to the victim's family. In many cases the guilty party is able to rehabilitate himself, but more commonly he is put to death and buried along with his victim.

Q: How do these Indians live?

A: In comfort unknown in the vicinity of European settlements. They do not cultivate the land. They wear less on their bodies than we do and hunt only with bows and arrows. But game is amazingly plentiful in their forests. I imagine that it was like this all the way to the coast before Europeans landed here. But the game is now being driven westward at an incredible rate. It has retreated more than a hundred leagues beyond the last white settlements. The Indian tribes in these parts would die of hunger if they did not do a little farming.

Q: Don't the Indians realize that sooner or later their race will be wiped out by ours?

A: They worry incredibly little about the future. The tribes that are already half destroyed, in whose footsteps we march, are desperately aware of the Europeans' westward progress, but resistance is no longer possible. The tribes that live farther west (who I've heard number more than three million) apparently have no inkling of the danger that awaits them.

Q: Is it true that the Indians like the French?

A: Yes, quite true. They will speak nothing but French. In the remotest forests the best recommendation one can have is to be a French citizen. They still remember how well we treated them when we were in control of Canada. And many of us joined them as allies and live almost as they do.[19]

Q: How do the French of Canada bear English rule?

A: As an inevitable evil. But we do not integrate. We remain two distinct peoples. The French population of Canada has grown quite large.[20]

* * *

Conversation with Major Lamard, 12 August 1831.

Major Lamard is a well-bred and sensible individual. He has been stationed

19. American Indians' perceived fondness for the French stemmed in part from the large mixed-race population that descended primarily from unions between French fur traders and native women.

20. France had ceded its North American colonies to Britain upon its loss of the Seven Years' War in 1763.

at Prairie du Chien for a year and a half. The region is a vast plain bordering the Mississippi.[21] There is a European outpost here, which the Indians regard as neutral territory where different tribes can meet in peace.

Q: Do you think the Indians will ever adapt to civilization?

A: I doubt it. They shun work and harbor certain prejudices that tie them to a barbarous way of life. Negroes try to emulate Europeans but cannot. Indians could but do not want to. The only things they value are warfare and hunting, and they view work as degrading. Far from desiring the comforts of civilization, they feel nothing but disdain and contempt for such things. I have seen Indians on the coldest days of the year clad only in blankets. Far from envying our furs and our overcoats, they pity us for wearing such garments. They cannot imagine why anyone would want more than a wigwam for shelter or cultivate a field when all the game needed for survival can easily be had with a rifle.

Q: Do you think they would ever consider joining forces to attack whites?

A: No. Some of them are clearly aware of the ultimate fate that lies in store for their kind and have fought to prevent it. In general, however, Indians are too preoccupied with their private wars to contemplate uniting in some common interest. I said earlier that the Indian character was *indomitable.* Here is evidence for this. I knew the son of an Indian chief who attended one of our best schools until he was twenty years of age, at which point he returned to the forest. Then came the war between England and the United States. The young man joined others of his tribe and marched in our ranks. The Americans had absolutely forbidden the Indians allied with them to take the scalps of dead enemies. After the first battle, the young man in question encountered one of our officers. In the ensuing conversation he could not prevent himself from showing off a scalp that he had placed between his jacket and his shirt so as to conceal it from his superiors.

Q: What sort of government do they have?

A: They are ruled by hereditary chiefs, who are powerless until they prove their mettle. In wartime, they choose a warrior chief known for his skill and courage.

Q: What sort of justice do they practice?

A: When a man kills another man, he is sometimes handed over to the family of the deceased. Usually the tribal authorities do not intervene. It is up to the victim's relatives to avenge his death. Frequently a compromise is worked out.

21. Prairie du Chien, located at the confluence of the Wisconsin and Mississippi rivers in present-day Wisconsin, had served as a French and then a British fur-trading post. American forces ousted the British during the War of 1812 and built Fort Crawford there in 1816. Various native tribes signed treaties with the American government there throughout the 1840s.

* * *

Conversation with Mr. ***, superior of the seminary of Montreal (24 August 1831).[22]

Mr. *** struck us as an amiable and enlightened ecclesiastic. He came from France a few years ago.

He: I do not think that there is a people in the world happier than the Canadian. Their customs are gentle, civil and religious strife do not exist, and they pay no taxes.

Q: But is it not true that vestiges of the feudal system remain here?

A: Yes, but essentially in name only. Most of Canada is still divided into *seigneuries.* Anyone who lives on or buys land belonging to one of these *seigneuries* is obliged to pay rent to the *seigneur,* or lord, in addition to transfer fees. But the rent is trifling. The lord enjoys no honorific rights or superiority of any kind over his tenant. In my opinion, there is less distance between lord and tenant here than between landlord and farmer in Europe.

Q: How are the expenses of the church paid for?

A: By tithe. In general the clergy owns no land. The term "tithe" refers to a twenty-sixth part of the harvest. It is paid without reluctance or difficulty.

Q: Do you have monasteries?

A: No. In Canada there are only nunneries. In addition, all nuns lead active lives caring for children or the sick.

Q: Do you have freedom of the press?

A: Complete, unlimited freedom.

Q: Has anyone ever attempted to use that freedom against religion?

A: Never. Religion enjoys too much respect for a journalist to dare to attack it.

Q: Are the upper classes of society religious?

A: Yes, quite.

Q: Is there animosity between the two races?

A: Yes, but not acute animosity. It doesn't affect everyday relations. Canadians maintain that the English government awards too many posts to people of English descent, while the English complain that the government favors the Canadians. In my opinion, both sides exaggerate. On the whole there is little religious animosity between the two nations, because the law provides for total tolerance.

Q: Do you think that this colony will soon escape English rule?

A: I do not. The Canadians are happy under the current regime.[23] They enjoy political freedom almost as great as in the United States. If they were to become independent, they would bear the burden of countless public expenses.

22. Joseph-Vincent Quiblier.

23. Lower Canada became a province in 1791, when Great Britain divided the province of Quebec into two parts. To the northeast of Upper Canada, Lower Canada stretched over present-day southern and eastern Quebec and Newfoundland and was populated mainly by

If they were to join the United States, they would have to fear the inundation of their population by a huge wave of emigration, and without English markets their ports, which are closed four months out of the year, would dwindle to nothing.

Q: Is it true that education is spreading?

A: The past few years have seen dramatic changes in this regard. A start has been made, and the Canadian race of tomorrow will be nothing like that of today.

Q: Are you afraid that such enlightenment will be inimical to the principles of religion?

A: It is too early to tell what the effect will be, but I believe that religion has nothing to fear.

Q: Will the Canadian race extend its dominion?

A: Yes, but slowly and little by little. It lacks the adventurous spirit and contempt for ties of birth and family that one sees in Americans. Canadians will abandon their villages and relatives only if absolutely forced to, and even then they will settle as nearby as possible. Still, there is considerable movement, as I said earlier, and it will increase a hundredfold as people acquire more education.

* * *

Conversation with Messrs. Mondelet, 24 August 1831.[24]

The Mondelets are lawyers in Montreal. They are intelligent and sensible young men.

Q: What is the ratio of the French population in Canada to the English population?

A: Nine to ten. But nearly all the wealth and commerce are in the hands of the English. They have family and contacts in England and can readily avail themselves of resources not available to us.

Q: Are there many French-language newspapers?

A: Two.

Q: What is the ratio of their subscribers to the subscribers of English papers?

French Canadians who continued to live in the area after France ceded the colony to Britain in 1763.

Quiblier's opinions reflected the most moderate, optimistic view of this situation. A more radical segment of the French Canadian population, called the Patriotes and led by Louis-Joseph Papineau, sought independence for Lower Canada. Papineau led an unsuccessful rebellion in 1837–38 and was exiled to the United States.

24. Spencer recommended that Tocqueville and Beaumont meet with Dominique (1799–1863) and Joseph-Elzéar (1801–1876) Mondelet. Dominique Mondelet was elected to the Legislative Assembly of Lower Canada as a representative of Montreal in 1831. In this capacity, he supported moderate reforms meant to increase the power of French Canadian citizens without creating a rift with England. He and his brother later became judges. Dominique Mondelet also conducted a study of penitentiaries based on Tocqueville's and Beaumont's model.

A: 800 to 1,300.

Q: Are these papers influential?

A: Yes, they have considerable influence, though less than people think in France.

Q: What is the position of the clergy? Do you find that the church has the political tendencies it is accused of having in Europe?

A: One could perhaps say that it secretly aspires to govern or rule, but that isn't saying much. On the whole, our clergy is eminently national. This is partly the result of the circumstances in which it finds itself. From shortly after the conquest to the present day, the English government has worked quietly to change the religious opinions of Canadians to blend more easily with those of the English. The interests of religion were therefore opposed to those of the government and in harmony with those of the people. So whenever there was a clash with the English, the clergy either took the lead or fell in with the rest of us. It was universally admired and respected. Rather than oppose the idea of liberty, it preached liberty itself. All the steps we took to promote public education, for which we battled hard and ran into opposition from the English, we took with the support of the clergy. In Canada, it is the Protestants who promote aristocratic ideas. Catholics are accused of being demagogues. What makes me think that our priests are special in Canada is the fact that the priests who occasionally arrive from France exhibit a tolerance of power and docility toward the government that we can scarcely imagine.

Q: Are morals pure in Canada?

A: Yes, very pure.

* * *

Conversation with Mr. *** in Quebec (merchant), 26 August 1831

Q: In your opinion, do you have anything to fear from the Canadians?

A: No. Among the French, it is the lawyers and wealthy who hate the English. They attack us vehemently in their newspapers and in the House of Commons. But it's all talk and nothing more. Most [French] Canadians are devoid of political passion, and nearly all the wealth is in our hands.

Q: But aren't you afraid that this large and unified population, though devoid of political passions today, might acquire such passions in the future?

A: Our numbers are increasing every day, and soon we'll have nothing to fear from that quarter. The [French] Canadians hate the Americans more than they hate us.

Note: in speaking of the [French] Canadians, Mr. ***'s phlegmatic features betrayed a very clear feeling of hatred and contempt. People seldom speak with so much passion about groups of which they are not afraid.

* * *

27 August 1831. Conversation with Mr. Neilson.[25]

Mr. Neilson is Scottish. Born in Canada, allied with Canadians, he speaks French as easily as he speaks his own tongue. Though a foreigner, Mr. Neilson can be regarded as one of the leaders of the Canadians in all their clashes with the English government. Though Protestant, he has been repeatedly chosen by the Canadians over the past fifteen years to represent them in the assembly chamber. All measures favorable to the Canadian population have found in him an ardent defender. In 1825, he and two other men were sent to England to present the grievances of the Canadians. Mr. Neilson has a vigorous and original mind. His birth and present social position, which stand in sharp contrast, sometimes color his ideas and conversation in unusual ways.

Q: In the current fiscal year, how much will Canada cost the English government?

A: Between 200 and 250 thousand pounds sterling.

Q: Does it provide England with any income?

A: None. Whatever customs duties are collected are used in the colonies. We would fight sooner than hand over one penny of our money to the English government.

Q: What, then, is England's interest in holding on to Canada?

A: The same interest that any great lord has in holding on to important possessions, which figure in their titles but cost them large amounts of money and often arouse ill will against them. Still, there is no denying that England has an indirect interest in holding on to us. In case of war with the United States, the Saint Lawrence is one route by which she can ship cargo and armies into the heart of America. In case of war with the nations of northern Europe, Canada would be an essential source of timber. And the costs are not as onerous as one might think. England is obliged to maintain control of the seas not for her glory but for her very lifeblood. The expenditures she must undertake in order to achieve that supremacy make the occupation of her colonies much less costly than it would be for a nation whose only goal was to hold on to those colonies.

Q: Do you think that the Canadians will soon get out from under English domination?

A: No, unless England drives us to it. Otherwise, it is completely against our interest to declare our independence. There are still only 600,000 of us in Lower Canada. If we were to become independent, we would soon be swallowed up by the United States. Our population would be crushed by an inevitable wave of emigration. We need to wait until there are enough of us to defend our nationality. Then we may become the Canadian nation. Left to itself, our

---

25. Beaumont reports a similar conversation in a diary fragment not translated for this volume, but he dates it a day earlier (*Lettres d'Amérique,* 131–35).

population is growing as fast as that of the United States. At the time of the conquest in 1763, there were only 60,000 of us.

Q: Do you think the French race will ever rid itself of the English race? (This question was put cautiously in view of our interlocutor's origins.)

A: No. I believe that both races will inhabit and share the same territory and that English will remain the official language as well as the language of business. Fortune has decreed that North America shall be English. But the French race will not disappear from Canada. Coexistence is not as difficult as you may think. What preserves your language here is above all *the clergy*. The clergy is the only *educated* and *intellectual* class that *needs* to speak French and that speaks it purely.

Q: Describe the character of the Canadian peasant.

A: The race is an admirable one, in my opinion. The Canadian peasant is simple in his tastes, very affectionate with his family, quite pure in his morals, and remarkably *sociable* and polite in his manners. At the same time he is very keen to resist oppression, as well as independent, courageous, and imbued with egalitarian spirit. Public opinion has incredible force here. There is no authority in the villages, yet public order is better maintained here than anywhere else in the world. If a man commits a crime, he is shunned. He must leave the village. If a man steals, no charge is filed against him, but he is banished in dishonor. No criminal has been executed in Canada for ten years. Children born out of wedlock are virtually unknown in our rural villages. There was one village (I've forgotten the name) where there had not been a single bastard for two hundred years. Ten years ago, an Englishman settled there and seduced one of the girls. The scandal was horrendous. Canadians are deeply attached to the land of their birth, to village and family. That is why it has proved so difficult to persuade them to seek their fortunes elsewhere. As I said earlier, moreover, they are eminently *social*. Friends meet, people gather for worship, crowds assemble at the church door—these are their only pleasures. Canadians are deeply religious. They pay the tithe without complaint. Anyone can avoid paying by declaring himself to be a Protestant, but no one has ever done such a thing. Here the clergy and the people are close. They share ideas and political interests and together do battle against the government. The clergy is recruited from the ranks of the people and exists only for the benefit of the people. Some people here accuse priests of being *demagogues*. I've never heard such a charge against Catholic priests in Europe. Indeed, the people here are liberal and enlightened yet deeply religious; their morals are exemplary. I am living proof of their tolerance: though a Protestant, Catholics have ten times elected me to our House of Commons, and I've never heard so much as a word of religious prejudice expressed toward me by anyone. French priests who come here from Europe have similar habits to ours but differ considerably from them in their political views.

I said earlier that Canadian peasants are highly sociable. Their sociability leads them to help one another at critical moments. If a farmer's field is damaged, the whole village will generally take a hand in setting things right. Recently, ***'s barn was damaged by lightning, and five days later the neighbors had rebuilt it without cost to the owner.

Q: Do any vestiges of feudalism remain?

A: Yes, but they are almost imperceptible. (1) The landlord to whom a land grant has been made receives a very small rent from his tenants, ranging for example from six to eight francs for ninety acres. (2) Tenants are required to have their grain milled at the landlord's mill, but he cannot charge more than an amount fixed by law, which is below the amount paid in the United States with its free market and competition. (3) There are dues known as *lods et ventes*, which means that when the owner of enfeoffed land sells, he is obliged to pay one-twelfth of the proceeds to the landlord. This would be a rather heavy charge if the population were not in the main so invincibly attached to the land. These are the only remaining traces of the feudal system in Canada. What is more, landlords here enjoy no honorific rights or privileges. There is no nobility now and never will be. Here as in the United States, a man must work in order to live. There are no tenant farmers, so landlords are themselves usually farmers. Yet despite this reduction in the status of landlords to a level of rough equality with everyone else, people are still somewhat afraid of them and envious of their advantages. Some of them have managed to win election to the House of Commons, but only by affiliating themselves with the people's party. Peasants here remember the subaltern status in which they were kept under the French government. Indeed, there is a word in their political lexicon that still sends shivers down their spines, and that word is *taille* [tallage]. They no longer know precisely what the word means, but it still stands for something intolerable. I am convinced that they would take arms if anyone tried to institute a tax bearing that name.

Q: What are the requirements for election to your House of Commons?

A: There are none.

Q: Who votes in rural areas?

A: Anyone who earns an income of forty-one livres from the land is eligible to vote.

Q: With such a broad suffrage is there nothing to fear?

A: No. Everyone here owns land. They are religious, are devoted to order, and make good choices, and although they take a great interest in elections, there is rarely any trouble connected with them. The English tried to import their corrupt system here, but they failed utterly on account of the morality and honor of our peasants.

Q: What progress has been made in primary education?

A: That is a long story. When the French ruled, there was no education. Canadians never put down their arms and could not afford to spend time in school. After the conquest, the English took care only of their own. Twenty years ago, the government tried to establish a school system, but they went about it clumsily, and religious sensibilities were offended. It appeared that the government wanted to use the schools to promote Protestantism, or at any rate that was what *we* said, and the project failed. The English said that the Catholic clergy preferred to keep the people in ignorance. Neither side told the truth, but that's what partisan language is like. Four years ago our House of Commons realized that if the Canadian population were not educated, it would eventually be dominated by a population of foreigners that would settle either in its midst or in close proximity. Speeches were made, advice was given, funds were appropriated, and school inspectors were appointed. I am one, and in fact I've just returned from an inspection tour. The report I shall make is a most satisfactory one. Things are off to a good start. The people are incredibly eager to learn. The clergy is pouring a great deal of effort into helping us. Half the children already attend our schools, on the order of fifty thousand of them. In two or three years I have no doubt that we will have *all* of them.[26] I hope that the Canadian race will then begin to move away from the riverbanks and into the interior. Until now we have settled both banks of the Saint Lawrence over a distance of 120 leagues, but the line of settlements seldom exceeds a breadth of 10 leagues. Yet there is excellent land farther from the river, and most of it sells for almost nothing (literally) and can be cultivated quite easily (the price of labor is three francs in the towns and less in the countryside). Food is very cheap. Canadian peasants themselves make almost everything they need: shoes, clothing, and woolens (*I have seen this*).

Q: Do you think that Frenchmen can come here and make homes for themselves?

A: Yes. Our House of Commons passed a law a year ago abolishing the so-called *aubaine*. After seven years of residence, a foreigner becomes Canadian and enjoys all the rights of a citizen.

We went with Mr. Neilson to see the village of Lorette, which is three leagues from Quebec and was founded by Jesuits.[27] Mr. Neilson showed us the old church that the Jesuits built and remarked that "the memory of the Jesuits is revered in these parts." The homes of the Indians are very well kept. They speak French and look almost European, although their dress is different. Nearly all are of mixed blood. I expressed surprise that they did not farm the land. "Bah!" Mr. Neilson exclaimed. "These Hurons are aristocrats. They would find it dishonorable to work. 'To scratch the earth like cattle is fit only for Frenchmen and Englishmen,' they say. They still live by hunting and the women's handicrafts."[28]

Q: Is it true that the Indians have a predilection for the French?

A: Yes, there's no doubt about it. As a people, the French may retain more of their original character than most others, yet they are also more apt for a time

26. Neilson's projection of the growth of public schools proved to be too optimistic. In 1836, Lower Canada's twelve hundred primary schools educated only about thirty-nine thousand students.

27. The Jesuits founded this village in the seventeenth century as a mission to convert the Hurons to Christianity.

28. The mixed-race population not only subsisted by these efforts but also controlled a great deal of the region's trade.

to embrace the mores, ideas, and prejudices of whatever people they live among. It was by becoming savages yourselves that you earned the savages' affection, which persists to this day.

Q: What became of the Hurons who were so steadfastly devoted to the French and who played such a large role in the history of the colony?

A: They slowly disappeared.[29] Yet they were once the largest Indian tribe on the continent, able to muster an army of 60,000 men. You see what remains. It is believed that nearly all the savages of North America come from the same stock. Only the Eskimos of Hudson's Bay clearly belong to a different race. There, everything is different: language, canoes, etc. I was just speaking of the French aptitude for adopting savage ways. In Canada there was once a species of man, now almost extinct, that distinguished itself in this, namely, the fur traders, known as *voyageurs*.[30] They were drawn from all ranks of the population. I don't believe that there was ever a bolder, more adventurous race of men. They went into the forests, where they astonished even the Indians and won their respect.

* * *

Boston, 16 September.

To Mr. Dwight,[31] a most zealous Protestant minister who spoke to me of the benign effects of education, I said that "there are people in France who are blindly in love with education. They imagine that merely by teaching a man to read, write, and do sums, you make him a good citizen and almost a virtuous man. Do Americans make the same mistake?"

He answered, "Probably not. No one here would argue what is often argued in Europe, that education can be pernicious. Implicit in our position is the idea that all education must be moral and religious. If anyone were to attempt to introduce a different system, it would provoke a general outcry, a sort of popular uprising, and everyone would say that it would be better to have no education than education of that sort. All our children learn to read by studying the Bible."

Mr. Dwight added that in his opinion religion was making progress in the United States. He told me that recently published reports showed that the number of people receiving Protestant communion had greatly increased in the year just past. He admitted, however, that there are (I believe) thirteen Unitarian churches in Boston.[32] In all of Boston there are sixty churches for sixty thousand souls.

29. The Hurons suffered a great defeat at the hands of the Iroquois in the mid-seventeenth century. This loss diminished the population and caused communities to disperse.

30. Beginning in the seventeenth century, these fur trappers pushed west and southwest from Quebec in search of game and sold their skins to large fur companies. They developed alliances with a number of native communities, but they disappeared at the beginning of the nineteenth century as relations with natives began to sour.

31. Louis Dwight, who opposed the Philadelphia system of solitary confinement, provided Tocqueville and Beaumont with numerous documents.

32. Unitarian churches experienced great growth in Boston during the second quarter of the nineteenth century. This faith emphasized the importance of reason in spiritual life

* * *

General Remarks. Boston, 18 September 1831.

I have thus far been surprised to discover how knowledgeable *educated people* in America are about French affairs. I have yet to meet one who thinks that we are ready to tolerate a republic or democratic institutions. It may be that, because they are such intimate witnesses to the effects of freely expressed popular passions in their own country, they are in a better position than we are to judge how difficult it is to obtain a good government, to say nothing of a stable government, from such elements. *All* believe that if a people is to be republican, it must be *level-headed, religious,* and *highly educated.* Many concede that, quite apart from these conditions, material prosperity is also essential, so that unsatisfied wants rarely lead to domestic disturbances. Some hint or even state forthrightly that America must eventually end in *monarchy* but that that time surely lies in the quite distant future. The educated classes feel no enthusiasm for M. de La Fayette. Nearly all think that the Restoration regime was the best arrangement for France and that the current revolution is a dangerous crisis that may prove fatal to liberty in Europe. By contrast, the middle classes, the people and the newspapers, representing the popular passions, are impelled by blind instinct to subscribe to all the principles of liberty that are professed in Europe and to all the men who profess them. That is why the most religious nation in the world has expressed its heartfelt wish for the success of the French political party that has most openly professed its hatred of all religion.

Non-alphabetic Notebooks 2 and 3

18 September 1831.

Today Mr. Clay (a Georgia planter, and seldom have I seen a man more amiable or better informed)[33] showed me a number of Boston's fine residences and told me that most of the men who had built these sumptuous homes were self-made and had started from very humble origins. He added: "Fortunes change hands here with incredible rapidity. People say that a wealthy father is almost always succeeded by a poor son and that families generally remain illustrious for only

---

and promoted the anti-Trinitarian belief in a single God and the humanity of Jesus. Unitarian churches operated as autonomous congregations within a loose association and often promoted social reform.

33. Nothing more is known about this Mr. Clay.

one generation." I asked what the reason for this was. I understand that your inheritance laws encourage the destruction of family fortunes. But in France the laws are even more democratic, and although fortunes there no doubt gradually shrink, they do not evaporate overnight as yours do. "The reason for the difference," Mr. Clay answered, "is that in France great fortunes are based on land, whereas in New England they are all commercial. Here, and indeed in America generally, tenant farmers are rare, because land is too cheap and its fruits sell for too little for anyone to cultivate the soil unless he owns it. Without tenant farmers you have no great landed wealth. But great commercial fortunes can be amassed and preserved only by industrious and talented individuals, and industriousness and talent cannot be bequeathed as easily as dollars; seldom do these qualities pass from father to son. By contrast, in the South, where our slaves do the work of your tenants, fortunes evaporate no more rapidly than they do in France."

This led us to speak of slaves. Mr. Clay said: "In our southern states there are many areas in which whites find it difficult to adjust to the climate but blacks thrive and prosper. Over time, I imagine that as the black population of the South gains its freedom, it will concentrate in those areas, while the white population will gradually abandon them. Thus a people of purely African descent will eventually form a nation of its own, with its own laws. I can see no other solution to the great issue of slavery. I do not think that blacks will ever mix with whites completely enough to form a single people. The introduction of this alien race to American soil remains, moreover, the one great blemish on America."

Note: Is the difficulty that Mr. Clay mentions, of establishing landed wealth in the northern states (which is undoubtedly the case), perhaps largely responsible for the commercial, industrial, and speculative spirit that is such a distinctive aspect of the people's character in this part of the Union? Only commerce and industry can assuage the passion for wealth in New England.

* * *

17 September 1831.
Today, Mr. Sparks (a distinguished Boston man of letters) told me that "the majority of educated people now recognize that General Jackson is not fit to fill the office of president. His lack of experience in matters of civilian government, as well as his advanced age, makes him unsuitable for the position. Yet he will be reelected."

"Why?" I asked.

"Our people," Mr. Sparks replied, "are not like yours. Public opinion here forms slowly and is unlikely to change suddenly, though it is only too prone to error. Much time and effort were devoted to persuading people that General Jackson is a great man and a credit to his country, and success followed. To persuade people otherwise will take time, and the general still commands a majority."

* * *

Today, Mr. Quincy, the president of the University of Cambridge [Harvard],[34] said: "The state of Massachusetts is a collection of small republics, which choose their own officials and take care of their own affairs."—But, I asked, what is the central bond?—"The legislature," Mr. Quincy answered. "The law fixes the sphere of action of each of these little republics, and beyond this they are completely subordinate to this larger political body, which represents the people. When individual communities violate the law, the state attorney general takes them to court. They can even be sued by any individual who deems himself to have been harmed by their actions. Suppose a town is responsible for repairing a road and fails to do so, and I damage my wagon while driving there. I can sue the town for damages."

Mr. Quincy also said: "I believe that, even more than to our constitution, we owe our good fortune to circumstances beyond our will. All man's material needs are satisfied here, and we are born free. We have known no other condition. In nearly all respects Massachusetts was as free before the Revolution as it is today. For the king's name we substituted that of the people, but nothing else changed."

Note: One of the most pleasant consequences of the absence of government (in the rare country fortunate enough to do without one) is the development of individual powers that infallibly ensues. Every man learns to think and act for himself without relying on any outside power, which, no matter how vigilant it may be, can never respond to every social need. A man accustomed to relying on his own efforts to secure his well-being exalts himself in his own eyes as well as in the eyes of others; his soul is thereby strengthened and enlarged. Mr. Quincy gave an example of this when he described the person who sued the town that had allowed a public road to fall into disrepair. One sees the same spirit at work everywhere. Suppose, for example, that a man has an idea for some social improvement: a school, a hospital, a highway. He does not think of turning to the authorities. He publishes his plan, proposes to set to work, calls on other individuals to join him, and tackles every obstacle head-on. Granted, he often does the job less well than if the authorities had done it in his stead, but, taken together, countless individual initiatives accomplish much more than any public administration could have done. What is more, the influence of this enterprising attitude on the public and moral character of the people more than makes up for any deficiencies. Yet it bears repeating that few nations can make do without a government. Only in two extremes of civilization has it been possible to do so. Savages, who have only physical needs to satisfy, also rely on no one but themselves. In order for civilized men to do the same, they must have

34. Josiah Quincy III had instituted a number of urban reforms and development projects to modernize the city when mayor of Boston from 1823 to 1828.

achieved a social state sufficiently enlightened to allow them to perceive clearly what needs to be done, and they must also have achieved sufficient control over their passions to do it. The primary concern of a good government should be to accustom people little by little to get along without it.

* * *

21 September 1831.

Conversation with Mr. Gray. Mr. Gray is a Massachusetts state senator. He is also a man of considerable talent.[35]

"Do you," I asked him, "have a set of laws that apply to municipal government?"

"No," Mr. Gray answered. "We have general principles. Everything else is a matter of habit."

Q. What are those principles, and how are they applied in practice?

A. The general principle is that the people[36] have the right, through their representatives, to govern the towns, but they must refrain from exercising that right when it comes to such internal town matters as maintaining law and order, administering tax revenues, and other strictly local affairs. The legislature never involves itself in such things. The towns themselves take care of local business through agents whom they select annually. The accepted rule is that as long as a town limits itself to local affairs and refrains from infringing anyone's rights, it is omnipotent within its own sphere. Thus it has the unlimited right to tax itself to pay for certain activities, and its budget is not subject to outside review.

Q. What happens if a town fails to abide by the law?

A. The attorney general summons it as an individual before the grand jury of the county in which it is situated. No resident of the town may sit on this jury. If convicted, the town may be required to pay a fine.

Q. How can a town be forced to pay a fine? In France, prefects are empowered to deduct penalties from the local budget.

A. We do things differently here. The law allows a person to whom compensation or damages have been awarded to make a claim against such residents of the town as he may choose. Residents against whom claims of this sort are filed then have claims of their own against the town and may act accordingly. But this is purely theoretical. In order to avoid such procedures, towns are always quick to pay claims against them.

Q. Do judges have much political power?

A. Our courts are the leading power in the state. Everyone concedes that they can refuse to enforce laws they deem unconstitutional, and in fact they do refuse to enforce such laws daily. I regard the grant of such power to judges as one of the greatest guarantees of liberty that a people can have. And the judges

35. And interests, including collecting rare engravings and sponsoring a museum of comparative zoology at Harvard.

36. That is, the people of the state.

do not misuse this power. They are careful to avoid provoking criticism. People know them and participate in the deliberations of the courts through juries. To my mind, one of the great benefits of having juries in civil cases is that they foster close relations between judges and the people, thus encouraging mutual confidence and greatly increasing the moral influence of the magistracy.

Q. While you're on the subject of juries, would you explain why it is that in America, or at any rate in the state of New York, you avoid juries in cases involving failure to honor good-faith agreements and other affairs of conscience? It seems to me that juries are especially useful in deciding such cases. What is the significance of your chancery courts?

A. I should first point out that chancery courts in Massachusetts are not organized in the same way [as in New York]. Here, cases of the sort you describe are heard, like all other cases, by a jury, unless the parties object. There are chancery courts in New York and many other states because the people in those states chose to follow the English model blindly. So the question is why the oddity you describe, which I concede to be odd indeed, exists in English law. And the answer is that in England, Roman law had at a certain point fallen completely into abeyance. All law was customary, and all cases were heard by juries. As the nation became civilized, however, the defects of customary law became increasingly apparent, and those defects were such that I do not believe that a people that remained subject to such law could ever have become enlightened. Little by little, elements of *written law* began to be invoked. The change began with the clergy, which was the best-educated and most enlightened class. Being enlightened and ambitious, the priests succeeded in attracting many litigants to their courts on one pretext or another. In general, these were cases of failure to honor good-faith agreements, which touched on matters of conscience. Now, in the ecclesiastical courts, where written law applied, there were no juries. Hence such cases were not heard by juries. Later, the chancery courts replaced the ecclesiastical courts, and although the reasons for excluding juries no longer existed, people continued to follow the old procedures out of habit. That is how an institution that originated in the power of the Roman Catholic Church survived and eventually established itself here, in a nation of Protestant republicans.

* * *

22 September 1831.

Mr. [Francis] Lieber (a young German banished for his liberal views, who has made a name for himself in the United States with a work entitled *Encyclopedia Americana*)[37] told me the following this evening: "We Europeans think we can establish a republic by organizing an immense political body of some kind. In

37. Born in Berlin, Francis Lieber (1798–1872) became a strong proponent of political liberty early in life. After fighting for Greek independence from Turkey and angering Prussian government officials, he escaped persecution by immigrating to Boston in 1827. He later became a professor at South Carolina College and at Columbia University in New York. He wrote *Political Ethics* (1838) and *On Civil Liberty and Civil Government* (1853), books foundational

TOCQUEVILLE'S TRAVEL NOTEBOOKS

fact, a republic is a form of government that depends more than any other on society as a whole. Take this country, for example. The Republic is everywhere, in the streets as well as in Congress. If some obstruction blocks a public way, the neighbors will form a deliberative body on the spot. They will appoint a committee and solve the problem by making sage use of their collective talents. If there is to be a public ceremony or banquet, you'll find that people come together, deliberate, and decide who is to take responsibility for what needs to be done. It would never occur to anybody that some preexisting authority ought to take charge. The people are republican in their very marrow."

On another occasion he said: "How can anyone who has seen America believe that it would be possible to transplant the American political system to Europe, much less to do so overnight? Having seen this country, I cannot believe that M. de La Fayette subscribes to his theories in good faith. It is impossible to go so seriously astray. As for myself, I am increasingly inclined to think that constitutions and political regulations are of no importance in themselves. Such creations are lifeless and inert until the mores and social situation of the people breathe life into them."

We asked: "Is it true that morals here are as pure as people say?" He answered that "the morals of the lower classes are less good than those of the educated classes but better, I think, than in the same classes in Europe. As for the educated classes, their morals are as impeccable as you might imagine. I do not believe that there is anything scandalous anywhere in Boston society. A woman whose reputation was suspect would be doomed here. Yet women are very flirtatious, bolder than in Europe, because they know that beyond a certain point they cannot go and no one would ever believe that they had gone. In the end, I prefer our European women with all their faults to the selfish and chilly virtue of the Americans."

Q. How do you explain the incredible control that people maintain over their passions here?

A. There are a thousand explanations: their physical constitution, the residue of Puritanism, work habits, the absence of an idle and corrupt class such as a garrison, early marriage, and even the way houses are built, which makes it almost impossible to keep an illicit affair secret.

Q. Some say that young men don't behave all that well before marriage.

A. True enough, and their tastes, like those of the English, can be quite crude, but like the English they distinguish radically between the society they normally live in and the company they keep for pleasure. It's as though there were two worlds having nothing in common. They would never try to seduce a respectable woman.

As we walked with Mr. Lieber, we passed a gentleman to whom he pointed and said, "That man is the sheriff. He was a colonel in the army. Yesterday we

---

to the development of political science; he also wrote Abraham Lincoln's General Orders 100, a classic codification of military engagement.

saw him at the home of the city's mayor, Mr. Otis.[38] (This was true.) Well, two months ago, I saw him hang two men."

Q. How can that be? we asked.

A. In America, sheriffs also serve as executioners.

Q. So no shame attaches to functions of that kind?

A. None whatsoever. The sheriff who executes a criminal is merely obeying the law, as did the magistrate who sentenced the man to death. People here respect the agents of the law because they have the utmost respect for the law itself (on account of having made it), so they feel no animosity toward police officers, tax collectors, or customs inspectors. All of these are honorable functions.

He also spoke to us about Germany. "We suffer from the fact that we are not a single people. There is a literary Germany but not a political Germany. It is far more difficult for a people to achieve political unity, in my opinion, than to acquire liberty. I would consider it a great boon if a single yoke could be placed upon all Germans, even if it were a yoke of iron. That way they would become a single people, and eventually they would gain their freedom."

Reflection: What is most troublesome in Europe is when men of inferior birth receive an education that gives them the desire to rise above their rank but not the means to do so. This flaw is almost nowhere to be found in America. Education *always* provides the natural means to acquire wealth and creates no social malaise.

* * *

28 September.

Today Mr. Gray said this: "To my mind, it is difficult to create large political bodies but even more difficult to establish municipal institutions. When I say municipal institutions, I refer not to formal entities but to the spirit that breathes life into them. The habit of subjecting all public business, even the most minute matters, to debate and majority rule is more difficult to acquire than any other. Yet this is what defines a truly free government. It is what sets New England apart not only from all the countries of Europe but also from the rest of the United States. Even our children, when they disagree, do not turn to their teachers but settle things themselves, and by the time a youngster is fifteen he has already sat in judgment in hundreds of disputes. I have no doubt that the lowliest man in Boston has a more parliamentary spirit and greater familiarity with public debate than most of your deputies. But two hundred years of effort have gone into shaping this spirit, and we began with English habits and a religion thoroughly republican in its inception."

Q. Do you think, then, that the political character of New Englanders doesn't have much to do with their nature?

38. Harrison Gray Otis (1765–1848) was mayor of Boston from 1829 to 1831, when he became embroiled in a property scheme undertaken to keep the state capital in Boston. Otis lived in a Beacon Street house designed by architect Charles Bulfinch.

A. Nature has something to do with it, but their political character is above all a consequence of laws and even more of habits.

* * *

29 September 1831.

This evening, Mr. (Alexander) Everett, a former United States ambassador to Spain and a distinguished writer,[39] said: "A people's point of departure is a matter of immense importance. The consequences for good or ill are so far-reaching that they constantly take us by surprise. Our English ancestors allowed imprisonment for proven debt. With far less justification they even allowed a debtor to be imprisoned before his debt was proven in court. We inherited this law, but lately it has come under attack, and several states have begun to modify it. In the state of New York, a new law will take effect next year abolishing imprisonment for debt completely. In Kentucky, imprisonment for proven debt has been abolished, yet a plaintiff may still insist that the defendant be jailed while judgment is pending." This example shows how difficult it is to break with customs that originated with the nation itself.

* * *

29 September 1831.

Today Mr. Sparks said: "Our provincial newspapers are all preoccupied with matters of national policy. They take positions for or against the federal government. Thus their influence may be compared with that of the two or three leading Paris newspapers in your country. Newspapers seldom disagree about the policies of state governments. They devote little attention to such matters and are mainly concerned with the petty interests of the localities in which they appear. That, at any rate, is how things are in Massachusetts."

Q. Representatives and senators are elected every year. Does this sometimes result in a complete change of legislative personnel?

A. No. In general, three-quarters of the members are reelected.

Q. Does the choice of governor stir much controversy, and are elections hotly contested?

A. The governor of Massachusetts has little power and is elected for one year. The post is therefore not passionately coveted, and the loser can always hope to replace the winner the following year, which moderates the ardor of the parties. In Pennsylvania, where the governor has much more power, including, for example, the power to *remove* as well as to appoint public officials, and where he remains in office for three years, elections are often hotly disputed.

Q. In order for the president of the United States to govern, is it necessary for him to have a majority in Congress?

39. Alexander Everett (1792–1847) had accompanied John Quincy Adams to Russia and had served as an ambassador to the Netherlands and to Spain. He published a book on the political state and future of Europe in 1822; five years later, he published a similar book about the United States. In 1831, he was editor of the *North American Review* and served in the Massachusetts legislature.

A. No. In fact, presidents have often not had the majority. General Jackson did not have a majority in the last Congress.

Mr. Sparks added: "In this country the political dogma is that the majority is always right. All things considered, we were right to adopt this principle, but there is no denying that experience has often shown it to be wrong. (He cited any number of examples.) Sometimes the majority has sought to oppress the minority. Fortunately, we have guarantees against the passions and errors of democracy in the governor's veto and above all in the power of judges to refuse to enforce unconstitutional laws."

He continued: "I believe that our government and mores are best explained by our origins. Upon arriving here we were already republicans and zealous Christians. We were then left to ourselves, forgotten in our little corner of the world. Nearly all societies, even in America, begin with government concentrated in a particular place and subsequently expand around that central point. But our ancestors founded *towns before there was a state.* Plymouth, Salem, and Charleston [Charlestown] existed before there was any government of Massachusetts to speak of. Only later did they join together, and then by an act of their own will. You will appreciate the extent to which such a point of departure must have strengthened not only republican principles but also the *town spirit* that is such a prominent distinguishing characteristic of New England, even among Americans. Those who wish to imitate us should note carefully that our history was unprecedented."

* * *

Boston, 30 September.
Today Mr. Coolidge[40] said: "Catholicism doesn't frighten us because we are convinced that it will adapt to our political mores rather than the other way around. Experience has shown that Catholics here always vote for the more democratic party. Of course they are also among the poorest of our people. Baltimore, where they dominate, is the most democratic city in the United States. Charles Carroll is Catholic."

Q. Do you ever notice the absence of government?

A. No, on the contrary, our greatest fear is that government will meddle where it is not needed.

* * *

Boston, 1 October 1831.
Interview with Mr. Adams (the former president). We met him at Mr. Everett's, where we were invited for dinner. He was received with all the politeness due an honored guest, but that was all. Most of the guests addressed him as "Sir," while a few used the honorific form "Mr. President." Mr. Adams is a man of sixty-two

40. Joseph Coolidge Jr. (1798–1879) had married Thomas Jefferson's granddaughter Ellen Wayles Randolph in 1825. The couple resided in Boston, although Coolidge traveled frequently as an agent in the China trade.

who seems still quite vigorous in mind and body. He speaks French with ease and elegance. I was seated next to him, and we had a lengthy conversation.

I expressed my astonishment at the degree to which Americans were able to do without government. Among other things, I remarked that people of every shade of opinion had the right to send others to represent them in conventions and public meetings advertised in advance. Mr. Adams replied "that five or six years ago such conventions were still a novelty. Today we hold them for all sorts of reasons. But if you want my frank opinion, I think they're dangerous. They usurp the rightful place of our representative institutions[41] and may ultimately interfere with their effectiveness."[42]

We talked about the American character in general, and he said that "there are two things that have had a great influence on our character. In the North, the religious and political doctrines of the original founders of New England, and in the South, slavery."

[Q.] Do you regard slavery as a great blemish on the United States?

[A.] Yes, certainly, it is responsible for nearly all our present difficulties and fears about the future.

Q. Are Southerners aware of this?

A. Yes, in their heart of hearts, but they will not admit the truth to themselves even though it is obvious that it worries them. Slavery has influenced every aspect of southern society, Mr. Adams added. The whites there constitute a class that has all the ideas, prejudices, and passions of an aristocracy, but, make no mistake, nowhere is equality greater among whites than in the South. Here we have great equality before the law, but when it comes to the customs of daily life, that equality disappears completely. There is an upper class and a working class. Every white man in the South is equally privileged, in that he has the right to put Negroes to work while doing none himself. You cannot imagine the degree to which Southerners have embraced the idea that labor is dishonorable. Any form of enterprise in which Negroes cannot be employed as inferiors has no chance of success in the South. All the major businessmen in Charleston and other southern cities came originally from New England. I can remember one occasion when a congressman from the South dined with me in Washington and could not refrain from expressing his surprise at the sight of white servants waiting on us. To Mrs. Adams he said, "I find the use of white servants degrading to the human race. If a white comes to change my plate, I'm always tempted to offer him my place at the table." The fact that southern whites live in idleness has had a major influence on their character. They devote themselves to

---

41. The original French text has *"corps politiques."*

42. Americans were holding these conventions to debate the merits and dangers of protective tariffs. The danger that Adams alludes to manifested itself in a South Carolina convention in 1832, during which representatives declared the protective tariffs of 1828 and 1832 null and void. After a tense conflict over nullification, South Carolina repealed these measures in exchange for a lower tariff.

physical exercise, hunting, and horse racing. They are men of vigorous constitution, brave, and prickly about their honor. Questions of honor are more delicate in the South than anywhere else, and duels are common.

Q. Do you think that the South really cannot do without blacks?

A. I am convinced that the opposite is true, Mr. Adams replied. Europeans work the land in Greece and Sicily. Why can't they do the same in Virginia and the Carolinas, where the climate is no hotter?

Q. Is the number of slaves increasing?

A. It is decreasing in all states east of the Delaware, where wheat and tobacco are grown, because for those crops Negroes are more of a burden than a benefit. Hence blacks are exported from those states to states where cotton and sugar are grown, and there their numbers are increasing. In the western states where slaves have been introduced, their numbers remain quite small. I know of nothing more insolent than a black, Mr. Adams added, when he is not addressing his master and is not afraid of being beaten. Indeed, if a master is weak, it is not uncommon for his Negroes to treat him quite badly. Negresses especially take advantage of the kindness of their mistresses. They know that corporal punishment is not customarily used on them.

We discussed religion, which Mr. Adams apparently regards as one of the most [important] safeguards of American society. I asked him if he thought that the religious impulse in the United States was on the wane. "If you compare the current state of religion to the state a century [ago]," he replied, "the answer is yes. But if you compare what exists today with what existed forty years ago, I think that religion has gained ground rather than lost it. Forty years ago, the philosophy of Voltaire in France and the school of Hume in England had undermined faith all across Europe. This had strong repercussions in America. Since then, the crimes of the French Revolution have left a deep impression on us. The intellectual revulsion is still felt today."

"Still," I replied, "ideas have come a long way since the inception of Catholicism. Don't you think that ideas about religion will continue to evolve, and don't you see your country's Unitarianism as the final stage in a movement toward natural religion?" Mr. Adams conceded that he did share this view. He added: "What is more, all the Boston Unitarians strongly resist the suggestion that their teachings will have this effect and adhere firmly to their extreme positions."

Mr. Adams apparently believes that one of the greatest guarantees of order and domestic tranquility in the United States lies in the westward movement of the population. "Many more generations will pass," he added, "before we begin to experience the consequences of overpopulation."

I then brought up more imminent dangers to the Union and potential reasons for its dissolution. Mr. Adams did not reply, but it was easy to see that on this point he had [no] more confidence in the future than I did.

Mr. Adams has just been elected to Congress. Many people are surprised that he agreed to fill this post. He is the first president to return to public life after leaving office.

* * *

2 October 1831.

I went today to see Mr. Channing, the most celebrated preacher and most notable writer (of serious works) in America today. Mr. Channing is a small man with an air of being worn out by his labors. His eyes are nevertheless full of fire and his manners warm. He has one of the most penetrating minds I know. He gave us a marvelous welcome, and we proceeded to have a lengthy conversation, from which I include the excerpts below.

We brought up the ebb of religion in France, and he responded: "I take a very lively interest in France, and I believe that its fate is linked to the fate of Europe generally. You have tremendous moral influence on your neighbors, and all the nations of the Continent will follow your lead. You hold in your hands a greater power for good or evil than any nation that has ever existed. I cannot believe that there is no hope for religion in France. Everything in your history demonstrates that you are a religious people. And besides, I believe that the human need for religion is so urgent that it is unnatural for a great nation to resist it. Indeed, I hope that you will take yet another step toward human perfection and not stop in midcourse as the English have done. They cling to the Protestantism of the seventeenth century. I am confident that France is called to a higher destiny and will discover a still purer form of religion."

We discussed Unitarianism with Mr. Channing and told him that many adherents of other Protestant sects had expressed to us their disapproval.

"The issue between them and us is whether the seventeenth century can be revived or has disappeared forever. They were the first to blaze a new trail and claim to have halted at precisely the place where the first innovator halted. We claim to be forging ahead. We insist that human reason has made progress and that what people believed in a century of crudeness and corruption is no longer tenable in the enlightened times in which we live now."

Don't you and your friends fear, I put it to him bluntly, that in seeking to purify Christianity, you will end up draining it of its substance? I am frightened, I confessed, by the turn that the human spirit has taken away from Catholicism, and I fear the end of the road will be natural religion.

"I believe," Mr. Channing replied, "that there is little reason to fear such an outcome. Man needs positive religion, and why would he ever abandon Christianity? The evidence for the Christian religion can withstand the most serious intellectual scrutiny."

"Allow me to raise one objection," I replied. "It applies not only to Unitarianism but to all the Protestant sects, and its political significance is enormous. Do you not believe that human nature is so constituted that, no matter how much improvement there is in education and the state of society, there will always be a large number of people incapable, owing to the nature of their position, of applying their reason to abstract theoretical questions and who will, if deprived of dogmatic faith, believe in absolutely nothing?"

Mr. Channing replied: "The objection you raise is indeed the most serious

challenge that can be raised against the fundamental principle of Protestantism. Nevertheless, I do not believe that it must go unanswered. (1) First, I do
not think that, for anyone of righteous heart, religious questions are as difficult
as you seem to believe, and I think that God has put answers to these questions
within everyone's reach. (2) Second, it seems to me that Catholicism leaves the
problem intact. I grant that once the dogma of the infallibility of the church is
accepted, the rest follows easily, but in order to accept that dogma, surely you
need to appeal to reason."

This argument seemed to me more specious than solid, but since our time
was limited, I decided to approach the question from another angle: "It seems
to me that Catholicism had established that ability should govern in religion—
religious aristocracy, if you will—whereas you introduced democracy. I confess
that the possibility of governing religious as well as political society by means
of democracy does not seem to me to have been proven yet by experience."

Mr. Channing responded: "I do not think that the comparison between the
two types of society should be pushed too far. I myself believe that everyone
can comprehend the truths of religion, while I do not believe that everyone can
comprehend political issues. For example, when the issue of the tariff, about
which the greatest economists are divided, is submitted to the judgment of the
people, my reaction is that one might as well submit the issue to the judgment
of my son over there (he pointed to a child of ten). No, I do not believe that
civil society is made to be governed directly by masses of people who remain
comparatively ignorant. I think we go too far."

* * *

2 October 1831.

I spent today with Mr. Clay (a very ardent Presbyterian).[43] He warmly pleaded
the case for democracy and religion. "We are in a very special and favorable position, I grant you. Yet I hold out hope that ultimately all enlightened nations
will follow our example."

"What!" I replied. "Do you really believe that a day will come when the
great nations of Europe will be able to tolerate unlimited democracy of the sort
you have here?"

"I hope so. Especially those that are already Protestant or may become so in
the future. I believe that Protestantism is indispensable to a republican people.
Religion is our best security for liberty. It enhances our freedom and sanctifies
its principles. If ever we were to abandon religion, we would find ourselves in
a very dangerous condition. All educated men here share this view. We know
that people who migrate to the West lose something of the religious habits of
their ancestors. This alarms us greatly. Indeed, we are so firmly convinced that
to allow a society without religion to grow up in our vicinity poses a political

43. This is the Mr. Clay whom Tocqueville identifies as a planter from Georgia.

danger that we spend enormous sums to help Westerners establish schools and churches. Many New England families have settled in the Mississippi Valley for no other reason than to establish a nucleus of religion there."

I said to Mr. Clay: "Your republic can flourish primarily because your country consists of small nations[44] that remain almost entirely separate within the larger nation." He answered: "That is truer than you know. Not only does each state constitute a nation, but each city within each state is a small nation, [and] each ward within each city is again a small nation, with its own special interests, its own government, its own representation—in a word, its own political existence. As long as France remains confined to Paris, you will have government by the rabble, not by the people."

* * *

2 October 1831.

Today Mr. Sparks said: "Real property is almost never divided anymore in Massachusetts. The eldest child almost always inherits all the real estate."

"And what becomes of the other children?" I asked.

"They migrate to the West."

Note: This is an extremely significant fact.

* * *

5 October 1831.

Today Mr. Dens, a judge in Hartford, said: "Last year I visited the Congress. There I found thirty-six members originally from Connecticut, which will give you an idea of how many people have migrated out of our state. Connecticut itself has only six representatives."

* * *

5 October 1831.

Mr. Winthrope [*sic*],[45] son of the lieutenant governor of Massachusetts and member of the legislature,[46] told me this today: "It is sad but true that our most enlightened states produce more criminals than other states." This statement stunned me. It was the first time I had heard anything of the kind in America.

"What evidence do you have for this?" I asked.

"Just compare the state of the population with the number of crimes."

Note: This observation deserves further investigation.

44. Meaning the several states.

45. Robert Charles Winthrop (1809–1894) was admitted to the Massachusetts bar in 1831 after studying with Daniel Webster. He served in state and national political positions throughout his life, most notably as the United States senator appointed to finish Daniel Webster's term in 1850.

46. That is, the state legislature.

* * *

Mr. Vaughan, Franklin's pupil and a highly respected Philadelphia elder,[47] discussed the penitentiary system this evening: "Our Walnut Street Prison is in terrible condition. This was not the case when the Quakers ran it, but when the political party opposed to the Quakers won the elections some time ago, the Quakers were forced out of all the posts they held."

"But what does politics have to do with the prisons?" I asked.

"Nothing, to be sure," Mr. Vaughan replied. "But people are eager for all kinds of jobs, and when a party wins, it seizes the opportunity to reward its supporters."

Mr. Coxe,[48] a Philadelphia judge who was present during the conversation, added that "this effect of the spoils system[49] is so well-known that, in order to remedy the ill, the legislature appointed a commission with a majority of judges to choose the warden of the penitentiary. The idea was that judges, being appointed for life, would be less inclined to allow politics to dictate their choice."

* * *

16 October 1831.

Mr. Richards (mayor of Philadelphia and a man who seems to be highly respected in these parts)[50] told me today that on the whole the people demonstrated a good deal of common sense in their choices.

"This has not always been the case in France," I replied. "In my country, there is an old antagonism between the people and the upper classes, so that whenever the people have been in charge, they have often voted for uneducated men of no social standing."

Mr. Richards continued: "We've seen nothing of the kind here. Of course in America what you might call the upper classes never enjoyed privileges and never set themselves visibly apart from the people in politics. You have to understand our situation, however. One might say that our republic represents the triumph of the middle classes, which dominate the government. For example, in the Mid-Atlantic states and New England, there is no real tie between the people and the truly superior classes. The latter show little faith in the wisdom

47. John Vaughn (1755–1841) was an Englishman who had immigrated to Philadelphia. He was a merchant and a leading citizen in Philadelphia society.

In 1790, the Walnut Street city jail became the first state penitentiary of Pennsylvania and of the United States. Under the influence of leading Quakers, prison reformers improved the cleanliness of the prison and instituted solitary confinement to give prisoners time to reflect on their crimes.

48. The son of Tench Coxe, Charles Sydney Coxe (1791–1879) was a Philadelphia lawyer and judge.

49. The original French text has *"système populaire."*

50. Benjamin W. Richards (1791–1851) served as mayor of Philadelphia from 1830 to 1831. He was also the inspector at Cherry Hill Prison, or Eastern State Penitentiary, and aided Tocqueville and Beaumont in their inquiry.

of the people and a certain contempt for the passions of the multitude, as well as disgust with popular manners. They are in fact cut off from the people. And for their part, the people, even if they feel little actual animosity, seldom choose members of the upper classes for public office. Usually they choose candidates from the middle classes. So it is actually the middle classes that govern."

Q. Do you think that is a good thing?

A. The middle classes are more useful to society, and we find that they are as capable of dealing with public affairs as anyone. What I have just told you, by the way, does not apply to the South. In the West as well, social change has been so rapid, and society is such a confused jumble of disparate elements, that my remarks do not apply there either.

* * *

27 October 1831.

Today Mr. Roberts [sic] Vaux said: "I regard manufactures as a social necessity, but a regrettable one. Factories deprave workers and often leave them in terrible need. There is especially good reason to be afraid of introducing the factory system into a country as fully democratic as this one. In France and England, when the manufacturing population finds itself in want and attempts to disturb the peace, an outside force can be called in to restore order. But where in this country does a force outside the people exist?"

I answered: "Are you aware of the far-reaching consequences of what you've just said? Once you admit that the majority can at times sow disorder and injustice, what becomes of the principle of your government?"

Mr. Vaux replied: "I will tell you frankly that I was never in favor of universal suffrage, which really does hand the government over to the most impassioned and least educated classes of society. Here we truly have no guarantees against the people. Our legislatures have no independence. I wish that the Senate were chosen by men of substance, but since the same voters who choose our legislature also choose our senators, that body offers no greater resistance to popular passions than the legislature does."

* * *

Idem.

Mr. ***, a distinguished Philadelphia lawyer, said: "We have a bankruptcy law, but even though bankruptcy has nothing to do with politics, the law was repealed when the party that had backed it ceased to command a majority."

* * *

27 October 1831.

Conversation with Mr. Duponceau. Mr. Duponceau is an elderly man and the author of several respected works, renowned for his learning. He is French but has lived in this country for nearly sixty years. Reasoning as if France were still as he remembers it, he said that "what shapes your morality is in part the fact that each Frenchman is confined within a certain sphere, from which he has no hope of escape. Here, by contrast, the road to wealth and power is open to everyone, no matter what his origins, with the result that there is a restlessness of spirit, an avidity for wealth, that you would find difficult to imagine. Imagine a country in which everyone wants to get rich and achieve a high rank and no one believes that he cannot do so. The result is ceaseless social activity, endless intrigue, constant agitation, and boundless desire to outdo one another."

"But amid all these passions," I asked, "what becomes of *equality*?"

"Equality exists only in the public sphere," Mr. Duponceau continued. "Money creates extreme social inequalities. To be sure, a man of talent can be received anywhere, regardless of his fortune, but you can be sure that he will be made to feel his lack of wealth, and his wife and children will not be admitted to society. 'We cannot frequent people of that sort,' the women will say, 'they have only two thousand a year, and we have ten.' Hence many families seek luxury in order to set themselves apart, and simplicity suffers. In state after state one finds the same desire for distinction. For vanity we throw money out the window!"

"I've also heard that you frequently choose incompetents to manage your affairs."

"That is true," Mr. Duponceau replied. "Men of talent are seldom selected. Politics governs all appointments. Connections and intrigue play as big a role here as in monarchies. Only the master is different."

At another point in the conversation Mr. Duponceau said: "You wouldn't believe how ignorant people are of the effects of their decisions. I have no doubt that if England had not conquered Canada in 1763, the American Revolution would not have taken place. We would still be English. The need to resist the French to the north and their natural allies the Indians to the west would have kept the colonies dependent on Great Britain. If they had tried to shake off the British yoke, France would not have dared to come to their aid for fear of setting off an insurgency in Canada. Yet never was any nation as intoxicated with victory as the English were back then."

He added: "The United States' gaping wound is slavery. It has grown steadily. The spirit of the age is to grant freedom to the slaves. I have no doubt that all the blacks will be free in the end, but I believe that one day they will vanish from our land."

"How can that be?" I asked.

"White blood will never mix with black here. The two races detest each other yet are obliged to share the same territory. Such a state is contrary to nature. It can only end in the destruction of the weaker of the two hostile peoples. Now, the white race, with the support it enjoys in the West and North, cannot perish in the South. The blacks will arm themselves against their enemy, and they will be exterminated. There is no way out of the situation our ancestors created when they brought slavery here other than massacre."

* * *

28 October 1831.

Conversation with Mr. Brown.[51] Mr. Brown is a distinguished lawyer, a very wealthy planter from Louisiana. He served for eight years as ambassador to France.

In discussing the Quakers, he said: "It's really unfortunate that the Quakers choose to wear ridiculous clothes and defend resistance to oppression in all circumstances. Otherwise their doctrine is admirable. Of all the religious sects, they are the only ones who have always *practiced* Christian tolerance and charity to the full. Amusements are forbidden to Quakers, their money goes uninvested, so *doing good* is their only pleasure. Unfortunately, their numbers are diminishing, and they are increasingly divided among themselves. For a long time they professed the doctrine of salvation by works rather than faith, but lately they have given up that salutary principle. Today they comprise two distinct churches, one of which has a lot in common with the Unitarians, including denial of the divinity of J[esus]-C[hrist]."

"As long as we're on the subject of religion," I said, "tell me what to think about the religious principle in this country. Does it exist only on the surface? Or is it deeply rooted in people's hearts? Is it a belief or a political doctrine?"

Mr. Brown answered: "I believe that for the majority religion is a respectable and useful thing rather than a demonstrated truth. Deep in people's souls I think there is a good deal of indifference to dogma. In church it is never discussed; morality is the issue. Yet I know no *materialists* in America. I am convinced that a firm belief in the immortality of the soul and in the theory of rewards and punishments is, one might say, universal. This is ground common to all the sects. I have been a lawyer for twenty years, and I've never seen anything but respect for the oath."

We discussed New Orleans, where he lived for twenty years. He said: "In New Orleans there is a class of women dedicated to concubinage. They are women of color. Immorality is their profession, as it were, and they pursue it faithfully. Girls of color are destined from birth to become the mistresses of white men. When a girl becomes nubile, her mother places her with a man in a sort of temporary marriage. Generally this lasts several years, during which time it is seldom necessary to reproach a girl who enters into this kind of relationship with infidelity. Concubines are passed from one keeper to another until they amass a certain fortune, at which time they marry in earnest a man of their own class; they then raise their daughters to follow in their footsteps."

"Now that," I observed, "is an arrangement truly contrary to nature. It must be tremendously disruptive to the social order."

51. A native of Virginia, James Brown (1766–1835) moved to New Orleans soon after the Louisiana Purchase. He was a Louisiana senator from 1813 to 1817 and from 1819 to 1823. After serving as minister to France from 1823 to 1829, Brown moved to Philadelphia.

"Not as much as you might think," Mr. Brown replied. "The wealthy young men are very dissolute, but their immorality is confined to women of color. White women of French or American descent are very pure in their morals. They are virtuous, I imagine, first because it pleases them and second because women of color are not. To take a lover would be to identify with colored women."

"Is it true," I asked, "that there is a vast difference between the northern and the southern character?"

"An immense difference," Mr. Brown replied. "Northerners are highly intelligent and energetic. The pleasures of the heart play almost no part in their lives. They are cold, calculating, and reserved. By contrast, Southerners are candid and passionate. The habit of command gives them a certain haughtiness of character and a quite aristocratic sensitivity to points of honor. They are much given to idleness and look upon work as degrading."

At another point I asked Mr. Brown: "Is it not often the case in America that the people are mistaken in their choices?"

"Yes, that often happens," he answered.

At yet another point, he told me this: "One bizarre fact is that in New Orleans men of color always make common cause with the whites against the blacks."

* * *

30 October 1831.

Conversation with Mr. Latrobe, a very distinguished lawyer from Baltimore.[52]

He said: "I believe that the constitution of Maryland is the most democratic in America. There are no property qualifications for voting. Any man who is a citizen of the United States and who has lived in the state for a year is eligible to vote."

"Are there no drawbacks to this universal suffrage?" I asked.

"There are a few," Mr. Latrobe replied. "The choices are not always good. Some say that we have fewer men of talent in our legislature than the Virginians have in theirs."

"So your laws are very democratic," I remarked, "but isn't it also true that the aristocratic spirit is more in evidence in Maryland than in other states?"

Mr. Latrobe answered: "True, our outward habits have retained something of an aristocratic cast, which is not to be found in our laws or even in our political customs. Luxury here is more apparent than it is in other places. In the streets you see coaches-and-four and servants wearing 'jackets,' a sort of livery, and certain families distinguish themselves by taking the names of their estates."

"Were your laws formerly as aristocratic as your mores?"

"Yes, Maryland was founded by English nobles, and the earliest immigrants

52. John Hazlehurst Bonval Latrobe (1803–1891), son of Benjamin Henry Latrobe, trained at West Point as an engineer and practiced law in Baltimore. He designed a number of buildings and practical inventions and was a writer, artist, and cultural leader. He was also a proponent of the colonization of free American blacks in Liberia.

professed the Catholic faith, which is itself favorable to aristocracy. They therefore divided the territory into large estates. But America is not propitious to landed wealth, since landlords cannot derive large incomes from their property. Until the Revolution, Maryland nevertheless looked a lot like an English province. Birth was as prized here as on the other side of the Atlantic. All power was in the hands of the great families."

"What changed things?"

"The inheritance laws. With equal division of estates, fortunes were quickly whittled down. A few families—that of Charles Carroll, for example—had only a single heir in each of several successive generations and therefore managed to preserve their wealth intact, but, generally speaking, the great estates were sliced into a thousand parts. Democracy was born with the advent of smallholders and commercial industry. The progress it has made since then is obvious."

"But how did members of the great families react to this change? How do they feel about the people, and what does public opinion say about them?"

"Contrary to what you seem to believe, the people are not hostile to the old families. Members of those families are routinely elected to office. For their part, the old families make no *show* of hostility to the present order. There are two reasons for this: when war broke out with Great Britain, the great families of Maryland ardently embraced the cause of independence. They shared the passions of the people and led them on the battlefield. After the war for independence, the Constitution became the divisive political issue. The nation fell into two camps: the Federalists, who wanted the Union to have a strong central government, and the Democrats or Republicans, who wanted the states to retain almost total independence. The latter party, which ultimately won, was the more popular of the two. And as it happens, the nobles of Maryland, who were fond of power and wished to preserve their local importance, nearly all embraced it. Thus in two major confrontations, the nobles marched with the people and thereby gained the people's favor. As I said a moment ago, there were Federalists and Republicans, and the Republicans ultimately emerged victorious. In other words, power was ultimately theirs. But once they took charge of the government, they ran it more or less as their adversaries might have done. They accepted a central government, a standing army, a fleet, and so forth. Opposition parties can never govern with the principles that brought them to power. At the moment there are no real parties in the United States. Everything comes down to a question of men. Some have power, and others want it: the ins and the outs."

"For which class do the people vote most often?"

"For lawyers. The United States is ruled by lawyers. They occupy nearly all government posts. The president is a military man, but look at his cabinet. Not a single cabinet secretary is anything other than a lawyer. Lawyers are even more dominant here than in the rest of the Union because here it is common practice for candidates to speak to the people before an election. Often a lawyer with a golden tongue will score an upset victory over an opponent whose genuine merit should have carried the day."

"Does slavery still exist in Maryland?"

"Yes, but we are working hard to get rid of it. The law permits slaves to be exported but not imported. As wheat growers, we can easily do without blacks. Our costs of production may even be lower without slaves."

"Is emancipation legal?"

"Yes, but we often find that emancipation causes a lot of trouble, and freed Negroes frequently find that they are more miserable and helpless as freemen than they were as slaves. Oddly enough, the black population is growing faster than the white west of the Chesapeake, while the opposite is true to the east. The reason for this, I believe, is that in the West large estates still dominate, and these do not attract free and industrious people to the region."

"Baltimore, which is today a city of eighty thousand people, had not thirty houses at the time of the Revolution. What caused the city to grow so rapidly?"

"The Revolution, first of all, plus the destruction of Santo Domingo, which caused many French families to flee here and become the colony's suppliers, and finally the revolutionary wars in Europe. England was at war with the whole Continent and ruled the seas. We became Europe's suppliers."[53]

"Is it true that Northerners are quite different from Southerners?"

"Yes, in Baltimore we like to think that we can spot a Yankee in the street or even a New Yorker or a Philadelphian."

"But what are the main traits that distinguish the North from the South?"

"I would put the difference this way. What distinguishes the North is the *spirit of enterprise.* What distinguishes the South is the *spirit of chivalry.*[54] The Southerner's manners are frank and open. He is excitable, not to say irritable, and highly sensitive to points of honor. The New Englander is cold and calculating, as well as patient. If you visit a Southerner, you're welcome to stay as long as you please, and he will share with you all the pleasures of his house. When a Northerner receives you, he immediately asks himself whether you're a person with whom he might do business." (Having drawn this portrait with brio, Mr. Latrobe seemed to worry that he had spoken too frankly and added several details to diminish the effect of his words.)

"But your current legislation, including your inheritance laws, is likely to change the look of your society, isn't it?"

"Yes, in the past we had a caste[55] of landowners who lived off their estates. Broadly speaking, they were the most distinguished men in their regions. They

53. In 1790, slaves revolted in Saint-Domingue, a French island colony in the Caribbean. In 1793, the revolutionaries, led by Toussaint-Louverture, gained rights within the French empire and managed to abolish slavery. Unrest continued through 1804, when residents of the colony finally founded the independent country of Haiti. Although white planters made up only about 10 percent of the island's population, most fled in the wake of the violent revolt.

After the disruption caused by the French Revolution between 1789 and 1799, Napoleon's imperial wars wreaked havoc throughout Europe between 1803 and 1815.

54. In English in the original; Tocqueville translates this phrase as *"l'esprit aristocratique."*

55. The original French text has *"race."*

were the beneficiaries of an excellent education and had the manners of the English upper class. We still have a certain number of these 'gentlemen farmers.' But the inheritance laws and democracy are killing them off. In two or three generations they will be gone."

"Do you regret that things are as they are?"

"Yes, in certain respects. Broadly speaking, this class was an excellent source of distinguished men for the legislature and the military. Our best statesmen and noblest characters sprang from it. All the leading revolutionaries in the South were of this class. Yet, all things considered, I am inclined to believe that the new order is superior. Our upper classes are less remarkable now, but the people are more enlightened. There are fewer distinguished men, but more people are satisfied. To put it in a nutshell, we are becoming more like New England with each passing day. Now, New England, despite what I said earlier, is far superior in everything to do with the economy of society. Someday I hope that the entire American continent will look like New England. This change is being hastened by the fact that the South is constantly importing men from the North. Their desire for wealth and enterprising spirit propel them southward. Little by little, all commerce will be in their hands, and they will be the leaders of society."

"Do you think that it might be possible to do without slaves in Maryland?"

"Yes, I'm convinced of it. Slavery is on the whole an expensive form of agriculture, but it is particularly expensive for growing certain crops. For instance, growing wheat requires a large amount of labor, but only in two seasons, for planting and harvest. Slaves are useful during those periods. The rest of the time they have to be fed and maintained even though they have nothing to do. What is more, every farm with slaves has a multitude of women and children, who have to be fed even if they don't work in the fields. Thus slavery is largely worthless in grain-growing regions, as is the case in most of Maryland. In the South, where plantation agriculture dominates, slaves are more useful."

"But if sugar and coffee yield more than wheat, and slave labor costs more than free labor, does it not follow that, although Southerners *can* stick with slave labor, their land would earn more if they cultivated it themselves or used free labor?"

"Perhaps, but southern whites would risk sickness or death if they attempted to do work that blacks can do without difficulty. What is more, some crops are cheaper to grow with slaves than with free workers. Take tobacco, for example. Tobacco requires constant care. Women and children can be set to these tasks. In a country where labor is as expensive as it is in America, it would be difficult to grow tobacco without slaves. Slavery is well suited to its cultivation. Tobacco is the only southern crop that is grown in Maryland. People will stop growing it as slavery disappears. It will be better to give up this source of income than to try to maintain it. What I am telling you is not just my own opinion but the opinion of the public at large. The past fifteen years have seen a complete revolution in public opinion in this regard. Fifteen years ago, it was unthinkable to say that slavery could be abolished in Maryland. Today no one would deny it."

"Don't you think that the inheritance laws will have a great influence on the existence of slavery?"

"Yes, an immense influence. The division of large estates creates a large number of small holdings and thus in short order a class of white workers, who will enter into competition with slaves. In Maryland, wherever fortunes were divided, slavery disappeared, and the white population grew rapidly."

"Does Maryland have a 'black code'?"

"No. The penal code applies to both races. There are, however, certain crimes that only blacks can commit. For example, no black, not even a freedman, is allowed to bear arms. A black slave cannot buy or sell on his own account without written permission from his master. Free blacks cannot assemble."

"Do freedmen have political rights?"

"No. In Pennsylvania they do, but in fact they are no freer to avail themselves of those rights than are freedmen in Maryland."

"Is it true that public education in Maryland is far less advanced than in New England?"

"Yes. We are only just starting down the path that Northerners have been pursuing for two hundred years. The greatest obstacle we face is public opinion itself. What is remarkable here, and has been so for a long time, is that the educated classes are aware of the need for public education and have worked steadily to make it available. But [the people], who do not yet see the need to pay for public schools, are loath to reappoint those who work for the benefit of the people without their support."

"Are you aware that what you've just said is a very strong argument against the principle of popular sovereignty?"

"No, not at all, at least not in my mind. The people are often blind. They make incredible mistakes. But in the end I find that they always see the light when it comes to their own interests. And then they accomplish more than the strongest government could do without them. For instance, with respect to public education, it was long impossible to accomplish anything, but lately public opinion has begun to shift in our direction. A start has been made, and nothing will now be able to stop it."

"What is happening to Catholics in America?"

"Their numbers are increasing at a remarkable rate, and they have conducted themselves very ably. Of the various religious denominations in the United States, only the Catholics have never suffered doctrinal division. They have maintained their unity and advance toward a common goal. For the past twenty years, they have shrewdly devoted all their efforts to education. They have established seminaries and colleges. The best educational institutions in Maryland are Catholic.[56] They have even established high schools in other states. Those high schools are full of Protestants. Of the educated young men in Maryland, I would

56. John Latrobe himself attended Saint Mary's College, a Catholic institution founded in Baltimore in 1791.

TOCQUEVILLE'S TRAVEL NOTEBOOKS

be surprised if even one were not schooled by the Catholics. Although Catholic teachers are careful not to discuss their beliefs with their pupils, you get the sense that they nevertheless exert a certain influence. Very adroitly, moreover, they have directed much of their educational effort to women. They believe that in families where the mother is Catholic, the children will almost always follow. The Catholic bishops of America are on the whole able men."

"What doctrines do American Catholics follow in regard to the government of the church?"

"They recognize the right of the pope to appoint bishops and of the bishops to appoint priests. As for matters of faith, they believe that the power to decide rests exclusively with the universal council in conjunction with the pope."

* * *

1 November 1831.

Conversation with Mr. Stewart.[57] Mr. Stewart is a distinguished Baltimore physician.

He said: "Physicians have some political influence in America. In small towns, they enjoy the trust of the people and are frequently elected to the state legislature or Congress. Clergymen can also be elected, but this very rarely occurs. People generally prefer to keep the clergy in their churches and separate from the state."

"What is your opinion of the religious spirit in the United States? I confess that I am tempted to believe that in all religions a vast indifference lies just below the surface of belief. As I see it, most educated people entertain many doubts about religious dogma, but they refrain from showing it, because they feel that positive religion is an important moral and political institution that must be preserved."

"Your picture is distorted. In the United States, the vast majority of the educated and, even more, of the people are true believers and hold firmly to the view that an un-Christian person cannot be relied upon as a member of society. This opinion is still deeply rooted, so much so that it gives rise to a level of intolerance that you can scarcely imagine. Because of it, the clergy exert considerable indirect influence. For example, if a minister respected for his piety were to state that in his opinion a man was an *unbeliever,* that man's career would almost certainly be ruined."

"Another example: take a skillful doctor who does not believe in the Christian religion. Thanks to his talent, his practice thrives. No sooner does he enter a home than some zealous Christian, a minister or a layman, will seek out the head of the family and say, 'Beware of this man. He may heal your children, but he will seduce your daughters or your wife. He is an unbeliever. But Dr. So-and-so is just as good a physician and is a religious man to boot. Take my word for it,

57. Richard Spring Stewart (1797–1876) had studied at Saint Mary's College and at the University of Maryland Medical School in Baltimore. He became a proponent of prison reform.

you should trust him with your family's health.' Such advice is almost always followed. Thus it isn't quite accurate to say that the clergy here is a civil authority, but there can be no doubt that *religion* exerts tremendous power beyond the confines of the church and has an immense influence on worldly affairs."

"Doesn't such a situation create large numbers of hypocrites?"

"Yes, but the worst thing is that it prevents people from talking. Public opinion here accomplishes what the Inquisition was never able to. I personally have known many young people who, after receiving a scientific education, came to believe that the Christian religion was not true. With the ardor of youth they made no secret of their opinion. Angered by the intolerance of certain zealous Christians, they did not hesitate to exhibit their hostility. Well, some of them were obliged to leave town or vegetate in idle poverty, while others were compelled to return, outwardly at least, to the religious fold or at any rate to hold their tongues. The number of people who were reduced to silence in this way is fairly large. Anti-Christian books are published here seldom, if at all. Still, irreligious views have begun to appear in a few newspapers. There is one such newspaper in Boston, another in New York, another in Jersey, and another in Cincinnati, but opinions of this sort make their way slowly. Yet a number of great Americans have shared them. Washington's views on Christianity are not known, but Jefferson, Franklin, and John Adams were definitely deists. By the same token, one has to admit that many talented Americans were and still are firm believers. But I imagine that the number is decreasing."

    ✳ ✳ ✳

2 November 1831. Conversation with Mr. Cranche.[58] Mr. Cranche is a Catholic priest and vice president of Saint Mary's School in Baltimore. Nearly all of the present generation graduated from this school. It was founded forty years ago by Mr. Dubourg, a French priest. Since then it has grown considerably.[59]

Me: How is the Catholic Church in the United States governed?

[A:] There is one metropolitan archbishop in the United States, who resides in Baltimore, and thirteen suffragan bishops. When a see becomes vacant, each of the remaining bishops sends the archbishop a list of three candidates. The pope chooses among them.

[Q:] Is this procedure a law or a custom?

[A:] A custom. In theory, the pope is free to choose as he pleases, but he always takes one of the bishops' candidates.

58. Possibly Father John Mary Joseph Cranche, who was at one time a bishop and missionary at Natchez.

59. Founded in 1791, Saint Mary's was the first Catholic seminary in the United States. The Sulpician Fathers, an order of diocesan priests, founded the adjacent college in 1800. The college began taking American students in 1803, under the guidance of Father Louis Guillaume Dubourg (1766–1833), who remained at the school until 1812. In 1805, Maryland chartered it as a civil university.

[Q:] How are the lower-ranking clergy appointed?

[A:] All *governmental* power is concentrated in the episcopate. In Europe, curates cannot lose their cures except for misconduct. America is regarded as an infidel country, where there are only missionaries and no resident clergy. The bishops choose these missionaries and may appoint or remove priests at will.

[Q:] So you have nothing like the former French *officialités* here?

[A:] No, we have no ecclesiastical courts of any kind.

[Q:] Is Catholicism spreading in the United States?

[A:] Yes, prodigiously.

[Q:] But is it spreading by conversion, and do you have any idea of the number of converts?

[A:] We have no idea of the number of converts, but we do know that there are a lot of them.

[Q:] I see many Protestant children in your school. Do some of them become Catholics?

Mr. Cranche answered rather vehemently in the negative. "In any case, such conversions are quite rare," he added. "We are careful not to say anything against their parents' religion. Children who talk among themselves about controversy with Protestants are punished. It is, however, true that we make all the students attend our religious exercises. But their parents know this before they send their children here."

"Still, it seems to me that, even though you refrain from speaking to your pupils about the Catholic religion, they cannot live as they do in an entirely Catholic atmosphere without coming away with a strongly favorable view of your teachings."

"Our influence is strong enough to overcome their prejudices against Catholicism but not strong enough to convert them. Marriages between Protestants and Catholics definitely have a greater effect. Such marriages are forbidden in Europe, but we encourage them here. We have noticed that when the mother is Catholic, the children always grow up to be Catholics, and often the husband will also convert. In Baltimore there are many institutions devoted to the education of women. It is not uncommon for young women to convert to Catholicism."

"I've been told that establishments like yours have sprung up elsewhere in America."

"This was the first. It has 180 pupils. There is another, similar school in Maryland, which is run by Jesuits, and a third in the District of Columbia."

"What is the opinion of American Catholics regarding the power of the pope and his independence from the general councils?"

"It's hard to say. In America as in Europe there are 'Gallicans' and 'Ultramontanes.'[60] The latter are led by the Jesuits. Up to now such questions have

---

60. Gallicans believed in the relative equality of civil authority and papal authority over the Catholic Church, while Ultramontanes believed that the pope had sole authority over the church.

been confined to the theological seminaries. The vast majority of Catholics take no interest in them, and it would be impossible to say what most people feel."

"Are American Catholics zealous in their beliefs?"

"Yes, I believe that America is destined to become the homeland of Catholicism. It is spreading here freely, without assistance from the civil authorities and without arousing hatred, thanks solely to the power of its doctrine, and in total independence from the state."

"Do people give generously to the church?"

"The clergy is not wealthy, but it has what it needs."

"Do you think that it is better to maintain the church in this way rather than by compulsory contributions?"

"Yes, certainly, in America."

* * *

3 November 1831.

I dined yesterday at the home of Mr. James Carroll.[61] Among the guests were the governor of Maryland, Mr. Howard, the son of Colonel Howard, the chief judge of the criminal court, Mr. Finley, and several others.[62] Most of these gentlemen belong to old Maryland families. There was much talk of this state's political constitution, and everyone agreed that the right to vote had been extended far too widely. As a result, according to these men, it is really the less educated part of the population that governs the rest. I took Mr. Finley aside and had the following conversation with him:

"I'm sorry," he said, "that you didn't come to Baltimore at the beginning of last month. That was when we had our legislative elections, and the spectacle would have been of great interest to you."

"Couldn't you describe them for me?" I replied.

"I could indeed," Mr. Finley answered, "and all the better for having participated in them myself. The Republicans, or anti-Jackson party, chose me as their candidate. My opponent was also one of my closest friends. Two days before the election we both went to Washington Square, where a platform had been erected for town meeting orators. I spoke first and started to explain to the crowd—which numbered at least ten thousand—the mistakes that General Jackson and the current administration had made since taking office. My opponent, on the other hand, defended the government. When I say that we did these things, I mean that we tried to do them, because while each of us spoke, the opposing party shouted us down. Several men in the crowd came to blows.

---

61. The identity of this individual is uncertain. Two men named James Carroll resided in Baltimore in 1830, neither of whom was Charles Carroll's nephew James (who lived in Ohio in 1830).

62. George Howard's father, Colonel John Eager Howard, had been governor of the state from 1789 to 1791.

Ebenezer L. Finley was a lawyer and prominent social figure in Baltimore. All of the men at this dinner belonged to old, elite Maryland families.

After some bones were broken, everyone went home to bed. The next day, my opponent and I set out for other parts of the county. We traveled in the same coach, ate at the same table, stayed in the same inns, and appeared as opponents on the same hustings."[63]

"But didn't such disorderly and tumultuous crowds make you afraid?"

"Personally, I find the whole business of speaking on the hustings quite distasteful. But it isn't as dangerous as you imagine. Our people are used to this sort of campaigning. They know just how far they can go and how much time they can devote to these events, which are like ancient saturnalia. Before an election, people beat each other with clubs, but on the night after an election, Baltimore is as quiet as Rome on Ash Wednesday. In a sense, democracy's excesses save us from its dangers. All public offices are up for reelection annually. The party that fails this year can hope to succeed the next. Why would it resort to illegal means?"

"You reason like a man who has never seen the people agitated by *deep* and *genuine* political passions. Everything here has thus far been on the surface. There are no great material interests at stake."

"That may be true. Note that I speak only of us and of the present time."

"I imagine that town meetings are convoked here as in New England, by the town authorities."

"That's the way it should be, but the custom here is different. In Maryland, any individual who wishes to do so may announce a public meeting in the newspapers, stating the date and purpose for which the meeting is to be held. In election season, I've seen tavern keepers advertise meetings in their own taverns in order to attract customers, and the ploy is frequently quite effective."

"Is it true that you have no property qualification for voting?"

"None whatsoever. I have seen elections carried by paupers from the almshouse turned out by one of the candidates."

"Do you approve of such tactics?"

"No. By pushing democracy to its utmost limit, we have in fact turned control of society over to people of no property and little education, who therefore have no interest in stability. What is more, we have erected a social order on ground that is constantly shifting beneath it. Not only do our officials change every year, but so do our governing principles and maxims. Parties rotate in and out of power with incredible speed. Social standing and wealth are inevitably affected by this universal agitation. Many projects are begun but never completed."

"But you of the upper classes made the current laws yourselves. Fifty years ago, you were in control."

"Yes, of course, but each party sought power by flattering the people and promising new benefits to secure their support. So by degrees the most aristocratic state in the Union became the most democratic."

63. A platform used for election speeches.

* * *

3 November 1831.

Today I said to Mr. ***, a criminal court judge in Baltimore: "In your civil courts you have two jurisdictions covering virtually the same cases, two procedural codes, two laws.[64] Don't you think that the system can be simplified?"

He answered: "Yes, I'm convinced of it. But how can we persuade the legislature to do the job? Politics gets mixed up with everything. All our laws are political. One party introduces them, another party opposes them. With party interests on both sides, it is not the public interest that makes things happen. How are good laws to be made in such circumstances?"

* * *

3 November 1831.

Today I said to Mr. Latrobe: "I grant for the sake of argument that democracy can deal with the less important affairs of a society, but I cannot believe that it is capable of conducting foreign policy. All the nations that have influenced the world, all that have accomplished great things outside their own boundaries, were led by powerful aristocracies. I am thinking of the Romans of old and of the English today."

Mr. Latrobe responded: "I agree with you on that point. This is indeed democracy's stumbling block. But we have thus far suffered no ill effects from this. We have no neighbors. *In general,*" he added, *"I find that America proves absolutely nothing as to the viability of the republican form of government."* He also said: "Too little attention is paid to habit in history—to the habits of nations as well as individuals. You can search far and wide for the reasons why we are able to endure republican government here. But in my opinion the most important reason is that we are *used* to it. What has to be explained is how we acquired that habit. Why was society so shaky here in the first ten years after the Revolution? Because we had not yet acquired the habit of governing ourselves as an independent state, even though we were already used to administering ourselves within each state individually."

* * *

5 November 1831.

Tonight we called on Charles Carroll.

Charles Carroll is the last surviving signer of the Declaration of Independence. He belongs to a very ancient English family and owns the largest estate in America. He lives on 13,000 acres of land and owns 300 Negro slaves. His granddaughter married the Duke of Wellesley. He is Catholic. Charles Carroll is 95 years old. He stands tall and suffers from no infirmity, although his memory is somewhat shaky. Nevertheless, he still converses quite easily and is an edu-

64. After American independence, Maryland retained a complicated colonial system of dual jurisdiction of state and county courts for criminal, civil, and equity cases. Many of these complications were not resolved until the Maryland legislature drafted a new state constitution in 1851.

cated and amiable man who was schooled in France. He received us with great warmth and kindness. The conversation was mostly concerned with the Revolution, the high point of Mr. Carroll's life. He reminded us with understandable pride that he had signed the Declaration of Independence and in so doing risked not only his life but also the largest fortune in America at that time. I ventured to ask him whether the idea of separating from Great Britain had arisen at the very beginning of the dispute between the colonies and the mother country.

"No," Mr. Carroll answered, "in our hearts we felt a powerful attachment to the mother country. But ultimately England forced us to go our own way." In a very friendly tone he added: "No, to be sure, we had no idea that things would go as far as they did. Even when we signed the Declaration of Independence, we thought that Great Britain would be sufficiently alarmed by our action to seek a rapprochement and ultimately we would return to being good friends. But the English stuck to their guns, and so did we."

We discussed the government of the United States. Charles Carroll admitted that he was sad to see Maryland's old aristocratic institutions go. On the whole, his conversational tone reflected that of the English aristocracy, as did his ideas, but at times modified in surprising ways by the habits of the democratic government under which he has lived and by glorious memories of the American Revolution. He concluded with these words: "*A mere democracy is but a mob.*[65] The government of England is the only one that suits you," he said. "We can endure ours because year in and year out we can send our upstarts out west."

In manners and cast of mind Mr. Carroll is a perfect specimen of a European nobleman. It is likely that the large southern landowners at the time of the Revolution were men of similar stamp. Individuals of this sort, of the stock from which America's greatest leaders sprang, are today rare. Noble manners are vanishing with them. The people are being educated, knowledge is spreading, and men of middling talent are ubiquitous, while great ability and great character are becoming rare. Society, though less brilliant, is more prosperous. These diverse effects of the progress of civilization and enlightenment, of which we catch only the merest glimpse in Europe, are readily apparent in America. What is their primary cause? I am not yet entirely clear about this.

* * *

5 November 1831.

Today Mr. James Carroll said: "One mustn't exaggerate the shortcomings of democracy here. To be sure, the people lack common sense about a whole host of details and a great many particular cases. On the whole, however, the machine works, and the state is prospering. There are no doubt dangers in universal suffrage, but it has one advantage: you don't have one class hostile to the others. A general satisfaction exists throughout the nation. Whatever the shortcomings of democracy may be, I believe that *when it can survive*, its benefits outweigh its evils. More than any other form of government, it stimulates activity and energy

65. In English in the original.

throughout society. Nevertheless, I am far from believing that it can survive everywhere. I believe that our circumstances here are unique and that our success proves nothing."

"What do the wealthy classes think of the current state of things?"

"The upper classes are very much aware of the people's blunders and passions. They believe that in many respects they could do a better job of leading society than the people can. But they recognize that, all in all, the state is prospering. They accept the present order of things, because they see that the final result is good even if they find fault with many details."

Note: Mr. James Carroll is a dispassionate and perceptive man on whom I think one can rely.

* * *

Philadelphia, 18 November 1831.

Mr. Biddle, president of the Bank of the United States, is one of the country's most distinguished men.[66] Today I said this to him: "What is most difficult for me to understand in America is the existence of political parties and their methods. In France and elsewhere in Europe, there are two or three leading ideas around which people with various positive interests and passions group themselves. In America I see nothing of the kind. It almost seems as though you have only coteries and not parties in the proper sense of the word. Individuals are everything, principles almost nothing."

Mr. Biddle replied: "I can understand that you find it difficult to fathom the nature of our parties and the way they work because we are no longer sure about them ourselves. The old parties have realigned themselves, and it would be impossible to say today what the political beliefs are of those who support the administration or of those who attack it."

"But hasn't it always been this way?" I asked.

"No, certainly not," Mr. Biddle replied. "This is quite new here. For many years we used to be divided between Federalists and Republicans. These two parties bore a close resemblance to your European parties. Their political doctrines appealed to certain passions and interests. They fought bitterly until finally the Federal[ist] Party, always smaller in number, was crushed by its adversary. Tired of losing, the Federalists eventually gave up on themselves. They either joined the winning party or organized around various minor issues and

66. Nicholas Biddle (1786–1844) descended from a prominent Quaker family that had come to Pennsylvania with William Penn in the seventeenth century. He served as president of the Second Bank of the United States from 1822 to 1839. In 1832, Biddle tried to renew the bank's charter four years before it expired. President Jackson refused to renew it, and after years of strife between the two men, the bank's charter expired in 1836. The state of Pennsylvania gave Biddle's bank a state charter, but a financial panic ensued. Biddle resigned in 1839, and the bank failed in 1841.

took some other name. But the party standard was lowered for good. This revolution was completed by General Jackson's accession to power. He pretended not to recognize any difference between the old parties in his choices. Since then, some people support the administration, and others attack it; some back a particular measure, while others denounce it. But there are no parties as such, permanently opposed to each other on the basis of contrary political beliefs. The fact is that there are today no two ways of governing this nation in practice, and political passions must inevitably attach themselves to details of administration rather than to principles."

Q: Can a majority of Congress oppose the head of state here without harm to the public's business?

A: Yes, certainly, our political machine is constructed in such a way as to run by itself. The situation you describe has arisen several times in the past. Right now, the president has lost the confidence of the Congress and the educated classes. His bills are not passed; his nominations are rejected by the Senate. Yet the public's business is proceeding as well as in the past, and no one fears for the future. For me, the most convincing proof of the goodness of our institutions is the ease with which we can do without government or carry on in spite of it.

* * *

Philadelphia, 20 November 1831.

Mr. Poinsett, who served for a long time as United States ambassador to Mexico and who enjoys the reputation of being quite a remarkable man,[67] said to me this evening: "If you want to judge the southern character, go to Kentucky and Tennessee. Kentuckians are descended from Virginians and have never mixed with foreigners. They have preserved the spirit and manners of Virginia better than the people of any other state. By contrast, Ohio, Illinois, and the West in general have drawn immigrants from all parts of the Union but especially from New England. These immigrants exhibit a restlessness of spirit that is quite extraordinary. Those who are the first to clear the land never keep what they have cleared. Once it begins to produce, the pioneers sell out and move further into the wilderness. It seems that the habit of moving, pulling up stakes, cutting trees, and laying waste has become one of life's necessities for them. Quite often the second owner of a property can't resolve to stay either. Once the land has been brought to the point of yielding a full crop, he too will sell out and move on to improve yet another farm. But a third round of immigrants settles on the land for good. They populate the new states. The others constitute the advance guard of civilization as it pushes its way into the American wilderness."

67. In his home state of South Carolina, Poinsett argued for the Union during the nullification crisis.

* * *

2 December 1831. Cincinnati.
Conversation with Mr. Storer, Cincinnati's leading lawyer.[68]

Q. Are your judicial institutions different from those of other states?

A. Yes, especially in one respect: our judges are appointed by the legislature and serve for only seven years. I believe that only one other state, Vermont, does as we do.

Q. Do you think this is a wise innovation?

A. I believe it to be quite pernicious. Judges should be independent of political passions. Therein lies liberty's greatest safeguard. Here they are all in the grip of the partisan spirit.

Q. Are most people aware of this evil?

A. I think so. We hope to be able to change that part of our constitution before long. But in order to do that, we need to organize a convention, and our fear is that with political passions as they are now, it won't have the proper complexion. The convention that drafted our 1802 constitution was very much unsuited to the task. At that time the people of Ohio were not a very savory lot, and the moral condition of the electorate had an impact on the outcome of elections. We've sacrificed too much to democracy here.

* * *

Id. Mr. Walker, a very distinguished young lawyer from Ohio.[69]

Q. Do you think that your system of electing judges is a good one?

A. I believe that it is very dangerous, and experience has already demonstrated some of its vices. Our constitution in general places too few limits on democracy. It has other defects as well: for instance, our legislature is not large enough. Some of its moral force is sacrificed as a result. One can never be sure that it really represents the will of the people.

Q. I have heard that the land in this part of the country is extremely fertile. Is that true?

A. Yes, I was born in Massachusetts and spent part of my life there. An acre there yields from 25 to 30 bushels a year. Here the yield is 70 to 80 bushels.

Q. Is it true that some former Ohioans have already moved west of the Mississippi?

A. Yes. This is how it works. People who own land here generally hold on to it and stay put. But their children seek their fortunes farther west, in states where there is still unclaimed land. In addition, large numbers of workers, proletarians, come to our cities from other states and from Europe. They remain here

68. Bellamy Storer (1798–1875) moved from his native Maine to Cincinnati to practice law in 1817. He was a fervent anti-Jacksonian and served in the U.S. House of Representatives from 1835 to 1837.

69. Timothy Walker (1802–1856) migrated from Massachusetts to Cincinnati in 1830 to practice law. He worked with Bellamy Storer, was a founder of the Cincinnati Law School, and wrote extensive intellectual tracts about the law.

for two or three years. The price of labor is so high (*one-third higher* than in New England) and the cost of living so low that in two or three years they can amass a sum of capital. When they have enough, they leave us and move west to buy land of their own.

Q. Is it true that no one in your cities is unemployed?

A. I don't know anyone without an occupation or a job.

Q. How is public education doing in Ohio?

A. The state of Ohio, which comprises some 25 million acres, is divided into townships, each of equal size. When Congress governed Ohio as a territory, it decreed that one thirty-sixth of the land of each township should not be sold and that the income from this land should be used for public schools.[70] A similar rule applied to religious institutions. These lands are currently our primary source of funds for public schools. What has slowed the progress of education here is the shortage of good teachers.

Q. Is the government involved in education?

A. Some basic distinctions have to be made. Anyone is free to start a primary school or high school. In that sense education is independent of the state. But the state also creates free public schools, and over these schools it does maintain supervision, albeit indirectly. School inspectors are appointed not by the state but by each locality, and these inspectors examine the teachers, their methods, and the progress of the pupils.

Q. With what state does your local school system have the most in common?

A. With the local school system in Pennsylvania, which is our nearest neighbor.

* * *

Id. Today, Mr. Chase, a Cincinnati lawyer,[71] said: "We have taken democracy here about as far as it can go. Universal suffrage is the rule. It has yielded some quite poor choices, especially in the cities. For example, the last four congressmen elected in the county in which Cincinnati is located were absolutely unworthy of the honor."

Q. But how did they gain their nominations?

A. By flattering everyone, as distinguished men will never do. By mingling with the dregs of the populace. By basely flattering the people's passions. [By] drinking with them. And the people don't just send such men to serve in the state legislatures. There are quite a few in Congress. Yet in spite of all this, the influence of talented men makes itself felt in our government.

70. These principles are outlined in the Land Ordinance of 1785, which reserved section 16 of each township in federal lands of the Northwest Territory for the support of public education.

71. Salmon P. Chase (1808–1873) moved from New Hampshire to Cincinnati in 1830 to practice law. He was a politically active abolitionist and associated himself with the Whig, Free Soil, and then Republican parties. Chase later became a U.S. senator, secretary of the treasury under President Abraham Lincoln, and chief justice of the Supreme Court.

Q. But don't you think that with such an extensive franchise, it is inevitable that the people will often choose badly?

A. Yes, I do think so, and I am convinced that there is not a distinguished man in the United States who does not regret the very broad suffrage we have here. But no one can fight the tide of public opinion, which has invariably pushed us in this direction. Take Virginia, for example. Virginia was a state in which until recently the owners of land were able to maintain a property qualification for voting. Last year, however, they were finally overwhelmed. They have begun to lower the bar. It is no longer within their power to reverse the tide. Only in New England, and especially Massachusetts—about which I can speak because my family was originally from there—are the people sufficiently educated and sufficiently in control of their passions always to elect the most noteworthy men. But Massachusetts is in my view the exception that proves the rule.

Q. What is the typical annual revenue of the state of Ohio?

A. About half a million francs. There are often unusual expenses, however. The state has already spent six million on canals, which it raised through loans.[72] In order to borrow that much money, moreover, the state had to turn to Europe, which shows the extent to which capital is still in short supply in America.

Q. Does Ohio have the same system of town government as New England?

A. No, our system is much closer to that of Pennsylvania. We have townships, but, unlike New England towns, our townships do not act as unified bodies, expressing a single will and governed by a single entity. Ohio townships often contain within them a town having its own separate government, independent of the government of the township. To my mind, the New England system is simpler and better.

Q. Do you not think that it was dangerous for Ohio to allow the legislature to choose judges and to limit their term to seven years?

A. Yes, I do believe that that was a dangerous measure. In America, judges are supposed to maintain a balance among all parties, and their special role is to counter the enthusiasms and errors of democracy. If they are merely an emanation of democracy and dependent on it for their future, they cannot enjoy the necessary independence. In fact, Vermont goes much farther in this direction than we do, because there judges are elected every year.

* * *

Id. Mr. McLean, justice of the Supreme Court of the United States.[73]

He told us the following: "In my view, what has helped most in establishing and maintaining republican institutions in this country is the fact that we

---

72. Ohio constructed two main canals between 1825 and 1847. The Ohio and Erie Canal stretched from Portsmouth to Cleveland, and the Miami and Ohio Canal went from Toledo to Cincinnati.

73. Although he was born in New Jersey, John McLean (1785–1861) moved to the West at the age of four. His family moved from Kentucky to Ohio in 1796, and in 1807 McLean started a law practice near Cincinnati. He served in the U.S. House of Representatives and on

are divided into several states. With our democracy, I do not think that it would be possible to govern the entire United States for long if they were only one people. The great nations of Europe face the same challenge. The federal form, I might add, contributes to the happiness of any people. The legislature of a large nation can never delve into the details of local interests, as the legislature of a small nation can. Our federal structure gives us the benefits of being a small people together with the strength of a great nation."

Q. Do you know how many people in Ohio are eligible to vote?

A. Around 150,000.[74] In the election that General Jackson won, 130,000 voted. An election is much less tumultuous than you might think because every effort is made to avoid large gatherings of people. Each township has its own electoral college. In six hours, the election is completed throughout the state, without fuss, travel, or expense.

Q. Do you know why there are so few banks in Ohio?

A. Ten years ago there were forty or so banks. But they all went bankrupt, and people very definitely lost confidence in them. What is more, they emitted large amounts of paper, which distorted the value of various commodities. Now virtually the only notes that are accepted are those of the Bank of the United States.

Q. Isn't there a move afoot to revoke the charter of the Bank of the United States?

A. Yes, some party men are exploiting for their own benefit the instinctive hatred that always attaches to the idea of a privilege or monopoly. I do not believe that the bank's enemies are acting in good faith. Its effects are obviously excellent, especially in the West, where its notes serve as a trustworthy and widely recognized form of currency. Apart from its other benefits, it also prevents unsound banks from doing business. If it refuses to accept the notes of any bank, that institution is immediately discredited.

* * *

3 December 1831.

Second conversation with Mr. Walker: *important.*

"Our constitution[75] was drafted at a time when Jefferson's Democratic Party was in the ascendancy throughout the United States. The influence of Jeffersonian political sentiments on its inception is unmistakable. It imposes no limits on democracy. The government it created here is weaker than that of any other state. The governor has absolutely no power and is paid only $1200. The people elect justices of the peace and exert control over ordinary judges. The legislature and senate change every year. In general, what sets our laws and those of

---

the Supreme Court of Ohio. In 1829, President Andrew Jackson appointed him an associate justice of the U.S. Supreme Court, which required him to ride a circuit to hear cases. He became known for his antislavery decisions.

74. According to the federal census, 937,903 people resided in the state of Ohio in 1830.

75. The Ohio state constitution.

the other new western states apart is the boldly innovative spirit in which they were conceived, the contempt for the past and for caution, the need to create anew and circumvent all legislative technicalities[76] in order to move quickly to the heart of things. The same unfettered spirit reigns everywhere. Here, nothing is settled, nothing is regulated, whether in civil society or religious society. Individual influence drives everything because there are no settled opinions about anything."

Q. Do the people often choose wisely?

A. No, their choices are almost always mediocre or bad. What you see in our democracy is a sort of permanent and pervasive jealousy, not of the upper classes—they do not exist—but of anyone who stands out by dint of wealth, talent, or service. We saw a striking example of this in the last election. General Harrison, a former congressman, well-known soldier, territorial governor, and two-time ambassador, ran for the state legislature.[77] He lost. His main adversary was a young man who three years ago was peddling bread on the street. True, he has since then joined a law practice as an apprentice. He won the election. In Massachusetts, which I regard as the perfect model of a republican government, no one runs openly for office. The people themselves nearly always choose the most outstanding men. In the West, candidates have to go give speeches at crossroads and drink with supporters in taverns.

Q. Doesn't this excessive development of the democratic principle frighten you?

A. Yes, I would not say so in public, but I'll confess it to you in private: I'm alarmed by what's happening here. The United States seems to me to be in crisis. We are experimenting with unlimited democracy. Everything is pushing us in that direction. But will we be able to tolerate it? It is too soon to tell.

Q. I recognize what is distinctive socially and politically about the western states. Don't they also introduce new interests of their own into the Union and thus threaten to upset the present equilibrium?

A. Before I can answer that, I'll need to expand on a number of points. The interests of the West are not contrary to those of the rest of the country, at least not to date, and there is no sign that they will ultimately become so. The North is almost exclusively a manufacturing region, the South almost exclusively agricultural. The West is both at the same time, and there is no reason to believe that its interests will collide with those of the other two regions in the future. Nevertheless, the growth of the West will necessarily change the face of the Union. Five million people already live in the Mississippi Valley. I have no doubt that twenty years from now the bulk of the population of the United States will live

76. Tocqueville wrote "technicality" in English.

77. William Henry Harrison (1773–1841) had earned notoriety fighting the Indians in the Northwest and solidified his fame with his victory at Tippecanoe in 1811. He served as the governor of the Indiana Territory, a representative and senator in the U.S. Congress, and a minister to Colombia. He returned to his Ohio farm in 1829. In 1840, he was elected president of the United States but served only thirty days before he died.

west of the Ohio. The greatest wealth and vitality in the nation are to be found in the Mississippi-Missouri basin. So it will be necessary to move the capital, which would otherwise lie at one extreme of the empire. The shift of vitality and wealth will inevitably result in new combinations, which are impossible to predict.

Q. Aren't you afraid that such a vast body will be impossible to maintain?

A. The country has prospered thus far, and in our heart of hearts we all feel a strong instinctive attachment to the Union. I am not altogether free of worry, however, about how long it can last. Various things weaken the federal bond. First, all the states are to some extent jealous of the central government. This is easy to see. The fact that in the West the democratic principle has been pressed so vigorously has made the new states even more impatient than the old with the federal yoke and the restrictions it imposes on their sovereignty. The tariff business still troubles me. South Carolina took a truly menacing stance, and it was supported by nearly all the southern states. The party leaders in the South seem determined to gain power, regardless of the cost, and they are stirring up passions, unwisely in my opinion. The growth of the North and weakening of the South have to some extent upset the equilibrium of the Union. One issue that threatens to erupt in the future is that of the public lands. As you know, Congress owns all uncultivated land. Thus it controls a vast amount of territory in the new states. Those states are beginning to insist that the land belongs to them. Indiana and Illinois have already pressed vigorous claims. On this issue the states may well collide head-on with the Union. And there are other such issues as well.

Q. Is it true that the central government distributes all government jobs to its supporters regardless of their abilities?

A. Yes. When General Jackson was elected, he removed 1,200 officials for no reason other than to replace them with his own supporters. Since then he has taken further, equally misguided steps in the same direction. Jobs have been used as rewards for services rendered to him personally. That is my main criticism of him: he has introduced corruption into the central government, and others will follow his example. Journalists who served the Jacksonian cause have been given jobs in the administration. He has even chosen friends of his to serve on the Supreme Court.

Q. To get back to Ohio, is it true that religious ideas are less influential here than in other parts of the Union?

A. There are many nonbelievers in Ohio, and what is more, they're more open about their views than nonbelievers elsewhere, because, as I said earlier, there is less need here to submit to prevailing opinion. People are more themselves. But the majority of people here are at least as steeped in religion as people in other states, including New England, and perhaps more so. To be sure, their religion is less enlightened. Because the residents of the new states live in the wilderness and must contend with harsh realities, education is more difficult to obtain than in the older states. Methodists predominate throughout the

Mississippi and Ohio valleys. But the absence of established rules and consistent methods is as evident in this area as in so many others. Many people don't belong to any church or regular congregation. Itinerant preachers travel about and preach the Gospel. Anyone who happens by can perform this service. Here, as opposed to rural New England, there are no pastors of proven ability with established salaries.

Q. Is it true that Ohio looks quite different from Kentucky?

A. The difference is prodigious, yet Kentucky was settled twenty years before Ohio, the land there is just as good, the climate is milder, and the scenery admirable. But Ohio has three times the population of Kentucky, and its farms are ten times bigger. Kentucky's population is growing, but its prosperity is not increasing. The only reason one can propose for this difference is that slavery exists in Kentucky and not in Ohio. Labor is dishonorable there but honored here. There you find idleness, here boundless activity. New settlers do not go to Kentucky. Ohio attracts industrious people from all parts of the Union. The South takes no one in but sends people to Ohio. Poor Southerners come here because no shame attaches to work. I see no reason for slavery to end in Kentucky. Although the people who live there now recognize the evils that slavery brings, they cannot learn to do without it. And new settlers do not go there.

Q. Ohio has passed some very harsh laws against blacks.

A. Yes, we try in every possible way to discourage them from coming here. Not only have we passed laws that allow us to expel them at will, but we also hinder them in a thousand other ways. A Negro has no political rights. He may not serve on a jury. He may not testify against a white. This last law in particular

Ohio, 26 November 31. "Is it true that Ohio looks quite different from Kentucky?" Tocqueville asked Mr. Walker on December 3. (GB1; GB2 *opposite top*)

TOCQUEVILLE'S TRAVEL NOTEBOOKS

has at times been the source of appalling injustices. Recently I was consulted by a Negro who had furnished the captain of a steamboat with a substantial amount of supplies. The white man denied that he owed the Negro any money. Since the creditor was black and the employees who might have testified in his behalf also could not appear in court, he could not even file suit.

Q. Are laws often changed?

A. Constantly. That is one of the great drawbacks of our democracy. But as a result, many sections of our legal code are in good shape.

* * *

3 December 1831. Mr. Drake, the leading physician in Cincinnati,[78] said this today: "Democracy here is unlimited, and I admit that the people's choices are not good. In general I've noticed that prominent men do not win the people's votes. Yet the state is truly thriving. Its activities are extensive and serve the general welfare. I've never heard a whisper of resistance against the existing laws. The people are happy and tranquil. If a single demagogue were in control, things would no doubt be going quite badly. But the demagogues keep one another in check. The ill effects of the people's choices are not as bad as you might think."

78. Daniel Drake (1785–1852) grew up in Kentucky and moved to Cincinnati in 1800. After studying medicine in Philadelphia, he became a well-known doctor in the West and taught at medical colleges in Ohio and Kentucky throughout his life. Drake had a great interest in the arts; he founded a number of cultural institutions and wrote several tracts promoting Cincinnati and the West.

* * *

Conversation with Mr. [Bowes Reed] MacIlvaine, one of the most important merchants in Louisville:[79]

Q. We've heard that Louisville has made tremendous progress over the past few years.

A. Enormous progress. When I came here seven years ago, the population of Louisville was just 3,000, and today it is 13,000.[80] I myself am doing more business today than all of Louisville did seven years ago.

Q. What accounts for such rapid growth?

A. It's mainly the unbelievable flow of migration to the West. Louisville has become an entrepôt for nearly all the merchandise headed up the Mississippi to supply the settlers. I believe that Louisville is destined to become a very large city.

Q. Is it true that Kentucky and Ohio differ greatly in prosperity?

A. Yes. The difference is striking.

Q. What is the cause?

A. Slavery. In my view, slavery does even more harm to the masters than it does to the slaves. In Kentucky slaves are treated very mildly and are well fed and well clothed. Seldom do they flee their master's household. But slavery discourages settlers from coming here. Thus we lack the dynamic and enterprising spirit of states where there are no slaves.

Q. Is it true that slavery prevents manufacturing from developing in a state?

A. Many people think that Negroes are incapable of becoming good factory workers. I disagree. When young blacks are sent to work in factories, they are as apt as young whites to become good workers. We have examples of this in Kentucky. A number of slave-run factories are doing well here. The reason why there is less manufacturing in the South than in the North is not that slaves cannot work in factories but rather that slavery discourages masters from developing the industrious spirit needed to build and run manufacturing businesses.

Q. Is it true that public opinion in Kentucky has begun to turn against slavery?

A. Yes, over the past few years there has been an incredible change in people's thinking. I am convinced that if opinions in Kentucky were counted by head, the majority would be in favor of abolishing slavery. But we don't know what to do with the slaves. Our ancestors did us a terrible wrong by bringing them here.

79. Tocqueville and Beaumont left Cincinnati on December 4, but their boat became stuck in ice on the Ohio River. They disembarked twenty-two miles north of Louisville and walked to the town through a winter storm.

80. In 1830, the total population of Kentucky was 687,917 people, of whom 165,000 were slaves.

Q. But if public opinion runs so heavily against slavery, why did Missouri so stubbornly refuse to abolish it when it would have been so easy?[81]

A. At that time, the revolution I just alluded to had not yet taken place. What's more, it's so convenient for new settlers to use slaves to cut down trees and clear land in places where free laborers are almost impossible to find that it's not difficult to imagine why Missourians didn't fully appreciate the rather remote benefits of abolition. But I think they've since recognized their mistake.

Q. Is the black population increasing much in Kentucky?

A. Yes, but it will never become large enough to endanger the white population. Kentucky is divided into small holdings. Each small farm is home to a white family and a few slaves. The division of the land and the type of agriculture practiced here, which requires few slaves, ensure that we won't see hundreds of slaves working in the fields of one white man, as is the case in states farther to the south. Here, slavery is a great evil but not a peril.

Q. What crops are grown in Kentucky?

A. Corn, wheat, hemp, and tobacco.

Q. For these crops, do you think that it is more economical to use slaves than free workers?

A. I believe the opposite. Slaves don't work as hard as free laborers, besides which the farmer must pay for their upkeep throughout the year. He also has to care for them when they're young and when they're old.

* * *

15 December 1831.

Conversation with our host, a farmer from Sandy Bridge.[82]

"I came from South Carolina and settled here some years ago."

Q. Explain to me why all the homes we've seen in this forest offer such inadequate protection against the weather. There are chinks in the walls big enough for wind and rain to enter easily. Homes like these must be uncomfortable and unhealthy for the owner as well as the visitor. Would it be that difficult to seal up the holes?

A. Not at all, but the people who live around here are generally lazy. They look upon work as an evil. As long as they have enough to eat and a roof over their heads, they're happy and think about nothing but smoking and hunting.

Q. What do you think is the main reason for such laziness?

81. Settlers who moved to the Missouri Territory had come mostly from the South and had brought slaves with them. When they applied for statehood, Missourians demanded that their state be admitted to the Union as a slave state. In an agreement known as the Missouri Compromise, the United States balanced Missouri's admission as a slave state with the admission of Maine as a free state, maintaining an equal number of slave and free states in the nation.

82. In Carroll County, about 96 miles south of Nashville.

A. Slavery. We're accustomed to doing nothing for ourselves. There's not a farmer in Tennessee so poor that he doesn't have a slave or two.[83] If not, he's usually obliged to work alongside the blacks in the fields. But if he's got ten or so slaves, which is common enough, he hires a white man to watch over them and does absolutely nothing himself but ride horses and hunt. There's not a farmer in these parts who doesn't own a good rifle and spend part of his time hunting.

Q. Do you think that farming with slaves is economical?

A. No, I think it costs more than using free labor.

* * *

New Orleans, 1 January 1832.
Conversation with Mr. Mazureau, one of Louisiana's leading lawyers.[84]

Q. Before you came under the jurisdiction of the American government, did you have any experience with free government of any kind?

A. No.

Q. Was it hard to make the transition from complete subjection to total freedom?

A. No. Congress took care to introduce independence by degrees. At first we were governed in a manner almost as absolute as that of our former rulers. Then we were governed as a territory. Finally, we joined the Union as an independent state. We are doing as well in that capacity as the other states of the Union, even though the majority here still consists of Creoles.[85] In my opinion, Congress could well have refrained from putting us through a trial period. A small state in our situation is always capable of governing itself. In small societies there is little need to fear the adverse consequences of popular sovereignty.

Q. Do you think that it would be possible for whites in Louisiana to farm the land without slaves?

A. No, but I was born in Europe, and I arrived here with ideas about this similar to those I suspect you have. Yet experience seems to contradict theory. I do not think that Europeans can endure the tropical sun when working the land. The heat here is always unhealthy and sometimes fatal. It's not that whites can't work at all here, but if they want to stay alive, they have to pace themselves to the point where they can barely scrape by. I can give you an example from the Arkapas district. Some time ago, Spain sent peasants from the Azores to that part

83. In 1830, 681,904 individuals lived in Tennessee. Of these, almost 142,000 were slaves.

84. Étienne Mazureau (1777–1849) had been exiled from France in 1803 when he opposed Napoleon's rule. He settled in New Orleans in 1804 and earned a great deal of money as a lawyer. At several points throughout his life, he served as attorney general and secretary of state of Louisiana.

85. Creoles were individuals of European descent born in the West Indies or European colonies in America. Spain had controlled the Louisiana Territory from 1763 to 1800, and France had owned it from 1800 to 1803, when Napoleon sold the territory to the United States. Many Louisiana residents in the 1830s had lived in New Orleans under European control or had emigrated from the Caribbean.

of Louisiana, and they worked the land without slaves. But today they're the poorest people in Louisiana.[86]

Q. But couldn't you say that their poverty is due to want of industry rather than to climate?

A. In my opinion, climate is the main reason.

Q. Is it true that the population of New Orleans is drawn from all the nations of the world?

A. Yes. What you see here is a mixture of all races. There is not a single country in America or Europe that is not represented here. N[ew] Orleans is a sample of the world's peoples.

Q. But in the midst of all this confusion, which race dominates and influences the behavior of the others?

A. To date I'd have to say the French race. It sets the tone and defines the manners of the city.

Q. Has yellow fever wreaked as much havoc here as we've heard?

A. I believe the damage has been exaggerated. From my experience, I'd say that for every ten foreigners who live within the bounds of moderation and refrain from all excess, only two will die. Of course I'm speaking of people who don't need to work with their hands in order to live. If you take the same number of people from the working classes and set them to work outside all day long, perhaps seven or eight will succumb to the disease. Remember, though, that yellow fever is confined to the city of New Orleans. Two miles north or south, no one ever gets it.

Q. How do Negroes fare in Louisiana?[87]

A. Fairly well. Harsh treatment is the exception. The condition of the Negro has changed markedly over the past twenty years. They used to live in wretched huts that offered almost no protection from the weather, their clothing was nothing more than covering for their bodies, and all they got to eat was a barrel of corn (about two bushels) a month. Now they generally get enough to eat, are fully clothed, and live in decent quarters.

Q. Does the law guarantee their right to live?

A. Yes, I recall that when I was attorney general, I obtained the death penalty against a master who had killed one of his slaves.

* * *

Id. Conversation with Mr. Guillemin, the French consul in New Orleans.[88]

Mr. Guillemin is certainly an intelligent man and, I believe, a man of means.

---

86. In 1778–79, Spain transported colonists from Spain and the Canary Islands (not the Azores) to the Attakapas district of Louisiana. The main settlement, New Iberia, was about 125 miles west of New Orleans.

87. In 1830, Louisiana had a total population of 215,529 people. Of these, nearly 110,000 were slaves and almost 17,000 were free persons of color.

88. J. N. François Guillemin had arrived in New Orleans in 1816. Before that, he had resided in Savannah and Baltimore.

In this he is the exception that proves the rule, which seems to be that French agents abroad are mostly incompetent. He has lived in New Orleans for fifteen to seventeen years.

"This region," he told us, "is still mainly French in ideas, mores, opinions, customs, and fashions. We clearly model ourselves on France. I have often been struck by the influence that political passions have here and by the similarity in this respect between the population of Louisiana and that of France. I've frequently been able to look at the impact of an event here and predict what impact it would have in France. Louisianans are more concerned with affairs in France than with their own."

Q. That attitude must be good for our commercial relations with the United States.

A. Very good. In my view, it is of the utmost importance for France's interests that French mores be maintained in Louisiana. This is the way to keep one of the main gateways to America open to us. It would have been very difficult for us to hold on to Louisiana as a colony, but we could at least have held on to it long enough, and expended enough effort, to establish a French population that could have sustained itself after we left. We are now in a rather weak position to maintain our presence against the pressure of the Americans. Nearly all of Louisiana's land is still in French hands, but the major trading companies have passed into the hands of Americans. There is no denying that the aptitudes of the two peoples for business differ in important respects. The French of Louisiana are not very enterprising. They don't like to risk what they've acquired on doubtful ventures, and they're afraid of incurring dishonor if they go bankrupt. The Americans who come down here from the North every year are consumed by desire for riches. They've abandoned everything to seek their fortunes. They arrive here with little to lose and have very few scruples when it comes to paying their debts, which is a point of honor with the French. It's interesting here to study the striking differences between the two races, each with its good points and its bad.

Q. It seems that the Americans and the French are locked in struggle in Louisiana. Doesn't this lead to bitterness between the two nations?

A. Each side is critical of the other, and they do not mingle much, but deep down there is no real antagonism. The French here, unlike the French in Canada, are not a conquered people. They live truly and completely on a footing of equality. They frequently marry Americans. And last but not least, the region is hugely prosperous and becoming more so every day. The future of New Orleans is very bright indeed. If the yellow fever can be banished or even just controlled, New Orleans is surely destined to become the largest city in the New World. In fifty years, the greater part of the population of the United States will be living in the Mississippi Valley, and the gateway to the river is here.

Q. Do you believe that this prosperity owes something to the free government that was established in Louisiana?

A. You have to observe closely, as I have done for the past fifteen years, the way in which business is conducted in a small and fully democratic repub-lic in order to convince yourself that prosperity is not due to political institu-tions but is rather independent of them. You have no idea of the kind of *bedlam* that reigns here. The people choose incompetent schemers to fill government posts. Prominent men are almost never elected. The result is a legislature that is constantly making, changing, and unmaking laws. It's Penelope's robe. Crucial clauses are quietly stricken from the books while nobody is watching. The gov-ernment is prey to any number of cliques. You've seen how shabby and filthy the city is, despite an annual revenue of a million francs, because public funds are lavishly squandered. People say that by expanding the right to vote, you in-crease the independence of the vote. I believe the opposite. Employers every-where influence their workers, and when workers' votes decide elections, what is called "the free choice of the people" is really determined by the intrigues of a few industrialists. Nevertheless, as I said earlier, Louisiana is remarkably prosper-ous, and its prosperity is increasing steadily. The government here has the merit of being quite weak, which keeps it from interfering with anyone's liberty. Here liberty poses no threat. This is true not only of Louisiana but of all the United States. To me, it's always been impossible to imagine how anyone could reason in general about American institutions. America is in such a special position.

Q. Is it true, as has been said, that religion has little influence here?

A. It doesn't have much influence, but I think that's partly because the priests sent here from Europe haven't been much good. We're inundated with Italians, who have nothing in common with the population and whose morals are detest-able. Nevertheless, there's no political or other animosity toward Catholic priests, who, for their part, never mingle in politics. Recently, some people smashed the windows of a priest who refused to bury a suicide in sanctified ground, but I'm convinced that the people involved were mostly imitating what happened at Saint-Germain-l'Auxerrois.[89] Based on what I've seen here and in other American states, I am absolutely convinced that for the sake of religion the clergy must be totally separated from the state and religion allowed to stand on its own.

Q. How are priests paid in Louisiana?

A. The state has nothing to do with paying them. Generally speaking, towns here have public lands that generate revenue for the purpose, in addition to which there are casual offerings, freewill offerings, payments for pews, etc.

Q. We understand that morals leave much to be desired, especially among the colored population.

A. Indeed, there is a great deal of immorality among the colored. But how could it be otherwise? The law in a sense condemns colored women to licen-tious ways. You've no doubt noticed the sections of theaters reserved for mulatto women, and elsewhere you've seen women as white as the most beautiful Euro-

89. On February 14, 1831, an anticlerical mob in Paris sacked the church as an archbishop celebrated a mass. The National Guard did not attempt to stop the crowd, and the church was closed for several months because of damage sustained by the building.

peans who are nevertheless classed among the proscribed race because African blood is said to flow in their veins. Many of these women, and others not quite so white, resemble Europeans in complexion and grace and have received an excellent upbringing. Yet the law prohibits them from marrying into the white race, which monopolizes all power and wealth. If women of mixed race want to wed lawfully, they have to marry men of their own caste and share their humiliation, because men of color are denied even the shameful privileges granted their women. Usually their color and manners give them away, but even if it were otherwise they would still be subjected to constant indignities. Even a beggar, should he happen to be white, can order a colored man out of his way and into the mud: "Stand aside, mulatto!" Should a colored man sign a contract, the law obliges him to sign as "a free man of color." I know many colored men who are virtuous and talented, yet they are not allowed to have any aspirations. By stubbornly cutting itself off from the rest of society, the white aristocracy (like most aristocracies) makes itself vulnerable in America and courts almost certain destruction in the Antilles. I'm not saying that whites should have given the Negroes rights, but if they had accepted men of mixed race—the colored closest to them by birth and upbringing—they could have enlisted their support, for the people of mixed blood are in fact much closer to the whites than they are to the blacks. They would have left the Negroes with nothing but brute force on their side. By rejecting the people of mixed blood, the whites have given the slaves the one resource they were lacking to gain their freedom, namely, intelligence and leadership.

* * *

Id. With a much-celebrated lawyer from New Orleans, whose name I've forgotten.

He said:

"When the legislature is in session, it's fair to say that all existing legislation is vulnerable. Our houses are composed largely of young lawyers, who are ignorant and prone to intrigue. (Everyone here thinks he has the ability to legislate.) They make and unmake laws and slash and cut with abandon. Here is an example: after the settlement with Spain, many aspects of our civil law were still governed by Spanish codes. At the end of the 1828 session, a bill was quietly passed that abolished those laws without putting anything else in their place. The next day, lawyers and judges were shocked to discover what had happened the day before. But the deed was done."

Q. Why are outstanding men never elected to the legislature?

A. I doubt that the people would vote for them. In any case, official posts are not highly prized, and prominent men do not seek office. (*This is why the state doesn't function well, but it also saves the state from revolution.*)

Another example of the same sort mentioned by the consul: "Three years ago, the legislature, on the final day of its session, quietly included in a bill having nothing to do with the subject a law stipulating that one-tenth of the estate of any foreigner who died in Louisiana should go to the state. This is tantamount to what is called the *droit d'aubaine* in French law. I raised some concerns," the consul said. "Many members seemed surprised themselves by what they had done. The law was revoked in the next session."

Fact to counterbalance the following:[90] the current governor of Louisiana is a man of talent and character.[91] The two senators from Louisiana, Mr. Johnston[92] and Ed. Livingston, are two of the most prominent men in the Union. They were elected, however.

* * *

Conversation with a lawyer from Montgomery (Alabama), January 6, 1832.

I spent two days traveling with this young man. I've forgotten his name, which was in any case not well-known. Nevertheless, I think his conversation deserves to be reported. It bore the stamp of good, practical common sense. Moreover, what he said was corroborated by subsequent information:

"An erroneous opinion is gaining currency among us every day, that the people are capable of doing whatever they please and of governing almost directly. The result has been an incredible weakening of anything that might be said to resemble executive power. This is a prominent feature of our Constitution, its chief defect, as it were, and it is a defect also found in the constitutions of all the new states of the Southwest. This has important consequences. For instance, many people were determined not to give the governor the right to appoint judges, which was granted instead to the legislature. What are the consequences of this? Responsibility for the decision is divided. Small coteries and groups of local intriguers are all-powerful. And instead of encouraging men of talent to become judges, you get minor party leaders, who control elections in the districts and whose loyalty members of the legislature seek to ensure or reward. Our judges are completely incompetent, and the people are as conscious of this as we are. So no one is tempted to call upon the regular courts. This is the way things are throughout much of Kentucky, Tennessee, Mississippi, and even Georgia, and in my opinion it is the primary reason for the violent ways for which the people of those states have been rightly reproached."

90. The original French text has *"les suivants,"* probably an inadvertent error for "the foregoing."

91. André Bienvenu Roman (1795–1866) was born in Louisiana to a French family and attended Saint Mary's College in Baltimore. He was governor of Louisiana from 1831 to 1835 and again from 1839 to 1843.

92. Josiah Stoddard Johnston (1784–1833) divided his early years between New England and the West. His family moved from Massachusetts to Kentucky early in his life; he attended school in Connecticut and graduated from Transylvania College in Kentucky. Johnston moved to Louisiana to practice law, and he represented that state in the United States Senate from 1824 to 1833.

"So is it true that the people of Alabama are as prone to violence as has been said?"

"Yes, there is not a person in the state who does not carry a concealed weapon. And they're quick to reach for the knife or pistol at the slightest provocation. Incidents occur all the time. Our social condition is close to barbarous."

[Q.] But when a man is killed this way, is his murderer not punished?

[A.] He is always tried and always acquitted by a jury of his peers, provided there are no seriously aggravating circumstances. I can't recall ever seeing a man of any reputation whatsoever paying with his life for such a crime. The violence has become habitual. Every member of the jury knows that when he leaves the court, he may find himself in the same situation as the accused and therefore votes for acquittal. Note that the jury is chosen from the list of all freeholders, no matter how little property they own. Thus the people judge themselves, and their prejudices on the subject of violence defy their very common sense. In any case, I was no better than anyone else in my day. You see the scars on my head (traces of four or five deep wounds were indeed visible). They're from knife wounds.

[Q.] But did you file charges?

[A.] My God, no! I tried to give as good as I got.

[Q.] Do the people choose good representatives?

A. No, in general they choose men they can understand and who solicit their votes. I haven't the slightest doubt that it would be a good idea to limit the suffrage. The choices would certainly be far better. But in a democratic state it is only natural and all but inevitable that the suffrage should be extended until everyone is eligible to vote, which is the case here. I predict that you won't be able to put that day off indefinitely in France either.

Q. But the results of such poor choices must be bad laws and bad government.

A. Not as bad as you might think, not by a long shot. There are always a few talented men in our legislatures. They outstrip the rest from the start and come to dominate the conduct of business absolutely. In fact, these few people are the ones who really debate the issues and make the laws. The others follow their lead. We have had representatives who could not read or write.

Q. Do you perceive a huge difference between the social condition of the North and that of the South?

A. An enormous difference. We Southerners may have more natural ability than Northerners, but we're far less active and, what is more, less persistent. We neglect education badly. There is no regular school system. A third of our population cannot read. We aren't as careful about attending to all our social needs or providing for the future.

Q. How strong is religious feeling here?

A. We pay far less attention to morality than people in the North, but the intensity of religious feeling here may be greater. In the North you have religion; here you have fanaticism. The Methodists are the dominant sect.

Q. What is the majority view of the tariff in Alabama?

A. The majority is strongly opposed to the tariff but strongly attached to the Union. The nullifiers of South Carolina have no support here.

Q. What do you think of trial by jury?

A. I think that juries are useful in criminal cases, and I regard them as useful in civil cases that turn on facts as opposed to matters of law or moral judgments. For instance, I think that all suits for damages and libel cases should be tried by juries. But when it comes to civil cases in the strict sense, involving questions of law or contract, I think that juries are awful, and I would much prefer that such cases be heard by a judge. One of the flaws of our jury system is that jurors are drawn from too small an area (counties). The jurors know the case before they hear the arguments in court. The verdict is reached in advance, in the tavern.

Upon arriving in Montgomery, we learned that a man had just been shot dead in the street with a pistol.

* * *

Conversations with Mr. Poinsett, from 12 to 17 July 1832.

"The future of maritime commerce in the United States is very bright indeed. We are surely destined to become the leading maritime power in the world. This is primarily due to what we grow here. We produce a wide variety of raw materials that are needed throughout the world. We are naturally in the best position to transport these goods. Given our national genius, moreover, we are destined to follow the English as traders with foreign nations. Look at what is happening already: hardly anyone but Americans carries American cargoes to Europe, and European goods come here on American ships. Our vessels clog the ports of Le Havre and Liverpool, while our harbors are virtually devoid of English and French ships."

Q. People say that it costs less to ship on American vessels than on the ships of other nations. Why is that?

A. There are intellectual rather than physical reasons for our lower costs. Because the cost of labor in America is very high, our ships cost more to build, and the wages of our crews are higher than in Europe. But the American sailor is industrious and thrifty, and he understands his interests especially well. No English or French vessel makes the Atlantic crossing in less time than our ships or spends a shorter time sitting idle in port. Thus we make up for our higher costs, and then some. Furthermore, Americans have qualities that make them unusually likely to succeed and prosper on both land and sea. The American is a very civilized man operating in a very new society; everything is still too new for him to have settled into a single occupation. Hence everyone here knows a little bit about many different things and has been used to doing a variety of jobs from childhood on. Our farmers make shoes, and their wives make cloth and carpets. When one of us encounters an obstacle, three words spring naturally to our tongues, and those three words describe us very well: "I will try."[93]

93. In English in the original.

Q. Some say that your ships aren't very durable.

A. You have to make a distinction between ships that are built to be sold and ships that are built to be used. In the North there is indeed a shipyard that produces vessels whose working life is relatively short. But if we want to build, for our own use, a ship to last, we have the best materials in the world, especially the green oak of Florida. One reason why our ships don't last is that when our merchants first start out, many of them have very little capital. So they take a calculated risk. As long as the ship remains afloat long enough to earn back their initial outlay plus a little bit more, they are satisfied. In any case, an attitude that is widely shared here discourages us from aiming for permanence: faith in progress is popular and universal. Everyone expects improvements in all aspects of life. And usually they're right. For example, a few years ago I asked the North River steamboat builders why they built such flimsy vessels.[94] Their answer was that they might actually be building their ships too well, because steam navigation was progressing by leaps and bounds. And sure enough, within a short time, boats that could do only eight or nine knots could no longer compete with newer vessels that could do twelve to fifteen.

Q. Don't you think that when the bulk of the American population is located in the Mississippi Valley, your maritime commerce will suffer as most capital investment turns to industry and agriculture?

A. I believe absolutely the opposite. The people of the Mississippi Valley need the United States to be a great maritime power just as much as the people of the Atlantic states, because the biggest market for their output is overseas. If we cannot protect our ports from being blockaded, what will become of our cotton, our corn, and our sugar, which grows on the banks of the Mississippi, Missouri, and Ohio and is shipped every year to South America and Europe? In such blunt terms did I answer Mr. Clay in Congress. Clay had spoken of "concessions" made by the western states to the commercial interests of the Atlantic states. I proved to him that what he called a concession was in fact in the West's own interest.

Q. Don't you think that without coercive measures such as impressment, it will be difficult for the Union to find sailors in time of war?

A. No. First of all, the large bonuses paid to sailors will always attract numerous foreign mariners, and, in addition, war harms commerce, leaving many sailors unemployed and therefore only too glad to serve aboard naval vessels.

Q. What principles guide the Union in maritime commerce and law?

A. Total commercial reciprocity. When we were able to obtain special privileges abroad, we found that the gain was insufficient to compensate for the harm done by the obligation to grant equivalent privileges here. Hence we never ask for special privileges in foreign ports, but by the same token we absolutely re-

---

94. The North River is about forty-five miles long and is contained within the state of Alabama. It runs through Tuscaloosa.

fuse to grant them here.[95] I know this from experience, because I was chosen to negotiate a commercial treaty with the nations of South America. As for maritime law, our position is that the flag covers the cargo, but in my opinion our embrace of this principle is a mistake. In the first place, I'm not sure that it is actually part of international law. What is certain, however, is that the opposite principle is highly beneficial to countries that rule the seas, and we will soon find ourselves in that position. We will then be obliged to disavow our current position, and to renounce a principle is always as damaging to a nation as it is to a man. The "flag covers the cargo" is a good rule only for those nations that can never hope to rule the seas. France is one of those nations. France will always be a great maritime power but never the leading power. It isn't even in France's interest to aspire to that role.

Q. What do you think of tariffs in general, and of American tariffs in particular?

A. I am not in favor of tariffs. I believe that they tend to impede commerce more than promote it. As for the tariff of the United States, I do not believe that it has done much harm or much good. Some people, frustrated in their ambitions, have taken it as a pretext, but I don't think that it has either the good or the bad influence that many people imagine. Its supporters say that it deserves credit for the immense progress that manufacturing has made here over the past fifteen years. I don't believe this at all. What encouraged manufacturing here was the War of 1812. Prohibitions are always inadequate in peacetime. Only war can truly shut off access to a country. It was the war that forced us to become manufacturers, and the growth would have continued without the tariff. Even with the duties, the volume of imported English goods increases every year. But we have on our own soil natural advantages with or without the tariff. The enemies of the tariff say that it's ruining the South. I don't believe a word of it. The tariff's only effect on the South has yet to be revealed, in my opinion. It is this: by refusing to allow English manufactured goods into our ports, we diminish the profits of English manufacturers. If they don't want to lose money, they are obliged to do one of two things: cut wages or cut the cost of raw materials. Now, in England, and indeed throughout Europe, it is *impossible* to cut the wages of workers without sending them to the hospital. They earn just enough to live on. So the cuts have to be made in the amount paid for raw materials. Therefore the result of the tariff has been to decrease the price paid for our cotton. (*Note:* this seems to me in contradiction with the rest and proves that the tariff is beneficial to the North.) I look at the usefulness of the tariff from only one point of view: a moderate tariff is a better basis for taxation than many other kinds of tax.

Q. Are American morals as good as people say?

95. This principle was established in 1815 by a commerce and navigation treaty with the English at the end of the War of 1812.

A. There has been some slippage in the lower classes, but everywhere else morals are excellent. In all my travels I have never encountered anything comparable. There's nothing similar in England. Morals there are quite irregular among both the common people and the upper classes; only in the middle classes does morality exist. Here, the bonds of matrimony enjoy such marvelous respect that a married woman's lover is more certain to forfeit his honor than the woman who gives in to him. He shuts himself off from public esteem and may even find it difficult to make his fortune. He should consider himself lucky if he is not murdered, for the woman's relatives may well feel a duty to avenge the family's honor.

Q. But what in your view accounts for such extreme purity of morals? I tell you frankly that I cannot regard you as a *virtuous* people.

A. I agree that we are no more virtuous than the people of other countries. The purity of our morals stems from peculiar circumstances, especially the total absence of a class of men with the time and means to attack the virtue of women. I believe, moreover, that American women are a remarkable breed. I find them far superior to American men.

Q. Do you believe that this moral condition has an influence on the political condition of society?

A. Certainly, a great deal. It instills in us habits of order and morality that serve as powerful restraints on political passions.

Q. What do you think of the influence of religion on politics?

A. I think that the state of religion in America is among the most important reasons why we are able to support republican institutions here. The religious spirit exerts a direct influence on political passions as well as an indirect influence by inculcating morality. Many educated Americans are convinced of this, which is why they not only conceal any doubts they may have about Christianity but are reluctant even to accept new sects such as the Unitarians. They are afraid that accepting innovations in religion might somehow lead to the demise of Christianity, which would do irreparable harm to humanity.

Q. What is meant in the South by nullification? It seems to me that nullification is in fact tantamount to destruction of the Union.

A. Eventually that is no doubt where it would lead, though the nullifiers deny it. They hold simply that individual states have the right to *suspend* laws passed by Congress and call for a convention.

Q. Do you fear for the future of the Union because of this doctrine?

A. No. The nullifiers constitute a party only in the state of South Carolina. Even there it is doubtful that they command a majority. And even if the whole state were behind them, what can the 700,000 whites who live there do against the forces of the Union?[96] The party of nullification, like so many other parties, originated with the personal ambitions of a few men, especially Mr. Calhoun

96. In 1830, the total free white population in South Carolina was only 257,863.

and Mr. Duke.[97] In the past the doctrine of nullification was preached without conviction, but now it claims true believers. (Mr. Poinsett is from South Carolina and a member of the state legislature.)

Q. Is the social state of the South as different as people say from that of the North?

A. Yes. The difference is obvious and entirely to the advantage of the North.

Q. What are the causes?

A. The first cause is slavery, the second, climate. The South is nevertheless making progress, yet it seems to be losing ground because the North and West are advancing so rapidly. Every ten years, the South loses a share of its representation, while the West and North gain votes. Power is rapidly shifting away from its old centers. Soon the thirteen original states will no longer command a majority in Congress.

Q. This will inevitably foster jealousy and suspicion in the South. The weak don't usually put much faith in the fairness of the strong.

A. That is true.

Q. Does the South have ships to carry its products?

A. None. The North sends ships to pick up southern cargoes and transport them all over the world.

Q. What accounts for this strange situation?

A. It's partly because the South still has no lower class. There is no place to recruit sailors.

Q. But why not employ Negroes?

A. There would be a risk of losing them. They would jump ship. The South also lacks industry.

Q. Do you see any way to get rid of the slaves?

A. No. The plan for the state to buy them and ship them elsewhere seems far-fetched to me.[98] All the wealth of the United States would not suffice for the purpose. As the number of slaves dwindled, their price would become exorbitant. In any case, need for their labor would lead to the importation of additional slaves. I do not share the fear that the growth in the number of blacks poses a threat to the safety of the white race. A slave revolt would never succeed.

---

97. John C. Calhoun (1782–1850) served as vice president of the United States under John Quincy Adams (1825–29) and Andrew Jackson (1829–32). In 1832, he resigned from his post to accept the nomination to become a senator from South Carolina. In the Senate, he was the most vocal proponent of the states' rights position, which held that states had the right to nullify any federal law.

Nothing more is known about Mr. Duke.

98. Some proponents of the gradual abolition of slavery promoted this strategy of colonization. In 1821, the American Colonization Society helped to found the colony of Liberia in West Africa. The society hoped that all free blacks would emigrate there, and by 1832, they had transported about twenty-five hundred persons to the colony. Despite the support of a number of influential Americans and the founding of similar societies, colonization failed to gain widespread support.

If they ever became intelligent enough to join together and create a powerful force, they would also be intelligent enough to see that, given their situation, ultimate success is impossible.[99]

Q. Do mulattoes side with the blacks?

A. No. They are disdainful of the blacks, and the blacks detest them in return. Mulattoes feel much closer to whites than to blacks. The most dangerous men are the emancipated blacks. Their presence upsets the slaves and makes them want to be free. I think that it is essential that masters be denied the power to free their slaves, especially when they do so posthumously by will. Washington set a very bad example by freeing his slaves when he died. The idea that slavery is a great evil and that we can do without it is increasingly gaining ground. I hope that in the natural course of things our slaves will somehow be taken off our hands. I know people old enough to have seen slavery in New England. In my lifetime I've seen it abolished in New York and Pennsylvania, and it is on the way out in Maryland. Already there is talk in the Virginia legislature of doing away with it. The black race is being pushed ever farther to the south owing to migration by whites.

Q. Do you believe that slaves are being smuggled into the United States?

A. Very few, but there is still large-scale trade in slaves.[100] Last year, the British House of Commons investigated this issue, and I read in its report that the number of blacks taken from Africa every year was as high as 300,000.

Q. What do you think of the Indians in the United States?

A. They are, I believe, a race that does not wish to become civilized, and they will perish. It may be possible to civilize the half-breeds, but not the rest. In any case, I believe that civilized people have the right to take the Indian land, which the Indians themselves are incapable of exploiting and where white men will prosper and grow rapidly in number.

Q. Do you think that the current banking system in the United States has contributed to the country's prosperity?

A. Yes. In a country as short of capital as this one, banks are enormously useful, but I don't know if the same can be said of France or England. Of all the state banks, I think the one in New Orleans is the soundest.

Q. Is it true that bankruptcy is not as rigorously condemned in the United States as in Europe?

A. Yes. As long as a failed merchant has not committed obvious fraud, people do not condemn him. A man can embark on the most hazardous ventures, start

99. Nat Turner's rebellion in Virginia in 1831 had renewed fears and discussions of slave revolts throughout the United States. About fifty free and enslaved African Americans killed fifty-seven white persons in two days. Turner was captured, tried, and executed, but his rebellion increased fear of black Americans across the Union.

100. Great Britain banned the slave trade in 1807, and the United States outlawed the importation of slaves in 1808. Brazil was the last country to ban the slave trade in 1831. However, the institution of slavery remained in place in many countries, and traders continued to smuggle slaves into these countries in small numbers.

a business without capital, or put his creditors' money at risk in any number of ways without doing significant damage to his reputation. After failing, he can immediately start over. Nearly all our merchants play double or nothing, which everyone finds to be quite aboveboard. Clearly, business ethics here are quite different from business ethics in Europe.

Q. How are roads built and repaired in America?

A. Whether or not Congress has the right to fund any roads other than those required for military purposes is a major constitutional question. I, for one, am convinced that it does have this right. But since the question is controversial, Congress refrains from acting. Many states pay to build and maintain roads within their borders. The costs are usually borne by the counties. In general, our roads are very badly maintained. There is no central power capable of forcing the counties to do their duty. Oversight of the roads is a local responsibility, hence inadequate and lackadaisical. To be sure, private citizens may sue towns that fail to repair their roads as needed, but no one wants to go to court against a town. The only passable roads are the turnpikes. The turnpike system is quite good, in my opinion, but it takes time for people to adapt to it. The turnpikes have to compete with free roads. If the turnpike is better maintained or shorter than the competing road, travelers will soon discover that it can actually save them time and money.

Q. Do presidential elections arouse real political passions?

A. No. Elections stir up a good deal of agitation among interested parties. The newspapers scream a lot. But most people remain indifferent. The president ultimately has so little influence on their happiness! It is really Congress that governs.

Q. Can you give me any information about Mexico?

A. Everything I've seen in Mexico leads me to believe that the people of that beautiful country had achieved a state of civilization *at least* as advanced as that of the Spaniards before the latter arrived. But Spanish superiority in the art of war followed by Spanish oppression totally destroyed it.

Q. What is the present composition of the Mexican population?

A. It consists of Spaniards, for whom white skin is a title of nobility, and poor and ignorant Indians, who cultivate the land. The Indians are free, and equal to the Spanish in the eyes of the law, but in reality have no political influence. There are virtually no Negroes or mulattoes.

Q. What do you think about the country's future?

A. I hope that Mexico will be able to establish itself on a firm foundation. There can be no doubt that it is making progress. One shouldn't judge the Spaniards of the New World too harshly. When the revolution came, they were still living in the sixteenth century, although they lacked the savage virtues that independence often bestowed on the people of that era. This idea has often served me well in doing business there. I frequently asked myself what men of the sixteenth century would have done or thought in a particular situation. Answering that question allowed me to predict what would happen with great confidence. A more thorough ignorance of all the discoveries of modern civilization is impossible to imagine. Like the South Americans, the Mexicans at first hoped to establish a single large republic. They did not succeed, and I, for one, do not believe that any large republic that is not a federation can survive. In the end, the Mexicans adopted the Constitution of the United States with minor variations. But they're not yet advanced enough to use their constitution as we use ours. It is a complex and difficult instrument.[101]

Q. Don't you think that the nations of Europe made a gross mistake in assuming that the independence of the Spanish colonies would open up a vast market for their products?

A. Yes, of course, Spanish America has yet to develop the needs that civilization fosters. That day will come, but it has not yet arrived.

Q. What is the position of the clergy in Mexico?

A. It is daily losing what little remains of its influence. It has already forfeited the support of the people almost entirely. Obviously, the situation bears no resemblance to the situation in Spain. The Mexican clergy retains its property, however. It is in possession of vast riches, which no one has yet dared to touch. In Mexico, it was the clergy that began the revolution: it was afraid that the Spanish Cortes would confiscate its possessions, so it stirred up the people. It wanted only a partial revolution, but once the movement was under way, it was impossible to stop it.

I ended the conversation by asking Mr. Poinsett how morals stood in Spanish America. He laughed and said: "That part of the picture is not pretty. I spent part of my life in Spanish America, and I can say that from Cape Horn to the thirty-fifth north parallel I never met a single woman who was faithful to her husband. Their notions of right and wrong are so topsy-turvy on this point that women consider it shameful not to have a lover."

* * *

24 January 1832. Mr. (Edward) Everett[102] told me today that nine-tenths of the members of Congress are lawyers. The number of landlords[103] is small.

---

101. The Mexican struggle for independence began in 1810 under the leadership of Father Miguel Costilla, a priest of Spanish descent. Costilla instigated revolts to encourage a return to the more conservative rule of the Spanish Bourbon monarchy, which Napoleon had deposed in 1807. Spain finally recognized Mexican independence in 1821, and the Constitution of 1824 established the United Mexican States as a federal republic. Modeled on the Constitution of the United States and amended in 1827, the Mexican constitution established twenty states, a bicameral legislature, an elected president and vice president, a supreme court with eleven justices, and individual state legislatures.

102. Edward Everett (1794–1865) served in the U.S. House of Representatives from 1825 to 1835. He was a Unitarian minister, a professor at Harvard University, and a prolific writer. Everett went on to serve as governor of Massachusetts, secretary of state, and a U.S. senator. He was the brother of Alexander Everett.

103. The original French text has *"propriétaires."*

* * *

Id. Mr. Serurier, who was ambassador from France twenty years ago, told me that he found the country much changed upon his return.[104] The men had shrunk, and great political talent was no longer to be found.

* * *

Id. Mr. Trist, a government employee and highly intelligent Virginian,[105] told me today that Virginia was but a shadow of its former self. There were no more great men or even notable men, and no new men were coming forward to replace them.

* * *

27 January 1832. Mr. Trist, a high-level employee in the State Department, told us today: Everything is published in this country, but there is perhaps no other country in the world in which it is more difficult to obtain documents pertaining to things that have happened in the past. Since nothing—neither men nor things—is stable, records vanish with incredible rapidity. For example, nothing is more difficult to obtain than records of congressional sessions. Recently, Virginia sought to print the records of its legislature from the time of the Revolution on, but it proved impossible to obtain full minutes of the debates. The project had to be abandoned.

* * *

28 January.

Today I asked Mr. Adams why there was such an obvious difference between the social condition of the new western states and that of New England. He answered: "New England was settled by men who were very well educated and deeply religious. The West is being settled by adventurers from all over the United States, mostly people without principles or morals, who have either been forced to leave the older states by poverty or misconduct or else have only one passion, which is to get rich."

104. When reappointed in 1831.

105. Nicholas Philip Trist (1800–1874) had graduated from West Point and studied law under Thomas Jefferson, whose granddaughter (Virginia Jefferson Randolph) he married. Trist served as a personal secretary to Andrew Jackson, and in 1833 he became ambassador to Cuba.

... They are not like the French Saint-Simonians, a bizarre mixture of the burlesque and the serious.[106] Here you have a philosophical sect, unpretentious and severe in manner, which breathes not a single word that could be mistaken for humorous.

Thus the same cause, indifference, drives people in two different directions. Men of ardent spirit or tender and lively imagination, together with others so wretched in this life that they have much to expect from the next, come together in the bosom of the most positive, the most imperious, and the most powerful of all religions. By contrast, those whose spirits are cold and logical, men of tranquil, meditative character, intellectual or scholarly in their habits, embrace a strictly philosophical faith, a pure deism that they are free to profess almost publicly.

Two great principles thus confront each other here in their simplest and most comprehensive form. Authority and liberty, both pushed to the limit, vie for supremacy. . . .

* * *

Utica, 6 July 1831.

One might say that the European is to the other human races what man in general is to all animate nature. When he cannot bend others to his purposes or make them contribute indirectly to his well-being, he destroys them and little by little banishes them from his sight. The Indian races are vanishing in the presence of European civilization as snow vanishes in the rays of the sun. Their efforts to thwart destiny are merely accelerating time's destructive ravages. Every ten years or so, the Indian tribes that have been driven into the western wilderness discover that retreat has gained them nothing, that the white race still advances more rapidly than they retreat. Vexed by a sense of their own impotence, or enraged by some new insult, they come together and launch an impetuous attack on the lands they used to inhabit, now occupied by the rustic huts of pioneers and, further on, the first villages. They tear through the countryside, burn homes, kill livestock, and take a few scalps. Whereupon civilization recedes, but only as the waves of the ocean recede as the tide is rising. The United States hastens to the defense of its latest settlers. The Confederation declares war on these wretched tribes ([maintaining] that they have violated the law of nations). An American army marches out to meet them, and not only do the whites retake their land, but, driving the savages before them, destroying their villages, and seizing their herds, the Americans also stake out a new boundary of their territory, a hundred leagues farther west than before. Deprived of their adoptive homeland by what learned and enlightened Europeans are pleased to call

106. Tocqueville compared the Saint-Simonians to the Unitarians in his June 29, 1831, letter to Kergorlay (part 1).

the *law* of war, the Indians resume their westward march, pausing only when they reach some new wilderness, where soon the white man's axe will be heard anew. In the region the Indians had only recently sacked, now safe from invasion, pleasant new villages appear, and these will soon grow to become substantial cities (or so the inhabitants believe). The pioneers, marching at the head of the vast European family, its avant-garde, lay claim to forests recently inhabited by savages. There they build their humble cabins and await the next war, which will open the way to yet another wilderness. . . .

Travel Notebook 2

. . . 18.[107] Departure from Canandaigua. Appearance of populated country as far as Batavia. Scattered houses after that. Swamp. Roadway of tree trunks. Arrived in Buffalo.[108] Walk around city. Many savages in the streets (pay day) giving rise to new idea. Their ugliness. Their strange look. Their bronzed and oily skin. Their long, stiff hair. Their European clothing, which they wear in a savage manner. Scene of drunken Indian. Brutality of his compatriots and of the Indian woman with him. Population stupefied by our wine and liquor. More horrible than equally stupefied populations in Europe. Plus something of the wild animal. Contrast with moral and civilized population among whom they live.

19. Second walk in Buffalo. Pretty shops. French objects. Refinement of European luxury. Second sighting of Indians. Effect less unpleasant than last night. Some of them bear a certain resemblance to our peasants (but with a savage complexion, the complexion of Sicilians). Not one passable Indian woman.

Departure for Detroit. Small steamboat. Nobody knows us. Notable change in manners of Americans toward us. Violent headwind. Agitation of the lake comparable to that of the sea in heavy weather.

20 July. At 9 in the morning we reach Erie, founded by the French under the name Presqu'Île (peninsula). What used to be a peninsula has now become an island. Erie visit in heavy downpour. A canal is currently being dug from Pitts-

107. Tocqueville began to record these notes in July of 1831. For a narrative account of his travels in the Great Lakes territories, see "Two Weeks in the Wilderness" in part 3.

108. Buffalo had sprung up as a trading village on the eastern tip of Lake Erie around 1789. However, its population grew quickly after the opening of the Erie Canal in 1825, and in 1830, over eighty-six hundred people lived in the town. The Indian Removal Act of 1830 had displaced a number of Native Americans and had opened their tribal lands in the area for purchase.

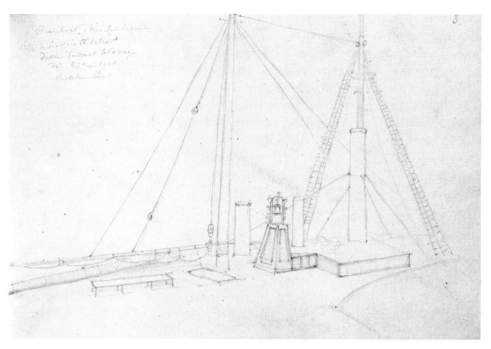

Steamboat on which we traveled from Buffalo to Detroit, drawn while aboard the steamboat on Lake Erie.
(GBI)

burgh (formerly Fort-Duquesne) to Erie.[109] It will join the Mississippi and the North River, the Gulf of Mexico and the Atlantic Ocean. We set off again after an hour's rest.

21 July. Quarrel with the captain. Arrival in Cleveland at 6 in the evening.[110] Thus far the lake has had a uniform appearance. Generally, to the right, the transparent waters of the lake, which resembles the sea, stretch as far as one can see. We sail close to the coast of Pennsylvania and Ohio, which lies to our left. The shore is generally flat, occasionally rising to a few feet in elevation, and seems to be lined almost everywhere by virgin forest, with immense trees reflected in the water that laps at their roots. The sight is impressive, not least for its uniformity. You can almost persuade yourself that the vessel you are traveling on is the first ever to have sailed these waters and that the land you see has yet to be claimed by man, but this is not the case. After hours of sailing close to a somber forest that ends only where the lake begins, suddenly you spot a steeple,

109. Begun in 1831, the Beaver and Erie Canal ran south through Pennsylvania, connecting Lake Erie with Pittsburgh and the Ohio River when it was completed in 1844.
   In 1830, about fourteen hundred people lived in the town of Erie.
   110. Although about ten thousand people lived in Cuyahoga County, Ohio, in 1830, only about a thousand lived in the town of Cleveland.

elegant homes, handsome villages, and evidence of wealth and industry. Nothing here is wild but nature, and everywhere man does battle with it, armed with all the resources of civilization. You pass without transition from wilderness to city streets, from the wildest of scenery to the most charming tableaux of civilized life. If nightfall does not force you to make your bed in the woods underneath a tree, you are certain to come to a place where you can find anything you want, including even the latest French fashions and caricatures from the Palais-Royal.

At 7 o'clock, we departed from Cleveland. Lovely night. Moonlight on the forest and reflected in the waters of the lake.

22 July. At sunrise, we are in the middle of the lake sailing northwest, with the shoreline in the distance but numerous small islands in our vicinity. We pass a small island known as Middle Sister, near the place where the English were defeated in a naval battle.[111]

Enter the Detroit River. An island, two passages. We take the English Channel. House at Fort Malden.[112] Village looks French. Catholic church. Cock on steeple. Scottish soldiers in full uniform on the bank, and on the other side, two savages, stark naked, in a canoe that circles our vessel like a whirlwind. Rings in their noses. Beneath the trees on the shore there are sheds of sorts with fires in the middle. Naked children run around them. On one bank, the ultimate in civilization, on the other, the exact opposite.

We reach Detroit at 4 o'clock.[113] A handsome American village. Many French names on the houses, French caps. We call on Mr. Richard, the curate of the Catholic church in Detroit.[114] We find him busy teaching. His story: schooled at the Irish school in Paris. Studied theology at Saint-Sulpice, ordained at the last ordination in 1791, went into exile, fetched up in Detroit. A few years ago, elected to represent the Michigan Territory in Congress. Elderly man whose religion seems ardent and sincere. Conversation rambling but interesting. Protestant population beginning to dominate in Michigan owing to immigration, but

111. During the War of 1812, the American naval fleet commanded by Commodore Oliver Hazard Perry engaged British ships in the Battle of Lake Erie. On September 10, 1813, Perry captured the fleet led by Captain James Lawrence, making this the first time that American forces had captured British ships.

112. Built in 1796, Fort Malden was the headquarters of British troops during the War of 1812. It sits in present-day Ontario, Canada, in the town of Amherstburg, located on the east bank of the Detroit River.

113. Founded in 1701 by Antoine de la Mothe Cadillac, Detroit had a population of just over two thousand residents when Tocqueville visited it. Yet at that moment, the town was on the brink of rapid growth. As a result of the advent of the canal system and Michigan's statehood in 1837, Detroit's population reached nearly ten thousand by 1840.

114. Gabriel Richard made enough of an impression on Beaumont to become the model for the good priest in *Marie.*

Catholicism winning converts among the better educated. Richard believes that the upper classes in America are extremely chilly in their attitude toward religion. This is one reason for their remarkable tolerance. Tolerance is total, moreover. Nobody asks what religion you are, only whether you are fit for employment. The greatest favor that can be done for religion is to separate it entirely from the temporal power. Barely perceptible dislike of popular government, intrigues, and cabals. Choices made by central government. System in the United States for the new states. Self-government introduced by degrees. Colonization of Christian savages around Michilimackinac. Their zeal, their ardor, their instruction.

Upon leaving Mr. Richard, we found ourselves at a loss as to where to go. All the Americans want us to take the prettiest roads and tour the oldest settlements. We want to see the wilderness and the savages but are reluctant to admit it.

Someone suggests Saginaw Bay, and, tired of protesting, we give in.

23 July. We purchase *cushions,* a *compass, brandy, sugar,* and *ammunition.* We rent two horses.

Conversation with Mr. Biddle.[115] We leave at 11 o'clock. Our costume. How we travel. Birds killed. Our pleasure at heading toward the wilderness at last. Perfectly flat land. One league around Detroit without trees and under cultivation. After that you plunge into thick forest, through which a fine road has been cleared. Occasional small clearing, surrounded by a circle of lovely trees interspersed with burned trees. A field covered with trunks, in the middle of which stands a log cabin. Often no windows. No sign of poverty. Well-dressed peasants. Cowbells in the vicinity. Air of comfort. Near Troy, at the door of a log cabin, a family taking tea. Houses thin out. Immediately thereafter the forest begins again. We pass through delightful swampland, like English gardens in which nature has done all the work. Dinner in Troy. Scene of French Canadians. We reach Pontiac at 8 in the evening. We want to change horses and are directed to the home of a man who lives a mile out into the forest. We set out alone. Nighttime scene. Incredible silence of the forest. Effect of moonlight on trees. Half an hour later, we spot a small clearing and a log cabin. We jump the fence but hear dogs and are afraid to move closer. Finally we arrive. We enter a room that fills the entire house. The fire is in one corner, utensils of all kinds, an excellent bed in another corner, a man and a woman asleep, the woman dressed like a lady. Strange mixture of comfort and poverty. Americans in their log cabins look like rich people who have decided to spend a season in a hunting lodge.

24 July. On leaving Pontiac, the width of the road gradually decreases as you move into the forest. Settlements become much more sparse. We had been told to look up a Mr. Williams, who earns his living by trading with the Indians

---

115. John Biddle (1792–1859) was a land registrar in Detroit from 1823 to 1837. After serving in the War of 1812, he became active in Michigan politics as a territorial delegate to the U.S. Congress and as a member of the Michigan House of Representatives.

and who might give us useful information. On reaching a settlement about four miles from Pontiac we inquire of an elderly man, who turns out to be Mr. Williams.[116] He tells us where we ought to go. We speak to him about the Indians. He praises them. Nothing to fear from them. You can trust them more than you can trust whites.

The cultivated fields seem to come to a complete end. Log cabins separated by increasingly greater distances. Very picturesque landscape. Wooded hillside, many lakes visible through the forest. Five miles from Little Spring, a lovely valley and a hillside covered with huge pines. A waterfall can be heard at the bottom of a ravine. We turn to admire the sight and see an Indian who has been running after us making no more noise than a wolf. Hair in tresses, bare head, earrings, a kind of blouse, red breeches without a seat, moccasins. A powder horn, a long carbine, two birds in hand. A moment of involuntary terror. Mr. Williams's words and the character of the Indian's face reassure us. We speak to him. He listens quietly to us and signals that he does not understand English. We give him brandy and buy his birds. We remount our horses. A short while later we look back, and the Indian is right behind us. We slow down, he slows down. We go faster, so does he, without the slightest sound. What a striking impression this silent and mysterious being makes as he flutters about us. A mile later, we spot a second carbine in the woods. We fear an ambush. It's a white man dressed almost like the savage. He's a European who has become half savage. He shows us his hut through the foliage. There he lives and hunts. He speaks to the Indian in the language of the Chippewa. To us he has nothing but praise for the Indians, whom he seems to admire both as individuals and for their way of life. He invites us to call on him on our way back. We canter off at a good pace, but the Indian continues to follow for two more miles. Reach a small clearing known as Little Spring. A temporary Indian camp. Men, women, children around the fire, eating apples and half-baked corn. Rather pleasant faces when they smile, awful when they turn serious. Rather handsome in profile, ugly head-on. Adam's apples too prominent. People say good things about them. Nothing to fear except when drunk. Otherwise honest and gentle. Proof of this is that the head man at Little Spring left his wife and six small children with this band of Indians and went off that very morning to hunt.

Lay of land from Little Spring to Grand Blank. Quite hilly. No thick forest, a sparse stand of tall trees showing the hand of man. Tall grass and especially ferns underneath. Virtually no more houses. Occasional band of Indians walking in the forest, or a fire. Dinner at Grand Blank. Only blacksmith. We set out again at 7 o'clock. We enter a forest of monstrous oaks. Thick woodland resumes. The road dwindles to a trail that is hard to follow. Night falls. Anxious that we will not reach Flint River. Wind dies down. Total calm. Deep darkness, impressive silence of forest. Disturbed only by the noise our horses make and the screech of a single bird that seems to be following us. The full moon rises. Lovely effects.

116. Major Oliver Williams.

On the forest floor grass turned silver by the moon like the waves of the ocean while shriveled trunks of fallen trees loom as black masses. Strange effects of moonlight on the thick trunks of the oak trees, tall columns of white marble. Moon glimpsed through withered forest on approaching a clearing. A small lake between hills glimpsed through the leaves. Very far off, Indian campfires. Icy cold. We come to the top of a hill. A clearing. A stream. We are uncertain of the trail. I go off alone to inquire at the houses I see in the clearing some distance away. I jump from tree to tree, rifle in hand. An immense oak lies on the ground. I cross the stream on a bridge of rough-hewn logs. Then I see in the moonlight that a crude dike has been erected across the stream, and someone has begun to build a small structure that is probably to become a sawmill. Unfinished houses. Nobody in sight. To find my way back to B[eaumont], I am obliged to shout like a madman. I am afraid that I will attract the attention of Indians. My cries echo through the wilderness, followed by silence. We find each other. We continue walking for another half hour. We hear the sound of dogs in the distance. We reach a clearing and see a light. B. goes to it. Woman alone, hides. Directs us to Mr. Todd.[117] He restrains his dog. His bear chained at door. He is harvesting oats by moonlight. He gives us a bed. I sleep on the ground.

25 July. We are provided with an Indian guide, a young man of twenty named Sagan-Kuisko of the Sauteurs tribe.[118] Bareheaded, with a kind of blue blouse fastened at the neck with a piece of tin. Tin earring. Seatless blue trousers, like the Indians. Moccasins. Leather belt. Tomahawk. Carbine. Not dirty. White teeth. Very pleasant smile. Wild look. A dog similar to a wolf. Nothing resembling politeness. But attentive to everything useful. He is accompanied by a child of twelve or thirteen. Unarmed. They walk, or, rather, run, ahead of us with the silence of their race, without looking back to see if we are following. We first cross the Flint River. Then we enter a vast clearing. Tall grass. Indians run about, crouching slightly, looking for wild fruit. Two or three miles farther on we enter the virgin forest. Scenery more or less the same all day long. Thick forest, copse, with occasional huge trees in the middle. Oaks of enormous thickness with no branches nearly all the way to the top, gigantic pines. As many trees down as standing. Huge trees broken by the wind form a kind of canopy. Uprooted trees that look like huge shields. Grass and ivy grow on all the debris. Trees suspended in the air. Others fallen across streams. Swampy areas triumph over the vegetation, a lovely lushness. Endless spectacle, striking for its duration, no more birds but for a few birds of prey and an occasional wood pigeon. Ideas of isolation, abandonment, more powerful even than on the ocean. Even harder to find one's location. Our Indians leap about ahead of us for four hours without stopping, never unsure about the path and apparently familiar

117. Major Todd and his wife "Aunt Polly" kept a small inn known as the half-way house to Saginaw.

118. The French called the Ojibwa (also known as the Chippewa) Indians by the name "Sauteurs."

TOCQUEVILLE'S TRAVEL NOTEBOOKS

with every variation in the terrain. One of them utters a strange, muffled cry. He points through the wood to the tallest tree: a famous "Bible tree." Picture they make. We set out again. The Indians stop. They draw a line in the sand. Point to one end, shouting: Flint. To the other: Saginaw. And then to the middle, to indicate that we are halfway and must stop. We make a sign for drinking to indicate that we don't want to stop until we reach a spring. They set off again at the double and lead us to a place where rainwater has accumulated. We unsaddle our horses and take our provisions. We had not been able to find any bread in Flint. Our meat is spoiled, and most of our eggs have gone bad. We have only sugar and some crackers. A swarm of mosquitoes drawn by the water soon make the neighborhood unbearable. We set out once more. At 5 o'clock we come to a rapidly flowing stream, not very deep but hemmed in by steep banks. We think we see a white settlement and breathe more easily. On the other bank, a cornfield and three abandoned wigwams. Beautiful site, tall trees on the right, and on the left the river, flowing slowly between empty woods on both sides.

The Indian points to the sun and indicates that it is too low in the sky to reach Saginaw before nightfall. He stretches out on tree trunks to make us understand that night will soon be upon us and to encourage us to make camp where we are. We had not yet dined. We urge him to continue on. He makes a sign to indicate that he is tired. We offer him the bottle covered with wicker. Then he takes off like an arrow. We pass through tall forest, occasionally passing near the river. Here and there we see lean-tos made of oak bark and the ashes of old fires. We encounter only one person: a woman lying with a child near a fire. Fixed stare. We kill some game and are ready to stop. The Indian signals that we must now finish the journey. Night falls. Many huge trees to be surmounted, swamps to cross. The Indian is obviously exhausted. He has a horrible nosebleed. We lay him across a horse's hindquarters. Strange look. We give him our horses, our rifles, and our bag of game and start walking. Dampness, silence of the forest. A rifle shot in the distance. The whole caravan stops. Trail almost impossible to find. Swarms of mosquitoes torment us. At 8 in the evening we reach a meadow. Grass four feet high. Our two Indians emit three savage cries, and voices answer from afar, as we catch sight of a fire. We soon find ourselves on the bank of a river almost as wide as the Seine in Paris, the Saginaw, which had been hidden from view by the grass. The last rays of the setting sun reveal a small Indian canoe, like a long black fish that is moving toward us. In it, a man we take to be an Indian is crouching. Half dressed like the Indians, moccasins, bare head. He speaks to them in their language. I try to hold my horse's bridle as I climb into the boat, but the supposed Indian says, "You've got to unsaddle it, sometimes they drown." Norman accent, almost unintelligible French. I take off the saddle and set it down in the canoe, then sit myself down alongside it. The big Indian sits at one end of the canoe, holding the bridle. The Canadian paddles while the horse swims. Striking scene. I speak to the boatman, a mixture of French and Indian blood. Half savage. The Indian, upon reaching the shore, wraps himself completely in his blanket and throws himself on the ground to keep from being eaten alive by the mosquitoes. I worry about B[eaumont]. Soon I hear the sound of the canoe returning. The full moon rises. It illuminates the forest, the river, and the entire scene. Impossible to describe my impressions. Two men approach us, speaking French. They are Canadians, and their speech resembles that of our peasants. They take us to one of the three houses that constitute Saginaw. Horrible night. Mosquitoes. I am obliged to wrap myself in my blanket, like the Indian, and sleep on the floor. Indians lie near the door with their dogs.

26 July. Saginaw. A cultivated spot amidst savage tribes and impenetrable forests.[119] Beauty of the solitary river that flows down below. We go to see Mr. Williams.[120] He does business with the Indians. Shows us a multitude of small items intended for them, for which they pay either with the money the United States pays them for their land or with furs. Obviously he robs them. What he and all other Europeans say about the savages: excellent people. Good and gentle. More trustworthy than whites. Unanimous testimony. On my return I enter the home of one of the French. His wife, who resembles an Indian, braids a rug. A redskin child beside her. I ask him if she is French. "No." English? "No." What blood? She looks down and answers, *"A savage."* The Frenchman was her husband and the father of several children by her. Extraordinary race, mixture of the savage and the civilized man, knows no language well, speaks English, French, Indian. Has penchant for the wilderness but still clings to cities. Common among the French, people say. Duck hunting with the young man. Squatting in an Indian canoe, we make our way up the Saginaw through impenetrable forest. Savages approach us. They envy my rifle, which is supposed to fire in the rain. Where are such rifles made? In the land inhabited by the fathers of the Canadians. Beavers. Insects.

In the evening, toward sundown, we proceed by ourselves in the canoe and proceed up a branch of the Saginaw. Rare evening. Still air, cloudless sky. Our canoe slides along without a sound. We paddle slowly and enjoy the spectacle. Transparent and still surface. Admirable vegetation along the way. Immense trees reflect in the water, setting sun shining through the branches and illuminating the trunks. In twenty years all of this will be replaced by villages, and the imminent change makes the present spectacle that much more grand. Sound of a rifle shot. We return in the dark of night. Strenuous efforts to protect ourselves from the mosquitoes.

27 July. We want to leave but are urged to stay. We hunt wild ducks in the meadowlands along the Saginaw. A Canadian guides us. Our conversation with the Indians. Their passion for strong liquor is irresistible. An Indian drinks as much

119. A few settlers were attempting to revive the town and sell city lots at the time Tocqueville and Beaumont visited.
120. Gardner D. Williams (1804–1858) was the son of Major Oliver Williams, whom Tocqueville met in Pontiac. Gardner Williams served as an agent for the American Fur Company in Saginaw.

as he can, even though he might die from it. Excellent people when sober. Their hospitality; in the wilderness, they share their food. Unfortunately it is no longer as easy as in the past to deceive them about the value of wares. Have no religion but believe in a god who is source of good, a devil who is source of evil, and another world where people play all the time. We come to a meadow. Unspeakable torment of mosquitoes. We see long snakes. We ask the Canadian why he does not follow us into the tall grass. His shoes are poor, he says, and he is afraid of rattlesnakes. So there are some. Many in the meadow. The Indians have a cure that keeps you from dying. We become more cautious. We see hummingbirds for the first time. During the day a storm. Beautiful sight. Calm preceding. Humming insects, thunderclaps echoing endlessly in the solitude that envelops us.

28 July. After a sleepless night, we leave Saginaw by ourselves at five in the morning. Feeling of solemnity after we take leave of our hosts and plunge into the forest without a guide. I am ill at ease. We easily find the Cass River and stop for lunch. Beauty, tranquility of the spot. Abandoned wigwam. Two trails. Uncertainty. We take the one on the right and cross the river. Trail seems little used. Distressing uncertainty for quite some time. We consult the sun and the compass. Eventually we come back to the place where we had lunch. At six in the evening we finally emerge from the forest, in which we saw no living thing other than deer and birds. Recollections of 28 July 1830 in the forest.

29 July. We reach Pontiac via the same trail. Nothing worthy of note.

30 July. Visit two small lakes, Orchard and Pine. Settlement of the year. Cabin of Doctor Burns.[121] Singular mixture of highly cultivated upbringing and current habits of a quite different nature. Books. Look of poverty, hovel. We find him hoeing his field. He gives us details.

31 July. Reached Detroit. Evening walk along the docks. Meet one of our fellow passengers from the *Ohio*. He tells us that the *Superior* is about to arrive, headed for Green Bay.[122] We immediately change plans and decide to go to Green Bay.

1 August. We embark at two in the afternoon. Detroit River. Cultivated lowlands. Numerous houses. Lake Saint Clair. Dancing on deck in the evening. American gaiety.

2 August. The next day we are in sight of ***, located at the outlet of Lake Huron. We sail on into that vast lake. The wind turns against us. We return to the fort and from there to the Black River, two miles further on, in search of wood. Visit the fort.[123] Appearance of officers and men. Drill. Insubordination.

121. Burns was a young doctor who had emigrated from Scotland.
122. A comfortable steamship that carried two hundred passengers from one end of Lake Michigan to the other.
123. Later known as Fort Gratiot; bad weather kept the two travelers here for two days.

3 August. At one o'clock I go out to hunt in the swamps on the other side of the Saint Clair River. We stop first at the fort. In the forest along the way, sound of a savage drum. Shouts. We see eight savages headed toward us, entirely naked except for a small loincloth. Six children, two men. Painted with colors from head to foot. Bristly hair with sticks inserted in a braid hanging down in back. Wooden clubs in their hands, leaping about like devils. Handsome men. They dance to amuse themselves and make money. We give them a shilling. This is the war dance. Horrible to watch. What degradation. Another dance on the knees with head on the ground. We have no idea how they got here. Huts in the swamp on the other bank. A canoe starts across. Terrifying crossing. Good hunting in the swamp.

4 August. We set out at six in the morning. Absolutely insignificant day. Toward evening we lose sight of land completely.

5 August. At 4 o'clock we reach the end of Lake Huron. We see several mountains in the distance. The lake is strewn with numerous small islands that poke their bushy tips through the surface of the water. Perfect solitude. Forest all around. Not the slightest trace of man, not a vessel in sight. Passing close to Saint Joseph Island, ruins of fort of that name.[124] Chimneys still standing. We enter the Saint Mary River. As broad as a lake at times, at other times squeezed between islands and spits of land covered with trees. Perfect solitude. Now and then an Indian family on the shore, sitting quietly around their fire, canoe drawn up on the bank. A large canoe with eight men aboard heads toward us. The Indians fire their rifles and shout for joy. They give us pigeons. We give them brandy. At sunset we enter a very narrow canal. Lovely view. Delightful moment. Waters of the river still and clear, reflecting the superb forest. In the distance blue mountains illuminated by the last rays of the sun. Indian campfires glow through the trees. Our vessel advances majestically amid this solitude, accompanied by fanfares that echo from the trees all around. At nightfall we lower the anchor. Dancing on deck. Astonishment and admiration of the Indians at the sight of the first steamboat "working in the water."[125]

6 August. A year ago today we made a king. Thick fog prevents us from leaving. It lifts to reveal hills and eternal forests. At 9 o'clock, arrival in Sault-Sainte-Marie.[126] Delightful sight. Admirable weather. Sainte-Marie: a square palisade,

124. After ceding Michilimackinac to the Americans, the British began to build nearby Fort Saint Joseph on an island at the northern tip of Lake Huron in 1797. It became a critical military point for the British during the War of 1812, but the Americans burned the fort in 1814, and the British never rebuilt it.

125. In English in the original.

126. Sault Sainte Marie was founded by French missionary Jacques Marquette in 1668, and towns grew up on both sides of the river of the same name, which connects Lake Huron and Lake Superior. In 1797, the boundary between the United States and Canada was drawn along this river; Tocqueville visited the town in the Michigan Territory.

with a flagpole and a huge American flag in the middle. Under the trees, wigwams. Between spits of land, rapids. Farther on, mountains and interminable forests. Further on, two spits of land covered with beautiful trees narrow the river. When we arrive, the whole population turns out to line the banks and rooftops. A vessel like ours arrives only once a year. The appearance of the people is striking, a mixture of every kind of blood. Most numerous are Canadians, *Bois-Brûlés* or half-breeds.[127] Every shade from European to savage. Gaudy painted faces. Hair tied up with feathers. Attentiveness of Indians to Mr. Mullon. Baptism in a stateroom on board. We set out for Lake Superior in an Indian canoe. About this canoe of painted bark. Eight people (including the two of us) sat in the bottom of this canoe, looking serious and remaining immobile. At either end a Canadian, half savage but with the good cheer of his ancestors, paddled while singing and telling jokes. How uncanny to hear French spoken at the end of the world with ancient turns of phrase and a provincial accent (*laridondaine, laridondon*). With occasional exclamations such as *Hou!* or *Marche!* We come to a spit of land covered with oak. A small Indian village. Their huts: twelve feet in diameter, six feet high. Their wild dogs. The chief asks to see my rifle (bolt-action). Chief's costume: red trousers, a blanket, hair piled on top of his head. Two feathers stuck in it. Old. I fire my rifle as he looks on. He admires it and says that he has always heard that the French were a nation of great warriors. I asked him about the feathers. He smiles and tells me that they indicate that he has killed two Sioux (he is a Sauteur, and the two tribes are always at war). I ask him for one of the feathers, telling him that I will take it to the land of the great warriors, where people will admire it. He immediately plucks it out of his hair and gives it to me, then extends his hand and grips mine.

We head back; downstream through the rapids. Unbelievable skill of the Canadians. Speed through the rocks like an arrow. The Johnson family (forgotten conversation) at the camp of the Indian traders. An Englishman, curt, cold, and taciturn amid a host of Canadians and savages he is taking up to Lake Superior to trade with the Indians. The Canadians crowd around us with the openness and affability of Frenchmen. We ask them for information about the Indians. They travel to the end of the lake every year, and all the Indians they know dress the same as the ones we have seen. Not thieves. Helpful and hospitable. Friends of Europeans who supply them with commodities that have become indispensable to them. Ferocious in war. Kill all indiscriminately. Scalp. Burn prisoners. The Sauteurs and the Sioux, the two great rival tribes. Chiefs have only nominal authority. No justice. Particular compensation or vengeance. No religion. Belief in God and in another world where those who have lived badly will be obliged to hunt in forests where there is no game. Others in forests full of game. Antipathy of Indians toward English language, their taste for French. Indians in the depths of the wilderness greet Europeans by saying, "Bonjour."

127. Literally meaning "burnt wood," the Bois-Brûlés were also known as *métis* (half-breeds).

Fort Howard, Green Bay, Lake Michigan, 9 August 1831; an "Iroquois Indian village farther on," Tocqueville recorded in his notebook. (GB1 *top* and GB2 *bottom*)

7 August. We leave at 5 o'clock in the morning. We cross the southwest tip of Lake Huron. Fleet of twenty-two Indian canoes passing in the opposite direction, returning home after receiving gifts from the English.

At 3 in the morning, after passing Bois-Blanc and the Île Ronde, we arrive in Mackinac.[128] Island three leagues around, rather elevated. At the summit, white fortifications of an American outpost. Near the coast, some fifty houses, several

128. This settlement had been an important military, trading, and missionary post for over a century. In 1830, the census counted just under nine hundred inhabitants.

of them rather beautiful, belonging to the American company.[129] On the shore, a number of Indian huts. They come from quite some distance to receive presents. Two churches. We hire a Canadian guide and go to see the caves in the rocks. Picturesque. Then to the pyramid, a rock formation unusual for its size and shape. We return at 5 o'clock. B. goes off to draw the cave. I wander around as usual. I go to see the curé,[130] but he is not home. Mme Framboise.[131] Indian blood. Interesting details about her life. Very respectable woman. Letter from a young Indian. Book of Indian prayers. A Canadian camp on the shore. A bivouac around the fire. A Canadian with a French appearance and manners. Gay, open, energetic. Some half-breeds. I sit by their fire and chat with them. Their chief, also a half-breed, a very intelligent man. He gives me details about the savages. Better in proportion to their distance from Europeans, unless they are Christians. In the depths of the northwestern wilderness, still armed with arrows. Happy there. Extraordinary abundance of wildlife. The animals invariably retreat a hundred leagues beyond the advance of civilization. Inability of the Indians to grasp that sooner or later the European advance will overtake them. They understand only when it is too late to do anything about it. Hereditary chiefs. Different from warrior chief. Kind of justice. A murderer is turned over to the [victim's] family, which either kills him or exacts a price for his head. No thieves. Terrifying in war. Iroquois and Hurons nearly gone. Hurons almost destroyed. Iroquois: remains scattered among the tribes on this side of the lakes. Many in Green Bay.

Catholic zeal. Ardor to combat the Presbyterians. Mr. Mullon sent out to respond to a challenge of sorts. Efforts of poor Canadians to support their church and create a school. Visit to Mr. ***.[132] Return to ship at 11 o'clock. On the way back a hut full of savages. Family singing a Catholic hymn in Indian.

8 August. Insignificant day on the water. Here and there, to the right or left, lowlands covered with forests.

9 August. Reach Green Bay at 8 o'clock. Fort. Village in the midst of a riverside meadow. Iroquois Indian village farther on. Large settlement. We don't know what to do. I go hunting alone. Swim across the river. Canoe. Grass on the river bottom. I lose my way briefly and return to the same spot without realizing it. After dinner I set out with an Englishman[133] for Ducks Creek: four miles.

129. The American Fur Company, founded by John Jacob Astor in 1808, held a near monopoly on the fur trade by the 1830s.

130. Parish priest.

131. The daughter of a French Canadian fur trader and an Ottawa Indian woman, Magdelaine Marçot La Framboise (1780–1846) was a prominent resident of Mackinac Island and Montreal. When her husband was murdered around 1806, she took over his fur-trading business and made large profits until her retirement in 1822. When Tocqueville met her, she lived in a large house on Mackinac Island and was an active member of the local Catholic church.

132. This was most likely Samuel Abbot, a wealthy agent of the American Fur Company.

133. Most likely this was Godfrey Thomas Vigne (1801–1863), a lawyer.

We paddle up a small, isolated stream in a canoe. Come to an Indian dwelling. Grass, good adventure. We return.

11 August. Conversation with a civilized savage, dressed like one of our peasants. Speaks English well. The savages prefer the French (he says): his ideas about civilized life; hopes that all Indians will adapt. Is not Christian. Religion of the Indians. God, immortality of the soul. Indian paradise. Obey commandments.

    Monotonous day on the lake.

12 August. Reach Mackinac at 11 o'clock.

    Sauvage pharo. European hat, black feather curled around. Tin ring around the top. Three *voltigeur* feathers at the peak. Immense earrings. Pierced nose with a ring through it. Black tie. Blue blouse. Large necklace of pieces of tin with animals engraved on them, rings of tin around the legs, red garters with hundreds of small glass pearls. Embroidered moccasins. A red cloak over his shoulders. Opinion of an old Canadian that they are more handsome in their savage costume, entirely naked but for a belt and headdress of feathers. Long braids often hanging to the feet. Entire body painted. Hunt for pigeons. Canadian pointer. Sermon by Mr. Mullon.

13 August. Depart Mackinac at 9 o'clock. Nothing interesting on the return trip. Reach Detroit on Sunday the 14th in the evening.

Travel Notebook 3

                      . . . 14 October 1831.
When the social state allows a people to elect its magistrates, the magistrates so elected can readily be invested with power that no despotic authority would dare to confer on them.

    So, for example, the selectmen of New England have the power to post the names of drunkards in taverns and impose fines on tavern keepers and others who supply these drunkards with wine. Such power to censure behavior would be rejected in the most absolute of monarchies. Here people submit to it easily. Once things are set up in this fashion, the power of the magistrate increases as electoral qualifications are lowered and the magistrate's tenure is decreased.

    Nowhere is arbitrariness greater than in a republic, because there is nothing to fear from it, but this is one reason why, when a republic turns to monarchy, it usually lapses into the cruelest of despotisms. The unelected and unremovable magistrate retains the prerogatives of the elected and temporary magistrate. . . .

    If I were assigned the task of classifying human miseries, I would rank them in this order:

1. diseases   2. death   3. doubt

Life is neither a pleasure nor a pain; it is a serious business for which we are responsible, and which we must conduct and conclude with honor.

Philadelphia, 25 October 1831.

When detractors of popular government claim that, in many aspects of internal administration, government by a single individual is better than government by all, they are undoubtedly correct, in my opinion. Seldom, in fact, does a strong government fail to exhibit greater consistency in its undertakings, more perseverance, a sounder overall conception, greater perfection in detail, and even greater discernment in its choice of men than does the multitude. A republic is therefore less well administered than an enlightened monarchy. Republicans who deny this miss the mark, but if they said that this was not the place to look for the advantages of democracy, they would regain the upper hand. What is admirable about republican government (where it is able to survive) is not the appearance of *regularity* or *methodical order* in the administration of a people but rather *the image of life*. Liberty fails to execute its projects with the same degree of perfection as does intelligent despotism, but in the long run it produces a greater result. It does not always, in all circumstances, give the people the most skillful and perfect government possible. But it does diffuse throughout the social body an activity, a strength, an energy that would not exist without it, and which works miracles. That is where its advantages are to be looked for.

Id.

The people are always right: this is the dogma of the republic, just as "the king is never wrong" is the religion of monarchical states. Whether one is more wrong than the other is an important question, but what is quite certain is that neither is true.

Mr. Washington Smith told me yesterday that nearly all crime in America was due to the abuse of distilled liquor. "But why don't you put a tax on brandy?" I asked.

"Our legislatures have given thought to this," he answered, "but they were afraid of rebellion, and in any case any member who voted for such a law would be sure of not being reelected, since drinkers are in the majority and temperance is unpopular."[134] . . .

29 October 1831. Baltimore.

We arrived here yesterday. Today we attended the fourth and last horse race to be run this season. The horses were handsome, but the jockeys wore a ridiculous get-up. There were many people in carriages and on horseback. On the whole,

---

134. George Washington Smith (1800-1876), member of the Philadelphia Society for Alleviating the Miseries of Public Prisons, wrote "Defense of the Pennsylvania System in Favor of the Solitary Confinement of Prisoners" (1829). Tocqueville reproduced the rest of this paragraph (a conversation with another Mr. Smith) in Alphabetic Notebook B (see p. 338).

however, the tone was not quite European. When a Negro took the liberty of entering the arena with some whites, one of the latter struck him repeatedly with his cane, a fact that apparently occasioned no great surprise in the crowd or, for that matter, in the Negro himself.

Yesterday, we attended a grand charity ball that is held to mark the occasion of the races. As foreigners we paid nothing, but the Americans paid five d[ollars] each. The guests were a glittering array, and the women remarkably pretty, though got up in a bizarre fashion.

This ball may give some idea of the state of society in America. Money is the only social distinction, yet it establishes the haughtiest of hierarchies among individuals. In France one would scarcely dare to charge so high a price to attend a public gathering. For the rich to separate themselves from everyone else in such a way would be seen as the most insolently pretentious display. . . .

1 November 1831.

How can anyone doubt the pernicious influence of military glory in a republic? Why did the people choose General Jackson, who seems to be quite a mediocre individual? Why do the people still vote for him, despite the opposition of the enlightened classes? The Battle of New Orleans.[135] Yet this battle was quite an unremarkable feat of arms, and the people whose enthusiasm it continues to arouse are the most antimilitaristic, the most prosaic, and the most coldly dispassionate people in the world. . . .

3 November 1831.

Birth retains a certain influence in America. Men who bear names celebrated for their role in the history of the colonies or made illustrious by the Revolutionary War are rather readily tapped for important offices, especially honorific ones. In Massachusetts, for example, Mr. Lionel Lincoln and the lieutenant governor, Mr. Winthrop, are both descendants of early governors of the colony.[136] In the state of New York, the lieutenant governor is Mr. Livingston, a scion of the greatest family in the state. In Maryland, the governor is Mr. Howard, the son of the celebrated Colonel Howard and a member of one of the oldest families.[137] All these gentlemen are quite ordinary individuals and clearly owe their

135. On January 8, 1815, Andrew Jackson defeated British forces led by General John Keane and captured the city of New Orleans. Although the Treaty of Ghent had declared an official peace two weeks earlier, Americans looked to the Battle of New Orleans as the final and decisive battle of the War of 1812.

136. Tocqueville refers to Levi Lincoln (1782–1868), governor of Massachusetts from 1825 to 1834. His father and brother were also politicians, and the family descended from Samuel Lincoln, who settled in Hingham, Massachusetts, in the seventeenth century.

Thomas Lindall Winthrop (1760–1841), lieutenant governor of Massachusetts from 1826 to 1832, was descended from John Winthrop (1587–1649), the first governor of the Massachusetts Bay Colony.

137. Both father and son served as governors. Until 1837, the state legislature chose the governor.

distinction solely to their names. The people are drawn to such intellectual distinctions, from which they sense they have nothing to fear. Birth speaks to the imagination of the people without arousing their envy. The same cannot be said of wealth. Wealthy men are rarely the people's candidates. The people do not persecute these men, but they do push them aside.

4 November 1831. Baltimore.

Mr. Howard, a very distinguished engineer from this part of the country,[138] told me that he had been sent (whether by the government or by some company I do not know) to look into the possibility of joining the Great [Lakes] to the Mississippi by way of a canal. His investigation yielded the following results: from Lake Michigan to the point where the Illinois River becomes navigable by steamboats is a distance of 95 miles. The level of the Illinois is 150 feet lower than that of Lake Michigan. In order to make the waters of Lake Michigan flow into the Illinois, one has only to excavate a hill twenty-five miles in length and only thirteen feet above Lake Michigan at its highest point. To be sure, one would have to cut through rock. Nevertheless, the job would rank among the easier canal construction projects. If this project is carried out someday, the Great Lakes, which already communicate with the Atlantic in any number of ways, would communicate just as easily with the Gulf of Mexico. From the end of the lake one would proceed easily to New Orleans, traversing a distance of 1,500 leagues via an interior route. . . .

4 November 1831.

Mr. Cruse, a very intelligent man and the editor of one of Baltimore's leading newspapers,[139] told me this today: "We have no power outside the people. Whatever the people want, everyone must accept. The militia itself is recruited from the people and is useless if it shares or condones the passions of the majority. We saw a terrible instance of this twenty years ago. It was during the war with England, which was very popular in the South. A journalist took the liberty of launching a vehement attack on supporters of the war. The people gathered, smashed his presses, and attacked his home, where he and his friends (who belonged to the leading families in the city) had taken refuge. There was a move to call out the militia, but it refused to march on the rioters and failed to respond to the call. The municipal authorities were able to save the journalist and his friends only by locking them up. The people still were not satisfied, however. That night, they assembled and marched on the prison. Another attempt was made to muster the militia, but once again it failed. The prison was attacked, and one of the prisoners was killed, while the others were left for dead. An attempt was made to prosecute the rioters, but jurors acquitted them."

138. William Howard was an engineer in the Topographical Bureau.
139. Peter Hoffman Cruse (1795–1832) had been the editor since 1822 of the *Baltimore American,* which was published under the name *American and Commercial Daily Advertiser* in the 1830s.

6 November 1831.

As far as I can judge, the republican social state is not as natural and appropriate in the South as it is in the North of the United States. Does this have to do with differences in education in the North and South or with physical differences and their effects on the character of the two sections? Or is it rather that the educated classes of the South, which are still not well suited to democratic government, are less able to conceal secrets that remain better hidden in the North? I still do not know the answers to these questions. What is certain is that my impressions of the two parts of the Union are not the same. The North strikes me, outwardly at least, as a place where government is strong, lawful, enduring, and perfectly adapted to the physical and moral condition of the region. In the South there is something feverish, chaotic, revolutionary, and impassioned in the way business is conducted, something that does not leave me with the same impression of strength and permanence.

Philadelphia, November.

Why, when civilization spreads, does the number of prominent men decrease? Why, when knowledge becomes the province of all, does great intellectual talent become more rare? Why, when there is no longer a lower class, is there no longer an upper class either? Why, when knowledge of government reaches the masses, does society want for great geniuses among its leaders? America clearly raises these questions. But who can answer them? . . .

25 November 1831. On the Ohio.

Although nature has not given each people an *indelible* national character, it nevertheless has to be granted that habits instilled in the spirit of a nation by physical or political causes are very difficult to eliminate, even after those causes cease to operate. In Canada we see Frenchmen who have lived under English rule for seventy years yet remain absolutely identical to their former compatriots in France. The English who live alongside them have lost nothing of their national character either.

It is at least sixty years since colonies of Germans came to settle in Pennsylvania. They have preserved intact the spirit and mores of their homeland. A nomadic population bustles around them, a population in which the desire for wealth knows no limits and which is tied to no place and tethered by no bond, being ready to go wherever the lure of fortune leads. Immobile amid all this activity, the German restrains his desire to improve his and his family's position. He works constantly but leaves nothing to chance. Slowly but surely he acquires wealth. He sticks to home and hearth, circumscribes his happiness within its horizon, and feels no curiosity about what lies beyond his last furrow. . . .

4 December 1831.

Apart from various other causes, what makes all the parts of the Union so similar is the high level of civilization that exists throughout. If the world ever becomes completely civilized, the human race will appear to consist of but a single people. Reason, like virtue, does not bend to different climates; it does not vary with the temperature and nature of different locales. It is uniform; it is inflexible. Everywhere it seeks the same goal and follows the same paths. All peoples that take reason as their guide must therefore resemble one another in substantial ways; they must think, believe, and feel the same things in a wide variety of circumstances. By contrast, when a people takes a certain social perfection peculiar to itself as its model, when it seeks to do as its forefathers did rather than to do the best that can be done, when it follows habit rather than reason, it remains entirely itself, and time only increases the distance between it and its neighbors. When change deprives a people of its distinctive and defining features, does it not also sap some of its peculiar nationality and vigor? That strikes me as an open question.

26 December 1831.

It occurs to me that what is called the character of a people is often nothing more than the character inherent in its social state.

Thus the English character might well be merely the aristocratic character. What suggests this to me is the immense difference that exists between the English and their descendants in America. . . .

3 January 1832.

Of all the European races in the New World, why is it the English race that has kept its blood the purest and mingled least with the indigenous races? Apart from powerful reasons derived from the national character and temperament . . . there exists a particular reason for the difference. Spanish America was populated by adventurers drawn by the lust for gold, and when they settled on this side of the Atlantic, they were in a way forced to couple with the women in the countries they were living in. The English colonies were populated by men who were driven from their homeland by religious passions or who came to the New World to settle there and cultivate the land. They came with women and children and were immediately able to establish a complete society. . . .

Travel Notebooks 4 and 5

. . . Knoxville, 8 January 1832.

There are two kinds of instability in political institutions, and one must be careful not to confuse them. One is associated with secondary laws, which change more or less as the will of the legislator changes. Even in an established and well-regulated society, such fluctuation in the will of the legislator may exist. Indeed, it is frequently a necessary consequence of the political constitution of a people. The other type of instability affects the basis of society itself, the *genera-*

tive principles from which the laws derive. Instability of this sort inevitably leads to trouble and revolution. A nation that suffers from the second kind of instability is in a violent and transitional state. America exemplifies the first kind of instability. For the past forty years, we have been tormented by the second kind. Because people often confuse these two kinds of instability, their hopes and fears are exaggerated, and they make inaccurate comparisons.

I should add that major political parties and dangerous factions emerge only where the second kind of instability exists. The first gives rise to coteries and not parties, to debates and not disputes, to noise and not war.

If you want to know whether a people is *settled* and may count on the future or not, examine it from this point of view.

Not far from Montgomery in the state of Alabama, I witnessed a small scene that made me think: near the home of a planter, a young Indian woman held an adorable white girl (the planter's daughter) in her arms and lavished maternal affection on her. With them was a Negress, who entertained the child. In her every movement the child betrayed the sense of superiority that, as her brief experience of life had already taught her, raised her above her two companions, whose caresses and attentions she received with an almost feudal condescension. Squatting in front of her and watching her every gesture, the Negress seemed clearly divided between devotion to her young mistress and respectful fear, while the Indian's effusive tenderness bore the mark of a certain freedom and even savagery, which made a strange contrast with the submissive posture and humble manners of her companion. Something I could not make out drew the Indian's attention to the woods, and she suddenly sprang to her feet, set the child down rather roughly, and plunged into the brush without a word. . . .

12 January. Oaths.

Americans make heavy use of oaths. There is no public official, no matter how minor the post, who does not swear to faithfully execute the duties of his office. The oath always includes the phrase "So help me God," which in a sense includes the deity among the parties guaranteeing the contract. Voters are not required to swear oaths, however, because of a strong belief that freedom of opinion must be respected in this fundamental political act.

Note, however, that because there exists in America a well-known legal means of amending the Constitution, obedience to the Constitution as it stands is a very strict obligation and entirely compatible with the dogma of popular sovereignty. To impose an oath of obedience to the Constitution on those who are to choose the delegates to a constitutional convention would be absurd, and a logical people [such] as the Americans would scornfully reject it. They would regard it, moreover, as a form of tyranny imposed by one party on another, and they understand the theory of popular sovereignty too well to permit such a thing.

In France, where the power superior to the Constitution is not clearly defined, where extraordinary means for remedying its flaws are not specified, and where the right to amend the constitutive laws (which must always exist some-where) is necessarily vested in the legislature, we are both a *legislature* and a *convention* at every election, yet we demand an oath that Americans do not require even of those who are only electing a legislature.[140] In other words, we ask a man to swear obedience to the law even as we permit him to choose someone to whom he may grant the legal mission to change or destroy the law. But the principles of liberty are still in their infancy with us, as poorly understood by those who propose them as by those who combat them.

Americans accept a sworn oath as evidence in civil cases so long as there is no written document to contradict it. The lawyers to whom I have spoken say that this rule does not lead to the serious abuses that one might fear. I am inclined to believe them. There is such complete confidence in the law that people tend not to abuse it. What is more, respect for truth thus becomes a social necessity of the first order, of which everyone is aware. If the law presumes depositions in certain cases to be false, it diminishes their value in all other cases. There is no better way to make men contemptible than to make it clear that one holds them in contempt. I regard it as most fortunate for a people if the truthfulness of sworn testimony is accepted as part of its habitual and customary ways, but it would be quite dangerous to make such an assumption where it had not always been the case. It also requires trial by jury in civil cases. The English owe the continued use of sworn testimony, along with many similar institutions, to the common law. . . .

12 January

. . . One of the most prominent features of American institutions is the way in which they are logically related to one another. This is a merit to which few peoples have been able to aspire, but upon close examination it turns out that this virtue does not contribute as much to the success of the Americans as a host of *profoundly* superficial minds contend. Logic and uniformity in the law are two things that are acclaimed not so much because of their excellence as because the most mediocre minds are so apt to bemoan their absence and create theories in which these two virtues are combined. The fact is that very few nations can be fully comprehended. What makes it possible to understand the Americans so thoroughly is the fact that they were able to start with [a] clean slate in designing their social edifice.

13 January 1832. If it is true that each people has a special character independent of its political interests, just as each man has a character independent of his social position, then one might say that America is, for both good and ill, the most perfect specimen of the special character of the English race. The American is the Englishman delivered unto himself. Follow with a portrait of what I mean by the English character. All that is brilliant, generous, superb, and sumptuous in the British character is aristocratic and not English. . . .

---

140. A law passed in France in 1830 required all public servants to swear an oath of loyalty to the king, the Constitution, and the kingdom.

... Political liberty is a hard-to-digest nutrient. Only the most robust constitutions can withstand it. But when it can be tolerated, even with pain, it gives the entire social body a vigor and energy that surprises even those who expected the most from it. . . .

Americans have not virtue but character. . . .

Alphabetic Notebook A

Causes of the social state and current government of America:

1. *Their origin:* excellent point of departure. Intimate mixture of religion and spirit of liberty. Cold and reasoning race.
2. *Their geographical position:* no neighbors;
3. *Their commercial and industrial activity:* everything, including their flaws, is now favorable to them;
4. *The material prosperity* they enjoy;
5. *The prevailing religious spirit:* republican and democratic religion;
6. The diffusion of *useful* knowledge;
7. Very pure morals;
8. Their division into small states. They prove nothing for a large state;
9. The absence of a large capital in which everything is concentrated. Careful to avoid it;
10. Commercial and provincial activity, so that everyone finds enough to do wherever he happens to be. . . .

NATIONAL CHARACTER OF THE AMERICANS

Restlessness strikes me as one of the distinctive character traits of the American people. The American is consumed by the desire for wealth. It is the sole passion of his life. He has no memory to connect him with one place rather than another, no deeply rooted customs, no devotion to routine. He is daily witness to the most abrupt changes of fortune and is less afraid than the citizen of any other country to risk what he has in the hope of a better future, because he knows that he can readily acquire new resources. He therefore enters the great lottery of human existence with the assurance of a gambler who risks only what he has already won. We are told that a man may try his hand at a dozen different walks of life. He may go from merchant to lawyer to doctor to evangelical minister. He may live in twenty different places without developing ties to any one of them. And how could it be otherwise?

The laws are constantly changing. Officials come and go in office. One system of administration follows another. Nature itself is changing more rapidly than man. In a striking reversal of the usual order of things, nature seems mutable and man immutable. A man may give his name to a wilderness that no one before him had ever explored. He may be the first to clear a forest for a solitary dwelling, around which will grow first a hamlet and then today a large city. In the brief expanse of a lifetime, he will have witnessed all these changes, and thousands like him will have done the same. In youth he may have lived among nations that have since vanished into history. He will have seen rivers change course or dwindle to a trickle. Even the climate is not what it was. And in his mind all of this is but the first step of a career whose end is not yet in sight. Time here flows with the power and impetuousness of a torrent, yet still the imagination races ahead of it. No canvas is big enough to capture it. There is no other country in the world where men are more confident of the future or prouder of their intelligence, which makes them masters of a universe that they can fashion at will. This mental revolution can only be compared with that initiated by the discovery of the New World three centuries ago. Indeed, one might say that America is being discovered a second time. Let no one think, moreover, that such thoughts are confined to the heads of philosophers: they are on the mind of the craftsman as much as the speculator, of the farmer as much as the city dweller. They envelop everything and color all sensation. They are palpable, visible, felt, and apparent to all the senses. The American—often born in a different clime, set down in the midst of an ever-changing environment, and driven by the same irresistible current that sweeps up everything in his vicinity—has no time to form bonds to anything. Change is the only thing to which he is accustomed, and in the end he comes to see it as man's natural condition. More than that, he feels a need for it and loves it, because instability seems to entail not disaster but miracles of the sort he sees wherever he looks. (The idea of a better possible world, of endless improvement of the social condition, is constantly before him in all its many guises.)

CANADA.

25 August 1831.

External appearance: Of all the parts of America we have visited thus far, Canada is incontestably the most comparable to Europe and especially to France. The banks of the Saint Lawrence River are beautifully cultivated and covered with houses and villages in every respect similar to ours. All traces of wilderness have disappeared, replaced by cultivated fields, steeples, and a population as numerous as that of our provinces.

The cities, and especially Montreal[141] (we have yet to see Quebec), bear a striking resemblance to our provincial cities.

---

141. Montreal was founded as a French mission at the confluence of the Saint Lawrence and Ottawa rivers in 1642. It became an important fur-trading post and was surrendered to

The population is basically French, and everywhere the French form the vast majority. But it is easy to see that the French are the vanquished people. The wealthy classes are mostly of English stock. Although French is nearly universally spoken, most newspapers, posters, and even the signs of French merchants are in English! Nearly all commercial enterprises are in English hands. The English are truly the ruling class in Canada. I doubt that it will remain so for long. The clergy and a good portion of the educated but not wealthy class are French, and they are beginning to be painfully aware of their second-class status. The French newspapers I have read maintain constant and vigorous opposition to the English. To date, the people, having few intellectual needs or passions and living quite comfortably in material terms, are only dimly aware of their situation as a conquered nation and have provided only limited support to the better-educated classes. In the past few years, however, the House of Commons, which is almost entirely Canadian,[142] has taken steps to introduce education everywhere. All signs are that the coming generation will be different from the present one, and if English immigration does not increase significantly and if the English already here do not succeed in bottling the French up in the space they already occupy, the two peoples will confront each other. I cannot believe that they will either mingle their blood or form an indissoluble union. I still hope that the French, despite the conquest, will someday create a beautiful empire of their own in the New World, more enlightened perhaps as well as more moral and prosperous than that of their forebears. For now, the division by race is singularly favorable to English domination.

27 August 1831.

The countryside between Montreal and Quebec seems as populous as the finest European provinces. The river is magnificent, moreover. Quebec is situated in a very picturesque location, surrounded by rich, fertile country. No region I know in Europe is more bustling than the area around Quebec.[143]

The entire working population of Quebec is French. Scarcely any language other than French is heard in the streets. Yet all the signs are in English. There are only two English theaters. The central city is ugly but has nothing in common with American cities. It is strikingly similar to the central sections of most of our provincial towns.

The surrounding villages are extraordinarily similar to our handsome villages. Only French is spoken in them. The people seem happy and comfortable. They are notably more handsome in aspect than the people of the United States.

---

the British in 1760 during the Seven Years' War. In 1831, Montreal had about forty thousand inhabitants; it was incorporated as a city the following year.

142. That is, French Canadian.

143. Quebec City had about thirty-two thousand residents in 1830.

These people are of robust stock; the women lack the delicate, sickly appearance of most American women.

The Catholic religion here has none of the accoutrements that it has acquired in the countries of southern Europe, where its reign is least contested. There are no monasteries, and convents of nuns are dedicated to utilitarian purposes and set examples of charity that even the English greatly admire. There are no roadside Madonnas, and no bizarre and ridiculous ornaments or devotional objects in the churches. The religion [is] enlightened, and Catholicism here neither arouses hatred nor draws sarcastic comments from Protestants. I confess that I find it more satisfying than I find the Protestantism of the United States. Here, the priest is truly the pastor of his flock and not an entrepreneur in the religious industry, like most American ministers. Unless one thinks it pointless to have a clergy at all, it should resemble the clergy of Canada.

Today I went to a reading room. Nearly all the printed newspapers in Canada are English. They are about the same size as London papers. I have not yet read any of them. In Quebec there is a half-English, half-French paper called *La Gazette* and a completely French paper called *Le Canadien.* These papers are roughly the size of our French papers. I carefully read numbers of each. They are vehemently opposed to the government and indeed to everything English. The masthead of *Le Canadien* reads: "Our religion, our language, our laws." It would be difficult to be more blunt. The content corresponds to the title. Anything likely to inflame passions great or small against the English is reported with relish in this newspaper. I read one article that said Canada would never be happy until it had a government of people Canadian by birth, principle, ideas, and even prejudices and that if Canada managed to free itself from England, it would not be to become English. The same newspaper contained several rather pretty examples of French verse. There were reports of prize competitions in which students had performed *Athalie, Zaïre,* and *La Mort de César.*[144] On the whole, the style of this newspaper is common, with an admixture of Anglicisms and bizarre turns of phrase. It is quite similar to the newspapers published in the canton of Vaud in Switzerland.[145] I have yet to meet a man of talent in Canada or to read a text offering evidence of talent. The man who is destined to stir up the French population against the English has yet to be born.

The English and the French are so unlikely to intermarry that only the latter are called *Canadians,* while the former continue to be called English.

144. These plays are *Athalie,* by Racine; *Zaïre,* by Voltaire; and *La mort de César,* Voltaire's adaptation of Shakespeare's *Julius Caesar.*

145. Vaud was a francophone canton of Switzerland. Like the newspapers from this Swiss region, the French Canadian newspapers published French prose and poetry in a region with competing languages and cultures.

Visit to a civil tribunal in Quebec.

We entered a spacious room filled with tiers of seats occupied by a crowd of people who by all appearances were French. At the far end of the room a large copy of the arms of Britain was painted on the wall. Beneath it sat a judge in robes and hood. The lawyers were arrayed before him.

When we came in, the court was hearing a libel case. The defendant was accused of calling another man a filthy scoundrel.[146] One of the lawyers was arguing in English: *"Pendard,"* he said, pronouncing the word with a very British accent, "means a man who has been hanged."[147] No, the judge replied gravely, "not a man who has been hanged but one who deserves to be hanged." With that the counsel for the defense leaped angrily to his feet and pleaded his case in French, while his adversary replied in English. Both men became rather heated in their respective languages, no doubt without fully understanding what the other had said. From time to time the Englishman endeavored to express his ideas in French, in order to respond more directly to his adversary. The latter occasionally replied in English. The judge attempted to restore order to the court, first in one language and then in the other. The bailiff shouted, "Silence!" sometimes with a French pronunciation, other times with an English. With calm restored, witnesses were introduced into the courtroom. Some of them kissed the silver Christ on the cover of the Bible and swore in French to tell the truth, while others took the same oath in English and, being Protestants, kissed the other side of the Bible, without the embossing. The customary law of Normandy was then invoked, Denisart was cited, and there was discussion of the decrees of the Parlement of Paris and the statutes of King George III.[148] The judge then gave his opinion: "Since the word *crasseux* connotes the idea of a man without morals, discipline, or honor, I sentence the defendant to pay a fine of ten louis or ten pounds sterling."

The lawyers I saw that day, who are said to be the best in Quebec, showed no talent for either the law or courtroom rhetoric. They particularly lacked distinction and spoke French with a middle-class Norman accent. Their style was vulgar and marked by *foreignisms* and English locutions. They say a man has been *charged* ten *louis* when they mean that he has been required to pay ten louis.

"Get in the box," they shout at the witness when they want him to take his seat on the bench where he is to testify.

There is something bizarre, incoherent, and even burlesque about the whole business. Yet the fundamental impression it left with me was sad. I have never

146. The original French text has *"pendard crasseux."*

147. The original French text has *"pendu."*

148. The government of Lower Canada, established by the Quebec Act of 1774, combined the civil law of France with the criminal law of England.

The legal works of the French writer Jean Baptiste Denisart (1713–1765) were frequently cited throughout the nineteenth century.

been more convinced than I was on leaving that courtroom that the most irreparable harm a people can suffer is to be conquered.

28 August 1831.

Mr. Neilson came today to take us on a tour of the region. (Regarding the character and position of Mr. Neilson, see the conversation with him.)[149] The result of this walk was to leave us with the most favorable possible impression of the Canadian population. We found well-cultivated fields and homes that breathed prosperity. We visited several of them. The main room is typically equipped with excellent beds, and the walls are painted white. Very clean furniture. A small mirror and a crucifix or a few engravings of biblical subjects complete the décor. The peasant is strong, solidly built, and well dressed. In his demeanor we find the frank cordiality lacking in his American counterpart. He is polite without being servile and receives you as an equal, but considerately. There was something distinguished in the manners of the farmers we visited that made a great impression on us. (To be sure, we were taken to see the leading families in the village.) All in all, this breed of men struck us as less well educated than the Americans but superior in regard to qualities of the heart. Here we sensed none of the *mercantile* spirit that is so obvious in the American's every word and action. Canadians do little to cultivate their minds, but they reason simply and directly. They undoubtedly have fewer ideas than their neighbors, but their sensibilities seem to be more highly developed. They go by their hearts, Americans by their heads.

29 August.

Today we set out on horseback to visit the countryside without a guide.

In the town of Beaufort, two leagues from Quebec, we saw people leaving a church. Its appearance hinted at considerable prosperity. People from a remote hamlet climbed into carriages for the trip home. We wandered the paths of the village and spoke with all the residents we encountered, attempting to turn the conversation to serious subjects. This is what we learned:

1. Things are currently quite prosperous here. The land around Quebec sells at an extremely high price, as high as in France. But it also yields a good income.

2. The people here have as yet done little to develop their thinking. Nevertheless, they are already quite well aware that the English in the vicinity are growing in number at an alarming rate, and they believe that they are wrong to remain within a limited territory rather than spread out across what is still free country. Their jealousy is aroused daily by the arrival of new settlers from Europe. They sense that in the end they will be submerged. Anything one says about this subject clearly arouses their passions. But they have no clear idea of the remedy. Canadians are too afraid of losing touch with home and hearth, and

---

149. This conversation is recorded in Non-alphabetic Notebook 1; see pp. 229–33.

they lack shrewdness. "Yes, you're right," they say, "but what can we do about it?" Such are their sentiments. They are clearly aware of their position as a vanquished people and do not count on the benevolence, not of the government, precisely, but of the English. All their hopes are invested in their representatives. For them, and especially for Mr. Neilson—"even though he is English," they say with surprise or regret—they have the same high regard that oppressed peoples generally have for their protector. It seemed to us that a number of them clearly understood the need for education and were quite pleased with the steps recently taken to secure it. All in all, these people seemed to us capable of being governed though still incapable of governing themselves. We are coming to a turning point. If Canadians do not overcome their apathy at some point in the next twenty years, it will be too late. All signs are that these people are on the verge of awakening. But if the intermediate and upper classes of the Canadian population abandon the lower classes and allow themselves to be drawn in the wake of the English, the French race in America is lost. And that would be a real pity, for you have here the elements of a great people. The French of America are to the French of France what the Americans are to the English. They have preserved most of the distinctive features of the national character and combined these with greater morality and simplicity. They, too, have rid themselves of a host of prejudices and faulty assumptions, which have been and may continue to be the source of Europe's woes. In short, they have in them everything it takes to establish an exalted image of France in the New World. But will they ever succeed in fully regaining their national independence? It seems likely but unfortunately not certain. A man of genius who understands and feels the national passions of these people and is capable of developing them might have an admirable role to play here. He would soon become the most powerful man in the colony. But I don't yet see such a man anywhere.

There already exists in Quebec a class of men who bridge the gap between French and English: English allies of the French,[150] Englishmen unhappy with the government, and Frenchmen in positions of power. This class is represented in the periodical press by *La Gazette de Québec*,[151] a mixture of French and English, and in political bodies by Mr. Neilson and probably a number of others whom we do not know. It is this class that I fear the most for the future fate of the Canadian population. It arouses neither the jealousy nor the passions of the Canadians; on the contrary, it is more Canadian in its interests than English, because it opposes the government. Yet at bottom it is English in mores, ideas, and tongue. If it were ever to assume the position of the educated upper class of the Canadians,[152] they would lose their national character permanently. They would vegetate, like the Lower Bretons in France. Fortunately, religion stands as an ob-

150. That is, the French Canadians.
151. Founded in 1764, this newspaper published both English and French editions through the 1830s.
152. French Canadians.

stacle to marriage between the two races and creates, in the clergy, an educated class with an interest in speaking French and absorbing French literature and ideas.

In our conversations with the people of this country, we have detected a good deal of jealousy and hatred of landlords.[153] Yet these landlords have no rights to speak of; they are as common as can be and nearly all reduced to cultivating the land in order to live. But the spirit of equality and democracy is as alive in Canada as in the United States, even if it is less argumentative. In the hearts of these peasants I have found the same political passions that gave rise to our Revolution and that are still the source of all our woes. Here they are harmless, or nearly so, because nothing stands in their way. We have also observed, we believe, the peasant's distress at the clergy's right to demand a tithe of its income and his envy of the wealth that this tax delivers into the hands of a few ecclesiastics. If religion ever loses its hold over Canada, this is the breach through which the enemy will have entered.

Like the French peasant, the Canadian peasant is cheerful and alert, and his answers nearly always have a certain bite. I once asked a farmer why Canadians were content with small fields when fertile but uncultivated land was to be found not twenty leagues away. "Why do you love your wife," he replied, "when your neighbor's wife has much more beautiful eyes?" To me, this answer seemed to have been prompted by deep and genuine feeling.

All the French newspapers in Canada publish snippets of literature and poetry, which one never finds in the more ample pages of the English papers. The poetry has the flavor of old French verse. It is simple and naïve in character, far removed from the pomposity, bombast, and affectation of our literature today, yet it thrives on insignificant or outmoded ideas.

31 August 1831.

Today we went with Mr. Neilson and a Canadian named Mr. Viger along the right bank of the Saint Lawrence to the village of Saint-Thomas, about 10 leagues from Quebec.[154] This is the spot where the Saint Lawrence broadens to a width of 7 leagues, which it maintains over the next 50 leagues. The area we traversed was admirably fertile throughout. Bounded by the Saint Lawrence to the south and the mountains to the north, the landscape was splendid and varied. The houses are *all* well built. All give out an air of prosperity and cleanliness.

The churches are richly decorated but in very good taste. Their interior

153. The original French text has *"seigneurs."*

154. A backbone of the Montreal elite, the Viger family had many members who might have accompanied the party to Saint Thomas. Louis Michel Viger (1795–1855), a lawyer and government official, and Jacques Viger (1787–1858), a journalist and future mayor of Montreal, are likely candidates. Neilson's good friend Denis Benjamin Viger (1774–1861) had left Canada in the spring of 1831 and therefore could not have been with the party in August.

Saint Thomas, south of Quebec, is about forty miles north of Montreal on the Saint Lawrence River.

decoration would not be out of place in a French city. It should be noted that towns tax themselves to build their churches. The population is exclusively French, yet when you come to an inn or shop, its sign is in English.

General remarks. 1 September 1831.

In conversations with several Canadians,[155] we noticed that their hatred was directed toward the government more than toward the English race in general. The people are instinctively hostile to the English, but many Canadians who belong to the enlightened classes do not appear to be as eager as we believed to preserve their original culture intact or to become a separate nation. A number of them seemed fairly willing to join the English so long as the English were willing to promote the interests of Canada. It is to be feared, therefore, that with the passage of time and, above all, the immigration of Irish Catholics, fusion of the two races will take place, and this can only be to the detriment of the French, their language, and their customs.

Nevertheless, it is certain [that]:

1. Lower Canada (fortunately for the French race) forms a separate state. In Lower Canada the ratio of the French to the English population is ten to one. The French form a compact group. They have their own government and their own parliament. They truly constitute a distinct nation. The parliament has 84 members, of whom 64 are French and 20 English.

2. To date the English have always kept to themselves. They support the government against the masses of the people. All the French newspapers are in opposition, while all the English papers are ministerial, with the exception of *The Vindicator* in Montreal, and it was founded by Canadians.[156]

3. In the cities, the English and the Canadians form two societies. The English make a great show of luxury. The largest Canadian fortunes are quite modest by comparison. This gives rise to small-town jealousies and annoyances.

4. The English control all foreign trade and dominate all domestic trade. This, too, is a source of jealousy.

5. The English are constantly seizing control of land that Canadians believed to be reserved for their race.

6. Finally, the English reveal all the traits of their national character in Canada, and the Canadians have retained all the traits of the French character.

It is therefore highly likely that Lower Canada will ultimately become an entirely French nation. But it will never be a populous nation. Everything around it will become English. It will be a drop in the ocean. I am quite afraid that, as Mr. Neilson said with his customary brusque candor, fortune has indeed decided that North America shall be English.

155. French Canadians.

156. Daniel Tracey, an Irish immigrant, founded the English-language *Vindicator* in 1828. The periodical promoted a republican government and criticized officials that were appointed rather than popularly elected.

2 September 1831.

We have seen a great many ecclesiastics since coming to Canada. To us it seemed clear that they constituted the leading class of Canadians. All the clergymen we have met have been educated, polite, and well-bred. They speak pure French. On the whole, they are more distinguished than most French priests. From their conversation it is apparent that they are *entirely Canadian.* They share the feelings and interests of the people and articulate their needs quite well. Yet in general they strike us as feeling *loyalty* to the king of England and generally supporting the principle of legitimacy. Nevertheless, one of them said this to me: "We have high hopes at present, the ministry is *democratic.*" Today they are in opposition and would certainly rebel if the government were to become tyrannical.

All in all, the people here are remarkably similar to the French people. Or, rather, they *are* French, feature for feature, and therefore entirely different from the neighboring English population. Cheerful, spirited, derisive, fond of glory and noise, intelligent, and eminently sociable. Their manners are mild and their characters helpful. The people in general are more moral, more hospitable, and more religious than people in France. Only in Canada can one find people who are what we call in France *bon enfant* [good-natured]. The English and Americans are either *coarse* or *cold.* . . .

2 September 1831.

Five or six years ago, the English government wanted to unify all of Canada in a single assembly. As there was no better way of dissolving the Canadian[157] nation entirely, the people rose as one, and since that time they have been conscious of their strength.[158]

Several priests have told me that in their towns there was not a single person who spoke English. They themselves did not understand the language and took us for interpreters.

The power to appoint officers of the militia belongs to the government, but the House decided that officers must reside in their place of command, and the result is that leadership of the military rests almost entirely in the hands of Canadians.[159]

A Canadian told me today that debate in the House was vigorous and heated and that resolutions were often passed in haste only to be rescinded when passions had cooled. It sounds a lot like the French chamber, does it not? . . .

157. French Canadian.

158. In 1828, British colonial officials renewed an appeal for the union of Upper and Lower Canada. This effort spurred sixty thousand Canadians to sign a petition opposing such a union, which John Neilson presented to the British parliament.

159. French Canadians.

PARDON.

Mr. Ingersoll, a lawyer and former member of the legislature in Philadelphia,[160] told us today (14 October 1831):

"The right to pardon is subject to far greater abuse in republics than in monarchies. This can be seen by comparing what happens here with what happens in France. Here, experience has shown that life sentences are illusory, because sooner or later the prisoner will obtain a pardon. Our sovereign is constantly changing, and with each change the prisoner gets a fresh chance. Furthermore, there is no intermediary between the sovereign and the relatives and friends of the prisoner. The attack is unrelenting and at close quarters. It is not in human nature to hold out indefinitely. In monarchies, by contrast, it is almost impossible to gain access to the sovereign, and his ministers can brush petitions aside by saying that the king refuses."

Note: In the prison records for Sing Sing from the year 1824 (I believe), I noted that of 180 freed prisoners, 95 had been pardoned. I observed that many repeat offenders were men who had been pardoned. Since that time, abuse of the pardon has greatly diminished.

PUBLIC EDUCATION.

Sing Sing, 1 June 1831.

Everyone I have met thus far, no matter what his social rank, has struck me as incapable of conceiving even the possibility of doubting the benefits of education. They never fail to smile when I tell them that this view is not universally shared in Europe. They agree that the spread of enlightenment, which is useful to all people, is absolutely necessary for a free people such as theirs, where there are no property qualifications for voting or holding office. This idea seems to have planted itself in everyone's head. Consequently, the states have spent a great deal to establish public schools (Beaumont has firm figures). I still do not know what people here think about the negative consequences of a semieducated population, which are so serious in France. Nevertheless, it seems to me that the strongest arguments that are raised against the excessive diffusion of enlightenment in Europe are not applicable here. For instance:

1. Religious morale suffers less from this here than anywhere else. There is absolutely no hostility between religion and knowledge.

2. There is less to fear here than anywhere else from the malaise that afflicts a state in which large numbers of people are educated beyond their station in life and become restless enough to disturb the tranquility of the society. Here, the resources provided by nature are still so far beyond man's ability to use them all that any moral energy or intellectual activity can readily be put to good use.

160. Charles Jared Ingersoll (1782–1862), a former U.S. congressman, had just finished serving as the U.S. district attorney for Pennsylvania. A Democrat, Ingersoll was reelected to the U.S. Congress in 1840.

19 July 1831, on Lake Erie, aboard the *Ohio.*
Even among those now confined to areas surrounded by Europeans, one still finds men whose superior intelligence is able to discern the ultimate fate of the Indian race and whose savage energy still seeks to fight against a future that has by now become inevitable. Red Jacket, who died in 1829 in a Seneca village near Buffalo, was one of these men, whom we might call the last of the Indians.[161]

Mr. Spencer told me the following anecdotes about him (18 July 1831): "Red Jacket was in recent times the greatest enemy of the white man, and his hatred of whites made him the greatest enemy of the Christian religion in the New World. Sensing that the time had passed when the Europeans could be fought openly, he nevertheless used all the moral authority he enjoyed among his compatriots to prevent them from mingling with us. Red Jacket was familiar with our customs and understood English, but he disdained to speak it. His influence on his compatriots was immense. It would be difficult, Mr. Spencer added, to find a man with greater or more appealing natural eloquence, who was also a master of irony. I remember an occasion ten years ago when an Indian from the vicinity of Buffalo was accused of killing an American. He was arrested and hauled before one of *our juries.* I was district attorney at the time and had to prosecute the man. Red Jacket took up his defense and, even though he was obliged to use an interpreter, won his case. After the trial he came over to me and with a great show of modesty said, 'No doubt my brother (referring to the accused) did you some great harm at some point in the past.' I said that until he was arrested I had no idea that he even existed. 'I understand,' Red Jacket replied. 'The white man he killed was your brother, and you wanted to avenge his death.' Once again I tried to disabuse him and explained the nature of my duties as district attorney. Red Jacket listened attentively and then asked if the elders among my people paid me to do what I had just explained to him. I said yes. Then, feigning outrage, he shouted, 'What! Not only did you try to kill my brother, who never did you any wrong, but you were paid in advance for his blood!'"

"I confess," Mr. Spencer added, "that I was dumbfounded by this attack."

Many years ago, the Presbyterians of Boston sent a missionary to the Mohawk Indians, who were at that time living in the valley that still bears their name. Red Jacket was one of them. The tribe gathered to hear the missionary. Afterward, there was a general discussion, and all the Indians agreed with Red Jacket that they should turn the missionary away. Red Jacket was deputed to deliver the news.

"My father has spoken well," Red Jacket said, "but my brothers would like to clear up one point that remains in doubt. Our ancestors taught our fathers that they had seen the Great Spirit, and we believe our fathers. We're told that white men believe in a book that the Great Spirit has given them, but we've also

---

161. Red Jacket (c. 1750–1830) was a Seneca chief from upstate New York. Noted for his oratorical skills, Red Jacket was the leader of the anti-Christian faction among the Seneca.

been told that each of the many tribes of white men interprets this book in a different way. Is this a false report that my brothers have heard?"

The missionary had to concede that there was some truth in what Red Jacket said, whereupon Red Jacket continued with an air of humility: "If the white men whose minds have been opened to all things by the Great Spirit who gave them the book are not sure they understand it, how can my father ask poor savages to attempt what they have failed to do?" The missionary attempted to explain to him that Christians disagreed about only a few points and agreed about all the rest. Red Jacket let him go on as long as he wished and then ended the conversation by saying, "These things are difficult for red men to understand. But we hope that my father will go and repeat them to our neighbors, the white men. And if his teaching prevents the white men from stealing our land and our livestock, as they do every day, then my father can come back to us, and you will find us more ready to receive your message."

First encounter with Indians, 20 July 1831.[162]

The first Indians we encountered lived in Oneida Castle, a village about 270 miles from New York.[163] They ran after our carriage begging for a handout, and we had little time to study them. On arriving in Buffalo on the evening of July 18, however, we ran into a substantial number of them. We were told that they had come to collect the payment due on land they had ceded to the United States, which paid them rent.

I don't think I've ever been as disappointed as I was at the sight of these Indians. My mind was full of memories of M. de Ch[ateaubriand] and of Cooper, and I expected to see in the natives of America savages, to be sure, but savages on whom nature had left traces of some of the lofty virtues to which the spirit of liberty gives rise. What I thought I would find was a race of men not very different from Europeans, with bodies developed by strenuous exercise in the hunt and at war and which would scarcely suffer from being viewed in the nude. The reader may judge my surprise by comparing this portrait with the one that follows. The Indians I saw that night were small in stature; their limbs, so far as one could judge beneath their clothes, were spindly and not muscular; their complexion, rather than red as is commonly believed, was dark bronze, so that at first sight they seemed not very different from Negroes. Their black hair hung stiffly about their necks, sometimes down to their shoulders. For the most part their mouths were unusually large, and their expressions were horrible and nasty. There was a great deal in their features that was European, but they resembled the lowest specimens of the dregs of one of our large cities. Their faces revealed a profound depravity of the kind that can only come from long abuse of the benefits of civilization. Yet they were still savages. To vices they took from us they added something barbarous and uncivilized, which made these

162. Tocqueville recounted much of the following narrative in his essay "Two Weeks in the Wilderness" (printed in part 3).

163. Oneida Castle is just east of the city of Oneida, in central New York State.

people a hundred times more repulsive. The Indians wore European garments but not in the way we do. Some wrapped themselves in blankets. Women [with] trousers and hats. Men with women's costumes. They were clearly not used to wearing these garments and seemed to be imprisoned in their folds. They combined European ornaments with barbarous luxury goods such as feathers, necklaces, and enormous earrings. Their movements were quick and chaotic, their voices sharp and discordant, their looks anxious and wild. At first sight it was tempting to think of them as a species of wildlife from the forest that had been brought up to present something of the appearance of human beings but that nevertheless remained in an animal state.

After proceeding some distance beyond the city, we encountered a large number of Indians on their way back to their village. Most of them were more or less drunk. An Indian woman rolled in the dirt and uttered savage cries. Not far from the last houses we caught sight of an Indian man asleep by the side of the road. He was a young man, and, as he lay there motionless, we took him for dead. When muffled moans emanated from his throat, however, we realized that he was still alive, a victim of the dangerous intoxication that often comes from drinking brandy. The sun had already set, and the ground was moist. It seemed likely that this poor wretch would breathe his last where he lay unless he got help. Now and then a group of Indians happened by. They approached him, turned him over, felt his heart to see if he was still alive, and then moved on without so much as deigning to reply to our observations. I shall never forget one young Indian female, who at first seemed to show some interest in the man; I believe that she was his wife or sister. She studied him closely, addressed him by name, felt his heart, and upon discovering that he was still alive tried to rouse him from his stupor. But when her efforts proved unavailing, she flew into a rage against the inanimate body in front of her. She banged the man's head against the ground, kneaded his face with her hands, and walked over his prostrate body. Throughout this ferocious performance, she uttered savage, inarticulate cries, which I can still hear ringing in my ears as I write these lines. At length we felt we had no choice but to intervene, and we peremptorily ordered her to go away. As she moved off, we heard her break out in barbarous laughter.

When we got back to town, we spoke to various people about the young Indian we had found lying by the road. We said that he was in imminent danger. We offered to pay for a room in an inn. Nothing came of our efforts. We could not persuade anyone to lift a finger. Some said, "These people are used to drinking too much and sleeping on the ground. They don't die from such mishaps." Others realized that the Indian probably was dying, and in their faces it was possible to read a thought that never quite made it to their lips: What is the life of an Indian worth? This was the idea that lay behind the sentiment that everyone shared. In the midst of American society, so well ordered, so moralistic, and so charitable, there reigned a chilling selfishness and total insensitivity to the plight of others, at least as far as the natives of the country were concerned. Americans do not set their dogs after the Indians, as the Spanish do in Mexico, but in the end the European race here is driven by the same merciless insensitivity as everywhere else. "This world belongs to us," they tell each other every day, "and the Indian race is doomed. Nothing can prevent it, and delay is undesirable. God did not make these people fit to be civilized. They must die. And anyway I don't want to get involved. I won't do anything to prevent their doom, and I shall limit myself to providing them with whatever is likely to hasten it. In time their land will be mine, but I won't bear any guilt for their demise." Satisfied with this argument, the American goes to church, where he listens to a minister of the Gospel repeat daily that all men are brothers and that the Eternal Being who made them all in his own image has made it their duty to help one another.

Quebec, 31 August 1831.

Mr. Neilson had this to say today about the Indians: "These tribes will disappear completely. But they will succumb as victims of the loftiness of their souls. The lowliest Indian thinks of himself as at least the equal of the governor of Quebec. They will not adapt to civilization, not because they are incapable of living as we do but because they despise our way of life and consider themselves our superiors." . . .

MASSACHUSETTS.

We have traveled the length of Massachusetts from Albany to Boston.[164] To us it looked quite different from the state of New York. Here there are no log houses, no burnt trees, no fields with tree stumps left in their midst—in short, not a trace of wilderness remains. The land is thoroughly cultivated, and the country looks old. Nearly all the homes are charming (especially in the villages), and the prevailing air of well-scrubbed luxury is astonishing. The countryside itself is more picturesque. There are many mountains.

20 September 1831: Boston is a pretty city, picturesquely situated on several hills surrounded by water.[165]

What we have seen of its inhabitants so far gives a completely different picture from what we saw in New York. Society—or at any rate the society into which we have been introduced, which I believe is the best—quite closely resembles the upper classes of Europe. Luxury and studied elegance are the norm. Nearly all the women speak French well, and all the men we have seen thus far have been to Europe. Their manners are distinguished, and intellectual subjects are the heart of their conversation. One feels liberated from New York's commercial habits and financial preoccupations, which make society there so vulgar. In Boston there are a fair number of people who have nothing to do and there-

164. Tocqueville and Beaumont traveled the 160 miles over the course of three days.

165. Boston, founded in 1630, was built on a peninsula connected to the mainland by a narrow isthmus (Boston Neck). By 1830, tons of land had been removed from the city's hills to create landfill to widen the neck. That year, over sixty thousand individuals lived in the city.

fore pursue the pleasures of the mind. There are a few who write. We have already viewed three or four quite handsome libraries, all literary. (It should be noted, however, that virtually everyone we have met is a distinguished person, though it should be added that the distinguished people here are of a different type from the distinguished people of New York.)[166] Furthermore, the prejudice against people who do nothing (which on the whole is quite useful) still appears to be quite powerful in Boston. As in all the states we have visited thus far, intellectual work in Boston is directed mainly to religious subjects. Of twenty-five semiperiodical works and brochures in the Athenaeum, twelve are more or less concerned with religious subjects.

PENITENTIARIES.

Sing Sing, 29 May 1831.

The penitentiary system that has been established at Sing Sing strikes me as dangerous to apply. My reasons follow. There is no denying that discipline at Sing Sing is far superior to that which can be found in any similar institution in France. Its effects are:

1. The health of the prisoners;
2. Their extreme dedication to work;
3. The income that the state derives from this work;
4. *Perhaps* the moral reform of a certain number of them.

How are these effects obtained? By complete *silence,* which keeps prisoners isolated from one another, and constant *labor,* which keeps their physical and moral faculties occupied.

How is the necessary degree of *silence* and *labor* achieved? By arbitrarily granting all the guards the power to inflict corporal punishment. But how do the guards use this power to produce the two effects I mentioned? This, it seems to me, is the paramount question, to which all others are subsidiary. Overseers are granted the power to beat *the convicts,* and they constantly make poor use of it (too little or too much). In any case, it surely does not have the same effect.

To make sure that the attention of the guards does not flag and to compel them to be both pitiless and just, the Americans see to it that maintaining discipline in the prison is a matter of urgent personal interest to each and every guard. The prisoners are unconstrained, they are armed [with axes and picks], they are not chained, and they are not surrounded by walls. Were they to concert their action, liberty would surely be theirs. Guards must therefore constantly remind themselves that their lives depend on thwarting plots, on keeping the prisoners diligently occupied, and even on refraining from inflicting unjust punishments for fear of provoking irritable characters, for one angry prisoner could inspire the rest to follow his lead. Guards will therefore be severe but

166. A combination of wealth, intellectualism, and descent from New England's founding families distinguished the segment of the city's elite known as the Boston Brahmins.

just, and they will be so not out of duty or fear but for reasons of self-interest. Americans thus court danger, they confront it directly, and by so doing I believe they have vanquished it. And that is why I believe that it would be dangerous to follow their example. As long as the machine runs smoothly, discipline in their prisons will be a thousand times better than in any prison in Europe. But no minor rebellion is possible. Thus the Sing Sing system in some ways resembles the steamboats of which the Americans are so fond. No other means of transportation is as convenient or rapid—as perfect, in short—as long as things are running normally. But if some part of the apparatus goes awry, vessel, passengers, and cargo may be blown to kingdom come.

Factual observation to add to the foregoing: Same day.

Three years ago, a man, who was pointed out to us, ran out of a workshop, axe in hand, and urged his fellow prisoners to rise in rebellion. They hesitated, and the man was placed under arrest. Clearly, the lives of the guards at Sing Sing hung by a thread that day. If one of them had neglected his duty long enough for five or six prisoners to communicate with one another and hatch a conspiracy, there is no doubt that they would have formed a vanguard and led the other prisoners in rebellion.

Another observation.

We saw 250 prisoners cutting stone in a shed. These men were under special watch because all had committed violent crimes suggestive of particularly depraved characters. Each held a stonecutter's wedge in his hands. Three unarmed guards patrolled the shed. Their eyes were in constant motion.

The same day—30 May 1831—we viewed several hundred prisoners at work in the stone quarry under a blazing sun (one of the hottest days of the year), and they seemed to work as hard as workers paid by the piece.

Id. 31 May 1831.

Mr. Prince, a minister at Sing Sing and house master there as well, told us that in his view prison guards were exposed to great danger and that experience thus far was still too limited to permit firm conclusions as to the obedience of prisoners. He compared the warden to a man who has tamed a tiger but who might one day find himself devoured by it. Mr. Prince seemed to me an intelligent man and in a position to have an opinion. He does not believe that the Sing Sing system has achieved a great moral reform. . . .

Auburn, 12 July 1831.

Conversation with Mr. Wainwright, Anglican minister.[167]

Mr. Wainwright appears to be an intelligent man. He has (what is rare in

167. Jonathan Mayhew Wainwright (1792–1854) was an Episcopal minister in charge of Grace Church in New York. He served at churches throughout New England and was instrumental in founding New York University in the 1820s.

America) the manners of the finest company and officiates at the most fashionable church in New York.

Q: Is there any point of contact here between religious ideas and political doctrines?

A: No. These are two entirely different worlds, and each of them lives in peace.

Q: What accounts for this?

A: The fact that ministers of the various sects have never become involved in politics and never claimed to wield political power. If we were to mingle in political matters, we would worry about diminishing the esteem in which we are held. Many of us even abstain from voting in elections. I, for one, always do so.

Mr. Smith, the chaplain of the Auburn prison, said the same thing to me.[168] He added: "I am convinced that if one proposed a political role to members of the Presbyterian clergy, they would refuse without a moment's hesitation." Mr. Smith is a young Presbyterian minister of rather common intelligence but quite eager and well-intentioned. . . .

UNCULTIVATED LAND. HOW TO CULTIVATE IT.

Information provided by a young Scottish physician, a "new settler," on 30 July 1831 near Pontiac.[169]

When a new settler arrives, he moves in with a neighbor, if there is one. If not, he erects a tent. The first order of business is to clear a field, which is done with hired hands. The cost of this (including clearing the land and building fences) is estimated at roughly 3 dollars per acre. Once the ground is prepared, the new settler plants an acre of potatoes, with the rest of his land reserved for either wheat or corn, depending on the nature of the soil. Corn can grow in wetter ground because planting is done in the spring. A new settler must come with enough supplies to last at least six months. Two barrels of flour and a barrel of salt pork are enough to meet his and his family's needs. A barrel of salt pork costs fourteen dollars. Tea serves as beverage. As a general rule, a man needs at least 150 to 200 dollars to establish himself. Of this, 100 dollars goes to buy the land, and for that amount you can get 80 acres. The rest is for initial household expenses and incidentals. With this money, new settlers also buy livestock, which can be maintained at relatively low cost. You put bells around the animals' necks and let them graze freely in the forest. A hired hand costs a dollar without board and six shillings with board. Plowing is done with oxen, which cost twelve shillings per day.

168. Tocqueville and Beaumont had extensive conversations with Rev. B. C. Smith, who believed in the potential of the prison system to reform the individual.

169. This is the Doctor Burns whom the travelers met in Michigan.

Information obtained from a resident of Detroit on July 22 on Lake Erie.

A rod is 16.5 (English) feet, and an acre is 20 rods long by 8 wide (smaller than the *arpent*[170]).

In the vicinity of Syracuse and Oneida Lake, uncultivated land sells for five to six dollars an acre, and cultivated land for 15 to 20 dollars (8 July 1831).

At Canandaigua, cultivated land sells for 18 to 20 dollars an acre and the best land for 25 dollars an acre. Prices at Buffalo are the same.

In the Michigan Territory, an acre of uncultivated land sells at a standard price of 10 shillings. The full price must be paid in one lump sum. This is true of all land sold by the state.[171] (This general policy was adopted because of the difficulty of recovering the money owed.)

The state believes that its interest and the public interest are best served by selling at a lower price but without a discount.

Purchasing the land is the easiest part of establishing a settlement when the land is uncultivated. The real expense comes in preparing the land for planting. This costs 5 to 10 dollars per acre (for cutting trees, removing the timber, building fences, and plowing the land), whereas the annual income from a cleared acre runs between 2 and 4 dollars. The price of a day of labor is 50 cents, not including food. If the laborer is not given board, the price is 6 shillings (this contradicts abundant information from other sources, according to which the price of a day of labor without food is 8 shillings or 1 dollar).

Information provided on 25 July 1831 at Pontiac by our host.

An acre of cultivated land is estimated to yield two dollars or more in annual income. The purchase of the land is nothing; the real expense is in preparing it, the cost of the labor involved.

This is what a man must do if he does not cultivate the land himself (which is rarely the case). Suppose I have someone clear twenty acres. I pay him five dollars per acre and provide him with a plow and a team of oxen. I also supply half the seed, and we then share the first year's harvest. If the harvest is good, my half pays more than my five-dollar expenditure. Subsequent harvests are entirely mine. . . .

Sing Sing, 29 May 1831.

Ancient republics operated on the principle that the particular interest was to be sacrificed to the general good, and in this sense one can say that these republics were *virtuous*. The principle of this republic seems to me to be to require the particular interest to serve the general interest. A sort of refined and intelligent egotism appears to be the axis about which the whole machine revolves. These people do not trouble to find out whether the public virtue is good, but they claim to prove that it is useful. If the latter is true, as I believe to some degree it is, this society can pass for enlightened but not virtuous. But to what degree are

170. A French unit of measure.

171. In 1820, the United States government set the price for all federal lands at a low $1.25 per acre and did not allow settlers to purchase on credit.

the two principles of individual good and general good compatible? To what extent can what one might call a reflective or calculating mind master political passions that do not yet exist but cannot fail to manifest themselves someday? Only the future can tell us.

Id. 1 June 1831.

When one reflects on the nature of this society, one discovers part of the explanation for the foregoing: American society consists of a myriad of different elements, all newly assembled.

The men who live under its laws are still English, French, German, Dutch. They have no common religion, mores, or ideas. To date, no one can say that an American character exists, unless it is not to have a character. Here there are no common memories, no national attachments. What, then, is the only bond that can possibly unite the various parts of this vast body? *Self-interest.*

Alphabetic Notebook B

ASSOCIATION.

10 October 1831.

The power of association has developed to the full in America. People associate for commerce as well as for political, literary, and religious interests. No one ever seeks success by recourse to higher authority; people rely instead on individual resources acting in concert.

The most recent form of association, I believe, is the temperance society, which is an association of men who mutually commit themselves to abstaining from a vice and who enlist their collective strength to aid them in resisting what is most intimate and personal in each of them, namely, their own individual penchants. The success of these temperance societies is one of the most remarkable things about this country.[172]

15 October 1831.

When a major crime attracts public attention, the residents of the place where the crime was committed come together, appoint a commission to find out who did it, and establish a fund to pay the expenses of the investigation. I have seen

172. The American Temperance Society was founded in 1826, and by 1833, over six thousand local chapters claimed about one million members who pledged to abstain from drinking any alcoholic beverage. The ATS often worked closely with church congregations to prevent drunkenness, idleness, and crime in American society, and alcohol consumption dropped significantly in the 1830s.

examples of this. What this shows is, first, that the investigative capacity of the police in America is limited and, second, that Americans know what associations can do for them. . . .

CONVENTION.

14 October 1831.

The right to hold a convention is the most extreme consequence of the dogma of popular sovereignty. An example of a convention that I saw in America will help more than anything else to understand what a *political* convention is, for there are conventions for all sorts of things. Everyone knows how agitated Americans are about the issue of the tariff and free trade. It is fair to say that the tariff arouses the only political passions that exist in the Union, because the tariff is supported and opposed not just by different shades of opinion but by very powerful material interests. The North ascribes much of its prosperity to the tariff, while the South blames the tariff for nearly all its woes.

About two months ago, Mr. Sedgwick, the brother of Miss Sedgwick, the author,[173] who lives in the small village of Stockbridge, Massachusetts, where I met him, had the idea of using newspapers to call upon all enemies of the tariff to send delegates to Philadelphia, where a convention would ponder the best ways to restore freedom of trade. This suggestion, relayed by the power of the press from Maine to New Orleans within just a few days, was taken up by all the states with interests for and against the tariff. The enemies of the tariff met throughout the nation and chose delegates to represent them at the convention. These delegates were nearly all very distinguished men, with names like Gallatin, Berian, and many well-known figures from the South. The Carolinas alone sent 63 delegates. On 1 October 1831 the convention met in Philadelphia with more than 200 delegates. Its debates were open to the public and from the first took on a legislative character. There was general debate, for example, about the extent of congressional power, fundamental debate about the theory of free trade, and, finally, pragmatic discussion of the various provisions of the tariff of 1828. After ten days of meetings, the convention adjourned indefinitely, having drafted a petition to the American people. This petition contended:

1. That Congress does not have the power to impose a tariff and that the existing tariff is unconstitutional.

2. That it is not in the interest of any people, and in particular of the American people, to impose limits on the freedom of commerce.

Nothing I have seen in America has made me more aware of the dangerous consequences of popular sovereignty and of the impracticability of the idea in France.

173. Theodore Sedgwick Jr. was an avid abolitionist and a free trader. Partisans of the tariff held a simultaneous convention in New York City.

Stockbridge, visit to Miss Sedgwick, 7 September 1831. (GB2)

Id.

Today I went to see Mr. Ingersoll, a lawyer and former legislator, to whom I expressed the sentiments I set forth above. He answered: "You exaggerate the dangers, in my opinion. When men can speak freely, there is a good chance that they will not act. Note, moreover, that the purpose of the convention is not to act but to persuade. It represents an opinion, an interest, and does not seek to represent the nation, which is fully represented in Congress. By contrast, the convention begins with the assumption that it does not represent the majority but rather seeks to influence public opinion and persuade the majority to change its views.—But, I said, the opinions and interests to which you allude can present their arguments in the press every day.—You must appreciate the vastly greater influence that a convention may exert compared to an obscure journalist or isolated man of talent, Mr. Ingersoll replied. I, for one, regard the right to assemble in convention as a rational consequence of the dogma of majority sovereignty. Take an opinion that is shared by the minority. For that very reason it would be eternally oppressed by the majority if there were not, in addition to public bodies expressing the all-powerful will of the majority, other forums expressing the moral force of numbers and pleading on behalf of the interests of the minority, forums acting not through laws but through discourse aimed at winning over the majority itself.—Very well, I replied, nothing could be more logical, for sure, but I hardly need cite other examples to prove that the immutable laws of logic cannot always be applied to the affairs of this world. Imagine a people not completely used to the government of laws and the rule of persuasion, and endow them with political passions and powerful political interests. Suppose that in addition to the majority that makes the laws, there is a minority that merely debates the pros and cons and stops short of ultimate decisions, and tell me what becomes of public order. Don't you see that in nearly everyone's mind it is but a short step from proving that a thing is good to actually doing it—a short step that is easy to take? Aren't there certain political issues where the majority is so much in doubt that any party might claim to be the majority party? You thus permit a second power to develop whose moral authority is as great as that of the ruling power, and yet you assume that even though this second power is aware of being sufficiently strong to contest the established order, it will nevertheless respect that order on the metaphysical grounds that the purpose of a convention is to inform the public, not to compel it, to advise rather than to act."

Mr. Ingersoll conceded that his answer applied only to the United States and only to the present time. "Since we may hold conventions without significantly endangering our principles, we are right to do so. In any case, it has always been my opinion that one must make laws for the people rather than attempt to mold the people through the law. I can imagine that a convention like the one in Philadelphia might pose a significant danger in France. Yet it seems to me that your association against the foreigner is in some ways similar to our use of conventions. What might make conventions more dangerous for you is the concentration of all of France in Paris. I suppose that a factious convention held in Paris might have the power to destroy the entire state. Nothing of the kind exists in America. On the general question, I am firmly convinced that until you restore a significant degree of independence to your provinces, you will never be sure of remaining free." . . .

DUELING.

Philadelphia, 22 October 1831.

Dueling on account of extreme sensitivity to points of personal honor—monarchical dueling—is virtually unknown in America. Laws that *oblige* a man in some parts of Europe to fight in certain specified cases do not exist here. Dueling does exist, however, but it is nothing more than an extralegal means of satisfying the most violent and implacable passions. In Europe, one rarely fights for anything more than to be able to say that one has fought. The offense is a sort of intellectual stain, which one wants to remove and which usually can be removed with little cost. In America one fights to kill. One fights because there is no hope of obtaining a death sentence against one's enemy. There are very few duels, but they nearly always end in death. The foregoing is not completely applicable in the South. . . .

MORES.

21 September 1831, Boston.

American mores are, I believe, purer than those of any other nation. This seems to me attributable to five main causes:

1. The physical constitution. They belong to a northern race, yet nearly all live in a climate warmer than that of England.

2. Religion still has great sway over people's souls here. They even cling to some of the traditions of the more severe sects.

3. They are normally absorbed by the pursuit of wealth. No one here is idle. They have the *disciplined* habits of people who work hard all the time.

4. There is no trace of the prejudices of birth that exist in Europe. And it is so easy to acquire wealth that poverty is never an obstacle to marriage. As a result, both men and women marry young and do so only when there is mutual attraction, so that they are bound to each other at a time of life when the man is almost always more susceptible to the pleasures of the heart than to those of the senses. It is rare for a man not to marry by the time he is twenty-three.

5. Women generally receive a rational (not to say argumentative) education. For the reasons set forth above, they can be allowed a considerable degree of freedom without serious difficulty. The transition from girl to married woman presents no dangers for them.

Mr. Clay,[174] who seems to have gathered statistics on the subject, told B. that there are roughly two thousand prostitutes in Boston. (I find this quite difficult to believe.) They are mostly country girls who have been seduced and then forced to leave their home and family and who find themselves penniless. Their clients appear to be young men of the city. But the activity is quite carefully hidden from view, and the evil is limited, never entering the home or disrupting families. Any man who was not even convicted but merely suspected of having an *affair* would be excluded from society immediately. All doors would be closed to him. Mr. Dwight told me that having a venereal disease was a mark of shame that was quite difficult to wash away.

In any case, the police do not interfere with prostitution in any way. Americans say that to police prostitution would be to legitimate the evil. Mr. Dwight told us (what we had already seen in prison reports) that of all prisoners, the most unlikely to be rehabilitated were women of low moral character.

Mr. Wood[175] told me today (24 October 1831) that there were a great many illegitimate children in Philadelphia. The law of England is in force here, and when a woman of the people becomes pregnant, the overseer of the poor interrogates her and compels her to reveal the name of the father so that the town can bring suit and avoid having to pay for the upkeep of the child. This practice is a redoubtable impediment to immorality. . . .

174. This is the Mr. Clay whom Tocqueville describes as a planter from Georgia.

175. The warden of Cherry Hill Prison, "a man of superior intelligence, whose religious beliefs led him to abandon a lucrative career to devote himself to the success of a useful institution," wrote Tocqueville and Beaumont in *On the Penitentiary System.*

27 September 1831.

In Massachusetts, blacks have the rights of citizens. They can vote in elections . . . but prejudice against them is so strong that their children are not accepted in the schools.

Phil[adelphia], 22 October 1831.

Many people in America, including some of the most enlightened, insist that Negroes belong to an inferior species. Many others affirm the opposite. The latter support their view by pointing to the aptitude of Negro children in their schools and to the example of those Negroes who, despite all obstacles, have managed to become independently wealthy. Mr. Wood of Philadelphia mentioned among other examples that of a Negro of this city who had acquired an enormous fortune and who owned several ships, of which the captain and crew were all black.

25 October 1831.

Mr. Smith, a very well-educated and capable Philadelphia Quaker,[176] told us today (24 October 1831) that he was completely convinced that Negroes belonged to the same race as we do, much as a black cow is of the same race as a white cow. Negro children demonstrate as much intelligence as white children. They often learn to read more quickly. We asked him if blacks had citizenship rights. He answered: "Yes, under the law. But they cannot turn up at the polls.— Why not?—They would be treated badly.—And what becomes of the rule of law in that case?—The law here is nothing unless it is backed by public opinion. Slavery has been abolished in Pennsylvania." We asked him how he thought the South might be saved from the woes he envisions. His answer was to attach Negroes to the land like medieval serfs. "Binding men to the land was a wicked institution," he added, "but it was infinitely better than slavery. It might be useful as a transitional state to complete freedom. But I am quite sure that Southerners, like despots everywhere, will never agree to give up any of their powers and will wait until someone takes them away."

In the Walnut Street Prison in Philadelphia I saw that blacks were kept separate from whites, even during meals.

In Philadelphia, blacks are not buried in the same cemetery as whites.

4 November 1831.

In Maryland, free Negroes pay the school tax, just like whites, but they cannot send their children to school. . . .

176. This is most likely the Quaker John Jay Smith, librarian of the Philadelphia Library and an abolitionist. He taught in a Sunday school for free blacks.

Notebook E: Various papers that cannot easily be classified; remarks, reflections, ideas

WHAT MAINTAINS THE REPUBLIC IN THE UNITED STATES.

14 January 1832.

A thousand things conspire to maintain republican liberty in the United States, but a few will suffice to clarify the nature of the problem.

In the United States, it is commonly said, society began with a blank slate. One finds neither vanquisher nor vanquished, neither commoner nor noble, neither prejudices of birth nor prejudices of profession.

But all of South America is in a similar situation, and yet republicanism thrives only in the United States.

The territory of the Union offers an enormous field for human activity. It provides inexhaustible resources for industry and labor. Love of well-being and wealth constantly takes the place of political ambition.

But where in the world can one find more fertile countryside, more admirable forests, more superb rivers, and more inexhaustible and untouched riches than in South America? Yet South America cannot sustain a republic.

The division of the Union into small states reconciles domestic prosperity with national might; it diversifies political interests and weakens party spirit by parceling it out.

But Mexico is a federal republic; it has adopted, virtually untouched, the Constitution of the United States; and yet Mexico is still a long way from prosperous. Lower Canada, like New England, contains boundless fertile land. Yet to this day the French population of Canada, for want of enlightenment, remains bottled up in a space much too small for it, and the price of land near Quebec is almost as high as the price of land near Paris, whereas adjacent land sells for ten francs an acre.

One factor dominates all the others and, all things considered, tips the balance: the American people, taken as a whole, are not only the most enlightened people in the world but also—and I count this as far more important—*the people whose practical political education is most advanced.*

This is the truth in which I firmly believe and the source of the only hope I have for the future happiness of Europe.

One great unanswered question remains, however: the material and special advantages of the United States would not suffice without its high level of civilization and experience, but would its high level of civilization and experience suffice without [its advantages]?[177]

---

177. A probable reading of the original French text is provided in square brackets. A definitive reading is rendered impossible by an apparent grammatical slip that leaves unclear the antecedent of the pronoun at this point in the original.

31 January 1832.

One of the greatest dangers the Union faces, which seems to be a result of prosperity itself.

The rapidity with which new nations[178] rise in the West and Southwest certainly subjects it to a harsh test.

The first result of this disproportionate growth is a violent change in the balance of power and political influence. Powerful states are becoming weak, and nameless territories are becoming dominant states. Wealth and population are shifting. These changes inevitably impinge on certain interests, though without arousing violent passions. The speed with which they are occurring makes them a hundred times more dangerous.

That is not all. A society of nations, like a society of individuals, is a hard thing to maintain. The more members there are, the greater the difficulty, and the greater the need for each of them to show moderation and wisdom in common councils. Not only do the new states of the Union by their mere existence increase the difficulty of maintaining the federal bond, but they also offer fewer guarantees of wisdom and moderation than the old ones. The new states are generally populated by adventurers, and social progress in them is so rapid, not to say impetuous, that everything is still chaotic in them. No aspect of mores, ideas, or laws shows any sign of order or stability. In short, the new states share the half-savage and uncultivated spirit of the pioneers who settled them but also have the power that is usually reserved to mature societies.

One thing that militates significantly in favor of the Union is the fact that all powerful men have an interest in maintaining it, and all the great political passions tend in the same direction. . . .

ON UNIVERSAL SUFFRAGE.

16 January 1832.

Universal suffrage, which has admirable advantages, can exist only in a nation where government, and especially good government, is a matter of subsidiary interest. By *government* I mean a power regulating society. Universal suffrage makes the absence of government easier to bear, because it decreases the number of malcontents. Although it reduces the obstacles to governmental action, it fills offices with less capable men. Witness all the western states [and] Louisiana.

It is possible to distinguish clearly between two different social states. In one, the people are enlightened enough to govern themselves and find themselves in circumstances that allow them to do so. Then society acts upon itself.

In the other, a power external to society acts upon it and forces it to move in a certain direction.

178. That is, states.

These two principles are clear, and their consequences can be easily deduced with strict logical rigor.

But there is a third social state, in which power is divided, being at once in society and outside it. This is difficult to understand in theory and painful and arduous to negotiate in practice.

The United States exemplifies the first of these social states; England and especially France exemplify the third.

For the latter two powers, this is a source of malaise, but it is not always within the power of a people to achieve the first social state, and if they try, they often end up in the second. This might be worthy of a prominent place in an anthology of puzzles.

COMMERCE.

16 January.

Is there any doubt that the Union will one day (fast approaching) become the world's leading maritime power? By itself and for itself it is already doing business on a vast scale and is destined for still greater things. The civilizing of Spanish America will only make it richer, moreover.

It is easy to see that all the imports and exports of the new republics will be carried by American vessels. The point is reinforced by the fact that the southern United States have no commerce. The northern states take it upon themselves to transport what the South produces. Yet the English race inhabits the South as well as the North. Is there any reason to believe that Spaniards living in the Tropics and near the equator are more industrious than Englishmen living near the thirty-fifth parallel?

England will be the only rival of the United States in supplying Spanish America (when that region develops the needs of a civilized people). But the Americans will easily win this competition, because they are closer and transport cargo more economically.

These commercial developments will postpone the day when America achieves *saturation,* which is always so dangerous, and therefore push the age of revolution far into the future.

Three factors contribute to the growth of maritime commerce:

1. Exportable *raw materials* or *manufactured products.*
2. Needs that the land cannot satisfy.
3. A maritime industry, without which the other two are insufficient.

A nation can be quite wealthy and prosperous without maritime commerce, but maritime commerce is a major component of wealth. It also has a political influence, in that it serves as a natural stimulus to mental activity for many people as well as a stimulus to passions that can prove disruptive to society.

GREAT AND MINOR PARTIES.

14 January 1832.

The parties that I call great are those that dedicate themselves more to principles than to consequences; to generalities and not particulars; to ideas and not men. Such parties generally have nobler features, more generous passions, more genuine convictions, and a franker, bolder manner than others. Private interest, which always plays a large role in political passions, is here more cleverly concealed beneath the veil of public interest. At times it even succeeds in concealing itself from those whom it animates and impels to act.

By contrast, minor parties are generally without political faith. Their character is of a piece and bears the stamp of selfishness, which is evident in all their ideas. They become hotly passionate for coldly calculated reasons. Their language is violent, but their course is timid and uncertain. Their methods are as miserable as their goals. Great parties turn society upside down; minor ones vex it more than they agitate it. The former often elicit pity for humanity; the latter provoke scorn. One feature is common to both: conscience almost never approves fully of the methods they use to achieve their ends. There are decent people in almost all parties, but it is fair to say that there is no party of decency.

America has had great parties, but they no longer exist. They have contributed greatly to its happiness but not much, I suspect, to its morality. I can scarcely imagine a spectacle more wretched than the one we see today when we look at the various coteries (they do not deserve the name "parties") that divide the Union. We see the whole panoply of petty and shameful passions that are normally kept carefully concealed in the depths of the human heart.

As for the national interest, no one gives it a thought, and if it is mentioned at all, it is purely for the sake of form. The parties inscribe it in the preambles of their charters, much as our forebears printed the king's imprimatur on the first page of their books.

It is distressing to read the crude insults, petty slanders, and impudent calumnies that fill the party newspapers and to remark their shameless contempt for all social proprieties as they daily arraign before the court of public opinion the honor of families and the secrets of private life.

REPORT ON THE PLANTATIONS OF LOUISIANA.

Today, December 31, 1831, I visited a beautiful sugar plantation situated on the Mississippi 50 leagues from New Orleans. It employs 70 slaves. Its revenue, I was told, is approximately 5 or 6,000 dollars per year, net of all expenses, or 25 to 30,000 francs.

Conversation with Mr. Houston,[179] 31 December 1831. This man's story is quite extraordinary. After a tempestuous and troubled youth, he finally settled in the state of Tennessee. There, his natural resources and perhaps also his obscure origins earned him the votes of the people. He was elected governor of the state.

Around that time trouble developed within his family. He blamed his wife; others said that he treated her badly. What is certain is that he left Tennessee, crossed the Mississippi, and went to live with the Creeks in the Arkansas Territory. There he was adopted by one of the chiefs and allegedly married the chief's daughter. Since then he has lived in the wilderness, half European, half savage.

We met him on December 27, at the head of the White River, where we had gone to see the Choctaws. He was riding a superb stallion that had been captured on the plains separating Mexico from the United States. Large herds of wild horses roam this range, and the Spaniards and Indians manage to capture some of them. They are of Andalusian blood, the horse not being native to America. Mr. Houston boarded our vessel to travel to New Orleans. He is a man of about forty-five, but the suffering and effort of a lifetime have as yet left only the slightest trace on his face. He is a man of athletic build, whose physical and moral energy is evident in his appearance.

We asked him a great many questions about the Indians, some of which follow:

Q.: Do the Indians have a religion?

A.: Some of them don't believe in the immortality of the soul. In general, though, the Indians believe in the existence of a God who metes out rewards and punishments in the next life for what a person does in this one.

Q.: Do they have an organized form of worship?

A.: The Osages, who live on the Mexican border, pray every morning to the rising sun. The Creeks have no organized ritual. Only in times of great calamity or on the eve of some major venture do they engage in public religious exercises.

Q.: Have you encountered many Christian Indians?

A.: Very few. My opinion is that it's a bad idea to try to civilize the Indians by sending missionaries to live among them.

Christianity is a religion for enlightened, intellectual people. It is beyond the intelligence of a people as little civilized as the Indians and as enslaved as they are to material instincts. In my opinion, one should first seek to woo the Indians away from their nomadic existence and encourage them to cultivate the earth.

179. Sam Houston (1793–1863) moved from Virginia to Tennessee at the age of fifteen. He served under General Andrew Jackson during the Creek War and studied law after he left the army in 1818. He served in Congress from 1823 to 1827 and as governor of Tennessee from 1827 to 1829. He then moved to the Indian Territory in present-day Oklahoma, became a trader and member of the Cherokee Nation, and traveled to Washington yearly to advocate for Indian causes in Congress. He moved to Texas in 1835 and served as a political leader of the state until his death.

Christianity would follow naturally from the change that this would entail in their social state. My observation is that only Catholicism is capable of making a lasting impression on the Indians. It strikes their senses and speaks to their imagination.

Q.: What kind of government do the Indians you've met have?

A.: A patriarchal government, broadly speaking. The position of chief is hereditary. In tribes that have become more enlightened through contact with European, chiefs are elected, however.

Q.: Do they have a system of justice?

A.: There is one idea that is deeply rooted in the minds of all Indians and that constitutes for many tribes the only penal code, namely, the idea that blood must be avenged by blood. In a word, the law of an eye for an eye. Thus, when a man has committed murder, he is left to the vengeance of relatives of the deceased, to whom he is handed over.

Q.: Does the law of *compensation* exist in the tribes you have seen?

A.: No. The Indians of the South would regard it as shameful to accept money in exchange for the life of a brother.

Q.: The notions of justice you describe are quite crude. What is more, they apply only to murder. What happens in a case of theft?

A.: Theft was completely unknown among the Indians before Europeans introduced them to objects designed to stimulate their greed.

Since then, it has proved necessary to institute laws to deter theft. Among the Creeks, who are beginning to become civilized and have a written penal code, theft is punished by whipping. The sentence is handed down by chiefs.

Adultery by a woman is punished in the same way. In addition, the guilty woman's nose and ears are usually cut off. The law of the Creeks also punishes fornication.

Q.: What is the condition of women among the Indians?

A.: Total servitude. Women must do all the hard work and live in a state of considerable degradation.

Q.: Is polygamy permitted?

A.: Yes. A man can have as many wives as he can feed. Divorce is also permitted.

Q.: Do the Indians strike you as having great natural intelligence?

A.: Yes. I believe that they have nothing to envy any other race in that regard.

What is more, I am also of the opinion that the same would be true of the Negro. The difference one sees between the Indian and the Negro is in my opinion solely the result of the difference in their upbringing.

The Indian is born free; he makes use of that freedom from the moment he takes his first step. No sooner can he act than he is on his own, barely aware of his father's power over him. Surrounded by dangers, spurred by needs, and unable to count on anyone else, he needs an ever-active mind to cope with these difficulties and maintain his own existence. Necessity obliges him to develop a subtle and often admirable intelligence. The Negro is ordinarily born into slavery. Having neither pleasures nor needs, he is of no use to himself, and he learns straightaway that he is the property of someone else, not responsible for his own future, and blessed with an intelligence that he lacks the freedom to use.

Q.: Is it true that traces survive in the Mississippi Valley of a race of men more civilized than the race that lives there today?

A.: Yes. I've often encountered fortified structures that indicate the existence of a people who had achieved a fairly high degree of civilization. Where did they come from? Where did they go? It's all a mystery. But there is no doubt that they existed, and there is no evidence that the Indians we see today are a residue of that nation.

The most likely explanation, I think, is that they came from Mexico and settled in the Mississippi Valley.[180]

Q.: Can you give me any information about the attitude of the American government toward the Indian tribes?

A.: Yes, of course. There were and are a number of semicivilized Indian tribes living in the southern United States. Their situation in relation to the governments of those states is ambiguous, and their presence is an impediment to the development of the region. In order to protect the interests of the southern states as well as the Indians, Congress therefore conceived the idea of moving them, with their consent, to a territory that is to remain essentially Indian territory forever. For this purpose it chose the northern part of the Arkansas district. The territory in which the Indians are to live begins at an imaginary line that you draw on a map from Louisiana to Missouri and that extends to the border with Mexico and the vast plains inhabited by nomadic tribes of Osages. The United States has solemnly pledged never to sell the land within the boundaries of this territory and never to allow whites to settle there.[181] There are already some ten thousand Indians living in the territory. I think that in time there will be around fifty thousand. The region is healthy and the land extremely fertile.

180. Americans had sustained an interest in American antiquities—earthworks and the objects excavated from within them—since westward expansion into the Northwest Territory in the 1780s. These features, which stretched throughout the Ohio and Mississippi valleys, generated debate over whether Native Americans or migrant Europeans had built the mounds and what had caused these populations to disappear. By 1831, travelers like Tocqueville and Beaumont had numerous books, pamphlets, and newspaper articles about the mounds at their disposal and could view artifacts collected from them in museums and galleries in Boston, New York, Philadelphia, and Cincinnati.

181. In 1830, despite vocal opposition, Andrew Jackson signed the Indian Removal Act into law. It required all American Indians to move west of the Mississippi River. Settlers in the Southwest were particularly supportive of the legislation because it would open large tracts of land held by the Five Civilized Tribes (the Cherokee, Choctaw, Creek, Chickasaw, and Seminole). Although the act stated that Indian leaders would agree to the terms of voluntary treaties and would be compensated for their lands, most tribes were coerced into moving west and were not paid adequately. The most egregious instance of forced removal, known as the Trail of Tears, occurred among the Cherokees in 1835.

Q.: Do you believe that this approach will save the Indians from the doom they apparently face otherwise? Don't you think that this arrangement is still temporary and that the Indians will soon be forced to retreat still farther west?

A.: No, I believe that the Indian nations of the South will find this a place of refuge and that they will become civilized, as long as the government takes steps to encourage them. The isolation in which these tribes will be living will make it possible to take effective steps to prevent spirit liquor from reaching them. Brandy is the major reason for the destruction of the aborigines of America.

Q.: But aren't you afraid that the various tribes will make constant war on one another?

A.: The United States will maintain an outpost in the territory to prevent this.

Q.: So you believe that it is possible to save the Indians.

A.: Yes, probably, if the government can act wisely for a period of twenty-five years, that should be long enough. Several of the southern tribes are already half civilized.

Q.: How do you rate the various tribes in terms of their degree of civilization?

A.: At the top I'd place the Cherokees. The Cherokees live entirely by farming. They are the only Indian nation with a written language.[182]

After the Cherokees I'd put the Creeks. They live by hunting as well as farming. They have a positive legal code and a form of government.[183]

Next I'd place the Chickasaws and the Choctaws. They haven't yet begun to civilize, but they have begun to lose many of their savage traits.[184]

Last I'd put the Osages. They live in nomadic groups, go almost entirely naked, make very little use of firearms, and have nothing to do with any Europeans other than fur traders.[185]

The Osages are the last southwestern tribe to sign a treaty with the United States.

Q.: But the Indian Territory in Arkansas that we were discussing a moment ago is intended exclusively for Indians from the South. What has been decided in regard to the Indians of the West and North?

A.: The Indians of the West and North are not surrounded by white settlers,

182. The center of the Cherokee population was in Appalachian Georgia. The Cherokees had adopted a number of European influences in their communities, in part as a way of garnering power with neighboring American communities. By the 1820s, they had formed a court system, drafted a constitution, and founded a newspaper in their own language. A number of Cherokees farmed using European methods, adopted Euro-American forms of housing and dress, and owned African American slaves.

183. The Creek Indians, also known as the Muscogees, were a migratory population centered in Alabama and Georgia. They were involved in a number of altercations with American military forces throughout the early nineteenth century.

184. The Chickasaws and Choctaws lived in Mississippi, Tennessee, and western Alabama.

185. The traditional lands of the Osage Indians were mainly in Missouri and Arkansas. The Osage were not considered one of the Five Civilized Tribes.

as the southern tribes are. They live beyond the borders of the United States and are being driven westward as the borders advance.

BANKRUPTCY

... 29 December 1831.

The large number of business failures and bankruptcies that occur in the various states of the Union, and above all the public's culpable indifference to the issue, constitute a major stain on the American character.

Well-informed individuals tell me that in Philadelphia there are roughly 800 bankruptcies every year.

Americans are known for their business acumen and enterprising spirit, but they are generally regarded as poor debtors.

When you see the purity of morals, the simplicity of manners, the diligent work habits, and the disciplined religious spirit that are characteristic of the United States, you are tempted to believe that the Americans are a virtuous people, but when you realize that the entire society is consumed by commercial fever, appetite for gain, respect for money, and ubiquitous bad faith in business dealings, you quickly conclude that this supposed virtue is nothing more than the absence of certain vices, and that if the range of human passions here seems limited, it is because all the passions are subsumed in one, namely, the love of riches.

UNION, CENTRAL GOVERNMENT.

28 December 1831.

Imperfection of the first American Union. Collapse of the state that resulted from it. On this point see *The Federalist,* no. 15, p. 60.[186] This whole subject is very ably dealt with.

The main difference between the new American Union and the old is this:[187]

The old Union governed *states,* not *individuals.* It was like an alien power subjecting inferior powers to its laws.

The new federal government is truly the government of the Union in everything that falls within its jurisdiction. It addresses itself not to *states* but to *individuals.* It gives orders to each American citizen, whether he be born in Massachusetts or Georgia, and not to Massachusetts or Georgia, and it has means of

186. Alexander Hamilton, author of *Federalist* no. 15 (1787), titled the essay "The Insufficiency of the Present Confederation to Preserve the Union." He listed a number of weaknesses in the Articles of Confederation, arguing for a more powerful federal government to keep the states strong and united. Hamilton's article was one of eighty-five essays written during the debate over the form of a new constitution for the United States.

187. The "old" American Union was governed by the Articles of Confederation (formally ratified in 1781) from 1777 until 1788. The ratification of the Constitution in 1788 ushered in the "new" American Union.

its own to compel each individual citizen to obey, without recourse to any authority other than its own.

Example to illustrate the difference.

Suppose the federal government imposes a tax:

In the old Union, each state was responsible for levying the tax and depositing the proceeds in the coffers of the central government.

The new federal power not only sets the tax but has its own officials to levy it on each American, independent of any other authority, and courts of its own to ensure the payment of sums due. In short, it governs, in the broadest sense of the word. All the rights of sovereignty are transferred to it, but its prerogatives are limited, and it may not go beyond them.

The practical differences that result from this new state of affairs are immense, even if they are not immediately apparent in theory.

In both cases, the federal power has the right to impose its laws on all members of the Union and to force them to obey. The only difference is in the method, but that difference is enormous.

When the central government addresses itself to a *state* and issues an order that is onerous or difficult to carry out, it will inevitably encounter great difficulty in obtaining the state's obedience. It finds in its subject power an adversary with an interest in resisting and substantial means to do so successfully. If a state does not wish to engage in open warfare, it still has a thousand ways to evade the order it has received. It may refrain from seeking obedience, feign impotence, and tolerate resistance to its laws with impunity. Civil war or anarchy is the usual consequence of such an order.

By contrast, when the central government not only imposes its laws but actually governs within its limited sphere of power, each time it issues an order it deals not with states but with individuals, each of whom is solitary and isolated vis-à-vis the Union and unable even to contemplate resistance. The action of the central government on each individual is thus direct rather than indirect. It proceeds in a straightforward rather than complicated way. It need not ask for anyone's support and has at its disposal all the force that is required.

To be sure, the national spirit, collective passions, and provincial prejudices of each state still tend significantly to diminish the extent of the central power thus constituted and to create centers of resistance to its will. Limited in its sovereignty, the central government cannot be as powerful as a government in full possession of its sovereign rights, but this is an inevitable defect of any confederation. Nevertheless, in an arrangement of this kind, each state has far fewer opportunities and far less temptation to resist, and if the thought of resistance arises, a state can act on it only by openly violating the laws of the Union, interrupting the regular procedures of justice, and raising the banner of revolt—in other words, by taking an extreme step, which men are always reluctant to do.

So great is the influence of laws, *by themselves,* on the destiny of nations that all previous confederations, both ancient and modern, ended in dissolution and ruin owing to ignorance of this principle.

It is an axiom of American public law that each power must be granted full authority within its own sphere, while the sphere itself must be so designed that the power cannot act outside it: this is an important principle, which deserves to be pondered carefully. The idea is expressed in the following passage from the *Federalist* (no. 23, p. 97):[188]

"If the circumstances of our country are such as to demand a compound, instead of a simple, a confederate instead of a sole government, the essential point which will remain to be adjusted will be to discriminate the objects, as far as it can be done, which shall appertain to the different provinces of departments of power; allowing to each the most ample authority for fulfilling those which may be committed to its charge."

29 December 1831.

What can be affirmed is that only a very enlightened people could have created the federal constitution of the United States, and that only a very enlightened people singularly accustomed to representative forms is capable of operating such a complicated machine and of maintaining within their separate spheres the various powers, which otherwise would not fail to clash violently with one another. The Constitution of the United States is an admirable contrivance, yet there is every reason to believe that its founders would not have succeeded had not a hundred and fifty years of history given the various states of the Union *the tastes and habits of independent provincial governing,* and had not a high degree of civilization *prepared them to withstand a strong albeit limited central government.* The federal constitution of the United States strikes me as the best and perhaps the only way to establish a vast republic, yet it cannot be imitated in the absence of the preconditions I mentioned above.

What aided in establishing the Constitution in America was the fact that the several states were still young and not accustomed to independence; hence, they had not yet fully developed the individual pride and national prejudices that make it so painful for old societies to yield the slightest bit of their sovereignty.

Examples of federal unions in antiquity and in modern history:
1. The Amphictyonic League.
2. The Achaean League.
3. The Germanic Corps.
4. The United Provinces of the Netherlands.
5. Switzerland.[189]

All of these confederations suffered from the defect of the first American

188. Alexander Hamilton wrote *Federalist* no. 23, "The Necessity of a Government as Energetic as the One Proposed to the Preservation of the Union" (1787). His argument rested on the consideration of three points: "the objects to be provided for by the federal government, the quantity of power necessary to the accomplishment of those objects, the persons upon whom that power ought to operate."

189. According to legend, the Amphictyonic League was founded in the twelfth century BC to protect and manage the temples at Delphi and Thermopylae in ancient Greece. City-

Union. They failed to make a single people out of the various united provinces that formed the union. They established a power but not a central sovereignty. All succumbed to civil war or decadence and anarchy, but none managed, as the American Union did, to see the light in time to devise a remedy for the deficiencies of their laws.

For a history of these confederations, see the able summary by Mr. Madison in *Federalist* no. 18 and others, p. 72.[190] . . .

SOVEREIGNTY OF THE PEOPLE

27 December 1831.

The principle of popular sovereignty often imparts an energy to nations that adopt it that other nations do not have. Yet the people are not always capable of imposing the necessary sacrifices on themselves.

"It is evident," Hamilton says in *The Federalist*, "from the state of the country, from the habits of the people, from the experience we have had on the point itself, that it is impracticable to raise any very considerable sums by direct taxation. Tax laws have in vain been multiplied; new methods to enforce the collection have in vain been tried; the public expectations have been uniformly disappointed, and the treasuries of the states have remained empty. The popular system of administration inherent in the nature of popular government, coinciding with the real scarcity of money, incident to a languid and mutilated state of trade, has hitherto defeated every experiment for extensive collections, and has at length taught the different legislatures the folly of attempting them."

(*The Federalist*, p. 50.)[191]

I have already noted similar examples in a number of places. It is difficult to pass onerous laws even when they are useful. All things considered, however, I

---

states began to leverage political power through this alliance by the sixth century BC, and the league disbanded in the second century BC.

The Achaean League was a confederation of Greek city-states in the northern Peloponnese that began in the fifth century BC. Roman forces defeated the league in 146 BC.

By "Germanic Corps," Tocqueville refers to the seven independent medieval kingdoms that later became a confederation to form a singular German state.

The United Provinces of the Netherlands, or the Dutch Republic, lasted from 1581 to 1795. Seven independent provinces enlisted in a confederation that built a strong navy, a successful economy and stock market, and a colonial empire. French forces conquered the declining confederation in 1795.

Switzerland has a long history of federal government, beginning with a confederacy of cantons in the thirteenth century.

190. James Madison and Alexander Hamilton wrote "The Insufficiency of the Present Confederation to Preserve the Union" (1787), which comprises *Federalist* nos. 15–20. They addressed the histories of these confederations in *Federalist* nos. 18–20.

191. This quotation is taken from *Federalist* no. 12, "The Utility of the Union in Respect to Revenue" (1787), by Alexander Hamilton.

believe that free peoples sacrifice much more money than others to social purposes. But this is especially true of aristocratic peoples; democracies live more from day to day and are far less capable of imposing arduous obligations on themselves with an eye to the future.

It is impossible to know precisely what degree of energy and what power over itself American democracy would prove capable of in a time of crisis. To date it has not been tested.

What is certain is that whenever the central government has tried to impose direct taxes, it was unsuccessful, and that even in the ardor of political passions stirred up by the Revolution, it was able to muster men and money only with the greatest of difficulty, and always in insufficient quantity.

Hence it will be impossible to judge what sacrifices democracies can impose on themselves until the nation some day finds itself compelled to *conscript* soldiers and levy *high taxes.* . . .

The generative principle of the English constitution is that Parliament is the source of all power and can do whatever it wants.

The principle of the various American constitutions is diametrically opposed to this. In America the source of all power lies in the Constitution, a law that preexists all other laws and that can be changed only by the authority from which it emanates, the people. The legislature, far from being the source of all power, is subject like everything else to this law of laws, from which it may not depart for a single moment without violating the first of its duties. . . .

SLAVES.

Legislation concerning them.

In Massachusetts, where slavery does not exist, a marriage between a white and a person of color is legally invalid.

How carefully the English race in America has endeavored to preserve the purity of its European blood.

K. C., v. 2, p. 205.[192] . . .

ELECTIONS.

Memphis, 20 December 1831.

When the right to vote is *universal,* and representatives are *paid* by the state, it is striking to discover how low the people's choice may go, and how far astray.

Two years ago, the inhabitants of the district of which Memphis is the capital sent to the House of Representatives an individual named David Crockett, a man with no education, who can barely read, who owns no property, and

192. Tocqueville is citing James Kent, *Commentaries on American Law.*

who has no permanent address but lives in the woods and spends his life hunting, selling game in order to live.[193]

His unsuccessful competitor was a man of some wealth and talent.

On the Mississippi, 27 December 1831.
We are traveling at the moment with Mr. Houston. This man was governor of Tennessee. Since that time, he has abandoned his wife, whom he is said to have treated very badly and caused to suffer. He sought refuge among the Indians, married one of them, and became one of their leaders. I asked him what might have persuaded the people to vote for him. The fact that he was one of them, he said, and that he raised himself *by his own exertions.*

Today I heard yet again that in the new states of the West, the people generally make very poor choices. Proud, uneducated voters want to be represented by men of their own ilk. What is more, in order to win their votes, a candidate has to engage in base maneuvers that men of distinction find distasteful. He has to frequent taverns and drink and debate with men of the people. In America this is called *electioneering.*

"The fittest men," Kent candidly states, speaking of judges, "would probably have too much reservedness of manners, and severity of morals, to secure an election resting on universal suffrage."

K. C., v. 1, p. 272.

In several state constitutions, voters are granted the right to demand that their representatives vote in a certain way. The best minds contest this principle.

Kent C., v. 2, p. 6.

If it were adopted generally, it would be a mortal blow to the representative system, that great discovery of modern times, which seems destined to exert a very powerful influence on the fate of mankind. It would then be the people themselves who acted, and representatives would be reduced to mere passive agents.

PATERNAL POWER.

27 December 1831.
Paternal power, which loomed so large in ancient republics that political theorists have seen it as the source of their greatness and longevity, has been reduced to almost nothing in American institutions. American laws seem to regard a father's power with as jealous and suspicious an eye as they regard any other power that might stand as an impediment to human liberty.

Customs, mores, and opinion accord with the law on this point. Paternal power is an aristocratic institution. It makes a privileged ruling class of older

---

193. David "Davy" Crockett (1786–1836), a native of Tennessee, served in the U.S. House of Representatives from 1827 to 1831 and again from 1833 to 1835. In 1836, he moved to Texas and died in the Battle of the Alamo.

men. It grants them a kind of patronage by making their offspring dependent on them. All of these things are antipathetic to democracy. . . .

PUBLIC EDUCATION.

Kent, in his *Commentaries,* states that in Connecticut, when parents do not educate their children, the selectmen have the right to take the children from them in order to provide the teaching they lack. "'This law,' said the late Chief Justice Reeve, 'has produced very astonishing effects, and to it is to be attributed the knowledge of reading and writing so universal among the people of that state.'" Kent adds: "During the 27 years in which that distinguished lawyer (Reeve) was in extensive practice of the law, he informs us he never found but one person in Connecticut that could not write."

K.C. vol. 2, p. 165. . . .

INTOLERANCE.

The rapidity with which religious tolerance has progressed in America is an incredible thing.

At the end of the last century, the state of New York passed a law stating that any Catholic priest who did not leave the territory of the colony within a specified period of time would be imprisoned for life or subject to a death sentence if he returned. The historian Smith, writing in 1756, stated that this law deserved to be kept in force in perpetuity.

Kent C. vol. 2, p. 63. . . .

EXPENSES OF A MISSISSIPPI STEAMSHIP.

Information provided by the captain of the *Louisville,* 26 December 1831.

The *Louisville,* which we are about to board, draws approximately 400 tons. It cost $50,000 to build and is expected to last only four years. The (average) expected lifetime of a freshwater vessel on the Mississippi is no more than this owing to "snags" and other dangers encountered on this river.

The (average) price of wood along the Mississippi is $2 per cord. The vessel consumes 30 cords per day, so that its daily fuel cost is $60.

Food for both passengers and crew plus the crew's wages comes to roughly the same amount, so that the daily operating cost of a vessel of this size is $120.

30 November 1831.

There is one thing that America proves incontrovertibly, which I doubted until now: that the middle classes can govern a state. I do not know if they will perform honorably in political situations of great difficulty, but they do well enough in dealing with the ordinary affairs of society. Despite their petty passions, their incomplete education, and their vulgar manners, they clearly bring practical intelligence to the table, and that turns out to be enough.

In France, the middle classes harbor some very narrow prejudices against the upper classes, but perhaps the upper classes also suffer unduly from an unfavorable impression due to the vulgarity of middle-class manners and ideas. From these incontestable facts they conclude that the middle classes are politically incapable, which is not true, or at any rate not as true as they believe.

Another point that America demonstrates is that virtue is not, as was long maintained, the only thing that can maintain a republic; what is more conducive to this social state than anything else is enlightenment. Americans are scarcely more virtuous, but they are infinitely more enlightened (I am speaking of the masses), than any other people I know. By this I do not mean simply that more of them know how to read and write (a fact to which more attention is paid than is reasonable, perhaps), but rather that large numbers of them understand public affairs, know the laws and precedents, and have a feeling for the nation's interest properly understood. Indeed, the ability to understand these things is greater in the United States than anywhere else in the world.

Id.

What is extremely interesting in America is to examine the penchants and instincts of democracy when left to its own devices and to see what social state is likely to emerge from a society in which democracy rules. This study is particularly interesting for us in France, where we may be headed toward despotism, or perhaps toward a republic, but certainly toward unlimited democracy.

ON EQUALITY IN AMERICA.

The relation among various social positions in America is fairly difficult to understand, and foreigners often make one of the following two errors: either they assume that there are no distinctions among Americans other than those of personal merit, or else, being struck by the high status granted to wealth here, they conclude that various European monarchies such as France exhibit a more genuine and complete equality than that which the American republics enjoy. As I said earlier, I believe that both of these ways of looking at things exaggerate the truth.

First, let us be clear about what we are discussing: not equality before the law, which is complete in America; it is not simply a right but a fact. Indeed, even if inequality exists outside of politics, the middle and lower classes are amply compensated in the political realm, for members of these classes share nearly all elective offices with members of historically illustrious families.

I am speaking of equality in the relations of social life, of the kind of equality that brings certain people to gather in the same places, to share their ideas and pleasures, to wed their families. It is in this respect that France is different from America, and these differences are becoming essential.

In France, no matter what anyone says, the prejudice of birth is still quite powerful. Birth still constitutes an almost insurmountable obstacle between individuals. In France, people are still classified to some extent by their occupations. These prejudices are more damaging to equality than any others, because they create permanent distinctions, which not even wealth and time can eradicate. Such prejudices do not exist in America. Birth is a distinction, but it does not assign those who have it to a class; it creates no right or incapacity or obligation to the world or to oneself. Classification by occupation is also virtually unknown. Occupation does create certain differences between individuals with respect to status and even more of wealth, but it does not create any radical inequality, for it does not prevent marriages from taking place (this is the great touchstone).

One should not assume, however, that in America all classes of society mingle in the same salons; this is not the case. People who share similar occupations, similar ideas, and similar educations choose to be with one another by a sort of instinct and gather in exclusive company. The difference is that no arbitrary and inflexible rule presides over these arrangements, so there is little shocking about them. No one is definitively excluded, and no one can feel hurt. In America, one therefore sees less than anywhere else the ardent desire of one class to share not only the political rights but the pleasures of other classes. This is what makes American society preferable to ours. Here is what makes it less preferable:

The primary social distinction in America is *money*.

Money creates a truly privileged class in society, a class that sets itself apart and blatantly asserts its preeminence.

This social preeminence is less damaging to equality than prejudices of birth and occupation. It is not permanent; wealth is within everyone's grasp. It is not radical, but perhaps for that reason it is more offensive. The display of wealth in America is infinitely more shameless than in France. Talent and merit, which in France ultimately trump wealth when in competition with it, are here obliged to defer to it. There are several reasons for this.

In France, inequality of rank used to be extreme. In order to combat imaginary distinctions, it proved necessary to invoke the one rational distinction, which is merit. In France, intellectual pleasures and gifts have always been held in high esteem.

In America, in the absence of all material and external distinctions, wealth stood out as a natural measure of merit. What is more, Americans are a people with little interest in the pleasures of the mind. Exclusively concerned with getting rich, they naturally feel a sort of veneration for wealth. It arouses their envy, but tacitly they recognize it as a supreme advantage.

To sum up, then, Americans, like Frenchmen, are ranked in the course of social life according to certain categories. Common habits, education, and above all wealth establish these classifications, but the rules are neither absolute nor inflexible nor permanent. They establish temporary distinctions and do not form classes in the proper sense of the word. They give no man superiority over any other, even in opinion, so that even if two individuals never see each other in the same salons, if they meet in public each can greet the other without pride or envy. At bottom they feel equal, and they are.

In order to measure the equality among various classes of a people, one always has to ask how marriages are made. This is the heart of the matter. A kind of equality, born of necessity, courtesy, and politics, can seem to exist and deceive the observer. But when it comes to putting that equality into practice in marriage, a sensitive spot is touched.

OHIO.

2 December 1831.

Ohio was admitted to the Confederation in 1802. At that time its population was between forty and fifty thousand, consisting of some Europeans, a certain number of people from the South and East, and many adventurers from New England, who were already beginning to migrate to less populous states. The population of Ohio could rise to as much as ten million without reaching a density greater than is found in many provinces of Europe.[194] The fertility of the land seems inexhaustible. It is admirably watered by three or four small rivers, tributaries of the Ohio, which can be followed upstream toward the Great Lakes.

As for the intellectual aspect of Ohio, one can say that its moral character resembles its physical character in that it is still growing and not yet set. Its population consists of nations that are thus far too heterogeneous to allow any particular spirit or specific mores to emerge. This territory has less national character than any other; it also has less national prejudice. In these two respects, it is at once above and below other portions of the Union. Its civil legislation demonstrates the degree to which it has freed itself from precedent. In criminal law, the state of Ohio has blazed a new path. In civil law, it has simplified English legislation to a surprising degree and seems, so far as I have been able to judge until now, to have freed itself almost entirely from the sway of tradition. I imagine that the same can be said of the *political realm*. Laws on blacks. *Political innovation,* not *bold and decisive.*

More than any other part of the Union, Ohio strikes me as a society totally occupied with its own affairs and, through work, with rapid growth. This is the place that one must visit above all to have an idea of this social state, which is so different from ours. In Boston, New York, Philadelphia, and all the large cities of the coast, there is already a class that has acquired much, adopted sedentary ways, and developed a desire to enjoy its wealth rather than make it. In Ohio, everyone has come to make money. Nobody was born here, nobody is keen to

194. In 1830, Ohio already had nearly one million inhabitants. The state had been admitted to the Union in 1803.

stay here, no one—absolutely *no one*—is idle, no one is engaged in intellectual speculation, and everyone is occupied with something, to which he dedicates himself with passion. Nobody yet has any notion of an upper class. The jumble is complete. All of society is a factory! In Ohio there are fewer general ideas than anywhere else, ranks are indistinguishable, and even the rules of politeness seem uncertain. No one has had time to establish a political or social position. Nothing has any influence on the people. Democracy is unlimited. In short, Ohio gives an impression of prosperity but not of stability. Its youthfulness is potent and vigorous, yet the very rapidity of its growth gives it the appearance of being in a transitory, temporary state.

One of the most interesting things about Ohio is the way in which democracy has been carried to extreme limits, which have rarely been seen before. In the states where we have witnessed the most extensive democracy, where there is no patronage of nobility or wealth, certain local influences remain. In one place it might be a name that calls to mind an important moment in history and speaks to the imagination of the people; in another it might be the prestige of a man of great talent; in still another, services rendered. In many places, it is the moral influence on the mind of the people stemming from their having witnessed a person in their midst who has devoted his entire life to doing good. But democracy in Ohio is devoid even of these weak local influences. The residents of Ohio are recently arrived. They came to the places where they live without knowing one another and bringing with them different mores and ideas. Most are here only temporarily. No common bond unites them. Not a person among them can tell his life story to a person capable of understanding him. None has had time to establish an existence, earn a reputation, or establish a more or less permanent influence based on personal service or virtue. As a result, democracy in Ohio is even more random and capricious in its choices than democracy in any other place I know. Someone happens by and flatters the people, often captures their vote, *and yet society prospers,* but does it prosper as a result of democracy or in spite of it? That is the point.

The new western states, and in particular the state of Ohio, strike me as standing in the same relation to the older states of the Union as those older states stand to Europe. Let me explain what I mean.

When the Americans came to America, they brought with them what was most democratic in Europe. They left most of the national prejudices they had been brought up with behind. They became a new nation and acquired new habits and mores and something of a national character. Today a new migration is beginning, and it is producing the same effects. The new migrants bring to their adopted homeland a still more unencumbered democratic principle, mores still less marked by tradition, and minds still freer of precedent. It is strange to see the traces of this intellectual and physical transformation in the laws of the new states. The first immigrants to America imported flawed English laws (of which there are many). They modified those laws and adapted them as best they could to their social state, but they still had a superstitious respect for them. They could not entirely get rid of it. Now a second migration is taking place. The same men are moving deeper into the wilderness. This time they have modified the law to such an extent that it has lost nearly all trace of its origin. A third migration will be necessary, however, before it ceases to exist. And if you recall that the English probably received their law from the Saxons, it is impossible not to be struck by the influence for good or ill that a people's point of departure has on its destiny.

Another remarkable fact about Ohio is that it may be the one state in the Union that offers the most striking and intimate view of the effects of slavery and liberty on the social state of a people. Ohio is separated from Kentucky by no more than a river. The land on either bank is equally fertile, the location is just as propitious, and yet everything is different. In Ohio the population is consumed by feverish activity, as people seek their fortunes by every possible route.

The people of Ohio may appear to be poor, because they work with their hands, but their labor is for them a source of wealth. Across the river live people who are served by others and display little compassion, people without energy, ardor, or a spirit of enterprise. On one side of the water, labor is honored and opens all doors; on the other, it is scorned as a mark of servitude. Those who are reduced to work in order to live cross into Ohio to seek their fortune without shame. Kentucky was first settled nearly a century ago, and its population has grown slowly.[195] Ohio joined the Confederation only thirty years ago, and it has a population of one million. In thirty years, Ohio has become a transit point for the wealth of goods that travel up and down the Mississippi. It has dug canals and linked the Gulf of Mexico with the Ohio River. Meanwhile, Kentucky, the older state and perhaps the more favorably situated, stood still. It is impossible to ascribe the differences to any cause other than slavery. Slavery numbs the black population and saps the energy of the white population. Its baleful effects are plain to see, yet the system remains in place and will remain in place for a long time to come. Slavery threatens the future of those who maintain it. It ruins the state. But it has become part of the habits and prejudices of the settlers, whose present interests are at war with their future interests and with still more powerful national interests.

In view of the comparison I have just drawn, what better proof could there be that human prosperity depends more on human institutions and will than on external circumstances? Man is not made for servitude: *the master is perhaps better evidence for this proposition than the slave.*

195. Kentucky entered the Union in 1792. By 1830, its rate of growth had slowed, and its population had been eclipsed by Ohio's. About 688,000 people lived in Kentucky, but 165,000 of those were slaves.

Civil and criminal laws: see article Law.

Banks.
Only two banks remain in Cincinnati. Ten years ago, all the banks in Ohio went bankrupt after issuing too many notes.

Political state.
All the people we have seen thus far seem to believe that the democratic principle has been extended too far in Ohio and that the people generally make poor choices.

Canals.
The state of Ohio has already constructed seventy miles of canal.[196] The rivers are not very navigable, and the roads are poor. In one year the canal linking the Ohio to Lake Erie will be finished. This will make it possible to travel from New York to New Orleans without setting foot on land.

Blacks.
Under the law, slavery is not tolerated in Ohio. Free blacks cannot even live in the state unless they post a bond. But this latter part of the law has never been enforced. In any case, we are told that there are no more than three thousand blacks in the state.[197]

CINCINNATI.

Cincinnati is striking to see. It is a city that seems in too much of a hurry to grow to bother with establishing any kind of order.[198] There are large buildings, cottages, streets blocked by debris, houses under construction, no street names, no numbers on the houses, and no external signs of luxury, but images of industriousness and labor abound at every turn.

It is always difficult to know exactly why cities develop and grow. Chance almost always plays a part. Cincinnati is situated in one of the most fertile plains of the New World, and because of this it began to attract settlers. Factories were built to supply the needs of these settlers and before long of a whole region of the West, and the success of these industries attracted new industries and more settlers than ever. Cincinnati was, and I believe still is, a transit point for many

196. This construction took place mainly on the Ohio and Erie Canal, which ran north–south through the center of the state. The state of Ohio, rather than private individuals or corporations, raised the funds for these internal improvements.

197. The 1830 census counted over ninety-five hundred free blacks in the state of Ohio.

198. In 1830, nearly 25,000 people lived in Cincinnati. In 1840, over 46,000 people lived in the city. In 1850, the population nearly tripled to over 115,000.

shipments to and from the Mississippi and Missouri valleys to Europe and for trade between New York and the northern states and Louisiana. For this purpose, however, Louisville is better situated and will soon have the advantage.[199]

KENTUCKY. TENNESSEE.

We traveled the length of Kentucky from Louisville to Nashville. We also traversed much of Tennessee on our way from Nashville to Memphis along the banks of the Mississippi. These two states struck us as quite similar in many respects.

The countryside is full of hills and shallow valleys with a great many small streams. There is natural beauty, but of a uniform kind.

In both states the land was still almost entirely covered by forests. At intervals a line of fences, some burned trees, a field of corn, a few animals, and a cabin built of rough-hewn logs piled one on top of the other revealed the existence of an isolated farm. There are virtually no villages to be seen. The farmers' dwellings are scattered throughout the woods.

Nothing in Kentucky is rarer than a brick house, and we saw no more than ten such houses in Tennessee, outside of Nashville.

In Kentucky and Tennessee, farmers' cabins are generally divided into two parts, as illustrated in the margin.[200] Around the cabin are a number of huts, which are used as stables.

The interiors of these houses indicate not so much the poverty of the owners as their indolence. There is usually a fairly clean bed, a few chairs, a good rifle, often some books, and almost always a newspaper, but the walls have so many holes in them that the outside air enters everywhere with [*illegible word in manuscript*].

The shelter is little better than in a cabin with a roof of foliage. Nothing could be simpler than to build a good roof and patch the holes in the walls, but the owners seem incapable of taking such steps. In the north, the humblest homes give off an air of cleanliness and intelligent upkeep. Here, everything seems rough and ready, and much is left to chance. The people seem to live from day to day, with absolutely no concern for the future.

In the parts of Kentucky and Tennessee in which we've been traveling, the people are tall and rugged. They look a great deal alike, and all seem robust and energetic. Unlike the residents of Ohio, they are not a jumble of all the American races. On the contrary, they all spring from a common stock and be-

199. Louisville never grew as quickly or as large as many people expected. In 1830, the town had a population of just over ten thousand people. In 1840, that number had grown to approximately twenty-one thousand. In 1850, the population numbered forty-three thousand. Louisville never approached the prosperity or size of Cincinnati.

200. Tocqueville's sketch is not reproduced here.

long to the great family of Virginians. To a greater degree than the Americans we saw previously, they therefore have an instinctive love of country, a love tinged with excess and prejudice, which is quite different from the rational sense of refined egoism that goes by the name of patriotism in nearly all the other states of the Union.

Nearly all the farmers we saw, including the poorest of them, had slaves.

The slaves wear rags but generally look strong and healthy.

For [a] foreigner, the sight of the interior of a [home] in Kentucky or Tennessee is quite extraordinary.

After passing through rough-hewn fences, not without risk of being devoured by the owner's dogs, you come to a cabin, through the walls of which it is possible to glimpse the flickering of a fire in the fireplace. You open a door, which hangs from leather hinges and has no lock. You then enter a sort of rudimentary hut, which seems to serve as refuge from a variety of miseries. In it lives a family of paupers, who live as if they belonged among the idle rich. As you enter, the master of the household rises to greet you with warmth and hospitality, but he does not go himself to get you anything you might need. In his mind, it would be degrading to serve you in that way. Instead, he has a slave poke the fire to warm the traveler. It is a slave who dries your clothes and brings your food. The master looks on and guides his servants with gestures as needed. He does nothing himself. If he opens his mouth, it is to call his dogs or tell you about their remarkable qualities. Even the most miserable of Kentucky and Tennessee farmers bears a remarkable resemblance to the country squire of old Europe.

Nothing in Kentucky or Tennessee gives the impression of a refined society. In this respect both states are quite different from those that have been settled in recent years by Northerners and bear the stamp of highly civilized New England. In Kentucky and Tennessee you see few churches and no schools; society seems not to look to the future any more than individuals do.

Yet these are not still-rustic people. They have none of the simplicity tinged with ignorance and prejudice that you find in agricultural peoples in inaccessible places. These people still belong to one of the most civilized, rational races in the world. Their mores have none of the naïveté of their fields. The philosophical, argumentative spirit of the English exists here as it does throughout America. There is an astonishing circulation of letters and newspapers in these untamed woods. We traveled with the mail shipment. From time to time we stopped in front of what they call the post office. It was almost always an isolated house in the middle of the forest. We dropped off a large packet of mail, no doubt containing letters for everyone in that neck of the woods. Even in the most enlightened rural districts of France, I do not believe that there is anything like the rapid and abundant circulation of ideas that you find here in the most remote wilderness.

Slavery has an enormous effect on the character and habits of slave masters in Kentucky and Tennessee. It makes them less industrious and discourages outsiders from coming to settle in these places, but it poses no threat to the future of those already here.

The black population is much smaller than the white, and in the future its proportion will diminish still further. There are natural reasons for this, which are easily stated.

In Kentucky and Tennessee, no crops are grown that require a large number of slaves, and virtually nothing that is grown produces [a great enough] income to yield a considerable [profit]. The land in [Kentucky] and Tennessee is therefore [divided into] small properties. On each of these, a white family lives with a very small number of slaves. Here, in contrast to the South, one does not see hundreds of slaves cultivating the fields of a single white man. In addition, Kentucky and Tennessee were settled by poor migrants, who did not have the means to assemble a large number of slaves on a single property, even if the nature of the crop had made this easy to do. In Kentucky and Tennessee, masters live all year on their land. They direct the work of their slaves, and the poorest of them work alongside their slave hands.

The foregoing proves that farming here would be feasible without slavery. Public opinion in these two states appears to be favorable to that idea. But slavery is an evil so deeply rooted that it is almost as impossible to be delivered from it after recognizing its harmful influence as before.

It would be ridiculous to try to judge a whole people after spending only a week or ten days among them. Hence I can only rely on "what people say."

Kentuckians and Tennesseans are celebrated throughout the United States for their violent ways. If what we've heard is true, they seem to deserve that reputation. We hear that their disputes frequently end in bloodshed and that elections rarely pass without stabbings and slashings.

It is possible to describe any number of causes that must have conspired to give Kentuckians and Tennesseans the character that is imputed to them.

The first of these is climate: it has been [found] long ago that passions are more ardent in southern than in northern climes.

The second is slavery, a cause that affects all Southerners and modifies their national character in the same way. The habit of giving orders without restraint instills a certain haughtiness that makes men impatient of opposition and irritable at the sight of obstacles to their will. Slavery makes work dishonorable. It turns the entire white race into a leisure class, which deprives money of some of its value. People of this class look to the resources of society and the pleasures of pride for their enjoyment. They constitute a kind of aristocracy, which is not guided by the respect for legality that defines commercial peoples but rather finds its virtues in conventional proprieties, delicacy of manner, and defense of honor. Southerners are brave, comparatively ignorant, hospitable, generous, quick to anger, given to violent grudges, and lacking in industriousness and enterprise.

Place these same men in a new country, put them in the midst of a wild region where they would be compelled to do daily battle against all of life's miseries, and you would make their passions still more irritable and violent and still more estranged from society. Any friction with society would be painful. Were they to become less civilized, they would experience even less need to dominate themselves.

Therein lies the key to the history of Kentucky and Tennessee. The people of these states are Southerners, slave masters made half savage by solitude and hardened by life's miseries.

MEANS OF INCREASING THE PUBLIC PROSPERITY

Nearly all political precepts are stated in such general, theoretical, and vague terms as to make it difficult to derive the slightest practical benefit from them. Nearly all are nostrums whose usefulness depends more on the temperament of the patient than on the nature of the malady.

I know only one way to make a people more prosperous. Its application is infallible, and I believe that it can be counted on in all countries and all locales.

What I have in mind is to increase the ease of communication among men.

In this respect, America is both curious and instructive.

Roads, canals, and the mails play a prodigious part in the prosperity of the Union. It is useful to examine the influence of these factors, the value attached to them, and the way in which they have been implemented.

America, which enjoys greater prosperity than has ever been granted to any other nation, has also done more to provide for the kind of free communication I have in mind (making allowance for its young age and limited means).

In France, there are numerous areas of very large and very dense population without any roads connecting them to the rest of the nation, from which they are more separate than one half of the world used to be from the other. I have no doubt that it takes longer and costs more to send ten sacks of wheat from certain towns in Lower Brittany to Paris than to send all the sugar of the colonies to the same place.

In America, one of the first priorities for any new state is to arrange for mail delivery. In the woods of Michigan, there is no cabin so isolated, no valley so wild, that letters and newspapers are not delivered at least once a week, as we had occasion to witness personally. It was above all in circumstances such as these that I felt the difference between our social state and that of the American people. There are few rural districts in France where proportionately as many letters and newspapers are received as in these still-untamed regions, where men are still struggling with all the miseries of life and enjoy only occasional glimpses of society.

No sooner do people give signs of wishing to settle a part of the country than an effort is made to build a road to reach it. Roads are almost always built before there are people to use them, but roads encourage the people to come.

On several occasions we saw large roads that literally opened a path through the wilderness.

America has planned and built immense canals. It already has more railroads than France. Everyone recognizes that the discovery of steam immeasurably increased the strength and prosperity of the Union by facilitating rapid communication among the various parts of this vast country. The southern states, where communications are less easy, lag behind the rest.

Of all the countries in the world, America is the one in which changes in thought and human industry are most constant and rapid. There is not one American who is unfamiliar with the resources of all parts of the vast country he inhabits. All the intelligent men in the Union know one another by reputation, and many know one another by sight. I have frequently been astonished to discover just how true this statement is. I can attest that I have never spoken to an American about one of his compatriots without finding him aware of the man's current position and life story.

I am aware that this extreme industrial and intellectual dynamism is strongly encouraged by education, by the type of government that Americans enjoy, and by the quite special situation in which they find themselves. People in America are not sedentary, not even those who come from old nations. Nearly all are true industrial entrepreneurs who feel an urgent need for means of communication and use them with a passion that one would scarcely expect to find in a French peasant wedded to his routine and slothful in his outlook. The effect of building a road or canal is more obvious and, above all, more immediate in America than it would be in France.

We should accordingly do in France as the Americans do in their new states in the West: build roads before there are travelers, with full confidence that sooner or later the travelers will appear.

As for the means used to open avenues of communication in America, my observations are recorded below.

In Europe it is generally believed that the leading maxim of government in America is *laisser faire:* that the government is purely a spectator, observing the progress of society, which is driven by individual self-interest. This is a mistake.

True, the American government does not involve itself in everything, as ours does. It does not seek to anticipate all needs and do whatever needs to be done. It distributes no bonuses, does not encourage commerce, and does not act as patron to arts and letters. But when it comes to projects of great public utility, it seldom leaves the job to private individuals but acts on its own. The great canal that joins the Hudson River to Lake Erie was built at the expense of the state of New York. The canal that links Lake Erie to the Mississippi River is the work of the state of Ohio. The canal that joins the Delaware River to Chesapeake Bay is a state enterprise. The highways that link two distant points are usually planned and built by states, not companies.

Note, however, that there are no rules. Companies, towns, and private individuals cooperate with the state in a myriad of ways. Projects of relatively small scale or limited interest are left to towns and companies. Turnpikes and other toll roads often run parallel to state roads. Railroads built by private companies take the place of canals in some sections of the country. Local roads are maintained by the districts in which they are located. There is no exclusive system here. America eschews the uniformity of system that certain superficial and metaphysical minds find so appealing of late.

On the contrary, difference and variety are the watchwords of American institutions, laws, government, and everyday life.

Everything is adapted to the nature of the people and the place rather than forcing people and places to adapt to inflexible rules. This variety gives rise to a prosperity that flourishes throughout the nation and in each of its parts.

To return to the subject of roads and other means of rapidly transporting the products of industry and thought from place to place, I do not claim to have made the discovery that these promote prosperity, for this is a universally accepted truth. I say only that America forces one to take note of this truth, which is more prominently demonstrated here than anywhere else in the world. It is impossible to travel across the United States without being convinced, not by argument but by the evidence of one's own senses, that the most infallible way to increase the prosperity of a nation is to encourage free communication among the people who inhabit it. . . .

IMPRESSIONS

First Impressions.

15 May 1831.

The Americans thus far strike us as having carried national pride to quite excessive lengths. I doubt that anyone can induce them to say anything at all unfavorable to their country. Most of them are undiscerning in their praise to foreigners, disagreeably self-assured, and largely unenlightened. On the whole, they exhibit a "small-town" outlook and tend to magnify what they see, as people do who are not accustomed to seeing great things. But we have yet to meet anyone truly remarkable.

All in all they seem to me a religious people. Clearly it never occurs to anyone to mock religious practice, and the goodness and even truth of religion are universally accepted *in theory.* To what degree do their beliefs govern their lives? What is the true power of religious principle over their souls? Why does the diversity of sects not lead to indifference, if not outwardly then at least inwardly? These questions remain to be answered.

What strikes me thus far is that the country exhibits the outward perfection of the middle classes, or, to put it another way, the entire society seems to have fused into one middle class. No one seems to possess the elegant manners and refined politeness of the European upper classes. On the contrary, one is initially struck by the vulgar tone of society, by a certain disagreeable lack of consideration for others. Yet at the same time no one is downright ill-mannered, that is, no one has what might be called *mauvais ton* in France. All the Americans we have met so far, right down to the simplest shop clerk, seem either to have been well brought up or to wish to appear so. Their manners are serious, poised, and reserved, and all dress the same way.

In all their customs Americans mix two conditions that Europeans take such care to keep separate. Women dress for the day at seven in the morning. By nine it is already acceptable to make visits. By noon one is received everywhere. Signs of a very busy life are everywhere. We have yet to see any "fashionable" people. It even occurs to me that the good morals here are a consequence not so much of severe principles as of the fact that young people find it impossible to think about love or to pursue such matters seriously. . . .

Notebook F: Civil and Criminal Law in America

Philadelphia, 15 November 1831.

I've just had a conversation of more than four hours about legal matters with Gilpin, a very intelligent young lawyer from this city.[201] Here is a summary of what I learned.

In order to understand American law, one has to know how the judicial system is organized in England and what the principles of English law are.

1. The chief and oldest source of English law is what is called the common law. The common law consists of two parts: (1) traditional customs that have never been collected into a corpus, as was done in France in the time of Beaumanoir,[202] but whose principles are contained in the records of judicial decisions spanning several centuries; (2) statutes, or laws passed by Parliament. Statute law is more recent than customary law, which dates back to the earliest days of the monarchy. Some statutes modified or attenuated earlier customs. Together, customs and statutes constitute a rather vague and incoherent body of law known as the common law. As we shall see, subsequent legislation was then grafted onto this common stock.

201. Henry D. Gilpin (1801–1860), a member of a well-known Pennsylvania Quaker family, was a successful lawyer. A supporter of Andrew Jackson, he was appointed to a number of government positions, including the board of the Bank of the United States and several state political offices. He served as U.S. attorney general for a year under President Martin Van Buren.

202. Philippe de Beaumanoir was a French government official in the thirteenth century. In 1283, he wrote *Coutumes de Beauvaisis;* it was not published until 1690, but it then became the definitive work about French customary law.

2. The Norman Conquest inaugurated the temporal power of the clergy. In England as on the Continent, the clergy was quick to assert jurisdiction over certain cases involving matters of conscience, such as those involving the execution of contracts with a sacramental element, such as marriages and wills. When the church asserted jurisdiction in such cases, it did not limit itself to applying the rules of any particular country. It accepted the universality of Roman law and rejected trial by jury. Under the cloak of the church, Roman law was thus introduced into English legislation. Its place was limited but quite important. In time, the ecclesiastical courts ceased to issue judgments yet continued to exist and in fact still exist today under the name *doctors' commons.*

3. Only at the inception of the Tudor dynasty did the inadequacy of customary and common law begin to make itself felt.[203] Society had become remarkably civilized. Social relations had become more complex, and with greater wealth and enlightenment came the need for a more perfect system of justice.

This need emerged in a period when royal power was at its height. Petitioners who wanted what the law would not give them therefore turned naturally to representatives of royal authority. This led to the creation of the so-called chancery or equity court, the device that the English adopted to remedy the defects in their laws without changing them. They preferred to embrace arbitrariness, to create a sort of judicial dictatorship, rather than to reform their ancient institutions. Chancery judges created a completely new body of law in the areas that fell within their jurisdiction. They took the principles of this new law in part from the common law, in part from Roman law, and in part from themselves and created a jurisprudence adapted to the times in which they lived.

Cases heard by the courts of equity can be grouped under four heads:

1. Cases involving "specific performance of contracts." Under the common law, when one party to a contract failed to perform, the other party could sue for damages in a trial by jury, but nothing more; this was an imperfect remedy, since the second party might need the thing promised in the contract and not the money offered in its place. Once a society attains a certain degree of civilization, it can no longer tolerate such a crude idea of equity.

The aggrieved party could therefore turn to the Court of Chancery seeking "a remedy to the deficiency of the law." The chancery judge could hear such a case without a jury and require the offending party to fulfill the terms of the contract. Note that this remedy applies only *to contracts* and not to *real actions in the strict sense.* Suppose that a man buys a piece of land and pays for it. Ownership is transferred, but the former owner refuses to deliver. In such a case, there is no need for a chancery judge. A jury can order that possession be awarded to the true owner. In this case, the contract has already been executed, as it were, so that the question comes down to an ordinary case of possession.

2. The second source of jurisdiction is what is called "trust states." Suppose

203. Henry VII was the first ruler from the House of Tudor. He became king of England in 1485, and the Tudors remained on the throne until 1603.

that a man makes a gift of land to another man but stipulates that payment shall be in the form of an annuity. The annuity is not paid. Under the common law, it was difficult for the aggrieved party to bring suit. The issue was more complicated than the law envisioned. There is no desire on the part of the donor to recover the gifted property and no claim that it is not the property of the donee. The suit is intended solely to force compliance with a commitment to perform subsequent to the sale but pledged prior to the transfer of property. When cases of this sort became common, the parties would turn to the chancery judge for a remedy.

3. The third area in which chancery courts have jurisdiction is bankruptcy. Rules governing the compensation of creditors and means of forcing the debtor to pay could not have been established in the semibarbarous society of the Middle Ages. But the need quickly arose as society became more civilized, and the chancery judge assumed responsibility for patching this loophole in the law.

4. Everything to do with minors, guardianship, and the property of minors fell within the purview of the chancery judge as a consequence of feudal notions about these matters. Under the laws of feudalism, the lord was the natural guardian of his minor vassals. By the same token, the king was the guardian of his minor subjects.

When the power of lords crumbled and the power of the monarch grew up on its ruins, it was the king who, through his chancellor, assumed responsibility for all matters involving guardianship and for hearing all cases involving the interests of minors.

It seems that when a party to a case in chancery refused to obey the order of the chancery judge, the judge could have him arrested and held until he gave in; this practice has survived.

This completes the outline of English law. It was necessary to clarify this before discussing what we learned in Pennsylvania.

It will be useful to begin by discussing the organization of the courts in Pennsylvania:

Pennsylvania is divided into one hundred counties, which are incorporated into twelve judicial circuits. There are twelve judges called judges of the inferior court. Every three months, they must hold court in each of the counties in their circuit, not alone but in the company of two clerks who live in the county and are not lawyers, so that the judge bears full responsibility.

This court hears all cases of undetermined value and all cases whose value has been determined to be less than five hundred dollars.

At the next higher level is the superior court. It consists of five judges. There are only five superior circuits in Pennsylvania, and every three months the five judges make a full circuit, just as the inferior court judges do. They have two duties:

1. They hear cases whose value has been determined to exceed five hundred dollars.

2. They hear cases on appeal (l' "appel," as we say improperly in French); we shall see in a moment what the word "appeal" means under English and American law.

Q. I see no chancery court or ecclesiastical court in this system.

A. Those courts have never existed in Pennsylvania.

Q. To whom have their prerogatives been assigned?

A. *In part to judges and in part to juries.* In many cases the courts refrain *altogether from doing what those courts would do elsewhere.*

Q. Explain those three ideas by examples.

A. Suppose that in a case of marriage (ecclesiastical court of Doctors' Commons) a question of fact and a question of law arise. An English court would settle everything. But here the judge would decide the point of law *by himself* and leave the question of fact to the jury by way of a special delegation known as "issue."

Q. In that case, why not just say that you've folded the ecclesiastical jurisdiction into that of "common pleas"? What you have just described is an ordinary trial.

A. No. In an ordinary trial under common law, the jury is judge of both law and fact. It follows the judge's instructions, but it is not the judge who pronounces the decision. Here the jury acts only by delegation. It decides a specific point but does not judge the case.

In nearly all matters pertaining to the jurisdiction of the courts of chancery, jurisdiction has simply been transferred to the court of common pleas. Questions of law are *instructed* by judges in accordance with precedents established by the courts of equity, and questions of fact are decided by the jury.

Nevertheless, there are numerous items within the jurisdiction of the courts of chancery that we have not included in our laws. For instance, in Pennsylvania, a party to a case cannot be questioned as to fact and article. In Pennsylvania, a defaulting party to a contract cannot be compelled to perform, and one is forced to impose excessive awards for damages in order to establish an indirect obligation to perform, whereas the court of chancery would have threatened him directly with imprisonment for failure to perform. Many people have been troubled by these gaps in the law and sought to establish a court of chancery here, but public opinion has always been against it. As you see, we cannot enforce what I earlier referred to as "specific performance of contracts."

Q. I am beginning to understand the jurisdiction of what you call the court of common pleas. Most cases gravitate toward it, but what I don't understand clearly is the procedure in these courts, the division of responsibility between judge and jury, and the way in which they operate.

A. To understand this properly, you have to see these courts in action. Nevertheless, I shall try to explain to you how they work in practice.

Once the judge and jury are seated, the plaintiff explains his case and produces evidence in the form of exhibits and witnesses. The defendant challenges the exhibits and produces additional witnesses or cross-examines those of his adversary. The judge then summarizes the evidence and sets forth the law under various theories of the case. The jury withdraws and returns with a unanimous verdict, which contains a crisply worded decision as to both the facts and the law. Suppose, for example, a man sues for property he believes he has inherited. The defendant invokes a twenty-year statute of limitations. When all arguments are said and done, the judge addresses the jurors: "The plaintiff has incontestable title to the property, but the defendant invokes a statute of limitations, which, *under the terms of such-and-such a law,* should invalidate the plaintiff's claim. It is up to you to decide whether the defendant has in fact been in possession of the property for twenty years, as he maintains."

The jury limits itself to stating that the property in question shall not revert to the plaintiff. With this verdict it is in effect declaring that: (1) the defendant has been in possession of the property for twenty years; and (2) the law entitles him to prevail in the suit that has been brought against him.

Q. So the jury never has to state the grounds for its decision?

A. No, never. This is a consequence of the institution of the jury. Nevertheless, the legal grounds noted by the judge in his instructions to the jury are recorded, and that record may be invoked on appeal.

Q. Do you allow the jury to examine written documents?

A. Yes. The jury decides all questions of fact, be it a simple fact, such as a physical document, or a complex fact, such as the will of the parties as attested in various documents emanating from them.

Q. But how can a jury deal with issues that demand so much experience and wisdom?

A. It receives help from the judge, who summarizes the arguments and supervises examination of the documents. Later, moreover, you will hear about various forms of appeal envisioned by the law.

Q. I thought that the jury could only order the payment of a sum of money. But I see that it can order possession of a piece of property.

A. Yes, of course. A jury can order that possession be restored to the true owner of a property.

Q. But the execution of such a judgment can lead to confrontation. Who is in charge then, since the court ceases to exist five minutes after handing down its judgment?

A. That sort of incident seldom occurs. In general, the parties will not be heard in court unless they agree as to the basis of the case, for example, the extent and limits of the litigation. If the execution of a judgment gives rise to an incident, that incident itself becomes the object of a new case, which is judged by a new jury.

Q. The jury undoubtedly has nothing to do with the execution of judgments?

A. No. No sooner is the verdict pronounced than the judge dismisses the jury, which has no further involvement in the case.

Q. When expert testimony is required, how does the court proceed?

A. When the parties foresee the need for expert testimony, they will call experts as witnesses before the jury, and these experts are then questioned in the same way as other witnesses.

Q. Are written depositions read in the presence of the jury?

A. This *may* be done if the parties agree to it. It *must* be done when the witnesses reside in another state. In that event the judge issues a warrant to the state in which the witnesses reside. They are heard, and the record of that hearing is presented to the jury.

Q. Do you allow witnesses to testify about all manner of subjects?

A. Yes, but we do not allow testimony contrary to the clear meaning of an act.

Q. In France, for example, one may not call a witness to prove what *may* be proved by a written document. In Pennsylvania, you may not call a witness to prove what *is* proved by a written document. In France, the *possibility;* here, the fact itself.

A. Exactly.

Q. I am beginning to understand your civil procedure. I see clearly that juries must constantly make huge mistakes in law and even in fact in cases where the facts are complicated. Explain to me now what the correctives are.

A. The corrective lies in the power of the judges, which is immense and arbitrary, but custom and public opinion have set the limits of that power in such a way that it is difficult to use it improperly.

In Pennsylvania we do not have what you properly refer to as appellate judgments, that is, judgments handed down by a superior court that may reverse, modify, or affirm the judgment of a lower court. Our system of appeal is quite [different] from yours. Note the gradation of means provided to correct the flaws resulting from the institution of the jury.

The judge who presides over the court of common pleas *always has the right to overturn a jury verdict while the court is still sitting, and he may order the jury to resume its deliberations.* That is the abstract principle, but as I said earlier, the verdict encompasses both law and fact. One therefore needs to look closely at actual practice. In order for a judge to overturn a verdict as unjust as to matters *of fact,* the injustice must be flagrant. Otherwise the judge takes an immense moral responsibility upon himself. Although the English do not have the same superstitious respect as the French for *jury verdicts as to fact,* they do admit that in principle such verdicts should not be tampered with except in extreme cases. By contrast, if the judge believes that the jurors have erred as to the law, it is virtually his duty to overturn the verdict, and judges do in fact quite frequently overturn verdicts for this reason.

So you see that in spite of appearances, judges here, like judges in France, have the last word on points of law, and here they also have some influence over the judgment of facts. That is one safeguard against incompetent juries. There is a second safeguard against the incompetence of judges as well as juries: what is called a "writ of error," which is a formal request for a new judgment.

This request may be made in two ways:

1. The losing party in a case may appeal the verdict to the judges of the lower court to which the presiding judge in the court of common pleas that heard the original case belongs.

The losing party explains to the whole court that the jury verdict in the case was either contrary to law or unjust in some way. He offers new evidence, proposes new witnesses, or develops a new theory of the case. The judge who first heard the case sits with his colleagues on the larger court and hears the appeal along with them.

If the court believes that the jury committed a flagrant injustice or that it erred in law, either because it followed the instructions of the judge or because it rejected them, it overturns the verdict but does not judge the case itself; rather, it remands the case to the lower court that heard it originally, with the same judge presiding but with a different jury.

If the jury returns the same verdict as before, a fresh appeal can be filed with the entire court, which can again order a new trial. In theory this process could continue forever, but in practice it seems that the court of common pleas accedes to the verdict of the jury after the second appeal.

2. A second means of appeal is available to the losing party. Instead of filing his appeal with the judges of the lower court, he may (*at his option, I believe*) choose to file it with the superior court, which then proceeds in the same manner as the lower court: if it overturns the verdict, it can send the case back to the original judge but with a different jury.

So you see that here, instead of a two-stage system, we have something like an appeal of the case to the same judge who heard it originally. Our superior court is not designed to correct the judgments of inferior judges but rather to judge more important cases. Its superiority is a question of enlightenment rather than of hierarchical position.

Q.: Are you aware that your judges wield immense power? It is far greater than the power we grant to judges in France.

A.: Yes, their power is immense, but they are equally answerable for their actions. In France, judges cannot be removed. Here, they can always be removed for "bad behavior." In any system of legislation, all the parts are interrelated.

Q.: But what do you mean by "bad behavior"? Does the judge have to commit a crime or misdemeanor specified in law? Or can he be removed for incompetence, bias, passion, or negligence—in short, for *deficiencies* (rather than *crimes*) that may be reprehensible in a magistrate but are not spelled out by law?

A.: The expression "bad behavior" is not defined, though it is limited to some extent by precedent and public opinion. It covers only actions pertaining to the profession, but these may be of many kinds.

Q.: But with such a broad definition, don't you worry that judges may gradually come to be swayed by public opinion and thus lose their neutrality and consistency?

A.: I have no idea what will happen in the future, but thus far these flaws in the system have not caused any problems. Wherever you locate the power to control judges, the fact remains that, for the good of the public, it always has to be placed somewhere. A completely independent judiciary strikes me as dangerous in principle.

Q.: Thus far we have dealt strictly with details of the jury system in civil cases. Let us turn now to a more general view of the institution. Tell me what you think of it.

A.: It seems to me that it is open to question whether the jury system is a superior institution for arriving at a correct judgment in each individual case, though I am still tempted to regard it as superior to permanent courts in this respect. I believe that justice through juries is more costly to the state than the other system. Nevertheless, I believe that the institution of the jury offers enormous advantages over any other system:

1. It ensures respect for justice. Not only is it impossible to corrupt a jury, it is also impossible to suspect that it has been corrupted. Hence decisions of the courts command considerable respect.

2. The jury system accustoms people to the practical administration of justice. Every person who participates in the act of judgment reflects that he may someday be judged in turn, and in similar circumstances.

3. It counters the individual selfishness that is the bane of society and teaches men to take an interest in affairs other than their own, to assume responsibility, to play a public role.

4. It performs an incredible service by fostering good judgment and enlightening the people. That, in my opinion, is its most important benefit. The jury is a school to which people come to learn about their rights; they come into contact with better-educated and more enlightened members of the upper classes; and they receive from the most intelligent minds practical instruction in the law, in a form they can understand. In this respect, I believe that civil juries are more important than criminal juries. The influence of civil juries on a nation's politics may be more indirect, but it is also more powerful.

Wherever the jury system takes hold, even in civil cases, despotism becomes impossible.

Q.: But do you think that the jury system can be instituted in a nation that has not long been accustomed to it?

A.: Yes, by having juries little by little assume responsibility for judging matters of fact apart from points of law, starting with those civil facts that are most analogous to *criminal* facts.

* * *

Conversation with the Philadelphia recorder, an extremely intelligent and capable young man.[204]

204. Tocqueville refers to Joseph McIlvaine, recorder of the city of Philadelphia in 1830, to be distinguished from the merchant Bowes Reed MacIlvaine, whom he met in Louisville.

Q.: Who sits on your juries?

A.: One has to distinguish between the right to sit on a jury and the use of that right. Any citizen of Pennsylvania above the age of *twenty-one* who pays taxes *may* sit on a jury. In fact, however, only about two-thirds of those eligible actually do serve.

Every year, the assessors (who set the amount of taxes due) draw up a list of those taxpayers whom they deem fit to fulfill this social duty.

They exclude men who are notoriously *incapable* or *unworthy* of serving and place the remaining names in a container, from which forty-eight names are drawn for each session.

Q.: Is the assessors' choice arbitrary?

A.: Yes.

Q.: Can their decision be appealed?

A.: No. Jury duty is a responsibility that people are happy to avoid, and in any case assessors serve for only one year and are elected to their post, so that there is a high likelihood that they will not act frivolously, which makes their decisions easier to bear.

Q.: Are jurors paid?

A.: Yes, in both the criminal and civil courts. They receive a dollar a day, without regard to travel expenses. This compensation is paid by the state, not by the parties. It is almost always insufficient to cover the cost of travel and lost time.

Q.: How far do jurors travel to sit in trials?

A.: At most eight to ten miles.

At this point I explained to the recorder how things work in France. My account seemed to surprise him greatly. He stressed the need to pay jurors, adding that trial by jury was perhaps more expensive than other methods.

Q.: But do you really believe it is useful in practice?

A.: All things considered, yes. Trial by jury ensures respect for the law. It gives people practical knowledge of the law and fosters the precious habit of reasoning and watching others reason. But I think that the jury is an institution that could be greatly improved. Questions of law could be left entirely to judges. Complicated questions of fact, such as those involving the examination of contracts, cannot be properly decided by juries either.

Q.: Do you think that juries can be introduced in civil trials in countries where the law does not provide for such an institution?

A.: Yes, with some changes, and provided that questions of fact are clearly distinguished and kept simple, for I believe that juries are better at deciding simple questions of fact than judges are.

Q.: In criminal cases, don't judges have considerable influence on the decisions of juries?

A.: Yes, provided the judge is skillful at handling the jurors. Some judges seem to make it their business to prosecute defendants and find them guilty. They fail. A skillful judge must seem to be impartial if he wants to guide the jury, and it is desirable for judges to do so, because juries often make serious mistakes.

* * *

. . . Conversation with Mr. Curtis, a distinguished Boston lawyer,[205] concerning civil legislation. 27 September 1831.

Q.: I've collected a great deal of information about matters of civil law, but my research was unmethodical, so I'm still rather confused. This time, if you'll allow me, I'd like to proceed in a more logical fashion.

When a person wishes to file suit against another person, what is the first step he must take?

A.: In each county there is an official called the sheriff. The sheriff acts as the agent of the civil authorities and executes their decisions.

If a person wishes to file suit against someone else, he goes to the sheriff. The sheriff then notifies the adverse party of the suit.

In New England any person who files suit to recover a debt he claims is owed to him must either seek to have the debtor locked up in prison or else force him to post a bond. In other states, the plaintiff must swear under oath that the debt is real in order to have the debtor put in prison (if he does not post a bond). That is not the case here. Without any such formality the creditor can ask the sheriff to imprison the debtor.

On the day appointed in the summons, the defendant or his attorney appears in court and, if he is not prepared to proceed, requests a postponement.

Q.: I see now what procedure is followed to get to court. Tell me what courts one can appear before and how jurisdiction is decided.

A.: The plaintiff chooses the jurisdiction at his own risk.

Q.: Can a judge declare himself incompetent to hear a case?

A.: Yes, but the parties can appeal that decision.

1. If the amount involved is less than 20 d[ollars] (100 F.), the case is heard by a justice of the peace, who renders his decision without the involvement of a jury.

2. If a will is involved, for instance if an heir files suit or a legatee wishes to invoke his rights, he appears before a judge of probate. This judge has both an *administrative* and a *judicial* function. He will not allow the heir or legatee to receive his share of the bequest until he has posted bond with the court to cover the value of any movable property.

If the will is contested, the probate judge decides without the assistance of jurors, but the parties may appeal his decision to a higher court.

3. There is a third type of court of first instance to which an aggrieved party

205. Charles Pelham Curtis (1792–1864), a graduate of Harvard College, was a well-known lawyer from a prominent Boston family. He held a number of city and state political offices throughout his life.

may turn, namely, the court of common pleas. Indeed, one might call this the usual jurisdiction, whereas the others exist to handle unusual cases.

The court of common pleas consists of one judge and twelve jurors. It meets four times per year, in sessions referred to as "terms."

Its jurisdiction includes all cases pertaining to property boundaries and all cases that can be reduced to suits for damages.

The court of common pleas proceeds as follows: Attorneys for both sides produce written as well as verbal depositions. They plead their case. The judge sums up, explains the points of law to the jurors, and lists the questions of fact. The jury withdraws to deliberate before rendering a verdict as to both the points of law and the questions of fact. But this verdict is not all of a piece. The decision of the jury as to the facts cannot be challenged (except before a higher court). The decision as to the law can be overruled immediately by the judge or overturned later on if one of the parties appeals and proves that the law was violated.

Furthermore, since verdicts never count as precedents, if the parties do not file an appeal, the judge leaves the verdict as it was rendered, even if it is contrary to the law.

It is the judge who decides if a question is a question of fact or of law.

Jurors are never asked to interpret a legislative act.

Before the jury one cannot interrogate the adverse party. Only the chancery court has the right to conduct such an inquiry.

I recently witnessed a trial that went on for nine days before the same jury. But such trials are quite rare.

4. The fourth and last court of first instance is the chancery court.

The chancery court is an English institution. It is only thirty years since it was introduced in Massachusetts. Its prerogatives are still more limited than in England and the rest of the United States. We have no chancellor. Before there was a chancery court here, we made up for the deficiency by assigning some of its prerogatives to other courts.

I regard the chancery court as a necessary institution when the jury is adapted to civil affairs.

Its competence is of two kinds:

1. It issues temporary orders in all cases of public emergency, disturbance, and violence. It issues summary judgments on an interim basis. It has no terms but remains in session throughout the year.

2. It judges all cases of conscience, all cases in which the good faith of one of the parties is questioned, and all cases that cannot be resolved by the payment of a sum of money and are therefore likely to give rise to decisions that are difficult to carry out or open to challenge.

The competence of the chancery courts is the most difficult thing for a foreigner to understand about our law. It is governed not so much by fixed rules as by subtle judgments. To avoid misunderstanding you have to recognize the role of tact in the practice of these courts.

In Massachusetts, a party is always free to turn to the court of common pleas, even when the case is of a nature that ought to be heard by a chancery court, provided only that the issue can be reduced to one that can be settled by payment of damages.

* * *

Reflections.

Summarized below are what I take to be the clearest implications of the foregoing conversation.

It is apparent that all English law, and therefore American law, is an old fabric stitched together out of pieces from different periods, so that there is no point in looking for any new idea, deduction from first principles, or methodical order.

As to the present, it seems to me that originally judgment by jury was the rule in all cases. Indeed, this was the sole judicial principle of our Germanic forebears, but such a judicial form can exist only in a society still in its infancy, where all cases are based on judgments of fact.[206]

As European societies became more civilized, the difficulty of relying on juries become increasingly apparent. On the Continent, and especially in France, where people have always been more apt to be struck by the advantages of a new state than by those of the old, juries were eliminated in favor of permanent tribunals.

In England, by contrast, where the human mind moves more slowly, where the need for logic is less of a concern than in France, and where everyday facts are more likely to serve as a guide and fears of a complete change are more likely to stand as an impediment, extraordinary efforts were made to maintain a place for juries in the legal system.

As the social state progressed from century to century, the impossibility of submitting certain kinds of cases to trial by jury became increasingly apparent. As difficulties arose, new expedients were invented to deal with them.

For instance, the increase in the number of cases (which grows as society becomes wealthier and more enlightened) made it clear that it would be impossible to try all cases before a jury. A minimum value of damages was therefore established below which a jury would not be called.

As the laws were perfected, people realized that a permanent tribunal was needed to prevent the parties from engaging in acts prejudicial to their rights while awaiting judgment. Such a tribunal was therefore created.

When people began to discern more clearly *the interests* involved in various kinds of legal action, they realized that justice was only partially served by reducing all cases to the payment of damages, and they also realized that whenever a court issued an order that something *be done,* there could be questions about the grounds for its judgment, and, furthermore, that the difficulties of

206. Tocqueville refers to ancient Germanic tribes, such as those described in Tacitus's *Germania* in the first century. These tribes were governed by councils, in which all free men could participate. Nineteenth-century historians recognized these tribes as the ancestors of the Germanic groups that moved to England in the fifth century and became the Anglo-Saxons.

carrying out the judgment could be resolved only by appealing to the judge who had rendered it. But a jury is a judge that is chosen for a particular case and that ceases to exist after its verdict is pronounced. Hence the institution of the jury was not abandoned but rather supplemented by a tribunal that was created specifically to judge cases of this sort.

Finally, even in cases where the issue was solely a matter of money, it was felt that as the law became more complicated, it became increasingly difficult to separate questions of fact from questions of law. People still clung to the hope that the jury could be preserved, but its *verdict* was now seen as having two elements, a judgment of fact and a judgment of law. The judge retained superiority in the latter and in the interpretation of legislative acts. Appearances notwithstanding, the jury in reality concentrated on questions of fact.

All in all, it is clear that the use of juries in civil cases is by its very nature an institution appropriate to a nascent society but not to the requirements of an enlightened and perfect legal system. English law demonstrates that it is almost impossible to adapt the jury system completely to an advanced social state and raises strong doubts about whether the role currently assigned to juries actually serves *justice.*

The political *utility* of the jury system is immense, however, and it is from a political point of view that it ought to be contemplated.

* * *

Continuation of the conversation with Mr. Curtis.

Q.: Don't you think that many parts of your procedure could be simplified, and can you give satisfactory reasons for all the rules you obey?

A.: No. Our legislation developed in stages. It was bequeathed to us by our ancestors. We have become accustomed to its spirit and familiar with its practices. Yet it would be impossible to apply our laws as they stand to another country. There is no logical system to them.

Q.: Do you think that, when all is said and done, juries are useful in civil trials?

A.: Speaking for myself, and for many others who think as I do, I believe that judges can more often be depended upon to make capable decisions than juries, even in regard to the judgment of facts.

The people are nevertheless surprisingly attached to trial by jury, and it would be absolutely impossible for us to get rid of it.

COMMON LAW

English customary law.

The subject of customary law—its advantages, drawbacks, and influence—is a most important one. Here I want only to set down a few ideas.

English customary law was never couched in written form, as some French customary law was. It is properly speaking the science of the past, knowledge of precedents. In English customary law there are examples, but there is no law.

As time went by, examples from the past grew in number, as did documents and other materials recording such examples. Kent, vol. I, p. 441, states that at the present time, the library of a legal scholar needs to contain no fewer than 648 volumes.[207]

Rendering justice in this way seems absolutely barbarous to people accustomed to codification.

I am nevertheless inclined to believe that either system would yield approximately the same result if employed by equally enlightened peoples.

I believe that respect for jurisprudence is greater where the number of written laws is smaller.

Vagueness in the law is such a palpable and widely recognized social evil that wherever there is no law, a conservative instinct ensures that magistrates will cling to precedent and reject any desire to demonstrate their power through innovation. With respect to the great principles of law, on which jurisprudence has spoken on thousands of occasions, judges therefore actually find themselves bound not by theory but by practice. It never even occurs to them to depart from the well-beaten track. Debate arises only as to the rare question, the relatively unimportant matter, or the novel issue, and on such occasions the judge is apt to believe that he knows the law well enough to venture an opinion of his own.

What an odd state of affairs! In a country where judges have the power to refuse to enforce laws they deem unconstitutional, they are bound even in the least important cases by the opinions of their predecessors and subordinate their own reasoning to that of another. Customary law seems to magnify the importance of the judge by raising him almost to the rank of legislator. In truth, however, it reduces his importance. Under customary law the judge obeys his predecessors; where there are written statutes, he obeys the law.

Isn't that almost what happens in nations with the best codes? Can even the ablest legislator foresee every conceivable case? Can he do more than lay down general principles, which give rise to endless litigation when applied?

Of course there are more vague points in customary law than in written legislation. But cases left in doubt under a code are more difficult to decide and take longer to resolve than those that arise under customary law, because jurisprudence has less power in countries where written law exists. Thus when applied by enlightened peoples, the two systems are more or less equivalent.

Proponents of customary law go further, however, and argue that it should be preferred. To me this position seems untenable.

Customary law, which was born in an age of ignorance and extended at various times by various hands, cannot be as comprehensive, as rational, and as logical as a written code produced by a legislature or an individual in a more learned age.

207. Kent, *Commentaries on American Law.*

All or nearly all the advantages of customary law are shared with written law, whereas written law has further advantages peculiar to itself.

The greatest of these is to make all the important points and general principles of the law accessible to everyone. Under customary law, only lawyers know what is permitted and what is prohibited.

The second advantage is that a written code reduces the law to a set of stable rather than shifting principles, which the lawyer can study at less cost and retain more easily.

Customary law is a dangerous weapon in the hands of a relatively unenlightened people.

One might say that customary law is a cause that results from its effect, a law that emerges from a judgment rather than serving as the basis of that judgment. Hence if the judicial body is poorly constituted and not subject to constant oversight by an enlightened public, the legal system can lapse into a state of almost total barbarism.

I see a special advantage in customary law, but one that is limited to monarchies and above all to absolute monarchies: namely, to involve the people *clandestinely* in the formation of the law. Under customary law, judges are in a sense legislators, especially in novel cases.

Now, judges are men of their times; they are immersed in public opinion; and they share a sense of the current needs of the nation with everyone of the same generation.

This is even more true if the judge regularly works in the presence of a jury. He will often incorporate his own ideas and those of his contemporaries into his judgments, which is to say, into the law, without being aware of what he is doing. In his hands, the law will inevitably be subject to changes, and he will become the interpreter of the opinions and needs of the age. But this advantage of customary law will not be apparent in states where the people participate in the making of the law. In such states there is no need to proceed in a roundabout manner.

The independence that distinguishes customary law from written law must be attributed to this flexibility as well as to its feudal origin.

It is fairly widely agreed that Roman law is more complete, more logical, more prudent, and more subtle than customary law, yet it is also argued, and rightly, that customary law reflects a respect for political rights and a libertarian spirit absolutely foreign to Roman law. Although this is true of Roman law, it cannot be used as an argument against written law in general. Kent, vol. I, p. 507, expresses this idea as follows: "The value of the civil law is not to be found in questions which relate to the connection between the government and the people, or in provisions for personal security in criminal cases. In everything which concerns civil and political liberty, it cannot be compared with the free spirit of the English and American common law. But upon subjects relating to private rights and personal contracts, and the duties which flow from them, there is no system of law in which principles are investigated with more good sense or declared and enforced with more accurate and impartial justice."

Born among barbarians, customary law is imperfect, like the civilization that witnessed its inception, yet it breathes the independent spirit of the centuries in which it first flourished. The answer to the question whether customary law is today preferable to written law is to my mind indubitably negative. Yet its abolition on the European continent was a great misfortune. By contrast, I believe that its preservation in England contributed significantly to keeping alive the ideas and principles of liberty, and thereby contributed indirectly, despite its imperfections, to the progress of civilization in the British Isles, whereas the introduction on the Continent of written law, though it might be thought more perfect, subtle, and civilized, contributed to the establishment of despotism in Europe and thus harmed the cause of civilization that it seemed to serve.

Independent of the political consequences of the preservation of customary law in England, I believe that its existence also contributed significantly to the shaping of the English mind.

It created in that nation what might be called the spirit of precedents, by which I mean a certain inclination to seek not what is reasonable as such but rather what was done in the past; not what is just but rather what is venerable; not general theories but particular facts. I have no doubt that familiarity with customary law, together with the role that lawyers and judges have always taken in political debate, lent powerful support to aristocratic institutions and, with them, helped to inspire in the English the superstitious respect for the works of their fathers and the hatred of innovation that set them apart.

In the United States, where laws and mores tend toward unlimited democracy, one still sees the influence of customary law on the human spirit. One sees it in the calm that reigns throughout the society, but its most obvious influence is on lawyers. Lawyers in the United States are the enemies of change, men attached to precedent. That would not be an accurate description of lawyers in France. What distinguishes our lawyers is the mania to generalize everywhere. In America the absence of general ideas among men of the law is quite apparent.

American lawyers are generally eloquent in their praise of customary law. They strenuously oppose codification for the following reasons:

1. If codification were to occur, they would have to begin their studies all over again;

2. Because the law would become accessible to the uninitiated, they would lose some of their importance. They would no longer be the sole interpreters of an occult science, like the priests of ancient Egypt.

Some distinguished Americans not belonging to the bar have also opposed codification, Mr. Poinsett among them. By contrast, Mr. E. Livingston is strongly in favor of it.[208] He told me today in no uncertain terms that lawyers who opposed codification were acting out of self-interest.

208. Tocqueville is likely referring to Edward Livingston (1764–1836), secretary of state, rather than the New York lieutenant governor Edward P. Livingston (1779–1843).

The fact is that unwritten constitutions often give rise to less debate than written ones.

It is easier to prove a prior fact than to discern the will of the legislator and the spirit of the written law. . . .

THE PROSECUTOR'S OFFICE IN THE UNITED STATES

The state prosecutor here occupies a position both below ours and above.

He is below: his position is not as high as in our society; he has no civil function and no permanent duties; in certain states his salary is decided by judges, while in others it is dependent on fines paid by those convicted of crimes.

The prosecutor is not a magistrate. He does not oversee the whole of society. He is not the guardian of criminal justice. He does not initiate criminal cases, nor does he direct them, and his participation in investigations is only indirect. Control of the police force for criminal investigation is divided rather than being concentrated in his hands.

He is above: His power in certain respects is unlimited. He cannot be enjoined to enforce the will of a civil party. He has absolute, unsupervised jurisdiction over public prosecutions.

He does not prosecute unless he wishes to do so, and he may prevent a jury from rendering a verdict if he terminates the case.

This aspect of American law seems ill digested and not very logical. It is a mixture of *arbitrariness* and *weakness*. I believe that the constitution of our prosecutor's office is preferable. . . .

PROSECUTOR'S OFFICE IN MASSACHUSETTS

Cincinnati, Walker, 2 December 1831.

The prosecutor's office in Massachusetts consists of two parts:

1. In each county there is a district attorney, who pleads before the court of common pleas, prosecutes even minor offenses, and acts on behalf of the state in less important cases.

2. There is an attorney general, who follows the court of oyer and terminer, prosecutes major crimes, and takes charge of important cases in which state interests are at stake.

There is no hierarchical precedence between these two officials. They are perfectly independent within *their spheres* (which seems to be the basic idea of the English prosecutor's office). Hence many states have felt that there was no need for this kind of redundancy in the branches of the prosecutor's office.

In Connecticut and Ohio, for example, there are only district attorneys.

Mr. Van Matre.[209] D. Att. Cincinnati, 4 Dec.

There are only district attorneys, no attorney general; the district attorneys are appointed by judges and do not receive regular salaries. The judges set the pay they are to receive each year. The salary of the district attorney of Cincinnati almost never exceeds five or six hundred dollars. This absolute dependence of the prosecutor's office on judges is regarded as a serious flaw in the system.

Its situation here is nevertheless more tolerable than in New England, where the ministry is paid a certain sum (three dollars, I think) for each defendant found guilty and nothing if the defendant is acquitted.

In Ohio the prosecutor's office has the power to prosecute any crime on its own, as well as to refrain from prosecution, and there is no need for a civil party to summon it to action. In general it chooses to prosecute only those crimes subject to imprisonment in a penitentiary.

Only the prosecutor's office can plead before a grand jury.

In Ohio, judges are allowed to sentence an accuser to pay court costs, but they rarely make use of this power.

Mr. Dallas.[210]

Quid felony and others?

CRIMES?

Quid? "No bills were found or were not prosecuted [*sic*]." What exactly is the power of the prosecutor's office to prevent a trial? What rule does it follow? What happens to cases that are not brought forward?

Quid executent a mare committed [*sic*].

CRIMINAL AND CIVIL LAWS OF OHIO

The criminal law of Ohio is quite unusual. It deserves close scrutiny. No milder criminal law exists anywhere. Yet Mr. McLean, a justice of the Supreme Court of the United States, assures us that crime has not increased under this system (the point remains to be verified).

Criminal law in Ohio is conceived on a completely different basis from ours. For instance, the *value* of a stolen object and the *outcome* of the attempt modify the magnitude of the punishment.

The most glaring defect of the law is to my mind the fact that it does not

---

209. Daniel Van Matre, a graduate of Yale College, was an Ohio district attorney.

210. George M. Dallas (1792–1864) was district attorney for eastern Pennsylvania and became a U.S. senator from Pennsylvania later in 1831. Dallas would later serve as vice president under James K. Polk.

punish *recidivism.* The problem with this is plain to see: the same individuals appear again and again in the defendant's box for petty crimes that they know are punished no more harshly no matter how often they are committed. This is to the detriment of both individuals and society. We have heard many complaints about this.

Penal law in Ohio treats sexual intercourse with a child under ten years of age as *rape,* even if consenting (a wise and moral law).

It punishes *fornication,* that is, cohabitation of a man and a woman not married to each other even if both are free. This law is common to most of the states of the Union. Even though it confounds ideas of vice and crime, of a sin against God and an offense against society, it shocks no one. It is justified by the strictness of morals, and it is also a consequence of Presbyterian customs that date back to the origins of America. In Ohio fornication is in theory automatically[211] prosecuted, but I believe that such prosecutions are rare.

The prosecutor's office can also prosecute adultery as a crime.

CIVIL LEGISLATION

Ohio seems to me to have escaped from English precedents and memories more completely than any of the other states of the Union we have visited so far.

Thus, not only has it eliminated the exceptional jurisdictions of the ecclesiastical and chancery courts, it has also transferred all the prerogatives of those courts to the courts of common pleas and superior courts.

In Pennsylvania, which failed to adopt this apparently quite simple and reasonable approach, the result has been a system of justice that remains incomplete and obscure. Many useful procedures cannot be employed there because under the common law they fall within the purview of exceptional tribunals that no longer exist.

It seems that in Ohio a new trial may be granted a maximum of two times.

Today I observed the court of common pleas in Cincinnati. The jury appeared to have been drawn from the lowest class of the population.

LAWYERS IN OHIO

There is no law school in the West. In order to become a lawyer, a man must spend two years in apprenticeship to a practicing attorney and pass an examination administered by a commission appointed by judges.

1. What officials are included in the prosecutor's office?
2. Who chooses its members?
3. Are they lawyers?
4. Can they be removed from office at will, and if so, by whom?

211. The original French text has *"d'office."*

5. Are all the members of the prosecutor's office subject to a central authority? In other words, does the attorney general or the solicitor general correspond with district attorneys or other officials of similar type? Are they regarded as hierarchical superiors, and do they have the power to give orders to subordinates?

6. What exactly are the functions of the prosecutor's office?

7. Are those functions often points of contact with politics?

For example, does the prosecutor's office have the power to prosecute towns, districts, or counties that refuse or neglect to fulfill their political obligations?

8. How does public opinion regard the prosecutor's office?

ON JURIES

1. What exactly are the functions of the grand jury? Does it not have administrative and political as well as judicial functions?

2. Who serves on grand and petit juries, and how are they chosen?

3. Do you not find that there are drawbacks to drawing jurors from the lower classes of society?

4. Do the same individuals serve frequently on juries? What compensation do they receive? How often are they required to perform jury duty?

5. Are people reluctant to serve as jurors? Do the upper classes attempt to avoid serving?

6. Do you not think that trial by jury in civil cases has more political than judicial utility? In other words, do you not believe that civil cases would almost always be decided as well or better by judges alone? In civil cases, isn't the advantage of the jury that it lends greater moral force to the judgment, familiarizes people with legal affairs, and induces them to consider society's business as their own?

7. Do you think that, all things considered, the rule requiring a unanimous jury is really useful? How do courts manage to abide by it in practice?

JUDGES

1. Judges can be removed from office, but by whom and in what circumstances? Are judges removed frequently?

Have they sometimes been removed for political reasons?

2. Have you noticed any drawbacks in granting judges the power to declare laws unconstitutional?

3. Are judges always drawn from the ranks of lawyers? Are they generally trusted? Do they usually enjoy the favor of the people?

4. Do judges not sometimes scorn prevailing opinion if they do not share it?

1. What are the functions of a justice of the peace?

2. Are justices of the peace regarded as a public institution, as they are in England?

In what respects do your justices of the peace differ from English justices of the peace?

3. Who chooses them? Who can remove them and for what reasons?

4. From what class of society are justices of the peace ordinarily recruited?

5. Do members of the upper classes willingly take on the role of justice of the peace?

Aren't they discouraged from doing so by the requirement to listen to tiresome arguments?

6. Do justices of the peace receive any kind of *compensation?*

GENERAL QUESTIONS

1. I have heard that your criminal procedures yield results at least as good as ours, in the sense that fewer crimes may go unpunished here than among us. Do you think that there is absolutely no possibility of obtaining documentation of this point? For example, are there district records showing how many crimes are committed whose authors remain unknown to the clerk of the criminal court, and what is the ratio of acquittals to indictments? Without such information no attempt can be made to reform our criminal laws.

2. How are court costs paid in criminal cases?

If the accused calls witnesses, is he required to pay them?

When the prosecutor's office calls witnesses, who pays?

When the victim of a crime sues for damages, is he required to pay court costs?

Are the costs of criminal justice substantial?

10 October 1831. Mr. Riker, recorder of New York,[212] told me the following: "In the state of Pennsylvania, it is a matter of principle that a person found guilty of a crime pays court costs. In my opinion, this is a salutary principle, but we have not adopted it. Here it is axiomatic that a person who pays with his body owes nothing more to justice."

In Connecticut there is no "state's attorney" as such, but in each county there is an officer who performs the same functions.

212. Richard Riker (1773–1842) was the New York City recorder from 1815 to 1838. He was appointed by the governor and, next to the mayor, had the most responsibility for civil matters in the city. Riker had given Tocqueville and Beaumont a general description of the crimes committed in 1830 and had shown them the difficulty of judging the success rate of prison reform programs.

Mr. Coxe, a Philadelphia judge, told me this today: "I am very much in favor of a reduction of penalties. I believe, and have observed in my practice as a judge, that milder but more certain penalties are a stronger deterrent to crime than penalties that are harsh but for that very reason less likely to be applied."

"On the other hand, I am positively opposed to total abolition of the death penalty. I believe that it is essential to dissuade criminals from going beyond certain limits, such as combining murder with robbery, as they would otherwise inevitably be tempted to do by fear of arrest."

"I therefore believe that the death penalty should be maintained but that it should be used only in extreme cases. I have always found that *executions* had a bad effect on the public."

"In all my years, I know of only four executions (for state crimes) in Philadelphia. Jurors are generally quite reluctant to return a verdict condemning a man to death. They opt for the second degree."

Note: In the general laws of Pennsylvania, there is no middle ground (for first offenders) between death and a prison term of only twelve years. In my view this is an unsatisfactory state of affairs. The penalty for repeat offenders is life imprisonment.

Mr. Barclay, a Philadelphia lawyer and secretary of the Prison Society,[213] told me this today:

"Everyone in Pennsylvania has the right to a trial by jury. Certain minor crimes are tried in what we call the mayor's court, but sentences handed down by this court can always be appealed to the court of sessions. The mayor's court was established to deal with delinquents, so that they would not have to remain in prison between sessions of the regular court."

Q.: What is the difference between the court of oyer and terminer and the court of quarterly sessions?

A.: The two are independent criminal courts on the same level. The court of oyer and terminer hears the most serious cases.

He added: "The grand jury hears only witnesses for the prosecution."

Q.: In a trial by petit jury, are witnesses paid?

A.: Prosecution witnesses are paid but not defense witnesses.

Q.: Is it true that if a witness for the prosecution cannot post bond to guarantee his appearance in court, he may be imprisoned?

A.: Yes. In my practice I saw a deplorable example of this.

A young Irishwoman was murdered at a dance in Philadelphia. Two friends who had witnessed the crime were arrested because they could not post bond. The court session was just ending when the crime was committed. It was three

---

213. James J. Barclay (1794–1885) was a member of the Philadelphia Society for Alleviating the Miseries of Public Prisons, known as the Philadelphia Prison Society. He later became president of the society, a post he held for nearly fifty years.

months before a hearing could be held, and at that point the case was postponed. All in all, these two young women were held in jail for six months even though they were accused of no crime.

Mr. Coxe, who served for a long time as attorney general, told me that although in America the prosecutor's office is less imposing than in France, in one respect it wielded immense power: it could decide not to pursue a case even after a grand jury indictment had been handed down. This, Mr. Coxe observed, was a much greater power than the power to grant a pardon.

The prosecutor's office always has the last word in America. Note that this is a bad thing.

Mr. Williamson.[214] Baltimore, 3 November 1831.

Judges may be removed only for "ill behavior," which means that in order to be removed, the judge must himself be judged. Criminal trials of this sort take the following form: A person wishing to file a complaint about a judge petitions the legislature. The petition is referred to a committee, and if, upon receiving the report of this committee, the legislature believes that there are grounds to prosecute, it votes to impeach and appoints a committee of prosecutors to try the case before the senate.

No specific offenses are indicated in the law. The complex provisions regarding the powers of judges are among the most curious features of American constitutions.

The prosecutor's office has the power to prosecute any kind of offense (in Maryland) without requiring any prompt from others. In fact, however, it prosecutes only serious crimes in this way. Furthermore, the prosecutor's office does not play as large a role in the investigation as in France. When a crime is committed, a complaint is filed with the justice of the peace, who on his own issues warrants and interrogates witnesses. A summary record is sent to the clerk of the court of sessions. Only then does the role of the prosecutor's office begin. On the basis of the record submitted to him, the prosecutor draws up an indictment and presents it to the grand jury. He also summons witnesses for the prosecution to appear before the grand jury.

If the grand jury returns a "bill of ignoramus," he orders the release of the accused. If the grand jury returns a "true bill," the prosecutor arranges for trial before the court of assize, subpoenas witnesses for the prosecution, and argues the case before a jury.

The presiding judge exerts a tremendous influence on the jury. He often abuses this power, however. In Maryland as in France one sees that men accustomed to judging ultimately cease to believe in the innocence of the accused and make it their business to ensure that the jury returns a verdict of guilty.

In theory, however, the judge is supposed to be impartial, restricting him-

214. This individual has not been identified.

self to the establishment of points of law while refraining from any attempt to influence the jury as to the facts. What often happens, however, is that the judge *pleads* the case against the accused.

In Maryland, when the grand jury returns a bill of ignoramus, its decision is final. Yet a kind of infallibility is granted to both grand and petit juries.

When a petit jury acquits, the invariable principle is that there is no appeal.

When a petit jury convicts, its decision may be overturned in two ways. The judge can overrule the verdict immediately if he is completely convinced that the accused is innocent or that the jury violated the law. If he does not overturn the verdict, the defendant may seek a writ of error. This is an appeal to a higher court (on this point there is more to be said).

In Maryland the governor may pardon prior to judgment.

Commitment is the act by which a judge orders that a person be imprisoned.

More than one indictment may be brought against an individual. If a person commits six small robberies, for instance, he may be sentenced to twenty years in prison.

SOME QUESTIONS ON THE JUDICIAL ORDER IN THE UNITED STATES OF AMERICA AND ESPECIALLY ON THE JURY IN CIVIL CASES

There exists a central judicial power, which resides, I believe, in the Supreme Court of the United States. What exactly are the prerogatives of the Supreme Court? I believe that it has nothing in common with our Cour de Cassation.[215] It cannot censure the courts of the several states, which issue *definitive judgments* of their own. It is concerned only with exceptional cases, such as lawsuits between citizens of two different states. It is essential, however, to clarify my understanding of the extent of its prerogatives.

Then the judicial organizations of each state must be examined, or at any rate the most important states, as well as those that may differ in significant respects from the systems of the most important states.

Is there an institution in the United States that corresponds in either name or fact to the justices of the peace of either England or France? Are there judicial officers whose mission is, like that of the justices of the peace, conciliatory?

Is there more than one degree of jurisdiction? Do two or more degrees of jurisdiction exist regularly or only exceptionally?

Is there in any of the states a judicial authority analogous to our Cour de Cassation, that is, a court that takes cognizance not of the facts of a case but only of violations or incorrect applications of the law? If this authority exists, are appeals to it filed by the parties and in their interest, and, if so, is judg-

215. The Court of Cassation is the highest court in France. Rather than ruling on disputes, the court judges whether lower courts have applied the law correctly in their decisions.

ment stayed while the appeal is pending? Or, alternatively, are appeals formulated purely in the interest of the law?

Extent of jury power.
Trial by jury exists only in certain kinds of cases, but what are the rules that determine the competence of the jury?

Is the jury's competence one of principle or exception? In other words, does it extend to all cases not declared exempt by some special law, or is it limited to cases in which jurisdiction is assigned by a special law?

Competence of the jury.
What judicial authority decides the competence of the jury? Is it the court in which the jury exercises its functions, or is it some independent judicial authority whose sole or principal prerogative is to decide the competence of juries?

Is there not some judicial authority with full jurisdiction, before which all cases must be tried unless it explicitly relinquishes competence in certain exceptional cases? Or else is the system like that in France, where the plaintiff decides at his own risk which judicial authority should hear his case?

Are juries totally excluded from deciding points of law? Can they not (as in England, at least in criminal cases) render a "general verdict," that is, a verdict covering both facts and law? Or may judges not grant them this power in certain cases?

As for the facts, is it always up to the jury to judge them in cases normally assigned to trial by jury?

There are judicial facts whose evaluation is simple and easy, and there are others whose evaluation is complex and arduous.

In general, purely *material* facts belong to the first category: facts of possession, violence, or the transfer of a sum of money or item of personal property.

Intellectual facts are generally less easy to evaluate. Generally these pertain to the characterization of stipulated material facts or the interpretation of clauses in a contract: for instance, is a fact of possession a matter of positive law or merely of tolerance? Was the transfer of a sum of money or item of personal property a loan or a gift? There may be debate as to the extent and effect of clauses in a contract of sale or a deed of gift.

If the jury is to judge all facts without exception (in cases it is assigned to hear), how can it be expected to evaluate questions that require knowledge and legal training it does not possess? Indeed, most *intellectual* judicial facts are so intimately intertwined with questions of law that it would seem impossible to separate them.

Looking at the matter from another angle, however, if the jury is excluded from judging certain facts, especially those complicated by points *of law,* then what rules govern such exclusion?

Are there general principles in this regard, or specific categories of issues that the jury may not judge?

Or, by contrast, is there some judicial authority invested with discretionary power, depending on the circumstances of each case, to deny juries the right to judge certain issues that might appear to be beyond their grasp?

This last hypothesis seems quite implausible: Such discretionary power would indeed be far simpler and easier to apply than general principles, but it would leave juries subject to the power of judges, who could arrogate the power of the jury to themselves. It is not credible that American institutions would permit such a significant delegation of the people's rights to any permanent authority whatsoever.

What I have set forth above in broad outline is a problem that remains to be resolved.

Here is another.

Deciding which of the parties has the better case is not the whole problem; it remains to decide how the judgment is to be carried out.

Execution of judgments.

Is the mode of execution decided by the judge?

In that case, it is easy to imagine that things will proceed smoothly, but once again the judge would perhaps wield more power than the spirit of American institutions would ordinarily allow.

The English, who were apparently afraid of bestowing too much power on judges in this way but who did not hide the fact that in many cases it might be beyond the ability of the jury to decide how the judgment ought to be carried out, sliced the Gordian knot rather than attempt to untie it.

According to one work on the administration of justice in England (by Mr. Cottu), all contractual cases subject to trial by jury are to be resolved by the payment of damages, that is, a fixed indemnity.[216]

This is a high price to pay for the benefits of extending the competence of the jury, because it legitimates the violation of virtually any contract.

In fact, some performances are purely personal and can never be ordered by a court. For example, if a playwright such as Scribe promises a vaudeville to the director of the Gymnase and refuses to write it, he can only be sentenced to pay damages.[217] That is and always has been the practice. *Nemo potest precise cogi ad factum,*[218] as Roman law puts it.

But many other promised performances can be materially compelled by the

216. Tocqueville is referring to *De l'administration de la justice criminelle en Angleterre et de l'esprit du gouvernement anglais* (1820), by Charles Cottu (1778–1849). A French counselor in a Paris court, Cottu wrote his work after conducting an inquiry into England's system of law during a tour of that country.

217. After Augustin Eugène Scribe (1791–1861) first found success as a playwright in 1815, he entered into a contract with the proprietor of the Gymnase Theatre to write plays for that venue. Scribe wrote approximately 150 scripts for the Gymnase by the time Tocqueville was writing, and he also wrote pieces for the Comédie-Française and the Opéra comique.

218. "No one can be forced to act."

courts, which do so compel them every day. For instance, if a person promises to sell me his country house and then refuses to hand over the deed, a court may order him to do so, and if he does not, the court order itself may stand as an equivalent for the deed. If my neighbor promises to deliver to my property water from a source lying within property he has inherited, a court may compel him to carry out the necessary construction or else authorize me to have the work done at his expense.

Well, in England it seems that in both cases I could expect to obtain nothing more than an indemnity compensating me for the damage I might be deemed to have suffered as a result of the failure to perform as promised.

It has always seemed to me that this was tantamount to a partial denial of justice, because I might have a heavy stake in seeing that the contract was materially executed. The monetary award I am obliged to accept cannot compensate me for all the damage I have suffered. In short, if a contracting party can be compelled to perform materially, and I request that he be ordered to do so and have an interest in seeing to it that he does, to deny my request is to do me an injustice. And that is certainly a fundamental flaw in the English judicial system.

I therefore find it difficult to believe that this resolution of all contract lawsuits by payment of damages is as general and absolute as the author claims. But it is a matter of very great interest to know what is practiced in the United States in this regard.

Appeal of jury verdict:

Is the decision of the jury subject to appeal? Is this appeal not limited to points of law in cases where the jury is permitted to decide these?

Extent of testimonial power:

Is testimonial evidence admitted to prove all facts? Are the exclusions as extensive and rigorous as in France?

If testimonial evidence is excluded in some cases, is it up to the judge to decide when? Or is it up to the jury in cases subject to jury trial?

In cases where testimonial evidence is admitted, it is far preferable that the arbiters of fact, whether judge or jury, decide (as in France) in accordance with their own conviction and without the impediment of legal proof. One should find out, however, whether there might not be some exceptions to this principle, especially in cases where judges evaluate the facts.

These questions involve the country's state of civilization and morality. The exclusion of testimonial evidence reveals a suspicion that the good faith of individuals called as witnesses cannot be relied upon. The establishment of a system of legal proofs reveals suspicions as to the consciousness or enlightenment of those who serve as judges and jurors.

Composition of the jury:

How are juries composed, and according to what rules? Are there property qualifications or other guarantees of ability? Do men of high social position feel the same reluctance to perform these duties as their counterparts in France, and do they seek to avoid serving by various subterfuges?

Investigation of these points may shed light on the prerogatives of the jury and account for its ability to perform or not to perform certain of its duties.

Are jurors chosen by lot or chosen as in England by the sheriff?

What is the general basis for the personnel organization of the magistracy?

Judges are appointed by the executive, I believe, but are they on a list of candidates chosen by the people?

Are judges appointed for life or for a limited period of time, and if the latter, for how long?

Tocqueville's Narration of Two Excursions

These two texts were published posthumously by Beaumont in his 1861 edition of his friend's writings. Tocqueville's narration of their trip to Frenchman's Island on Oneida Lake is an extension of a long letter he had written to his sister-in-law Émilie on July 25, 1831. Tocqueville predicted that the mystery of the island would keep Émilie daydreaming for a week after reading his letter.

Tocqueville wrote his longer narrative of their fortnight in the wilderness, an account of their trip to Saginaw, while taking a steamboat excursion to Sault Sainte Marie, Mackinac Island, and Green Bay, Wisconsin.

Tocqueville had intended to publish this second text as an appendix to volume 2 of *Democracy in America* in 1840, but he refrained from doing so out of regard for Beaumont. Tocqueville's beautiful narration might have competed with Beaumont's description of the same landscape in *Marie*.

One discovers in these two texts that the austere classicism of much of *Democracy in America* was far from Tocqueville's only stylistic register. We see instead the full impact of Romanticism on the young Tocqueville, who was capable of a lush, descriptive lyricism reminiscent of Chateaubriand.

The Journey to Oneida Lake

At sunrise on July 8, 1831, we left the small village known as Fort Brewerton and set out toward the northeast.[1] About a mile and a half from our host's home, we found the trail leading into the forest and hastened down it. The heat was becoming bothersome; an agitated night had given way to a muggy morning. Soon we found ourselves shielded from the sun's rays in the midst of one of those profound forests of the New World, whose somber and savage majesty grips the imagination and fills the soul with a sort of religious terror. How to describe such a spectacle? Across a swampy terrain, where a thousand streams not yet imprisoned by the hand of man run free as far as the eye can see, nature with incredible profusion has scattered seeds of nearly all the plants that creep over the earth or rise above it. Above our heads stretched a vast dome of green. Beneath this thick canopy, in the moist depths of the woods, an immense confusion beckoned the eye from afar, a sort of chaos. Trees of all ages, foliage of all colors, grasses, fruits, flowers of a thousand species mingled—all entwined in a single place. There, generations of trees had succeeded one another without interruption down through the centuries, and the earth was littered with their debris. Some seemed to have been felled only yesterday. Others, already half buried in the earth, were reduced to but a hollow and spindly surface, while still others had turned to dust that served as compost for the last of their offshoots. Interspersed among them, a myriad of diverse plants vied for the light. They slithered among the motionless cadavers, crept across them, made their way under decaying bark, and displaced or dispersed their powdery remains. It was as if life and death vied for supremacy. Here and there we encountered an enormous tree that the wind had uprooted, but the forest is so dense that often, despite the weight of these fallen giants, they cannot clear a path for themselves all the way to the ground. Their desiccated branches continue to sway in the breeze.

In the midst of this solitude, a solemn silence prevailed. Few if any animate creatures could be seen, man was nowhere to be found, yet this was no wilderness. On the contrary, nature displayed a vigor unmatched anywhere else on earth. Everything was alive, and the smell of vegetation seemed to pervade the

---

1. The British built Fort Brewerton in 1759 on the Oneida River at the west end of Oneida Lake. The village that grew up around the fort is about fifteen miles north of Syracuse, New York.

air. A sound from within seemed to reveal the work of creation, and one could almost see the sap of life circulating through still-open channels. For several hours we made our way through this imposing solitude, illuminated by an uncertain daylight, without hearing any sound other than that our horses made as they trampled the accumulated leaves of several winters and cut a difficult path for themselves through the withered branches. We maintained our silence. Our souls were filled with the grandeur and novelty of the spectacle. At length we heard the first axe blows heralding from afar the presence of a European. Felled trees, scorched and blackened trunks, and a few plants useful to humans sown amidst a jumbled mass of debris led us to the pioneer's dwelling. In the center of the rather tight circle that iron and fire had drawn around it stood the crude home of civilization's precursor, like an oasis in the middle of a desert. After conversing for a moment with the inhabitant of this place, we resumed our course, and a half hour later we reached a fisherman's hut at the edge of the very lake we had come to visit.

Oneida Lake sits amid low hills at the center of still-virgin forests. A thick girdle of foliage surrounds it completely, and its waters lap the roots of trees whose reflections gleam in its tranquil, transparent surface. A lonely fisherman's cabin is the sole structure to grace its shores. There was not a sail in sight, nor could so much as a trace of smoke be seen above the woods, for although Europeans have yet to take full possession of the lake's edge, they have come close enough to exile the numerous and warlike tribe that gave these waters their name. A mile from the shore on which we stood lay two islands, oval in shape and equal in length. These were covered by forest so thick that it entirely hid the earth beneath. It seemed almost as if two thickets of wood floated peacefully on the surface of the lake. No road passes near the spot. No great industrial plant or picturesque site exists in the vicinity. Yet it was not by chance that we came to this lonely lake. On the contrary, it was the purpose and destination of our journey.

Many years ago, I had chanced upon a book entitled *Voyage au lac Onéida*.[2] The author told the story of a young Frenchman and his wife, who had been driven from the country by the violent upheavals of our first revolution and had come to the lake seeking asylum on one of its islands. There, cut off from the entire world, far from the tempests of Europe, and cast out by the society into which they had been born, these two unfortunate souls lived for each other and consoled each other in their woe. This book made a deep and durable impression on my soul. Whether this effect on me was due to the talent of the author, the authentic charm of the events recounted, or the influence of the age, I cannot say. But I could not erase from my mind the memory of those two French people at Oneida Lake. How often I envied the tranquil pleasures of their solitude. Domestic happiness, the charms of marriage, and love itself mingled in my mind with the image of the lonely isle, on which my imagination had created a

2. See Tocqueville to his sister-in-law Émilie, July 25, 1831 (part 1, pp. 85–88).

South Bay village seen from Frenchman's Island on Oneida Lake, 8 July 1831. (GB2)

new Eden. When I recounted this story to my traveling companion, he too was deeply moved by it. We spoke of it often, and inevitably we ended our conversations, whether in laughter or sadness, with the words, "There is no happiness in the world except on the shores of Oneida Lake." When unforeseen events impelled the two of us to go to America, this memory took hold of us with even greater insistence than before. We promised ourselves that we would visit those two French people if they were still alive or at least explore the place where they had dwelled. Behold the strange power of the imagination over the mind of man! To us these wild places, this still and silent lake, these verdant islands did not seem new. On the contrary, we felt that we had returned to a place where we had spent a part of our youth.

We entered the fisherman's hut straightaway. The man of the house was off in the woods somewhere. An elderly woman was the sole occupant. She hobbled to the door to greet us. "What is the name of the verdant island in the lake a mile from this spot?" we asked. "It is called Frenchman's Island." "Do you know why it was given that name?" "I was told that it has that name because a Frenchman built his house there many years ago." "Was he alone?" "No, he came with his young bride." "Do they still live there?" "Twenty-one years ago, when I first settled here, the French couple was no longer living on the island. I remember being curious enough to row out to visit it. It was still a beautiful place back then, even if it looks wild from here. The central part of the island was carefully cultivated. The French couple had set their house in the middle of an orchard, so that it was surrounded by fruit and flowers. A huge grapevine climbed the walls and wound around the house, which was already falling down because no one lived there anymore." "What had become of the French couple?" "The woman died, the man left the island, and nobody knows what became of him." "May we borrow the boat tied up outside to go out to the island?" "Of course, but it's a long way to row and hard work if you aren't used to it, and in any case what's so interesting about a place that the forest has reclaimed?" We did not answer but hastened to push the skiff into the water. "I see what you're up to," the woman said. "You want to buy the island. The soil is good, and land in this county is still cheap." We told her that we were merely travelers. "Well, then," she went on, "you're probably relatives of the Frenchman, and he sent you here to look over your inheritance." "That's even farther from the truth," we replied. "We don't even know his name." The old woman shook her head incredulously while we worked the oars and began to move rapidly toward Frenchman's Island. Throughout the brief crossing we maintained total silence, as our hearts were filled with emotions both sweet and painful. As we drew near, it became more difficult to understand how this island could ever have been inhabited, for the difficulties of access were formidable. We came close to thinking that we had been taken in by a made-up tale. At last we managed to reach the shore by slipping beneath the immense branches that hung out over the lake, and then we began to move inland. We first passed through a ring of ancient trees that seemed to defend the approaches to the place. Beyond this leafy rampart a very different sight greeted us: the center of the island was entirely taken up by a span of sparse saplings and then a cluster of tall young trees. In the forests we had traveled through that morning, we had seen frequent signs of man's struggle with nature, where by dint of great effort he had managed to tame the savage energy of the natural world and bend it to his laws. Here, however, we saw that the forest had reasserted its dominion, sallying forth to conquer the empty space, defying man and rapidly erasing the fleeting traces of his victory. It was easy to see that a diligent hand had once cleared the place at the center of the island now occupied by the saplings I mentioned a moment ago. Here, no fallen trunks stretched across a forest floor littered with debris. On the contrary, everything felt young. Nearby trees had clearly sprouted offshoots in the midst of abandoned fields. Grass had grown on land that had once supported the exile's harvest. Brambles and parasitic plants had reclaimed possession of their old domain. Here and there one could barely make out a trace of a fence or field. For an hour we searched in vain amid the trees and brush that filled the former clearing for vestiges of the abandoned home. The Arcadian splendor that the fisherman's wife had earlier described, the gardens and flowers and fruits, the products of civilization that tender ingenuity had introduced into the heart of the wilderness—all had vanished along with the couple who had lived here. We were about to give up our search when we spotted an apple tree half dead from old age. This discovery put us on the right track. Nearby, a plant that we took at first for a runner climbed the highest trees, twining around their soaring trunks and draping itself over their branches like a garland of green. On closer examination this turned out to be a grapevine. Thus we were certain that we were at the precise spot that our two unfortunate compatriots had chosen forty years earlier as their final refuge. Then, digging down through the thick bed of leaves that covered the ground, we found a few items all but crumbled to dust, which in no time at all will have ceased to exist. As for the remains of the woman who had not been afraid to exchange the pleasures of civilized life for a grave on a deserted island in the New World, we were unable to discover the slightest trace. Had the exile left this precious treasure in his wilderness? Or had he carried it with him to the place where he himself ended his days? No one can say.

Perhaps those who read these lines will be unable to conceive of the feelings they describe and will find them exaggerated or strange. I must nevertheless add that it was with hearts filled with emotion, stirred by hopes and fears, and animated by a sort of religious feeling that we conducted our minute search for traces of this man and this woman, whose names and families we knew not, and much of whose history remained a mystery to us. All that recommended them to us was that on this very spot they had felt the pains and joys that move the hearts of all mankind, because it is in the heart of man that they find their source. Is there a fate more wretched than the one that this man experienced!

Here was a man so unfortunate as to have been bruised by society. His fellow men rejected him, banished him, forced him to cut off all contact with them and flee into the wilderness. Only one other person accompanied him, followed him into solitude, soothed his soul's wounds, and made up for the lost pleasures of society by sharing with him the deepest of human emotions. Thus was he reconciled to his fate; he forgot revolutions, parties, cities, family, rank, and fortune. At least he breathed. Then his wife died. Death came for her but spared him. The wretch! What was to become of him? Would he remain alone in the wilderness? Would he return to a new society, which had long since forgotten him? No longer fit for either solitude or society, he could live neither with men nor without them. He was neither a savage nor a civilized man. He was nothing but a fallen vestige of what once was, like those trees in the forests of America that the wind has had the power to uproot but not to bring down. Like them he continued to stand though he had ceased to live.

After scouring the island in every direction, inspecting every scrap we could find, and harkening to the glacial silence that now reigns over its dusky woods, we headed back for the mainland.

It was not without a pang of regret that I watched that vast green rampart recede into the distance, a rampart that had for so many years defended the two exiles against the European's lead and the savage's arrow yet been unable to protect their humble cottage from death's unseen hand.

Two Weeks in the Wilderness

Written on the steamboat *Superior*.
Begun August 1, 1831.

One of the things that piqued our curiosity most acutely in coming to America was the idea of exploring the outer limits of European civilization and even, if time allowed, visiting some of the Indian tribes that had fled into the vast open spaces of the continent rather than submit to what the whites called the pleasures of life in society. It is more difficult than many people think, however, to find the wilderness today. We left New York City and headed northwest, yet the closer we came to our destination, the further ahead it seemed to flee. We visited places celebrated in the history of the Indians, we explored valleys they had named, we crossed rivers that still bore the names of Indian tribes, yet everywhere the hut of the savage had given way to the house of the civilized man. The woods had fallen, and solitude had come to life.

Yet it seemed that we were following in the footsteps of the native peoples. Ten years ago they were here, we were told; five years ago they were there; two years ago, there. "On the spot where the most beautiful church in the village now stands," one man told us, "I cut down the first of the forest's trees." "Here," another man told us, "the Iroquois held the Great Council of the Confederation." "And what has become of the Indians?" I asked. "The Indians?" our host went on. "I'm not sure where they went, somewhere out beyond the Great Lakes. They're a dying race. They're not made for civilization. It kills them."

Man gets used to everything—to death on battlefields, to dying in hospitals, to killing and suffering. He accommodates himself to every spectacle: an ancient people, the first and legitimate ruler of the American continent, is melting away like snow on a sunny day and vanishing from the face of the earth, before our very eyes. In the very places from which the natives are disappearing, another race is even more rapidly expanding its presence. This other race fells the forests; the swamps are drained, and lakes as broad as seas and vast rivers are as nothing in the face of its triumphal march. Year after year, wasteland turns into villages and villages into cities. The American, who witnesses such marvels daily, sees nothing astonishing in them. The incredible destruction and the still more amazing expansion strike him as nothing out of the ordinary. He is as used to such things as he is to the immutable order of nature.

And so it was that, still in search of savages and wilderness, we traveled the miles that separate New York City from Buffalo.

The first thing we saw was a large group of Indians who had come to Buffalo looking for money owed them in exchange for land surrendered to the United States.

I do not think I have ever been as disappointed as I was at the sight of those Indians. Memories of the works of M. de Chat[eaubriand] and Cooper filled my mind, and I expected to see in these native Americans savages on whom nature had left traces of the proud virtues that the spirit of liberty fosters. I expected to find men with bodies made robust by hunting and warfare and no less impressive for their nakedness. By comparing this portrait with the one I am about to give, the reader will be able to judge my astonishment. The Indians we saw that evening were small in stature. Their limbs, so far as one could judge beneath their clothing, were spindly and not well muscled. Their skin, rather than being of coppery complexion, as is widely believed, was dark bronze, so that at first sight they seemed not very different from mulattoes. Their shiny black hair hung quite stiffly about their necks and shoulders. Their mouths were in general inordinately large, and the expressions on their faces were base and nasty. Their features spoke of that deep depravity that can come only from long abuse of the boons of civilization. These people resembled the dregs of the populace of a large European city. Yet they were still savages. Along with the vices they had taken from us were signs of something barbarous and uncivilized, which made them a hundred times more repulsive. These Indians bore no arms. They wore European clothing but did not use it as we do. Clearly not yet accustomed to these garments, they seemed imprisoned in their folds. In addition to European trinkets, they decorated themselves with items of barbaric luxury: feathers, enormous earrings, and necklaces of shells. Their movements were abrupt and chaotic, their voices shrill and discordant, their gazes anxious and wild. At first sight, it was tempting to see them as animals of the forests: education had given them the appearance of men, yet they remained beasts. Yet these feeble, depraved creatures belonged to one of the most celebrated tribes of colonial America. It is a pity to say it, but what we beheld before us was what remained of the celebrated Iroquois Confederation, tribes that had been as famous for their virile wisdom as for their courage and who for many years had held the balance of power between the two greatest nations of Europe.

It would be a mistake, however, to judge the Indian race by this unrepresentative sample, this stray offshoot of a tree of the forest that had somehow taken root in the muck of our towns. But this was the mistake we made ourselves, as we did not realize until later in our journey.

That night we left the town, and shortly beyond the outermost houses we caught sight of an Indian lying beside the road. It was a young man, and as he lay there motionless we thought he was dead. But a few muffled moans escaped from his throat, letting us know that he was still alive and struggling against a dangerous intoxication of the sort that comes from drinking brandy. The sun had already gone down, and the ground was becoming increasingly damp. There was every likelihood that this poor wretch would breathe his last breath on this spot unless help arrived. It was the hour when Indians were leaving Buffalo to return to their village. From time to time a group of them passed close to where we stood. They would approach their compatriot's body, brusquely turn it over to see who it was, and then proceed on their way without so much as deigning to respond to our entreaties. Most of these men were themselves drunk. At last, a young Indian woman arrived, and at first she seemed to take a certain interest in the dying man. I thought she might have been his wife or sister. She studied him attentively, called him by name, placed her hand over his heart, and, having assured herself that he was still alive, tried to rouse him from his slumber. But when her efforts proved unavailing, we watched as she flew into a rage against the inanimate body lying at her feet. She slapped the man's face, twisted it in her hands, and stomped on it. In venting her ferocious rage she uttered a series of inarticulate and savage cries, which I can still hear reverberating in my ears as I write these lines. At length we felt obliged to intervene and peremptorily ordered her away. She obeyed, but as she strode off we heard her burst out in a barbarous peal of laughter.

Returning to town, we spoke to several people about the young Indian. We explained that he was in imminent danger. We even offered to pay the expense of an inn. All our efforts proved fruitless. We could not persuade anyone to lift a finger. Some told us that "these people always drink too much and often stumble on their way home. Accidents like that don't kill them." Others acknowledged that the Indian would very likely die, but on their lips it was possible to read a thought they hesitated to express out loud: "What is the life of an Indian worth?" This was the basis of the general sentiment. In the midst of this most orderly, most prudish, most pedantically moralistic and virtuous society, one encountered an almost impenetrable insensitivity, a sort of cold and implacable egoism, when it came to native Americans. The inhabitants of the United States do not hunt Indians down like animals, as the Spanish did in Mexico. But here as elsewhere it is the same pitiless sentiment that drives the European race.

How many times in the course of our travels did we encounter respectable citizens who, seated quietly of an evening next to the fireplace, told us "that the number of Indians is decreasing daily. But the reason isn't that we are wont to go to war with them. The brandy we sell them at a bargain price claims more of them every year than our weapons ever could. This world belongs to us," they added. "God deprived the original habitants of what it takes to become civilized and thereby condemned them to certain destruction. The true owners of the continent are those who know how to take advantage of its riches."

Pleased with this argument, the American goes off to church, where he listens to a minister of the Gospel tell him that all men are brothers and that the Almighty who shaped each of them from the same mold made it the duty of all to help one another.

On July 19 at ten in the morning, we boarded the steamship *Ohio,* which set a course for Detroit. A stiff breeze blew from the northwest and whipped up the waters so that Lake Erie looked like the Atlantic Ocean. To our right the horizon stretched without limit. On the left we hugged the southern coast of the lake, often within shouting distance of the shore. The coastline was perfectly flat, quite different from any lakeshore I had visited in Europe. Nor did it resemble a seacoast. It was shaded by immense forests, which formed a thick and virtually continuous girdle around the lake. Now and then, however, the aspect of the countryside changed abruptly. We would pass a stretch of wood, and suddenly an elegant steeple would loom ahead, flanked by well-kept houses of dazzling white and some shops. A short distance further on, the primeval and apparently impenetrable forest would reassert its dominion and once again display its foliage in the reflecting surface of the water.

Anyone who has traveled around the United States will find in this description a striking emblem of American society. Everything in America is startling and unforeseen. Everywhere the utmost extreme of civilization finds itself virtually face-to-face with untouched nature. In France this is unimaginable. I came with my own traveler's illusions—what class of men is entirely without illusions?—and had imagined something quite different. I had noticed that in Europe, the location of a province or city, whether remote or not, its wealth or poverty, and its size, large or small, exerted a tremendous influence on the ideas, mores, and entire civilization of its inhabitants and often made a difference of several centuries between different parts of the same country.

I imagined that it was the same in the New World only all the more so, and that a country incompletely and sparsely populated like America ought to exhibit all conditions of life and exemplify the society of all ages. In my view, therefore, America was the only country in which it should be possible to study all the changes in man induced by his social state, the only country in which it would ever be possible to discern the vast chain of being descending link by link from the most opulent urban patrician to the savage of the wilderness. There, in short, I expected to find the entire history of humanity compressed within a few degrees of longitude.

Nothing in this portrait is accurate. Of all the countries in the world, America is the least apt to illustrate what I had come to find. In America, even more than in Europe, there is but a single society. It may be rich or poor, humble or brilliant, commercial or agricultural, yet everywhere it is composed of the same elements. It has been subjected to the leveling blade of an egalitarian civilization. The man whom you left in the streets of New York is likely to turn up again in the depths of an almost impenetrable wilderness: the same clothes, the same mind, the same language, the same habits, the same pleasures. There is nothing rustic about him, nothing naïve, nothing that smacks of the wilderness, nothing even that resembles one of our villages. The reason for this singular state of affairs is easy to understand. Those parts of the territory that were settled earliest and most completely achieved a high degree of civilization; education was laid on in abundance; and the egalitarian spirit, the republican spirit, lent a remarkably uniform color to life's inner habits. Now, these are the same people who set out each year to populate the wilderness. In Europe, each man lives and dies on the land where he was born, but nowhere in America does one encounter the representatives of a race that multiplied in solitude, ignored by the world and left to its own devices for a lengthy period. The people who live in isolated places arrived in them only yesterday. They came with their mores, ideas, habits, and civilized needs. They sacrifice to the savage life only that which the imperious nature of things demands. The most bizarre contrasts result from this. You pass without transition from wilderness to city street, from the most savage scenes to the most felicitous tableaux of civilized life. If night doesn't take you by surprise and compel you to make camp under a tree in open country, you are more than likely to come upon a village in which you can find anything you want, including the latest French fashions and caricatures by boulevard artists in Paris. The merchant in Buffalo or Detroit is as well stocked as the one in New York. The factories of Lyons labor for the former as well as the latter. You leave great highways for barely blazed trails. At length you come upon a cabin made of split logs, with but a small window for daylight, and you think that you've finally stumbled upon the home of an American peasant. Wrong. You enter what had seemed to be a shelter for all of life's miseries, but the owner of the place wears the same clothes you do, speaks the language of the town, and has piled his rough-hewn table with heaps of books and newspapers. He hastens to sit down with you so that he can find out what exactly is going on in old Europe and ask what has struck you most about his country. He will draw you a map for an invasion of Poland and tell you in the gravest of tones what needs to be done to ensure the prosperity of France. He could almost be a wealthy landowner spending a few nights in a hunting lodge. And indeed, the log cabin is but a temporary shelter for the American, a concession to circumstantial necessity. When all the surrounding fields are producing and the new owner has the leisure to enjoy life's pleasures, he will replace the log cabin with a more spacious house, better suited to his way of life, and this will serve as home to his many children, who will one day set out in their turn to build homes for themselves in the wilderness.

But to get back to our journey, we sailed within sight of the coast of Pennsylvania and later Ohio, making headway with difficulty. We stopped briefly at Presqu'Île, today called Erie. This will eventually become the terminus of a canal stretching all the way to Pittsburgh. This project, for which the financing is now assured and which I am told will be relatively easy to build, will connect the Mississippi to the Northern River, and the wealth of Europe will flow freely across the five hundred leagues of land that separate the Gulf of Mexico from the Atlantic Ocean.

That night, the weather turned favorable, and we proceeded rapidly toward Detroit across the middle of the lake. The next morning we were in sight of the small island known as Middle Sister, near which Commodore Perry won a celebrated naval victory over the English in 1814 [1813].

A short while later, the flat Canadian coast seemed to hasten toward us, while ahead the Detroit River beckoned and the houses of Fort Malden loomed in the distance. This was originally a French settlement and still bears many traces of its origins. In shape and location its houses resemble those of our peasants. In the center of the hamlet stands a Catholic spire topped by a cock. The village resembles any village that one might see in the countryside around Caen or Evreux. As we contemplated—not without emotion—this image of France, our attention was distracted by an unusual sight: on the riverbank to our right, a Scottish soldier stood guard in dress uniform. He wore the outfit made famous on the fields of Waterloo. The feathered cap, the jacket—nothing was missing, and the sun glinted from his regalia and weapons. To our left, as if to provide us with a standard of comparison, two quite naked Indians, their bodies daubed with color and rings in their noses, departed from the opposite bank. They crossed in a small skiff of bark with a blanket for a sail. In this flimsy vessel, driven by the wind and the current, they shot toward our ship like an arrow and in an instant had sailed around it. Then they set off to fish quietly at a spot not far from the English soldier, who, still glinting in the sun and standing motionless, seemed to have been planted there as a representative of Europe's impressive and heavily armed civilization.

We arrived in Detroit at three o'clock. Detroit is a small town of two or three thousand souls, which the Jesuits founded in the middle of the woods in 1710 and which is still home to a good many French families.

We had crossed the entire state of New York and traveled a hundred miles on Lake Erie and had by now reached the limits of civilization. But we had absolutely no idea where we ought to go next. Gathering information was not as easy as one might think. An American thinks nothing of hacking his way through a nearly impenetrable forest, crossing a swift river, braving a pestilential swamp, or sleeping in the damp forest if there is a chance of making a dollar: that is the whole point of the exercise. But to do such things out of curiosity confuses him utterly. Since he lives in the wilderness, moreover, the only thing he prizes is the work of man. He is quite happy to send you off to see a highway, a bridge, or a fine village. But the urge to gaze upon huge trees and commune in solitude with nature utterly surpasses his understanding.

So finding someone capable of understanding you is an incomparably difficult task. "If it's woods you want to see," our smiling hosts advised us, "just follow your noses and you'll find all the woods you could possibly want. In fact, there are some new roads and well-marked trails not far from here. As for Indians, you'll find no shortage of them right here in town. No need to travel far. The ones you see around town have at least begun to civilize themselves and don't look quite so much like savages." We soon realized that the direct approach to the truth would get us nowhere and we'd have to adopt a more roundabout method.

We therefore went to see the official in charge of selling unclaimed public land, which is still quite plentiful in the Michigan Territory. We described ourselves as people who had not yet made a firm decision to settle in the region but who might have a vague interest in finding out more about the price and location of available lots. Major Biddle,[3] as this official called himself, had no trouble grasping what we were after and immediately offered up a wealth of de-

3. John Biddle.

tails, to which we listened avidly. Pointing on the map to the Saint Joseph River, which follows a long, meandering course before emptying into Lake Michigan, he said, "This part here strikes me as the most suitable for your purposes. The land is good there, some fine villages have already gone up, and the road up that way is so well maintained that public carriages run back and forth every day." Good! we said to ourselves. Now we know which way not to go, unless we want to travel to the wilderness by postal coach. We thanked Mr. Biddle for his advice, and then, feigning indifference bordering on contempt, we asked him what part of the district had thus far drawn the fewest immigrants. "Over this way," he said, attaching no more interest to his answer than we had to our question, "up in the northwest. Recently some fine settlements have sprung up as far out as Pontiac and thereabouts, but you mustn't think of settling any farther out than that. The territory is blanketed by virtually impenetrable forest, which runs off interminably to the northwest, and out that way you'll find nothing but wild animals and Indians. The federal government is planning to build a road up that way any day now. But the work has only just begun and goes no farther than Pontiac, as I was saying. You'd best cross that district off your list." We thanked him again for his excellent advice and left his office determined to do precisely the opposite of what he had recommended. We were beside ourselves with joy finally to have learned of a place that had not yet been inundated by the flood of European civilization.

The next day, July 23, we hastened to hire two horses. Since we planned to keep them for ten days, we tried to leave a deposit with the owner, but he refused to accept it and said we could pay when we returned. He had absolutely no qualms. Michigan is surrounded on all sides by lake and wilderness. He was letting us loose into a corral whose gate he guarded. So we purchased a compass and some ammunition and set out on our way with rifles slung over our shoulders, as carefree and lighthearted as a couple of schoolboys setting out for home on a school holiday.

Indeed, if we had only wanted to see woods, our Detroit hosts were right to say that we needn't go far, because a mile from the city the highway entered the forest for good. The terrain it covers is perfectly flat and frequently swampy. New clearings appear occasionally along the route. Since these settlements all look exactly alike, regardless of whether they happen to be located in the depths of Michigan or just outside New York City, I shall try to describe them here once and for all.

From the clang of the bells that the pioneers fasten about the necks of their livestock so that they can find them in the dense forest, you know well before reaching it that a clearing lies ahead. Soon you hear the sound of an axe striking a tree, and as you draw near, signs of destruction herald the presence of man still more unmistakably. The trail is paved with cut branches, and tree trunks scorched by fire or mutilated by axes line your route. You continue on and come eventually to a patch of wood where all the trees seem to have been struck dead at one fell swoop. It is the middle of summer, yet their withered branches give the impression of winter. On closer examination it emerges that a deep cut has been made in the bark to stop the flow of sap, causing the trees to perish soon thereafter. This is usually the planter's first step. Since it is impossible to cut down all the trees on his property in the first year, he plants corn beneath their branches and then kills the trees to prevent them from cutting off the light to his crop. Passing beyond this makeshift cornfield, which marks civilization's first foothold in the wilderness, you catch sight of the owner's hut. It usually stands in the center of a patch of land more carefully cultivated than the rest of the property, even though the owner may still be waging his unequal battle with nature. In this patch only stumps remain, cluttering land that now-vanished trees once shaded. Around the lifeless stumps grows a hodgepodge of wheat, oak shoots, and plants and grasses of all kinds, a riot of vegetation on an inhospitable and still half-wild stretch of soil. In the center of this thick and varied growth stands the planter's house, or log cabin,[4] as it is known locally. Like the adjacent field, this rustic home shows signs of recent and hurried labor. The house is rarely more than thirty feet in length. It is twenty feet wide and fifteen feet high. Its walls and roof are made of rough-hewn logs packed with moss and dirt to keep out the cold and rain. As the traveler approaches, the scene comes to life. Alerted by the sound of hoofbeats, children who had been rolling on the ground suddenly get up and flee into the house, as if frightened by the sight of a man, while two large, half-wild dogs with straight ears and long muzzles come running out of the house, growling in defense of their young masters in headlong retreat.

Then the pioneer himself comes to the door of his home. He casts an appraising eye on the new arrival, signals his dogs to come back inside, and hastens to set an example for them while showing neither curiosity nor concern at our appearance.

Standing on the threshold of the log cabin, the European cannot help being astonished by the sight.

Generally, the cabin will have but a single window, sometimes covered by a muslin curtain, for even in places where necessities are commonly in short supply, luxuries can often be found. On the hearth of packed earth crackles a resinous fire, which illuminates the interior better than the light from outside. Above this rustic hearth are trophies of war or the hunt: a long rifle, a deerskin, some eagle feathers. To the right of the chimney there is often a map of the United States, which flaps and waves in the breeze that enters the cabin through chinks in the walls. Nearby, on a lone shelf of rough-hewn board, stands an odd assortment of books: a Bible, its cover and spine already worn from use by two pious generations; a prayer book; and occasionally a poem by Milton or a tragedy by Shakespeare. Along the walls are ranged a few crude chairs, the work of the owner's own hands; trunks in lieu of cabinets; farm implements;

4. The original French text has "log house."

and samples of the harvest. In the center of the room stands a rickety table, its legs still sprouting leaves, so that it seems to have grown out of the very ground on which it stands. Here the family gathers every day to take its meals. You also see a teapot of English porcelain, spoons, usually made of wood, a few chipped cups, and some newspapers.

The master of the premises is no less remarkable to look at than the place that serves him as shelter.

Etched muscles and slender limbs reveal a New Englander at a glance. This man is not a native of the solitude he now inhabits. His constitution alone makes this clear. He spent his early years in an intellectual and rational society. It was an act of will that brought him to the wilderness and to a life of labor for which he seems not particularly well suited. Yet even if his physical resources appear to fall short of what the undertaking requires, his features, deeply etched by life's worries, are dominated by an air of practical intelligence, of dispassionate and persevering energy, which strikes you immediately. His gait is slow and formal, his words are measured, and his mien is austere. Even more than habit, pride gives his face a stoic rigidity that his actions belie. To be sure, the pioneer is contemptuous of the more violent passions that rock the heart of man. He would never risk life and property on a throw of the dice or the fate of a woman, yet in search of comfort he has braved exile, solitude, and the countless miseries of life in the wild. He has slept on the bare ground and exposed himself to the fevers of the forest and the tomahawks of the Indians. One day he set to work, and he has been at it now for years and may still be at it twenty years from now without discouragement or complaint. Is a man capable of such sacrifices a cold, insensitive person, or should we see him rather as a man in the grip of a quite ardent, tenacious, and implacable passion of the mind? Intent on a single goal—to make his fortune—the emigrant ultimately succeeds in making a wholly individual life for himself. Even family feeling has been absorbed into a vast egoism, and it is doubtful that he sees his wife and children as anything other than a detached part of himself. Deprived of regular relations with his fellow men, he has learned to take pleasure in solitude. When you turn up on the doorstep of his isolated home, the pioneer comes out to meet you. He extends his hand in the customary manner, but his face expresses neither kindness nor pleasure. He speaks only to question you, and the need that he must satisfy is of the head rather than the heart. No sooner has he gotten from you the news he wishes to know than he lapses again into silence. You have the sense that this is a man who has fled importunate people and the world's bustle and retired to his home for the evening. Question him in turn and he will intelligently provide you with information. He may even attend to your needs and ensure your safety as long as you remain under his roof. Yet he does all this with such reluctance and such haughtiness that you sense in him a deep indifference to the result of his efforts, and your gratitude freezes on your lips. Yet the pioneer is in his own way hospitable, although his hospitality in no way touches you because in extending it he seems to be subjecting himself to a painful necessity of the wilderness. He sees it as a duty imposed on him by his position rather than a pleasure. This anonymous individual is the representative of a race to which the future of the New World belongs: a restless, calculating, adventurous race that acts with cool detachment in ways that only the ardor of the passions can explain and that traffics in everything, not excluding morality and religion.

A nation of conquerors that is willing to subject itself to life in the wild without ever being distracted by its allure; that loves only those aspects of civilization and enlightenment that are useful to well-being; and that plunges into America's solitudes with an axe and newspapers; a people that, like all great peoples, has but one thought and marches toward the acquisition of wealth, the only purpose of its labors, with a perseverance and a scorn for life that might be called heroic if that word applied to anything other than virtue; a nomadic people, whose progress neither river nor lake can halt, before whom forests fall and prairies are made to bask in shade; and after reaching the Pacific Ocean, this same people will retrace its steps in order to disrupt and destroy the society it created as it went.

In speaking of the pioneer, one cannot forget his companion in misery and danger: the young woman who, at the other end of the hearth, sees to the preparation of dinner as she dandles her youngest son on her lap. Like her husband, this woman is in the prime of life and can still recall the comfort of her early years. Indeed, her dress indicates that her taste for finery has not been entirely extinguished. Yet time has dealt harshly with her. In her features, prematurely lined with age, and in her spindly limbs, it is easy to see that life has been a heavy burden for her. Indeed, this frail creature has already been exposed to unbelievable miseries. Barely embarked on life's way, she was obliged to wrench herself away from her mother's affection and from the sweet fraternal bonds that no young woman relinquishes without tears, even if she is leaving to share the opulent abode of a new husband. The pioneer's wife was wrenched away from the innocent cradle of youth suddenly and without hope of return, yet it was for the solitude of the forests that she gave up the charms of society and the pleasures of home. Her nuptial bed stood on the bare forest floor. To accept harsh duties, to submit to unfamiliar privations, to embrace an existence for which she was not intended—such was her lot in the prime of life, such were the pleasures of her marriage. Destitution, suffering, and boredom affected her fragile makeup but left her courage undaunted. From the deep sadness evident in her delicate features one easily divines a religious resignation, a profound peace, and I know not what quiet native firmness of character, able to endure all of life's woes without fear or rebellion.

Her children press around her, half naked, glowing with health, and careless of tomorrow, true children of the wilderness. From time to time their mother gazes at them with eyes full of sadness mingled with delight. To judge by their vigor and her feebleness, one would say that she had exhausted herself that they might live yet harbored no regrets about the cost.

The emigrants' home has neither inside walls nor attic. In the evening the whole family must gather in the single room for shelter. The house is a world unto itself. It is the ark of a lost civilization in an ocean of foliage, a sort of oasis in the desert. A hundred paces away the shadows of the immemorial forest resume, and solitude begins anew.

It was evening, after sunset, by the time we reached Pontiac. Twenty very neat and quite pretty houses, enclosing an equal number of well-stocked stores, a clear stream, a square clearing a quarter of a league on a side, and the eternal forest all around: there you have a picture of the village of Pontiac, which in twenty years perhaps will be a city. The sight of this place reminded me of what Mr. Gallatin said in New York a month earlier: "There are no villages in America, at least not in the sense you use that word in France. Here the homes of the farmers are scattered among their fields. The only reason people come together is to set up a market to serve the region. The only people you find in these would-be villages are lawyers, printers, and merchants."[5]

We had someone show us the way to the finest inn in Pontiac (because there are two), and as usual we were ushered into what is called the "bar room." This is a room in which drinks are served, and where anyone, from the humblest worker to the wealthiest merchant in town, can come to smoke, drink, and talk politics on a footing of absolute equality, at least to judge by appearances. The landlord of the inn was, I won't say a coarse peasant, because there are no peasants in America, but in any case a very coarse man who wore on his face an expression of guileless simplicity of the sort you see in Norman horse traders. Here was a man who, for fear of intimidating you, never looked you in the eye when speaking but rather waited to get a good look at you while you were engaged in conversation with someone else. Yet he was a subtle politician and, as Americans are wont to be, a pitiless interrogator. Along with the rest of the company, this worthy citizen at first found us a puzzling sight. Our traveling clothes and rifles were hardly the marks of industrial entrepreneurs, and the idea of traveling to a place just to see it was absolutely foreign. In order to avoid a lengthy explanation, we announced straightaway that we had come to buy land. No sooner was the word uttered than we realized that in trying to avoid one difficulty we had run headlong into another far worse.

To be sure, people stopped treating us as though we were bizarre aliens of some sort, but now they all wanted to do business with us. To ward them off and put an end to the descriptions of their farms, we told our host that, before we came to any decision, we would need some practical information from him about the price of land and methods of cultivation. He immediately led us off to another room and with appropriate gravity spread out a map of Michigan on the oak table in the middle of the room. Then, setting a candle down between us, he waited impassively for us to say our piece. The reader, who is no more likely than we were to want to settle in the American wilderness, may neverthe-

5. See Tocqueville's conversation with Gallatin in Non-alphabetic Notebook 1, pp. 212–13.

less be curious about how the thousands of Europeans and Americans who go there every year go about finding a place to live. I shall therefore set down the information our Pontiac host provided. We later had ample opportunity to verify the accuracy of what he told us.

"It's not like France here," said our host, after listening in silence to all our questions and snuffing out the candle. "Where you come from, labor is cheap and land is dear. Here, the price of land is nothing, but the cost of labor is out of sight. I say this so that you'll understand that if you want to settle in America, you'll need capital, just as you do in Europe, although you'll put it to different use. I wouldn't advise anyone to settle in the wilderness in the hope of making a fortune unless he has 150 to 200 dollars (800 to 1,000 francs) at his disposal. An acre in Michigan never costs more than 10 shillings (approximately 6.5 francs) if the land is uncultivated. That's roughly a day's labor. So a worker can earn enough in a day to buy an acre of land. But once he owns it, that's when the difficulties begin. Now, this is how you go about dealing with them. The pioneer goes to the place he's just bought with a few animals, some salt pork, two barrels of flour, and some tea. If there's a cabin nearby, he can go there for temporary shelter. If not, he has to set up a tent at once in the middle of the woods where he wants to put his field. His first order of business is to cut down the nearest trees, and out of these he builds a rudimentary cabin of the sort you've already had a chance to examine. Here it costs almost nothing to keep livestock. The emigrant ties a bell around the animals' necks and lets them run free in the woods. Seldom do the animals stray far from the vicinity of the house. The biggest expense is for clearing land. If the pioneer arrives with a family able to assist him in the early stages of the work, his task is relatively easy. But this is rarely the case. Emigrants are generally young, and if they have children, they are usually infants. In that case he has to provide for all of his family's initial needs or else hire the services of his neighbors. It costs 3 to 4 dollars (or 15 to 20 francs) to clear an acre of land. When the land is ready, the new owner plants an acre of potatoes and the rest in wheat or corn. Corn is our salvation in these parts. It grows in the marshes and does better in the shade of our forests than in the open sun. Without corn the emigrant's family would face inevitable disaster if poverty, illness, or incompetence were to prevent him from clearing a sufficient amount of land in the first year. The first years after the clearing are the most difficult. Then comes prosperity and finally wealth."

So said our host, and we listened to these unadorned details with almost as much interest as if we had intended to profit from them for ourselves. When he stopped talking, we posed our questions.

"All the forests in this area are naturally marshy and unhealthy. If the settler is willing to brave the miseries of a life of solitude, can he at least be sure that he needn't fear for his life?"

"Land clearing is always a dangerous enterprise," the American replied. "And virtually no pioneer family is untouched by forest fever during the first year. If you travel in these parts in autumn, it's not uncommon to come upon a cabin in which everyone is down with the fever, from the pioneer himself to his youngest child."

"What becomes of these poor folks when Providence sends such afflictions their way?"

"They resign themselves to their fate and hope for a better day."

"But can they expect help from their neighbors?"

"Not much."

"Can they at least get help from a doctor?"

"Often the nearest doctor is sixty miles away. They do as the Indians do: die or recover as God wills."

We continued: "Does the voice of religion ever reach them?"

"Very seldom. We still haven't been able to provide facilities for public worship in these parts. Nearly every summer, though, a few Methodist preachers visit the new settlements. News of their arrival spreads incredibly quickly from cabin to cabin. It's big news. When the day arrives, the pioneer travels with his wife and children to the appointed place along the merest of forest trails. People come from fifty miles around. The worshippers gather not in a church but outdoors, right in the middle of the forest. Their rustic temple is bare of ornament but for a pulpit of rough-hewn logs and rows of felled tree trunks pressed into service as benches. The pioneers and their families camp out in the nearby woods, and for three days and three nights they eat, sleep, and drink religion. You have to see how ardently these folks pray, how intently they listen to the preacher's solemn voice. It's in the wilderness that you see real hunger for religion."

"One last question. At home, most people think that the American wilderness is being settled in part by emigrants from Europe. So why is it that in all the time we've been traveling in this area, we have yet to meet a single European?"

On hearing this question, our host could not prevent a smile of superiority, an expression of smug pride, from appearing on his face. His reply was emphatic: "Who but Americans would have the courage to subject themselves to such misery and pay such a price for prosperity? The European emigrant gets no farther than one of the seacoast cities or the countryside around them. There he finds work as a craftsman, a farmhand, or a servant. He lives better than he did in Europe and is content to bequeath no more than that to his children. The land belongs to the American. It's his privilege to occupy the vast solitudes of the New World, to subject them to man's dominion, and thus to secure a bright future for himself."

With those words our host stopped talking. He exhaled a long column of smoke and sat back to listen to what we had to say about our plans.

We first thanked him for his invaluable advice and wise counsel, of which we assured him we would one day make good use. "Before settling in your district, sir, we'd like to visit Saginaw and hope to consult with you about our trip." At the sound of the word Saginaw a most striking change came over the American's face. It seemed as though we had wrenched him violently from real life and forced him against his nature into the realm of the imagination. His pupils dilated, his jaw dropped, and his face betrayed the most complete surprise. "You want to go to Saginaw!" he exclaimed at last. "To Saginaw Bay!" Two rational men, two well-bred foreigners, want to go to Saginaw Bay? He could scarcely believe such a thing.

"But why not?" we answered.

"Do you have any idea what you're in for?" our host resumed. "Do you know that Saginaw is the last inhabited place between here and the Pacific Ocean? That between here and Saginaw there's nothing but wilderness and trackless waste? Have you given any thought to forests rife with Indians and mosquitoes? Do you realize that you'll have to spend at least one night sleeping on the damp ground? Have you thought about the fever? Can you find your way in the wilderness, or will you lose yourselves in the labyrinth of our forests?"

At the conclusion of this tirade he paused to gauge the impression he had made. Undaunted, we continued: "All that may be true. But we're leaving tomorrow morning for Saginaw Bay."

Our host weighed this for a moment, nodded, and then resumed in a slow, clear voice. "Two foreigners like you wouldn't undertake such an adventure unless you expected to make a lot of money. You probably figure that there's a big advantage to setting yourself up as far as possible from the competition, but you're dead wrong." We did not answer. He continued: "Maybe the Canadian fur company has sent you here to strike a bargain with the frontier tribes?" Again, silence. With no more conjectures to offer, our host fell silent but continued to puzzle over our bizarre plan.

"Have you ever been to Saginaw?" we asked.

"I had the misfortune to go up there five or six times, but I had my reasons, and I don't see that you have any."

"Please bear in mind, sir, that we're not asking you if we ought to go to Saginaw but only what the best way to get there might be."

His mind focused once again on the matter at hand, our American recovered his sangfroid and clarity of vision and in few words and with admirable practical common sense explained to us how we ought to proceed; he went into great detail and anticipated any number of difficulties that might arise. When he had done with his recital, he paused again to see if we might at last be prepared to reveal the secret of our journey, but recognizing that neither of us had anything more to say, he picked up the candle, led us to our room, and after shaking our hands quite democratically returned to the common room to end the evening.

We rose at the break of day and prepared for our departure. Our host was soon up as well. The night had not revealed to him the reason for what he regarded as our extraordinary behavior. Nevertheless, since we seemed absolutely determined to ignore his advice, he dared not offer any more of it. He hovered around us instead. I heard him mutter, "Damned if I know why two foreigners would want to go up to Saginaw." He repeated this several times, until finally,

Beaumont, self-portrait on his horse: *straw hat, jacket gray, gamebag white, wicker bottle hung around neck, Indian pipe in hand, portmanteau black, trousers gray, horse bay.* (GBI)

as I put my foot in the stirrup, I said, "There are many reasons, sir." On hearing these words he stopped short and looked me in the eye for the first time, as if preparing to hear a great secret revealed. But I calmly mounted my horse and ended the conversation by giving him a friendly wave as I rode off at a rapid trot. After fifty paces I looked back and saw him standing still as a millstone in front of his door. Then he turned and, shaking his head, went inside. I suppose he was still muttering to himself, "Damned if I know what two foreigners are going to do up in Saginaw."

We'd been advised to look up a Mr. Williams, who had long traded with the Chippewa and had a son living in Saginaw, in the hope that he might provide us with useful information. After riding a few miles through the forest, we were beginning to think we'd missed his house, but just then we spotted an old man at work in a small garden. We approached him, and it turned out to be Mr. Williams himself.[6] He received us warmly and gave us a letter for his son. We asked him if we had any reason to fear the Indians whose territory we'd be crossing. Mr. Williams dismissed the suggestion almost indignantly. "No, no!" he shouted, "you can travel freely. As far as I'm concerned, I sleep more easily among Indians than among whites." This was the first favorable opinion of Indians that I'd heard since arriving in America. In the more populous regions,

6. Major Oliver Williams.

TOCQUEVILLE'S NARRATION OF TWO EXCURSIONS

people speak of them with a mixture of fear and contempt. And in those places I believe that the description is merited. The reader will have seen earlier what I myself thought when I encountered Indians for the first time in Buffalo. As you read further in this diary and follow me as I visit European frontier settlements and Indian tribes themselves, your idea of America's first inhabitants will change, and you will come to see them in a more honorable as well as more accurate light.

After leaving Mr. Williams, we resumed our route through the woods. From time to time a small lake (this region is full of them) would appear in the form of a silvery patch of water visible through the foliage. It is hard to imagine the charm of these beautiful places, where no man has yet settled and profound peace and uninterrupted silence still reign. I have visited hideous Alpine wastes where nature, having refused man's labors, nevertheless displays midst all her horrors a grandeur that moves the soul and stirs the passions. Here the solitude is no less profound, yet the impression it makes is not the same. While exploring this flourishing wilderness in which, as in Milton's *Paradise,* everything is ready for man, you feel only quiet admiration, a gentle, melancholy emotion, and a vague disgust with civilized life. With a sort of savage instinct, it pains you to think that soon this delightful solitude will have been utterly transformed. Indeed, the white race is already pushing its way through the surrounding woods, and within a few years Europeans will have cut down the trees whose images shimmer in the limpid waters of the lake and will have forced the animals that inhabit its shores to flee to new homes in some other wilderness.

Continuing on our way, we came to a region of quite different aspect. The ground was no longer flat but marked by hills and valleys. Several of these hills looked quite wild. It was in one of these picturesque passes that we turned back to look at the impressive spectacle we had left to our rear and saw, to our great surprise, an Indian hard on our horses' tails. He was a man of about thirty, tall and admirably proportioned, as nearly all of them are. His shiny black hair hung down to his shoulders, except for two braids fastened atop his head. His face was painted black and red, and a very short blue tunic covered his upper body. He wore red *mittas,* a kind of trouser that ends above the knee, and moccasins on his feet. A knife hung at his side. In his right hand he held a long carbine, and in his left two birds he had just killed. At first the sight of this Indian was rather disagreeable. The place was ill chosen to ward off an attack. To our right was a forest of immensely tall pines. To our left lay a deep ravine, at the bottom of which a stream roared among the rocks, which the foliage hid from view and toward which we descended blindly via a steep trail. It took only an instant to grab our rifles and turn to face the Indian. He halted as well. We remained as we were, in silence, for half a minute. His features exhibited all the characteristics that distinguish the Indian race from the rest. His deep black eyes shone with the savage fire that one sees even in the gaze of half-breeds, and which persists down to the second or third generation of white blood. His nose was hooked in the middle and slightly flattened at the end. His cheekbones were quite high,

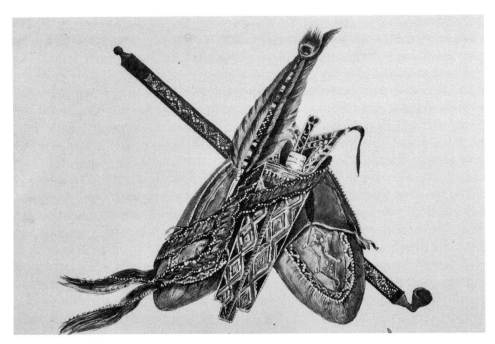

Indian accoutrements. (GB2)

and his mouth, wide open, revealed two rows of shining white teeth, evidence that the savage, unlike his less fastidious American neighbor, did not spend his days chewing on tobacco leaves. As I said, the moment we turned around and grabbed our weapons, the Indian stopped. He remained absolutely impassive, with a fixed, steady gaze, as we looked him up and down. When he saw that our intentions were not hostile, he began to smile. He probably realized that he had alarmed us. It was my first opportunity to observe how completely an expression of gaiety changes the appearance of the savage. I have made the same observation a hundred times since. A serious Indian and a smiling Indian are two completely different people. A savage majesty predominates in the stillness of the former, to which one reacts with an involuntary feeling of terror. Let the same man smile and his whole face takes on a simple, kindly expression that lends it real charm.

When we saw the man's face brighten, we spoke to him in English. He allowed us to rattle on for quite some time before signaling that he hadn't understood a word. We offered him a little brandy, which he accepted without hesitation or thanks. Still communicating with signs, we asked if we could have the birds he was carrying, and he gave them to us in exchange for a small coin. Having thus made his acquaintance, we waved farewell and rode off at a quick trot. After proceeding at a good pace for a quarter of an hour, I turned again and was surprised to find the Indian still there, right behind my horse. He ran with the agility of a wild animal, without uttering a single word or appearing to lengthen his stride. We stopped, he stopped. We started off again, he started off again.

We rode at a full gallop. Our horses, raised in the wilderness, easily cleared every obstacle. The Indian effortlessly doubled his pace. I spotted him now to the right, now to the left of my horse, hurdling bushes and landing without a sound. He reminded me of the wolves of northern Europe, who will follow a rider in case he falls from his horse and becomes ready prey. The sight of his impassive face, which would disappear for a time into the obscurity of the forest only to reappear in broad daylight as he seemed to buzz around us like a fly, eventually became irksome. Unable to imagine why this man would want to follow us at such a rapid pace (and thinking that he may well have been at it for a long time before we first noticed his presence), it occurred to us that he might be leading us into an ambush. As this thought gnawed on our minds, we spotted the barrel of another carbine in the woods ahead of us. In a few moments we had closed the gap between us and the man with the gun. At first we took him to be an Indian. He wore a short jacket tucked in at the waist, revealing a man with a trim physique and upright posture. His neck was bare, and he wore moccasins on his feet. When we approached and he lifted his head, we saw at once that he was a European, and we stopped short. He came toward us and cordially shook our hands, and we launched into conversation. "Do you live in the wilderness?" we asked.

"Yes," he answered, "that's my house over there." He pointed through the trees to a log cabin more wretched than most.

"Alone?"

"Alone."

"So what do you do here?"

"I hunt in these woods and shoot any game I see, but the hunting's not very good right now."

"You like this way of life?"

"More than any other."

"But aren't you afraid of the Indians?"

"Afraid of the Indians! I'd rather live among them than in white society. No! No! I'm not afraid of the Indians. They're better than we are, except when we reduce them to a stupor with our liquor, the poor wretches!"

At this point we called the attention of our new acquaintance to the man who had been following us so persistently and who stood now only a few steps from where we were standing, as impassive as a milestone. "That's a Chippewa," he said, "or as the French call them, a Sauteur. My guess is that he's on his way home from Canada, where he received his annual gift from the English. His family must be nearby."

With these words the American signaled to the Indian to come toward us and began speaking to him with considerable fluency in his own language. It was remarkable to see the pleasure that these two men, so different in birth and mores, took from their exchange of ideas. The conversation obviously involved the respective merits of their weapons. The white man carefully examined the savage's rifle and said, "That's a fine carbine. The English no doubt gave it to him to use against us. And he won't hesitate to do so when the next war breaks out. That's how the Indians get themselves into such trouble. But the poor folks don't know any better."

"Are the Indians good at using such long, heavy rifles?" I asked.

"Nobody can shoot like an Indian," our new friend replied in the most admiring of terms. "Take a good look at those birds he sold you, sir. You'll find only one bullet in each, and I'm quite sure he fired no more than two shots to get them. You know, no man is happier than an Indian lucky enough to live in a place where we haven't yet driven out all the game. But the bigger animals can smell us coming three hundred miles away, and when they flee in advance of our arrival, what's left is like a desert, and the poor Indians are done for unless they take up farming."

As we resumed our route, our new friend called out to us. "When you come back this way, knock on my door. It's a pleasure to see white faces out here."

I have recounted this conversation, though its content is unremarkable, in order to familiarize the reader with a type of man we subsequently encountered quite often on the fringes of inhabited territories: Europeans who, despite their upbringing, have discovered ineffable charms in the freedom of the wilderness. Attached by taste and passion to the empty spaces of North America and by religion, principles, and ideas to Europe, they combine love of the savage life with pride in civilization and prefer Indians to their own compatriots, yet without acknowledging the savages as their equals.

We continued our rapid progress and half an hour later came to the house of a pioneer. An Indian family had made camp in the front yard. An old woman, two girls, and several children crouched around a fire, around which were arrayed the remains of a large deer. A completely naked Indian lay on the grass a short distance away, warming himself in the sun, while a small child rolled in the dirt beside him. Our silent companion stopped here. He left us without a word of farewell and gravely took up his place among his compatriots. What had compelled this man to follow us for two leagues? We could not even hazard a guess. After stopping here for lunch, we remounted and continued on through a not very dense forest of tall trees. The woods had been burned some time earlier, as was apparent from the charred remains of trees lying amid the grass. Today the ground beneath the forest's canopy is covered with ferns as far as the eye can see.

A few leagues further on, my horse threw a shoe, which caused us no end of worry. Fortunately, we ran into a farmer a short way down the road, and he managed to replace the shoe. Had it not been for this fortunate encounter, I doubt that we could have continued, because we were coming to the outer limits of settlement. This same man not only enabled us to go on but also encouraged us to pick up the pace, because the day was drawing to a close and we still had two leagues to travel before reaching Flint River, where we hoped to spend the night.

Indeed, a thick darkness soon began to envelop us. The night was peaceful but quite cold. In the depths of these forests the silence is so profound and the stillness so complete that all the forces of nature seem paralyzed. All we could hear was the annoying buzz of mosquitoes and the sound of our horses' hooves. Every now and then we would glimpse an Indian fire in the distance, and through the smoke we could make out an austere and immobile profile. After an hour we came to a fork in the trail. Two paths diverged ahead. Which of the two to take? The choice was tricky. One path led to a stream of unknown depth, the other to a clearing. By the light of the rising moon we could see ahead of us a valley littered with fallen trees. A little farther on we saw two houses. It was so important not to go astray at such a place and such an hour that we decided to make inquiries before proceeding on. My companion stayed behind with the horses, while I, slinging my rifle over my shoulder, clambered down into the draw. I soon realized that I had entered a patch of forest that had only recently been cleared. The ground was covered with huge trees that had yet to be stripped of their branches. By leaping from one to another I managed fairly quickly to move close to one of the houses, but I was prevented from reaching it by the same stream that we had encountered earlier. Fortunately, the stream was bridged at this point by several huge oak trees, no doubt felled by the pioneer's axe. By inching my way along the trunks of these trees, I at last made it across to the other bank. Cautiously, I approached the two houses, afraid that they might be Indian wigwams. They were still unfinished. I found the doors open, and no voice answered mine. I returned to the bank of the stream, where I could not resist spending a few minutes admiring the sublime horror of this place. The valley seemed to form a vast arena, enclosed on all sides by a black curtain of foliage. A few rays of moonlight illuminated the center of this arena, casting a thousand fantastic shadows, which played in silence over the fallen trees. Otherwise, not a single sound or other sign of life emerged from the emptiness. At last I remembered my companion and called out to him to apprise him of my findings and urge him to cross the stream and rejoin me on the other side. My voice echoed for quite some time in the surrounding emptiness, but there was no response. I gave another shout and listened again. The same deathly silence reigned over the forest. Gripped by anxiety, I raced along the bank in search of the trail that I knew crossed the water farther downstream. Upon reaching it, I heard hooves in the distance and soon caught sight of B[eaumont] himself. Concerned by my long absence, he had decided to move down toward the stream. He had already descended into the valley when I called to him, so he had not heard me. He told me that he, too, had tried to hail me and, like me, had become frightened when he heard no response. Had the ford not served as an obvious rendezvous, we might have spent much of the night searching for each other. We continued on, promising ourselves that for the rest of the journey we would stay together, and in three-quarters of an hour we at last came to a clearing with two or three cabins and, to our great delight, a light. A violet ribbon of water stretching across the far end of the valley signaled that we had reached Flint River. Before long the woods resounded with the barking of dogs, and we found ourselves in front of a log cabin, from which we were separated by no more than a fence. As we were about to pass through the gate, the moonlight revealed a large black bear standing on its hind legs and tugging on its chain to indicate as clearly as it could that it intended to greet us with a friendly hug. "What the devil kind of country is this," I said, "where they use bears as watchdogs?" "We must first call out," my companion replied. "If we pass through that gate, my guess is that we'll have a hard time explaining ourselves to the gatekeeper." So we shouted at the top of our lungs instead, and eventually a man came to the window. After looking us over in the moonlight, he said, "Come in, gentlemen. Down, Trinc. Get back in your kennel. These aren't robbers." The bear waddled off, and we passed through the gate. Our [horses] were half dead with fatigue, so we asked our host if we could have some oats. "Sure," he said, and with the usual American equanimity he immediately took a sickle to the nearest field as readily as if it had been the middle of the day. Meanwhile, we unsaddled our horses and, since there was no stable, tied them to the fence we had just passed through. After taking care of our traveling companions, we turned to our own sleeping arrangements. There was only one bed in the house. Fate assigned it to B[eaumont], so I wrapped myself in my cloak and lay down on the floor, whereupon I fell into a deep sleep, as befits a man who has just traveled fifteen leagues on horseback.

The next day, July 25, our first order of business was to inquire about a guide. Fifteen leagues of wilderness separated Flint River from Saginaw, and the road is little more than a narrow trail barely visible to the eye. Our host approved of our plan and took us to see two Indians in whom he assured us we could place our confidence. One of the Indians was a child of thirteen or fourteen, the other a youth of eighteen. The latter had yet to acquire the vigorous physique of maturity, yet already his appearance suggested agility combined with strength. He was of medium height, taut and slender, and his supple limbs were well proportioned. Long braids hung from his bare head. He had taken care, moreover, to paint his face with black and red lines arranged in a highly symmetrical pattern. He wore a ring in his nose, with a necklace and earrings to complete his accoutrement. His martial paraphernalia were no less remarkable. First there was his battle-axe, the celebrated tomahawk. On the other side he carried a long, well-honed knife, which the savages use to remove their victim's scalp. Around his neck hung a bull's horn, which he used as a powder horn, and in his right hand he held a rifle. As with most Indians, his gaze was fierce and his smile kindly. Trotting alongside him, as if to complete the portrait, was a dog with straight ears and a long muzzle, much more like a fox than any other animal, and a fierce look in perfect harmony with his master's countenance. After examining our new companion with an attention which he gave no sign of noticing, we asked how much he wanted for the service he was about to perform. The Indian answered with a few words in his native tongue, and the American, hastening to intervene, informed us that what the savage was asking was the equivalent of two dollars. Our host then charitably added that "since these poor Indians don't know the value of money, you can give me the dollars, and I'll gladly take it upon myself to supply him with the equivalent." I was curious to know what this worthy fellow considered to be the equivalent of two dollars, so I very quietly followed him to the place where the transaction was to be completed. I saw him hand our guide a pair of moccasins and a handkerchief, certainly not worth half the sum we had paid. The Indian went away quite satisfied, however, while I withdrew without a sound, repeating to myself the words of La Fontaine: "Ah, if only lions knew how to paint!"[7]

What is more, it was not only Indians whom the American pioneers took for dupes. We were daily victims of their inordinate greed. To be sure, they do not steal. They are too enlightened to take such risks, but I've yet to see an innkeeper in a big city more shameless about overcharging than these denizens of the wild, in whom I had expected to find the primitive honesty and simplicity of ancestral ways.

Everything was ready. We mounted our horses, and, fording the river that marks the outermost boundary of civilization, we entered the solitude of true wilderness at last.

Our two guides walked, or rather leapt, ahead of us like two wildcats, negotiating all obstacles in our path. Whenever we encountered a fallen tree, a stream, or a swamp, they pointed out the best way around, went on ahead, and never looked back to see if we'd made it through the difficult pass. Self-reliant by habit, the Indian has a hard time imagining that anyone else might need assistance. He will help you out if the need arises, but no one has ever taught him how to show thoughtfulness and consideration and thus curry favor for services rendered. We might have offered a few observations on this point had we been able to make ourselves understood. And in any case, we felt that we were completely in their power. Here, the tables were turned. Plunged into darkness and forced to rely on his own strength, the civilized man proceeds blindly, incapable of negotiating the labyrinth or even preserving his own life. Faced with the same challenges, the savage triumphs. For him the forest holds no mysteries. He is at home there. He walks with his head held high, guided by an instinct more trustworthy than the navigator's compass. Hidden in the treetops or in the densest of foliage, prey that the European would have passed by reveals itself time and time again to his unerring eye.

Occasionally our Indians would stop, put a finger across their lips to warn us to be silent, and signal us to get down from our horses. With their guidance we would then proceed to a spot where at last we were able to see the game they had spotted long before. As they led us by the hand, like children, their smiles seemed almost contemptuous.

---

7. This quotation refers to La Fontaine's fable "The Lion Brought Down by Man." In this tale, a lion walks by a painting of a man single-handedly killing a lion. Upon seeing the canvas, the lion exclaims, "With more reason, we would have the advantage, if my fellow lions knew how to paint."

The further we went, the fewer traces of man we saw. Before long even signs of the savage's presence disappeared, and we beheld what we had been seeking for so long: the virgin forest.

Through a rather sparse patch of woods it was possible to see a fairly considerable distance, and what we glimpsed ahead was a cluster of tall trees, nearly all pines and oaks, shooting skyward. Confined to a fairly limited area and almost entirely deprived of sunlight, these trees had taken the shortest path to air and light. They rose as straight as a ship's mast, high above the surrounding vegetation, and not until they reached a substantial height did they serenely extend their branches and bask in the shade of their own foliage. Each tree that reached this lofty height was quickly joined by others, which wove their limbs together to form a huge dais high above the forest floor. Beneath this damp, motionless canopy everything changes; an utterly different scene confronts the eye. High aloft, a majestic order reigns. Nearer the ground, all is confusion and chaos. Some trunks have collapsed under the weight of their branches and split down the middle, leaving only a sharp and jagged tip. Others, buffeted by the wind, have been hurled to the ground in one piece. Ripped from the earth, their roots form a kind of natural rampart large enough to shield several men. Huge trees, held up by surrounding branches, remain suspended in the air as they turn to dust. In France there is no region so unpopulated that a forest can remain untouched long enough for trees to grow unmolested to maturity and eventually fall and decay. Man cuts them down in their prime and rids the forest of their debris. In the emptiness of America, by contrast, all-powerful nature is the only destructive agent as well as the only reproductive force. As in forests under man's dominion, death here strikes repeated blows, but no one is responsible for removing the remains. Day after day their number grows; trees fall, one upon another, and there isn't time enough to reduce them all to dust and make room for new ones. Generations of the dead lie side by side. Some, in the final stages of decay, are little more than long streaks of red dust in the grass. Others, though half consumed by time, still retain their shape. Still others have fallen only yesterday, and their long branches still sprawl across the trail, confronting the traveler with unanticipated obstacles. In the midst of all this debris, the work of reproduction continues without letup. Shoots, climbing vines, and grasses of many varieties surmount all obstacles to reach the light of day. They slither along fallen trunks, creep amid the dusty residue, and lift and crack the bark that still remains. Life and death here look each other in the face, seemingly keen to mingle and confound their works.

While sailing on the Atlantic, we often enjoyed evenings of serene calm, when the sails flapping tranquilly on their masts hid from the sailors the direction of the breeze. Nature's repose is no less impressive in the emptiness of the New World than on the immensity of the sea. In the middle of the day, as the sun beams down on the forest, one can frequently hear what sounds like a long sigh in the depths of the woods, a plaintive cry echoing in the distance. This is the last gasp of the dying wind. All around the forest then subsides into a silence so deep, a stillness so complete, that a kind of religious terror grips the soul. The traveler stops; he looks. The trees, pressed one against the other, their branches intertwined, seem to form but a single being, an immense and indestructible edifice, beneath whose vaults an eternal darkness reigns. Whichever way the traveler looks, he sees nothing but a field of violence and destruction. Broken trees, torn trunks, and countless other signs indicate that here the elements are perpetually at war. But the struggle is suspended, the restless energy comes suddenly to a halt at the instigation of some unknown power. Half-broken branches still hang from a trunk that seems no longer to offer them any support. Uprooted trees, arrested in their fall, hang suspended in midair.

The traveler listens. Trembling, he holds his breath, the better to hear the least sound of life, but not a whisper, not a murmur can be detected. In Europe I have lost my way in a forest more than once, but inevitably some sound of life reached my ears. Perhaps it was the peal of a nearby village bell, the footsteps of a traveler, the sound of a woodsman's axe, the sharp report of a firearm, the barking of a dog, or simply the vague buzz of a civilized land. Here, not only is man absent, but even the animals are silent. The smaller ones have left the deep woods to be closer to where people live, while the larger ones have headed in the opposite direction. Those that remain lie hidden, safe from the rays of the sun. Thus in the woods everything is still, everything silent beneath the forest canopy. It is almost as if the Creator has for a moment turned his face away from this place, paralyzing the forces of nature.

This was not the only time we remarked on the striking similarity that exists between the ocean and the wild forest. An idea of immensity takes hold of you as you gaze upon either. The endless, not to say monotonous, repetition of the same scenes astonishes and overwhelms the imagination. In the solitudes of the New World I felt an even stronger and more poignant sense of isolation and abandonment than had oppressed me in the middle of the Atlantic. On the ocean, at least, the traveler contemplates a vast horizon, toward which he directs his gaze with hope. But in this ocean of foliage, who can point the way? Where should one direct one's eyes? In vain you climb the tallest trees, only to find yourself surrounded by others still taller. To no avail you climb the hills, for the forest climbs with you everywhere, and this same forest stretches from where you stand all the way to the North Pole and the Pacific Ocean. You can travel thousands of leagues in its shade and all the while think you're still in the same place.

Back to the Saginaw trail. We had been traveling for five hours in utter ignorance of where we were when our Indians stopped, and the older one, whose name was Sagan-Kuisko, drew a line in the sand. He pointed to one end of the line and exclaimed, "Miché-Couté-Ouinque"—the Indian name for Flint River—and then to the other end and pronounced the name of Saginaw. Then, marking a point in the middle of the line, he showed us that we had reached the

Saginaw forest, 25 July 1831, with Indian guide. Tocqueville is reclining against the fallen tree. (GB1 *top* and GB2 *bottom*)

halfway point and that it was time to take a short rest. The sun was already high on the horizon, and we would have accepted the Indian's invitation with pleasure had we noticed any water in the vicinity. But not seeing any, we signaled to the Indian that we preferred to rest when we stopped to eat and drink. He understood immediately and resumed his course at the same fast pace as before. An hour later, he stopped again and indicated a spot thirty paces off into the woods where he indicated with a sign there would be water. Then, without awaiting our response and without helping us to unsaddle our horses, he headed for the water himself. We hastened after him. The wind had recently brought down a tree at the spot. In the hole formerly occupied by its roots, a little rainwater had collected. This was the fountain to which our guide led us, and he gave no sign of imagining that one might hesitate to drink such a beverage. We opened our knapsack. Another stroke of bad luck! The heat had completely spoiled our provisions, and all we had for dinner was a very small piece of bread, the only loaf we had been able to find in Flint River. On top of that, the puddle had attracted a swarm of mosquitoes, which had to be warded off with one hand while lifting the bread to the mouth with the other: now you have an idea of rustic lunch in a virgin forest. While we ate, the Indians sat with arms crossed on the trunk of the fallen tree I just mentioned. When they saw that we had finished, they signaled to us that they, too, were hungry. We showed them our empty knapsack. They nodded and said nothing. Indians have no idea what it means to eat at fixed hours. They gorge themselves when they can and then fast until another opportunity to assuage their appetite presents itself. Wolves in similar circumstances behave the same way. Before long we were ready to mount our horses once more but were alarmed to discover that they had disappeared. Bitten by mosquitoes and spurred by hunger, they had wandered from the trail where we had left them, and we had a hard time picking up their tracks. Had we remained oblivious a quarter of an hour longer, we would have awakened like Sancho with our saddles between our legs. With a heartfelt benediction to the mosquitoes that had given us the idea of parting so soon, we resumed our journey. Soon the trail became harder and harder to see. Our horses had to force their way continually through thick undergrowth and hurdle the trunks of enormous trees that blocked our way. After two hours of extremely difficult travel, we came at last to a river that was not very deep but had quite steep banks. We crossed at a ford and, as we mounted the opposite bank, discovered a field of corn and two structures quite similar to log cabins. As we drew nearer, we realized that we were in a small Indian settlement. What we had taken for log cabins were actually wigwams. The solitude here was as profound as that of the surrounding forest. Sagan-Kuisko stopped in front of one of the abandoned dwellings. He carefully examined all the objects in the vicinity, then put down his carbine and came over to us, where he first drew another line in the sand to show us that we had still completed only two-thirds of the journey. Then he got up and pointed to the sun, indicating by sign language that it was going down very rapidly. He then looked at the wigwam and closed his eyes. This language was perfectly intelligible. He wanted us to make camp at this spot. I confess that his proposal surprised us greatly and pleased us scarcely at all. We had not eaten since that morning, and we didn't much like the idea of going to bed without supper. The dark and somber majesty of the scenes we had witnessed during the day, the utter isolation in which we found ourselves, and the fierce countenances of our guides, with whom it was impossible to strike up any kind of relationship, were hardly of a nature to inspire confidence. What is more, there was something odd about the behavior of the Indians, which we did not find reassuring. The route we had been following for the previous two hours seemed even less traveled than the one we had followed earlier. No one had mentioned an Indian village on the trail, and everyone had assured us that you could travel from Flint River to Saginaw in a single day. So we could not imagine why our guides wanted to spend the night in the wilderness. We insisted on continuing. The Indian indicated the woods would soon be engulfed in darkness. To force our guides to continue against their will would have been dangerous. We decided to tempt their greed. But the Indian is the most philosophical of men. He has few needs and consequently few desires. Civilization has no hold on him; either he knows nothing of its pleasures, or he holds them in contempt. I had noticed, however, that Sagan-Kuisko had shown particular interest in a small, wicker-covered bottle that hung at my side. A bottle that cannot be broken. This was an object whose usefulness he grasped at once and which had elicited his genuine admiration. My rifle and my bottle were the only items of my European equipment that seemed to arouse his desire. I indicated by signs that I would give him my bottle if he took us directly to Saginaw. At this the Indian seemed greatly distressed. He looked again at the sun and then at the ground. Finally, he made up his mind, grabbed his carbine, put his hand over his mouth and twice uttered the cry, "How! How!" before striking out into the brush in front of us. We followed at a fast trot, forcibly opening a path for ourselves, and soon we had left the Indian dwellings behind. For two hours our guides ran even faster than before. Yet night fell, and the last of the sun's rays had just vanished behind the trees when Sagan-Kuisko began to bleed profusely from his nose. As used to physical exercise as this young man and his brother appeared to be, it was obvious that fatigue and lack of nourishment were beginning to take their toll. We were afraid that they might give up and decide to make their bed underneath a tree. We therefore invited them to take turns with us on horseback. The Indians accepted our offer without surprise or humility. It was strange to see these half-naked men solemnly seated on an English saddle with our game bags and rifles slung over their shoulders while we struggled along on foot ahead of them. At length night fell, and a damp chill began to spread through the forest. Darkness altered the appearance of the woods and made them terrifying. The eye could make out only vague masses scattered hither and yon, bizarre, misshapen forms, incoherent tableaux, fantastic images that seemed to have sprung from some feverish imagination. (As in today's literature, the gigantic and the ridiculous were closely related.) Never had our footsteps awakened so many echoes. Never had the silence of the forest seemed so daunting. The hum of mosquitoes seemed the only sign of life in this slumbering universe. As we pushed on, the darkness thickened, and the only light to be seen was the streak of the occasional firefly darting through its depths. Too late, we recognized the wisdom of the Indian's counsel, but there was no question of turning back. We therefore continued to move ahead as rapidly as our strength and the darkness allowed. After an hour we emerged from the woods and found ourselves in a vast prairie. Our guides let loose three savage whoops, which resounded like the discordant notes of a tom-tom. An answer came from far away. Five minutes later we came to the bank of a river, but it was so dark that we could not see the opposite shore. Here the Indians halted. They wrapped themselves in blankets for protection against mosquito bites, lay down on the grass, and soon were little more than a barely visible ball of wool that betrayed nothing resembling a human shape. We dismounted and patiently awaited whatever was to happen next. A few minutes later, a faint noise could be heard, and something approached the bank. It was a canoe about ten feet long, strangely colored and fashioned from a single tree. The man who was crouching in the bottom of this frail bark wore Indian dress and in every respect appeared to be an Indian. He spoke to our guides, who at his command hastened to remove our horses' saddles and deposit them in the canoe. As I made ready to step into the canoe myself, the supposed Indian came toward me, placed two fingers on my shoulder, and, in a perfect Norman accent that gave me a start, said, "Watch you don't be too quick settin' your feet, times are people been known to drown right about this spot." Had my horse spoken to me I don't think I could have been more surprised. I stared at the speaker, whose face, illuminated by the first glimmer of moonlight, shone like a copper pot. "Who are you?" I asked. "French seems to be your language, but you look like an Indian." He answered that he was a *Bois-Brûlé,* that is, the child of a Canadian father and an Indian mother. I shall have occasion to speak often of this singular race of half-breeds, who are numerous throughout the Canadian and much of the American frontier. At the moment I had no thought other than the pleasure of speaking my mother tongue. Following the advice of my savage compatriot, I set myself down in the bottom of the canoe and tried to balance myself as much as possible. The horse plunged into the river and began to swim, while the Canadian paddled and quietly sang an old French tune, of which I caught only the first two lines: *"Entre Paris et Saint-Denis / Il était une fille . . ."*[8]

We reached the other bank without incident. The canoe immediately went back for my companion. I will always remember the moment it approached the shore for the second time. The moon, which was full, was at that moment rising above the prairie we had just crossed. Only half of its disk appeared on the horizon. It was like a mysterious door, through which light streamed from some other sphere of existence. The shimmering rays reflected from the river held my eye. Along the very line marked out by the moon's pale light the In-

8. "Between Paris and Saint-Denis / There was a girl."

dian canoe advanced. The paddles could not be seen, and there were no creaking oarlocks, so that the canoe slid rapidly and effortlessly across the water, long, narrow, and dark like an alligator in the Mississippi pointing toward the bank and ready to seize its prey. Sagan-Kuisko sat crouching in the bow, his head resting on his knees, so that only his glistening braids were visible. At the other end of the boat, the Canadian paddled in silence, while behind him the powerful horse churned up the water of the Saginaw as he thrust his way forward. There was a savage grandeur in this spectacle that made a deep impression on me at the time and that has not vanished since. Having safely reached shore, we hastened toward a house that the moon had revealed a short distance from the river, where the Canadian assured us we could find a bed. Indeed, we settled in quite comfortably, and we would probably have fallen into a deep, restorative sleep had we not had to ward off the myriad mosquitoes that filled the room. We never did manage to do this successfully. The insect known in English as *mosquito* and in Canadian French as *maringouin* is a small creature quite like the French *cousin,* from which it differs only in size. It is generally larger, and its proboscis is so strong and sharp that wool is the only thing that can protect you from its bite. This little bug is the scourge of the American wilderness. Its presence would be enough to make a long stay unbearable. I have never been subjected to torture equivalent to what I experienced throughout this journey and especially during our stay in Saginaw. During the day the mosquitoes prevented us from drawing, writing, or remaining in one place for even a moment; at night thousands of them hovered about us. Any part of the body left uncovered immediately became their gathering place. Awakened by the pain of a bite, we would cover our heads with sheets, but they could pierce right through them. Hunted down and pursued by these small insects, we got up and went outside for some fresh air until at last we succumbed to fatigue and slept intermittently and badly.

We got up very early, and the first thing that struck us on leaving the house was the sight of our two Indians, who had wrapped themselves in blankets and were sleeping near the door, alongside their dogs.

We then beheld for the first time in daylight the village of Saginaw, which we had come so far to see.

For now, this nascent town is no more than a cultivated plain bordered on the south by a beautiful, tranquil river and on the east, west, and north by forest.

Near us stood a house whose construction suggested that the owner was well-to-do. This was the house in which we had spent the night. A similar type of dwelling could be seen at the far end of the clearing. In the interval, along the edge of the woods, two or three log cabins were half hidden by foliage. On the opposite bank of the river, the prairie stretched without limit, like the ocean on a calm day. A column of smoke rose calmly above it into the air. By following the column back to the ground, you could just make out two or three wigwams, whose conical shapes and sharp peaks blended with the prairie grass.

An overturned plow, oxen returning to their labors on their own, and a few half-wild horses completed the picture.

Log House. Saginaw, 26 July 1831. (GBI)

Whichever way we looked, we searched in vain for a Gothic spire, a wooden cross marking the wayside, or the mossy threshold of a presbytery. No such venerable vestiges of the old Christian civilization had been imported into the wilderness. There is as yet nothing to awaken an idea of either past or future. There are not even tombs to shelter the remains of those who are no more. Not even death itself has had time to stake its claim or mark the extent of its territory.

This is still a place, apparently, where a child enters this world by stealth. Generations of elders do not gather around the baby's cradle to express extravagant hopes for its future or to rejoice in premature anticipation of its accomplishments. Its name is not recorded in the town registers. The family's solicitude for the newborn must make do without religion's impressive solemnities. A mother's prayers and a few drops of water dripped on the child's head by its father must suffice to open the gates of heaven.

The village of Saginaw is the northwesternmost point of the vast Michigan peninsula to be occupied by Europeans. It can be seen as an outpost, a sort of sentry box that the whites have stationed amidst the Indian nations themselves.

Only occasionally do the revolutions of Europe, the tumultuous upheavals that erupt constantly in the world of law and order, reach this place, and then only as the echo of a sound whose nature and origin the ear can no longer make out.

It might be an Indian who happens by and in the poetic idiom of the wilderness recounts a few of the sad realities of social life. Or it could be a forgotten newspaper in some hunter's knapsack, or just one of those vague rumors spread by strangers through which people come to learn of just about everything extraordinary that happens anywhere in the world.

Once a year, a vessel sails up the Saginaw, restoring this lost link to the great European chain that already circles the globe. It brings the diverse products of industry to the new settlement and in return takes away the fruits of the soil.

At the time of our visit, thirty individuals—men, women, elders, and children—constituted this tiny society, this barely formed embryo, this seed recently sprouted in the wilderness and obliged to live on whatever the wilderness can provide.

Chance, self-interest, and passion had conspired to bring these thirty individuals together in this diminutive patch of earth. No common bond unites them, moreover, and they differ profoundly from one another. Among them are Canadians, Americans, Indians, and half-breeds.

Some philosophers hold that human nature is the same everywhere and that variation among human beings is due solely to the different institutions and laws that exist in different societies. This opinion would appear to be contradicted by every page of world history. Every nation, like every individual, appears in those pages with a distinctive physiognomy. Its characteristic features persist through all the transformations it undergoes. Laws, mores, and religions may change; empire and wealth may shift from place to place; outer appearances may vary, the cloak may change, prejudices may vanish or be replaced by others. Despite these various transformations, you can always recognize the same unchanging people. In the midst of human variability, something invariable remains.

The people who inhabit this small cultivated plain belong to two races that have occupied American soil for nearly a century and are subject to the same laws. Yet they have nothing in common. They are still English or French, just as you find them on the banks of the Seine or the Thames.

Enter this cabin of leaves and you will find a man whose cordial welcome, frank features, and smiling lips immediately signal a taste for the pleasures of society and a carefree attitude toward life. You may at first take him to be an Indian. Exposed to the savage life, he has voluntarily adopted the dress, customs, and one might almost say the mores of the savage. He wears moccasins, an otter-skin cap, and a wool cloak. A tireless hunter, he remains alert even when asleep and lives on wild honey and buffalo meat. Yet he is still a Frenchman: cheerful, confident, proud of his origins, eager for military glory, more vain than self-interested, moved by instinct and impulse more than reason, and preferring reputation to money. Before departing for the wilderness he seems to have broken all bonds with the living: he appears to have neither wife nor children. To live like this runs counter to his mores, yet he adapts readily to his new situation as to everything else. Left to himself, he would naturally remain close to home. No one takes more pleasure from the domestic hearth. No one rejoices more in the sight of his ancestral chapel. Yet he was lured away from his tranquil habits. Novel images fired his imagination. He was transplanted to a new climate, and suddenly this same man became possessed by an insatiable desire for violent emotions, adventure, and danger. The most civilized of Europeans became a worshipper of the savage life. He prefers savannahs to city streets and hunting to farming. He will risk his life and live without a thought of tomorrow.

"The white men from France are as good at hunting as we are," the Indians of Canada used to say. "Like us, they scorn the conveniences of life and brave the terrors of death. God made them to dwell in the hut of the savage and live in the wilderness."

Just steps away from this man lives another European, who, when confronted with the same difficulties, stiffened his back against them.

This man is cold, tenacious, and pitiless in argument. [He] clings to the land and takes whatever he can from the wild. His struggle is constant, and not a day goes by when he does not claim another of nature's prizes. Little by little he brings to the wilderness his laws, his habits, his customs, and, when possible, the latest discoveries of his advanced civilization. The American immigrant values the victory solely for its results. Glory is but idle rumor in his estimation, and he holds that man lives only to acquire wealth and the conveniences of life. He is brave, but brave by calculation, brave because he has discovered that there are any number of things more difficult to bear than death. He is an adventurer who surrounds himself with family yet attaches little value to intellectual pleasures or the charms of social life.

Ensconced on the other side of the river, amid the reeds of the Saginaw, the Indian now and then casts a stoic eye on the dwellings of his European brethren. Do not think that he admires their works or envies their lot. For nearly three hundred years the American savage has struggled against the civilization that is pushing him back and surrounding him, and still he has neither knowledge of nor esteem for his enemy. Generations of both races come and go, to no avail. Like two parallel rivers, they have flowed for three hundred years into a common abyss. The space between them is narrow, but their waters do not mingle. Although the native of the New World does not lack for natural aptitude, his nature seems stubbornly refractory to our ideas and our arts. Lying on his blanket in his smoky hut, the Indian looks with contempt on the European's comfortable abode. He revels in his poverty, and his heart swells with pride at symbols of his barbaric independence. He smiles bitterly when he sees us torment ourselves to acquire useless riches. What we call industry, he calls shameful subjection. He likens the farmer to the ox who strains at his furrow. What we call the conveniences of life, he calls children's toys or women's trinkets. The only thing of ours that he envies is our weapons. When a man can spend the night beneath a tent of foliage, when he can light a fire to chase away the mosquitoes in summer and the cold in winter, when his dogs are good and game is plentiful, then what else can he ask of the Eternal Being?

On the other bank of the Saginaw, near the Europeans' clearing and on the border, as it were, between the Old World and the New, stands a rustic cabin more comfortable than the savage's wigwam yet coarser than the home of the civilized man. This is where the half-breed lives. The first time we called at the door of this semicivilized hut, we were quite surprised to hear a soft voice inside singing psalms of repentance to an Indian tune. We stood there for a moment. The modulations of the music were slow and deeply melancholy. We recognized at once the plaintive harmony that is so characteristic of songs of the wilderness. We went inside. The master was absent. Seated in the middle of the room, legs crossed on a rug, a young woman made moccasins, while with her foot she rocked the cradle of a child whose bronze complexion and features signaled its dual parentage. The woman was dressed like one of our peasants, except that her feet were bare and her hair hung loosely about her shoulders. At the sight of us she fell silent with a sort of respectful alarm. We asked if she was French.

"No," she answered with a smile.

"English?"

"Not English either," she said. Then, lowering her eyes, she added, "I am only a savage."

A child of two races, brought up to speak two languages, nourished by diverse faiths and soothed by contradictory prejudices, the half-breed constitutes a composite as inexplicable to himself as to others. The world reflected in his primitive mind is but an inchoate muddle from which he cannot escape. Proud of his European origins, he despises the wilderness, yet he loves the savage liberty that there reigns supreme. He admires civilization yet cannot submit fully to its dominion. His tastes are in contradiction with his ideas, his opinions with his mores. With but a dim light by which to divine his way forward, he cannot decide which way to turn; wrestling painfully with inexpugnable doubt, he adopts contradictory ways: he prays at two altars. He believes in the Redeemer and in the amulets of the medicine man, and by the time he reaches the end of his road, he still will not have managed to penetrate the riddle of his existence.

Here, in this obscure corner of the world, the hand of God has already sown the seeds of diverse nations. Several different races, several distinct peoples, here confront one another.

A few exiled members of the great human family have come together in these vast forests. Their needs are common. Together they must struggle against the animals of the woods, the hunger, the inclemency of the seasons. There are barely thirty of them in the midst of a forest where everything resists their efforts, yet they regard one another with hatred and suspicion. The color of their skin, their poverty or their wealth, their ignorance or enlightenment have already established indestructible classifications. National prejudices, prejudices of education and birth, divide and isolate them.

Where else can one find in such a compact setting a fuller portrait of the wretchedness of human nature? One trait is missing, however.

The deep divisions that birth and opinion have established among these people extend beyond life into the grave. Six different religions or sects vie for the faith of this nascent society.

Catholicism, with its formidable immobility, its absolute dogmas, its terrible anathemas, and its immense rewards; the religious anarchy of the Reformation; ancient paganism—all are represented here. The One Eternal Being who created all men in his image is already worshipped in six different ways. There is passionate dispute about heaven, which each sect claims to be its exclusive heritage. Amid the miseries of solitude and the woes of the present, moreover, the human imagination spends itself in efforts to imagine future suffering beyond words. The Lutheran condemns the Calvinist to eternal flames, the Calvinist condemns the Unitarian, and the Catholic reproves them all.

More tolerant in his primitive faith, the Indian confines himself to banishing his European brethren from the blessed provinces he claims for himself. Wedded to the obscure traditions handed down to him by his forebears, he consoles himself easily for this life's woes and dies in peace, dreaming of evergreen forests safe forever from the pioneer's axe and full of deer and beaver for him to hunt through all the numberless days of eternity.

After lunch we went to see the wealthiest man in the village, Mr. Williams.[9] We found him in his shop selling a variety of cheap trinkets to Indians, including knives, bead necklaces, and earrings. It was pitiful to see how these wretches were treated by their civilized European brothers. What is more, all the Europeans we met in Saginaw had strikingly positive things to say about the Indians. They were good, inoffensive people and a thousand times less likely to steal than whites. The only problem was that they were beginning to get a better sense of what things cost. What was wrong with that? we asked. The problem was that it meant that the profits of doing business with them were declining daily. Does this exchange give you a better idea of the civilized man's superiority over the savage? The Indian in his primitive simplicity would have said that he was finding it daily more difficult to deceive his neighbor. But the white man, with his firmer grasp of language, has hit upon a felicitously subtle way to say the same thing without making his actions sound shameful.

On the way back from Mr. Williams's store, we had the idea of following the Saginaw upstream a way to shoot the wild ducks that live along its banks. As we were hunting, a canoe moved out of the reeds, and some Indians paddled toward us in order to examine my rifle, which they had glimpsed from a distance. I had noticed that this weapon, which was by no means extraordinary, always drew particular attention from the savages. A rifle that can kill two men in one second and disappear in a cloud of its own smoke is in their eyes an incomparable wonder, a priceless masterpiece. The Indians who approached our boat were as usual quite admiring. They asked where my rifle came from. Our young guide responded that it had been made on the other side of the Great Water by the fathers of the Canadians, which, as one might imagine, did not diminish its value in the Indians' eyes. They pointed out, however, that since the sights were not positioned in the center of each barrel, you couldn't be as certain of your aim, and I confess that I had no clear answer to this.

When evening came, we returned to our canoe and, trusting in the experi-

9. Gardner D. Williams.

ence we had acquired that morning, set out by ourselves up one branch of the Saginaw, which we had only glimpsed earlier.

There was not a cloud in the sky, and the air was pure and still. The river flowed through a vast forest, but so slowly that it would have been almost impossible to say which way the current ran. We had long felt that in order to appreciate the forests of the New World, we would have to follow one of the rivers that run through them. The rivers are like great highways that Providence was careful to provide when the world was created so that man could find his way into the wilderness. As you make your way through the woods on foot or horseback, your view is usually quite limited. What is more, the very trail you are following is the work of man. By contrast, the rivers are roads that retain no tracks, and their banks offer free access to the variety of strange and magnificent spectacles that profuse vegetation can create when left untouched.

The wilderness we beheld before us was no doubt just as it appeared six thousand years ago to our earliest ancestors: a delightful, fragrant solitude filled with blossoms, a magnificent abode, a living palace built for man, though he had yet to take possession of the premises. Our canoe skimmed the surface of the water silently and without effort. Serenity reigned all around, and all was quiet. We ourselves were quickly overcome by the sight. Our words grew fewer and fewer, and before long we were expressing our thoughts in whispers. At length we fell silent, and as we lifted our paddles out of the water we both fell into a quiet reverie, contemplating the ineffable charm of our surroundings.

Why is it that human languages can find words for every pain yet cannot manage to convey the sweetest and most natural emotions of the heart? Will anyone ever give an accurate account of those rare moments when physical well-being offers a foretaste of moral tranquility, when the universe stands in perfect equilibrium before your eyes? When the soul, half asleep, hovers between present and future, between the real and the possible? When, surrounded by natural beauty and quiet warmth, man, at peace with himself amid universal peace, can hear the beat of his own heart, each pulse marking the passage of time as it flows drop by drop into the eternal river? Many will live long lives, perhaps, without once experiencing anything like what I have just described. They will not understand what I have written. But I am sure that there are some who, upon searching their memories and the depths of their hearts, will know how to lend color to my images, and who in reading will feel awakening within themselves memories of fleeting hours not quite erased by the passage of time or the concerns of everyday existence.

We were wrenched from our reverie by a rifle shot, which rang out suddenly in the woods. At first the noise seemed to ricochet between the riverbanks, but then it rumbled off into the distance until it was completely lost in the depths of the surrounding forest. It was as if civilization in its advance had let loose a long and terrifying war cry.

One night in Sicily, I chanced to lose my way in a vast swamp near the place where the city of Hymera once stood.[10] The sight of what had once been a famous city now become wasteland made a deep and lasting impression on me. I had never before encountered a more splendid monument to the instability of human affairs and the wretchedness of human nature. Here was another empty place, but now the imagination, instead of searching in the past, looked ahead to a vast, imponderable future. By what peculiar caprice of fate, I wondered, had I, the son of an ancient people, who had seen the ruins of empires that no longer exist and explored wildernesses made by man, been brought to witness scenes from the primitive world and discover the still-empty cradle of a great nation? To say this is not to engage in rash philosophical speculation; it is to state a truth as certain as if it were already accomplished. In a few years these impenetrable forests will have fallen. The rumble of civilization and industry will disrupt the silence of the Saginaw. The whisper of its waters will no longer be heard echoing in the woods. Quays will imprison its banks, and currents that today flow through a nameless wilderness unheeded and undisturbed will find themselves parted by the bows of ships. Fifty leagues still stand between this place and the major European settlements, and we are perhaps the last travelers who will have been allowed to contemplate this solitude in all its primitive splendor—so great is the impetus that drives the white race to conquer the whole of the New World.

It is, I think, this idea of destruction, this nagging thought of imminent and inevitable change, that makes the American wilderness such a unique and touchingly beautiful sight to behold. One takes it in with a pleasure tinged with melancholy. One must admire it, as it were, in haste. This savage natural grandeur is about to meet its end, and the idea of it mingles in the mind with the superb images to which the triumphant march of civilization gives rise. One feels proud to be human, yet at the same time one somehow feels bitter regret that God has granted man so much power over nature. The mind is assailed by contradictory ideas and sentiments, yet no impression is without grandeur, and all leave an indelible trace.

Our intention was to depart Saginaw the next day, July 27, but one of our horses had been cut by its saddle, so we decided to stay another day. For want of any other way to pass the time, we went hunting in the prairies along the Saginaw, below the clearings. These prairies are not marshy, as one might expect. They are fairly broad plains on which the forests have not encroached, despite the excellent soil. The grass is sharp edged and three or four feet high. Finding little game, we turned back early. The heat was stifling, as if a storm were approaching, and the mosquitoes even more bothersome than usual. A swarm of them enveloped us as we walked, and we had to wage constant war against them. Woe unto anyone who might be obliged to stop, for he would then find

---

10. Hymera, an ancient city on the northern coast of Sicily, was destroyed by Hannibal's Carthaginian forces in 409 BC. Tocqueville visited the spot in 1827.

himself defenseless before a merciless enemy. It was so difficult to stand still that I recall having to load my rifle while on the run.

As we made our way back across the prairie, we noticed that our Canadian guide was following an existing trail and watching carefully where he stepped. "Why are you being so careful?" I asked. "Are you afraid of getting wet?"

"No," he answered. "But I'm in the habit of watching my step whenever I'm walking through a prairie so as not to step on a rattlesnake."

"What the devil!" I replied, jumping back onto the path. "Are there rattlesnakes around here?"

"Definitely," my imperturbable Americanized Norman replied, "there are plenty of them."

I scolded him for not having warned us sooner. He said that since we were wearing good boots, and since the rattlesnake never bites above the ankle, he hadn't thought we were in much danger.

I asked him if the rattlesnake's bite was fatal. He replied that victims always died within twenty-four hours unless they got help from the Indians. They know a remedy which is supposed to save the victim if administered in time.

Be that as it may, for the rest of our hike we followed our guide's lead and were careful about where we put our feet down.

The night that followed this scorching hot day was one of the worst I've ever spent. The mosquitoes had become so bothersome that even though I was dead tired, it was impossible to get any sleep. Toward midnight, the storm that had been threatening for some time finally arrived. With no hope of falling asleep, I got up and went to open the door of our cabin so that I might at least breathe a little of the cool night air. It was not yet raining, and the air seemed calm, but the limbs of the trees were already swaying, and deep moans and persistent growls emerged from the forest. An occasional flash of lightning lit up the sky. The quiet flow of the Saginaw, the small clearing along one of its banks, the five or six cabins, and the girdle of foliage that enveloped us suddenly emerged from the darkness—a fleeting image of what the future would hold for this place. Then all receded once more into the blackest night, and the terrifying voice of the wilderness could once again be heard.

I was watching this impressive spectacle and feeling moved when I heard a sigh alongside me and by the light of a lightning bolt I saw an Indian leaning as I was against the wall of our cabin. The storm had no doubt interrupted his sleep, for he was taking in the surroundings with an agitated eye.

Was he afraid of thunder? Or did he see the clash of the elements as something other than a passing convulsion of nature? Did the fleeting images of civilization that erupted out of the commotion in the wilderness hold a prophetic meaning for him? Did the moans from a forest that seemed locked in an unequal struggle strike his ear as an occult warning from God, a solemn revelation of the ultimate fate awaiting his savage race? I could not say. But his trembling lips seemed to whisper a prayer, and his face betrayed a superstitious terror.

At five o'clock in the morning, it was time to leave. All the Indians from the surrounding region had vanished. They had gone to receive the gifts that the English bestow on them every year while the Europeans are busy with the harvest. We were therefore forced to make our return trip through the forest without a guide. A journey of this sort is not as difficult as one might think. Usually there is only one trail through these vast empty tracts, and all it takes to reach your destination is to avoid losing the trail.

At five in the morning, we crossed the Saginaw once more to bid our hosts farewell and hear their last words of advice, and then we turned our horses around and found ourselves alone in the middle of the forest. It was not, I confess, without a sense of gravity that we plunged into its moist expanse. To our rear, the same forest that now engulfed us stretched all the way to the North Pole and the Pacific Ocean. Only one settlement stood between us and wilderness without end, and we had just left it. These thoughts only encouraged us to ride faster, and after three hours we came to an abandoned wigwam on the lonely banks of the Cass River. A grassy spit of land shaded by tall trees jutted into the stream, and there we dismounted to eat our lunch and enjoy the view of the river, whose crystal-clear waters snaked their way through the woods.

On leaving the Cass River wigwam we came to a place where several trails diverged. We had been told which one to take, but it was easy to forget or misunderstand certain details in such explanations. And that was indeed our experience on this particular day. We had been told that there were two trails, but we found three. True, two of the three joined back up a short while later, as we learned afterward, but we did not know this at the time, and we were thoroughly confused.

After carefully evaluating the situation and talking things over, we did as great men nearly always do and made our choice almost at random. We forded the river as best we could and moved off rapidly toward the southwest. More than once the trail seemed close to vanishing in the thick forest. At other places it seemed so little traveled that we had a hard time believing that it led anywhere but to some abandoned wigwam. True, our compass told us that we were still headed in the right direction. Nevertheless, we were not completely confident until we came upon the place where we had dined three days earlier. We recognized the spot because of a giant pine, whose trunk, lacerated by the wind, we had admired. We did not slow down, however, because the sun was beginning to set. Soon we came to the clearing that usually marks the approach to a farm, and as night was about to fall, we caught sight of the Flint River. A half hour later we pulled up at our host's door. This time the bear welcomed us as old friends and reared up on its hind legs only to celebrate our happy return.

Throughout that entire day of travel we had not encountered a single human being. The animals, too, had disappeared. No doubt they had sought refuge in the shade from the heat of the day. The only living thing we had seen was the occasional sparrow hawk perched on one leg and slumbering tranquilly in the sun at the top of some dead tree, seemingly sculpted out of the very wood on which it stood.

It was in the midst of this profound solitude that we suddenly remembered the Revolution of 1830, the first anniversary of which had just passed. I cannot tell you how insistently memories of July 29 assailed our minds.[11] The shouts and smoke of combat, the roar of the cannon, the volleys of musket fire, the terrible clang of the tocsin—the memory of that terrible day seemed suddenly to erupt in flames out of the past and come to life before my eyes. It was but a sudden flash, a fleeting dream. When I looked up and glanced around me, the apparition had already vanished. But never had the silence of the forest seemed more chilling, its shadows darker, or its solitude more complete.

11. July 29 was also Tocqueville's twenty-sixth birthday.

part 4

Tocqueville's and Beaumont's Texts
on the Penitentiary System

The full text of the penitentiary report is available in English only from the initial translation Francis Lieber produced in 1833, *On the Penitentiary System in the United States and Its Application in France: With an Appendix on Penal Colonies, and Also, Statistical Notes.* Tocqueville was quite dissatisfied with that translation, as Lieber attempted to turn the work into a plea for the Philadelphia system of cellular isolation several years before Tocqueville and Beaumont were willing to take the same stand publicly.

We provide here selections from the report and its appendices, as well as letters preceding and following its publication.

Beaumont was the primary author of the report. For his part, Tocqueville wrote to French officials on the progress of their mission from Sing Sing, Auburn, and Philadelphia. He continued his dialogue on prison systems with American reformers long after the publication of the report, gaining insights he could use in his fight to reform the French prison system.

Indicative of the depth of the American research are the one-on-one interviews with inmates at the Philadelphia penitentiary that are reproduced in full here. "Save for sleeping in a cell and being whipped," we live practically like the inmates, Tocqueville wrote, tongue in cheek, to his cousin Le Peletier d'Aunay, who had been instrumental in getting the study assignment for the two travelers.

Letters from America

From Tocqueville | To Félix Le Peletier d'Aunay[1]

[Sing Sing, June 7, 1831]

... We have found in America such a spirit of hospitality and enlightened benevolence that we have found it easy to carry out the mission that was entrusted to us and conduct all the research that it requires. We have already availed ourselves of this warm reception to visit the prisons of New York. For the past week, we have been living in the tiny village of Sing Sing, the site of the largest penitentiary in the United States. Except for sleeping in a cell and being whipped with a rope, we are leading almost the same life as the inmates. In other words, we have thrown ourselves wholeheartedly into the penitentiary system.

As you will no doubt appreciate, our investigation to date has not been extensive enough to form any firm opinions about what we have seen thus far. Nevertheless, we have already formulated any number of ideas and registered a variety of impressions that I should like to impart to you at once. To do this as efficiently as possible, I can think of no better way than to summarize for you the pros and the cons, leaving it to you, my dear cousin, to draw the definitive conclusions that have thus far eluded us. As you can see, I have not forgotten my legal training.

To date we have visited penitentiaries of two kinds: those for juveniles below the age of sixteen and those intended for the correction of older criminals. The former are known as reform schools [*maisons de refuge*], and so far our opinion of them has been entirely favorable. The youthful inmates we have seen appear to be in good health, obedient, and studious. The atmosphere is that of a school rather than a prison, and from the official reports we have been given, it is clear that since the reform schools were established, the number of young delinquents in New York has decreased by nearly half. Of all the institutions we have seen in this country, these schools would, I believe, be the easiest to transplant to France. The idea is simple, is easy to put into practice, and does not re-

1. Félix Le Peletier d'Aunay (1782–1855), a cousin of Tocqueville, served as a deputy and prefect. He was able to maintain political favor through the empire, the Bourbon Restoration, and the July Monarchy by supporting the majority in each case. Le Peletier d'Aunay was interested in prison reform and helped Tocqueville to secure support for his study of American penitentiaries.

quire any costly construction. Yet I doubt that the effects to be expected in Europe would be as good as those obtained in America. Here, the need for labor is so urgent that the children who are released from reform school each year immediately find employment. Hence the work of reform is never undone by idleness and want. With us, the prejudice associated with a history of criminality would probably have greater influence.

As for the penitentiaries proper, it is more difficult to give a satisfactory account of those we have seen thus far. In some respects they have exceeded our expectations; in others, they have fallen well short. What can be said in general is that those who criticize them in Europe know very little about them, as do those who praise them. At first glance they appear to be more than satisfactory. Here at Sing Sing we find ourselves in the midst of 900 prisoners living under the watchful eye of just 22 guards, without chains or walls to confine them during the day and without hope of putting any money aside, and yet they work from morning till night without uttering a word. We have been watching them constantly for ten days and have yet to divine a furtive glance between inmates or to hear a single word spoken. In short, they seem to have renounced, utterly and irrevocably, any claim to a will of their own. I have witnessed something of the sort among Trappists, yet I would never have believed that such obedience could be obtained by force alone had I not seen it with my own eyes.

In addition to this extraordinary result, consider the following: *there is no doubt* that mortality among the prisoners is lower than in the free population. *There is also no doubt* that prisons administered in this way *earn revenue* for the state rather than costing it money. We had doubted that this could be true, but official documents have now convinced us that it is indeed the case.

So much for the positive elements of the picture. Here is the rest:

First, I doubt that the discipline that yields these very surprising results can be applied in France, even if one were to assume that the physical state of our prisons were such as to allow solitary confinement at night, which is an indispensable requirement of the system. In order to obtain such complete obedience with so few actual means of repression while at the same time requiring the prisoners to do useful work, the Americans have sought to isolate the inmates from one another to such a degree that each man must rely solely on his own individual strength and must therefore feel weaker than the guards watching over him. They achieve this by means of *silence* and *constant work:* silence separates the inmates from one another, and work absorbs all their physical and moral energy and keeps them out of mischief. That is the whole secret of the system, but there is more to it than meets the eye, for if constant labor is one condition of the silence, how does one get the inmates to labor constantly? It was this point that puzzled us in France when we studied the penitentiary system in books. The authors who described the prisons of America always struck me as rather like the Hindus who place the world on a tortoise, the tortoise on a horse, and the horse on an elephant yet never manage to describe the ultimate base on which everything rests.

The system of work and silence—in short, the admirable discipline we have observed—ultimately rests on nothing other than the unlimited arbitrary power to inflict corporal punishment, a power that is vested in men whose everyday interest is not to abuse it and to use it only to maintain strict order in the prison. This power rests virtually in the hands of the head of the institution, who may delegate it, and who does in fact delegate it (at Sing Sing, at least), to the members of his staff, all of whom are authorized to administer whippings without supervision or oversight by higher authority. Such practices are a long way from what people imagine in Europe.

All this is worthy of reflection, however, because I doubt that this kind of disciplinary power, on which the prosperity and security of the institution depend, can be maintained, and, furthermore, I am not sure that it is very humane or even very safe to place such power in so many hands. Finally, I have great difficulty believing that in the current state of mores and public opinion in France, the government would be permitted to take such a course even if it had the will to do so.

You may well be thinking, moreover, that even if we were to countenance such extraordinary power, it would still be hard to believe that guards can pay close enough and persistent enough attention to the inmates to ensure that they work constantly and remain silent at all times. I confess that we are still puzzled by this question, and although we daily witness the effects of the disciplinary regime here, we do not yet have a very clear idea of the cause. But this is what we think.

In the first place, all responsibility is concentrated here in one man, the director of the institution, who is called the agent. He is obliged by law in a vague and general way to maintain order and ensure that the prison is productive, *by whatever means seem appropriate to him.* Indeed, there are no written regulations. All administrative details are decided by the head man, who has the power to choose all the employees of the institution. Add to this the fact that in a society as small and peaceful as this one, the public pays close attention to its prisons; that the number of penal institutions is quite small; that experience with the penitentiary system is still quite limited; and that there is a lively rivalry among the states regarding it; and you will understand that prison administrations here are required to work more diligently than it would be prudent to expect elsewhere.

That is not all. I believe that there is also a more general cause, but one that I do not find it easy to explain. The Americans seem to me to have chosen a very dangerous but very effective way to ensure that their prison guards remain vigilant at all times, as their disciplinary system requires. They assemble hundreds of vigorous individuals outdoors, in open fields, and equip them with lethal tools. It is obvious that if the disciplinary system did not prevent these men from plotting together and if their time were not completely occupied by work, then not only would the institutional order be in imminent danger, as in Europe, but so would the lives of the guards. Thus it is fair to say that the guards are obliged on pain of death to be demanding, vigilant, and just, and I assure you that, watching them on the job, you see readily that they are not working solely for the love of God.

In general, what is most striking in this society thus far is the artfulness with which particular interest and general interest are induced to work together toward a common goal. One thus contrives to draw from men nearly all the good of which they are capable, often without their even being aware of it.

But to get back to the penitentiary system, do you not think, my dear cousin, that such means of discipline can be dangerous in practice? In the end, what the Americans do is nothing other than to court danger in the hope of avoiding it. As long as the machine runs properly, their prisons will clearly operate in admirable fashion. But should any cog in the mechanism seize up, I greatly fear that a terrible catastrophe could ensue. Should a government adopt a system whose success depends on conditions that are difficult to satisfy and whose failure would be so perilous? Will the American government itself be able to persevere on a path on which it embarked only a few years ago?

One very important question preoccupies us constantly, and yet we find it very difficult to answer: the question of recidivism. Does the penitentiary system reduce the number of crimes? As you reminded us prior to our departure, the answer to this question is indeed the proof that a system is good or bad. Would you believe that we have as yet been unable to find a single comprehensive official document dealing with this issue, and that the government of New York has set out to change all its prisons and has pursued this project for years without any reliable data regarding the effectiveness of the new system? We had read in the work of Mr. Charles Lucas and mentioned in our memorandum the fact that Auburn had achieved a recidivism rate one-sixth that of prisons in France. We see now that in order to arrive at this result, Lucas counted only those inmates who *returned* to Auburn after initially being incarcerated there. But Auburn is not the only prison in America or even the only central prison in the state of New York, so it is obvious that such a method of calculating is totally unsatisfactory. In an attempt to obtain a more accurate figure, we have begun to examine the records of all the central prisons of New York and neighboring states. In this we have made considerable progress for the state of New York, so the most difficult part of the job is done.

I also hope that by the time we return we will be able to state quite accurately what it costs the state to build a new prison here or to improve an existing one, and that we will also be able to provide data for comparison and, more broadly, documentation sufficient to allow people in France to take advantage of this knowledge.

In doing the research that is indispensable to find out what we need to know about this and many other subjects, we daily become more aware of the fact that the Americans and the French are guilty of opposite excesses. At home people complain of the abuse of centralization; here, the government is not in evidence at all, and, despite what people say, things are not always the better for it. Seldom do we find a general idea guiding a project undertaken in the public interest; one searches in vain for the central point from which an administration might set its course. What is more, those in whom what seem to us such limited and incomplete powers of administration are vested succeed one another so quickly that we find it impossible to detect any enduring views in their plans or continuity in their efforts.

That is where things stand, my dear cousin. I hope to have furnished you with enough information to judge as soundly as we are able to. At any rate, I have tried to do so.

To summarize:

1. We are certain of the following:
   a. That the American penitentiaries we have visited thus far cost the state nothing and in many cases earn a profit despite the very high salaries of prison staff.
   b. That the mortality rate is virtually zero.
   c. That discipline is extremely strict and designed to isolate each inmate within the population, in the hope that inmates will not leave prison worse than when they went in.
2. We believe (but we cannot yet prove) that the American system decreases the number of recidivists.
3. Finally, we do not believe that it has been proven that the system as it exists today can be maintained, and we doubt that one could or would even want to adopt the discipline on which it depends in France, even if we were willing to undertake the initial expenditures that such a system would require.

Our thinking on these various points should soon be clarified. In a week we leave for Boston, where there is a well-known prison, and from there we go to Philadelphia, but New York will continue to be our headquarters, and letters should still be addressed to us there.

As we work on the penitentiary system, my dear cousin, you may rest assured that we remain curious about many other things that we encounter in our travels. People talk so much about America in France, and it occupies such an important place in public opinion and so frequently influences our political decisions, that we take a very lively interest in everything that has to do with the life of society here. Since our arrival we have become the world's most implacable investigators. Yet the results of our research have not been uniformly happy. Some of our investigations have yielded fairly clear findings. This is the case when the general principles of a subject are familiar to us, or when we know enough about the state of affairs in France that we can clarify our thinking by way of comparison. Yet on numerous other points we must proceed in almost total darkness. To confine our attention to matters of public administration, for instance, we can see in a general way that everything here is different: the number of administrative powers, their extent, their attribution, and their means of action. Unfortunately, we have no idea which details would be useful to explore in order to understand the reasons for these differences. What is better here than in France, what is worse, and what is simply different? If by any chance you were to find yourself with a spare moment without anything useful to do—a rare circumstance, I know—and if it isn't too much trouble for you to offer us a few words of advice to guide us in our research, we would have one more reason to be grateful to you, in addition to those of which I hardly need remind you. The difficulties that arise in any administration, as well as the theoretical and practical questions to which the art of governing civil societies may give rise, are familiar to you. More than anyone else, you have the discerning eye to identify which points would be most interesting for a Frenchman to study in America. The fact that it is so easy for you to provide us with the advice we need not only encourages us to ask you for it but also doubles its value to us.

I shall close, my dear cousin, where I should have begun, by congratulating you on the choice of the new member you have just added to your family. I have not yet had the opportunity to meet M. Séguier, but his reputation as a man of distinction is such that I can only rejoice in anticipation of having him for a kinsman.[2] I beg you to share with him my warmest regards.

From Tocqueville and Beaumont | Letter to the Minister of the Interior[3]

Auburn, July 14, 1831

Monsieur le Ministre,

In the letter that it was our privilege to address to you on June . . . , we reported on what particularly attracted our attention in the penitentiaries of the state of New York, Sing Sing prison and the reform school for young delinquents.

In the same letter we told you of our intention to visit next the penitentiary at Auburn, the first institution of its kind in America and still the most famous both here and in France.

During this visit we made very detailed observations of the prison over a considerable length of time, and we must now submit to Your Excellency a report of our findings.

Auburn is the model on which the Sing Sing penitentiary was based. Because the two institutions are therefore similar in many respects, we will describe the points of similarity quite briefly, referring to our first report for fur-

2. Armand Pierre Séguier (1803–1876) was the son-in-law of Le Peletier d'Aunay. He served as a magistrate and was a member of the French Academy of Sciences.

3. Casimir Pierre Périer (1777–1832) served as minister of the interior and prime minister of France from 1831 to 1832. A member of a wealthy French banking family, Périer was active in politics during the Bourbon Restoration and reluctantly supported the ascension of Louis-Philippe, duc d'Orléans, during the July Revolution in 1830. He served as president of the Chamber of Deputies for a few months in 1830, and during his terms as minister of the interior and prime minister, he set aside many of his liberal leanings in favor of restoring peace and stability to France.

View of Auburn prison from the Belvedere American Hotel, 14 July 1831. (GB2)

ther details. Note, however, that there are also significant differences between the two prisons, and it is to these differences that we particularly direct the attention of Your Excellency.

The administration of Auburn is the same as that of Sing Sing. Power is concentrated in the hands of a warden (the agent) appointed by the state government. His authority is great, but he is required to post a substantial bond to ensure that he does his job conscientiously. The warden is assisted by the clerk, who monitors all his work and who, as the overseer of the institution's accounts, is in a good position to restrain unnecessary spending.

Above the warden is a commissioner of inspectors, whose legal powers are extensive but whose actual powers are in fact quite limited. Below him are the guards, who are appointed by the inspectors on the warden's recommendations. At Sing Sing, the warden was free to choose the guards himself.

As at Sing Sing, certain general principles of discipline are followed: Prisoners are separated at night but work together throughout the day, and total silence is observed at all times. As in the other two institutions, the only disciplinary measure here is whipping. The number of strokes is unlimited, and the decision is made by the guards at the moment of the infraction, without any need to seek the permission of the warden. There are, moreover, slight differences in the prisoners' schedules and the details of the daily agenda that it would be pointless and tedious to recount here.

These common features establish between Auburn and Sing Sing a family resemblance that is impossible to miss, yet each institution has certain distinctive traits that are readily apparent to the attentive observer.

At Sing Sing, the serious difficulties that arise from the harshness of the discipline are compounded by certain special circumstances. Several hundred prisoners are dispersed during the day across a considerable expanse of country without chains or walls to restrain them, and they are issued implements of iron and steel that could easily be put to pernicious use if the inmates so chose.

At Auburn, by contrast, the type of work that has been chosen to keep the inmates occupied allows for a simpler and more natural approach. As in most of our prisons, the courtyard is surrounded by high walls. Armed guards constantly patrol catwalks atop these walls. This physical arrangement has yielded good results. Since the inmates always work at fixed posts in assigned workshops, it has been possible to equip each shop with a wooden platform from which guards can observe what is happening and hear what is said without being seen or heard themselves. This simple and relatively inexpensive innovation has led to noticeably improved discipline. No prisoner can expect to outwit the guards, and the warden's surveillance is feared all the more because it is omnipresent yet invisible. We found these platforms quite useful ourselves for gauging the state of discipline in the institution. Because of these arrangements, the prison at Auburn looks much less unusual than the one at Sing Sing, and one is less aware of the severity of the discipline; these differences would make it easier to imitate the American system and would increase the likelihood of achieving durable success.

In our opinion, however, what distinguishes Auburn most clearly from Sing Sing is, first, the system of contract labor that has been established there and, second, the very careful attention that is paid to moral reform of the prisoners. Our investigation therefore focused on these two points especially.

Sing Sing found a way to use the prisoners' labor for the benefit of the state. Initially, the men were put to work in an immense stone quarry, and the product of their labor was used to build the prison itself. The state thus availed itself of a source of abundant raw material while making good use of the prisoners' time. The work it demanded of inmates was simple and easy to learn, and almost anyone is capable of it.[4]

At Auburn things were not quite so simple. With respect to inmate labor, Auburn was in much the same situation as our central prisons. It was therefore necessary to set up a much more complicated system to meet the diverse needs of the surrounding population. A diverse range of occupations had to be accommodated. The authorities accordingly established first shops that employed weavers in the manufacture of textiles, then shops that made barrels, locks, shoes, etc. There are at present 13 different workshops employing 462 workers. In addition, 158 inmates work directly for the state or the prison itself.

In theory, the work is managed by the prison authorities. At first, the war-

4. The previous passage replaces the following, which is crossed out in the manuscript: "At Sing Sing, which stands adjacent to immense granite quarries and where the prison itself had yet to be built, the inmates have thus far been employed solely in work on behalf of the state. They built the vast prison that holds them and to which another story is currently being added. At Sing Sing it was therefore easy to find productive use for the labor of criminals. The only need was for masons and stonecutters, two types of manual laborers."

den purchased the raw materials himself, provided overseers and tools, and marketed the manufactured products. This system was abandoned several years ago, however. Some officials seemed to prefer it to the current system, but direct management has been replaced by contractual agreement with outside entrepreneurs. The system is nevertheless quite different from the contractual systems in use in French prisons.

In France it is common for the same person to provide food to the inmates, to supply them with raw material and tools, and, finally, to pay the state or the workers themselves for their labor. The prison thus becomes more or less dependent on the contractor, and discipline inevitably suffers, often irreparably. That, at any rate, is what we have observed in numerous cases.

At Auburn, by contrast, the authorities have been careful to enter into multiple contracts. Each workshop is serviced by a different contractor, so that no single individual can obtain more than a limited and temporary influence over the prison. We met men with experience of this system who were critical of certain aspects of it: for instance, contractors are frequently present in the shops and can develop regular relationships with inmates that are sometimes detrimental to prison discipline and ultimately compromise the rigor of the regime. In particular, Mr. Elam Lynds, the former warden of Auburn and principal founder of the penitentiary system in America, is of this opinion. In his day, contractors were prohibited from entering the workshops by the terms of their contracts. The prison agreed to supply them with items made according to specifications for which they paid an agreed price. Two of these contracts are still in force, and we asked to examine them. As a consequence of this arrangement, Mr. Elam Lynds was obliged to hire guards with a knowledge of various trades. He was able to do so. Several of these men are still in the prison and for the most part seem remarkably intelligent.

Whatever ultimate results may be feared from the contractual system now in force at Auburn, it is in any case certain that it has not prevented the institution from prospering financially. There is no denying that it has contributed significantly to the prison's material success.

We have documented proof that in 1829 the state earned a profit on the prison above its costs and that in 1830 the revenue nearly covered its expenses. This prosperity is remarkable in more than one respect. The reasons for this are not specific to America, because the official accounts, which the comptroller general of the state of New York allowed us to examine in Albany, showed that the prison that preceded Auburn and that was operated under the old system cost the state approximately . . . annually.

The prison's earnings have increased as discipline has improved. Upon our return we will provide the government with proof of this assertion in the form of tables of receipts and expenditures. Far from complaining about the work of the prisoners, the contractors, with whom we met frequently, assured us that inmates produced more in a year than free workers and that there was no difference in the quality of the work. It was not in the interest of these men to exaggerate the productivity of the convicts, so the fact that they were unanimous in their opinion seemed worth calling to Your Excellency's attention.

We cannot, however, hide the fact that this astonishing financial performance is due in part to circumstances that need to be made explicit. In France, it is difficult to find markets for prison-made items. By contrast, Auburn is located in a vast country whose prosperity is growing by leaps and bounds and where consumption is growing faster than production. In France, inmates receive a significant portion of the price of their labor. At Auburn they receive nothing, and the state takes the profits. All the Americans with whom we have had the opportunity to discuss the prison system thus far, including both practical men and philanthropic theorists, have expressed strong opposition to the practice of allowing prisoners to retain part of their earnings. They argue that this would constitute a sort of bonus for crime. It deprives prison of its penal character and almost inevitably hurts discipline by allocating to prisoners sums of money that they almost invariably put to bad use. Without entering into a theoretical discussion of this subject, which can be rather complicated, we cannot refrain from pointing out that while it may be useful to allow prisoners to retain some of what they earn, Sing Sing and Auburn prove that it is not necessary. To judge by the reports of contractors as well as our own close and thorough observation of these two prisons, it is clear that, even without pecuniary compensation, it is possible to extract all the work that it is reasonable to expect from the inmates. In Massachusetts prisoners are still allowed to retain a portion of their earnings. After visiting the institutions where this practice is allowed, we will be in a better position to offer a final judgment on this point. If we ultimately determine that American discipline makes inmates much more productive than they are in France even without pecuniary compensation, this would of course be an important argument in favor of adopting the American system.

The second feature that distinguishes Auburn and Sing Sing from other prisons is the importance attached to moral reform. At Sing Sing everything is clearly sacrificed to the need to maintain the material order so necessary to the very existence of the prison and to the lives of its guards. Literary and religious instruction is dispensed parsimoniously, and the directors of the institution apparently do not count on reform and have not tried to determine whether it actually occurs.

This is not the case at Auburn. There, by contrast, everything that is done seems to be done with an eye to achieving moral reform. In addition to public religious services, the prison chaplain visits the prisoners' cells every night in an effort to awaken their sense of honor and virtue. A Presbyterian, this minister assures us that on the whole the inmates seem to trust him and to heed his advice. On Sundays there are also classes. At Sing Sing these last for an hour, and only 80 students are admitted, but at Auburn they continue for two hours, and 200 inmates receive the benefits of instruction. We are assured that most of these men have been making rapid progress. All will know how to read by the time they leave prison.

Further evidence of the importance ascribed to moral reform at Auburn is the extreme care that is taken there to monitor progress. In 1827 prison officials wrote to various places where they believed former inmates had gone after their release. The purpose of these letters was to compile concrete documentation of the former prisoners' subsequent behavior. A similar survey was conducted in 1828. It is regrettable that it was not continued longer. The results were overwhelmingly favorable to the reform system: of 160 individuals about whom information was obtained in 1827, behavior was entirely correct in 112 cases, 12 had improved, 10 were doubtful, and 26 were unreformed. Of 142 freed prisoners investigated in 1828, 80 were found to exhibit good behavior, 19 were more good than bad, 18 were doubtful, and only 19 remained in the grip of crime. It is regrettable that this useful effort was not continued.

Despite these impressive results, which deserve to be known, we must not hide from Your Excellency the point about which we remain most in doubt: Does the American system of discipline possess as great a power to reform the souls of those subjected to it as many people in both the United States and France assume?

What we have learned thus far is that an admirably orderly environment has been achieved in the penitentiaries we have visited to date, that the inmates are in incredibly good health, and that they are highly productive. We are fairly certain, moreover, that convicts sent to these prisons never emerge in worse condition than when they went in. But do they improve? Are the authorities able to achieve a complete and lasting revolution in the convicts' habits and ideas? We have not yet reached any firm conclusions on this point. Broadly speaking, Americans themselves seem to be divided on the question. Most of the practical men we have encountered thus far are rather skeptical of radical reform. They refuse to believe that the number of "corrected" former inmates is as large as the results of the surveys discussed above would seem to indicate. According to these people, many of the individuals covered by these surveys have been out of prison for too short a time to reach any definitive conclusions about their behavior. Furthermore, some of the testimonials to their good behavior may have been given out of fear or indulgence. More reliable if less satisfactory evidence is to be found in the dockets of the criminal courts, which every year include the names of a certain number of ex-convicts. These contradictory assertions suggest that it is best to withhold judgment for the time being. Neither side in this debate has reliable documentation on which to rest its case. We will now concentrate all our effort on trying to obtain such documentation. We first tried to find out from the clerks of the criminal courts how many defendants were repeat offenders, but we soon realized that the judicial authorities were completely unequipped to provide us with such data. Half of the defendants in the criminal courts of the state of New York are citizens of other states, and nothing is known about their criminal records. Furthermore, it is quite easy for a resident of New York to conceal his real name, because there is no real equivalent of our investigative police in America. The only way we found of obtaining the vital information we were after was to examine the books of various prisons. We have determined the number of prisoners who, after serving time at Sing Sing or Auburn, were later returned to one or the other. We intend in a similar way to examine New York State records from the time of the old prison, before the penitentiary system existed.

Without seeking to compare the number of repeat offenses committed in France with the number in the United States, one can try to compare a particular prison in America with another in France to see what useful lessons can be drawn from the parallel. If, as we hope, we can manage to do the same in all the states of the Union where the penitentiary system has been established, we will then be in a position to compare the old methods with the new and thus perhaps to derive a substantive argument in favor of the American reform and a probable argument in favor of achieving similar results in France.

In sum, Monsieur le Ministre, the Auburn penitentiary exceeded our expectations in more respects than it disappointed them. We found it to be both the best we have seen thus far and the easiest to imitate. The disciplinary system, tested by ten years of practical experience, now functions smoothly and easily. It does not attempt to do the impossible, as Sing Sing seems to want to do, but it does aim high and yet appears to attain its goal readily. Sing Sing is unlike any other prison we know, whereas Auburn strikes us as a more perfect version of one of our own prisons.

Nevertheless, we must mention in closing that we are still reluctant to recognize the necessity of allowing guards to inflict corporal punishment, especially without supervision. To be sure, at Auburn this right is not abused. Although punishment was frequent in the early days, when inmates had to be persuaded to accept the new order, it has become increasingly rare. We have evidence that in certain workshops no corporal punishment has been meted out in four months. Incontrovertible proof of this can be seen in the fact that the health of the prisoners is excellent (there is approximately one death per year), as we learned from our interviews with the prison physician. Consequently, public opinion in New York State is strongly in favor of the disciplinary system, which is based on corporal punishment. We did not meet a single proponent of the opposite system, even though it enjoyed majority approval ten years ago.

Nevertheless, there are penitentiaries which appear to have adopted the Auburn system of discipline and yet have not found it necessary to support it with corporal punishment. Weathersfield [sic] is a successful example of this new system.

Therefore we will concentrate much of our attention in the future on institutions of this type. We are convinced that the adoption of the American system in France will hinge in large part on the questions of discipline and cost, so most of our effort will be devoted to resolving these two issues. We know that public opinion in France is in general strongly opposed to corporal punishment as a means of discipline. We have already collected a great deal of information on what it costs in America either to build a penitentiary or to convert an older prison to the new method. We hope that we will also be able to provide information about the value of labor and materials in this country in order to compare costs here and in France and provide the government with the data it needs to decide whether or not to attempt a reform.

After our visit to Weathersfield, it will be our privilege to write once again to Your Excellency.

From Tocqueville and Beaumont | To the Minister of the Interior

> Letter written in Philadelphia on November 10, 1831, concerning
> the penitentiary system adopted in Pennsylvania

Monsieur le Ministre,

In the various reports that it has been our privilege to convey to you to date, we limited ourselves to calling Your Excellency's attention to the penitentiary systems currently in use in the states of New York and New England. You will have noticed that in the various prisons that we have had the opportunity to examine thus far, disciplinary rules and construction methods were by and large similar, and the differences that could be observed had to do with the ways in which principles were put into practice rather than with the principles themselves. From our study of all these institutions, we were therefore led to propound a general theory, which one might call the New York penitentiary system. The task before us now is different, and today we embark on a new path.

Rather than follow the lead of the northern states, Pennsylvania attempted to blaze an entirely new trail. Although this system has as yet found no imitator in America, it nevertheless deserves special and detailed examination.

The basis of the New York system was partial solitary confinement combined with common labor for the benefit of the state.

In Philadelphia the basic principle is solitary confinement both day and night: in other words, total isolation of the criminal. In order to put this principle into practice and achieve the desired goal, it was first necessary to build a new type of prison, which we must now describe before examining the disciplinary system that has been adopted there and the physical and moral effects that may be expected of it.

In the Philadelphia system, the prisoner is cut off from the entire world. His only contact with society is limited to that which is indispensable for his instruction and maintenance. Day and night, the prisoner remains in his cell. Hence the cell must be spacious enough for the inmate to live and work in and comfortable enough to satisfy all his needs.

Each cell in the Philadelphia penitentiary is . . . feet wide by . . . feet long.[5] Each cell contains a water faucet and a latrine constructed so as to eliminate all

---

5. Eastern State Penitentiary, or Cherry Hill Prison, was built in 1829 and had hallways of individual cells, each with a private walled yard attached, that radiated out from a central watchtower. A large wall encircled the entire complex. The prisoners were allowed visits only from guards, inspectors, and chaplains.

odor. In front of each cell, moreover, is a small exercise yard, where the prisoner can see the sun and breathe outside air for one hour each day.

Cut off in this way from his companions in misfortune, whom he will never see and whose voices will never reach his ears, the prisoner is initially abandoned for several days to all the terrors of solitude. Only then is he allowed to engage in work, whose necessary isolation and boredom will have brought him to recognize. At the same time he is provided with a number of religious tracts, which he seldom has the strength to read but which are usually accepted as a boon.

In the Philadelphia penitentiary, corporal punishment is never used. It is incompatible with the basic principles of the institution, and in any case order is not very difficult to maintain in an institution of this type. Left to their own devices and isolated from one another, the inmates cannot break the rules of the institution, and if they do somehow violate them, they can be reduced to obedience by depriving them of work, diminishing their rations, or preventing light from entering the cell. Yet the solitude to which inmates in Philadelphia are condemned is not so severe as to deprive them completely of the pleasure of seeing and at times communicating with other human beings. Four times a day, a guard brings the prisoner whatever he requires, and he can always call a guard if necessary. Every Sunday, moreover, a minister is allowed to visit the cells and bring consolation and advice to the inmates.

This, Monsieur le Ministre, is an overview of the Philadelphia penitentiary.

What criticisms can be made of the current system, and what results can it reasonably be expected to produce? We will try to answer these questions briefly in what follows.

Nearly everyone concerned with prison discipline in both Europe and America agrees that solitude cannot fail to harm the health, or at the very least the reason, of the inmate subjected to it. That is why systems based on solitude are almost unanimously condemned.

Monsieur le Ministre, we are obliged to say that nothing in our examination of the Philadelphia penitentiary would seem to justify these apprehensions. We visited all the cells and spoke with all the prisoners. Nearly all appeared to be in remarkably good health, although several have been in prison for as long as two years. Nothing in their conversation suggested mental derangement of any kind. Their ideas are generally grave and even melancholic but by no means incoherent or bizarre. We consulted with the prison physician, who is also the physician for all the other Philadelphia prisons. He stated that the health of the penitentiary inmates was better than that of inmates elsewhere. The fact is that solitary confinement in Philadelphia does not have the harsh character that is generally imputed to it in books. Most of the writers who have dealt with this subject show us an inmate perpetually confined within four walls, deprived of all contact with other human beings, and utterly without distraction or hope. Granting these points, they have no difficulty proving that a man reduced to such a wretched state must soon lose either his reason or his life. But in Philadelphia

The Cherry Hill or Eastern State Penitentiary outside Philadelphia. Designed by Philadelphia architect John Haviland and built between 1822 and 1829, the building has a Gothic facade. (GB2)

solitude does not have this terrifying and homicidal character. To begin with, it is not total. The inmate is sufficiently isolated to induce him to forget the perverse society in which he had been living previously, but he is not totally cut off from human society. He is allowed to enjoy intellectual relationships that do not threaten his reformation and may in some cases help him to endure the monotony of his existence.

In Philadelphia, the prisoner is not tormented by his own lugubrious thoughts. His life is not idle. His time is divided between reading and work. It is enough to speak with a few of these unfortunate individuals, Monsieur le Ministre, to understand the degree to which the introduction of work in a prison of this kind softens its rigors. The inmates never speak of work without a sense of gratitude. They tell us that work alone makes their lives bearable. By contrast, they describe the horrors of idleness with such energy and often such eloquence that it is clear how much they suffered from it in the early days of their incarceration.

The typical Philadelphia inmate is not serving a long sentence. Because the punishment is so rigorous, it has been possible to shorten its duration. What is more, paroles, which are granted far more often in America than in France, offer real hope of future salvation, so that the inmate's imagination is always filled with hopeful thoughts and impervious to despair.

We do not claim, however, that the inmate condemned to live in his cell day and night is as healthy and vigorous as the prisoner who is confined alone only at night while working all day long in the open air alongside his companions in misfortune. We recognize, for example, that a term in Sing Sing, where the mortality rate is far lower than in free society, will always be more conducive to the health of the prisoner than a moderately long sentence in the Philadelphia penitentiary. Yet if the man confined in the latter has a lower chance of dying than in almost any other prison we know of, if he is not subject to more dangers in prison than outside it, and if he even leads a healthier life than most people who earn their living in freedom, has society not fulfilled all its obligations to him, and can anyone reasonably expect it to do more? That is precisely what happens in Philadelphia. The rates of illness and death relative to the number of inmates are no greater than the rates outside the prison walls. Out of . . . inmates, there are . . . illnesses and . . . deaths each year.

It has been said that solitary confinement is an unequally apportioned punishment, that its intensity might well depend in large part on the physical and mental habits, the cast of mind, and the age of the prisoner subjected to it. This is true, but the same reasoning can be applied to any punishment. The effect of any punishment varies radically according to the physical and intellectual condition of the person on whom it is inflicted. A law based solely on general principles is often unjust and unequal in its application. This is an evil inherent in our nature and entirely unavoidable.

In France as well as in America, any number of writers have maintained that solitary confinement makes it impossible to achieve positive results from prison labor. They argue that there are very few occupations in which a person can work alone or in which a person working alone can succeed. The example of Philadelphia proves that this argument is usually couched in far too general terms. We concede readily that collective labor enjoys enormous advantages over solitary labor. Nor can it be denied that one person working alone simply cannot succeed in many lines of work, so that inmates may not be able to provide for their daily needs or for the even more variable needs of commerce. No matter what one does, Auburn and Sing Sing will always be more productive than the Philadelphia penitentiary. It is no less certain, however, that the range of work that can be done in solitude is broad enough that inmates can be kept busy. Their work may not be as profitable as the work done in other prisons, but it is always useful. From our examination of this prison's accounts, it has emerged that each inmate earns almost enough to cover the cost of his upkeep, so that the state has only to pay the wages of the guards and the costs of maintaining the institution.

To what extent has the penitentiary system met the expectations of its founders and contemporary supporters? Whatever its benefits may be, can its successes be imitated? These questions remain to be answered. One of the greatest benefits of the penitentiary system is the ease with which good discipline can be established. We know of no prison in which it is easier to maintain order than in the Philadelphia penitentiary. As we observed above, it is almost impossible for a prisoner held in total isolation even to conceive of disturbing the prison's order, much less to do so in fact. In a prison where solitary confinement is the norm, there is no need to fear offenses of the kind that can result from

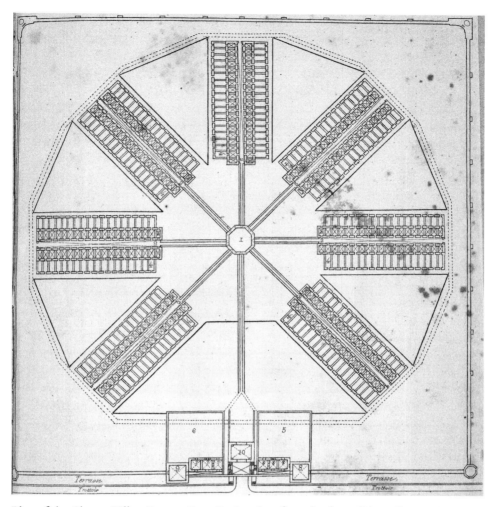

Plan of the Cherry Hill or Eastern State Penitentiary from the first edition of *Du système péni-tentiaire* (1833). A radial design with an observatory in the center intended to offer a panopti-cal view; seven wings with from 100 to 136 cells in each.

a conspiracy among the inmates, and, in addition, it becomes easier to control each prisoner than it would be if the inmates did not live in solitude.

In this kind of prison, the work of the guards is simple. No special talents are required, nor is constant effort necessary—constant effort of a sort that it may be dangerous to expect from most people, no matter how carefully they are chosen. In Auburn and especially Sing Sing, the guards must not only be honest and loyal; they must never relax their vigilance. A single moment's lapse can lead to a collapse of order. The basic principles of the system cease to be respected. The reform process is interrupted. And if this state of affairs continues, the entire prison is soon plunged into total confusion.

This cannot happen in Philadelphia. A bribe or an administrative error may well have a negative effect, but in order for the benefits of the system to be destroyed, management of the prison would have to be placed in truly corrupt hands, and it is reasonable to hope that such a thing could never happen.

Since the size of the staff is relatively small, moreover, it is that much easier to choose the personnel carefully.

So discipline is easy to maintain under the penitentiary system, but does it ultimately lead to reform and to a decrease in the number of crimes? Does it achieve the principal goal that the various penitentiary systems are intended to achieve?

Proponents and adversaries of the Philadelphia system differ on these questions, but neither group has thus far been able to present solid facts to bolster its opinions. The Philadelphia penitentiary has been in existence for only two years. It still has only ninety prisoners, and only ten have been returned to society. If they have not yet committed new crimes, it is impossible to credit the system itself. An argument based on this fact would not withstand a moment's scrutiny. Nevertheless, to the extent that one can see into the future, there is reason to believe that the Philadelphia penitentiary will turn out to be the most powerful and complete instrument for the reform of criminals ever created.

The sole purpose of the New York system is to prevent inmates from influencing one another. Experience in both America and Europe has shown that convicts left the prisons that were supposed to correct their behavior more dangerous and perverse than when they went in. New buildings were therefore built and new systems of discipline instituted for the purpose of preventing contact among inmates. Constant effort is required to attain this goal, and we have reason to believe that even then the desired result is not always fully achieved. There is no doubt that in several penitentiaries, inmates were able to establish relations that, while they may not have been corrupting, nevertheless delayed reform and potentially threatened internal discipline.

Even if the goal was met, it was just as fully achieved in the Philadelphia penitentiary and at lower cost. But the Philadelphia system aimed at achieving other important results that the New York system never even contemplated.

Indeed, it is not enough to prevent inmates from corrupting one another. One would like to prevent them from having any contact with one another, for if punishment fails to achieve correction and the convict leaves prison with the intention of committing new crimes, he will easily find among his companions in misfortune some wretched individual willing to follow his example and help him break the law. The most cunning robberies and most atrocious crimes are nearly always committed by criminal associations of this type. A few days ago, a New York State judge told us that criminals convicted in the same court and sentenced to identical terms were often implicated in joint crimes after their release. Because they were released on the same day and knew one another in prison, they were able to enter into conspiracies at the prison gate.

Let us assume, however, that the convict leaves the penitentiary determined to behave himself. He is nevertheless at the mercy of other convicts whom he came to know in prison. The more he wishes to reform himself, the more concerned he is about public opinion, and the more strenuously he seeks to hide his criminal past, the more vulnerable he becomes to former companions who wish to enlist him as an instrument in new crimes or merely to take advantage of his fears.

None of these things need be feared under the Philadelphia system. If the prisoner has not been corrected by his punishment, he returns to an entirely different world. His former companions are either dead or dispersed. Though he might find help or support among those who lived under the same roof, he no longer even knows their names. Free, he is therefore reduced to his own devices to do wrong, as he was in prison.

If, on the other hand, he wishes to begin a new life, no obstacle stands in his way. He need not fear an encounter with vexatious witnesses to his past, men who might be indiscreet or greedy enough to deprive him of the public esteem he seeks and has begun to earn.

It is our belief that the convicts themselves are keenly aware of the advantage of being able to remain invisible. For many of them, the torment of solitude is markedly reduced by the hope that their shame will not become known and that they will be able to return to society without fear of rejection.

In this respect, it is therefore possible to say that the Philadelphia system readily obtains everything that the New York system sought to accomplish, and, what is more, it attains a result that the latter cannot hope for.

Not only do convicts released from the Philadelphia penitentiary find themselves completely free to begin a new life, but it is also reasonable to believe that the system of imprisonment to which they have been subjected has taught them the usefulness of reform and instilled in them a firm resolve to attempt it.

Eager to know their attitude in this regard, we asked for and obtained permission to interview them without witnesses. The warden saw to it that every cell was open to us, and we were able to speak freely with each and every inmate. The results of this moral survey deserve to be brought to the attention of Your Excellency.

To be sure, it would be dangerous to place much faith in what prisoners say, but when a great many individuals who have not been able to communicate among themselves report similar impressions and express similar ideas, and when they speak without self-interested purposes and therefore without ulterior motives, it is very likely that they speak the truth.

In our investigation, we attached no importance to what the inmates told us about their reform projects. In their position, words of this sort prove nothing. The religious ideas they spoke of had little effect on us, because it is in their interest to exhibit religious sentiments they may not actually feel. What did impress us, however, was their tranquility of mind, as well as the serious and reasonable character of their thoughts.

All the prisoners insisted that after a certain period of time, the solitude became less difficult to bear, that work shortened this period of adjustment, and that the habit of living alone reduced the need for contact with others. Thus the duration of the sentence, rather than making the convict bitter, actually makes him more amenable to his punishment. In visiting inmates who had entered the prison at different times, we were able to see for ourselves that this was indeed the case. A prisoner who has only recently been placed in his cell is usually mired in despair. He cries; solitary confinement terrifies him. He berates society for its injustice and sees no hope of surviving his punishment.

The inmate who has been in his cell for a month is already calmer. He has savored the consolations of work and reading. He no doubt finds his position very hard but not unbearable. Though still depressed, he has begun to hope.

The prisoner who has served a year is perfectly calm. He speaks of the past without bitterness and of the future without terror. The most serious subjects consume his imagination. He exhibits none of the heedlessness of consequences that marks the hardened criminal. Indeed, he reasons about everything and has clearly acquired the habit of reflection. In fact, we were often surprised to see the degree to which solitude had fostered in some inmates an ability to relate ideas and analyze impressions.

What we saw when we examined the Philadelphia cells from inside was totally new and quite interesting. The inmates are generally in good health, well clothed, well fed, and supplied with comfortable bedding. Material comforts not available to them outside the prison are within their reach inside, as the inmates themselves are quick to recognize. Nevertheless, they are profoundly unhappy. The mental suffering to which they are subjected is more terrifying than chains or blows. Is this not how an enlightened and humane society ought to seek to punish? Punishment here is at once milder and more terrifying than any other punishment yet invented. It aims solely at the prisoner's mind but achieves incredible power over it. In Philadelphia, the prisoner works from morning till night without hope of compensation and does so of his own free will. He occupies his mind with serious and edifying literature, although no one forces him to do so. Is this not the form of punishment that an enlightened and human society would want to impose on those whom it convicts of crimes?

We devoted particular attention to those inmates who had previously been imprisoned for other crimes. They vividly described for us what they had endured in other prisons. Although the work they were forced to do was not as constant as the work they did voluntarily in Philadelphia, it was still unbearable to them. The food was insufficient, the discipline violent and brutal, and the accommodations unhealthy, and yet they were tempted to long for the time when they were so unhappy. In their opinion, their current misfortune is greater still. Some of them were surprised by some of the changes they had undergone. For example, they found it difficult to understand why they experienced work as pain in their former institution but as pleasure here. They readily acknowledged, moreover, that never before had they devoted so much thought to the things that most regularly occupy their minds today.

Insofar as it is possible to judge a man's future attitude by his present state of mind, then, most of the inmates incarcerated in the Philadelphia penitentiary today will emerge with the proper mental habits to avoid relapsing into a life of crime. Whether as a result of terror or of reform, there is reason to believe that nearly all will leave prison firmly resolved to do nothing that might put them back in.

Will they maintain their resolve, however? It is at this point that a serious objection to the Philadelphia system can be raised, and it is an objection that only the future can dispel. The Philadelphia system places the inmate in an isolated situation that is absolutely contrary to his nature. It subjects him to a most painful privation by cutting him off from his fellow human beings. Is there not reason to fear that once he returns to society he will be carried away by immoderate love of the pleasures it has to offer? In other words, might not the very severity of the punishment make its effects less durable? There is no hiding the fact that there are reasons to fear that this might be the case. Only experience can show what power such temptations might have over a man who has been kept away from the world for many long years and who in all that time has had no opportunity to develop habits of self-control.

In any case, it is our duty not to hide from Your Excellency our conclusion thus far: we are strongly inclined to believe that the Philadelphia system is superior to the New York system as well as to all the other systems that have been tried at one time or another in the United States.

Nevertheless, we are far from convinced that we should attempt to imitate this system at home. Its success is still problematic, but it is already clear that to establish it in France would require expenditures on a level that a nation is seldom prepared to undertake and that might well exceed the benefits to be expected.

Indeed, the influence of the penitentiary system on the social economy should not be exaggerated. The system no doubt prevents inmates who are subjected to it from becoming more perverse and thus diminishes the number of crimes, and especially the number of major crimes. It may completely reform some young delinquents, but it is doubtful that it will have much power over the souls of hardened criminals. Together with good preventive laws, it may enhance the well-being of the society that adopts it, but to sacrifice millions that might be devoted to more useful innovations in order to obtain this result would no doubt be to pay more than the benefits warrant.

The Philadelphia penitentiary has already cost the state of Pennsylvania . . . for just 150 cells. To be sure, in building the prison the state indulged in certain architectural excesses that are quite useless and therefore inexcusable. In all of America there is no more splendid building than the Philadelphia prison. There is no doubt that for half the cost one could build a penitentiary to house the same number of prisoners under the same disciplinary system. Upon our return we will be in a position to offer detailed figures on this point.

No matter what one does, however, a penitentiary suitable for the Philadelphia system will always cost far more to build than a penitentiary based on the Auburn plan, and operating costs will also be much higher.

This difference is inscribed in the very nature of the two systems: The Auburn inmate occupies his cell only at night. The place where he sleeps can be quite small. In Philadelphia, the prisoner spends the whole time of his sentence in his cell. Each inmate must therefore be given a full apartment equipped with all the necessities of life, and it must open on to a yard spacious enough for the prisoner to exercise from time to time and breathe the outside air.

True, there is talk at present of eliminating this exercise yard. But what would the effect of such a change be? It is difficult to say, but many people think that such an innovation would be harmful to the prisoners' health, and we are inclined to agree with them.

The initial costs of a penitentiary based on solitary confinement are therefore inevitably substantial. In such a prison, moreover, the convicts' labor will always be less productive than in a prison where joint labor is allowed. To be sure, the moral effects will in all likelihood be more thoroughgoing, but this point has yet to be established empirically, and even if it should eventually be demonstrated, it would still remain to be seen whether the benefits were worth the cost. Nations, like individuals, are often reduced to aiming not at what is most perfect but at what appears to be most practical.

Our intention on leaving Philadelphia is to go to Pittsburgh, where an attempt was made to establish a system of complete solitary confinement without labor.[6] It seems that this experiment did not succeed, but it would be useful to find out why. In Europe, the Pittsburgh system is confused with the Philadelphia system, and the same criticisms are applied to both. This is an error that may be worth refuting.

After Pittsburgh we intend to visit the penitentiary in Baltimore. This institution enjoys a good reputation in America. It earns more revenue for the state than any other prison we know of. It earns a substantial annual income.[7]

Finally, we shall end our study with the Washington penitentiary. We are in any case very eager to visit the city of Washington, where the most notable men in the Union will be gathered at the time of our visit. Among other people we will see the celebrated Edward Livingston, the current secretary of the interior, whose work on prisons and penal legislation has been well-known in Europe for some time. From these distinguished men we hope to obtain a political perspective and other general observations on the various penitentiary systems in

6. The Western State Penitentiary opened in 1826. Although the penitentiary was built to keep prisoners in solitary confinement, that principle was abandoned and the building demolished in 1833 because the cells proved to be too small and not soundproof.

7. The Maryland State Penitentiary opened in 1811. Both male and female convicts were put to work at a variety of jobs, many of them beyond the penitentiary walls. By 1830, the prison earned a profit of approximately ten thousand dollars per year.

the United States, which they are well placed to observe by virtue of the high offices they hold.

From Washington we will dispatch a final letter to Your Excellency. It will be sent a short time before our departure for Europe. Upon our return our first order of business will be to present the many documents we have collected to the minister of the interior, together with a general report containing all our observations as well as the detailed findings of the mission with which he was good enough to entrust us.

From Tocqueville and Beaumont | To Richard Riker

January–February 1832[8]

. . . Queries proposed to Richard Riker, Recorder of the City of New York, by M. Tocqueville and M. Beaumont.

1. What is the average time that is spent between the commitment of a man accused of an offense and his trial? I speak of the time employed in criminal proceedings and not of the time during which the man is detained in prison because the session is not yet begun.

2. Is it sometimes perceived that the rapidity and simplicity of your criminal proceedings prevent the complete reunion of proofs in favor of or against the prisoner and cause the guilty to escape?

3. To what extent is carried the right to be judged by a jury?

4. Before and since the Revolution, the penal code of the state of New York has undergone various modifications. Is it possible to know at what dates these different changes took place?

5. What crimes were formerly punished more severely than they now are?

What has been the effect of this change of the criminal law?

Has the commission of any crime become more or less frequent in consequence of a milder punishment?

Such documents would be particularly valuable for the cases of crimes which were formerly punished, but which are not any longer punished, by death.

6. Is the number of offenders not prosecuted very numerous, particularly in cases of small offense?

8. This letter is in English in the original.

Excerpts from Beaumont and Tocqueville,
On the Penitentiary System in the United States
and Its Application in France

PART I: "PENITENTIARY SYSTEMS IN THE UNITED STATES,"
CHAPTER 3: "REFORM"

... When seeking to ascertain the influence of the penitentiary system on society, the question is usually posed as follows: Did the number of crimes increase or decrease since the penitentiary system was established?

The answer to all questions of this sort is extremely difficult to ascertain in
the United States, because it is impossible to obtain the necessary statistics. No
central authority exists in either the Union or the several states to collect them.
With difficulty it is possible to obtain statistics for a single city or county but
never for an entire state.

Pennsylvania is the only state where we were able to determine the total
number of crimes. In the year 1850, 2,084 individuals were sentenced to prison
in Pennsylvania, which, compared to a population of 1,347,672, gives a ratio of
one inmate for every 655 inhabitants.

In the other states, we obtained very accurate information about the numbers of some crimes but not all crimes. For instance, in the states of New York,
Massachusetts, Connecticut, and Maryland, we know only the number of cases
that resulted in state prison sentences.

If we count only those crimes about which statistics are available, we see
that in New York, Massachusetts, and Maryland, the number of criminals has
decreased relative to the size of the population. In Connecticut it has increased,
while in Pennsylvania it has remained stable.

Can we conclude from this that the prison in Connecticut is very bad, while
only the prisons in New York, Massachusetts, and Maryland are good, and the
prisons of Pennsylvania are better than those of Connecticut but not as good as
those of the latter three states?

This would be a strange conclusion to draw, because the penitentiary in
Connecticut is certainly better than the prisons in Maryland and Pennsylvania.

If we look closely at the political situation and other circumstances in each
of these states, we see that the number of crimes, and the tendency of that number to increase or decrease, may be related to causes having nothing whatsoever
to do with the penitentiary system.

The number of crimes must first of all be distinguished from the rate of increase. In New York there are more crimes than in Pennsylvania, but the number
of crimes has held steady in the latter, whereas it has decreased in the former. In
Connecticut, where crime is on the rise, there are all told half as many crimes as
in the other states.

Furthermore, in order to establish proper points of comparison among the various states, foreigners should be subtracted from the population, and only crimes committed by the settled population should be compared. Proceeding in this manner, we find that, of all the states, Maryland is the one in which the settled population commits the most crimes. This is due to a cause peculiar to the southern states, namely, the presence of the black race. It has been observed in general that in states where there is one Negro for every thirty whites, the prisons hold one Negro for every four whites.

States with many Negroes must therefore be responsible for more crimes. This alone would suffice to explain the elevated crime figure for Maryland. It does not apply to all southern states, however. It affects only those in which the emancipation of blacks is permitted. It is a serious error to believe that setting Negroes free stops them from committing crimes. On the contrary, experience teaches that in the South, freed slaves commit far more crimes than actual slaves. Slavery seems to be headed for collapse, moreover, so that the number of freed slaves in the South will continue to rise for some time to come, and so will the number of criminals.

While the southern states must contend with this prodigious source of additional crime, various political factors in such northern states as New York and Massachusetts have tended to decrease criminal behavior.

First, the black population is steadily decreasing in size relative to the white population, which is constantly growing.

Furthermore, although foreigners who arrive from Europe without the means to support themselves are a source of crime, the influence of this factor is decreasing.

In fact, as the population grows, even though the number of foreigners arriving is not decreasing, they represent a smaller fraction of the total population. The population has doubled in thirty years, but the number of immigrants is virtually the same. Although the foreign population in the North seems to be holding steady, the influence of this factor on crime seems to be decreasing year after year. The absolute size of the foreign population is constant, but its relative importance in the steadily growing population is smaller.

Some people in the United States also think that education, which is so widespread in the northern states, has contributed to the decrease in crime.

In the state of New York, out of a population of two million, 550,000 children are being educated in the schools, and the state alone spends nearly six million francs a year on education. It would seem that an enlightened population not lacking for opportunities in agriculture, commerce, and manufacturing should commit fewer crimes than a population with similar opportunities but without the educational advantages needed to exploit them. Nevertheless, we do not believe that education deserves credit for reducing crime in the North, because in Connecticut, where education is even more widespread, we observe that crime has increased extremely rapidly. Although education cannot be blamed for this prodigious increase, one is nevertheless forced to acknowledge that it does not have the power to stop it either. In any case, we do not claim to explain these strange anomalies, which we find in states with quite similar political institutions and yet very different crime rates. Such difficulties never fail to arise in any kind of statistical work. The facts set forth above nevertheless prove that crime has many serious causes that are independent of the penitentiary system.

In some cases, an industrial crisis, the disbanding of an army, or other, similar causes suffice to explain a temporary increase in the crime figure.

For example, in 1816, the number of inmates in all American prisons grew unusually large. Was the penitentiary system responsible for this? No, it was simply a consequence of the war between the United States and England. When the war ended, many soldiers were sent home and no longer had the means to earn a living.

Another difficulty exists. Even if there is agreement about the causes of crime, we do not know exactly why crime increases.

What evidence do we have of the number of crimes committed? The number of convictions. But in fact any number of causes can explain why convictions become more frequent without any increase in the number of crimes.

For example, the police can pursue crimes more zealously and energetically, as often happens when public attention is focused on the issue. Even though the number of crimes committed does not increase, more crimes are investigated. Criminal courts can also mete out harsher sentences. Repression often increases when criminal penalties are made milder. Fewer defendants are acquitted. The number of crimes remains steady, but there are more convictions. The penitentiary system itself, which is supposed to decrease the number of crimes, initially results in an increased number of convictions. Indeed, just as judges are often reluctant to sentence criminals to prison when they fear its corrupting influences, they will sentence more readily when they know that prison is not a school of crime but rather a place of penitence and reform.

In any case, the foregoing shows clearly that the increase or decrease in the number of crimes stems from both general and accidental causes and is not directly related to the penitentiary system.

If we reflect on the purpose of the penitentiary system and its natural consequences, it becomes clear that it cannot have the influence that is generally ascribed to it and that to evaluate the system purely in terms of an increase or decrease in the crime rate is to commit an error of method. Prisons can have an influence, whether for good or ill, only on those who have been confined in them. Very good prisons can exist in countries where there is a great deal of crime, and very bad prisons in countries where crime is quite rare. For example, in Massachusetts, where there are fewer convicts than in New York, the prisons are deeply flawed, whereas in New York, which has more crime, their quality is high. A bad prison can no more corrupt those who have not been exposed to its baleful influence than a good penitentiary can reform those who have not been subjected to its beneficial regime.

Institutions, mores, political circumstances—these are the things that influence the moral character of any society. Prisons affect only the morality of their inmates.

The penitentiary system therefore does not have the extensive influence that is sometimes ascribed to it. Limited to the prison population, its direct influence is important enough that there is no need to credit it with an influence it cannot possibly possess. Although the portion of the social body to which the prison regime applies is small, it is also the most gangrenous; it is there that the canker is most contagious and most urgently in need of cauterization.

When it comes to judging the value of a prison or prison system, therefore, we must be careful to observe not the morality of society in general but only that of individuals who, after serving time in prison, return to society. If they commit no new offense, we may conclude that the influence of prison on them was salutary. If they lapse into recidivism, we may conclude that the prison regime did not improve their condition.

Although it is indeed the case that the number of recidivists is the only evidence that a prison is good or bad, it should be said as well that precise information about the rate of recidivism is hard to come by.

In fact, it is very difficult to determine for sure whether freed prisoners abide by the law after being released. The authorities are not always aware of any new crimes they may commit.

In addition to the foregoing remarks, which we believe necessary to frame the question properly, we would add one further comment, which we think it is equally important to bear in mind. If one is to judge the penitentiary system properly, one must consider not the period in which it was created but subsequent periods. Although it might seem unnecessary to state this point explicitly, it has frequently been forgotten by very respectable authorities. Let us cite one example.

We mentioned previously that a new system of imprisonment was established in Philadelphia in 1790. As a result, the Walnut Street Prison was established there in accordance with a plan that we found to be full of flaws. Nevertheless, owing to fortuitous circumstances, or to causes unknown, the number of crimes committed in Pennsylvania in the period 1790–93 was far smaller than in previous years. Mr. Livingston and Mr. Roberts [sic] Vaux in the United States and the duc de La Rochefoucauld-Liancourt and M. Charles Lucas in France took this decrease in crime as evidence of the effectiveness of the new system. In order to credit the new prison regime with this result, however, they would have had to show that prisoners released from Walnut Street did not commit new crimes. But no such proof could be given. Indeed, the new system did not go into effect until 1790, yet these authors looked for effects in the years 1791, 1792, and 1793, before most of the inmates of the new prison had been released.

It is easy to understand that the effects of the penitentiary system can be judged only after a certain number of years and only after inmates released at the conclusion of their sentences have had time either to commit new crimes or to become law-abiding citizens.

We should therefore take no account of the results obtained by the new penitentiaries in Philadelphia, Sing Sing, Boston, and Baltimore. If we eliminate arguments that might be drawn from these various prisons, we narrow the range of discussion, to be sure, but we gain the benefit of reasoning on a solid foundation.

Let us therefore compare the effects produced by the older prisons of the United States with those of the new system established at the penitentiaries of Auburn and Wethersfield, the only ones that have been in existence long enough to permit an accurate assessment of their influence.

In the old New York prison (Newgate), one out of every nine inmates was a repeat offender. In the Maryland prison, it was one out of every seven inmates. In the Walnut Street Prison, one out of six, and in the old Connecticut prison, one out of four. In Boston, one-sixth of released prisoners returned to prison after committing new crimes.

The recidivism rate is much lower in the new prisons of Auburn and Wethersfield. In the former, recidivists account for one-nineteenth of the population, and for every one hundred individuals released from the latter since its creation, only five have returned after committing new crimes, for a rate of one-twentieth.

At Auburn, officials did not limit themselves to tallying up recidivists who had previously served time in the penitentiary. They also attempted to verify the conduct of freed prisoners who did not commit new crimes and remained in society. Of 160 individuals about whom it was possible to obtain information, 112 had behaved well, while the rest had resumed their former bad or dubious habits.

As conclusive as these figures may seem, the number of years on which they are based is too small to yield incontrovertible proof of the efficacy of the system. One is nevertheless forced to admit that they are extremely favorable to the new penitentiary prisons, and the presumptive conclusion in their favor is all the stronger in that the effect observed is in perfect agreement with what the theory promised. It should be noted, too, that although it is impossible to derive any proof from the penitentiaries at Sing Sing and Boston and other prisons of similar nature, because they are too new, it cannot be denied that the success of Auburn and Wethersfield makes it very likely that these establishments, which are based on absolutely the same model, will also succeed.[9] . . .

PART 3: "REFORM SCHOOLS" (*MAISONS DE REFUGE*), CHAPTER I

. . . Reform schools in New York and Philadelphia are based on a simple fundamental principle: children are separated at night in solitary cells but allowed to communicate during the day. The nighttime separation appears to be necessary to maintain good morals. It is not necessary during the day. Complete isolation would be fatal for some children, and silence could not be maintained without severe punishments, which must be rejected as too violent. There are also very

9. The Massachusetts State Prison was built at Charlestown, just north of Boston, in 1805. It later adopted the Auburn system of management.

serious drawbacks to depriving the children of all social relations, for this would impede their intellectual progress.

In Boston, children are not separated either during the day or at night. We did not find that nocturnal communication in this institution had any negative effects. Nevertheless, we believe that the potential danger is high, and it is averted in Boston only thanks to a quite extraordinary level of zeal and vigilance, which one cannot expect to find even in the most dedicated public officials everywhere.

The children's time is divided between classroom instruction and physical labor. They are taught basic subjects that may be useful to them in later life, and in addition they learn a trade, which may help them to earn a living. Their intellectual endeavors lend the institution a certain resemblance to a primary school, while their activities in the workshop are similar to those found in adult prisons. These two features are typical of reform schools.

Education is not limited to training hands and developing minds. The primary goal is to shape the children's hearts and inculcate principles of religious morality. Mr. Hart, the warden of the New York reform school, told us repeatedly that without the help of religion, he did not think that his efforts could possibly succeed.

When the young delinquent arrives at the school, the warden ensures that he is apprised of the rules of the institution and of two remarkably simple precepts: (1) never lie, and (2) do the best you can. The warden records the name of the new inmate in the register of conduct, in which notes on the child's moral condition are regularly entered. These notes include information about the child's prior life and about his behavior while confined as well as after his release from the institution. The child is then assigned to a class appropriate to his age and moral condition. According to Mr. Hart in New York, the top class is reserved for children who do not swear, never lie, and never use any obscene or inappropriate expression, and who are also diligent in school and in the workshop. In Boston, according to Mr. Wells,[10] the top class consists of those who make a positive, regular, and consistent effort to do well.

In Boston, the circumstances surrounding a child's admission to reform school are worth noting. The institution is a small society in the image of the larger one. In order to be admitted, a child must not only know its laws and submit to them voluntarily but must also be accepted by all existing members of the society. Admission is therefore preceded by a trial period, at the end of which the candidate is either admitted or rejected by majority vote.

In each reform school, inmates are assigned to classes on the basis of their behavior. The classes for the good inmates enjoy certain privileges that are denied to the others. Conversely, the bad classes are subject to certain privations not inflicted on the good classes.

10. The Reverend E. M. P. Wells, an Episcopal minister, ran the House of Reformation in South Boston.

At least eight hours a day are devoted to shop work, where the children do useful labor as cabinetmakers, shoemakers, tailors, carpenters, etc. Four hours are spent in the classroom. Prayers are said after rising in the morning and before going to bed at night. A half an hour is set aside for each of three meals. All told, the day lasts around fifteen hours. Night and sleep consume nine hours. With few differences, the same program is followed in both New York and Philadelphia. The order is the same each day and varies only with the changing of the seasons, which affects the time of waking and retiring. Boston is different: there, much more time is devoted to moral education. In the Boston reform school, only five and a half hours are set aside for shop work. In addition to four hours in the classroom, an hour is given to religious instruction, and all the children have two and a quarter hours of recreation daily. These hours of leisure are not the least beneficial to the young inmates. Mr. Wells, the warden, takes part in all their games, and while they develop their physical strength through exercise, their moral character is formed under the influence of a superior man, whose presence may be visible but who is in reality hidden among them, and whose authority is never greater than when it is felt the least.

In the classroom the children are taught to read, write, and count. They are also taught the rudiments of history and geography. Lancaster's method of mutual instruction is used.[11] The children generally exhibit great facility in grasping the ideas laid before them by their teachers. It has often been remarked in America that reform school inmates are on average more intelligent than other children. The explanation may lie in the very nature of these institutions. The children assigned to them have for the most part been abandoned by their families or fled the parental home. Hence they were forced to live on their own at an early age and obliged to rely on their intelligence and natural gifts in order to survive. It should therefore come as no surprise that they succeed in learning. Furthermore, most of them have restless, adventurous minds and are eager to learn. The very penchant that led them initially to ruin becomes an asset in the classroom. If they ask for sound books in order to educate themselves, their requests are seldom denied. In Philadelphia the reform school library contains more than 1,500 volumes, all of which are available for use by the children.

Working hours are fixed for all inmates, and no one is exempt. If a more energetic child finishes his assigned task ahead of time, however, he may begin his recreation sooner.

The surveillance to which the children are subjected in classroom and shop continues during their leisure time. They may play together freely, but games of chance (gambling) are strictly prohibited.

11. Joseph Lancaster (1778–1838), a British immigrant to the United States, developed a pedagogical method popular in the first half of the nineteenth century. Also known as the mutual or monitorial system, the Lancasterian system of education divided students into small groups determined by skill level and age. After the main lesson, students would break into smaller groups to recite and review their lesson with the help of an older peer.

Everything in the inmates' regime is intended to foster good health. The children are required to wash their hands and feet daily. They are always properly dressed, and their food, though plain, is abundant and healthy. No one may eat anything but what is prescribed in the institution's regular diet, and the only beverage served is water. There is no cafeteria where the children might find additional food or drink, and they are carefully watched to prevent them from obtaining food or drink from persons outside the institution.

Young inmates are supplied with food, clothing, and bedding by the administration. Only the children's labor is contracted out, and contracts for their services are carefully designed to make sure that the outside contractor cannot acquire any influence over the institution itself.

In New York and Philadelphia, contractors are granted eight hours a day of work; in Boston, only five and a half hours. The contractor or his agents may enter the institution to teach the various trades that are practiced there. They may not engage in conversation with the children, however, or keep them in the workshops one minute more than the time allotted. Clearly, under such conditions, the contracts with outside contractors are not particularly lucrative, but the children are not put to work in order to derive a profit from their labors. The only purpose is to inculcate the habit of hard work and teach a useful trade.

It should therefore come as no surprise that the cost of maintaining reform schools is higher than the cost of other penal institutions. For one thing, the young inmates are better fed and better clothed than adult convicts, and more money is spent on their education. For another, their labor is as profitable as that of criminals who are incarcerated for long periods. As we shall see, young inmates are released as soon as they can be advantageously placed elsewhere. They are set free as soon as they have learned a trade, that is, as soon as their labor begins to earn revenue for the institution.

Reform schools in the United States are almost always publicly administered. It is rightly believed that private management would be incompatible with the institution's function as a moral preceptor.

Although the upkeep of young inmates is in general costly, everything possible is done to keep expenses down. The schools house both boys and girls, who, though living under the same roof, are kept strictly apart. But this proximity makes it possible to assign to the girls many chores that would have to be paid for if done by others. For instance, they wash linen, mend clothing, and sew most of the garments worn by the boys as well as by themselves. They cook for the entire institution. In this way the institution not only saves on expenses but also provides useful work to girls whom it would otherwise be difficult to employ productively.

Order is established and maintained by various disciplinary measures, which we shall now examine. Two influences are used: punishments and rewards. In applying this principle, however, the reform schools in New York and Philadelphia must be distinguished from the one in Boston.

In the former two institutions, the following punishments are administered to children guilty of disciplinary infractions:
1. Loss of recreation time
2. Solitary confinement in a cell
3. Reduction of food and water rations
4. In serious cases, corporal punishment, namely, whipping

In New York, the regulations explicitly authorize whipping. In Philadelphia, they do not explicitly allow this practice but do not prohibit it either. The meting out of punishment is the responsibility of the warden, who has discretionary powers within the institution.

While uncooperative young inmates are subject to these punishments according to the seriousness of their infraction, rewards of various kinds are given to children who behave well. In addition to the honor of being assigned to the top classes, those who distinguish themselves wear badges of honor, which everyone recognizes. Finally, the warden chooses some of the best inmates to serve as monitors, to whom some of his own surveillance functions are assigned. This mark of confidence is highly prized by the inmates.

In Boston, corporal punishment is prohibited in the reform school. Discipline in this institution is entirely moral and is based on the highest philosophic principles.

Everything possible is done to elevate the souls of the young inmates and make them covet their own esteem and that of their fellow inmates. To do this, the authorities pretend to treat them as grown-up members of free society.

We consider this theory from a disciplinary standpoint because it seemed to us that the high opinion that the child is induced to form of his own morality and social condition is not only well calculated to bring about reform but also a very clever way of obtaining total obedience.

To begin with, it is a well-established principle in the institution that no one can be punished for any fault not forbidden by the laws of God, the state, or the institution. The reform school thus upholds the first principle of criminal justice. The regulations also lay down the following principle:

"Since it is not in man's power to punish lack of respect toward God, anyone guilty of such an infraction will simply be barred from participation in all religious services, thus leaving the criminal to the justice of God, who awaits him in the next life."

In the Boston reform school, the child barred from religious services endures, in his own as well as his comrades' eyes, the most terrible of all punishments.

It is also stipulated that the children are not allowed to denounce each other's failings. In the next paragraph it is added that no one will be punished for any infraction if a sincere confession is made. We know public institutions in France where denunciations are encouraged and where good inmates participate in the practice.

In Boston, too, each inmate's merits and demerits are recorded in a moral ledger, but what distinguishes this from the records kept in other reform schools is that in Boston each child grades himself. Every evening the young inmates are questioned one by one. Each one is summoned to judge his conduct during the day just ended. A mark is entered in the record book on the basis of the inmate's declaration. Experience has shown that inmates always judge themselves more severely than they would be judged by others. There is frequently a need to moderate this severe judgment, to diminish the injustice of the sentence.

When difficulties arise concerning merits and demerits, or when young inmates commit disciplinary infractions, judgment must be rendered. Twelve jurors are chosen among the children of the institution, and they decide whether to convict or absolve the accused.

When a judge or monitor needs to be chosen, the community assembles and holds an election, and the candidate who obtains a majority is declared the winner. These ten-year-old voters and jurors discharge their functions in the most serious way imaginable.

We beg the reader's indulgence for having described the system at length and in minute detail. Needless to say, we do not take these child citizens seriously. We nevertheless thought it important to analyze this remarkably original system carefully. Indeed, in these political games, which accord so well with the institutions of the country, there is greater depth than one might think. Childhood impressions and early use of liberty might contribute later to making these young delinquents more obedient to the law. Leaving aside this hypothetical political benefit, one can at least say that such a system is a powerful means of moral education.

Indeed, it is easy to sense the moral force of which these young souls are capable once sentiments with the power to lift them above themselves have been set in motion.

When the moral means described above prove insufficient, however, other disciplinary weapons are available.

Children whose behavior is good enjoy significant privileges.

They alone vote in elections and are eligible to run as candidates. Indeed, the votes of members of the top class count double. The others cannot be envious of this privilege, because it is within their own power to earn it for themselves. The good inmates are entrusted with the institution's most important keys. They are free to leave when they wish and can walk out of meetings without permission. Their word is accepted as true in all circumstances, and their birthdays are celebrated. Not all good children enjoy these privileges, but anyone who is a member of a good class is entitled to some of them.

The punishments imposed on the bad class are:

Forfeit of the right to vote and to run for office. In addition, bad inmates may not enter the warden's office or speak to him without his permission and may not speak with other young inmates. Finally, when necessary, punishments are inflicted that affect the delinquent physically. He may be forced to wear manacles or to go blindfolded or be confined in a solitary cell.

This is the system employed in the Boston reform school.

Although the system used in New York and Philadelphia is less noteworthy, it may be better. Not that we do not believe that the Boston reform school is admirably administered or that we do not find it superior to the other two. But its success seems due not so much to the system itself as to the distinguished man who administers it.

As mentioned earlier, the indiscriminate mixing of children during the night is this institution's most serious flaw. The system in operation here is based on a noble theory, which runs the risk of being imperfectly understood at times, and its utilization might lead to serious trouble if the warden lacked the considerable resources needed to make it work successfully.

By contrast, in New York and Philadelphia, the theory is simple. Isolation at night, classification by day, work, instruction: such a system is easy to understand and execute. It takes no great genius to invent and can be maintained without constant resourcefulness.

To summarize what has been said on this point, discipline in Boston is based on a much loftier intellectual conception than discipline in New York and Philadelphia, but it is difficult to put into practice.

In the latter two institutions, the theory of the system is simpler and can be readily grasped by anyone. Wardens capable of administering the Philadelphia system can no doubt be found fairly readily, but one should not expect to find men of Mr. Wells's caliber very often.

Despite the marked differences between the two systems, one of which can be implemented only by superior minds while the other is within the reach of ordinary intelligences, we should note, finally, that in both cases success depends essentially on the warden. He is the one who implements the principles on which the system is based, and if he is to succeed, he must possess many qualities as rare as they are necessary.

If one were searching for a model reform school warden, one could do no better, perhaps, than Mr. Wells, who heads the Boston school, or Mr. Hart, who heads the school in New York. Constant zeal and tireless vigilance are the least of their qualities. Both men combine distinguished minds with even tempers, and both can be firm yet also tolerant. Both believe in the religious principles they teach and have confidence in the efficacy of their efforts. Blessed with deep sensitivity, they obtain more from the children by touching their hearts than by educating their minds. Finally, both men look upon the young delinquents as their own children. They see their work not merely as doing a job but also as discharging a duty.

We have seen how young inmates come to reform school and what regime they discover inside.

Let us now examine how they come to be released and what happens to them after they return to society.

The principle set forth above—that reform is not punishment—remains paramount. Since the child has been sent to reform school solely in his own interest, he can be released as soon as his interest requires it.

Therefore, when he has learned a trade and acquired the habit of good morals and hard work for a year or more, it is time to think of restoring him to his place as a useful member of society. But he is not simply set free, for what would become of him in a world in which he found himself alone, without support, and bereft of family and friends? He would find himself in precisely the same situation as before he was sent to reform school. To avoid this unfortunate outcome, the warden waits until an opportunity arises to place the child in apprenticeship with some craftsman or as a servant with some respectable family. He avoids releasing him into a city where he would resume his bad habits and renew his connections with erstwhile companions in crime. Farm employment is preferred whenever possible.

When the child leaves the institution, he is given a tract offering advice about how to behave along with a Bible.

It is generally agreed that it is not a good idea to restore young inmates to liberty before they have spent at least a year acquiring the habit of discipline.

When the child leaves the reform school, he does not end all ties to the institution: as an apprentice he remains its ward. If he quits the master to whom he has been assigned, he is by law subject to being returned to custody, where he remains subject to the institution's rules until he has once again proven himself and been found worthy of freedom. Indeed, he can be returned to the institution and set free as often as its governors deem appropriate. Their power over him does not end until the day he turns twenty; in the case of a girl, until the day she turns eighteen.

During his apprenticeship, the institution does not lose sight of the child. The warden corresponds with him and offers advice intended to keep him on the straight and narrow. The child also writes to the warden, and often these letters attest in a touching way to the child's gratitude.

What results have been achieved? Do these institutions really succeed in reforming the child? Are there statistics to back up the theory?

If we consider the system by itself, it would seem quite difficult to deny its effectiveness. If any human being can be reformed, these young inmates would seem to be among the best prospects, for they are guilty not so much of crime as of inexperience. One might therefore hope to arouse in them all the generous passions of youth. In criminals whose corruption is long-standing and deeply engrained, the sentiment of honesty cannot be revived, because it has long since been extinguished. In the child, this sentiment still exists but has yet to be sufficiently exercised. We believe, therefore, that a system that strives to correct wicked inclinations and develop positive motivations; that gives a protector to a child who had none; that teaches a trade to the individual without one; that instills discipline and industry in the vagabond and beggar corrupted by idleness; and that bestows an elementary education and religious principles on a youth whose education has been sadly neglected—we believe that such a system should yield many benefits.

Yet some young delinquents are almost impossible to reform. For instance, experience has taught the wardens we consulted that it is fantasy to believe that girls with corrupt morals can be reformed and pointless to try. Among boys, the most difficult to correct are those who have become habituated to theft and drunkenness. Yet their regeneration is not as hopeless as that of girls who have been seduced or become prostitutes.

In the United States it is generally believed that boys above the age of sixteen and girls above the age of fourteen should not be admitted to reform school. Above these limits it is difficult to achieve reform with the system in force in these institutions, and the harsher discipline of the prisons is more appropriate.

In Philadelphia, it is estimated that more than half the children released from the reform school have behaved well.

Seeking to verify for ourselves the effectiveness of the New York reform school, we undertook a complete analysis of the moral register. For each child released from the institution, we tried to determine what sort of behavior was observed after release and return to society.

Of 427 young male delinquents released from the institution, 85 behaved well and 41 were rated excellent. Information on 34 of the released prisoners was negative, and 24 received very negative reports. Information regarding 37 others was ambiguous or contradictory; 24 were deemed more good than bad and 14 more bad than good.

Of the 86 girls released from the institution, 37 behaved well; 11 were judged excellent; 22, bad; 16, very bad. Information about 10 others was ambiguous; 3 seem to have been more good than bad, and 3 others more bad than good.

Thus of the 513 children who returned to society after being confined to the New York reform school, more than 200 were saved from otherwise certain ruin and renounced lives of mischief and crime in favor of an honest and law-abiding existence. . . .

APPENDIX 2: PUBLIC EDUCATION

In our judgment, the system of public education in all the states of the Union is based on similar principles, which are easily enumerated.

In the United States, as in other countries, schools are divided into secondary schools devoted to more advanced studies and elementary schools.

Prominent among the secondary schools are institutions that either charge fees or are subsidized by the state, which participates indirectly in their administration.

Most elementary schools are also subject to oversight by the public authorities. Under the terms of the law, each town is required to provide a primary school that is open to the children of all residents. This school is usually overseen by local authorities. In some cases, however, the government reserves the right to inspect the schools.

Outside this system of national education complete freedom reigns. Everyone is free to enter into competition with the state in regard to education, and families are free to judge what is in their own best interest. In some parts of the Union, however, it has been thought wise to insure against the abuse of this liberty by requiring that all teachers obtain from the local authorities and the town pastor a certificate of good morals.

In the United States, therefore, the government does not relinquish control of public education, but it does not reserve a monopoly for itself. . . .

APPENDIX 4: IMPRISONMENT FOR DEBT IN THE UNITED STATES

Early American laws on imprisonment for debt were extremely severe. Like all English institutions, they were especially harsh on the poor and gave short shrift to the pauper's freedom.

For instance, imprisonment for debt was sought regardless of the amount of the debt. It preceded the judgment, so that debtors were imprisoned before their obligation was proved in court. A promissory note in the hands of the creditor was enough. It is surprising to note that, in general, the English emphasized liberty in their political laws more than any other modern nation while making greater use of imprisonment in their civil laws.

For almost ten years now, this oppressive legislation has come under vehement attack in America. Several states of the Union have already amended or abolished it. For example, the states of Kentucky, Ohio, and New York have entirely abolished imprisonment for debt in cases where the debtor has acted in good faith.

In many other states, women have been exempt from physical restraint. In still others, such as New Hampshire and Maryland, the minimum debt required for imprisonment has been set at a fairly high level.

In the majority of states, however, the old law is still in force. Thus in Philadelphia one finds a substantial number of prisoners whose debt is less than one dollar (5 fr. 30 c.). In 1830, a man was arrested for a debt of 19 cents (roughly 1 fr.). He was held in prison for nine days and was finally released only after paying 8 francs in fees above the original amount of the debt. A law like this does creditors no good; it merely sanctions private violence and vengeance.

It is believed that the number of people arrested in Pennsylvania for debt is seven thousand. If we add this to the number of people sentenced to prison for crimes and misdemeanors, which we have estimated to be 2,074 for 1830, we find that roughly 1 in every 144 residents of Pennsylvania goes to prison every year. . . .

APPENDIX 5: IMPRISONMENT, WITNESSES

In the United States, when a witness cannot post a bond, he is put in prison and remains there with the guilty and the accused until the proceedings are finished and the court is ready to hear his testimony.

In Philadelphia we heard the story of two young Irishwomen who had arrived in the country too recently to find sponsors and who were too poor to post bond and who were therefore held in prison for an entire year until the courts were ready to take their deposition.

An itinerant merchant was robbed in a Baltimore inn. He lodged a complaint, but because the thief did not leave him enough to post bond, he was arrested. So in order to find out who had robbed him of a part of his fortune, he was forced to await justice in prison and to give up his business, which demanded his presence in the West.

We could easily cite many similar examples.

In Europe one often hears complaints about the onerous burdens sometimes imposed by law on the indigent and about the obstacles they face in seeking to enforce their rights.

In America, the condition of the poor man is harsher still. If by chance he should witness a crime, he must hasten to avert his eyes, and if he is himself the victim of a crime, he has no choice but to flee lest the legal system undertake to avenge the wrong.

As monstrous as such legislation may seem, people have become so accustomed to these injustices that only a small number of enlightened people understood our objections. Most lawyers see nothing in such procedures that is at odds with their ideas of the just and the unjust or even with the principles of the democratic constitution that presides over them.

In what might appear to be a rather strange anomaly, the Americans altered the political laws of the English but kept most of their civil laws.

These laws were generally conceived for the convenience of the wealthy and provided virtually no protections for the poor. In a country where the person who brings charges against a thief can be put in prison, the thief himself remains free if he can post bail. Murder is the only crime whose author does not enjoy the protection of the law. . . .

APPENDIX 6: TEMPERANCE SOCIETIES

No country in the world has derived greater benefit from associations than America. In a country where equality of wealth is the rule, association has made it possible to amass enormous sums of capital with which to sustain the most extensive commercial and industrial development to be found anywhere. It is through political association that minorities successfully resist oppression by the majority, obtain a foothold in public opinion, and eventually gain power themselves. In America, people unite for a variety of purposes, including pleasure, knowledge, and religion. The support that weak individuals derive from association is so well-known that large numbers of people conceived the idea of associating to combat a purely intellectual enemy, a passion whose effects are more damaging in the United States than anywhere else, namely, intemperance.

When the residents of a given town or county wish to form a temperance society, they gather in a designated place. There they pledge in writing to abstain from all "ardent spirits" and to see to it that their subordinates also abstain. Anyone who takes the pledge becomes a member of the new society. They appoint a board, which is responsible for accepting new pledges. The members of the board are responsible for monitoring the level of spirit consumption in the town or county in which the society was organized. They also attempt to determine the influence of the abuse of spirits on the morality and well-being of the population and try to assess the past success of the society and likelihood of future success in reducing liquor consumption. An annual report of their findings is read to members of the society.

All the local societies in a state are usually affiliated with a state society, which analyzes and publishes the overall findings.

The most influential men in America have been quick to join temperance societies. They hope to enlist public opinion on their side, to engage vanity in the cause of morality, and thereby to effect a revolution in the habits of their compatriots.

It is impossible to assess precisely the degree to which these efforts have been successful. There can be no doubt, however, that important results have already been achieved. In the state of New York, the temperance society boasts more than 100,000 members, and there is reason to believe that the consumption of spirits has diminished by half. In Pennsylvania, the number of society members is not known, but it has been estimated that spirit consumption has already been reduced by 500,000 gallons per year. In 1831 there were 140 temperance societies in Maine, 96 in New Hampshire, 209 in Massachusetts, 202 in Connecticut, 20 in Rhode Island, 727 in New York, 61 in New Jersey, 124 in Pennsylvania, 5 in Delaware, 38 in Maryland, 10 in the District of Columbia, 13 in Virginia, 31 in North Carolina, 16 in South Carolina, 60 in Georgia, 1 in Florida, 10 in Alabama, 19 in Mississippi, 3 in Louisiana, 15 in Tennessee, 23 in Kentucky, 104 in Ohio, 25 in Indiana, 12 in Illinois, 4 in Missouri, and 13 in Michigan, for a total of 2,200. Membership numbered 270,000. Note that these figures include only those societies that published reports of their operations. It is believed that the total number of temperance societies in the United States may be as high as 3,000. . . .

APPENDIX 7: STUDY OF THE PHILADELPHIA PENITENTIARY
(OCTOBER 1831)[12]

No. 28. The inmate is able to read and write. He was sentenced for murder. He states that his health, though not bad, is worse than it was outside of prison. He

12. Tocqueville and Beaumont interviewed prisoners and employees at Eastern State Penitentiary, or Cherry Hill Prison.

strongly denies having committed the crime for which he was sent to prison. He nevertheless readily admits that he was a drinker and troublemaker and had no religion. Yet he adds that his soul is no longer the same. He finds a kind of pleasure in solitude and is tormented only by a desire to see his family again and give his children a moral and Christian upbringing, something to which he had given no thought prior to entering prison.

Q. Do you think you could live here without working?

A. I think work is absolutely necessary to survive. Without it I would die.

Q. Do you see your guards often?

A. About six times a day.

Q. Is it a consolation for you to see them?

A. Yes, sir. We are very glad to see their faces. This summer, when a cricket came into my yard, it looked like company to me. When a butterfly or any kind of animal comes into my cell, I never harm it.

No. 36. The prisoner previously served time at the Walnut Street Prison. He says he prefers the penitentiary to the old prison. His health is very good, and he doesn't find solitude unbearable.

When asked if he was forced to work, he said no but added that work here should be seen as a great privilege. Sunday always seems like the longest day of the week, because work is prohibited on Sundays.

Q. In your opinion, what is the main advantage of the new system of imprisonment?

A. Here, no prisoner knows any of the other prisoners, and they don't know him. It was a friend from Walnut Street who enlisted me in another crime when I got out.

Q. Do they give you enough food?

A. Yes, sir.

Q. Do you think that the yard adjacent to your cell is essential for your health.

A. I am convinced that you can't do without it.

No. 41. This prisoner is a young man. He admits that he is a criminal. He cried throughout the interview, especially when we spoke about his family. Fortunately, he says, no one can see me here. He therefore hopes to be able to return to the world without shame and without being rejected by society.

Q. Do you find your solitude difficult to bear?

A. Oh, sir, it's the worst torture you can imagine!

Q. But your health has not suffered from it?

A. No, my health is very good, but my soul is quite ill.

Q. What do you think about most?

A. Religion. Religious thoughts are my greatest consolation.

Q. Do you ever see a minister?

A. Yes, every Sunday.

Q. Do you enjoy speaking with him?

A. It's a great pleasure to be able to have a conversation with him. Last Sunday we had an hour together. He promised to bring me news of my father and mother tomorrow. I hope they are still alive. In the year that I've been here, I've had no news of them.

Q. Do you feel that work eases the burden of solitude?

A. It would be impossible to survive here without work. Sunday is a very long day, I assure you.

Q. Do you think that the yard adjacent to your cell could be eliminated without harming your health?

A. Yes, if there were air circulation in the cells.

Q. What is your opinion of the usefulness of the system of imprisonment under which you are confined?

A. If any system can bring men to look into their souls and change their ways, this is it.

No. 56. This prisoner has already been sentenced three times. His constitution is weak. He was ill during his first several months in the penitentiary, for which he blames lack of exercise and inadequate ventilation. He was transferred to the penitentiary at his own behest. He says he likes solitude. He would like to avoid all contact with his former friends and form no new attachments. He shows us his Bible and assures us that he derives his greatest consolations from it.

Q. You seem to have no difficulty working here. You said that this was not the case in the other prisons in which you were held. What accounts for the difference?

A. Work here is a pleasure. Our condition would be much worse if we had nothing to do, although if forced to do without it, I think I could manage.

No. 46. This prisoner is fifty-two years old. He was sentenced for burglary. He is in good health. For him, solitude is an extremely harsh punishment. The mere presence of guards pleases him, and he looks forward to occasional visits from clergymen. Work is his greatest consolation. He denies committing the crime of which he was convicted.

No. 61. This inmate was convicted of horse stealing; he claims that he is innocent. No one can understand what torture uninterrupted solitude can be, he says. When asked how he spent his time, he answered that he had only two pleasures: working and reading his Bible. The Bible is his greatest consolation. (This prisoner seemed quite agitated by religious ideas, perhaps even religious passions. His conversation was animated. He quickly became emotional and teary-eyed. We've noticed the same thing in all the inmates we have seen thus far.) He is of German origin, lost his father when still quite young, and had a bad upbringing. He has been in prison for a year. Good health. According to him, the yard adjacent to the cell is absolutely necessary for the health of the prisoners.

No. 65. This prisoner is thirty years old, has no family, and was sentenced for forgery. He has been in prison for seven months but is quite healthy. He is not very communicative. He complains of suffering in solitude, from which work is his only relief. He does not appear to be very concerned with religious ideas.

No. 32. This prisoner is a Negro aged twenty-two. He has no education and no family. He was sentenced for burglary and has been in the penitentiary for fourteen months. His health is excellent. He states that work and visits from the chaplain are his only pleasures. This young man seems to have a very dull mind and could barely name the letters of the alphabet before going to prison. He nevertheless learned on his own to read the Bible easily.

No. 20. This prisoner was found guilty of murdering his wife. He has been in the penitentiary for eighteen months. His health is excellent. He seems intelligent. He says that solitude was initially unbearable but that you slowly get used to it. Work becomes a distraction and Bible reading a pleasure. Furthermore, the isolation is tempered by the daily visits of the guards. He learned the weaver's trade in prison. This prisoner is unusually serious and devoted to religious ideas. We previously observed similar attitudes in nearly all the prisoners we have visited.

No. 72. This prisoner is a Negro of twenty-four, sentenced for the second time as a thief. He seems quite intelligent.

Q. You were a prisoner at Walnut Street. What difference do you see between that prison and the penitentiary in which you are now incarcerated?

A. The inmates at Walnut Street were free to communicate and therefore not nearly as unhappy as the prisoners here.

Q. You seem to enjoy your work. Was it the same at Walnut Street?

A. No. There, work was a punishment that you tried to escape in any way possible. Here, it is a great consolation.

Q. Do you ever read the Bible?

A. Yes, quite often.

Q. Did you also read it at Walnut Street?

A. No. I never enjoyed reading the Bible or listening to sermons until I came here.

The prisoner has been in prison for six months; excellent health.

No. 83. This prisoner is thirty-three years old. He is a repeat offender. In the Baltimore prison, where he was held previously, discipline was very harsh, and every prisoner was required to do a significant amount of work.

Q. Do you prefer being held here?

A. No, I would much rather be back in Baltimore, where there was no solitary confinement.

The prisoner has been in the penitentiary for only two months. He came down with a fever but has since fully recovered.

No. 64. This prisoner is a Negro of twenty-six. He was sentenced for burglary. His intelligence seems quite limited. He has learned the weaving trade in prison.

No. oo. This prisoner was convicted of attempted murder. He is fifty-two years old and has seven children. He seems to be well educated. Before his conviction he was incarcerated at Walnut Street. He painted a terrifying picture of that institution as a place where vice flourishes. He nevertheless believes that most prisoners would rather serve their time at Walnut Street than in the penitentiary, so great is their fear of solitude.

When asked his opinion of the system of imprisonment employed in the penitentiary in which he is now confined, he answered that it cannot fail to make a deep impression on every inmate's soul.

No. 15. This prisoner is twenty-eight. He was convicted of manslaughter. He has been in the penitentiary for nearly two years. His health is excellent. He learned the weaving trade in his cell. Solitude, he says, at first seems unbearable, but one gets used to it.

No. 54. This prisoner is thirty-five. He was convicted of murdering his wife. He has been in the penitentiary for a year and is in fine shape.

This man's thoughts about the ill effects of solitude show how much he has suffered from it, but he is beginning to get used to the way of life it requires and no longer finds it so hard.

No. 22. This prisoner is a thirty-four-year-old Negro. He was convicted once before of theft. He has been in the penitentiary for eighteen months. His health is fairly good.

Q. Do you find the prison regime here as rigorous as people say?

A. No, but everything depends on the prisoner's frame of mind. If the convict reacts badly to solitary confinement, he succumbs to irritation and despair. On the other hand, if he immediately sees how he can turn the situation to his advantage, it no longer seems unbearable to him.

Q. Were you ever held in the Walnut Street Prison?

A. Yes, sir, and I cannot imagine a worse sink of vice and crime. It takes only a few days there for a petty criminal to become a hardened scoundrel.

Q. So you believe that the penitentiary is better than your former prison?

A. It's as if you asked me whether the sun is more beautiful than the moon.*

* We thought it best here to reproduce the prisoner's exact words.

No. 68. This individual is twenty-three years old. He was sentenced for theft. He has been in the penitentiary for six months. His health is excellent. This young man is chilly and not very communicative. He comes alive only when speaking of the ills of solitude. He ardently throws himself into his work. Not even the presence of a visitor interrupts him.

No. 85. This individual has been in the penitentiary for just two months. He was sentenced for theft. His health is good, but his mind seems to be in great turmoil. When his wife and child come up in conversation, he collapses in tears. On the whole, prison seems to have made a very deep impression on him.

No. 67. The prisoner is thirty-eight years old. He was convicted of theft and has been in the penitentiary for eight months. His health is good. He has learned the cobbler's trade in prison and makes six pairs of shoes per week.

Nature seems to have given this man a serious and meditative cast of mind. His time in prison has markedly accentuated this natural tendency. His thoughts are quite lofty. He seems preoccupied with philosophical and Christian ideas.

No. 52. This prisoner is thirty-nine. He is a repeat offender. He first served time at Walnut Street, which he describes as a horrible place: you cannot come out of it an honest man. If I had been in a prison like this one from the beginning, I would not have been convicted a second time.

Q. Did you find it easy to adjust to solitude?

A. Initially the solitude terrified me. Little by little I adjusted to it. But I don't think I could live without working. Without work, there is no sleep.

This man has been in prison for nearly two years. He is in very good health.

No. 1. This prisoner, the first to be sent to the penitentiary, is a Negro. He has been here for more than two years. His health is very good.

This man works very hard. He makes ten pairs of shoes per week. He seems calm, and his attitude is excellent. He seems to look upon his incarceration in the penitentiary as a gift of Providence. Broadly speaking, his thoughts are religious. He read us the parable of the good shepherd from the Gospel, and its meaning, which he grasped fully, had touched him deeply, even though he was born to a degraded and oppressed race and had never experienced anything but the indifference and cruelty of other human beings.

No. 17. The prisoner is a mulatto sentenced for theft. He has been in the penitentiary for twenty months and has never been sick there. Volunteer teachers have taught him to read. While in prison he has also learned the cobbler's trade. He felt such a powerful need to work that after a week he was already skilled enough to make a crude pair of shoes.

No. 50. This convict, age thirty-seven, is a repeat offender. He drew a vivid portrait of the vices that flourish in the Walnut Street Prison, where he was previously incarcerated.

If I had been sent here after my first crime, he said, I would never have committed a second, but people always leave Walnut Street more corrupt than when they went in. This is the only prison where a man can reflect on things and look into his own heart.

Q. But isn't the penitentiary regime quite harsh?

A. Yes, sir, especially at the beginning. During the first two months I came close to despair. But reading and work eventually consoled me.

The inmate has been in prison for twenty months. He is in marvelous health.

No. 62. This prisoner is a well-bred man of thirty-two. He was formerly a practicing physician.

Solitary confinement seems to have made a profound impression on this young man. He cannot speak of the early days of his detention without a sense of terror. The memory of that time reduces him to tears. For two months, he says, he lived in despair, but his desperation gradually eased. Now he is resigned to his fate, as harsh as it might be. He was given the freedom to do nothing if he so chose, but idleness in solitude is such a horrible thing that he works all the time. Since he has no special skill, he cuts leather for use in making shoes. His greatest sorrow is that he cannot communicate with his family. He ended the conversation by saying that although solitary confinement is very difficult to bear, he believes that it is eminently useful to society.

The health of this inmate is good. He does not complain about the physical regime to which he is subjected.

No. 4. This man, age twenty, was previously held in the Walnut Street Prison. He attributes his recidivism to the pernicious influence of that institution. The prisoners here are much happier, he says, but not because the penitentiary regime is mild—far from it. The first months here are especially awful. I thought I would die of despair. But I have never been sick here, and I have been here for two years now.

No. 35. This inmate is more than eighty years old. When we entered his cell, he was reading the Bible.

No. 73. This cell is occupied by a Negress of twenty, a repeat offender. The penitentiary is far better than the Walnut Street Prison, she says.
Q. Why so?
A. Because it makes you think.
This woman has been in her cell for seven months. She is in very good health.

No. 63. This inmate, age 22, was sentenced to thirteen months in prison.[13] He has been in his cell for nine months. His health is excellent. His attitude seems good. He is glad to have been sent to the penitentiary.

No. 6. This individual has been in prison for two years. He was sick when he arrived but has since regained his health.

No. 69. This individual is thirty years old. He was convicted of theft. He has been in prison for five months. His health seems quite good, but his spirits are flagging. I do not think I will get out of here alive, he said. Solitude is terrible for a man's constitution, and it will kill me.
Q. What consolations do you have?
A. Only two: work and reading my Bible.

13. The first edition of Tocqueville and Beaumont's penitentiary report specified "for fornication" as the cause of imprisonment.

No. 51. This prisoner, age forty-four, has been convicted before. He bitterly resents having been sent to Walnut Street. He says that this is the only place where a man can reflect on what he has done.

He has been in his cell for ten months and has never been in better health.

No. 47. This man has been in the penitentiary for a year. He seems to be in excellent health.

His attitude seems good, but it is difficult to attach much importance to what he says in view of the fact that he hopes to be freed soon.

No. 66. This prisoner is twenty-one. He is unusual in that initially he refused to work and had to be placed on reduced rations for quite some time in order to bring him around. Now he seems to be completely submissive. He has recognized the usefulness of work in solitude and is diligent in what he does. He quickly learned the cobbler's trade and now makes eight or nine pairs of shoes a week.

He has been in his cell for eight months. Excellent health.

No. 00. This prisoner is forty years old. He was convicted of armed robbery on a public highway. He seems quite intelligent. This is how he tells his story:

I was fourteen or fifteen when I arrived in Philadelphia. I was the son of a poor farmer in the West, and I came looking for a way to earn my living in a big city. Being without recommendations, I found no work, and lacking shelter, I was forced the very first night to sleep on the deck of a ship in the harbor. The next morning they found me there. A constable arrested me, and the mayor sentenced me to a month in jail as a vagabond. During that time I was thrown together with criminals of all ages, and I forgot what my father had taught me about the importance of honesty. On leaving jail, one of my first acts was to join up with several young criminals of my own age, with whom I committed several robberies. I was arrested, tried, and acquitted. After that I thought the law couldn't touch me, and confident in my abilities, I committed other crimes that landed me in court yet again. This time I was sentenced to nine years at Walnut Street.

Q. Didn't that punishment convince you of the need to mend your ways?

A. Yes, sir, but not because the Walnut Street Prison made me repent my crimes. I confess that I never did manage to repent, nor did the idea even cross my mind, during my time there. But I soon observed that the same individuals ended up in jail again and again, and no matter how clever, strong, or bold these thieves were, they always got themselves arrested in the end. This made me take a serious look at myself, and I firmly resolved to give up this dangerous way of life for good when I got out. Having come to this conclusion, my conduct improved, and after seven years in jail I was freed. I had learned the tailor's trade in prison and soon found a good job. I married and began to earn a fairly good living. But Philadelphia was full of people I had known in prison, and I was constantly afraid that one of them would betray me. One day, two of my former cell mates turned up at my employer's shop and asked to speak to me. At first I pretended not to recognize them, but they soon forced me to admit who I was. They then asked me to lend them a large sum of money, and when I refused, they threatened to reveal the story of my life to my employer. I then promised to meet their demand and proposed that they return the next day. As soon as they had left, I followed and, together with my wife, left Philadelphia for Baltimore. Once again I easily found a job, and for a long time I lived fairly comfortably, but one day my employer received a letter from a Philadelphia constable informing him that one of his workers was an ex-convict from Walnut Street. I have no idea why this man did what he did. It's his fault that I'm here. Immediately after receiving this letter, my master fired me in the most humiliating way. I looked for work with all the other tailors in Baltimore, but they had been warned and refused to interview me. Penniless, I was forced to take a job with the railroad that was being built at the time between Baltimore and Ohio.[14] The work was so demanding and arduous that I soon succumbed to a violent fever. I lay ill for quite some time and used up all my savings. When my condition improved, I arranged to be taken to Philadelphia, where once again I contracted a fever. When I began to recover, I realized that I was penniless, with nothing to feed my family, and I saw how difficult it would be to earn an honest living. I dwelt on all the unjust persecution to which I had been subjected and became more exasperated than I can say. So I said to myself, "All right, since they've forced me into it, I will go back to being a thief, and if there is a dollar to be had anywhere in the United States, even if it's in the president's pocket, I'll take it." I called my wife and ordered her to sell all the clothes we could do without, and with the money I had her buy a pistol. Armed with this weapon but still too weak to walk without crutches, I headed for the outskirts of town, stopped the first person who happened by, and forced him to give me his wallet. But I was arrested that very night. The man I had robbed had followed me at a distance, and since in my weakened condition I had been obliged to rest not far from the scene of the crime, the police had no trouble finding me. I confessed my crime straightaway and was sent here.

Q. What are your resolutions for the future at this time?

A. I will tell you frankly that I have no intention of blaming myself for what I did or of becoming what people call a good Christian, but I am determined not to steal anymore, and I think I can stick to this resolution. When I get out in nine years, nobody on the outside will know who I am. Nobody will know that I've been in prison. I will not have made any dangerous acquaintances. I will be free to earn my living in peace. That, to my mind, is the great advantage of this penitentiary, and it is the reason why I would a hundred times rather be here than in Walnut Street despite the harshness of the discipline.

In prison for a year. Health very good.

14. Construction of the Baltimore and Ohio Railroad began in 1828, and the first span of track opened in 1830.

No. oo. This prisoner is forty years old. He has been in the penitentiary for a week. I found him reading the Gospel. He seemed calm and almost pleased. He told me that for the first few days the solitude had seemed unbearable. He was not allowed to read or work.

Yesterday, however, he was given some books, and since then he finds that his situation has changed completely. He showed me that he had already read almost all of the volume containing the Gospels. From this reading he had taken a number of religious and moral themes on which to reflect. He has no idea why he never reflected on these themes before.

No. oo. This prisoner has been in the penitentiary for two years. His sentence will expire in a few days. His health was excellent. His face was full of hope and joy, which was a pleasure to see. He had much praise for the way he had been treated in prison. He assured us that he was resolved never to commit another crime. All signs are that this young man's intentions are indeed good and that he will keep his resolution. He was convicted of a violent crime. His behavior in prison has always been exemplary.

Nos. oo and oo: These two individuals are crazy. The warden assures us that they were mad when they arrived. Their madness is quite calm. Their speech is incoherent, but there is no indication that their illness is a result of their imprisonment.[15]

No. oo. This inmate is seventy years old. He entered prison in the final stage of a pulmonary phthisis. He is wholly preoccupied with thoughts of the other life.

No. oo. This inmate was a physician before his conviction. He is responsible for the prison pharmacy. He speaks intelligently and discusses the various systems of imprisonment with an open-mindedness made extraordinary by his situation. On the whole, he finds the discipline of the penitentiary to be mild and conducive to reform. For a well-bred man, he says, it is better to live in absolute solitude than to be mixed indiscriminately with people of the most wretched sort. Isolation encourages all prisoners to reflect on their situation and is therefore conducive to reform.

Q. Have you noticed any harmful effects of solitary confinement on health? Since you are a physician as well as an inmate, you are in a better position than most to judge.

A. I find that, all things considered, there is no more illness here than in society at large. I do not believe that the health of prisoners suffers unduly.

No. oo. The individual in this cell is fifty-five years old. Before his conviction, he was well-to-do and was a justice of the peace in his county. He was convicted of killing his wife's lover.

15. With no mental health hospital wards or asylums in existence, many individuals with mental disabilities ended up in prisons, either picked up as vagrants or handed over by their families.

This inmate, who speaks French, appears to be preoccupied by an *idée fixe*: to win a pardon. We were unable to get him to speak about anything but his trial and the circumstances leading up to it. He is drafting a letter to the governor. We had to listen to him read a portion of it and examine documents from the case. He is serving a long sentence. He feels old and lives only in the hope of imminent release. In our judgment, this man seemed to believe in the effectiveness of the type of imprisonment to which he has been subjected. He believes that it is quite well adapted to the reform of the guilty, among whom he does not count himself, however.

Very good health.

No. oo. This prisoner is a young man of twenty. He is English by birth and arrived in America only a short while ago. Convicted of forgery. He seems intelligent, mild, and resigned. His health is excellent. His outlook for the future seems positive.

No. oo. This prisoner is the same age as the previous one and also English. He seems irritated by his punishment rather than resigned to it. Our visit seems to annoy him. He does not stop working to talk to us and barely responds to our questions. He shows no signs of repentance and no interest in religious ideas.

Good health.

No. oo. This prisoner is thirty-eight. He has been in the penitentiary for only three weeks, so he is in a state of real despair. The solitude will kill me, he says. I will never survive my punishment. I will die before I regain my freedom.

Q. Don't you take any consolation from your work, at least?

A. Yes, sir. Solitude without work is a thousand times worse. But work doesn't stop you from thinking and feeling wretched. This place torments the soul, I assure you.

The poor man sobbed while speaking of his wife and children, whom he believed he would never see again. When we entered his cell, we found him crying as he worked.

No. oo. The prisoner is twenty-five. He comes from the upper class. He expresses himself with ease and warmth. He was convicted of falsely declaring bankruptcy.

This young man seemed very pleased to see us. Solitude is clearly a terrible torment for him. The need for intellectual relations with his peers seems to preoccupy him more acutely than it does less well-educated inmates. He is eager to tell us his story. He spoke of his crime, his position in the world, his friends, and above all his family. Family feeling seems quite well developed in him. He cannot think of his parents without collapsing in tears. From under his bed he took a packet of letters that his family had managed to get through to him. The letters were nearly in shreds from having been read so often. He reread them for us, commented on them, and lingered over any expression of interest in him, however small, the letters contained.

Q. I see that you find your punishment extremely harsh. Do you believe that it will result in reform?

A. Yes, sir, I believe that, all things considered, this type of imprisonment is better than any other. It would be more difficult for me to be confined with all sorts of riff-raff than to live alone here. In any case, a punishment like this cannot fail to make you think.

Q. But do you think that it may prove fatal to reason?

A. I think that the danger is real. In my own case, I recall that I had some strange visions during my first months in solitude. For several nights in a row, for instance, I thought I saw an eagle perched on the foot of my bed. But now I'm working and am accustomed to this way of life. I am no longer tormented by such ideas.

One year in prison. Good health.

Letters Following Publication of the Penitentiary Report

From Tocqueville | To Gustave de Beaumont

Paris, May 26, 1837

. . . A first matter of importance is the return of M. de Metz, whose report, while not exactly contrary to ours, nevertheless alters the state of the question significantly.[16] M. de Metz found 400 prisoners in the Philadelphia prison. It has now existed for nearly eight years. He claims to have *proof* that this mode of imprisonment does no harm to the sanity or health of the prisoners and is a powerful agent of regeneration. Crawford and Julius were of the same opinion.[17] Furthermore, M. de Metz states that repeated, arbitrary use of the whip has become customary in all prisons built on the Auburn model. It proved necessary to permit use of the whip at Wethersfield, because without it neither silence nor even order could be achieved. All of this leads to the conclusion that the Philadelphia system, which we were inclined to favor if the penitentiary idea was to be acted on, is ardently advocated by the new commissioners. I for one see no great harm in this. If the nation wants to pay the price of such a system, if the chambers are willing to make the changes in the penal code that the system requires, and, finally, if public opinion is prepared to accept it—all quite doubtful things—

16. The French government sent magistrate Frédéric de Metz (1796–1873) and architect Abel Blouet (1795–1853) to study American prisons in 1836. One of their main objectives was to determine whether the Auburn system or the Philadelphia system of managing prisons was the better model for France to adopt.

17. William Crawford (1788–1847) published the *Report on the Penitentiaries of the United States* in 1835. Doctor Niclaus Heinrich Julius (1783–1862), a German prison reformer, traveled to America from Prussia in 1835.

there is no doubt that it is possible to have a simpler, more efficient prison system that reforms more prisoners. This is the position I have adopted vis-à-vis M. de Metz (who, by the way, is deathly afraid of us and therefore quite obsequious). I think we ought to stick to it. According to the documents he has brought back, it seems certain that, *if the penitentiary system is chosen,* the Philadelphia system is preferable. Yet it remains quite difficult to establish and quite costly. M. de M. claims that in England the government is returning to this system. He intends to write you with questions about this. I thought it would be worthwhile to let you know my impressions in advance.

The same M. de Metz has returned from America, moreover, with the most violent, the most unintelligent, and, as *Le Corsaire* would say, the most *fulchiron* hatred imaginable.[18] He saw everything, judged everything, and condemned everything in three months. He also learned everything but the language, of which he has not brought back a *single* word. . . . He has also judged England from the top of a coach while traveling at full gallop from Liverpool to Dover. There he saw, judged, and admired everything in a week, still without knowing a word of the language. As you can see, it gets better and better. He says that America is nothing but a wretched copy of England, a botched imitation of a splendid original. All of this is of course as amusing as it is pitiful. But what is truly serious is what is happening right now in America itself. Never has any country at any time experienced such a terrible commercial and industrial disaster. I cannot believe that it will not lead to a major political upheaval, and then just imagine the shouts of joy among the *juste milieu* rabble in France and the enemies of liberty everywhere. . . .

From Tocqueville | To Honoré Langlois[19]

Tocqueville, August 17, 1838

My dear Monsieur Langlois,

You ask for my opinion on the question that has been submitted to you by the minister of the interior. It is a pleasure for me to summarize very briefly

---

18. *Le Corsaire,* a satirical literary periodical, was published from 1822 to 1852. The term *fulchiron* referred to a conservative deputy from Lyon, M. Fulchiron.

19. Honoré Langlois was the *conseiller général* for La Manche, Tocqueville's home department in western Normandy. In anticipation of prison reform in France, the minister of the interior, the comte de Montalivet, had circulated a questionnaire regarding the treatment of prisoners to all of the counselors on August 1. The questionnaire focused on issues related to solitary confinement and revived the debate between proponents of the Auburn system and the Philadelphia system of incarceration. Langlois sought out Tocqueville to learn his opinion on the matter, and the press widely published Tocqueville's letter in support of the Philadelphia system. As Tocqueville revealed in a letter to Beaumont on October 19, 1838, his letter to Langlois was a hasty response not intended for publication. Tocqueville apologized for not crediting Beaumont by name or consulting with him before composing his thoughts on the American prison system; Beaumont responded on October 25 by affirming his agreement with Tocqueville's opinions.

what I learned from my trip to America and several years of studying the subject. As you will see, it all comes down to a small number of rather clear and simple propositions.

Statistics published by the Ministry of Justice tell us that the number of repeat offenders in France is growing steadily and rapidly. Furthermore, reports issued by the courts tell us that nearly all major crimes are committed by ex-convicts.

Our present prison system is therefore unsatisfactory. It constitutes a danger to law and order and a threat to the security of each and every one of us. It must therefore be changed. This is an incontrovertible fact. The administration in charge of the prisons is aware of this fact and has stated publicly that it is the case.

Few issues have stirred more thought in America or Europe these past ten years than that of what new system of imprisonment should replace the one we have.

Many different systems have been proposed. They differ from one another in a multitude of small ways, yet all this variety comes down to two basic systems: either one can isolate the inmates at night while obliging them to work together in silence during the day, or one can require each inmate to live and work in his own separate cell.

I call the first the Auburn system and the second the Philadelphia system. I use these names for convenience in what follows and not to suggest that one should copy exactly what is done in Auburn or Philadelphia. When it comes to penitentiaries or any other institution, I do not believe that nations should servilely copy one another, nor do I believe that a system that is successful in one place can be adopted without change in another.

The Auburn system totally prevents nocturnal conversation and all the acts of depravity that usually accompany it. It also prevents communication during the day to a certain extent, but it does not prevent inmates from getting to know one another or from getting together after leaving prison. It can be maintained, moreover, only by means of close and constant surveillance. To work well it requires quite frequent and arbitrary punishment. Indeed, there is reason to doubt that it can be introduced into our prisons without allowing the beating of prisoners, which public opinion in France rightly rejects.

The Philadelphia system is as completely opposed to nocturnal communication as the Auburn system, but in addition it also prevents daytime communication. It prevents the inmates not only from speaking to one another but also from seeing one another. This in itself is a very important fact. As a result, when a man is released from prison after serving a term of several years, all the bonds that might have tied him to the world of crime in spite of himself are broken. He will have lost track of his former companions without making new ones. He will therefore find himself isolated and helpless in the midst of a society organized by honest men and women.

In the Philadelphia system, discipline is simple and easy, because it relies on walls rather than men. An honest and intelligent prison warden is enough to establish and maintain such a system even in a large institution. Because inmates are isolated from one another, they cannot mount any resistance to the system. They are always alone against the rest of society.

Of all the systems of imprisonment, the Philadelphia system is the one that makes the greatest impression on the convict's imagination. This is a great advantage. People nowadays have lost sight of the need to make prisons *intimidating*. The inmate must not suffer physically in prison, but he must be made unhappy enough about the consequences of his crime that fear will prevent him from breaking the law again and deter anyone who might be tempted to imitate him.

Finally, of all known penitentiary systems, the Philadelphia system offers by far the greatest chance of reform. I have shown you how it absolutely ensures that inmates will not become *worse* while in prison (as they invariably do in our current prisons and sometimes do in the Auburn prison). Very frequently, moreover, the Philadelphia system must change the inmate's habits and modify his ideas.

What leads most criminals to crime is laziness. Among diligent workers thieves are rare. The Philadelphia system not only forces inmates to work but makes them need and love their occupations. Idleness is so difficult to bear in solitude that the inmates would rather do without bread than without work. I have seen Philadelphia inmates beg for permission to work as the greatest favor one could do them. The cruelest punishment one can inflict is to deprive them of their tools. In Auburn inmates are beaten in order to make them work. In Philadelphia they would rather be beaten than remain idle. They thus naturally acquire the habit, taste, and need of an occupation, and their occupation turns them away from crime.

In the Philadelphia system the inmate is carefully isolated from the vicious portion of society and protected from all its corrupt emanations, but this is done in order to expose him to honest influences. The Americans leave edifying reading material in each cell. Inmates generally read these tracts and often learn them by heart even without being told to do so. Indeed, it would be a punishment to prevent them from absorbing the lessons offered. I have seen prisoners who taught themselves to read for the pleasure of studying the one volume they were permitted to possess. Had these same men been in one of our prisons, they would have spat on the very tracts that these American prisoners find so precious.

Edifying lectures are no different. The men in the common workshops do not listen to them. They make fun of them. In the cells, however, prisoners welcome them eagerly. Morality and reason thus quietly penetrate each man's soul.

My experience, moreover, leads me to believe that solitude is the only path to reform, so long as it is not absolute. I visited all the cells of the Philadelphia penitentiary. I conversed with all the inmates, and I can tell you that I found these men in a more satisfactory state of mind than any other group of prisoners

I have ever seen. Their thoughts were grave and calm, their words simple and reasonable. I found that isolation had greatly intensified those sentiments that contribute the most to the development of moral judgment. I saw few inmates who did not have tears in their eyes when they spoke of their families and children, the places where they were born, and their early childhood.

From all this, my dear Monsieur Langlois, I conclude without hesitation that the Philadelphia system is infinitely easier to establish and maintain, more intimidating, more likely to achieve reform, and, in general, more useful to society than its competitor. To me this is perfectly clear. But since I am not writing a brief in favor of the system, and since I have promised to tell you what I know about the subject that concerns us both, I turn now from the positive aspects of the system to a rehearsal of its drawbacks.

It costs more to establish the Philadelphia system than the Auburn system.

Bear in mind, however, that even though cells in the Philadelphia system need to be much larger and also need to be equipped with various fairly costly fixtures, there is no need for dining halls, workshops, hospitals, exercise yards, high double walls, or even an abundance of bars—all items that are very costly and, under the Auburn system, essential.

Bear in mind, too, that if the Philadelphia system were adopted, all sentences would certainly be of shorter duration, so that the cost of guards and upkeep would be lower. Finally, remember that nothing is more expensive than a bad prison system that leads to repeated prosecutions of the same criminals as well as to a steady increase in the number of delinquents. Do not forget that every thief levies a double tax on society. He deprives his victim of his property and compels other citizens to bear the cost of prosecuting and punishing him. A bad prison may cost little in the way of upkeep but still be very expensive if it causes crime to increase. What is saved in the budget of the minister of the interior is added to the budget of the minister of justice. Society squanders on the latter much more than it saves on the former.

The second objection, which is more serious, is that under the Philadelphia system it is more difficult to employ prison labor productively. This is true. There are many types of work that can be done only by a fairly large number of people working together or that can only be performed outdoors.

Note, however, that this objection does not apply to jails in which defendants are held pending trial, because society has no right to force a person who has not been convicted to work. It has little relevance, moreover, to jails that hold convicts whose sentences are under one year, because it is difficult for the authorities to organize regular workshops or require sustained labor in such a place. The number of prisoners is too small, and their sentences are too short. That leaves prisoners serving longer terms. Clearly, under the Philadelphia system it becomes more difficult to employ such inmates productively. The effects of this should not be exaggerated, however. Many types of work can be carried on in solitude, and some are highly lucrative. All the inmates I saw in Philadelphia were occupied, and any number of them earned a fairly substantial revenue for the prison. It is in any case an important and difficult question whether it is appropriate for the state to employ the criminals entrusted to its safekeeping as industrial workers whose competition may in many cases prove ruinous to honest free labor. To maintain a prison with convict labor is arguably to compel the working classes to bear the full cost of criminal justice. I will not pursue this discussion further here, because it would take me too far afield. To give you an idea of its gravity, I will simply say that in England the idea of using convict labor to defray the cost of prison seemed so dangerous that the decision was made to employ inmates in useless or relatively unproductive tasks.

I come now to a third and final objection: it is by far the most serious. Some say that solitary confinement destroys the prisoner's health and puts his life in danger. This is an important point, and it demands the full attention of the legislature. I was concerned about this point myself and raised the issue in America. In Philadelphia I saw prisoners who had been in their cells for more than a year (the length of time the prison had been in operation) without ill effect. I was afraid, however, that a longer detention might eventually affect their health, and I concluded that before adopting a similar system in France, it would be wise to await the results of the American experiment. As you know as well as I, my dear Monsieur Langlois, a single fact is worth more than the finest and most elaborate argument. It was in 1831 that the royal government sent me and my colleague M. de Beaumont to America. Seven years have passed since then. A table of mortality summarizing the results of the past eight years has been established. From this it emerges that although the mortality rate in Philadelphia was a little higher than in Auburn, it was much lower than in France's central prisons and workhouses and has always been lower than the mortality rate in the city of Philadelphia itself. In France, a person is more likely to die in prison than outside. Reflection reveals the reason for these favorable results: solitary confinement as I conceive of it is not total isolation, since the inmate has frequent communications with his guards, the chaplain, and even the good and charitable citizens who take an interest in his reform. He is not separated from his family, which he can see with the permission of the authorities and under their supervision. He is not kept in a dungeon but rather in a healthy, well-ventilated, well-heated room, where he is well fed and well clothed and where he can work, read, and write. Conceived in this way, solitary confinement torments the soul, to be sure, but it spares the body, thus achieving two goals that every system of imprisonment must seek to attain. A man confined in this way is segregated only from the corrupt portion of society and prevented from indulging his vicious habits.

I do not deny, however, that it is healthier to live in society than confined to a cell. Yet it must be granted that a prison is not a hospital. We do not put our fellow human beings in prison for their pleasure or for the sake of their health. We do so to reform and punish them, and a person who has violated the laws of his country and offended the entire society must expect to suffer certain discomforts and inconveniences for his crime.

I will end with one last reflection and an example.

None of the European observers who object to the Philadelphia system have witnessed it in operation. Those who have been to America favor it.

When I went to the United States, I was strongly opposed to this system. I came back convinced that we should adopt it if experience proved that it did not ruin the lives of inmates. Eighteen months later, Mr. Crawford, who was sent to America by the English government on a mission similar to ours, returned with the same opinion. Some time later, the Prussian government entrusted Herr Julius with a similar mission. He began full of prejudices against the Philadelphia system and returned a warm partisan. The same thing has recently happened to the honorable M. de Metz, a learned and humane gentleman. Thus the longer the system endures and develops, the greater the number of its proponents and the more enthusiastic their support. Only those who do not know the Philadelphia system attack it. Does this not strike you as significant?

When I went to America seven years ago, the system of day-and-night isolation had as yet been adopted nowhere other than in Philadelphia, where it originated. Nearly all the other states were in the process of copying the Auburn prison. Since then, some new prisons have been built on the Philadelphia model. What is even more impressive, however, is that England, which has been concerned with the prison issue for half a century and which in that time built some of the finest and most costly prisons to be found anywhere in Europe, has recently decided to change course. It is either tearing down or renovating all the prisons that it built at such great expense and adopting the Philadelphia system throughout the country.

In sum, my dear Monsieur Langlois, I believe that the system of day-and-night cellular confinement is not workable in the jails. On this point, nearly all the members of the commission appointed by the minister of the interior, of whom I was one, agreed.

As for the central prisons and workhouses, I have no doubt that the Philadelphia system, if modified in accordance with French customs to suit our needs and habits as much as possible, is greatly preferable.

I will end here, because my hand is very tired. I hope that this long and hastily scrawled letter will have answered all your questions. If you want to hear more, I would be glad to oblige. All my knowledge of this issue is at your disposal.

Farewell, and please accept my sincere best wishes.

Alexis de Tocqueville

P.S. I recall that you spoke to me yesterday about the portion of the prisoners' earnings that is set aside as savings for their personal use. Here is my thinking on this point:

I regard the idea that prisoners have a right to a portion of their earnings as mistaken. The convict has not only harmed society by his crime but compelled it to bear a substantial burden to maintain him in prison. It seems to me immoral and contrary to reason for this same convict to claim a portion of what he earns.

In working for the state without pay, he is simply discharging a debt. He is paying for his room and board.

Hence I would not want to see prisoners legally entitled to a portion of their earnings. I would, however, like the prison authorities to use all of the inmates' excess earnings to help those who behave well in prison and especially those who behave well outside. The money should be paid out gradually, as evidence of genuine reform accumulates.

From Tocqueville | To Nathaniel Niles[20]

[June 15, 1843]

I thank you profusely for the document you sent me, which I regard as important.[21] I also want to thank you for your kind offer in connection with your stay in the United States. As you know, nothing interests me more than matters connected with that great and powerful nation. Documents that might shed light on its internal situation or, especially, tell me about its relations with England and ourselves would be immensely valuable to me, and I would be particularly grateful to you if you could let me know of their existence.

I also have a more specific request. As you know, I am *rapporteur* on the law concerning prisons, a very important bill in connection with which we have learned a great deal from studying the American experience.[22] The debate will not take place this year, but it will probably begin in the next session. You will have gathered how important it is for me in the meantime to obtain any American documents I can that might shed light on this important question. In particular, I need the last two "Reports of the State Prison of Philadelphia (Cherry Hill prison)." I also need the last two "Reports of the Prison Discipline Society of Boston."[23] These documents are essential, and I would be most grateful if you could obtain them for me. *Any other* important document concerning this issue would be of great interest to me.

I have allowed my connections to the United States to lapse. I regret this and would like to reestablish them. This is not only something dear to my heart but also a matter of patriotism, because one of the foundation stones of my politics is that in spite of prejudices and quarrels over minor issues, France and the United States are such natural and necessary allies that they should never lose touch with each other. . . .

20. Nathaniel Niles (1791–1869) served as an American diplomat in Paris from 1830 to 1833.

21. The contents of this document remain unknown.

22. Tocqueville had been named to this commission in April.

23. The Prison Discipline Society of Boston argued against the effectiveness of the Philadelphia system on the grounds of mortality and dementia rates. This debate continued, in America and in France, for several more years.

From Tocqueville | To Charles Sumner[24]

[Tocqueville, August 6, 1847]

My dear Sir,

I read in the *Daily Advertiser* of June 1 a report of the meeting in which you proposed that the Boston Prison Society ought not to be regarded as "the pledged advocate" of the Auburn or any other system, and it was decided that all systems should be judged without preconception or prejudice. I have since learned from the same newspaper that the society refused to adopt the resolution. This vote surprised and distressed me. I am very keenly interested in prison reform and have always maintained my respectful devotion to the society, which did me the honor of accepting me unbidden as a member and which is so justly renowned in the world of philanthropy. These two sentiments impel me to write.

I do not hesitate to say that the vote to which I refer will come as an unpleasant surprise to nearly everyone in Europe who is concerned with the prison issue. They will interpret it as a formal commitment by the society to become the champion of the Auburn system and the systematic adversary of individual imprisonment. It will be seen to have abandoned the role of judge and to have become a party to the case.

I hardly need remind you that in Europe today, deliberation and experience have persuaded nearly everyone to adopt the system of individual imprisonment and to reject the Auburn system.[25] Most old-world governments came to this position not overnight but after serious examination and lengthy debate. I shall speak here only of the two great free nations of Europe, those which I know best and which deserve their authority because they make up their minds only after open debate and in obedience only to public opinion, namely, France and England. I can assure you that in both of these countries the Auburn system is almost unanimously rejected. Most who formerly favored it have renounced it either following debate or after seeing it in operation and have adopted instead, either in whole or in part, the system of individual imprisonment. Both governments have moved in the same direction. As you know, the French government a few years ago introduced a law based on individual imprisonment. After a five-week debate, the longest and most thorough debate on any issue in the history of our parliament, this law was approved by a *vast majority*. Although the law has

24. In 1847, Charles Sumner (1811–1874) was a Boston lawyer who was beginning to achieve great influence in the Whig Party. He opposed war with Mexico and advocated prison reform and abolition. Sumner later became a senator and a leader of the Republican Party. In 1856, he gained notoriety when Preston Brooks, a South Carolina congressman, beat him with a cane on the Senate floor to protect the honor of South Carolina senator Andrew Butler, whom Sumner had insulted in his Senate speech entitled "The Crime against Kansas." While traveling in Europe to recover from this attack, Sumner visited Tocqueville in France.

25. Prussia and Italy were notable exceptions and had come to the same conclusions that Louis Dwight had in the annual reports of Boston's Prison Discipline Society. Charles Lucas used these examples to build a case against Tocqueville's support for the Philadelphia system.

not yet been debated by the Chambre des pairs, that is because of circumstances having nothing to do with the penitentiary question.[26] The Chambre des pairs will take up the issue at the beginning of the next session, and among the leading men in that chamber, most have already openly declared their approval of the measure in principle. As for the press, nearly all the newspapers support the system of individual imprisonment. The one paper that had most intelligently and forcefully opposed that system recently declared itself to have been persuaded of its soundness. This change came about in part because of experience gained in a large number of our prisons over the past several years. Thus there is reason to doubt that when the law is reported to the Chambre des députés there will be anyone who opposes it *in principle.*[27]

Given these circumstances, the vote just taken by a society as enlightened and celebrated as the Boston Prison Society will not be understood here, and I confess that I cannot help fearing that it may damage the society's honorable reputation on this side of the ocean or at the very least diminish its authority. I would be very sorry to see this happen, not only for the sake of an organization to which I am honored to belong but for the sake as well of humanity, whose cause it might do so much to serve.

Please, sir, accept my most respectful consideration.

Alexis de Tocqueville,

Member of the Institut and of the Chambre des députés

26. The Chambre des pairs (Chamber of Peers) was the upper house of the French parliament. The king appointed members of the French nobility to serve.

27. The Chambre des députés (Chamber of Deputies) was the lower house of the French parliament and was elected by popular suffrage.

Beaumont's *Marie; or, Slavery in the United States: A Novel of Jacksonian America,* 1835

"The racial taint remains even if the color is bleached out." This declaration from one of the protagonists in Beaumont's novel, *Marie,* captures the drama surrounding the forbidden love of a French traveler for an American woman who is marked forever by the stigma of her distant black ancestry.

In selecting excerpts from the novel, we chose a few vivid scenes and reflections that convey the author's intent to denounce racial oppression in America and take up the cause of the victims.

Of the several appendices, we have selected the one on African Americans—slaves and freemen—as a model of Beaumont's concise mastery of the issues. We have not included his appendix on Native Americans, which is primarily a review of the ethnographic literature on Indians available in the 1830s.

As with *Du système pénitentiaire,* the Académie française recognized *Marie* with its prestigious Montyon prize.

The excerpts begin with some consideration of dating and marriage in France and America. Then merchant and minister David Nelson tells French traveler Ludovic how his wife's black ancestry—as well as that of their children, Marie and Georges— was exposed by a spurned suitor in New Orleans. The revelation led to the extreme chagrin and death of Theresa Spencer and forced the rest of the family to flee to Baltimore. Nelson, Ludovic, and Georges debate slavery and race, with Nelson trying to persuade Ludovic that he can never marry Marie.

When Ludovic remains determined in his love for Marie, Nelson tells him to spend six months in the American North so that he can better gauge the strength of white prejudice against interracial marriage even in states where blacks presumably enjoy the same civil rights as whites.

Ludovic's observations reveal the indignation of even the most progressive whites toward his planned union. After their secret is also revealed in Baltimore, the Nelsons flee to New York City, where Ludovic and Marie are to be united. Beaumont gleaned the episode of rioters intent on preventing an interracial union from accounts of a real riot in New York following his return to France. The mayor dutifully called out the militia but refused to order them to fire on the white rioters, since the mob also represented his potential constituents.

As Ludovic and Marie flee Manhattan the following day, this time to Michigan, their nuptials still uncompleted, they witness the flames rising from the black schools and churches destroyed by rioters.

They journey to Michigan along with David Nelson, who fled New York following the riot. Meanwhile, Georges is killed leading an unsuccessful rebellion by Indians and black slaves in the South. In a dramatic reenactment of her mother's fate, Marie succumbs to a broken heart.

Chapter Excerpts

[FROM CHAPTER 2]

For any girl above the age of sixteen, marriage is the most important thing in life. In France, she wants to marry; in America, she seeks to do so. Since the American girl becomes mistress of herself and her behavior at an early age, she makes up her own mind about whom to wed. Clearly, the task of the young woman responsible for her own destiny is a delicate one, fraught with peril. She must look out for her own welfare as a father or a mother would look out for the welfare of a daughter in France. In general, it must be said that she acquits herself of her task quite soberly. In this very down-to-earth society, where everyone works, American women have a job of their own: to find a husband. In the United States, the men are cold and chained to their labors. A woman must go to them, or else attract them with some powerful charm. So do not be surprised if a young woman who lives among such men lavishes them with studied smiles and tender looks. Her flirtatiousness is nonetheless enlightened and prudent. She has taken the measure of her freedom and knows the boundaries she must not cross. Although her wiles may be deserving of censure, her goal at least is irreproachable.

There is no lack of opportunity for young men and young women to make known their affections and mutual attraction. Girls are accustomed to going out alone, and if a young man joins them, no proprieties are violated. The only formality they must respect is to walk apart, for a gentleman may not offer his arm to a young lady unless they are engaged. The same liberty reigns in the salon. Mothers rarely meddle in their daughters' conversation. Girls may receive whomever they please in their own homes. They are at liberty to give private audiences and in some cases to invite young men whom they have met in society but whom their parents do not know. In behaving thus, they do no wrong, because these are the country's mores.

Flirting in America is of a rather special kind. In France, a flirtatious girl is eager not so much to marry as to please. In America, she is eager to please only in order to marry. With us, coquetry is a passion; in America, it is a calculation. If a young woman who is engaged continues to flirt, it is not because she is flirtatious but rather because she is prudent. It is not unheard-of for a fiancé to break his word. If a girl anticipates such a misfortune, she may try to win hearts not in order to possess several at once but in order to replace the one she is in danger of losing.

In such circumstances, and indeed in all circumstances, she is entirely free to entice, encourage, or reject suitors as she pleases.

In America, the freedom that is granted to young women so early in life is quickly withdrawn. In France, a young woman passes directly from the swaddling of infancy to the bonds of matrimony, but the chains of wedlock are very light. By taking a husband, a French girl earns the right to make a gift of herself to the world. By pledging herself, she becomes free. At that point she embarks on a life of parties, pleasures, and conquests. In America, by contrast, it is the young girl who enjoys the brilliant life. When she marries, she dies to worldly pleasures in order to be reborn to the austere duties of the household. Men previously paid homage to her not because she was a woman but because she might become a spouse. Her flirtatiousness, having found a husband, is of no further use, and once she has given her hand, there is nothing more to ask of her.

In the United States, a woman ceases to be free on her wedding day, whereas in France that is the day on which she gains her freedom. . . .

[FROM CHAPTER 8]

He quietly spread the rumor that Theresa was a mulatto by her great-grandmother, and in support of this allegation he named all of Marie's ancestors back to the woman whose impure blood he blamed for the debilitation of all her offspring.

His slander was odious, but it was true. The origin of the stain on Theresa Spencer had been lost in the night of time. Fernando's voice awakened long-dormant memories. The human heart is capacious when it comes to the misery of others. The public was aroused. An investigation of sorts was launched. The local elders were consulted, and it was determined that sometime in the last century, Theresa Spencer's family had been tainted by a drop of black blood.

Over subsequent generations this mixture had become imperceptible. Theresa was distinguished by her lovely white complexion, and nothing in her face or features revealed her tainted past. Yet tradition condemned her.

From that day forward, our life, which had been tranquil and pleasant, turned bitter and cruel. Because we had stood high in society's esteem, the shame of our downfall was all the more glaring. What I had thought were solid bonds of affection at once proved tenuous. Only one friend stood by me in misfortune, and he was obliged to hide his face.

This generous friend, to whom you are related by blood, was a Frenchman and therefore more generous toward the black race and less prejudiced against it than Americans generally are. In my misfortune he alone reached out a helping hand and saved me from the shame of bankruptcy. The blow to my social position had also undermined my credit. People in this country will tolerate bankruptcy but show no mercy to those who marry improperly.

FROM *Marie; or, Slavery in the United States*

Nevertheless, the ill was beyond all remedy. I struggled against my fate, because we are raised never to give up hope. But no man could overcome so great an obstacle. . . .

Nelson:

The black race is despised in America because it is a race of slaves. It is hated because it aspires to be free.

In our mores as well as our laws, the Negro is not a man. He is an object.

He is a commercial commodity, a superior type of merchandise. A Negro is worth ten acres of cultivated land.

No record is kept of the birth, marriage, or death of a slave.

The child of a Negro belongs to his master, just as the fruits of the earth belong to the owner of the land. Love between slaves leaves no more trace in the records of civil society than do the plants in our gardens, and when a slave dies, one thinks only of replacing him, as one would replace a useful tree that succumbed to age or the elements.

Ludovic:

In other words, your laws prevent Negro slaves from exhibiting filial piety, paternal feelings, and maternal affections. What, then, does the slave have in common with other human beings?

Nelson:

The principle, once accepted, has numerous consequences. A child born in slavery has no more a family than an animal does. A slave mother feeds her child as a wild animal suckles its young. The relations of mother to child, child to father, brother to sister are meaningless to slaves and have no moral significance. And a slave cannot marry, because he is the property of another man and cannot give himself to anyone else.

Ludovic:

But how is it that a nation as enlightened and religious as the American does not recoil in horror from an institution that offends the laws of nature, morality, and humanity? Are not all men created equal?

Nelson:

No people is more devoted to the principle of equality than we are, but we do not allow an inferior race to share our rights.

At these words, Georges's face turned red, and his lips trembled. He came close to shouting out in anger, but with great effort he managed to restrain himself.

I responded to Nelson: People in the United States believe that blacks are inferior to whites. Is that because whites in general are judged to be more intelligent than Negroes? But how can you compare a species of men raised in slavery, whose legacy from one generation to the next is abjection and misery, with people who can boast of fifteen centuries of uninterrupted civilization and whose education begins in the cradle? In Europe we do not share your American prejudices; we believe that all men are equal and belong to the same family.

Nelson:

No doubt slavery is an offense to God's morality and law, but don't judge the American people too harshly. Greece had its helots; Rome, its slaves; the Middle Ages, their serfs. Today we have Negroes. And these Negroes, whose brains are naturally limited, attach little value to freedom. For most of them, emancipation is a poisoned gift. Ask one and he will tell you that he was happier as a slave than in freedom. Left to their own devices, they cannot sustain themselves. Fifty percent more freemen die in our cities than slaves.

Ludovic:

When a slave is suddenly set free, he is naturally incapable of making good use of his independence or enjoying it. A man who has been bound hand and foot since early childhood will totter if suddenly told to walk. Freedom in his hands is a dangerous weapon, and he may use it to wound others in his vicinity; usually he himself is the first victim. But does it follow that once slavery is established in a place, it must be maintained forever? Surely not. It is nevertheless accurate to say that the generation that benefits from emancipation will not be the one to enjoy it: the blessings of liberty will accrue only to subsequent generations. I will never accept your so-called laws of necessity, the effect of which is to justify oppression and tyranny.

Nelson:

I think as you do. But do not assume that Negroes are treated inhumanely, a charge that is routinely leveled against all slaveholders. Most slaves are better clothed, better fed, and happier than your free peasants in Europe.

"Stop!" Georges suddenly exclaimed (for at this point anger overcame his filial respect). It is wicked and cruel to say such things! Yes, you care for your Negroes as well as you care for your pack animals! Better, in fact, because a Negro earns more for his master than a horse or mule. And true, when you beat your slaves, you do not kill them: a Negro is worth $300. But you cannot boast that a slave master is humane because he takes care of his slaves. To kill with cruelty would be better than to calculate the value of an odious existence! To be sure, according to your laws, a Negro is not a man. He is a chattel, a thing. But he is a thinking thing, a thing that can act and wield a dagger. You say "inferior race"? You've measured the Negro's brain and determined that there is no room inside for anything but suffering, and then you condemn him to suffer perpetually. But you are wrong. Your measurements are inaccurate. In the brute's brain there is a chamber you have missed, in which a powerful faculty resides: the faculty of vengeance—implacable, horrible, but intelligent vengeance. If he hates you, it is because your whip has flayed his body, your injustices have bludgeoned his soul. Is he so stupid to detest you? The most intelligent animal licks the cruel hand that beats it and rejoices in servitude. The stupidest man, this brutalized Negro, may be chained like an animal, but his mind is free, and his soul suffers as nobly as the soul of the Martyr who died that the world might be free. He submits, but he is conscious of his oppression. Only his body obeys; his soul rebels. He grovels! Yes, for two centuries he has groveled at your feet, but one day he will rise up, look you in the eye, and kill you. You call him cruel, but you forget that he has lived his whole life in suffering and hatred. He has only one thought, vengeance, because he has only one feeling, pain. . . .

Georges:

Do you know why the Americans are tempted to abolish slavery? Because they have begun to think that slavery is harmful to industry.

They see that the slave states are poor, while nonslave states are rich, and they condemn slavery. They say to themselves: the free worker, who works for himself, works harder than the slave, and it is more profitable to pay a worker who works well than to feed a slave who works badly. And they condemn slavery.

Then they say: Labor is the source of wealth, but servitude dishonors labor. Whites will be lazy as long as they have slaves. And they condemn slavery.

Their self-interest reinforces their pride. The emancipation of blacks makes free men in name only. The emancipated Negro cannot compete with Americans in commerce or industry. He can become one of two things: a beggar or a servant. Custom blocks his path to other occupations. To free the Negroes in the United States is to establish an inferior class, and any pure-blooded white will then belong to a privileged class. White skin will become a mark of nobility. . . .

Nelson:

Confronted with two races different from their own, the Indians and the Negroes, Americans have not mingled their blood with either. They have preserved their ancestors' blood intact. To prevent all contact with these other nations, their reputation had to be destroyed. Thus the racial taint remains even if the color is bleached out. . . .

Nelson:

New Orleans is populated mainly by Americans from the North who move south to get rich and leave as soon as they've made their fortune. These temporary residents seldom marry. Here is the reason why.

Every summer, New Orleans is ravaged by yellow fever. Anyone who is not tied down leaves town and travels up the Mississippi and Ohio into the northern and central states or perhaps on to Philadelphia and Boston in search of a healthier climate. When the summer heat has passed, they head back south and return to their businesses. These annual migrations are no problem at all for unmarried men but would be inconvenient for a family. So in New Orleans men avoid trouble by refraining from marriage and forming illegitimate couples. As mistresses they always choose free women of color, on whom they bestow a kind of dowry. The women are honored to be part of an arrangement that gives them a status closer to that of whites. They know that they can never marry a white, but it is still something to be loved by one. Under our law, these colored women could marry a mulatto, but this would not improve their status. In any case, a mulatto husband could not offer them any kind of protection. For a colored woman to marry a colored man is to perpetuate her degradation, but she can improve her position by prostituting herself to a white. These prejudices are part of the upbringing of all colored women, whose parents prepare them for a life of corruption from early childhood. There are public dances to which only white men and colored women are admitted. The husbands and brothers of the colored women are turned away, but their mothers are not, and most attend. They witness, encourage, and rejoice in the compliments addressed to their daughters. When a white falls in love with a colored girl, it is her mother whom he asks if he may have her. The mother drives the hardest bargain she can, and the price depends on how much of a novice the child is. No mystery surrounds these transactions. Monstrous as these unions are, they are contracted without any of the shame that attaches to vice and drives it into the shadows, just as virtue hides itself out of modesty. The girls exhibit themselves to any man who wishes to look, and no infamy or blame attaches to the men who initiate them. When the Northerner has made his fortune, he has achieved his goal. One day he will leave New Orleans and never return. Neither his children nor the woman with whom he lived for ten years as man and wife means anything to him thereafter. The colored girl then sells herself to someone else. Such is the fate of women of the African race in Louisiana. . . .

[FROM CHAPTER 9]

The Negro is by law equal to the white in every respect. He has the civil and political rights. He can be president of the United States. In fact, however, the exercise of all these rights is forbidden to him, and he is lucky if he can achieve a social status above that of domestic servant.

In the so-called free states, the Negro is no longer a slave, but he is a free man in name only.

I am not sure that his new condition is not worse than servitude. As a slave, he had no rank in human society. Now he is counted as a human being but occupies the lowest rank among men.

It is not uncommon to see whites in the South treat Negroes kindly. Because the distance between the one and the other is immense and uncontested, free Americans are unafraid that by making contact with a slave they might raise him to their level or lower themselves to his.

By contrast, in the North, where equality is proclaimed, whites hold themselves apart from Negroes so as to maintain their distinction. They shun the black man as if in horror and mercilessly reject him in order to avoid any humiliating assimilation, thus maintaining in custom a distinction that no longer exists in law. . . .

In Philadelphia there is a reform school to which boys and girls are sent if they commit an offense whose gravity lies somewhere between a mistake and a crime. Their families do not have sufficient influence over them. A term in prison would be too harsh a punishment. The reform school, more severe than the one but less cruel than the other, is well suited to these young but not yet hardened delinquents. I once visited this institution and was surprised to see not a single child of the black race. I asked the principal the reason for this, and this was his answer: "It would degrade white children if we were to mingle them with others whom the public despises."

On another occasion, I expressed my astonishment at the fact that Negro children are excluded from public schools reserved for whites. I was told that no American would want to send his child to a school with even a single black student.

Then I remembered these words, which Marie had once uttered in desperation: "Whites and Negroes are kept apart everywhere: in churches, where humanity prays; in hospitals, where it suffers; in prisons, where it repents; in cemeteries, where it sleeps the sleep of eternity."

Everything in this portrait was true, although I had initially taken it to be a picture distorted by her own pain.

Hospitals segregate patients and jails segregate inmates by color. Whites everywhere receive care and attention that is denied to poor Negroes.

In every city I saw separate cemeteries: one for whites, the other for people of color. What a strange thing, human vanity! When nothing remains but dust and corruption, human pride refuses to die; it lives on in the blackness of the tomb! . . .

[FROM CHAPTER 10]

When Americans realized that cleverness and cunning were of no avail, they resorted to violence—not the violence of arms but that of legislation. Faced with ignorant savages, these lawmaking people waged war on their enemy in the courts. Hiding their iniquity behind a simulacrum of justice, they expelled the Indians from their homes *by due process of law.* The Georgia legislature declared that the Indians did not own their land but only enjoyed the use of it and that it was within the sovereign power of the state to determine when their usufruct expired. Deciding that the usufruct had run out, the legislature then authorized citizens of the state to take the Indian land. The Indians, not well versed in the legal distinction between ownership and usufruct, failed to grasp the meaning of the law apart from the fact that it deprived them of their land and put others in their place. They protested yet again. The dispute was submitted to judgment by the Supreme Court of the United States.[1] This august tribunal, standing at the top of the social hierarchy in a realm inaccessible to vulgar passions, solemnly found in favor of the native Americans and declared that the state of Georgia had no right to take their land. The debate seemed to have been re-

1. In *Worcester v. Georgia* (1832), the U.S. Supreme Court ruled that Georgia state law did not apply to Cherokee lands, as they were the property of "dependent domestic nations." President Andrew Jackson openly defied this ruling and supported the corrupt Treaty of New Echota in 1835, which led to the forced removal of the Cherokee from their lands in 1838.

solved. But good businessmen never lack for legal arguments, even for disobeying the law, so the Georgians contemptuously rejected the decision of the Supreme Court on the grounds that it had no jurisdiction in the matter. This was not a declaration of war, but it did make war inevitable. . . .

At length I experienced in the depths of my soul a feeling of happiness, as the contentious din of the assembly reached my ears. I looked down and saw thousands of threatening gestures directed to the place that I occupied next to Georges. Then we heard shouts: "Get him out of here! He's colored!" All eyes were riveted upon us. The shouting would cease for a moment, then resume with still greater force. The crowd moved from calm to agitation and agitation to calm, as if the cause of its irritation were at once clear and ambiguous. Among the multitude of faces I made out one that seemed to be that of the leader, a man who tried hard to communicate to the others his indignation, whether feigned or real. "It's an outrage!" he shouted. "A mulatto here with us!" As he said this, he pointed straight at Georges. The whole crowd then erupted as one: "Get him out of here! He's colored!"

From the outset I realized that this incident would not end well, and my heart was racing. Georges stood still and remained silent. His eyes radiated fury. The shouts grew louder. The outbursts became general. Then a man stood forth in the middle of the crowd and with a wave of his arm reduced it to silence. He indicated that he wanted to speak, and the clamor immediately ceased. I never knew the name of this American, whose philanthropic views might have suggested that he was a Quaker if Quakers did not shun the theater. "Why," he asked, "compel this man to leave the hall? There is no evidence that he's black. People say he's colored, but there's no proof." Uttered calmly, these words were greeted with a quiet murmur of approval. No one came forward to contradict them. The instigator of the disturbance was no longer standing where I had first spotted him. Calm in Americans has something of the character of a violent passion, and it had suddenly reasserted its dominion over them. The awful storm had almost passed when Georges, whose long-suppressed rage needed to find an outlet, blurted out in a loud voice, "Yes!" He stared defiantly at the crowd. "Yes, I am colored!" This declaration was met with a thunderclap of protest. "Get the scoundrel out of here! Blackguard!" The screams came from every direction. . . .

[FROM CHAPTER II]

In the United States one finds neither the pride of one class [the aristocracy] nor the wrath of the other [the people].

This is not because Americans have polite manners. A majority of them exhibit neither elegance nor distinction, but their coarseness is never intentional. It stems not from pride but from a deficiency in their upbringing. Hence no one is less susceptible to a slight than an American; he will never believe that you wish to offend him.

FROM *Marie; or, Slavery in the United States*

When a Frenchman is coarse, it is because he wants to be; an American would always be polite, if he knew how....

I also admired in Americans a quality that is invaluable to a free people, namely, common sense. I do not believe that reason is more universally shared anywhere than it is in the United States.

In certain European countries, there can exist a thousand different and contradictory solutions to the same moral or political problem. By contrast, you can be sure of finding Americans in agreement as to nearly all the principles of public and private life. You will not find a single one who denies the usefulness of religious beliefs or the obligation to abide by the law.

Each and every one of them knows everything that is happening in the country, judges it wisely, and speaks of it only cautiously and upon reflection.

Americans like to travel and are accustomed to it. Nearly all of them have at some point in their lives explored the region between the Canadian border and the Gulf of Mexico. In this way they acquire experience on top of the natural rectitude that they derive from common sense. They do not reserve their admiration for ancient things exclusively, nor do they succumb to foolish astonishment at novelties or suffer from inveterate prejudices or ridiculous superstitions.

Their superb common sense may be a consequence of the rarity of their passions. One reason to believe this is that when in the grip of national pride, the most exalted of all their sentiments, they utterly lose their hold on reason.

Their lack of taste for poetry, fine arts, and speculative science also encourages common sense. Man is less likely to stray from the straight and narrow if he resists sudden flights of the imagination and dazzling flashes of genius.

Neither the philosophical dreamer, the contemplator of the heavens, nor the artist moved by nature's touching harmonies is likely to comprehend the practical business of life.

The power of reason and superiority of common sense over the passions account for the admirable stolidity of most Americans. Great joy eludes them, but no misfortune can shake them either. An unexpected blow leaves them impassive, as does an imminent danger. What a strange contrast! They pursue wealth with the greatest of passion yet calmly withstand every adversity. Nothing can impede them in their enterprises; nothing can discourage them. No matter how great the obstacle, no American will ever say, "I cannot overcome it." Bold, patient, indefatigable, he will try his luck. To the end the American people are faithful to their origins, for this is a nation born in exile, and you can be sure that people who crossed two thousand leagues of ocean in search of a homeland did not lack for energy.

No one, I assure you, admires the American people in this respect more than I. Reason, practical common sense, and enterprising audacity gave birth to American industry, whose prodigies have astonished the world. Behold their canals, man-made rivers that are destined one day to join the Atlantic to the Pacific. Behold the railroads, which insinuate themselves into the sides of mountains, and above which steam rises in clouds swifter and mightier than those that gather above the surface of the sea. Behold the manufactured goods that pour forth from every point of the compass. Behold the merchants whose stores contain the wealth of all nations. Behold the ports at which a thousand vessels call. Everywhere there is wealth and abundance: Where once there was virgin forest, now one finds fertile fields. Where once there was wilderness, now there are magnificent cities and pleasant villages, sprung from the soil by I know not what magic, as if the old American soil, so long barbaric and savage, were at last pregnant with a civilized future, as if from its fecund bosom harvests now flow without cultivation and cities rise without labor where forests formerly flourished.

As witness to this peerless prosperity, which no other nation can match, I admired it and admire it still, but everything about it is material, and it was a moral world that I required.

Ah! Why don't the Americans have as much heart as head? Why so much intelligence without genius, so much wealth without splendor, so much strength without grandeur, so many miracles without poetry?

Perhaps the industrial character that sets this society apart is intimately entwined with whatever order it is that decides the fate of nations. . . .

[FROM CHAPTER 12]

VI.

Material utility: that is the goal toward which all modern societies tend. In Europe, however, this tendency vies with memories, habits, and mores. The present is still subject to the influence of the past.

We are not religious, but we have magnificent churches. Although materialist positivism is taking hold of us, we still choose splendid palaces to house our libraries, museums, and academies. In our country the most vulgar minds and most indolent souls pay homage to genius and virtue. In our cities the man who has forfeited all honor still bows before the statue of Bayard.[2]

America is unfamiliar with these fetters. It pursues its material interests without hindrance from any prejudices or diversion by any passions.

VII.

Do not look for poetry, literature, or art in this country. The universal equality of conditions casts a monotone over the whole society. No one is completely ignorant, and no one knows much. What could be duller than mediocrity? Poetry exists only in extremes: in great wealth or great poverty, in celestial clarity or infernal night, in the lives of kings or the burial of paupers.

VIII.

In American society there is neither shadow nor splendor, neither heights nor depths. Therein lies the proof of its materialism: Wherever the soul reigns, it

---

2. Known as the "Good Knight," Pierre Terrail, seigneur de Bayard (1476–1524), was a French knight renowned for his chivalry.

FROM *Marie; or, Slavery in the United States*

either rises or falls. Brilliant geniuses soar above dull minds, enthusiastic hearts above benumbed souls. An even level can be achieved only in matter. . . .

XIII.

In fact, there exists in America something that resembles the feudal aristocracy.

The factory is the manor; the manufacturer is the suzerain lord; the workers are the serfs. But what splendor does this industrial feudalism exhibit? The crenellated castle with its deep moats and noble lady and devoted knight was not without poetry.

What harmony will the modern poet find in countinghouses, distilleries, steam engines, and paper money?

XIV.

In the United States the masses reign always and everywhere, jealous of anyone who stands out and prompt to destroy those who raise themselves up, for average intelligences reject superior minds, just as weak eyes, which thrive in darkness, shrink in horror from the light of day. So do not look for monuments in honor of illustrious men. I know that this nation has heroes, but I did not see their statues anywhere. For Washington alone are there busts, inscriptions, and a column. That is because in America Washington is not a man, he is a god.

XV.

The American people seem to have been congenitally condemned to do without poetry. In the darkness surrounding the birth of a nation there is something fabulous, which encourages audacity of imagination. Obscure times are always heroic times. In antiquity there was the Trojan War; in the Middle Ages, the Crusades. Now that enlightenment has come to nations, there are no more demigods. The Americans are perhaps the only nation without a childhood shrouded in mystery. The enlightenment of maturity enveloped them at birth; they themselves wrote the history of their early years. And the printing press, which existed before they did, was charged with recording the swaddled infant's every cry. . . .

XVII.

No sooner was the American nation born than public life and industry absorbed all its moral energy. Its institutions, fertile in liberty, granted rights to all. Americans have too many political interests to concern themselves with literature. Toward the end of the last century, when twenty-five million Frenchmen were governed by the whims of a loose woman, they could rest easy about the country's affairs, amuse themselves with frivolous things, and throw themselves body and soul into a quarrel between two musicians.

Unwilling to place much trust in powerful men, Americans govern themselves. Public life is not limited to salons and the opera. It takes place on the podium and in clubhouses.

XVIII.

When political life ends, commercial life begins. In the United States everyone is industrious, because industry is essential to all. In a society of perfect equality, work is the common lot. Everyone works in order to live; no one lives in order to think. There are no privileged classes that enjoy, along with a monopoly of wealth, a monopoly of leisure. . . .

XXIII.

In America, science is respected solely for its applications. People study the useful arts but not the fine arts.

Germany and France invent theories. In the United States theories are put into practice. Here, no one dreams; everyone acts. Everyone aspires to the same goal, material well-being. And since money is its source, it is money alone that people pursue.

XXIV.

When people in this country make literature, it is still an industry. There is neither a classic school nor a Romantic school. There is only the commercial school, consisting of writers who write newspapers, pamphlets, or advertisements and who sell ideas as another man might sell fabric. Their study is a shop, and their minds are commodities. Every item has its price. They will tell you exactly what a printed enthusiasm costs. . . .

XXXI.

Although there are few authors in America, no other country in the world prints as much. Every county has its newspaper. In fact, newspapers are the country's only literature. Businessmen without much wealth need something they can read quickly that doesn't cost much. Primary schooling and religion account for the enormous consumption of books. This is bookselling rather than literature. The education of children is purely utilitarian. It does not aim to develop lofty faculties of soul and mind. It trains people for the business of social life. . . .

XL.

Religion, so fertile in poetic harmonies, brings neither inspiration nor enthusiasm to American hearts. What Americans love in religion is not that which speaks to the soul but only that which is directed to reason. They love religion as a source of order rather than of pleasant emotions. Italians are artists of religion; Americans are disciplined parishioners.

XLI.

In any case, the various Christian sects are too divided to provide the arts with subjects of general interest. The simple, modest Quakers will never build sumptuous palaces for themselves. What do the admirable sermons of Mr. Channings [sic], the Unitarian minister,[3] mean to the Methodist Church? If the Baptists erect a monument to their faith, what interest would it have for Presbyterians? . . .

XLII.

Protestant congregations have no magnificent temples full of statues and paintings to bring them together. They meet in simple homes, built without luxury at little cost. The most splendid of their religious edifices turn out to be supported by columns of painted wood: such is their Parthenon. Take away from America its Capitol, the poetic expression of its national pride, and the Bank

---

3. William Ellery Channing (1780–1842).

FROM *Marie; or, Slavery in the United States*

of the United States, the poetic expression of its passion for money, and not a single monumental edifice will remain. . . .

XLIV.

Let this society grow, some say, and you will see illustrious men appear in letters and the arts. Nascent Rome did not listen to the poems of Horace and Virgil, and it took fourteen centuries for France to bring forth Racine and Corneille.

Those who speak this way confuse two distinct things: political society and civilization. American society is young; it is not yet two centuries old. By contrast, its civilization is as ancient as that of England, from which it descends. The former is a work in progress; the latter is in decline. English society is regenerating itself in American democracy; English civilization is dying there. . . .

LI.

But Americans wonder what good it does to know what the Indians did in the past and what they are up to today, how they lived in their forests once and how they are dying now. The savages are paupers from whom nothing is to be had in the way of riches, instruction, or labor. Their forests must be taken away from them—that is all there is to it. Taken and held not to make poetry out of them but to cut them down and plow fields where soaring oaks once stood. . . .

[FROM CHAPTER 13]

In New York, as in other northern cities, the friends of the blacks are divided into two quite distinct parties.

In the judgment of some, slavery is bad for the country and perhaps contrary to the Christian religion, so they insist on the emancipation of the black population, but being full of the prejudices of their race, they do not regard freed Negroes as the equals of whites. Hence they think that colored people should be deported once they are granted their freedom and keep them in a state of debasement and inferiority as long as they remain in America. Many of these friends of the Negro are opposed to slavery solely for reasons of national pride. They find foreign criticism on the issue painful and are loath to hear slavery described as a barbaric relic of another era. Some attack the evil simply because it pains them to see it. Emancipation for them changes little: They destroy slavery but do not grant freedom. They deliver themselves from sorrow or embarrassment, from the suffering of vanity, but they do nothing to heal the slave's wounds. They work for themselves, not for the slave. Still bearing his chains, the slave is cast out of free society.

The other champions of the Negroes love them sincerely, as a Christian loves his brothers. They not only want the abolition of slavery but also welcome freed slaves into their company and treat them as equals.

Such zealous friends of the black population are rare, but their ardor is indefatigable. For a long time it yielded little in the way of results, although they did overcome certain prejudices and whites married women of color.

As long as pro-Negro philanthropy ended in futile declarations and nothing more, Americans tolerated it without difficulty. What did it matter to them if a few people proclaimed the theoretical equality of blacks, as long as blacks remained inferior to whites in fact? But on the day an American married a woman of color, the experiment with mixing the two races took on a practical character. This was an attack on the dignity of whites. American pride rose up in protest everywhere. . . .

My mind filled with a myriad of cheerful thoughts of the future as Marie and I, prostrate before the altar, received the blessings of the church. Just as the priest, having offered us the touching counsel of his heart, took our hands to join them together in holy matrimony, a great tumult erupted at the door of the church. "Riot!" a sinister voice cried out. One person after another took up the cry. Then a depressing silence filled the sacred vault. At that moment the sound of a raucous multitude could be heard outside, like the rumbling of an approaching thunderstorm. Driven by a violent wind, the thundercloud approached rapidly, and lightning filled the sky. "Kill the colored! To the church! To the church!" These awful cries resounded on all sides. Terror gripped the congregation. The priest turned pale, his knees buckled, and the wedding ring that was to have united us fell from his hands. Marie, transfixed with terror, felt faint and began to swoon, so I reached out to support the falling woman who, a moment later, was to have become my beloved wife.

A few intrepid Negroes had rushed to the doors of the church to defend it against the invaders, but soon the sacred edifice was being pelted with thousands of projectiles. The doors strained against their hinges. The assailants urged one another on to violence. Each new success was met with tumultuous applause. The blows intensified, the walls shook, the floor trembled. Already those prodigious destroyers, the people, had burst through the gates into the church courtyard. Inside the church the scene was one of terrible chaos and confusion. Children wailed, and women screamed. The thought of bloody massacre filled their souls with horror, for the rabble of all countries are the same: stupid, blind, and cruel. Men, or, rather, monsters with no respect for the sanctity of the place and no pity for the infirmity of sex or age, hurled themselves upon the pious congregation and committed the most brutal and violent acts, sparing neither women nor children nor the elderly.

I was in a state of extreme anguish. Appalled by this spectacle of vandalism and sacrilege, Nelson was torn between paternal solicitude and national pride. "Oh, my God!" he shouted. "The sacrilege! Shame on my country!"

The danger was imminent and terrifying. I turned to Nelson and said, "I beg of you, let me take care of Marie," whereupon I took her in my arms. How forcefully I took hold of my beloved! How strong I felt holding her against my bosom! But no sooner had I lifted my precious burden than I heard several voices cry out: "John Mulon! John Mulon! Kill the Catholic who dared to marry colored and white!" I felt all eyes turn in our direction. I understood that we had been betrayed and that terrible dangers awaited us. How could I save Marie?

How could I make my way through the ranks of our enemies, with such terrible passions unleashed?

I saw a glimmer of hope. "The militia! The militia!" shouted some of the rioters. "Who cares?!" responded others. "The militia wouldn't dare fire on Americans!"

A group of militiamen had indeed arrived with orders to quell the disturbance, but it was made up entirely of whites, who didn't much care for people of color. Instead of quelling the popular furor, they stood by and watched its outrages. The impassive troops only increased the furor of the assailants, who roamed the inside of the church, smashing and overturning everything: furniture, religious symbols, the pulpit, even the altar. All the exits were watched so that no one could escape the violence. . . .

By that evening, the insurrection had abated. The New York philanthropic society that favored the emancipation of Negroes published a statement intended to restore calm: "We have never contemplated the insane project of mixing the two races. We would never compromise the dignity of whites to that extent. We respect the laws that allow slavery in the southern states."

For shame! What sort of free people is this, that will not tolerate the hatred of slavery? The Negroes of New York were not asking for freedom for themselves: they were all free. They were calling upon Americans to pity their slave brothers—and their prayers and the prayers of their friends were crimes for which they had to beg for pardon! . . .

[FROM CHAPTER 14]

It is indeed strange in the midst of savage nature's still almost intact empire to be distracted by the sonorous names of cities reminiscent of the most ancient and brilliant of civilizations: here a Thebes, there a Rome, and there again an Athens. Why rob all the peoples of the world of their glories and memories? Is the intent to draw a parallel or underscore a contrast? The city of a hundred gates is a village. The queen city is a clearing. The birthplace of Sophocles and Pericles is a trading post. . . .

When a man bids farewell to his country, it is profoundly sad, but when an entire people leaves for exile, the scene is as solemn as it is painful.

The faces of these wretches were impassive, yet one could detect signs of great misfortune.

When the departure signal was given, we noticed a group of Indians heading toward the port. They were even more serious and meditative than the others and walked more slowly. One of them seemed to stoop, as if he were carrying a heavy burden. As he approached, the others stepped aside to make it easier for him to pass. In the midst of the crowd we then spotted a decrepit old man bent by the weight of years. His bald head, withered arms, and unsteady gait made him look more like a ghost than a living human being. On one side, two other old men held him up, even though their slumped and trembling shoulders seemed less apt to lend support than to receive it. On the other side, he leaned on two women, one with white hair and another, younger one with a child at her breast. This man was the tribe's patriarch. He was 120 years old. What a strange and cruel fate! This man, so close to the grave, would not leave his bones to rest alongside the bones of his ancestors. Cast out of his homeland on the eve of death, he was on his way to find another in which he might be buried. Five generations accompanied him on his journey. Their combined misfortune could not rival his. What does exile mean to a newborn? For a person with a future, a new world is as good as a fatherland. . . .

Appendix 1: On the Social and Political Condition of Negro Slaves and Freed Men and Women of Color[4]

The existence of two million slaves in a nation where social and political equality has reached its highest stage of development; the influence of slavery on the mores of free men; the oppression that it causes to weigh on the wretches subject to servitude; the danger it represents to those for whom it was established; the color of the race that supplies slaves; the phenomenon of two populations that live together and touch one another without ever blending or mingling; the serious clashes to which this contact has already given rise; the more serious crises that it may engender in the future—for all these reasons it is clearly important to understand the lot of slaves and freed men and women of color in the United States. In the course of this work I have tried to depict the moral consequences of slavery for people of color who become free. I would now like to offer a glimpse of the social condition of those who are still slaves. To do so I must describe the nature of American slavery.

After explaining how slavery is organized, I will explore whether this social wound can be healed. Where does public opinion in the United States stand on this question? What means of emancipating blacks have been proposed, and what objections have been raised? Finally, what is the probable future of American society in this regard?

1. The Condition of the Negro Slave in the United States

It might seem that nothing could be simpler than to define the condition of the slave. Instead of enumerating the rights he enjoys, shouldn't it be enough to say that he has none? Because he is nothing in society, has the law not done

4. Beaumont's citations of specific law codes and constitutions of several states, including Tennessee, South Carolina, and Louisiana, are not included in this translation of the appendix.

all it needs to do by declaring him a slave? The subject is not as simple as it might appear at first glance, however. In any society, many laws are needed to assure free men of their independence. By the same token, the lawmaker has much to do in order to create slaves, that is, in order to strip human beings of their natural rights and moral faculties, alter the condition that God created for them, and substitute for their perfectible nature a state of constant degradation in which a body and soul destined for freedom are bound in chains.

The rights that man may claim in any lawful society are of three kinds: political, civil, and natural. Laws are made to guarantee free men the enjoyment of these rights and to deny slaves the same.

Plain common sense suggests that slaves must be entirely deprived of political rights. One cannot have participating in government and lawmaking a person whom government and laws are intended to subject to unremitting oppression. On this point, the task of the legislator is as easy as his course is clear. However extensive political rights may be, they are in all countries a kind of privilege. Not all free citizens enjoy them; hence, it is *a fortiori* easy to deny them to slaves. It is enough not to prescribe them.

In all American states where slavery is lawful, the law is therefore silent about the political rights of slaves: silence is tantamount to exclusion.

It is no less indispensable to strip the slave of all his civil rights.

Hence the slave, because he is the property of his master, cannot marry. How could the law allow him to form a bond that his master could break at will? The slave's children belong to his master, like the spawn of animals. Hence the slave cannot be granted any paternal authority over his children. He cannot be the legal owner of any property, because he is the property of another man. Hence he may not buy or sell, nor may he enter into any contract for the ownership or maintenance of property.

American law generally limits itself to declaring any contract to which a slave is a party null and void. In some cases, however, this prohibition is reinforced by a penalty. In South Carolina, for example, a contract for the sale or purchase of property by a slave is not only invalid under the law; the property mentioned in the contract is also subject to confiscation. The law of Louisiana contains a similar provision. Tennessee law provides for the whipping of any slave who enters into a contract, while a free man who is party to such a contract is subject to a fine.

Despite the rigor and scope of the provisions of the law that impose civil death on the slave, it is clear that lawmakers have no difficulty adopting them. This is true of rights embodied in law. In fact, the principle of such rights preexists the legislation that consecrates them. The law does not create them; it proclaims them. In recognizing that free men possess such rights, however, it is easy to strip others of the same rights.

Thus far the lawmaker has encountered few obstacles in his path. He has nevertheless accomplished a great deal, since already the slave has no fatherland, no society, and no family. But his work is not yet done.

Having deprived the Negro of his rights as an American, a citizen, a father, and a husband, the lawmaker must still divest him of rights that stem from nature itself. It is at this point that serious difficulties arise.

The slave is in chains, but how can his love of liberty be rooted out? Though he may not employ his intelligence in the service of state or city, how can the intelligence he might use to smash his fetters be eliminated? Though he may not marry, he will have sexual relations, whatever name may be given to them; this cannot be prevented. In any case, the slave's relations add to the wealth of the master, since every child born is an additional slave. Without the affections and interests that family ties create, how can one ensure that there will be a mother and children, a father and sons, brothers and sisters? In other words, how can one make sure that the slave can no longer be a man?

The lawmaker's difficulties increase as he moves from proscription of civil rights to proscription of natural rights, thereby passing from the realm of fiction into the realm of reality. His first order of business in declaring the Negro to be a slave is to classify him as a material object: the slave is movable property under South Carolina law, immovable property under Louisiana law.

Of course the law may declare that a man is a chattel, a commodity, or a good; he nevertheless remains a thinking, intelligent commodity. The law may treat him as a material thing, but it cannot destroy his moral qualities. Yet the development of the intellectual and moral faculties must be halted. All laws of slavery prohibit the education of slaves. Not only are public schools closed to slaves, but masters are forbidden to impart the most elementary forms of knowledge. A South Carolina law provides for a fine of one hundred pounds sterling for anyone who teaches his slaves to write. The penalty for killing a slave is scarcely more severe. Perfectibility is the most noble of the human faculties, but the slave is denied the opportunity to perfect himself and thus to discharge the duty incumbent upon every intelligent creature to strive always for moral improvement.

The law seeks to degrade the slave, yet his instinctual craving for dignity ensures that he will hate his servitude. A still nobler instinct causes him to love liberty. Though cast in chains, he breaks his fetters and becomes a free man! In other words, he enters into a state of open rebellion against society and the laws that made him a slave.

All the states of the American South agree that the fugitive slave is an outlaw. South Carolina law says that anyone can apprehend a fugitive slave, arrest him, and whip him forthwith. Louisiana law states explicitly that half-breed slaves who do not halt on command may be shot. Tennessee law stipulates that it is lawful to murder a slave for whom an arrest warrant has been issued. The law adds that a slave in such a position may be killed with impunity by any person whatsoever and in any way that person chooses without fear of legal repercussions. The same laws provide for rewards to be paid to any citizen who arrests a fugitive slave. The law also pays people to turn in fugitive slaves. South Carolina law goes further: it imposes the death penalty on both any slave who flees and any person who abets his escape.

FROM *Marie; or, Slavery in the United States*

All the powers of society are bent to the task of recapturing fugitive slaves. If a fugitive manages to evade capture and reach free territory, he might be tempted to believe that he has regained possession of his natural rights. But any such hope will soon be dispelled. The northern states, which have abolished servitude, nevertheless refuse to admit fugitives; they return fleeing slaves to the masters from whom they have fled.

Thus society employs all its harshest weapons and most extravagant powers to seize the slave and punish him for harboring in his bosom man's most natural and inviolable feeling: the love of liberty.

Suppose the slave restored to his chains. He has been punished for the crime of coveting independence. He will make no further attempt to smash his fetters. He will work for his master, who has succeeded in breaking his spirit. But now the lawmaker and the slave owner must overcome a great many more obstacles and difficulties. The slave's two noblest faculties, moral perfectibility and love of liberty, have been snuffed out, yet the man himself has not been entirely destroyed.

In vain does the master prohibit all contact between his Negro and civil society. In vain does he seek to degrade and brutalize his slave. All such prohibitions and degradations must end at a certain point, namely, the point at which the master's interest begins. The master, having bound the slave hand and foot, must unbind him so that the slave can work. Having brutalized the Negro, he must allow him some measure of intelligence, because it is intelligence that makes him valuable property. Without it, the slave would be worth no more than any other livestock. Finally, even though the master has declared the Negro to be a material object, he maintains personal relations with him, for such relations are the very essence of servitude. And the slave, who has been forbidden to engage in any form of social life, is nevertheless forced, in order to serve his master, to entertain relations with a social world in which, to be sure, he is nothing, in which he appears only as another man's representative, but in which he is nevertheless compelled to bear the moral responsibility that is incumbent on all intelligent beings.

Here, again, the man reemerges—so concede the very people who tried to crush him. No matter how degraded the slave may be, he needs physical freedom in order to work, intelligence in order to serve his master, and social relations with the master and with society in order to discharge the duties of servitude.

But if he does not work, if he disobeys his master, if he rebels, and if, in his relations with free men, he breaks the law, what should be done? Should he be punished? How? According to what principles? With what punishments?

With these questions the lawmaker begins to face a host of difficulties.

Because the law makes one man master and the other slave, thereby creating two beings totally different in nature, the idea arises that it is impossible to establish relations between slave and master or between slave and free men on a basis of reciprocity. But since reciprocity is the only equitable foundation for human relations, rejecting it leads to complete arbitrariness and the violation of all principles. For instance, the crime of the master who kills his slave is no longer the equivalent of the crime of the slave who kills his master. The same difference will exist between the murder of any free man by a slave and the murder of a slave by a free man.

American state laws all stipulate the death penalty for a slave who kills his master, but several states impose nothing more than a fine on a master who kills his slave.

Violence by the master against the Negro is authorized under American law, but a Negro who strikes his master is punishable by death. The law of Louisiana provides the death penalty for a slave guilty of merely striking a white child.

The same distinctions can be found in relations between slaves and free persons. For example, in South Carolina, a white who seriously injures a Negro is subject to a fine of forty shillings. But a Negro slave who injures a free man is punishable by death. If a Negro injures a white while defending his master, he incurs no penalty, but if he injures a free man while defending himself, he is subject to punishment.

There is no law to punish a free man who insults a slave. It is of course conceivable that such a minor infraction was considered unworthy of repression. But Tennessee law provides for the whipping of any slave who dares to pronounce any verbal insult whatsoever against a white person.

These differences are not anomalies. All are logical consequences of the principle of slavery. Oddly enough, the law seeks to turn the Negro into a brute yet inflicts punishments on him more severe than those inflicted on the more intelligent being. He is less guilty because less enlightened, yet one punishes him more. This is necessary, however: it is obvious that the scale of offenses cannot be the same for the slave as for the free man.

The scale of punishments is no less different, and the legislator's task in this regard is still more difficult.

The degrees of punishment established for free men cannot be applied to slaves, because society has more to fear from those whom it oppresses than from those whom it protects. We shall see, moreover, that wherever slaves are concerned, the very nature of punishment must change.

Under American laws, free men are subject to three kinds of punishment: fines, imprisonment either for a term or for life, and death. The first attacks a man's property, the second his liberty, and the third his life.

It is clear, to begin with, that a slave cannot be fined, because he owns nothing and therefore cannot be attacked through his property.

Imprisonment, by its very nature, is also a punishment not well suited to the condition of the slave. What can deprivation of liberty mean to a man already in servitude? A distinction is in order here, however. Is it a question of temporary imprisonment for a short term? A slave will be little daunted by such a punishment. He will see it simply as a material change in his position, which a man in misfortune will always seize upon as a kind of hope. He will also prefer idleness to arduous labor from which he derives no benefit. Indeed, the punishment will affect only the master, who will be deprived of the labor of his slave, and the longer the sentence, the greater the damage.

What about life imprisonment? Perpetual incarceration is clearly a serious punishment, even for a slave who has no freedom to lose. But here another obstacle arises: life imprisonment deprives the master of his slave. To impose such a penalty on a slave is to punish his master.

The objection to the death penalty is even more serious. To inflict such a punishment on a slave is to destroy his master's property. In other words, none of the punishments to which the law has recourse in dealing with free men can be applied to slaves. Even death, an instrument of which every tyranny avails itself, is of no use to the owner of Negroes.

Frequently, however, we do find the death penalty and life imprisonment in American slavery laws. Sometimes, these penalties are imposed by the courts, but such cases are quite rare. Only when a slave commits a crime that seriously disturbs the peace of the community does society insist on reparations for the injuries it has suffered. It then seizes the Negro and sentences him either to death or to life in prison. And since, in doing so, it deprives the master of his slave, it compensates him for the loss. The law states that "any slave sentenced to death or to life in prison will be paid for by the public treasury. The amount may not exceed three hundred dollars." Here, incompatible outside interests influence the judgment of the courts in unfortunate ways. Before delivering his Negro up to public justice, a master will carefully consider the slave's offense and turn him in only if he believes it to be a capital crime. In view of the conditions on compensation, it is in his interest to turn the slave over to the authorities only if he is to be condemned to death. Meanwhile, since society must pay for the right to judge the criminal, it will be extremely cautious about exercising that right. It will be reluctant to shed blood for reasons of thrift rather than humanity, and although it is in the master's interest to be strict in punishing his Negro, society's interest favors leniency. A master will be quick to deliver up his slave in one case only: when the slave is old and infirm. In that case, he may hope that the death sentence meted out to the invalid Negro will earn him an indemnity equivalent to the price of a good one. If society suspects fraud, however, it will acquit the slave in order to avoid paying the indemnity. The slave, whose misfortune fails to move either society or his master, is protected by the calculations of greed.

The foregoing explains the remarkable Louisiana law that stipulates that no slave may be subject to a term of imprisonment longer than one week unless it is a life term: "Except for cases in which slaves are to be sentenced to life in prison, juries summoned to judge crimes and misdemeanors committed by slaves shall not be authorized to imprison them for a period of more than one week."

The grounds for this provision are easy to understand. Temporary imprisonment, which deprives the master of the labor of his Negroes and causes him damage without compensation, is in his eyes the worst of all punishments. To be sure, life imprisonment takes the slave away from the master, but in that case society compensates him for his loss.

It should now be clear why it is impossible to inflict death or a long prison term on slaves very often. Repeated punishments of this severity would either harm the interests of slave owners or prove costly to society.

Punishment of slaves is necessary, however—severe punishment that can be imposed whenever required. What is to be done?

Now we are in a position to understand why the need to punish slaves leads to corporal punishment, that is, punishment that can be imposed instantly, without loss of time, and without cost to either master or society. After being subjected to cruel suffering, the slave can return immediately to work. Whipping, branding, the pillory, and mutilation of a limb—all these punishments are used. To be sure, the legislator's ability to use the last of these methods—mutilation of a limb—is inherently limited, since the slave's arms must be left intact if he is to be able to work.

So much for the punishments peculiar to slavery. They are indispensable accessories of the institution, without which it would die. American law had no choice but to incorporate them. Apart from death, Tennessee law envisions only three forms of punishment for slaves: whipping, pillory, and mutilation. The punishment for perjury is worth noting: the perjurer is placed in the pillory, and one of his ears is nailed to the beam. After an hour, that ear is cut off, and the other is nailed to the beam. An hour later, the second ear is also cut off.

Pillory, mutilation, and branding are not the most common punishments in the slave states, however. They require a certain amount of preparation, risk complications, and result in loss of time. The whip avoids these drawbacks. It flays the body of the slave without threatening his life. It punishes the Negro without harming the master. It is truly the punishment best adapted to servitude. Hence American slavery laws consistently rely on whipping.

As we have seen, the legislator is compelled to define crime differently for slaves and free men. We have also seen that none of the punishments authorized for free men were suitable for slaves, so that the authorities were obliged to envision the cruelest penalties to chastise the latter.

Once crime has been defined for slaves and their punishments determined, who is to apply those punishments? By what principles is the Negro to be judged? Will he be protected during his trial by the guarantees that civilized peoples everywhere have established to protect those accused of a crime?

Let us review American law with these questions in mind. When we do, we find that necessity after necessity has compelled the legislator to violate, one by one, all his basic principles. The first rule of criminal law is that no man may be judged except by his peers. Clearly this maxim of fairness cannot possibly be applied to slaves, for this would place the fate of the master in the hands of slaves. In all cases, therefore, the juries charged with judging slaves are composed of free men. Not only must the accused Negro fear the prejudice of free men against the slave; he must also fear the white man's antipathy to the black man.

FROM *Marie; or, Slavery in the United States*

It is an axiom of jurisprudence that any person accused of a crime is presumed innocent until proven guilty. In Louisiana and Carolina laws I find a different principle at work. Under Louisiana law, "if a black slave shoots another person with a firearm or strikes or injures another person with a lethal weapon and with the intent to kill, said slave, upon conviction for said crimes, shall be punished by death, *given that the presumption of intention is always against the accused slave unless he proves the contrary.*"

Another salutary principle, respected by all wise criminal codes, is that punishments should be fixed by law. American laws generally leave the punishment of the slave to the discretion of the judge, however. Sometimes they say that the judge may sentence a slave to be whipped without specifying a minimum or maximum number of lashes. Other times they leave it to the judge to choose the form of punishment, beginning with the whip but excluding the death penalty. The slave is thus subject to the arbitrary will of the judge.

There is another principle even more sacred than the previous ones: that no one may impose justice on his own, and that a person who has been injured by a crime must appeal to magistrates charged by the law with deciding between the plaintiff and the accused.

This rule is peremptorily violated by the laws of South Carolina and Louisiana pertaining to slaves. The laws of both states give a master discretionary power to punish his slaves either by whipping, beating with a stick, or imprisonment. The master evaluates the offense, judges the slave, and inflicts the punishment: he is at once party, judge, and executioner.

Such are the laws governing slaves, and so they must be. Here, the principles of common law would be harmful and the usual forms of justice impossible. Must every one of the Negro's infractions be brought before a judge? The master's life would be consumed in court. In any case, the judgment of a tribunal is sometimes uncertain and always slow. Is it not necessary that a terrible and inevitable punishment always hang over the slave's head? Must it not strike at the guilty in the shadows, at the risk of harming the innocent?

Justice and the courts are therefore almost always alien to the repression of slave offenses. Punishment is between the master and his slaves. When the latter are docile, the master enjoys the fruits of their labor and brutalization in peace. If the slaves do not work hard enough, he whips them as he would whip a beast of burden. These punishments of the moment are not recorded by the clerk of any court. They are not worth the cost of an investigation. Anyone who consults court records will find very few judgments pertaining to Negroes. Let him travel through the countryside, however, and he will hear cries of pain and misery: no other record exists of the punishments meted out to slaves.

Thus, in order to establish servitude, man must not only be deprived of all civil and political rights; he must also be stripped of all natural rights, and the most inviolable principles must be trampled underfoot.

The slave retains only one right: to practice his religion. This is because religion teaches courage and resignation. Yet, even here, South Carolina law imposes many prudent restrictions. For instance, Negroes can pray to God only at designated times of day and may not attend the religious services of whites. The slave must not be allowed to hear the prayers of free men.

What a testimonial to human freedom, that servitude cannot be established without violating all the sacred laws of morality and humanity.

2. The Character of Slavery in the United States

It has now been shown that slavery in the United States has relied on harshness and cruelty to establish itself and survive. I believe, moreover, that there is nothing specifically American about this harshness and cruelty. Servitude is the same everywhere, and wherever it exists, the same iniquities and the same tyranny follow.

Those who accept the principle of slavery yet argue that its rigors should be lessened and that the slave should be allowed a little freedom, that his body should be granted some respite and his mind some enlightenment—such people seem to me to be endowed with more humanity than logic. To my mind, there is but one alternative: either abolish slavery or maintain its utmost rigor.

To soften the slave's lot is only to make him feel all the more the cruelty that remains. The improvement in his condition becomes for him a sort of incitement to revolt. Why educate him? To make him feel his misery all the more? To cultivate his intelligence so that he can seek better ways to break his chains? When slavery exists in a country, the slave's bonds cannot be loosened without endangering the life of both master and slave: the master must face the possibility of a slave rebellion, while the slave must fear the master's punishment.

Thus all the outcry against the barbarity of slave owners in the United States and elsewhere is not very rational. Americans should not be blamed for mistreating their slaves; slavery itself should be blamed. Once the principle of slavery is accepted, its deplorable consequences become inevitable.

There are people, eager to excuse servitude and its horrors, who praise American slave masters for their humanity toward their slaves. Such people are both illogical and untruthful. If a slave owner were humane and just, he would cease to own slaves. His dominion over his Negroes is a persistent and inevitable violation of all the laws of morality and humanity.

American slavery, which rests on the same foundation as all other forms of human servitude, nevertheless exhibits several peculiar traits of its own.

Among the peoples of antiquity, the slave was attached to the master's person rather than to his estate. He was a luxury good, one of the external signs of power. By contrast, the American slave is more closely tied to the master's estate than to his person. He is never an object of display for the master but merely a useful instrument. In the past, the slave contributed as much to the master's pleasures as to his fortune. In America, the Negro serves only the material interests of his owner.

Jefferson, though not a proponent of slavery, sought to prove that the lot of the Negro was a happy one compared to that of the Roman slave. After depicting the gentle ways of American plantation owners, he cites the example of

Vedius Pollionus, who fed one of his slaves to the eels in his pond as punishment for breaking a crystal glass.[5]

I do not know how good Jefferson's evidence is. It is true that an American slave master would be relatively indulgent toward a slave who broke a luxury item, but would he be equally indulgent toward a slave who destroyed a useful implement? I am not sure. What is certain, however, is that South Carolina law provides the death penalty for a slave who damages a field.

I believe, moreover, that the lives of Negroes in America are not subject to the same dangers as the lives of slaves in the ancient world. In Rome, the wealthy did not attach much value to the lives of their slaves, no more than one attaches to a surfeit of luxury or an item of fashion. A whim, a moment of anger, or even a depraved instinct of cruelty was enough to put an end to more than one life. These passions are not found among American slave owners, for whom the slave has the material value that we ascribe to useful things. Devoid of violent passions, these American planters feel nothing when they see a Negro in their employ other than an instinct to preserve what belongs to them.

The American slave owner does not live in high style on his plantation and never goes to town with a cortège of slaves. The exploitation of his plantation is an industrial enterprise. His slaves are tools for cultivating the land. He has chosen each of them as carefully as a manufacturer chooses his machines. He feeds and takes care of them, just as the manufacturer keeps his factory in good working order. He calculates the strength of each slave and keeps the strongest moving relentlessly while allowing those who would break down if pushed harder to rest. This is not tyranny enforced by blood and torture. It is the coldest, most intelligent tyranny that any master in history has ever exercised over a slave.

Yet from another point of view, is it not true that American slavery is harsher than ancient slavery was?

The calculating, positive spirit of the American slave owner impels him toward two distinct goals. The first is to get as much work out of his slave as possible. The second is to spend as little as possible to get it. Two problems must be solved: how to preserve the life of the Negro while feeding him little, and how to make him work hard without depleting his strength. Clearly, the master is faced with an embarrassing dilemma: he does not want his Negro to rest, yet he fears that constant work will kill him. The American slave owner frequently makes the same mistake as the manufacturer who runs his machine so hard that it breaks. Since these greed-driven calculations cost human beings their lives, American law was forced to prescribe the minimum daily ration that a slave must receive and to impose severe punishment on masters who failed to respect this necessity. Such laws prove the existence of the evil, moreover, but cannot remedy it. How can the slave subjected to a tyrannical master obtain justice? If

5. Thomas Jefferson (1743–1826) wrote about slavery and the African race most notably in query 14 of his *Notes on the State of Virginia,* published in 1784 in French and in 1787 in English.

he complains, he is usually treated even more harshly. And if by chance he gets his day in court, he finds that his judges are both his natural enemies and friends of his adversary.

It therefore seems to me fair to say that in the United States slaves do not have to fear the murderous violence to which the slaves of antiquity often fell victim. Their lives are protected, but their ordinary condition may be worse.

Here is yet another dissimilarity: among the ancients, the slave often abetted the master's vices. His intelligence lent itself to immoral activities.

The American slave never has to render such services. He rarely leaves the land, and his master's morals are pure. The Negro is stupid. He is more brutish than the Roman slave but less depraved.

3. Can Slavery Be Abolished in the United States?

It is impossible to discuss slavery without recognizing that the institution is a stain upon any nation in which it exists, as well as a misfortune.

The canker exists in the United States, but it cannot be blamed on today's Americans, who inherited it from their forebears. Part of the Union has already managed to rid itself of this scourge. The New England states, New York, and Pennsylvania no longer have slaves.[6] Can the abolition of slavery now take place in the South, as it did previously in the North?

Before attempting to answer this important question, let us begin by acknowledging that public opinion in the United States generally favors the emancipation of the black race.

There are several moral reasons for this opinion.

First, religious belief is universal in the United States.

A number of denominations ardently favor the cause of human freedom. Religious people have been tireless in support of the cause, and if their influence is almost imperceptible, it is nevertheless felt. Can slavery long endure in a Christian society? Christianity means moral equality among human beings. Once this tenet is accepted, it would seem impossible not to proceed to social equality, and from social equality to political equality. The legislators of South Carolina clearly sensed the full implications of the moral principle contained in Christianity. In one of the first articles of their code of laws pertaining to slavery, they explicitly stated that a slave who is baptized does not thereby become a free man.

It is undeniable, moreover, that the progress of civilization has led to the condemnation of slavery. Indeed, Europe has influenced America in this regard. Americans, though too proud to acknowledge any superiority in other nations, suffer grievously from the stain on their honor owing to the negative judgment of American slavery elsewhere.

Finally, perhaps the most powerful moral reason to emancipate the blacks

6. Article 6 of the Northwest Ordinance of 1787 also prohibited slavery in the states formed from the Northwest Territory: Ohio, Indiana, Illinois, and later Michigan, Wisconsin, and Minnesota.

is the opinion, increasingly widespread in American society, that the states in which slavery has been abolished are richer and more prosperous than those in which it remains in force. This opinion has a real basis in fact, moreover: people have finally begun to recognize that in slave states, free men do not work, because work, being the attribute of slaves, is debased in their eyes. Hence in these states, whites are idle, and only blacks work. In other words, the most intelligent and energetic portion of the population, the people most capable of enriching the country, remain inert and unproductive, while productive labor is left to another portion of the population, which is coarse and ignorant and unenthusiastic about its work because it has no interest in the results.

I have more than once heard southern slave owners themselves deplore the existence of slavery for this reason and express the wish that it might be destroyed.

It is undeniable, therefore, that public opinion in the United States is increasingly leaning toward the complete abolition of slavery.

But is abolition possible? How could it be accomplished? To respond to these questions, let us examine various objections that have been raised against the idea.

First objection. Some people regard Negro slavery as a matter of fact rather than principle. They contend that the African race is inferior to the European race, so that blacks are destined by their very nature to serve whites.

I will not discuss here the question of the superiority of whites to Negroes. This is a point about which many good minds are in disagreement. To say more, I would need more information about the subject than I possess. I will therefore offer only a few brief observations.

Generally speaking, the question of superiority is settled on the basis of a simple test: a particular white is compared to a particular Negro, and the observer says, "The former is more intelligent than the latter." But this is a fundamental error: the race is confused with the individual. Even if I assume that Europeans today are intellectually superior, the difficulty is not eliminated.

Indeed, is it not possible that the Negro is in principle as intelligent as the white but that his intelligence has degenerated for accidental reasons? If the black population lives for centuries in a social state that subjects it, generation after generation, to a degrading condition, to a wholly material existence that is destructive of human intelligence, will this not result in a progressive alteration of the moral faculties? At a certain point, the very structure of those faculties will be affected, and people will take this altered structure to be the natural condition of the Negro, whereas in fact it is merely a deformation of his natural condition. This question, which I merely adumbrate here, is treated in great detail in a two-volume work by Richard, entitled *Natural and Physical History of Man*.[7]

So it is an error to compare two races that have been following opposite

---

7. Beaumont gives the title in English. This work has not been identified.

paths for many centuries, one toward moral perfection, the other toward brutalization. It is no less misleading to compare individuals. How can one expect a Negro who, throughout his life, has encountered nothing that might awaken his intelligence to exhibit the same development of his faculties as a white, whose progress is the fruit of a liberal education from early childhood?

In addition, there is much to be learned about this question by looking at what is going on now in those American states that have abolished slavery. In Boston, New York, and Philadelphia there are public schools for the children of blacks, based on the same principles as schools for whites. Wherever I went, I found people who were of the opinion that children of color demonstrate as much of an aptitude for work as white children and are equally capable. For a long time people in the United States believed that Negroes lacked the intelligence necessary to engage in business. Yet one finds in the free northern states at the present time a good many colored people who have established commercial fortunes of their own. Indeed, it was long thought that the Negro was destined by his Creator to toil on the land and that he lacked the intelligence and skill necessary for the mechanical arts. Yet a wealthy industrialist in Kentucky told me once that this was now recognized to be an error and that Negro children who are taught a trade work just as well as whites.

Hence the question of white superiority over the Negro admits of no clear answer at the present time. But even if this superiority were incontestable, would it lead to the consequences that are currently drawn from it? If one were to grant that the European is a shade more intelligent than the African, would it necessarily follow that the latter is destined by nature to serve the former? Where would such a theory lead?

Unequal intelligences also exist among whites. Is servitude the punishment to be meted out to everyone who is less enlightened than the average? And who is to determine what the average intelligence is? No, man's moral value does not lie entirely in his mind; it is above all inherent in his soul. If it were proven that the Negro's understanding is inferior to the white's, it would still be necessary to show that his feelings are less keen, that he is less capable of generosity and virtue.

Such a theory cannot withstand scrutiny. If it were applied to the comparison of white with white, it would seem ridiculous. Limited to Negroes, it is more odious still, because it affects an entire race of men, all of whom are subjected to the most dreadful misery.

Hence the first objection must be rejected.

Second objection. But others say: "We need Negroes to cultivate our land. Only Africans can stand such harsh labor in the burning sun. Since we cannot do without slaves, we must maintain slavery."

The American planters who speak this way clearly reduce the question to one of their own self-interest. To be sure, their self-interest would coincide with the prosperity of their region if it were correct to say that the southern states cannot be cultivated except by Negroes.

On this point there is a wide variety of opinions in the southern United States. There is no doubt that the closer whites are to the tropics, the more dangerous labor in the heat of the sun becomes for them. But how serious is that danger? Would it disappear if they became accustomed to such work? At what degree of latitude does it begin? Is it in Virginia or Louisiana? At the fourth parallel or the thirty-first?

To these vexed questions the Americans offer a variety of contradictory answers. In traveling through the southern states, I often heard it said that if the slavery of blacks were abolished, the agricultural wealth of the southern regions would vanish.

Yet what is happening today in Maryland is enough to shake one's faith in any such assertion.

Maryland, a slave state, is situated between the thirty-eighth and thirty-ninth parallels. It occupies a middle ground between the northern states, where there are only free men, and the southern states, where slavery remains in force. As recently as a few years ago, it was universally believed in Maryland that the labor of the Negro was indispensable to the cultivation of the soil. Anyone who contradicted this opinion would have been silenced. Yet by the time I visited the state (in October 1831), a complete reversal of opinion had taken place. I can give no better account of this revolution in the public mind than to report verbatim what a man of noble character and distinguished rank in American society said to me in Baltimore:

There is at present no one in Maryland who does not want to see the abolition of slavery as eagerly as they used to want to see it maintained.

We have recognized that whites can do agricultural work with no problem, work that we previously believed could be done only by Negroes.

Based on this experience, a great many free workers and white farmers settled in Maryland, and we then made an equally important discovery: namely, that once there is competition between slaves and free men, the ruin of slave owners becomes certain. The farmer who works for himself, as well as the free worker who works for wages, produces half again as much as the slave who works for his master without self-interest. As a result, the products of free labor sell for half the price. Thus an item that cost two dollars when all our workers were slaves now costs just one dollar. A farmer who uses slaves to produce that item must nevertheless sell it at the same price, so that he loses money. His income falls to half of what it was previously, while his expenses remain the same, because he must still feed his Negroes and their families and care for them in childhood, sickness, and old age. Yet in the end he still has slaves doing half the work of free men.

I cannot leave this subject without taking note of what Charles Caroll [*sic*], a justly celebrated American, said to me about black slavery.[8] Caroll, who signed

8. In a footnote, Beaumont noted that he had met Carroll late in 1831, only a year before Carroll died at the age of ninety-six.

the Declaration of Independence, has lived to enjoy his glorious work longer than any other signatory.

It is wrong to think that Negroes are necessary for the growing of certain crops, such as sugar, rice, and tobacco. I am convinced that whites could easily get used to it if they tried. They might suffer initially from the need to alter their habits, but they would soon overcome this obstacle, and once accustomed to the climate and to the work done by blacks, they would be twice as productive as slaves.

When Mr. Charles Caroll told me this, he was living on a plantation that had three hundred blacks.

The foregoing remarks do not lead me to the conclusion that the objection raised to white labor in the South is entirely without foundation, but can we conclude that a number of southern states, which have hitherto considered slavery to be a necessity, will one day recognize their error, as Maryland is doing now? Communication among the states is steadily becoming easier and more frequent. Is it not likely that the moral revolution that has taken place in Baltimore will spread to the South? The southern states, once purely agricultural, are beginning to become more industrial. Manufacturers who establish themselves in the South will need to compete with those in the North, and that will mean that they must produce as cheaply as the latter. They will no longer be able to use slave labor, since it has been shown that slave labor cannot compete with free labor. Wherever free workers appear, slavery collapses. Last but not least, what has been shown is that (economically speaking) slavery is harmful when it is not necessary, and it has been judged so by those who formerly believed it to be indispensable. Nevertheless, there are far more serious objections to the abolition of slavery than the question of how useful the labor of Negroes is to whites.

Third objection. Suppose that the principle of abolition were accepted. How would it be carried out?

Here, two systems are possible: either all slaves can be emancipated immediately, or else just the principle of slavery can be abolished and all unborn children of Negroes be declared free. If the first course of action were chosen, slavery would vanish overnight, and on the day the law was passed, American society would consist exclusively of free men. If the second course were chosen, the status quo would be maintained. Those who are slaves now would remain slaves. Only the future would be affected. The effect of the law would be felt in future generations.

Both systems are simple in theory, yet both would face certain common difficulties if put into practice.

First, if present slaves or their offspring are declared free, equity requires that the government pay their owners what they are worth. Indemnity is the first condition of emancipation, because the slave is the property of his master.

How would such compensation be made?

Some say that the American government is in the best possible position to carry out such an operation. The public debt of the United States has been retired. The annual revenue of the federal government is 159 million francs. Of this sum, 74 million francs are absorbed by the expenses of the federal administration. That leaves 85 million, which sum was formerly devoted to the retirement of the public debt and could not be used to redeem enslaved Negroes.

I have often heard this proposed as a way to achieve general emancipation, but many obstacles remain. First, the assumption about revenue is flawed. To be sure, the United States no longer has a public debt to service. But having freed themselves of debt, Americans have also considerably reduced the tax that was the source of their revenue. It is therefore incorrect to say that the federal government takes in 85 million annually that could be used to redeem Negroes.

But let us assume that such a sum were in fact available and ask whether it would indeed be possible to hope that it might be used as proposed.

According to the most recent census, carried out in 1830, there were 2,009,000 slaves in the United States. Now, assuming that the average value of each Negro, counting women, children, and the elderly, is 100 dollars, it would cost more than a billion francs to redeem these two-million-odd slaves. To that sum we would have to add the price of the at least 200,000 slaves born since 1830, which would add 111 million francs to the billion already mentioned. Assuming that the federal government were able and willing to spend 85 million francs per year on the redemption of Negroes, it could purchase only 160,000 slaves a year with that sum. It would therefore have to spend the same sum for the same purpose for fourteen years to redeem all the slaves who exist today. But that is not all. The 2,009,000 slaves who exist at present multiply daily, and assuming that their annual increase in the future is proportionate to what it has been in the past, the number of slaves will increase by about 60,000 annually. Thus 47 million francs would be absorbed each year not to diminish the number of slaves but simply to prevent its increase. That sum of 47 million is more than half of the amount destined for redemption.

Clearly, the government of the United States would have to impose on itself a pecuniary sacrifice matched only by its lack of efficacy. Is it possible to believe that the American government would ever undertake such a task by such means?

I do not know whether a people that governs itself would ever make such an enormous sacrifice in the absence of an urgent need. The masses, which are resourceful and capable when it comes to remedying present and palpable ills, have little ability to anticipate future woes. Slavery, which may in fact someday become a cause of trouble and instability for the entire Union, currently affects only a portion of the United States to any considerable degree, namely, the South. Why would the North, which at the moment does not suffer from the ills of slavery, devote such considerable sums to the redemption of southern slaves for the benefit of the South, and perhaps also in anticipation of uncertain perils to come, when the same sum, if used for the benefit of all, could yield immediate present benefits? To hope for such a sacrifice on the part of the federal government of the United States would be to overlook the laws of self-interest and take no account of the American character or of the principles on which democracy is based.

The exorbitant price of redemption is not the only obstacle to overcome, however.

Let us assume that this difficulty is somehow dealt with.

Fourth objection. Once the Negroes are emancipated, what will become of them? Will breaking their chains be the end of it? Will they be allowed to remain free alongside their former masters? If yesterday's slaves and yesterday's tyrants confront one another in more or less equal numbers, are not bloody clashes likely to result?

Clearly it is not enough to redeem the Negroes. Once they are emancipated, a way must be found to remove them from the society in which they once lived as slaves.

Two systems for accomplishing this goal have been proposed.

The first is Jefferson's.[9] He suggested that, once slavery was abolished, a portion of American territory should be assigned to the Negroes, and there they would live separate from whites. This is a seriously flawed and politically unrealistic idea. Its immediate consequence would be to establish on American soil two distinct societies made up of two races that have covertly hated each other and whose hostility would now burst into the open. It would be to create an enemy of the United States within its borders, whereas it has until now been the country's good fortune to have neither enemies nor neighbors.

Since Jefferson first suggested this peculiar means of separating Negroes from whites, however, another method has been found that does not suffer from the same drawbacks.

A colony of emancipated Negroes has been founded on the coast of Liberia (6 degrees north latitude). Philanthropic societies have been established to oversee the settlement and maintenance of this colony, which is currently prospering. At the beginning of 1834, its colonists numbered 3,000. All were emancipated Negroes who had emigrated from the United States.[10]

To be sure, if it were possible to emancipate all blacks and transport them to Liberia, it would be an unalloyed good. But can such a vast exodus of emancipated slaves from America to Africa ever be carried out? Even if the redemption costs are covered, the transportation costs alone would be considerable. The cost of transporting a single Negro has been estimated at 30 dollars (160 francs), which for 2 million Negroes would add another 318 million francs to the 1,200

9. See Jefferson's *Notes on the State of Virginia* (1787), query 14.

10. The American Colonization Society was founded in 1816 and counted a number of prominent Americans among its members, including a number of slave owners, such as James Madison and Henry Clay. In 1821, the group founded the colony of Liberia on the western coast of Africa and organized the transport of freed slaves to this colony. A number of motives propelled white American support for this project, ranging from prevention of discrimination against free blacks to the security of white Americans. Liberia grew slowly and became a financial drain on the ACS, but it survived and became an independent country in 1847.

million already mentioned. Thus, the deeper one delves into the question, the more obstacles one encounters.

Assume next that these initial difficulties are somehow overcome. Grant that the government of the Union is willing to make the immense sacrifice required to emancipate the Negroes and that the northern states, which have little to gain from such a sacrifice, refrain from opposing it. Grant further that there exists a practical way to transport the emancipated population outside of American territory. With these obstacles out of the way, the most insuperable of all would still remain: namely, the will of the southern states in which the slave population resides.

Fifth objection. Under the American Constitution, the abolition of slavery in the southern states can be accomplished only by a sovereign decision of those states themselves. Or else, if the federal government were to attempt to emancipate the slaves, the individual states affected by the decision would have to give their consent. Of course I have no idea what the southern states may think or do in the future, but it seems clear to me that as things stand now, with minds and interests made up as they are, all the southern states would oppose emancipation even with a promise of indemnity.

To begin with, there can be no doubt that a sudden transition from black servitude to black freedom would mark a dangerous moment of crisis for slave owners.

To the objection that the freed Negroes would have no further grounds for complaint against the society or their former masters, I reply that they would have their memories of tyranny. It is the common lot of the oppressed to submit as long as they are weak and to seek vengeance once they become strong. The slave becomes strong on the day he becomes free.

It is not likely that the Americans who reside in slave states would willingly run the risk that emancipation of the Negroes would pose for them in order to avoid the risk of a race war in subsequent generations.

They would be even less likely to run that risk because their material interests would be harmed. All the wealth and resources of the South are today based on slave labor. No monetary indemnity could replace the slaves lost. The former masters would find themselves with capital that they would have no idea how to put to use. Eventually, new enterprises and new forms of exploitation would no doubt emerge, but for the present generation the elimination of slavery would represent a profound disruption of existing material interests.

Is it plausible to think that an entire generation would accept ruin for the benefit of future generations? No. Indeed, it is doubtful whether it would submit to such a fate even in the face of present dangers. Nothing is more difficult to imagine than a large number of people willingly sacrificing their own material interests in order to avoid some danger. The present danger is nothing more than an anticipation of future misfortune, whereas the sacrifice would be a misfortune here and now.

Someone may say that these objections can be circumvented in large part if emancipation is limited to the unborn children of slaves, while slaves born prior to the act of abolition remain in servitude. That way, the people who agree to abolish slavery get to keep their slaves, and the generation that is to suffer from emancipation will not have known anything better.

Granted, this system weakens the objections raised, but it does not entirely overcome them. If unborn children are declared free while their fathers remain enslaved, will slaves not be given grounds for insurrection? Much effort is expended in persuading the Negro slave that he is not the white man's equal and that this inequality is the reason for his slavery. What would become of this fiction if it were to be contradicted by reality? Why would the Negro slave obey, when his child has been granted the right to resist?

To assume, moreover, that southern Americans would preserve their own rights while sacrificing the rights of their children would be to exaggerate their selfishness. As surprising as it would be if they were to sacrifice their own interests for the sake of remote future generations, it would be equally surprising if they were to sacrifice the interests of their immediate offspring in order to preserve their own, because paternal feelings are almost selfish in their strength. It is therefore certain that fathers would be as reluctant to take steps that would be ruinous for their children as they would be to ruin themselves.

At this point one might object that the northern states abolished slavery for the future, that is, for still-unborn children, while leaving those who had been slaves prior to abolition in servitude. Why couldn't the southern states do the same?

The answer to this objection is easy. Large-scale slavery never gained a foothold in the North. When Pennsylvania, New York, and the other northern states abolished slavery, the number of slaves residing within their borders was small. To cite just one example, New York abolished slavery in 1799, at which time there were just three slaves per one hundred inhabitants.[11] One could emancipate the Negroes or declare their unborn children free without fear of the consequences of suddenly exposing slaves to the prospect of freedom. Slave owners constituted only a tiny fraction of the population, so there was nearly universal interest in eliminating slavery so that no dishonor would attach to labor, the source of all wealth. In abolishing black servitude for the future, the northern states made no sacrifice. The majority, which benefited from abolition, imposed its law on the small number of people whose interests were different.

How can the northern states be compared to the southern, in which the number of slaves is equal to if not greater than the number of free men, and the majority if not the totality of citizens have an interest in maintaining slavery?

11. New York used Pennsylvania's plan for emancipation as a model. The New York law declared that all children born to slaves after July 4, 1799, would gain their freedom in adulthood, males at age twenty-eight and females at age twenty-five. Although slaves born before that date were to remain "indentured servants" for life, an 1817 law declared that all slaves would become free on July 4, 1827.

Clearly the dissimilarity is complete in regard to the present time, but is there no reason to hope for some change in the situation of the southern states in the future? Are there no grounds for thinking that today's interest in maintaining slavery might someday develop into an interest in abolishing it? I am firmly convinced that sooner or later abolition will take place, and I have already set forth the reasons for my confidence. But I also believe that slavery will last a good while yet in the South. It is useful, I think, to summarize the material differences that make it impossible to compare what will happen in the South to what did happen in the North.

There is no denying the fact that the cold climate of the northern states is hostile to the African race, whereas the warmth of the South is favorable to it. In the North the race languishes and diminishes in number, whereas in the South it prospers and multiplies.

Thus the black population, whose numbers tended naturally to dwindle in states where slavery was abolished, is growing today in the southern states.

In the North, slavery was clearly harmful to the majority. Southerners are still in doubt about whether or not they need slaves. Slavery in the North was never more than a luxury. Till now in the South it has at the very least been useful. For Northerners it was an accessory. In the South it is linked to customs, habits, and interests of all kinds. To eliminate slavery, the free states had only to pass a law. To abolish slavery in the slave states would require changing the whole of society.

Many factors in the North were hostile to slavery: the bustling economy, the Northerner's taste for work, the religious zeal of New England Presbyterians, and the austerity of Pennsylvania's Quakers, to say nothing of a highly advanced civilization. The South is different. The southern states have religious beliefs but not religious passions. Some of them, including Alabama, Mississippi, and Georgia, are semibarbarous, and their inhabitants are, like those who live in southern climes everywhere, given to indolence and idleness. Thus none of the causes that led to the ruin of slavery in the North exists thus far in the South.

Hence the southern states are a long way from emancipating the slaves.

Yet however much Southerners cling to slavery in the present, they are frightened for the future. The steady increase in the number of slaves living in their midst is genuine cause for alarm. In South Carolina and Louisiana, the number of blacks is already larger than the number of whites, and the reason for the increase may be cause for greater concern than the fact itself. Because the importation of slaves from abroad has been prohibited throughout the Union, not just by the federal government but by all the states, the increase in the number of slaves can only result from births. Since the number of whites is not increasing in the southern states in the same proportion as the number of Negroes, it is clear that the black population will eventually be much larger than the white.

Although the southern states see the growing danger gathering, they are doing nothing to ward it off. Each of them opposes or favors an increase in the number of slaves depending on whether it currently has an interest in owning more or fewer of them. In Maryland, the District of Columbia, and Virginia, where free labor has begun to infiltrate, many slaves are being emancipated, and as many as possible are sold to states farther south. Louisiana, South Carolina, Mississippi, and Florida, which to this day derive huge profits from the use of slaves to exploit their land, do not emancipate their slaves and constantly seek to acquire more. Because these states are frightened of the future, it is common for them to pass laws to prohibit the purchase of Negroes in other parts of the Union. When I was traveling in Louisiana in 1832, the legislature had just passed a law prohibiting the purchase of Negroes in border states. In general, however, such laws are not enforced. Legislators themselves are often the first to break these laws. Their private interest as slave owners causes them to buy slaves, even though they have prohibited such transactions in the general interest.

In short, when you consider the intellectual reaction against slavery around the world; the public disapproval of slavery in many nations; the rapid progress that the idea of freeing the slaves has made already in the United States; the steady progress of emancipation in both the North and the South; the need to substitute free labor for slave labor that the southern states will sooner or later face if they wish to remain on a par with the northern states—given all these facts, it seems inevitable that sooner or later slavery will disappear entirely from North America.

But how can such emancipation be achieved? What means will be used, and what will be the consequences? What will become of masters and emancipated slaves? No one dares to make firm predictions on any of these points.

A more serious question for America than slavery, perhaps, is the question of race. American society, with its Negroes, finds itself in a situation quite different from ancient slaveholding societies. American slaves are colored, and that fact influences all the consequences of emancipation. An emancipated white retained virtually none of the characteristics of a slave. An emancipated black acquires virtually none of the characteristics of a free man. In vain is the black man freed; he remains a slave in the eyes of public opinion. Mores are more powerful than laws. The Negro slave was taken to be an inferior or degraded being. The freed Negro retains the degradation of the slave. His black skin perpetuates the memory of servitude and stands as an eternal obstacle to the mixing of the two races.

The nature of these prejudices and repugnances is such that in the most enlightened northern states, the antipathy between the races remains intact. Indeed, it is worth noting that several of these states have inscribed the inferiority of blacks in their laws.

It is easy to understand why emancipated Negroes in the slave states are not treated entirely as free white men. So it is not surprising to find a Louisiana law which states that "free colored people must never insult or strike whites or claim to be their equals. Indeed, they must step aside to allow whites to pass everywhere and address them respectfully on pain of imprisonment for a term proportionate to the gravity of the offense."

Nor is it surprising to find that the slave states prohibit marriage between whites and freed colored people or slaves.

What is more extraordinary, perhaps, is that even in the northern states there were for many years laws against marriage between whites and colored. For example, Massachusetts law declared such marriages null and void and imposed a fine on any official who performed one. This law was not rescinded until 1830.

Even when the law does not forbid such marriages, moreover, mores still bar the way. An ironclad barrier remains between whites and blacks.

Although the two populations inhabit the same territory and the same cities, each has a distinct civil existence. Each has its own schools, its own churches, and its own cemeteries. When both must be present in public places at the same time, they do not mix; distinct places are assigned to each. They are therefore kept separate in courtrooms, hospitals, and prisons. The freedom that Negroes enjoy does not bring them the benefits of society. The same prejudice that leads to their being held in contempt bars access to most professions. It is difficult to judge just how difficult it is for a Negro to make his way in the United States. He finds obstacles everywhere and support nowhere. Most free Negroes are therefore all but compelled to work as domestic servants.

In political life the separation is even greater. Although eligible for public jobs in theory, they have none. There is not a single Negro or mulatto in public office anywhere in the United States. The laws of the northern states generally acknowledge that the political rights of free colored people are the same as those of whites, but nowhere are the colored allowed to enjoy those rights. Some time ago in Philadelphia, free blacks who tried to vote were violently ejected from the polls and had to forgo the exercise of a right whose legitimacy no one contested. Since then, they have not tried to assert their legitimate right. It is sad to say, but the only option for the oppressed black population is to submit to such tyranny without a murmur. Recently, some well-intentioned philanthropists tried to arrange for marriages between blacks and whites in the hope of achieving a fusion of the races. These efforts flew in the face of American pride, however, and led to uprisings in New York and Philadelphia in July 1834. Anytime that emancipated Negroes indicate a direct or indirect intention to pose as the equals of whites, the latter rise up as one to beat back such impudence. Yet these things take place in the most enlightened and most religious states of the Union, where slavery has long been abolished. Would anyone now doubt that the barrier between the two races is insurmountable?

Broadly speaking, the free Negroes of the North patiently bear their misery, but would they submit to such humiliation and injustice if there were more of them? In the northern states they are a barely perceptible minority. What would happen if they were equal or superior in number to whites, as they are in the South? What is happening today in the North may give us some idea of the future of the South. If it is true that generous efforts to transport freed Negroes from America to Africa are doomed to partial success at best, then it is unfortunately all too certain that the southern states will one day be home to two hostile races distinguished by the color of their skin and kept apart by invincible prejudice, and that the contempt of one race will earn it the hatred of the other. This is surely the great open wound in American society.

How can this important political problem be resolved? Will the future bring a crisis of extermination? When? Who will be the victims? Southern whites are in possession of the forces of civilization and have the habit of power. They are also certain of finding support in the North, where the black race is dwindling. Does it follow that the Negroes are destined to lose this fight if it comes to war? No one can answer these questions. We see the storm clouds gathering. We hear the distant thunder. But no one can say where lightning will strike.

Note Excerpts

NOTE ON AMERICAN WOMEN[12]

The most striking trait in the women of America is their superiority to the men.

The American man plunges into business at a tender age. No sooner does he learn to read and write than he becomes a merchant. The first sound he hears is the sound of money. The first voice he hears is that of self-interest. From birth the air he breathes is industrial, and his earliest impressions persuade him that a life in business is the only life suitable for a man.

A girl's fate is different. Her moral upbringing does not end until the day she marries. She acquires knowledge of history and literature. She generally learns a foreign language (usually French). She knows a little about music. Her life is intellectual.

Eventually this young man and young woman, so different from each other, join in matrimony. The male, yielding to habit, spends his time at the bank or in his store. The female, who goes into isolation the day she takes a husband, compares the real life that befalls her to the existence of which she once dreamed. Since nothing in this new world of hers speaks to her heart, she thrives on her imagination and reads novels. Not being very happy, she is quite religious and reads sermons. When she has children, she lives among them, takes care of them, and lavishes affection on them. In this way she spends her days. At night, the American male returns home, anxious, worried, and dead tired. He brings his wife the fruit of his labor and has already begun dreaming of tomorrow's specu-

12. Beaumont's heading; headings in square brackets have been supplied by the editor.

FROM *Marie; or, Slavery in the United States*

lations. He asks for dinner but has nothing else to say. His wife has no knowledge of the business that preoccupies him. Even when her husband is at home, her isolation does not end. The sight of wife and children is not enough to rescue the American man from the material world, and so rarely does he show his family any sign of tenderness or affection that the Americans have a word for families where the husband kisses his wife and children when he returns home after an absence: they call them "kissing families." For Americans, a wife is not a companion; she is a partner, who helps her husband spend the money he earns in business for his greater well-being and comfort.

The sedentary and withdrawn lives that women lead in the United States, together with the rigors of the climate, explain their pallid complexions. They seldom leave the house or take any exercise, and they live on a light diet. Nearly all of them have large families. It should come as no surprise that they age quickly and die young.

American life is a life of contrasts: agitated, adventurous, almost feverish for men, melancholic and monotonous for women. It unfolds uneventfully until the husband announces to his wife that they have gone bankrupt. Then they must pull up stakes and begin the same life anew in a different place.

Every American family thus encompasses two distinct worlds: one entirely material, the other entirely moral. However intimate the bond between husband and wife, one always finds between them the barrier that separates body from soul, matter from mind. . . .

"It is she who makes the choice": A woman's parents will seldom contradict her on this point. If they do raise an objection, a girl can usually win by sticking to her guns. Society would censure a father who held out too long against the wishes of his child. Not that paternal authority is without weapons in the land of liberty. The law allows parents to disinherit their children to whatever extent they choose, but they do not use that right in these circumstances, because mores, always more powerful than laws, protect freedom in marriage.

"At birth, great wealth": Occasionally one meets young people who by some accident of inherited wealth and polite upbringing show some aptitude for social intrigue and amorous flirtation, but there are too few of them to do much harm, and if they give any hint of disturbing the peace of a family, all of society will unite to crush the common enemy. That is why unmarried Americans of wealth and leisure do not remain in the United States and come to live in Europe, where they find intellectual men and corrupt women.

"No difference in rank": Thus anyone who seduces a young woman is obliged to marry her. If he does not, his reputation is ruined, and he is banished from society.

In England, a young man of aristocratic background can seduce a young woman of the middle class without causing much of a scandal. People of his own class will readily forgive him for the damage he does among the lower ranks. This cannot happen in a society where conditions are equal and ranks are not clearly differentiated. . . .

"He detested the English": To say that Americans hate the English is to misrepresent their true feelings. The inhabitants of the United States were once subject to English rule, and the memory of independence is mingled with that of the wars that had to be fought to win it. This reminds Americans that there was once deep antipathy between them and the English.

England's advanced civilization also inspires very deep feelings of jealousy in all Americans. Yet the moment they forget the rivalry between them and the English, it is clear that they are proud to descend from a nation as great as England and that feelings of filial piety still attach the colonies to the mother country long after they have obtained their freedom.

The memory of old disputes grows fainter every day, but the jealousy increases. The material prosperity of the United States has grown prodigiously, and the English look upon this with an anxious eye. Despite America's rapid progress, moreover, the Americans cannot hide from themselves the fact that they are still inferior to England. The feelings of both peoples are entirely legitimate in principle, but national pride, spurred on by the press in London as well as New York, poisons the relationship.

The English papers are contemptuous of the United States, which they depict as a savage country. One English magazine, published in London, asks its readers to "compare the morality of England and America, as if any parallel can be drawn between a country crowded with people, with six million individuals involved in commerce and industry, in which the eye is drawn to countless objects that invite larceny; and America, where there is nothing to steal but grass and water; where the soil is the only thing on which a person can live; where everyone must be his own tailor, his own carpenter, and so forth; where all savoir faire consists in knowledge of how to grow corn and potatoes; where to eat a pudding is the height of luxury; and where the sight of a mirror is so rare that it can excite the entire population of a state." Many similar observations follow. (*Daily Commercial Gazette,* Boston, September 28, 1831.) Similar invective can be read in the English papers any day of the week. It is only natural that this sort of thing should irritate Americans, whose resentment is proportionate to the injustice of the English.

Another cause yields a similar effect. The English who travel in America are perfectly welcome there for three reasons. First, Americans are naturally hospitable to foreigners who speak their language. Second, although they are jealous of England, they take real pleasure in welcoming any English visitor, whom they treat as a representative of the nation from which they themselves are descended. Third, they want to be judged favorably by the English both as individuals and as a nation, precisely because they are rivals. They therefore try to be polite to prove that Americans are not savages, and since they sincerely believe that they have some very beautiful things in their country, they make it their duty to show all the moral and material wealth of the United States to the insular British.

Yet the Englishman, full of his own national prejudices and, even without bias, likely to find America inferior to his own country, returns home to write of his trans-Atlantic travels and produces a volume or two of satire. In some cases he doesn't even bother to disguise proper names and exposes to the ridicule of his fellow Englishmen the worthy foreigners whose hospitality he accepted. Even those whose style is the most reserved are still insulting and cutting. Soon after publication in England, the book arrives in the United States, where its appearance comes as a thunderclap to American vanity.

The rivalry between the Americans and the English is not limited to industry and commerce. The two nations share a common language, and each claims to speak it better than the other. I believe that both are right. In England, the upper class possesses a delicacy of tone that is unknown in America except for a small number of salons that are utterly exceptional. In the United States, where there is neither an upper class nor a lower class, the entire population speaks English less well than the English aristocracy but as well as the middle class and far better than the lower class in England. . . .

[NOTE ON FREEMASONRY]

"Anti-Mason": The word indicates that there are Masons in the United States, that is, societies of Freemasons.[13] In a country of universal unlimited liberty, these societies are neither useful to citizens for obtaining or preserving their rights nor dangerous to the government, against which there are innumerable legal and open means of attack. Accordingly, Masonry to date has not become the symbol of any political party. General Jackson, the president of the United States and representative of the Republican Party, is a Freemason, as is Mr. Clay, his opponent in the last election, whose opinions are considered to be less democratic.[14]

The creation of a Freemasonry in the United States can be explained only

13. Freemasonry originated from medieval artisans' guilds, which protected their members by regulating skill, quality, and prices and by relying on secret codes and handshakes to prove membership. As craft guilds lost capital and influence in the open market of the seventeenth century, stonemasons' guilds in Great Britain began to offer membership to nonmasons who were interested in fellowship and academic discussion. Freemasonry became an elite voluntary society in the early eighteenth century and continues to exist as a semisecretive international fraternal organization, with local chapters called lodges. Though Freemasonry is not a religion, the group encourages its members to be active worshippers in their chosen religions, and it upholds a moral code that is centered on a Supreme Being and represented by symbols of masonry.

14. The Democratic (or Old Republican) Party nominee, Andrew Jackson (1767–1845), defeated the National Republican candidate, Henry Clay (1777–1852), and the Anti-Mason nominee, William Wirt (1772–1834), in the presidential election of 1832.

by the American penchant for imitating Europe whenever doing so is compatible with the nature of their government. Americans wanted the institution on their shores because they admired the relations of philanthropy and fraternity that develop among Masons.

In any case, they themselves attach little importance to the Masons: "Only one thing is more absurd than the Masons," a clever Bostonian once said to me, "and that is the anti-Masons."

In 1827, however, a deplorable event focused public attention on Masonry and changed people's opinions about membership in this society. A man named Morgan, who was affiliated with Masons in New York State, suddenly quit the group and joined the anti-Masons. It seems that he even stated his intention to divulge the group's statutes and secrets. A few days later, he disappeared from his home, and for a time no one knew what had become of him. A short while later, however, his body was found floating in Lake Erie, and there was every reason to believe that he had been murdered and thrown into the lake. An investigation was launched and evidence collected. But the witnesses from whom information might have been gleaned were so terror-stricken that they refused to say anything against the suspects in the case.

The case triggered a revival of the Anti-Masonic Party. Many people not involved with the Masons rejected what they believed to be a group that had been if not the cause then at least the pretext for an odious crime. Others hastened to profit from this turn of events to advance their own ambitions and organize an anti-Masonic party, ostensibly on moral grounds but in reality for the sole purpose of currying favor with the public. In a country without political parties, ambitious men have a hard time gaining attention. In the place of real interests, they are obliged to create imaginary ones. Any incident or idea can be turned to account and donned as a costume by an actor playing a role.

[NOTE ON MORES]

"Austerity of the Puritans of New England": This austerity is not only evident in mores. One sees it also in laws: drunkenness, games of chance, fornication, blasphemy, failure to observe Sundays—in Massachusetts these are crimes punishable by fine or imprisonment. Puritanism, which is dominant in New England, still exerts an influence on nearly all the states of the Union. For instance, the penal code of Ohio prescribes imprisonment for relations between unmarried men and women. In Cincinnati I saw people sentenced for this crime and consigned to foul cells with no ventilation.

In New York, all games of chance, such as cards, dice, and billiards, are prohibited in public places, inns, taverns, ships, etc., with a fine of $10 (55 francs) for innkeepers and ship captains who violate the law. Any person who wins money in a game of chance is subject to a fine of five times the amount won. Win or lose, anyone who bets a sum of 25 dollars (152 francs) is guilty of a misdemeanor and subject to a fine that must be equal to at least five times the amount won or lost. The law of the same state punishes oaths and blasphemy. It prohibits the sale of strong liquor within two miles of a church. The laws of Pennsylvania contain similar provisions. Drunkenness is punishable by fine or imprisonment, while the keeper of the inn where the infraction takes place may lose his license. An individual known for habitual drunkenness may be assigned a guardian, as if he were incompetent, and anyone—innkeeper, distiller, or grocer—who sells him spirits or wine is subject to a fine of 10 dollars (55 francs).

"When Sunday came": The celebration of Sunday is not limited in America to a service as it is in France. It lasts all day. After the service, each person returns home, and soon the streets are empty of carriages, men, women, and children. To block carriages, streets adjacent to churches are barred with chains at a height of two feet. The city becomes so silent that one might think an enemy had passed through the night before and left everyone for dead. New York State law bans all amusements on Sunday including hunting, sports, horse racing, etc. No innkeeper or distiller may dispense any spirits, and no merchant may sell merchandise of any kind. (See revised statutes of New York State, vol. 1, pp. 675–6.)

It seems quite certain that many Americans who are confined to their homes on Sunday do not read the Bible much but rather take advantage of the opportunity to engage in work that is anything but pious. Some freely indulge their passion for gambling, which is all the more damaging in America because the most innocent public games are banned, so that gamblers privately engage in the most dangerous activities. Others imbibe spirits. Many of the working class go to sleep immediately after services. The same thing can be observed in England, where the cause is also the same. Protestantism, which recommends silence and meditation on Sundays and prohibits all sorts of pleasures, took into account only the condition of the upper classes of society. Such wholly intellectual observance of the holy day is suitable for cultivated people and apt to ennoble souls capable of meditation, but it is unsuited to the lower classes. You will never get a man who works all week with his body alone to spend his Sundays thinking. If you deny him public amusements, he will retire to the shadows on Sunday and indulge in the coarsest of pleasures without inhibition.

"Whoever traveled on Sunday": There is a law in Massachusetts (New England) that allows anyone who travels on Sunday to be arrested and fined. Anyone who has an urgent need to travel on the holy day must seek authorization. The driver of a public carriage who ventures onto a road on Sunday without permission can lose his license for three years. (See the general laws of Massachusetts, vol. 1, p. 535, and vol. 2, p. 403, 1815, chap. 435.) New York law contains a similar but less severe provision. (See revised statutes, vol. 1, p. 676.)

"The mail carriage": In the past, postal service was entirely suspended on Sundays. The mail carriage was obliged to park for the day. This restriction was relaxed some years ago. Most people approve of the change, but the Presbyterians are bitterly opposed to the law and consider it sacrilegious. . . .

[NOTE ON POLITICAL PARTIES]

"Because there are no parties": There are no political parties in the United States, in the sense that everyone accepts the fundamental principle of government, which is popular sovereignty, and the form of government, which is republican. In America, therefore, we see nothing like what we see in Europe, where some people want despotism, others constitutional monarchy, and still others a republic. Nevertheless, parties have formed in the United States around the consequences and applications of the universally accepted principle. These are at bottom disputes among personalities, but private interest must cloak itself beneath the general interest. The question of *political parties in America* is treated in the work that M. de Tocqueville is going to publish on democracy in America (see vol. 2, chap. 2).

[NOTE ON NATIONAL PRIDE]

"These exaggerations": I blame this blindness on American national pride, which makes them admire everything that takes place in their country, but I like even less the attitude of people in some other countries, who are disposed to find fault with everything that happens. Political institutions explain both tendencies, which are equally exaggerated. In the United States, the people are responsible for everything and can never praise their own work enough. In European countries, by contrast, the people do nothing and can never get their fill of satire attacking the actions of the minority that governs them.

Writers who want to find readers in the United States are obliged to praise everything American, even their harsh climate, which they are certainly powerless to change. For instance, Washington Irving, clever as he is, feels compelled to admire the temperate heat of North American summers and the mildness of North American winters.[15] . . .

NOTE ON BANKRUPTCIES

"Indulgence for a bankrupt . . . no pity for mismarriage": I'm not sure that any country could be more commercially prosperous than the United States, and yet in no country on earth is the number of bankruptcies greater. There are two main reasons for this. First, business conditions in the United States are the most favorable that can be imagined: a vast, fertile territory, huge rivers to serve as natural means of communication, numerous well-placed ports, and an enterpris-

---

15. Washington Irving (1783–1859) gained acclaim in the United States and Europe for his fictional stories, such as "Rip Van Winkle" and "The Legend of Sleepy Hollow," set in historic New York State. Later in his life, he also published popular nonfiction, such as his biographies of Oliver Goldsmith and George Washington.

FROM *Marie; or, Slavery in the United States*

ing people with a calculating spirit and a genius for the maritime. All these circumstances conspire to make America a commercial nation. That is the source of its wealth. But precisely because success is likely, it is pursued with frenetic ardor. The sight of fortunes being made overnight intoxicates speculators, who race blindly toward their desired goal: that is the cause of ruin. Thus all Americans are traders, because everyone sees trade as a means to riches. Everyone goes bankrupt, because their desire for wealth is so impatient.

Shortly after my arrival in America, I joined an elite company in one of the largest cities in the Union. A Frenchman who had been living in the country for some time caught my ear. "Be sure not to say anything bad about bankrupts." I followed his advice and was wise to do so, because among the wealthy men to whom I was introduced, there was not one who had not gone bankrupt once or twice in his life before striking it rich.

Since all Americans are in business and all have failed to one degree or another, it follows that going bankrupt in the United States is not a matter of great moment. In a society where everyone commits the same crime, it ceases to be a crime. Tolerance of bankruptcy stems first of all from the fact that it is a common misfortune, but even more important is the fact that it is extremely easy for a bankrupt to get back on his feet. If a man who failed in business were lost forever, he would be abandoned to his misery. People show far greater indulgence toward the unfortunate when they are sure that misfortune is a temporary condition. This is not a generous sentiment but a consequence of human nature.

It should now be clear why there is no law punishing bankruptcy in the United States. Voters and lawmakers—everyone, in short—are in business and vulnerable to failure. No one wants to punish the universal sin. If there were a law, it would seldom be enforced. The people, who make the law through their representatives, may enforce or refuse to enforce it in the courts, where they are represented by juries. Under these circumstances, nothing protects American business from fraud and deception. Anyone can do business without keeping books or records. There is no legal distinction between the businessman who is merely unlucky and the bankrupt who is reckless, spendthrift, or fraudulent. Businessmen are in all respects subject to common law. . . .

[NOTE ON FRENCH MORALS]

"Morality of Frenchwomen": In the United States it is widely believed that French morals are still what they were in the eighteenth century. Many people think that vice is still in fashion in France and that the French spend their time in amorous banter, salon intrigue, and other frivolities. Americans believe this mainly because of the influence of certain widely read English novelists who are themselves a half century out of date because their only knowledge of France comes from books. . . .

"The Indian custom of taking several wives": The substance of the Oneida episode is entirely true. (See *Voyage du major Long aux sources de la rivière Saint-Pierre, au lac Winnepek, au lac des Bois, etc., etc.*, vol. 1, pp. 300 and 280.)[16]

Polygamy exists among all the savage tribes of North America. Every Indian has as many wives as he can find. These women are really in a state of servitude. They prepare the Indian's food, take care of his clothing, and do not leave his hut while he is out hunting or making war. Relations between an Indian and his wives are entirely material; no moral or intellectual element enters in. It is not uncommon to see three sisters serving the same man as wives. The condition of Indian women is the most wretched imaginable. They enjoy none of the prerogatives of women in civilized societies, nor any of the sensual pleasures afforded women under the mores of the East, where they are slaves.

I said that an Indian has as many wives as he can find. It might be more accurate to say that he finds as many as he can feed, because Indian families live in such poverty that parents are willing to give their daughters to any man who can feed them. Thus everything depends on a man's skill as a hunter. A renowned hunter will ordinarily have a large number of wives, because he can provide all of them with what they need to survive.

An Indian marriage takes place without ceremony, and sometimes it is dissolved within days. This is fairly uncommon, however. An Indian who breaks off a marriage that easily would damage his standing with his tribe, and thereafter no family would be inclined to ally itself with him.

As one might imagine, this life of fatigue, misery, and contempt disheartens and disgusts many Indian women, among whom the suicide rate is high (see Major Long, p. 394, vol. 1, 2nd journey, and Tanner's Narrative, New York, 1830).[17] The anecdote that I included in the text of the book was for me one of the most striking examples of the despair into which their wretched lives can plunge these poor women. I describe some tragic funeral scenes, which were not pure figments of my imagination. Indians certainly display great sorrow when a friend dies. They will blacken their faces, fast, forgo the use of red face paint, and abandon all ornament in their dress. They make incisions in their arms and legs and bodies. These outward signs of mourning will often be maintained for quite some time. Major Long reports an encounter with an Indian who had

---

16. Beaumont refers to a story of an Indian leader who, upon taking a second wife, assured his first wife that she would always remain superior to the second wife. Nevertheless, the first wife left home and drowned herself and her children in the rapids of a river.

Narrative of an Expedition to the Source of St. Peter's River, Lake Winnepeek, Lake of the Woods, Etc., by William Hypolitus Keating, was published in Philadelphia in 1824. It was based on the notes of a number of men, including Major Stephen H. Long, taken during an expedition in 1823.

17. John Tanner published *A Narrative of the Captivity and Adventures of John Tanner . . . during Thirty Years Residence among the Indians in the Interior of North America* in 1830 in New York.

given up red face paint for fifteen years in honor of a dear friend and who said that he intended to continue in this way for another ten years. These marks of suffering will be proportionate to the Indian's degree of affection for the deceased. (See Long's *Expedition to the Rocky Mountains,* vol. 1, p. 281. See also Tanner's Narrative, p. 288.)[18] . . .

NOTE ON AMERICAN SOCIABILITY

"American sociability": Although I could cite a thousand examples of the extremely sociable nature of Americans, I shall limit myself to one. In 1832, when M. de Tocqueville and I set out from New Orleans for Washington via an overland route, we first crossed Lake Pontchartrain on a steamboat. Upon our arrival in Pascagoula, where we were to take the stagecoach, we found that all the seats were occupied. This was an occasion for great disappointment, because we were keen that our departure not be delayed. Noticing our consternation, two Americans, whom we did not know at all, stepped down from the coach and offered us their seats in such a kind and straightforward way that it was clear they genuinely hoped we would accept their offer. In many other situations my traveling companion and I observed similar behavior in Americans. Anyone who judges the people of this country on the basis of first impressions risks going seriously wrong. If you ask an American a question, he will answer yes or no without looking at you, or he may not answer at all. You would be tempted to conclude that he was not sociable. You would be wrong. He may be silent, but he is thinking about the question you asked him. He will reflect for some time. If his memory fails him, he will consult someone else, and half an hour later you will have the answer to your question, which you may have forgotten in the meantime. And the answer will be not the half-baked sort of answer that people often give but a full briefing, organized point by point and set forth in chapter and verse. To be sure, this manner of answering is not very polite, but it is surely sociable, because mutual respect is the first condition of sociability. In similar circumstances, how many Europeans would answer the question offhandedly or let you know in the most urbane way that they cannot possibly be of any use to you?

American sociability is chiefly a product of their commercial customs. They need to rely on one another constantly. Business requires them to engage in constant communication. Hence they take it on principle that people should always be ready to do favors for one another. Equality of conditions also helps. All Americans have the same respect for one another that members of the same class have in Europe. This sociability, of whose value the European is keenly aware, sometimes loses part of its charm. People say that New Englanders view social relations purely as an opportunity for business and commerce. Whenever

---

18. First published in Philadelphia in 1822, *Account of an Expedition from Pittsburgh to the Rocky Mountains, Performed in the Years 1819 and '20* was compiled by Edwin James from the notes of a number of men on the expedition, including Major Stephen Long.

they see a newcomer, their first question is: "Is there some business I can do with this man?"

American sociability should not be confused with hospitality. *In general,* Americans are not very hospitable. Hospitality requires leisure, which the businessman does not have. I say "in general" because there are many exceptions to this rule. I have personally experienced some of them, but here I am reporting observations that apply to the majority.

On this point the southern states must be distinguished from the northern. All the southern states have slaves. This has a tremendous influence on southern mores. Because the slaves work, free men are idle. Southerners therefore enjoy a leisure that Northerners do not. They can receive guests without neglecting their affairs. Nearly all Southerners live in relatively isolated dwellings far from cities. A visit from a friend or the arrival of a stranger can be a happy event for the isolated farmer. For people with nothing to do, any pastime is precious. Broadly speaking, moreover, one can say that in town people *see* one another whereas in the country they *receive.* Because relations among Southerners are less self-interested, they are more agreeable than relations among Northerners. Northerners, who always entertain hopes of profiting from their acquaintances, are universally kind. Southerners, who are less calculating in their relationships, are more sincere. Northern manners are so strict that there is something legalistic about them. Southern manners are less stiff and therefore more frank and loose. Since the existence of a slave population establishes an inferior class, all southern whites consider themselves to be members of a privileged class. They think of themselves as superior to all others (the Negroes). The exercise of their rights as masters over slaves further encourages these ideas of superiority and fosters a sense of pride. In the South, whiteness is seen as a title of nobility. Whites are therefore kinder and more respectful to one another because they live in proximity to others whom they hold in contempt. Southern mores thus acquire a certain aristocratic element, which gives rise to certain distinctive formalities and a more exclusive form of sociability than one finds in the North.

"The crudeness of Americans": English exaggerations on this score should not be accepted. Mistress Trolloppe [*sic*] says, vol. 1, p. 27: "I sincerely believe that I would rather live under the same roof as well-tended pigs than be confined to one of these cabins."[19] (She was speaking of a Mississippi steamboat.) This is a *crude* insult. To be sure, Americans, with their habit of chewing tobacco and consequent need to spit, can seem shockingly uncouth to anyone accustomed to polite manners. It is no less certain that their total lack of gallantry is displeasing to women. Finally, anyone who looks to them for elegance of manners or urbanity of forms will be sorely disappointed. But that is where criticism should end.

19. Frances Trollope (1780–1863) was an Englishwoman who, in the wake of her husband's financial decline, traveled to America in 1827. After a short stay at a failing utopian community, she moved to Cincinnati, Ohio. In 1832, she returned to England and published the widely read *Domestic Manners of Americans,* a scathing review of American society.

Americans do not court women, but they do respect them, and this feeling of respect, which does not reveal itself outwardly, is far more profound in the United States than it is in our countries of civilization and gallantry.

Aboard the steamboats of which Mistress Trolloppe speaks, it is true that society is not very polite. The company consists of merchants traveling from Ohio and Kentucky to Louisiana or to the territories west of the Mississippi. These people are not disgusting in the way the English writer supposes, however. The steamboats are on the whole enormous, clean, and elegant. More than two hundred of them navigate constantly up and down the great river. The food is abundant and healthy and the price of travel incredibly low. You can go from Louisville to New Orleans, a distance of five to six hundred leagues, for 120 francs, including food. Having made this voyage, I know whereof I speak. The passenger cabin is comfortable enough to read, write, and work in as though you were in your own home.

In any case, American crudeness also has its good side. Our polite manners and linguistic refinements are often no more than pleasant masks that hide our egoism. Self-interest is no doubt as common among Americans as it is among us, but in the United States there is less hypocrisy of formal manner.

NOTE ON EQUALITY

"Universal equality": A great many writers, English writers in particular, have said that the laws of the United States stipulate a degree of equality higher than is actually found in the country's manners. In the United States, as in any number of European countries, they argue that there exists an arrogant aristocracy contemptuous of the classes that stand below it, and that the Americans, who perfected the theory of equality, do not practice it. I confess that in my travels in the United States I formed a very different impression. Not only did I find political equality realized in action through the participation of all citizens in the affairs of the country, but I also saw social equality everywhere, in wealth, in occupations, and in habits of all sorts.

There exist few great fortunes. The hazards of commerce, which sometimes create them, also destroy them, and in any case they do not survive the equal division of estates required by the inheritance laws.

Occupations, which are highly diverse, do not create dissimilarities of position among those who exercise them. I am not speaking here only of Pennsylvania, where the influence of the Quakers made equality among occupations into something like a religious dogma. I am referring to all the states of the Union. Occupations, jobs, and trades are everywhere looked upon as forms of labor. Commerce, literature, the law, public offices, and religious ministries are all occupations. The people who practice these callings may be more or less happy and more or less wealthy, but all are equal. They do not all do the same thing, but everyone works. From the servant who serves his master to the president of the United States, who serves the nation; from the machine worker, whose brute strength turns a wheel, to the man of genius, who creates sublime ideas, all perform a task and discharge a similar duty. That is why white household *help* in America are said to *assist* their masters rather than *serve* them. It is also one explanation for the way business is done in the United States: to be sure, the American merchant makes as much money as he can. Indeed, I believe that he often deceives the buyer. But he would never take a penny more than he asks, not even if he were the poorest of innkeepers. This is true of the industrial worker, the hired hand, and the domestic servant. All will insist on their *legitimate* salary, the price of their labor, and nothing more. To take more than one is due would be to accept a handout and therefore behave as an inferior. Now we can see why the president of the United States in Washington receives guests of all stations as equals. Anyone who comes to see him begins by shaking his hand. All Americans do the same when they visit the various states of the Union. I have often heard eminent men—chancellors, governors, secretaries of state—speak of "my brother the *grocer*" or "my cousin *the merchant*" as though such a thing were perfectly natural.

To complete the proof that practical equality exists in the United States, I will mention just two facts.

One day, on my way to visit a county jail in New York State in the company of the district attorney, he recounted for me the circumstances of a terrible crime committed by a person I was about to meet. He described the murder for me in the darkest terms, adding that he was the prosecutor who had sent this man to prison. My head was therefore full of the most sinister thoughts by the time we reached the prison, so that I recoiled in horror when I saw the district attorney himself approach the prisoner and shake his hand.

Another time, in a brilliant salon where some of the best people in one of the largest cities of the Union had gathered, I was introduced to a very well-dressed gentleman with whom I chatted briefly. Afterward I asked who he was. A very good-humored fellow told me that he was the county sheriff. When I asked what a "sheriff" was, I learned that he was the executioner. (Note: In the United States, the office of executioner does not have the same shameful connotations as it does in France. Since people there are more respectful of the law, they are more indulgent toward the man who enforces the law. They also try to elevate his office by assigning him other important functions that are in no way ignoble: the sheriff is the chief law enforcement officer.)

Why is it that despite such facts as these, which one encounters in a myriad of forms wherever one turns, there are still people who doubt that Americans practice equality?

The answer has to do with a number of points that are not well understood as well as with certain appearances that a hasty observer is likely to mistake for realities.

In the United States, where wealth and status are uniform, you constantly see people who measure their worth in terms of fortune and attach very great value to birth. People do not say: "This man is worthy of respect because he is honest and just, and this other man is distinguished for his mind and his eloquence." They say: "Smith is worth $10,000, while Jones is worth only half that much."

Within this democracy, the mistress of society, one sometimes encounters instincts that are by nature quite aristocratic. By law children divide their parents' estate equally, but the parents are free to assign different shares to each child as they see fit. They can give everything to one child and disinherit the others. It is common for Americans to use this right to award a very large dowry to a firstborn son, not to reward him for behaving better than his brothers but to establish a designated heir whose position in society feeds his father's pride.

The same Americans you see mingling with people of all estates are often childish in their veneration of their ancient lineage or noble ancestry. Some will rehearse their genealogy for you at length. Sometimes they bend the truth to impress you with the illustriousness of their forebears. It is not unknown for those with genuine aristocratic ancestry to affect a sort of contempt for those who pretend to similar birth without justification. One time, a resident of *** said to me, "You see that gentleman over there who is so proud of his vast fortune? He's nothing but an upstart. His father was a shoemaker."

Americans, who by custom as well as Constitution recognize no nobility, nevertheless afford great respect to noble titles. A foreigner is certain to be greeted enthusiastically, very warmly, merely warmly, or coldly depending on whether he is a duke, marquis, count, or nothing at all. A title immediately attracts attention and creates respect in America. Whether the person who bears it is worth anything at all is a secondary matter. Because their political institutions and social state do not allow them to take noble titles, you find them clinging in every possible way to the smallest aristocratic distinctions. Here I am not speaking of the title of "gentleman," which is claimed by every stagecoach driver and tavern keeper. But anyone who acquires even a modest fortune, whether in business, law, or any other profession, does not fail to add the title "esquire" to his name. Many adopt coats of arms, which they use on their seals and carriages. In Maryland, which is one of the most democratic states, you find ardent democrats attaching an "of" to their name and linking it to the name of an estate.

What can we conclude from these facts? That no real equality exists in the United States and that there is an aristocratic tendency in the country's mores? Certainly not. What is happening in this regard is not a progression from present to future but a remembrance of things past.

When you study either institutions or mores in America, you must never forget that the ancestors of the Americans were English. This point of departure exerts an influence on their laws and habits that, while no doubt steadily diminishing, will never entirely disappear. In England, two things take precedence in shaping opinions about individuals: birth and wealth. This is the true source of the Americans' respect for wealth and birth. It is a tradition that has been transmitted from generation to generation, an old memory, an ancient prejudice that does battle by itself with all the combined power of law and mores. But the battle is not serious: this love of titles, this taste for coats of arms, these family pretensions are merely tricks and expressions of vanity. Wherever there are human beings, their pride seeks distinctions. But the best proof that these distinctions have no real substance among Americans is that common people do not seem to mind them. All power in the United States comes from the people and must return to them. There, you must either be a democrat or be treated as a pariah. The mores of democracy are not to everyone's liking, but everyone is obliged to accept them. Some Americans might be tempted to live more nobly, to adopt less coarse manners, and to create a class superior to the single class that exists. Some suffer at having to shake hands with their shoemaker. Others find it painful that they cannot find anyone willing to work as a lackey and ride at the back of their carriage, no matter how much they are willing to pay. (Note: No white domestic is willing to submit to such service.) Some of these people are pained that the country's public affairs are governed by relatively uneducated masses. Others are indignant that many public offices are filled by mediocre men. They must suppress these sorrows and passions, however. Anyone who exhibited such feelings would immediately incur the wrath of the populace. They must also renounce forever any hope of a political future. Elections are the only route to public office, and on election day the voice of the masses makes itself heard and crushes any hint of resistance or hostility toward the power of the people.

I was surprised to see an English author (Hamilton), who has written with talent about the mores of the United States, fall into the errors I have just outlined by alleging that in practice there is no more equality in the United States than in England.[20] Among other arguments in support of his opinion, he relates an evening he spent in a New York salon, where people of various walks of life had gathered. He writes: "A lady seated next to me was as shocked as I was to see women of such a common sort in a brilliant salon. 'That young woman is certainly pretty,' she observed, 'but she's the daughter of a tobacconist. That one dances well but has had no education.' And so on." From this Mr. Hamilton concluded that conditions in the United States are not equal. Yet he might have responded to the lady who made these observations that "you and those vulgar, common women are equals, because you are together in the same salon."

The only real challenge to social and political equality in the United States involves the black race. But Americans do not think that this violates the principle of equality, because they regard the Negro as belonging to an inferior race. In slave states, where inequality between blacks and whites is most marked, equality among whites is perhaps still more perfect than it is elsewhere. As I said earlier, whiteness is for them a title of nobility, and they treat all whites with the respect and distinction that the members of a *privileged class* show toward one another.

"No inveterate prejudices": In many European countries, it is assumed that

20. Thomas Hamilton published *Men and Manners in America* in Edinburgh and Philadelphia in 1833.

FROM *Marie; or, Slavery in the United States*

the moral and political sciences and even the arts have attained a degree of perfection beyond which nothing remains to be discovered. That is why all the creation of art and industry in Europe bears the distinctive stamp of splendor and duration. Everything on the Continent—laws and constitutions as well as monuments—is made with an eye to eternity. The opposite is true in the United States. No one there believes that anything is definitively fixed. The most beautiful science, the wisest laws, the most marvelous inventions are all regarded as mere trials. Hence everything that is done bears the stamp of the provisional.

Americans will build a building to last twenty years. Who knows if a better means of construction might not be discovered before then? A law may pass that is obscure and poorly drafted. What good would it do to polish the text? Perhaps the flaw will be discovered within a year.

[NOTE ON SELF-CONTROL]

"American sangfroid": During my stay in the United States, I had many opportunities to witness the sangfroid of Americans. I will cite only one example. While traveling down the Ohio on a steamboat along with a number of merchants together with their merchandise, our ship, named the *Fourth of July,* hit a reef known as Burlington Bar, three miles upstream from Wheeling.[21] This is not the place to recount the details of that accident or its dangers, which readers may suppose to have been magnified by the traveler's imagination or memory. I shall simply say that, the vessel having been submerged, all the commercial goods aboard were spoiled or ruined. For some of the men on board, this entailed a considerable financial loss; for others it meant complete ruin. Yet not one of these American businessmen uttered a cry of sorrow or despair. . . .

[NOTE ON LITERATURE]

"Everyone writes and speaks, not without pretention but without talent": The reader should rest assured that I do not entirely agree with the person I am describing.

Would I say that there are no talented writers in a country that can boast of Washington Irving, whose works combine grace of style, delicacy of ideas, and finesse of perception; Cooper, whose genius Europe admires; Edward Livingston, who is both a statesman and a profound philosopher; Robert Walsh, who combines a marvelous facility of style with brilliant conversational barbs and sallies; Jared Sparks, the author of the remarkable *Life of Gouverneur Morris;* and many others whose names must go unmentioned? Would I say that there are no talented orators in the United States, where I have met Daniel Webster, whose Senate speeches, models of style and logic, also reveal a noble and lofty

21. For a fuller account of this incident, see pp. 173 and 175–76.

soul steeped in love of country; Henry Clay, who stands out at the podium for his brilliant delivery and extraordinary talent for improvisation; Edward Everett, whose speeches in the House of Representatives recall the Roman school and the ancient manner; Channings [*sic*], whose sermons contain much of the style and soul of Fénelon;[22] etc. etc.?

Finally, would I say that it is impossible for a man with literary and oratorical talent to be a politician in America when I see John Quincy Adams, who may be more well versed in ancient literature than any European and yet became president of the United States; Albert Gallatin, whose ornate mind and great ability did not prevent his country from calling on him to fulfill diplomatic functions of the highest order, etc. etc.?

Nevertheless, it should not be forgotten that the speaker may be expressing ideas that, despite these and other exceptions, are nevertheless true in general. It is true in general that in the United States one finds not orators but merely lawyers; not writers, but merely journalists.

"Forbidden entertainments": I have already described the austerity of Puritan mores and explained what happens on Sundays. The entertainments that are forsaken on Sunday are not made up on other days of the week. In some states, the law does not rely on the people's natural aversion to games and amusements; it strictly prohibits them. The law of Connecticut strictly prohibits plays as offensive to good morals, and there is no exception even for large cities such as Hartford and New Haven. In New Jersey, horse racing is not allowed, because it is said to be an occasion for large gatherings, gambling, wagers, luxury, disorder, and disruption of habits, all immoral consequences. In Boston it is forbidden to play the organ in the street, because it is said to frighten horses. In New York, the law prohibits public amusements of the sort one sees in Paris on the Champs-Elysées, such as swings, balloons, quoits, etc. Such diversions are a waste of time and a public disturbance.

"Theater": There are three theaters in Philadelphia, two of which are of a high order, in which tragedies and comedies are performed. The third, which is quite inferior to the other two, is given over to crude farces.

The two large theaters are open only during the winter, when nights are long. The third never closes. Even during the winter, the first two theaters are not well attended. The audiences generally comprise the following: foreigners who come to the theater because they don't know what else to do with their evenings; prostitutes, who are attracted by the presence of foreigners; young Americans of dissolute morals; and finally, families of businessmen, whose frequentation of the theater does their reputation no good in American society. People distinguished to any degree by wealth or position do not usually go to the theater. It takes an extraordinary event, such as a visit by a famous actor, to attract them. Then everyone goes, out of fashion rather than taste. To tell the

---

22. François Fénelon (1651–1715) was a French Catholic priest who ministered to the royal family of Louis XIV and was also a prominent writer elected to the Académie française.

truth, nobody in the United States likes the theater, and nearly everyone who goes does so out of boredom. They pay no attention to the play. Americans who go to plays in France are astonished by the silence of the audience and the emotional response to the performance. In America, the audience ignores what is happening on stage. People talk, argue, move about, and use the play as an occasion to drink with their friends. They take no interest whatsoever in the play itself.

The Quakers who founded Pennsylvania strictly prohibited theater for religious reasons. Since they are no longer in the majority, they do not make the law, but traces of their moral outlook remain. The same can be said of the Presbyterians in New England. In Boston, their rigid principles were set aside in order to establish theaters, but most people have no taste for theater and are not in the habit of attending plays. I omit New York, whose American inhabitants seem no fonder of the pleasures of the theater than people in other cities. To be sure, there are more frequent performances, but this is because there are always 20,000 foreigners in New York for whom theater is almost a need. Several theaters could prosper in New York without justifying the conclusion that the Americans there actually enjoyed going to plays.

[NOTE ON THE AMERICAN ARMY]

"Inspire respect in hordes of savage Indians": The army of the United States consists of 6,000 men, all volunteers. The American population reaps the benefits of not being subjected to compulsory recruitment. The disadvantage for the country, however, is that its army is made up of men with no morals who take up the career of arms out of self-interest rather than patriotism, as a means of subsistence rather than of achieving glory.

This situation, which is an evil in itself, has additional unfortunate consequences in the United States. Since the United States does not have to fight many wars, there are very few desertions in its military, because volunteers who take up arms as a way of earning a living desert only in the face of peril. When there is combat with Indian raiding parties, the desertion rate increases, but there is no danger to the country, because the outcome of these battles is hardly in doubt, given the vast inequality between the two sides. Far from the frontier, the danger is perhaps even less.

Six thousand men dispersed across a territory half the size of Europe are hardly noticeable, and they are permanently removed from the civilized population. They occupy forts on the northern and western frontiers of America and move deeper into Indian forests as the American population draws closer. There is not a single American city with an American regiment in garrison. Such an army therefore poses no threat inside the country to either morals or liberty. There is a military school (West Point), which trains officers. All officers are recruited among its graduates. No soldier or noncommissioned officer ever rises through the ranks to become an officer. Admission to West Point is by favor, but to graduate as an officer one must pass an examination. A captain receives a fixed salary of $1,200 (6,260 francs), and counting allowances for housing, stable, etc., this comes to $1,800 (9,540 francs) in all.

Soldiers who leave the military receive no retirement allowance, no matter how long they have served. When they go on leave, however, nothing is deducted from their pay. . . .

[MISCELLANEOUS NOTES]

One of the main reasons why mores are so uniform across America is the enterprising spirit of New Englanders, who have spread throughout the Union as intrepid and tireless pioneers, taking with them the civilization of their native region.

Think of the diverse tribes that cover Africa and Asia. Though in contact with one another, they remain isolated. Separated by a mountain or valley or stream, each preserves its distinct mores and peculiar character. It is therefore striking to find 12 million people spread across a territory that could easily support 150 million, yet all of whom look the same, mingle constantly with one another, and who, thanks to the perfect identity of their tastes, passions, and habits, form but a single family. Such is the power over the mores and fate of a people of the bond created by a common origin, a shared language, a common religion, and similar political institutions. . . .

Every year the English distribute a certain number of rifles, carbines, powder, and lead to the Indians. Their apparent goal is to maintain their friendship with the savage tribes who live close to them in Canada. Their real ulterior motive is to arm the Indians, who are natural enemies of the Americans, and thus enable them to help England in case of war with the United States. At a certain time of the year, close to July, Indians come from all over to take part in this distribution, which takes place on the Upper Canadian frontier. . . .

"Road in a wild forest": The Americans do not wait for people to move into a region to build roads there. They begin by building roads. The roads attract the people. . . .

FROM *Marie; or, Slavery in the United States*

part 6

Tocqueville's Letters on the Writing and Publication of *Democracy in America*

Shortly before the publication of the first volume of *Democracy in America,* a tormented Tocqueville, always afraid of being misunderstood, wrote to his cousin Camille d'Orglandes, "It would be best for me if no one read the book, and I have not yet lost hope that this happiness will be mine."

This part is exclusively devoted to Tocqueville's correspondence on the meaning of his work on America. Among these important letters are several revealing ones in which Tocqueville clarified his intent for his British translator, Henry Reeve. He also engaged in self-criticism, as when responding to a glowing review by another British friend, the young philosopher John Stuart Mill.

From Tocqueville | To Camille d'Orglandes[1]

November 29, 1834[2]

. . . I am not disputatious by nature. When an opinion that I do not share leaves me indifferent, or I am not completely convinced of the opposite, I remain silent. So I have been able to live for quite some time with people who in the end were quite surprised to find me resolutely pursuing a course that they had assumed was quite remote from my preferences. Thus it was not without mature reflection that I decided to write the book that I am about to publish.[3] I do not hide what may be troubling about my position. It is not likely to enlist the active sympathy of anyone. Some will find that at bottom I do not like democracy and treat it rather severely. Others will think that I am incautiously encouraging its spread. It would be best for me if no one read the book, and I have not yet lost hope that this happiness will be mine. I know all that. But here is my answer. It is ten years since I conceived most of the ideas that I recently explained to you. Since they did not please me, I examined them from every angle before accepting them. I went to America only to remove my remaining doubts. The penitentiary system was a pretext. I took it as a passport. In the United States, I found a thousand things that fell short of my expectations, but I also saw several that vividly illuminated my thinking. I discovered facts that struck me as useful to know. I did not go there with the idea of writing a book; the idea of the book came to me there. I believe that each of us owes society an account of our thoughts as well as our strengths. When we see our fellow human beings in peril, our obligation is to go to their aid. The strong do a great deal, the weak little, but just because one is weak is no reason to fold one's arms and refuse one's assistance. I therefore told myself this: If what I am about to publish is no good, no one will even notice the book's existence. My self-esteem will suffer and nothing else. If, on the other hand, the book contains something useful, the danger that I may personally incur in writing it is in no way an argument that I should refrain. If, finally, it should somehow do harm, which I cannot believe, I would surely be in despair, but I would have nothing for which I feel I should reproach myself.

Now, have I chosen the most suitable form in which to express my ideas? You tell me, dear friend, that I am wrong to show my hand fully from the very

1. Camille d'Orglandes (1798–1871) was a cousin of Tocqueville; his father was a peer of France.

2. A draft of this letter was published in Tocqueville's correspondence with Louis de Kergorlay, who had been incorrectly identified as the intended recipient (see O.C., XII, 1, 373–75).

3. Tocqueville is referring to the first volume of *Democracy in America,* which he published in 1835.

first words. There is much truth and justice in this observation. I made up my mind to take the course I did for the following reasons: It would have been impossible to find a place in the remainder of the book for the set of ideas that form the introduction, yet I did not want readers to be unaware of the basis of my thinking. I would probably have preferred to place this section somewhere in the body of the text, but I chose to put it at the beginning rather than leave it out altogether.

You also feel that I have not been artful enough or cautious enough in setting forth my ideas. I do not think I could have followed your advice without doing myself a disservice. The book's only merit is the fact that it was dictated by what I truly and deeply feel. This will perhaps entitle me to indulgence for any errors the work may contain. I would be afraid of forfeiting this advantage if I were to veil my thought behind some more or less obvious disguise. In any case, it would have been very difficult for me to do so. Although it is very easy for me to remain entirely silent, as I told you earlier, once I open my mouth I cease to find words clear enough to express my ideas, even though ours is the clearest language in the world. This is a habit that I have sometimes sought to correct when I was obliged to speak in public, but I never managed to do it. . . .

From Tocqueville | To John Stuart Mill[4]

Saturday night [June 1835]

My dear Mr. Mill,

I received your letter the day before yesterday, in the evening. I wanted to reply yesterday, but various circumstances prevented me from doing so. I will not tell you that your letter, as to its form, would do honor to a Frenchman or that few Frenchmen can write as well in their own language as you do. I will not tell you all that because we are not at the stage of compliments, and in any case I have too much gratitude to express as to the *substance* of your thoughts. I can think of no higher flattery than the opinion of me that you express in your letter. My only fear—and I say this in all sincerity—is that it may be exaggerated. I love liberty by taste, equality by instinct and reason. These two passions, which so many people pretend to have, I believe I truly feel and am prepared to make great sacrifices for them. These are the only advantages I grant myself. They have far more to do with the absence of certain common vices than with the possession of any rare qualities.

To return to the principal subject of your letter, I will tell you that the longer I stay in England, the more inclined I feel to accept the role in your journal that its principal editors have seen fit to assign me, and I will explain frankly why I feel this way increasingly.

4. John Stuart Mill (1806–1873), a liberal English intellectual, befriended Tocqueville in 1835, when he reviewed the first volume of *Democracy in America.* Mill became most famous for his theories of political economy, particularly his revision of Jeremy Bentham's theory of utilitarianism.

I confess that when I came to this country, I had fairly substantial prejudices against the Democratic Party. I compared it to the party that occupies an analogous position in France, and that comparison was not favorable to it. You know France well enough to know that one of our greatest miseries is the exploitation of democratic ideas—the only ideas with any future in our modern societies—by a great many people who do not understand them and whose efforts serve only to alienate from democracy many good minds that would otherwise be drawn to it. A French democrat is in general a man who wants to place exclusive control of society in the hands not of the people as a whole but of a certain portion of the people and who, to achieve that end, clearly comprehends only one means: physical force. Unfortunately, there are many other traits that might be added to this portrait, but these are the principal ones.

Everything that I have seen of English Democrats leads me to believe that although their views are often narrow and exclusive, their goal is at least the true goal that friends of democracy ought to adopt. In reality, their ultimate purpose seems to be to put the majority of citizens in a position to govern and to make them capable of governing. Faithful to their principles, they do not claim to be forcing the people to be happy in the way they deem most appropriate, but they want to put them in a position to recognize that way and then to adopt it. I myself am a Democrat in this sense. To bring modern societies to this point by degrees seems to me the only way to save them from barbarism or slavery. All the energy and will I possess will always be in the service of such a cause, when represented as it is in this country by educated and honest men. As you know, I am not one to overestimate the ultimate outcome of the great Democratic Revolution that is taking place in the world at this moment. I do not look upon it as the Israelites looked upon the Promised Land. But all things considered, I regard it as useful and necessary, and I move toward it resolutely and without hesitation, enthusiasm, or, I hope, weakness.

There are no doubt many other things to say on this subject. But I write in haste and leave everything that escapes me for now until we are able to chat freely. I asked you to let me know what you wanted from me for your review, because I wasn't very clear about what I could do.[5] Your letter does not dispel my doubts, but it does induce me to put my mind to dispelling them. I positively promise to do so as soon as I am in a position to think seriously about things. Give some thought to this yourself and share your ideas with me. In the meantime, please accept my esteem and friendship.

Alexis de Tocqueville . . .

5. Tocqueville eventually contributed an essay entitled "Political and Social Condition of France Before and Since 1789," which Mill published in the *London and Westminster Review* in April 1836.

From Tocqueville | To M. le comte Molé

Paris, August 1835

... I always thought that a year was too short a time to properly appreciate the United States, and it is infinitely easier to formulate clear ideas and precise thoughts about the American Union than about Great Britain. In America, all laws in a sense originate from the same thought. All of society is based, as it were, on a single fact. Everything derives from a unique principle. One might compare America to a large forest traversed by a number of straight roads all culminating in the same point. If you find that hub, everything becomes clear in an instant. But in England, all the roads cross, and it is only by following each of them that it becomes possible to formulate a clear idea of the whole. ...

From Tocqueville | To John Stuart Mill

December 3, 1835
Château de Baugy,

My dear Mill,

I've just received from Paris the third issue of the *London Review* and your letter dated the 19th of last month.[6] I read both carefully, and now all that remains is to discuss them with you.

Your article in the *Review* contains more praise of me than an author could possibly want, no matter how much pride he may have been endowed with by his Creator, and as you know, pride is something with which He has liberally endowed the authorial breed. But I must tell you that there is something in your article that gave me even more pleasure than your praise. Of all the writers who have been kind enough to bring my work to the attention of the public, you are the only one who has understood me *entirely,* who has been able to grasp my ideas as a whole and divine the purpose for which I have been striving, and who has at the same time kept the details clearly in view. It would be too easy to be a writer if there were many readers of your caliber! Your article therefore filled me with real joy. I will treasure it as proof to myself that I can indeed be understood. I needed such proof to console me for all the erroneous judgments that I see my work has occasioned. The people I come across either want to reduce me to some opinion I have expressed or claim to share with me opinions I do not hold. The material success of the book is holding up nicely, but I really do not know when the public will pronounce its definitive judgment of the work.

To get back to your article, I repeat that nothing else that I have read about my work is so thorough. You have penetrated more deeply into my thinking than anyone else and, having seen clearly what is to be found there, you freely choose what is worthy of your approval and what deserves your blame. I am not exaggerating when I say that I read your critiques with as much interest as your

6. Mill's favorable review of volume 1 of *Democracy in America* appeared in the *London Review* 1 (*Westminster Review* 30) (October 1835): 85–129.

praise. The friend is everywhere in evidence beneath the censor. Your criticism is therefore instructive and does not wound. I would like to respond to all of your objections, my dear Mill, but in that case I would send you a book rather than a letter. A conversation—and I hope to converse with you soon—will shed more light on the questions that divide us than a voluminous correspondence. I do nevertheless want to put forward a few remarks.

Paris, December 5.

I had written this much of my letter, my dear Mill, when I learned that my mother, who lives in Paris, was in grave danger. As you can imagine, I hastened to her side. I found her somewhat improved, but we are still quite worried about her. I hope that you will forgive me if, in my present state of mind, I postpone the rather lengthy discussion promised by the last words I wrote in Baugy. Yet I am still not done responding to your article, which I reread attentively on my way here. Several passages seemed quite brilliant. I know of no other friend of democracy who has yet dared to make so sharp and clear a distinction between *delegation* and *representation* or who has better defined the political meaning of these two words.[7] Rest assured, my dear Mill, that you have thereby put your finger on the most important question—that, at any rate, is my firm belief. The challenge for the friends of democracy is not so much to find means to govern the people as it is to induce the people to choose those most capable of governing them and to give them enough power to supervise the general conduct of their governors without subjecting every governmental action or method to minute scrutiny. That is the problem. I am deeply convinced that the future of modern nations depends on its solution. But how few people even see it, and if they do see it, how few call it to the attention of the public! Yet I believe that if the problem were plainly stated, many people who still waver would become sincere friends of democracy, and the most dangerous weapons would be snatched from the hands of democracy's enemies.

The favorable notice I have just received from the *London Review* is further incentive to write the articles I promised. The first is well advanced. But both the beauty and the difficulty of the subject seem to increase with each passing day. You probably think that it is taking me a long time to finish. You would forgive me if you knew how difficult it is for me to be satisfied with my work and how impossible to leave things in an unfinished state. I have always believed that the public was entitled to expect the utmost of authors, and I try to live up to this expectation in my own work. I am therefore toiling over your article as if it were to appear in French under my own name. I would count myself quite happy if, as reward for my effort, I were to produce something that pleased you and the enlightened readers of your *Review*.

As for the author's name, I would be glad if it were not overtly mentioned.

---

7. Mill reported that Tocqueville's distinction between these concepts had prompted him to develop his own political thinking, particularly in regard to moderating the degree of his radical beliefs.

As you can imagine, writing about *my country* in a *foreign* journal, I must maintain a certain reserve, and it may be useful to me should the need arise not to be the acknowledged and avowed author of certain ideas, and especially not to appear to have resorted to an English intermediary to publish them. Furthermore, it seems to me that if you persist in thinking that my name might somehow be useful to you, it would be very easy to circulate the information without publishing it openly. . . .

From Tocqueville | To an American correspondent

This Monday evening [1835 or 1836?]

. . . Are there statistical documents similar to those published by the newsletter of the book trade in France that would reveal the number and subject matter of works published each year in the United States in science, the arts, philosophy, religion, and literature in the strict sense? If there is no such document for the Union as a whole, as may well be the case, might there at least be one for the major states? If so, what must I do to obtain it?

If there is no statistical document, what English or American work would be most useful for finding out more about the movement of ideas in the United States and the literary consequences of those ideas?

Finally, sir, would it be too great an imposition to ask for your personal opinion on this important and interesting subject? In France we are quite familiar with Messrs. W. Irving and Cooper and somewhat familiar with Dr. Channing.[8] We have heard of a few other writers but have never been in a position to judge them. We have scarcely any knowledge of the reputation of your poets, your philosophers, your economists, your politicians, and even your scholars. This is a gap in our knowledge that I would like to repair, but I confess that on this point I am almost as much in the dark as my readers. My sense, which may be wrong, is that Americans have until now acted more than they have written, which is to be expected in a young and vigorous society in which all the powers of intelligence can be put to use outdoors. For nations as for men, youth is the time for action rather than reflection. The love of theoretical studies and the taste for literary pleasure come later. I offer you these reflections, sir, though I am quite prepared to be told that I am wrong if you are willing to take the trouble to prove it to me, for on this point you are a far better judge than I. I would therefore be most grateful if you would share your ideas on this subject with me. You are familiar with all the American authors either personally or through their writing. Could you let me know which are the most prominent, what the nature

8. French translations of the fictional works of Americans Washington Irving (1783–1859) and James Fenimore Cooper (1789–1851) began to appear in France in 1822. Cooper became particularly popular for his descriptions of American Indians and landscapes. Most Frenchmen familiar with William Ellery Channing (1780–1842), the famous Unitarian minister, knew of him through the French translation of his book *Remarks on the Life and Character of Napoleon* (1827).

of their talent is, and what particular cast of mind they exhibit? I would not ask this of you, sir, without adding that I beg you not to inconvenience yourself to meet my request. A short note supplemented by verbal explanations would suffice, and if you find the idea tiresome, I urge you not to bother. . . .

From Tocqueville | To Henry Reeve[9]

Château de Baugy
June 5, 1836

My dear Reeve,

Your news that a new edition of my *Democracy* is needed in England touched me greatly. I was afraid for the fate of the first edition, since Mr. Senior[10] and other clever people who were also my friends predicted that it would not sell and that the editor would lose money. But in this century of Democratic Revolution, everything written on democracy in any language sells.

As for your questions, which I am obliged to answer in haste because time is short, I must first tell you that my third volume has doubled in my mind since we last saw each other. Rather than a single volume, I shall be *forced* to publish two. I say *forced* because on this point I do not share the opinion of the booksellers and am determined to publish in the smallest possible format. Ultimately, however, there are limits to concision, and I have found it impossible to fit what I had to say in a single volume. Since the book is to be longer, it will cost me more in time and effort. I am sure that it will not be ready for publication before the end of next spring, or almost a year from now. Indeed, I will have to make great haste to meet that deadline. At that time, I think I will publish the two new volumes separately, postponing until later the correction of the first two and the coordination of the whole, which I will not be able to do without a long period of leisure that I cannot anticipate for some time to come. Hence you should not wait to do your translation or, rather, to reprint the one that exists. I ask you only to obtain one of the latest of the published French editions. You will find two or three small corrections of no great importance but of which you should take advantage. Among other things the one concerning the good Franklin, to whom I devoted as much attention as to a patriarch. I have no doubt that you can easily obtain copies of the latest editions in London.

Since the translator can be considered up to a certain point an extension of the author, so that their interests are never entirely distinct, I will share with you the news I have just received: the Académie française, at its meeting last Thursday, awarded me the grand prize of 8,000 francs established by M. de Mon-

---

9. Henry Reeve (1814–1895) was an English lawyer and journalist. He met Tocqueville in Paris in 1835, and they quickly became good friends. Reeve translated into English the two volumes of *Democracy in America* in 1835 and 1840 and *The Old Regime and the Revolution* in 1856. Reeve became editor of the *Edinburgh Review* in 1855.

10. Nassau William Senior (1790–1864) was a professor of political economy at Oxford whom Tocqueville had first met in 1833.

thion for the most useful book published in the past year. I had two-thirds of the votes, although the discussion was quite stormy and from the beginning took on an entirely political character. Royer-Collard, Lamartine, and Villemain spoke at length in my favor; Viennet, Michaud, and Lacretelle spoke at even greater length against me. The deliberation lasted three days. I have just learned that in the end I carried the day. But the result of the deliberation is not yet public, so do not speak of it.[11]

Forgive me for this hastily scribbled note. I am very pressed and fear that you may not be able to read me. I cannot close, however, my dear Reeve, without assuring you once again of my sincere affection.

Alexis de Tocqueville

P.S. Please give my regards to your mother and Mrs. Austin. I *authorize* you to do a second edition only on condition that you send me a copy. I tell you without reproach that I received only the first volume of the first edition.

I almost forgot two criticisms that I received recently from an Englishman, which I send to you, my dear translator, because you deserve them. On page 165 of the second volume I say something about the *Monarchies absolues de l'Europe* and you say *the Monarchical states of Europe*. Before that, on page 152, I said: *les monarchies absolues avaient déshonoré le despotisme,* but you say, *monarchical institutions have thrown an odium upon Despotism.* I beg you to observe, dear sir, that you make me out to be even more of a scoundrel than I am, because what I said about *absolute monarchies* you have me saying about monarchies in general. This is a peccadillo to which awareness of my other crimes has not left me insensible.

From Tocqueville | To Captain Basil Hall[12]

Château de Baugy, June 19, 1836

... In your opinion I portrayed the *domestic happiness* of Americans too indulgently. Since it is very important to me to clarify this delicate issue, to which I shall be obliged to return in my final two volumes, I hope you will allow me to offer a few observations. I did not argue that American households were places ruled by great tenderness of feeling. What I wanted to say was that they are places of great order and purity, and that this is an essential condition of order and tranquility in political society itself. I felt that this was due in part to the principles and character that American women brought to marriage, and it was in that sense that I said that women exerted considerable indirect influence on

11. Tocqueville and Beaumont had won the Montyon prize in 1833 for their book, *On the Penitentiary System in the United States, and Its Application in France.*

12. After retiring from the British navy, Captain Basil Hall (1788–1844) devoted himself to literary and scientific pursuits. He visited America in 1827 and 1828 and published his *Travels in North America* in 1829, in which he critiqued American manners. Hall had asked Tocqueville to send him a copy of the English translation of *Democracy in America* for review in the *London Quarterly Review.* Tocqueville's letter is a response to a second letter from Hall, in which he expressed a number of criticisms amidst his praise for the work.

politics. In the United States more than in any other country I know, it seemed to me that it was agreed by *universal consent* that a woman once married owed herself entirely to her husband and children. It was for that reason that I said that *no higher or more just ideal of conjugal happiness ever existed anywhere.* The extreme purity of morals in marriage ultimately seemed to me to be the primary though not the sole condition of such happiness, and in this respect America seems to me to have the advantage even over England. My conduct has demonstrated the high ideal I held of Englishwomen.[13] But if virtue is, as I doubt not, the general rule for Englishwomen, it seems to me that there are still fewer exceptions to that rule on the other side of the Atlantic. On this point I would offer the following remark: in the United States I never heard a married woman spoken of in jest. American books assume that all women are chaste. Even foreigners, whose tongues are not tied by custom, admit that there is nothing to controvert this fact. Indeed, I met some foreigners corrupt enough to express regret about this, and I took those regrets as incontrovertible proof. No such unanimity is evident in England. In England I met conceited young men who had few kind things to say about the honor of their female compatriots. I met moralists who complained that the morality of women, especially in the lower classes, was no longer what it once had been. Finally, your writers have been known to take it for granted that conjugal vows are sometimes violated in England. In America, so far as I know, one finds none of this. . . .

From Tocqueville | To Henry Reeve

Château de Baugy by Compiègne
November 21, 1836

My dear Reeve,

I've just received your letter, and I want to respond without delay.

I shall speak to you first about the matter that interests us both most particularly, which is neither more nor less than democracy, the great affair of the modern world. (I beg you to believe that I do not mean to say that my book interests the modern world but only its subject matter.) Having given the brief explanation that my statement required, I return to the subject. As you may know, I was obliged to accompany Madame de Tocqueville to the baths at Baden in Switzerland, and I lost two months there, and I have been working like the devil ever since to make up for it. Though I have worked *twice* as hard as usual since my return, I realize that those two months are gone forever, and I must reconcile myself to the fact. The consequence of this is that I will not be able to publish *this* winter, and that being the case, I am no longer interested in going to press before the end of next summer. As you will have gathered, you must not count on me to occupy your long evenings in Hampstead, and you have at least six months ahead of you if not more. I hope, moreover, that the book will not

---

13. Tocqueville had married Mary "Marie" Mottley, an Englishwoman, eight months earlier.

lose anything for waiting. I have never worked at anything with so much ardor. I think about my subject day and night, and I flatter myself that, because of this, I have become absolutely antisocial. I would never have imagined that a subject that I have already considered from so many angles could present itself to me in so many new guises. In the end, it may be the mountain that gives birth to a mouse. But if my book fails to satisfy the public, at least it will have kept me going full tilt for nearly a year, which is already a great boon as far as I am concerned.

I have been extremely happy for the past two days because of an article I read in the July issue of the *North American Review.* My book is reviewed in the most flattering of terms. The author, whom I do not know, says several times that I am the first European to have grasped the spirit of American institutions and offered an accurate description of them.[14] I read this with genuine pleasure. I spent so little time in the United States and had so little leisure to delve deeply into things, and in my text I so often reasoned by analogy, as Cuvier did in his study of animal fossils,[15] that I was truly afraid of having committed one of those gross errors that immediately destroy your credibility with knowledgeable readers. Thank God this was not the case.

You beg my pardon for providing me with so many details about the northern states. I will not excuse you for their brevity. Nothing could interest me more. Absolute governments are *terra incognita* for me, and I daily recognize that I may need these ideas. My mind is too confined within a narrow sphere, so as soon as I can escape, I shall hasten to do so. I intend to travel extensively in Germany in one year. The trouble is that I do not know the language, and unfortunately my mind has always been highly resistant to words. . . .

From Tocqueville | To Gustave de Beaumont

Baugy, November 22, 1836

. . . A few days ago I was truly happy to read an article about my book in the *North American Review.*[16] The article was in general quite flattering, but what particularly impressed me was the praise for my impartiality and above all for the great *truthfulness* of my portraits. As you know, I worked on America in almost the same way that Cuvier worked on his antediluvian animals, making constant use of philosophical deductions and analogies. I was therefore afraid that I might at times be making monumental errors, principally in the eyes of the people of the country. As you can imagine, it is very pleasant to hear them say that no other writer has plumbed the spirit of American institutions more deeply than I or rendered their detail more accurately. . . .

14. The unsigned review was written by Edward Everett and was published in the *North American Review* 43, no. 92 (July 1836): 178–206.

15. Georges Cuvier (1769–1832) was a French scientist best known for his zoologic studies, published most famously in *Le règne animal.*

16. See Tocqueville's November 21, 1836, letter to Reeve, above.

From Tocqueville | To Henry Reeve

Paris, March 22, 1837

My dear Reeve,

I was extremely pleased to receive your letter. You gave me news both of yourself and of your translation, and both interest me greatly. Indeed, I believe that I am sufficiently unselfish to prefer the prosperity of the former to that of the latter. Praise the Lord that both are doing well. I previously received Sir Robert Peel's speech and the brochure of an American citizen.[17] I don't know if I'm in your debt for either of these. You would be doing me a favor if you were to keep me informed of similar publications, if there are any. Quite apart from my keen interest in judgments of me, I am delighted to see the various ways in which I am portrayed by people of diverse political passions. I would like to compile a collection of such portraits. Thus far I haven't found any that are a perfect likeness. They are all determined to make me out to be a party man, which I am not. They impute passions to me, whereas I have only opinions, or, rather, I have only one passion: love of liberty and human dignity. To me, all forms of government are merely more or less perfect means of satisfying this sacred and legitimate human passion. People attribute either democratic or aristocratic prejudices to me. I might have had either had I been born in another century and another country. But the accident of my birth made it quite easy for me to avoid both. I came into the world at the end of a long revolution, which, after destroying the old state, created nothing durable in its place. Aristocracy was already dead when my life began, and democracy did not yet exist. Instinct could not therefore impel me blindly toward one or the other. I lived in a country that for forty years had tried a bit of everything without settling definitively on anything; hence, I did not easily succumb to political illusions. Since I belonged to the old aristocracy of my country, I felt no hatred toward or natural jealousy of the aristocracy, and since that aristocracy had been destroyed, I felt no natural love for it either, because one forms strong attachments only to the living. I was therefore close enough to know it well yet distant enough to judge it dispassionately. I would say as much about the democratic element. No family memory or personal interest gave me a natural or necessary inclination toward democracy, but I had suffered no personal injury from it. I had no particular grounds to love or hate it apart from those provided by reason. In short, I was so perfectly balanced between past and future that I did not feel naturally and instinctively drawn toward either, and it took no great effort for me to contemplate both in tranquility.

17. Sir Robert Peel (1788–1850), British prime minister from 1834 to 1835, was a conservative politician in the Tory Party. In one of his published speeches, he cautioned his audience not to take British travel accounts at face value and argued that any intelligent American would advise Britons not to try to "improve" their society by introducing more democratic principles into Britain. The American author of the second pamphlet refuted Peel's characterization of American society and Americans' opinions on democracy. Both pamphlets were published in 1837.

But enough about me. Let us discuss the principal purpose of your letter. You want to know when you might expect the first pages of the two new volumes. I do not think that I will be in a position to go to press before December. Indeed, I have no interest in doing so sooner. It is best for a literary work not to appear during the summer, but once into the winter, the month makes little difference.

As for the difficulties that Gosselin may raise in connection with the proofs, I hope that we can eliminate them. You are aware of what makes him so nervous on this score. Counterfeiters from Brussels went so far as to *steal* Lamartine's proofs from his printer.[18] You may have heard about this affair. In any case, I am confident that we will be able to do what we want to do. . . .

From Tocqueville | To Jared Sparks

At the Château de Tocqueville, August 21, 1837

My dear Mr. Sparks,

I recently received the two letters you were kind enough to send on June 6 and July 5 of this year. I am enormously grateful for all the trouble you have taken with the translation of the second part of my book. I am in your debt for many other things as well. Nevertheless, I cannot accept the proposition you mention from the commercial house in Boston, because I've promised an English friend of mine to send him the proofs of my book to translate and publish in England. Hence I am no longer free to meet the conditions on which the American publisher insists. So let us drop this project, which I valued as proof of your interest in my work. I am most devoted to all the friends I left on the other side of the Atlantic, and I always take great pleasure from any token of their remembrance.

Recently, I had as guests in my home M. de Corcelle and his wife, who, as you may know, is a granddaughter of General La Fayette.[19] I showed them the part of your letter dealing with the excerpt from Morris's diary that you were told had displeased the general's family.[20] M. and Mme de Corcelle asked me to thank you for your kind and warm words about their grandfather and to assure you that no member of the family holds you responsible for the excerpt in question and that all regard you as a true friend. M. de Beaumont and his wife, who

18. Charles Gosselin, a Parisian publisher, had published works of the French poet Alphonse de Lamartine (1790–1869).

19. Francisque de Corcelle (1802–1892) was an aide to Lafayette in 1830, and like Beaumont, he married one of the general's granddaughters. Corcelle had reviewed the first volume of *Democracy in America* in 1835 and had subsequently developed a close friendship with Tocqueville. He held a number of political appointments throughout his life and served as an ambassador to the Vatican in 1849 when Tocqueville was minister of foreign affairs.

20. Jared Sparks had published *The Life of Gouverneur Morris* in 1832 and had heard that certain passages from Morris's journal regarding Lafayette had offended Lafayette's family. As he was preparing his volume for a French translation, Sparks considered omitting these passages so as not to call into question Americans' respect for Lafayette.

is also a granddaughter of La Fayette, begged me to convey similar sentiments. They arrived here yesterday on their way back from England. While here, Beaumont intends to finish or at least make good progress on a major work on Ireland, on which he has been working for the past two years and for which I have very high hopes.

I am pleased to learn that business is improving and that the unprecedented crisis that you have just experienced will soon be over. I regard the calm and determined way in which your country extricated itself from its distress—a consequence, I believe, of your own errors—as evidence of the nation's and of its constitution's significant strengths. My impression is not widely shared in Europe, however. There is, my dear Mr. Sparks, no blinking the fact that what has been happening in America for the past three years has done major damage to your country's reputation on this side of the ocean and noticeably slowed the development of liberal ideas and institutions.[21]

Once again, my dear Mr. Sparks, I beg you to accept my thanks and the assurance of my sincere friendship.

Alexis de Tocqueville

From Tocqueville | To John Quincy Adams[22]

Paris, December 4, 1837

. . . It was only upon my return from the country a few days ago that I discovered the letter you did me the honor of writing on June 12, along with the three volumes you kindly enclosed. Hence I was unable to thank you sooner. I now do so belatedly.

It is with deep gratitude, sir, that I receive the three speeches you were good enough to send me. I have already read all three and admired them as they deserved. Coming from you, however, they are all the more precious to me. I have

21. Widespread speculation, a year of bad harvests, and the dynamics of the international economy put the American economy in a precarious situation in the 1830s. Andrew Jackson's refusal to renew the charter for the Second Bank of the United States and the widespread recall of banknotes when specie was scarce exacerbated economic problems and spurred the Panic of 1837, during which the failure of thousands of banks and businesses caused a five-year depression.

To the French, the Panic of 1837 seemed to demonstrate the dangers of widespread credit and the destabilizing effects of a democratic government in a diverse society.

22. Adams wrote to Tocqueville on June 12, 1837, complimenting him on the French and English editions of *Democracy in America* and thanking him for a copy of Tocqueville and Beaumont's prison report. However, Adams also asked Tocqueville to make a correction in future editions of *Democracy* (see *Tocqueville on America after 1840,* ed. Craiutu and Jennings, 496–98). Tocqueville had written that Adams dismissed many civil servants upon his election to the presidency; Adams stated that he had removed only two civil servants from their positions after they committed crimes. Andrew Jackson, who defeated Adams's bid for reelection in 1828, was the first president systematically to dismiss civil servants appointed by previous presidents, thus creating what critics called the spoils system of political patronage. Tocqueville made this correction in future editions of his text.

long been among your admirers, sir, and I have always considered it my good fortune to have had the opportunity to make your acquaintance.

I was most pleased to receive the request you were kind enough to make regarding a sentence in my book concerning you. Rest assured that this sentence will disappear from the sixth edition, which is to appear, I believe, this winter. I am delighted that you have given me this opportunity to do you a service by correcting an error that I regret having made. The information to which you object and which you say is incorrect was imparted to me in America (as my notes confirm) by a man whose veracity I believed I could count on.

The flattering things that you say about my book touched me deeply, sir. They gave me great pleasure not only for themselves but also for the source of the admiration. My work is intended for men, like you, of lofty character and spirit, and their approval is precious to me.

The book that you have read is, incidentally, only the first part of the work that I want to publish about America, which is to comprise four volumes. I am now working on the last two, which will deal with mores and how democratic institutions influence them. I truly hope that this second part, which will appear, I think, in about a year, will meet with your approval as much as its predecessor.

Even as I remain preoccupied with the United States in a theoretical way, I am, as you might imagine, constantly mindful of the daily news from your country. I will not hide from you my deep distress at what has been happening in America over the past few years. The deplorable unrest that has affected various parts of the Union in regard to blacks; the violent and illiberal principles put forth and supported by many of your statesmen in these circumstances; the dispute between the president and the bank; and, finally, the commercial crisis from which you have only just emerged—all these things have singularly diminished the moral authority of the United States in Europe. All sincere friends of humanity and liberty among us bemoan this result, even as all proponents of despotism rejoice in it. Americans are insufficiently aware of the attention that their faults attract around the world and of the advantage that the enemies of freedom in all corners of the globe derive from them. If they knew these things, I believe that they would exhibit greater self-control.

It is up to men like you, sir, to teach your fellow citizens what great power they wield and how to make use of it.

I beg you, sir, to accept my most respectful wishes.

Alexis de Tocqueville

From Tocqueville | To Henry Reeve

Baugy, January 3, 1838

. . . The present situation in Canada seems to me to be an extremely serious matter that calls for very close attention from your lawmakers.[23] The Canadians are

23. Tocqueville is referring to the declaration of martial law in Montreal in December of 1837 to quell the rebellion of the French Canadian Louis Joseph Papineau and the Patri-

a distinctive people in America, a people with a distinct and firmly implanted nationality, constituting a new and sound nation with a martial past and a language, religion, laws, and mores all its own and a population that is more composite than any other in the New World. It may be possible to conquer it, but it cannot be forcibly dissolved into the Anglo-American race. Such a result can be achieved only by time, not by legislation or the sword. At the time of my visit, the [French] Canadians were full of prejudices against the English who lived among them, but they seemed sincerely devoted to the English government, which they regarded as an honest broker between themselves and the English population, which they feared. How did they become enemies of this government? I do not know. But I find it difficult to believe that the colonial administration has not made some major errors for which it needs to reproach itself, if not in substance then at least in form. In the past England's position seemed to me a singularly happy one, so much so that I was inclined to believe that if your country retained possession of Canada, it was solely because of the coexistence there of two different peoples on the same soil. Had there been only English, they would soon have become Americans. How did you lose that unique and favorable position? I do not know.

In sum, my dear friend, be wary of what English settlers in Canada and enemies of the United States tell you about the [French] Canadian population. Their vision is distorted by unbelievable prejudices, and they will lose control of the government if it sees through their eyes alone. Rest assured that if the civil war in Canada ever becomes an all-out and prolonged battle between races, the colony will be lost to Great Britain. The [French] Canadians are much inferior to their neighbors in the art of producing wealth. They are merchants and above all pioneers, and less enterprising, and sooner or later they will be surrounded by men of the English race and confined within certain limits. Yet they still constitute an energetic tribe capable of enthusiasm, commitment, and sporadic but vigorous effort. Traditions passed down since the time of the American wars still exist among them, and no one will ever be able to force them to remain attached to the metropolis for very long against their will. . . .

From Tocqueville | To Louis de Kergorlay

Baugy, February 2, 1838

. . . It seems to me that the natural effect of a social state that makes all conditions almost equal is to make everyone eager to change places while not encour-

---

ote party. In Upper Canada, the Scottish Canadian journalist William Lyon Mackenzie (1795–1861) led a simultaneous revolt based in Toronto. It was put down much more easily than the one in Lower Canada.

Despite tensions between inhabitants of French and British descent, both revolts included anglophone and francophone participants who wanted a republican government in Canada. Though the Canada Act had created a Canadian assembly, all legislation had to be approved by the British government. In 1841, the Union Act merged the two provinces into the single Province of Canada, but tensions surrounding colonial governance continued for decades.

aging anyone to go very far. It makes ambition (understood in the broadest possible sense) universal but decreases the number of great ambitions, so that what is lost in grandeur is compensated by what is gained in extent. Desires grow more numerous and perhaps more intense, but they attach to smaller objects. Such is the general theory, whose outlines seem fairly clear. Upon reflection, however, various theoretical and practical objections give me pause, and I want to avoid vagueness.

When I consider what is happening in America, the theory seems to me to coincide exactly with the facts. Nearly everyone is absorbed by the desire to get ahead, to improve his lot, to increase his well-being or fortune. Yet occasionally I come across people whose ambitions may not seem very great in comparative terms but are immense to the individuals who entertain them. For instance, the ambition to amass a fortune often takes on colossal dimensions here. The idea of governing the state sometimes grips the imagination of the humblest of citizens. What becomes of my theory in light of these exceptional cases, which exist not in spite of equality but because of it? . . .

From Tocqueville | To Pierre-Paul Royer-Collard[24]

Tocqueville, August 30, 1838

. . . Now that I can envision nearly the whole of the book, I see that it is much more about the general effects of equality on mores than about the particular effects that equality has produced in America. Is that a flaw? Have my previous readers become so attached to what I have already said about the United States that they will be reluctant to follow me onto new ground? In short, will they prefer America to me? This is a difficult problem, the solution to which has given me a great deal of trouble, because the flaw, if it exists, is now irreparable. . . .

From Tocqueville | To John Canfield Spencer[25]

[September 20, 1838]

My dear Sir,

I have only received in the country where I usually pass the summer, the book and the letter you have been good enough to send me.[26] I cannot thank you too much for the one and the other.

---

24. Pierre-Paul Royer-Collard (1763–1845) was a member of the French parliament during the Bourbon Restoration and the July Monarchy. As a leader of the Doctrinaire party, Royer-Collard believed that France could increase individual liberties under its monarchy, and he sought to establish a constitutional monarchy under the Bourbon regime. Although he did not meet Tocqueville until 1835, Royer-Collard became a close mentor to the younger man. Royer-Collard was active in the Académie française and avidly defended *Democracy in America* upon its publication.

25. Tocqueville wrote this letter in English.

26. Tocqueville refers to Spencer's notes and introduction to Reeve's English translation of *Democracy in America*.

I have never read anything on my work which have [*sic*] given me so much pleasure as that you have said in the preface prefixed to the translation by M. Reeve for I have always set the greatest value on the judgment of enlightened Americans and I could not presume to hope it would have been so favorable.

I owe you also much gratitude for the notes you have joined at the end of the book. A great number of your critiques appear to me to be just and I purpose taking advantage of them in the seventh edition of my work which will come out, I think, in about year from this [*sic*]. I hope you will permit me at that epoch to enter again in communication with you and to ask you for such circumstantial informations and explanations as will enable me to render the work more perfect.

As you have been told, I am occupied at the present moment in a work which will be the continuation and the end of the one you are acquainted with. I think I shall have terminated it by the beginning of the next spring. I accept then most willingly your offer concerning an American translation. If I could find an opportunity of making a suitable arrangement in the United States, I would send successively to the person with whom I had treated the *proof sheets* of my work as soon as corrected, so that the translation could appear in America at the same time as the original in France. This arrangement would preserve the American translation from any competition either American or English. Without doubt, my work will be translated in England. If an American translator should present himself who would be inclined to treat on these grounds, I would thank you to inform me of it. My address is at Paris *rue de Bourgogne no. 12.*

I will not conclude this letter, Sir, without telling you again how much I am flattered by your remembrance. I have not forgotten the obliging manner in which I was received by you and by your family during my short stay in your fine country and I am delighted to have found such a good occasion to express once more my gratitude.

Believe me, Sir, your very obedient servant.

Alexis de Tocqueville.

At the Château de Tocqueville, September 20, 1838

From Tocqueville | To John Canfield Spencer[27]

> At the Château de Tocqueville, near St. Pierre-Église, département de la Manche, Sept. 12, 1839

My dear Sir,

I have many apologies to make for having so long delayed answering the letter I received from you seven months ago. I hope however you will accept my excuses when I have made them known to you.

In the month of March last, precisely at the moment I was putting the

---

27. Tocqueville wrote this letter in English.

last strokes to my work on America, I was elected Deputy.[28] Immediately after my entrance in the chamber, I took part in several important affairs which demanded the sacrifice of all my time. I was obliged in consequence and greatly to my regret to abandon for some time my philosophical and literary pursuits. It was not till lately that I was able to return to them. My intention is to push them with the greatest activity until the next session, at which epoch I hope they will be terminated. Our session will begin, I think, in December. Such are the circumstances which have prevented me in the first place from thanking you for the interest you have shown in my affairs and, in the second, for the precious documents you have sent me. My gratitude is not less lively for have been so tardively expressed [sic].

With regard to the principal affair upon which you were good enough to write to me, this is exactly as the matter stands: M. Benjamin, whom you mentioned to me in your letter dated of the 14th of November, having retired from business, it seems that M. Adlard has undertaken to do what the former intended.[29] In consequence, it was he who transmitted to me your letter 19th last December, to which he added the following proposition:

He offers me a third of the clear profits of my new work on condition that I should send him the proof sheets at the same time that they appear here and that I should delay the publication in France the time necessary for allowing the book to appear simultaneously in New-York and in Paris.

I have no hesitation in acceding to these conditions, if instead of remitting to me the third of the clear profits he would give me immediately a sum of money which may be considered an equivalent. You will easily conceive that it would be extremely difficult for me to establish a running account with a librarian [sic] in America. That would demand more time and attention than it would be in my power to bestow. I should prefer then to receive a little less but in ready money. It is probable the first proof sheets would be sent about January 1840.

I have already made known my wish on these points to M. Adlard through one of his friends and partners who is now in France, Mr. Flash,[30] but I own, Sir, it is on you chiefly that I have founded my hopes of terminating this little affair to my satisfaction. Be then good enough, I beg of you, to enter into a negotiation in my name with M. Adlard and to inform me on what terms you think it advisable for me to treat with him. I have the most perfect confidence in your judgment.

28. Tocqueville served as a representative in the Chamber of Deputies from 1839 to 1848. During this time, he advocated for Algerian colonization, the abolition of slavery, and the guarantee of basic civil rights to French citizens.

29. George Adlard was the New York publisher who had printed an English edition of the first volume of *Democracy in America* in 1838. G. H. Langley of New York published both volumes in 1840. Tocqueville actually never earned any money from the American editions of his book.

30. Alexander Flash was a publisher and bookseller in Cincinnati, Ohio.

If an engagement was entered into, I hope you would not refuse to do me the honour of joining a preface and notes to this new work. I should be most happy if you would consent to do both.

The same cause which prevented me from writing to you earlier has also prevented me from making the changes which I had intended to in my first book. I have not yet been able to occupy myself with the seventh edition, though the sixth is nearly out.

I hope, my dear Sir, the high functions to which I know you have been called and my parliamentary duties will not interrupt our occasional correspondence, to which, for my part, I attach a high value; for I have never ceased to remember you as one of the most distinguished men I met with in your country.

I am, Sir, with the highest consideration,
Your sincere friend
Alexis de Tocqueville.

P.S. I send you by the same courier a copy of my first speech in the Chamber of Deputies on the eastern question and of which I beg your acceptance.[31]

From Tocqueville | To Henry Reeve

Paris, September 15, 1839
11, rue Castellane

My dear Reeve,

I am sending you under separate cover a copy of my report on the abolition of slavery.[32] I believe that you will find in it a real taste for liberty but none of the revolutionary passions that sometimes agitate my colleagues, the abolitionists. In any case, please accept this gift in the spirit in which it is offered, with friendship.

I arrived in Paris yesterday with my complete manuscript.[33] My book is fi-

31. The "Eastern Question" refers to the debate among European powers about a sovereignty dispute between the leaders of the Ottoman Empire and Egypt. Mehemet Ali, the ruler of Egypt, had established his independence from the Ottoman Empire and had conquered Syria in 1832. In July 1839, in his first speech to the Chamber of Deputies, Tocqueville urged support for the Egyptian leader; one year later, British foreign minister Lord Palmerston led Great Britain, Russia, Austria, Prussia, and the Ottoman Empire in signing a treaty that declared Ottoman sovereignty over Egypt and demanded that Mehemet Ali withdraw from Syria. French officials felt insulted by these countries' exclusion of France from the London treaty conference, and the chamber passed measures to prepare for war. Seeking to avoid armed conflict, Louis-Philippe dismissed foreign minister Adolphe Thiers, appointing François Guizot in his place. In another speech to the chamber in late November 1840, Tocqueville criticized Guizot as a weak accommodationist looking to appease British leaders. It shocked many of Tocqueville's associates to see him urge opposition to England, a country that he admired.

32. In July of 1839, Tocqueville had made a report to the Chamber of Deputies advocating the immediate abolition of slavery in all French colonies. After receiving Tocqueville's pamphlet, Reeve wrote his own article on the slave trade.

33. Tocqueville refers to the second volume of *Democracy in America.*

nally finished, definitively finished. Hallelujah! I think that I will send it to press in the first week of next month. Let me know therefore without delay whether you are ready and willing to begin work on the translation immediately.

I am upset that your business or antiaquatic instincts prevented you from coming to see us at Tocqueville, where we could have talked quietly and at length about this book and its spirit and the way in which I think it ought to be translated. That would have made your work easier. For now I will limit myself to just one preliminary observation. This work is ultimately written primarily for France, or, if you prefer the modern jargon, from the French point of view. I write in a country and for a country in which the cause of equality has triumphed, precluding any possibility of a return to aristocracy. In these circumstances, I felt that it was my duty to dwell particularly on the evil tendencies to which equality *might* give rise in order to prevent my contemporaries from succumbing to them. That is the only honorable task for those who write in a country where the battle is over. I therefore state some very harsh truths about contemporary French society and about democratic societies in general, but I say these things as a friend and not a censor. Indeed, it is because I am a friend that I dare to say them. Your translation must preserve this character. I ask this not only of the translator but of the man. It seemed to me that in the translation of the last book, without intending to and merely by following the instinct born of your opinions, you very vividly colored what was hostile to democracy and toned down anything that might reflect badly on aristocracy. I beg you urgently to wrestle with yourself on this point and preserve the character of my book, that of genuine impartiality in the theoretical judgment of the two societies, old and new, coupled, moreover, with a sincere desire to see the new society established on a firm footing.

That, my dear friend, is all I have time to tell you today. Please give my regards to your mother and believe in my sincere affection.

From Tocqueville | To John Stuart Mill

Paris, November 14, 1839
11, rue Castellane

My dear Mill,

It has been quite some time since I've had news of you, and this saddens me, because you are among the Englishmen of whom I retain the fondest memories. Beaumont has heard that you were feeling better. If this good news is true, please let me know, I beg you.

I will today send you by post a copy of the report that I have just published on behalf of the committee appointed by the chamber to abolish slavery in our colonies. You will see that, contrary to most of my colleagues, I did not seek to make a show of *eloquence* on this issue. I was even careful to avoid irritating colonial passions, which did not prevent the colonial newspapers from saying many unpleasant things about me. But you know colonists: They are all alike, no matter what nation they come from. They become enraged the moment they are asked to treat their blacks justly. But try as they might, they will not succeed in irritating me or in inducing me to inject violence into a debate in which I think it would be dangerous for the country.

I arrived in Paris two days ago to oversee the printing of the book on which I have been working for the past four years and which is the sequel of the other, that is, the *Influence of Equality on Man's Ideas and Sentiments.*[34] I will send you a copy as soon as it appears, which should be around next February. In reading it, you will not forget that it was written in and for a country in which equality has definitively triumphed and aristocracy has totally disappeared, so that the imperative task henceforth is to combat the unfortunate tendencies to which the new state of things might give rise and not to bring this new state into being. Hence I often say harsh things to the new American and French society, but I say them as a friend. Indeed, it is because I am a friend that I dare to say them and want to say them. Among us, equality has flatterers of all kinds but hardly any staunch and honest counselors. You will decide whether I have fulfilled the task I set myself.

I cannot write at greater length today because of all the little things I must take care of now that I am in Paris.

Please believe in my sincere friendship.

Alexis de Tocqueville

From Tocqueville | To Henry Reeve

Paris, February 3, 1840

My dear friend,

I am in despair and humiliated by the way in which I acted with regard to your friend Mr. Chorley.[35] He must take me for a real boor. He came to see me twice and wrote me once. I did not answer, and yesterday when I went to the Canterbury Hotel at four o'clock, he had just left to catch a stagecoach. I beg you to convey my apologies to him and urge him to accept them. I hope that he will find a way to overcome the poor opinion that this trip must have given him of me and that he will allow me to prove to him that, though a Democrat, I do not wear wooden sandals. The fact is that I am so overwhelmed with work of all sorts that I am behaving unpardonably toward everyone.

I laughed at your embarrassment in regard to general ideas. I am sure that, no matter what you say, you will find some marvelously clever way of overcoming the difficulties you mention. As to the basis of your opinion in the matter, I believe that you are wrong. I think that the realists are mistaken. More than that, I am sure that the political tendency of their philosophy, which is always dangerous, is particularly pernicious at present. Rest assured that the great peril of any democratic age is the destruction or excessive weakening of *the parts* of the social body as compared with the *whole.* Everything that reinforces the idea of the individual today is healthy. Everything that confers a separate existence on

---

34. Tocqueville refers to the second volume of *Democracy in America.*

35. Henry Fothergill Chorley (1808–1872) was a British writer, music critic, and social commentator. Reeve had roomed with him a few years earlier.

the species and enlarges the notion of the genus is dangerous. Contemporary thinking inclines naturally in this direction. In politics, the realist doctrine encourages all kinds of abuses of democracy. It facilitates despotism, centralization, contempt for individual rights, the doctrine of necessity, and the institutions and doctrines that permit the social body to trample on individuals and treat the nation as everything and the citizens as nothing.

This is one of my central opinions, to which many of my ideas lead. On this point I am totally convinced, and the principal purpose of my book was to bring the reader to share my conviction. . . .

From Tocqueville | To Henry Reeve

Paris, February 28, 1840

My dear friend,

Do not be surprised by the delay in sending the proofs, and don't blame the post office. The blame lies with the printer, who was forced to suspend work for five or six days owing to minor problems that it would take too long to explain. Work starts up again Monday.

I cannot tell you how happy I am that you approve of my work. This reassures me greatly. I am happy that this is your impression, and I thank you for sharing it with me. I hope that the second volume will strike you as better than the first. That is how I judge it.

What you tell me about Milton is distressing, particularly since, contrary to my habit, I spoke in this instance on the faith of someone else, so that I have no certainty that I was right. I took the point that shocked you in Chateaubriand's translation of the *Paradise*.[36] I had thought that on a subject to which he had devoted so much time, he would not have ventured such an important assertion without evidence. I should have known that one should always be wary of poets, even when they pose as scholars, or, rather, whenever they pose as scholars. Be that as it may, I am not yet certain that he was wrong. Unqualified though I am, the *Paradise* seemed to me to bristle with learned words that I do not find elsewhere. In any case, I authorize you to eliminate the assertion from the English edition if you think it appropriate; as for the French edition, it is too late.

I will not say anything about our politics. Time is short, and in any case the subject does not interest me. The present makes me sad, and the future worries me. . . .

From Tocqueville | To John Stuart Mill

[Paris, May 3, 1840]

My dear Mill,

Perhaps you have already read my book. I nevertheless want to send it to you so that you may have one from me directly. I have therefore just arranged

---

36. Chateaubriand translated John Milton's *Paradise Lost* (1667). He claimed that a handful of words in Milton's text did not appear in any English dictionary.

TOCQUEVILLE'S LETTERS ON *Democracy in America*

for a copy to be transmitted to you. I have entrusted it to M. Guizot, who I hope will pass it on to you. In any case, you could have it picked up at the embassy. I do not know what you will think about the value of this book, which has cost me such a great deal of effort. In any case, I beg you to consider it a token of my high esteem and sincere affection for you.

A thousand thanks.

Alexis de Tocqueville

Paris, May 3, 1840

From Tocqueville | To John Stuart Mill

Paris, December 18, 1840

11, rue Castellane

My dear friend,

I have much to reproach myself for not having written you sooner. I hope you will forgive me when you learn of the great pressure of public affairs under which I have been living for the past two months. Nothing less than that could have prevented me from writing to you immediately after reading the article you published in the *Edinburgh Review*.[37] I cannot tell you all the various ideas that your most remarkable piece brought to mind: it would be too long for a letter, especially the kind of letter that I have time to write just now. But there are a few things that I should have found time to tell you long ago, including this: of all the articles that have been written about my book, yours is the *only one* whose author has mastered my thought perfectly and found the words to explain it to the public. I hardly need tell you that I took great pleasure in reading your review. At last I saw my work judged by a man of lofty intellect who had taken the trouble to investigate my ideas and subject them to a rigorous analysis. I repeat: you *alone* have afforded me this pleasure. Apart from you, all who have praised or blamed me have struck me as men of inadequate intelligence or distracted minds. I am having your article bound with a copy of my book. The two should go together, and I want always to have both available. Thank you, my dear Mill, for what you have written. You have afforded me one of the greatest satisfactions I have experienced in a long time.

The second volume of *Democracy* has been less of a popular success in France than the first. In the present day I do not much believe that the public errs in its literary judgments. I am therefore very diligently pondering where I must have gone wrong, for there is likely to be some rather major flaw in the work. I think that the defect I am looking for lies in the very premise of the work, which is obscure or problematic in some way that the average reader cannot grasp. When I spoke simply about democratic society in the United States, people understood immediately. Had I spoken of our democratic society in France as it is emerging

37. Mill's review of the second volume of *Democracy in America* appeared in the *Edinburgh Review* 72 (October 1840): 1–47. The *Edinburgh Review* was a British periodical with a large circulation and prominent contributing writers.

today, that, too, would have been understood. But starting with notions that I took from American and French society, I wanted to describe the general traits of democratic societies of which no complete model yet exists. It is here that I lose the ordinary reader. Only readers quite accustomed to seeking general and speculative truths care to follow me down such a path. I believe that the relatively smaller impact of this book must be attributed to this original sin in its subject matter rather than to the way in which I treated this or that aspect of it.

You must have moaned as I did, as any sensible person must have done, at the rupture of the close alliance between our two countries. No one was a warmer partisan than I of the union of our two peoples, but I hardly need tell you, my dear Mill, that in order to maintain any nation, and especially a nation as fickle as ours, in the state of mind required to do great things, it must not be allowed to believe that little account is taken of its views. After the way in which the English government acted toward us, for our statesmen not to have taken offense would have been to wound and perhaps extinguish a national passion that we will someday need.[38] National pride is the greatest sentiment that we still possess. We must no doubt seek to regulate it and moderate its excesses, but we must be careful not to diminish it. Your ministry's conduct toward us was inexcusable, in my opinion, and I was greatly pained to see that the English people allowed its government to behave in such a manner. A reaction in favor of the alliance with France might perhaps have cemented it permanently. I am afraid that the moment has passed, however. The people themselves have begun to be irritated, and I am saddened not only for the good of our two countries but for that of all Europe, because all of this is energetically prompting us to enter into the projects of the most redoubtable of all powers.

But enough, indeed too much, of this sad political business. Farewell? Does this mean that you will never come to France? I would have a great deal to discuss with you. In the meantime, please accept this token of my sincere and eager devotion.

Alexis de Tocqueville

From Tocqueville | To Louis de Kergorlay

October 18, 1847

. . . I was delighted to hear that the politicians you see generally share your view of German affairs. Two days ago, I saw in Paris a very worthy Englishman by the name of Senior. He has just been in Germany. After chatting with him, I was pleased to discover that he seemed as impressed as you are by what is happening in Prussia. That, at any rate, was how it seemed to me. For me, this is real evidence that you are on the right track. The difficulty will be to make the accuracy of your assessment plain to the French reader and to paint a portrait that the reader will be able to grasp of a society and of individuals so different not only from what we imagine but from what our sense of ourselves inclines us to

38. Tocqueville refers to the "Eastern Question." See note 31 on p. 581.

TOCQUEVILLE'S LETTERS ON *Democracy in America*

imagine.[39] The great difficulty of the subject is not our ignorance but the natural prejudice that stems from contemplation of our own country and of memories of our own history. Unfortunately, on this point I have no advice to offer, other than to review what you write constantly and ask yourself what you spontaneously thought about Germany before you began to study it and what route you took in moving from your instinctive opinions to your considered ones, and then try to make your readers follow the same path. I am sure that this is what you want to achieve. But how to do it? Only the author can judge. Should you explain the differences and similarities between the two countries or simply lay them before the reader? I do not know. In my book about America, I almost always chose the second method. Although I very seldom spoke of France in that book, I did not write a page without thinking about France or without having France in a manner of speaking before my eyes. And what I tried to bring out about the United States and make people understand was not so much a full portrait of that foreign society as it was the contrasts with ours, as well as the similarities. I always began with one in order to bring out a contrast or an analogy with the other. I tell you this not as an example to follow but as information that will be useful for you to know. The constant, unspoken comparison with France was in my opinion one of the main reasons for the book's success.

On the subject of religious passions you ask a question that I believe cannot be answered, at least not in the form of a general and absolute truth. To my mind, there is no denying that political liberty has at times damped down religious passions, at other times animated them. Many circumstances influenced the outcome, such as the nature of the religion or the maturity of either religious or political passion at the time of their encounter, because passions, like everything else in this world, grow and know a period of virility and a period of decadence. When religious passion was in its decline and political passion was just beginning to flourish, the latter overshadowed the former. These circumstances, along with many others that I do not mention here, may help to ex-

---

39. Kergorlay had been working on an essay about the state of the German government for some time, though he never completed and published it. At this time, residents of a number of the German Confederation's thirty-nine states were beginning to meet and draft petitions to demand a national republican government, popular freedoms, and free elections. In France, revolutionary successes in the early months of 1848, along with King Louis-Philippe's unceremonious abdication on February 24, incited similar turbulence across the Rhine. In the "March Revolution," urban centers across the west and south of the German lands, including the Habsburg Empire, fell prey to mass demonstrations and demands for liberalization. These efforts culminated in the convergence of more than a hundred popularly elected deputies on Frankfurt. The Frankfurt National Assembly convened for a year, debating the nature of its envisioned nationalist project, and produced the Paulskirche Constitution, which called for a constitutional monarchy and a new united German empire. By the spring of 1849, when the parliament offered the crown of a united German state to King Friedrich Wilhelm IV of Prussia, the forces of conservatism and monarchy had largely regained their traditional authority, quashing revolution and routing opposition. The Prussian king declined the crown, citing the revolutionaries' lack of legitimacy to tender such an offer.

plain why times and places vary so markedly in this regard. Yet if I were obliged to abstract from all the individual cases and state what is most commonly and generally true in this regard, I would tend to agree with your Germans rather than with you. As a general rule, I believe that political liberty animates religious passions more than it extinguishes them. In the first place, I think that the family bonds between political and religious passions are more numerous than you imagine. In both one finds general and to a certain extent immaterial goods. In both one pursues an ideal of human society, a certain perfection of the species, the image of which raises the soul up above the contemplation of petty individual interests and carries it away. Speaking for myself, I find it easier, for instance, to understand a man animated by both religious passion and political passion than by political passion and the passion for well-being. The first two passions can coexist and fuse in a single soul, but not the latter two. There is another less general and less noble but perhaps more persuasive reason why the two passions go together and reinforce each other. Each is often called upon to assist the other. Free institutions are the often natural and sometimes indispensable instruments of religious passion. Nearly all the effort that the moderns have invested in liberty has been a consequence of the need to express or defend their religious beliefs. It was religious passion that drove the Puritans to America and made them seek to govern themselves. The two English revolutions came about because people yearned for freedom of conscience. The same need caused the Huguenot nobility in sixteenth-century France to entertain republican views. In all these cases, religious passions spurred political passions, and political passions helped to foster the development of religious passions. If religious passions were never thwarted, this effect might not occur. But they almost always are. When they obtain the satisfaction they desire, the effect may also cease. Your theory might be applicable in a society that was religious without being agitated by religious controversy or passion. It is possible that public affairs would then come gradually to all but monopolize the attention of citizens. I am not sure that this would occur, however, unless public political circumstances were unusually favorable. It will usually be the case that the same agitation that fosters and sustains political liberty in the souls of men also encourages religious ferment, which may then persist in the country and spur an uprising. In my opinion, this is what is happening in the America of which you speak. To my mind, the march of time and the increase of well-being have deprived the religious element in America of three-quarters of its original power. Yet what remains is truly in a state of turmoil. All religious men in the United States meet, talk with one another, and act in concert far more commonly than elsewhere. I believe that the habits fostered by political liberty, and the energy it imparts to everything else, play a large part in the distinctive dynamism of the religious element that still exists in the country. These circumstances cannot restore religion to its former omnipotence, but they can protect it and derive from it all the force of which it is still capable. Care must be taken to avoid conflating political liberty with certain of its occasional side effects. When well established in a tranquil environment, political liberty stimulates a desire for well-being and the means to achieve it, a passion to get rich. Then these tastes, needs, and desires extinguish religious passion. But these are remote and secondary consequences of political liberty and are scarcely less harmful to political passion itself than to religious passion.

That is what I have to say on this particular point, which I am far from having considered with all the attention it deserves. The only absolute truth I see in this regard is that there is no absolute truth. It is therefore wise, in my opinion, to study particular circumstances with great care. . . .

Tocqueville's and Beaumont's Views of America after 1840

Beaumont appears only occasionally in this last part, as it was Tocqueville who nurtured enduring friendships with a close-knit network of Americans. Tocqueville remained abreast of American political developments and feared the potentially negative consequences of lawlessness and the extension of slavery in the territories for the cause of freedom worldwide.

In addition to letters, this section includes occasional political speeches. At a public banquet during his successful campaign for the Chamber of Deputies in 1848 (the first election in France to allow universal male suffrage), Tocqueville praised the American Republic as "liberty itself." The following year, Tocqueville served briefly as foreign minister of the Second Republic.

After he retired from political life, Tocqueville remained a major presence in the work of the Institut de France. He had over the years brought to the Académie des sciences morales et politiques the work of American authors he admired, such as George Bancroft, Edward Everett, Samuel Prescott, and Francis Lieber. Here he formally introduces that of his younger friend Theodore Sedgwick.

From Tocqueville | To Jared Sparks

At the Château de Tocqueville, October 13, 1840

My dear Mr. Sparks,

I beg your pardon for not having previously responded to the letter you sent me early last month. The letter went initially to Paris, which I had already left. It was then forwarded to me here but arrived while I was temporarily absent. Thus it was impossible for me to answer until a few days ago.

I am very happy that you approved of my report on the abolition of slavery and that it was translated in the United States.[1] I have little hope, however, that it will have any useful effect in that country (I am speaking of the South). Slavery is more deeply and tenaciously rooted in your soil than anywhere else. Neither you nor I will see the end of it. It is for me a very melancholy thought that your nation has so incorporated slavery that you and it have grown up together, so that humanity can only bewail your rapid progress, which without slavery would have been reason for all civilized peoples to rejoice. It is hard to think of a single case in which slavery was abolished by the master class. Only a power that dominated both master and slave has been able to accomplish this feat. That is why slavery will endure longer in your country than anywhere else, because you are entirely independent.

It is good news to hear that you plan to come to Paris in November. I will be there then to take part in the deliberations of the Chamber of Deputies, of which I am a member. I hope, my dear Mr. Sparks, that you will call on me. My wife will be delighted to make your acquaintance. I live at 11, rue Castellane. You can rest assured that I will do my best to assist you in your historical research, the value of which I know so well.

Please believe in my esteem and sincere devotion.

Alexis de Tocqueville

---

1. Tocqueville had sent a copy of his report advocating the abolition of slavery, delivered in July of 1839, to Jared Sparks. Mary Crowninshield Sparks, Jared Sparks's wife, translated Tocqueville's report into English; it was published in Boston in 1840 as "Report Made to the Chamber of Deputies on the Abolition of Slavery in French Colonies."

From Tocqueville | To John Canfield Spencer

[Tocqueville, November 10, 1841]

... I have learned, sir, with the greatest satisfaction of your accession to the ministry.[2] I rejoice not for you—I have been close enough to public affairs to know that one derives little pleasure from directing them—but for your country and even for world affairs generally. The United States already plays a large enough role among nations that every country has an interest in whom Americans choose to lead them. This interest is particularly keenly felt in France among those who know and think. All rightly regard the Union as our natural and necessary ally. Although separated by the ocean, we have in fact a common interest in the freedom of the seas. When we fail to find ways to act in concert, both of us suffer, and are increasingly obliged to suffer, from England's maritime predominance. Great Britain today is for all the nations of the world that have not given up on the oceans what Louis XIV was for seventeenth-century Europe. It has destroyed most of them and to one degree or another threatens all the rest with the same fate. I foresee that sooner or later this state of affairs will become so intolerable that it will instigate a new League of Augsburg, and all the navies of the world will ultimately unite against such a dangerous and troubling supremacy.[3] This would already have occurred in Europe if the French Revolution had not diverted the attention of princes and peoples and raised questions of government and domestic politics that divided nations whose common interests would otherwise have joined together in action. Fortunately, no issues of this sort can arise between the American Union and France. These two great states are therefore free to follow their natural inclinations, and these inclinations encourage them to form a close alliance. Though the hazards of circumstance and the caprices of men may try to separate them, a permanent and irresistible force will always draw them together.

Among the incidents that might temporarily divide two nations that have such great need of each other, I mention with utmost regret the recent bill that has deprived French commerce of the advantages it previously enjoyed in your marketplace.[4] I dare say that no matter how strong the reasons that American statesmen had for taking these steps, they strayed from the fundamental law of politics in their country as well as in ours, as experience will one day show them, and I am doubly glad to see a man as supportive of his country and as enlightened as you entering government at such a moment. . . .

2. President John Tyler (1790–1862) had just appointed Spencer to be secretary of war. Spencer would serve until 1843, when he was appointed secretary of the treasury.

3. The League of Augsburg was formed in 1686 when nearly a dozen European states allied against France, which was ruled by Louis XIV from 1654 to 1715. It was sometimes known as the Great Alliance after England joined in 1689.

4. The Tariff of 1841 set a duty of 20 percent on imported items, of which luxury items like wine and silks were the most popular. Though this high duty angered the French, heavy trade between France and the United States proved that French fears of a great decline in export trade were unfounded.

From Tocqueville | To Odilon Barrot[5]

Tocqueville, September 16, 1842

. . . Our country errs in any case in thinking that an opposition can survive only if it wants to make major changes to existing laws.

The parliamentary histories of England and America very clearly demonstrate the opposite. These countries sustained powerful and brilliant oppositions that distinguished themselves only by their intent to implement existing laws and carry out routine actions of government differently from the majority. The same legislation can sometimes be harmful or beneficial depending on whether it is applied in one spirit rather than another, and this simple question of conduct is sufficient to divide political men deeply and create very marked differences between them. When the opposition adopts or at any rate declines to overturn most existing laws, if only to show that it can get something else out of them than the majority, or that it would apply them in a more national sense, it may still play an important role, a role more liberal than the majority and certainly more effective than if it appeared ready to change the law itself. Do you not agree that what is delaying the development of free institutions in France is the fear inspired by those who advocate them? . . .

From Tocqueville | To Francis Lieber

Tocqueville near Saint-Pierre Église (Manche)
Sept. 18, 1844

My dear Lieber,

I received the letter you sent me from Paris a few days ago. I would far rather have met you in person and shaken your hand before you returned to America, but our respective commitments made this impossible. In any case, please accept my sincerest wishes, and those of Madame de Tocqueville, for your happiness, as well as for your imminent and permanent return. You are not made to live in America. Europe is the true homeland of your intellect, and you would need to live here even if you hadn't been born here. Knowing you, I am sure you find it difficult to breathe in the atmosphere of American society. As you say, a free European country is your theater. I would like that country to be ours. This nation is not the freest in the world politically, but it is certainly the one in which the individual is least aware of the restraints that the state of society imposes on his everyday actions. If the Institut does not soon create a new bond between you and France, I assure you that it will not be for lack of effort

5. Odilon Barrot (1791–1873) was a liberal lawyer who promoted political and social reforms throughout his life. Though he supported the ascension of Louis-Philippe after the abdication of Charles X, he was a center-left member of the Chamber of Deputies who argued for rule by popularly elected leaders. As a moderate proponent of republicanism, Barrot served under Louis-Napoleon as prime minister of France in 1848 and 1849 when Tocqueville was minister of foreign affairs.

on my part. Beaumont is keen to make this happen as well, and I believe that Mignet is also in favor of the idea.[6]

I have a proposition to make to you, and I would be happy if you were to accept. I have considerable influence with a major Paris newspaper called *Le Commerce,* and I am very keen for this paper, which is the principal political organ of which my friends and I avail ourselves, to gain a good reputation among serious people.[7] The best way to do this is to emulate what is most praiseworthy in the English papers but entirely lacking in ours, namely, interesting pieces by foreign correspondents. I have already managed to obtain an English correspondent for the next session of Parliament: a distinguished member of the House of Commons has agreed to write two articles a month for us.[8] You can well imagine how eager I am to conclude a similar arrangement for the United States. You would be in a better position than anyone else to perform this service for us, should you be willing. Once a month, or more often if you deem it appropriate, you would write us a letter long enough to fill two or three French newspaper-sized columns, in which you would report what is happening in the Union in politics, business, industry, and the arts. Several individuals have already proposed themselves for this position, but to do the job correctly one needs enough tact and familiarity with Europe to sense not only what is interesting in itself but also what would be interesting to Europeans and to the French. You are the only person who could do this really well. Would the position suit you? If you prefer to keep your identity secret, rest assured that the secrecy would be absolute. I would be the *only* person to know. It goes without saying that a foreign correspondent does not work for free. We can discuss this point later if the idea appeals to you.

Meanwhile, you could do us a real favor in another way. Our search for good German correspondents, chiefly in northern Germany and especially Prussia and the Hanseatic cities, has thus far yielded nothing. Yet what is happening in Prussia, as well as what touches on the German Customs Union, Baltic commerce, and the general direction of thinking in northern Germany, is of the utmost interest to us. Information of a commercial nature is especially valuable to a newspaper that specializes in commerce as well as politics. So if you could find

6. The Institut de France comprised five learned societies, including most notably the Académie française. Tocqueville had nominated Lieber for membership in the Académie des sciences morales et politiques.

François Mignet (1796–1884) was a prominent French historian and a member of both the Académie française and the Académie des sciences morales et politiques.

7. *Le Commerce* was a four-page newspaper published daily between 1837 and 1848; at times, it had a circulation as high as five thousand. In the fall of 1844, Tocqueville had organized a group of political allies and investors to purchase the newspaper as an outlet for their views, providing an alternative to *Le Siècle,* a popular paper whose content was under the control of minister Adolphe Thiers.

8. Charles Buller (1806–1848), a British lawyer and friend of John Stuart Mill and Henry Reeve, wrote letters for the newspaper in 1845.

us some good correspondents, either in Prussia for general politics or in Hamburg for north German industrial and commercial affairs, you would be doing us a great service. I should repeat what I said above: if secrecy is wanted, *it can be guaranteed,* because I would be the only intermediary. As for other terms, we should have no difficulty in reaching an agreement. For politics, I think a university professor might be preferable. But would it be possible to find one?

I end this long letter by wishing you a pleasant journey and begging you not to forget the good and loyal friends you leave behind in France. My wife wishes particularly to be remembered to you.

Alexis de Tocqueville

From Tocqueville | To Francis Lieber

Paris, November 13, 1844

My dear Lieber,

The letter I received from you yesterday gave me a great deal of pleasure, all the more so because I had begun to worry, or, rather, I blamed the post, thinking that you had left Europe before receiving the letter I sent you from Tocqueville. I had written a second letter addressed to you in America. Your last arrived on the very day I was going to post it, so I threw it in the fire instead. Now I will answer your questions in the order in which you asked them:

I took it for granted that your communications would be in English. So no difficulty on that score.

I understand that it would be better if you were in New York rather than South Carolina. But that is a drawback I anticipated and always thought mattered less than having a correspondent of your caliber.

As for the secrecy, I give you my word that it will be absolute. *Nobody* at the newspaper will know your name. Beaumont, who shares my political interest in the success of *Le Commerce,* and my wife will be the only people who know that you are writing for us, and I am as certain of their discretion as I am of mine.

As for the regularity of the dispatches, it would be desirable to have them as regular as possible, so that not a month would go by without readers being able to follow what is happening in America. Nevertheless, punctuality in such matters is impossible. In addition, events will inevitably have some influence on the timing of dispatches. If something important were to happen in the interval between two letters, there would be no reason to wait for the next regular dispatch date to let us know about its significance. Such judgments would be entirely up to you.

What we would ask of you would be an article of two or three columns. I will send a copy of the paper to you in Hamburg so that you can judge approximately how long that is. It is more difficult to specify in advance how those two or three columns should be filled. On that point I am perfectly willing to rely on your judgment. Never forget that you are speaking to France, and choose those aspects of America that are likely to interest us most. Remember, too, that you will be writing for people who are not very familiar with the people, history, institutions, or social state of the United States and with whom you must therefore be clearer and more explicit than if you were writing for Americans or even Englishmen.

Anything pertaining to the behavior of the American people toward other nations, particularly *the English* and Mexico, would naturally capture our attention. But we would also be keenly interested in all internal events and intellectual developments, as well as in the growth of the country's social prosperity, industrial and commercial importance, etc. As a resident of the Union, you will know better than I what should appear in this kind of monthly review of its affairs, and I imagine that you will be able to do the job without difficulty.

You ask me to send you a copy of the newspaper. That is quite reasonable, but how can I do so without revealing your name to the management of the paper? Can't you have one sent to one of your friends or to yourself under a different name? Send me your instructions on this score.

As for remuneration, the paper usually operates as follows. We have in England a very distinguished man, a member of Parliament, who, like you, wishes to keep his identity secret and who has agreed to do what we are asking you in regard to America. He asked to be paid two guineas or roughly fifty francs per article. Tell us frankly if this basis seems suitable to you. If not, state your terms, and I think I will be able to persuade the owners of the paper to accept them. As for the manner of payment, it seems to me that it would be quite easy to arrange for a banker to receive the payment and pass it on to you.

I would like you to become our correspondent for any number of reasons, among them because this would inevitably lead to more frequent and closer relations between us and you. I hardly need remind you that I would be obliged to write you often to indicate what we would like to know. Bear in mind, moreover, that Beaumont and I will be at your disposal to provide you with any information you may need.

Did you learn anything in Germany, and in Prussia particularly, that might be useful for us to know in regard to the penitentiary system? If so, we would be grateful if you could let us know, because the debate on this important issue will surely resume in the next session.[9]

Farewell, my dear friend. It is with sadness that I watch you depart once again from this European continent, in which you were made to live. Know that our good wishes and friendship will follow you across the sea. Madame de Tocqueville remembers you most warmly, as she would tell you herself if she were here. But she left me three days ago to visit one of her aunts, who lives in

9. In his response, Lieber reported that the king of Prussia favored solitary confinement but that many of his ministers opposed this position thanks to the reports of Johann Tellkampf (1808–1876). Tellkampf was a German professor who had taught in America and who critiqued the American penitentiary system in part by arguing that the solitary confinement used by the Philadelphia system was cruel and did not work to reform the prisoners. See his *Essays on Law Reform, Commercial Policy, Banks, Penitentiaries, Etc.,* published in 1859.

the country. She had added a word for you in the letter I mentioned at the beginning of this one, which I tossed in the fire. I hope that we will soon have occasion to resume our correspondence. Meanwhile, please accept this assurance of my sincere devotion.

Alexis de Tocqueville

P.S. I hope that you were able to find the German correspondent we need in Hamburg. In any case, I should think it would be easy to find a merchant there who could send us commercial news.

From Tocqueville | To Francis Lieber

[December 14, 1844]

My dear Lieber,

I have just received your letter and hastily dispatch this brief reply. You ask me (1) if you should send letters via England and steamship. My answer is yes, if I am correct in thinking that this is the quickest way. Send your letter not to me but to M. Scheffer, the editor in chief of the paper, at 6, rue Saint-Joseph.[10] Do not sign it, because he does not know your name. If you have something for me in particular, enclose it in a sealed envelope inside a larger envelope. M. Scheffer will be notified and will transmit the inner envelope to me, and in this way the newspaper will pay the postage. If you think that there would be the slightest danger in allowing M. Scheffer to see the postmark on the letter, you should send it to me directly. (2) You ask if you can send me documents from either Hamburg or America without paying postal fees. While the chamber is in session, which is until the end of July, you can send them to me in care of the president of the Chamber of Deputies. Place the letters or documents in a sealed inner envelope with my name on it. Upon reflection, it occurs to me that this route is also the best for sending your monthly letters during the session. So use this method instead of writing to M. Scheffer.

As for the pamphlets, after the session you should send them to me in care of the Ministry of the Interior, taking care to mark the envelope for me "penitentiary documents."

You would do well to speak to Herr von Humboldt about the Institut.[11] There will be discussion about you in Paris, and he can help us enormously.

Write us as soon as possible after arriving in America. As you know, this is a very interesting moment. The beginning of the new administration, its domestic and foreign policy, the state of the country, its attitude toward England, and

10. Francisque de Corcelle had made Charles-Arnold Scheffer (1796–1853), a fellow former secretary to the marquis de Lafayette, the editor of the newspaper.

11. Alexander von Humboldt (1769–1859), a well-known German naturalist, often served as a diplomat in the court of Louis-Philippe and shared a personal friendship with the French king.

the decisions it is likely to make in regard to major issues such as Texas, Oregon, and the tariff—all these things arouse considerable curiosity here.[12]

Farewell, my dear friend, I leave you, but not before wishing you prosperity in all your endeavors. My wife joins me, and both of us beg you to believe in our sincere friendship.

Alexis de Tocqueville

December 14, 1844

P.S. Tell me how we can send the small sum that you have kindly agreed to accept.

If you can find us a German correspondent, you would be an admirable fellow.

From Tocqueville | To Francis Lieber

July 22, 1846

... I am right now deeply immersed in African affairs, which daily assume greater importance.[13] For us, the war has become, and will remain as long as we have no quarrels in Europe, the less important aspect of our enterprise. The primary concern today is colonization. How can we attract and above all keep a large European population of farmers in Algeria? We already have 100,000 Christians in Africa, not counting the army, but almost all have settled in the towns, which are developing into large and beautiful cities, while the countryside remains empty. It is impossible to contemplate the colonization of Africa without thinking of the powerful examples set by the United States in this regard. But how to study them? Have there been books or documents of any kind published in the United States that might shed light on this point and explain how things happened? Might such information be found in official or unofficial reports? I would be most grateful to receive anything you can find on this subject. ...

From Tocqueville | To Edward Everett

[Paris, February 15, 1850]

Sir,

M. de Bois-le-Comte, our new ambassador to the United States, asked me for two or three letters of recommendation to distinguished individuals with

---

12. James Knox Polk (1795–1849) had just been elected the eleventh president of the United States; he would be inaugurated in March of 1845. A Jacksonian Democrat, Polk promised to annex Texas (which became a state in early 1845 under President John Tyler), gain total sovereignty over the Oregon Territory (which the United States ruled jointly with England), and reduce the high tariff rates enacted by President Tyler.

In his letters to Tocqueville, Lieber had consistently expressed his concern that it was more difficult to get American news and to express his views on these events from his residence in Charleston, South Carolina, than it would have been from a northern city.

13. France had spread along the coast of Algeria after the conquest of Algiers in 1830 and expanded its control of the interior. In 1847, Tocqueville published a report on Algeria that

whom he might, in my view, establish useful and agreeable relationships.[14] I naturally thought of you. This should come as no surprise to you. My personal recollections were bound to influence my choice. I therefore urge you to receive M. de Bois-le-Comte as he deserves, namely, as a worthy man who has recently rendered excellent service for us as ambassador to Sardinia and who will, I am sure, do even greater service in the post that has now been entrusted to him. I was the one who recommended him to the president, when, even before I was aware of Mr. Clayton's rather unfair attack on me, I ordered M. Poussin's recall.[15] M. de Bois-le-Comte is a man as respectable in his private life as in his public life, and I hope he will gain the sympathy of all enlightened Americans. Here he belongs to the republican party, but he would prefer the republic of Washington, not that of Robespierre.

I thank you, sir, for all that you were kind enough to do for my compatriot M. de Cessac and for his parents, who seem to me more deserving of pity than of wrath.[16] I believe that the American courts will come to this judgment.

Our country is calm and more prosperous than one might think after such violent crises. But confidence in the future is still lacking, and although sixty years of revolution have made the feeling of instability less harmful to social

---

encouraged French officials to seek a colonization policy based more on accommodation than on militarism.

14. André-Ernest Olivier Sain de Bois-le-Comte (1799–1862) had served as a French minister to Turin in Sardinia in 1848 and 1849 before serving in Washington, D.C., from 1849 to 1851. As French minister to America, he replaced Guillaume Tell Poussin.

15. Guillaume Tell Poussin (1794–1876) served as the French minister to the United States in 1849. Born in France, he moved to America during the Bourbon Restoration and became an American citizen. However, he returned to France to live and in 1841 published a book about American democracy (*Considérations sur le principe démocratique qui régit l'Union américaine*), in which he claimed to understand America and its institutions better than Tocqueville. Poussin published another book on America two years later, and both the French and American governments anticipated excellent relations with each other when Poussin was appointed as French minister to America in 1849.

However, soon after assuming his post, Poussin used abrasive language in two letters to Secretary of State John Middleton Clayton (1796–1856) demanding the censure of an American navy commander. The commander had rescued a French boat in the Gulf of Mexico but detained it for a few days in a vain hope for an award for salvage. Tocqueville disapproved of Poussin's conduct. But a comedy of errors ensued. Clayton, not sure whether Tocqueville would actually recall Poussin, dismissed him under instructions from Zachary Taylor. This move made it impossible for Tocqueville officially to receive the new American minister, William Cabell Rives. The dispute was resolved, and Rives installed as minister, only after Louis-Napoleon's change of heart abruptly put an end to the Barrot ministry and hence to Tocqueville's brief tenure as foreign minister in October of 1849. Tocqueville remained hurt and embarrassed by the whole affair and feared that his reputation would suffer in America.

16. At the instruction of his mother-in-law, the comtesse de Montesquiou, vicomte Gérard de Cessac (1812–1885) was traveling to Saint Louis, Missouri, to arrange a criminal defense for his brothers-in-law Raymond and Gonsalve de Montesquiou, who were accused of killing a man. Edward Everett helped Cessac to retain a prominent lawyer, Edward Bates, who

progress and less painful for us than it would be for other nations, it has nevertheless had most unfortunate consequences. This great nation is entirely in the grip of a state of mind common to the sailor at sea or the soldier in the field. It is doing the best it can every day without worrying about the day after. But such a state is precarious and dangerous. What is more, it is not peculiar to us. Throughout continental Europe, with the exception of Russia, society is in turmoil, and the Old World is in the final stages of collapse. Rest assured that all the restorations of old powers that are taking place all around us are merely passing phenomena, which will not prevent the great tragedy from playing itself out. That tragedy will result in the complete destruction of the old society and the edification in its place of I know not what human concoction whose shape cannot yet be clearly made out.

Farewell, my dear sir, and know that I hold you in high esteem and will always value your correspondence.

A. de Tocqueville

Paris, February 15, 1850

From Tocqueville | To Theodore Sedgwick

Paris, December 4, 1852

30 rue de Courcelles

. . . Nowhere are you more welcome than in Paris, where people say that you're the most amiable and witty American conversationalist ever seen in France. And as you know, the French, who still credit themselves with a quality that few nowadays possess, find it hard to admit that wit exists anywhere except in France.

You are right to thank me for lending you Ampère.[17] He is one of the best and most agreeable men I know, and one whose attractiveness is most universally acknowledged, because, as a man interested in everything, he is always ready with conversation for every companion. What is more, he has come home enthusiastic about your country and says so openly even though this is not the most propitious moment to admit it. His lively taste for America is yet another bond between us, because as you know I am half an American citizen, which al-

---

successfully argued for Raymond de Montesquiou's acquittal and Gonsalve de Montesquiou's acquittal by reason of mental handicap.

Cessac's father, Jean-Gérard Lacuée de Cessac (1752–1841), was a military and political leader in France. Upon his death, Tocqueville was elected to fill Cessac's seat in the Académie française.

17. Jean-Jacques Ampère (1800–1864) first met Tocqueville in 1835, and the two quickly became close friends. Ampère was an avid traveler and scholar of languages, literature, and history. He taught at the Collège de France and was appointed to the Académie française in 1847.

In a letter dated May 20, 1852, Sedgwick had reported very much enjoying Ampère's visit to him in New York. Sedgwick used Ampère as a messenger to send a copy of the last volume of George Bancroft's *History of the United States* to Tocqueville.

lows me at least to be a citizen of some place. As a compatriot, I have felt rather uneasy about the spirit of conquest, not to say plunder, that has emerged in your country over the past few years. This is not a sign of good health in a nation that already has more territory than it can fill. I confess that I would be most unhappy to learn that your country had embarked on an adventure against Cuba or, what might be even worse, allowed itself to be manipulated by its lost children.[18] If this whole business is not handled very carefully, you will have to deal with the powerful nations of Europe. On that you can count.

I do not need to tell you that you do not enjoy a saintly reputation on our continent. Governments revile you. They regard the United States as the pit of the abyss from which only pestilence emerges. And the people reproach you for having led them to believe in a Democratic Republic. There has never been a time when the two have been so ready to join forces to create real trouble for you and show you that you are not as completely safe from the blows of the Old World as you might imagine. . . .

From Tocqueville | To Jared Sparks

[Paris, December 11, 1852]

Dear Mr. Sparks,

I wanted to add to the official letter that I have written you as president of the university a word of friendship to remind you of our acquaintance. I particularly wanted to let you know that I could not have been more touched by the demonstration of esteem that you and your colleagues showed me on this occasion. What I say in my public letter about Harvard's [*sic*] college I feel deeply, and I can think of no greater pleasure or honor than to acknowledge my feelings about this great and beautiful institution. No literary distinction is worth more to me.[19] I have abandoned public life entirely since December 2, 1851, and I am determined not to return as long as the prevailing order in my country is so contrary to what I hoped and wished for it. Today I am therefore living a wholly literary life surrounded by a small number of friends and a great many books. From my retirement I often turn my attention, with much pleasure mingled at times with a certain anxiety, toward your America, of which I consider myself almost a citizen, so strong is my desire that your country prosper and become a great nation. It no longer has anything to fear but itself—the abuse of democracy, the spirit of adventure and conquest, an exaggerated sense

18. The United States had embarked on a number of expansionist campaigns in the previous decade, annexing Texas and Oregon and fighting the Mexican War to gain more territory to the southwest. To keep a balance between slave and free states, many Southerners pressed the Polk administration to buy Cuba from Spain. After failed negotiations and an unsuccessful expedition to Cuba under Polk, Franklin Pierce was elected to the presidency in 1852, and Tocqueville expected him to continue to press for the annexation of Cuba.

19. In 1852, Harvard presented Tocqueville with an honorary doctorate of law degree. The formal letter to Jared Sparks as Harvard president is printed in *Tocqueville on America after 1840: Letters and Other Writings,* ed. Craiutu and Jennings, 140–41.

of and pride in its own strength, and the enthusiasm of youth. To such great fortune I cannot but preach the utmost moderation. Nations need this no less than individuals. Avoid entering into disputes with Europe lightly. People here take a very dim view of you at the moment and would gladly seize any opportunity to demonstrate their ill will. As great and strong as you are, a conflict with Europe could entail grave dangers, or at the very least serious inconveniences, and might have grave and unpredictable repercussions on your internal affairs. Pardon me for speaking to you at such length about your country, which I left so long ago, and take my words solely as a token of my continued interest.

I have received the small pamphlet in which you respond to English criticisms of your important edition of Washington's letters. These criticisms have not made their way to France, and your work, as translated by M. Guizot, continues to enjoy a very well-deserved reputation.[20]

Beaumont, who is in Paris right now, asks me to add his greetings in particular to mine. And please remember both of us to Mr. E. Everett if you are still in touch with him, and tell him that he has friends in Paris who have not forgotten him. . . .

From Tocqueville | To Theodore Sedgwick

St.-Cyr-près-Tours (Indre-et-Loire)
November 7, 1853

My dear Mr. Sedgwick,

I should like to have your opinion on a point that I think it quite important to clarify. It has to do with the true state of industrial affairs in America and with what Europeans who have invested a part of their fortune in the United States may actually have to fear. Here is my position: in 1848, when I was somewhat anxious about the financial condition of France, I bought a number of American bonds, which I continue to hold. They are: (1) New York and Harlem Railroad bonds; (2) Galena-Chicago Union Railroad bonds; (3) Michigan Central Railroad bonds.[21] [These] investments have paid good interest, and I had no reason to believe that the capital might be in any danger whatsoever. But the newspapers are full of more or less alarming news about the state of affairs in America. Many people have begun to be afraid that the country will soon suf-

20. Lord Mahon had accused Jared Sparks of changing text in Washington's letters and omitting many documents. In 1852, Sparks published his response in a pamphlet about the "mode of editing" of the Washington papers. He explained that Washington himself had edited a number of his letters and that it was impossible to compile a complete edition of his works. Sparks's dozen volumes of the Washington papers were very popular, and François Guizot (1787–1874) translated an abridged six-volume edition into French.

21. The New York and Harlem Railroad was incorporated in 1831 to build tracks running north from Lower Manhattan. By 1853, the railroad reached Chatham, New York, 153 miles north of New York City.

Incorporated in 1836, the Galena and Chicago Union Railroad sought to connect the lead mines at Galena, on the western edge of Illinois, to the budding city of Chicago on Lake

fer from yet another industrial crisis similar to those that have afflicted it in the past. These rumors have somewhat alarmed me, for although my fortune is equal to my desires, so that I consider myself independent, I am not wealthy, and the loss of a portion of what I own in America would be most unpleasant for me. In this situation, I felt that there was no one to whom I could turn in the United States in whom I had more confidence than you. Would you, therefore, be good enough to answer the following questions: (1) Do you believe that fears of a crisis are well-founded? (2) Do you believe that if there is indeed a crisis, the funds I mention would be at risk? (3) What do you advise me to do in the present circumstances?[22] I hardly need tell you how grateful I will be for any information you might provide. I beg you, in answering, to say nothing about French political matters, which might well prevent your letter from reaching me, for the post here can no longer be assumed to be private to any degree. But do please tell me about your country, in which I take an increasing interest as my interest in other places wanes. . . .

From Beaumont | To Alexis de Tocqueville

Paris, July 31, 1854, 23, rue de Miromesnil

. . . On the way from Bonn to Mainz, pay close attention to the banks of the Rhine, which are more admired in this area than in any other. No doubt the people who feel this way are largely correct. But don't you think that, all things considered, the banks of the Hudson have it all over the banks of the Rhine? Take away the memories associated with the forests of Germania and the castles of the Burgraves, whose ruins do indeed offer some wonderful views, and don't you find that the evergreen hills of the North River are far superior to the enclosed vineyards that line the Rhine nearly everywhere?[23] I confess that I don't attach much value to the memories of the Prince von Metternich that Johannisberg calls to mind.[24] And the *hoch* itself, which I have always felt fell far short of

---

Michigan. Construction began in 1848, and the rail lines reached Galena just under six years later.

Conceived in 1830, the Michigan Central Railroad began construction in 1836. The railroad originally sought to connect Detroit to Saint Joseph, Michigan, but was later extended to Chicago. After years of financial difficulties and construction delays, the railroad lines finally reached Chicago in 1852.

22. Sedgwick replied that the high price of silver created financial woes mainly for speculators and bankers but that the cotton market, northern agriculture, and railroads remained stable. Sedgwick thought that Tocqueville's investments were wise and judged the newspaper reports exaggerations.

23. Beaumont is comparing the Rhine River in Germany to the North River, or the lower Hudson River, in New York as he and Tocqueville viewed it during their trip to America.

24. Johannisberg, in Hesse, was the site of a well-known castle. Francis, emperor of Austria, gave the castle to Prince Klemens Wenzel von Metternich in 1814, in part because of his valuable participation in the Congress of Vienna. Though Metternich fled to England during the revolutions of 1848, he returned to the estate in 1851.

its reputation, fails to touch my heart at all. I much prefer Anthony's Nose to all that, especially when we were perched on the heights opposite in Mount Pleasant, contemplating it together.[25] . . .

From Tocqueville | To Gustave de Beaumont

Bonn, August 6, 1854

. . . The other day I had what I thought was quite an interesting conversation with a Prussian who is just back from the United States, where he served for ten years as ambassador. His chief business was to keep an eye on emigration. He stunned me when he said that last year, German emigration to the United States reached the incredible figure of 140,000 individuals. And it is continuing at that rate. Previously only the poor came, but today many well-off and even wealthy families are arriving. Relatively few come from Prussia. There were only 10,000 Prussians among the 140,000 Germans. But nearly all were well-bred and well-off. The rest came chiefly from the small states of central Germany, along with large numbers from Baden, Würtemberg, and Bavaria. According to the person I was speaking to, all these people take their ideas with them to the United States, and they hold on to a certain number of them once they are there. They preserve their language. They do not mix much with the natives, they generally stay together, and although they ultimately acquire some American political customs through emulation, especially in the second generation, they remain a distinct and foreign element. In short, what he told me confirms what I have always thought, namely, that the rapid introduction into the United States of men alien to the English race was the greatest danger that America faced, and for this reason the ultimate success of democratic institutions remains an unresolved problem. I forgot to mention that my interlocutor said that most of the families who leave Germany to go to America today do so in response to the urgings of relatives and friends who have already emigrated. But what *German* cause drove them to emigrate? I was unable to elicit a clear statement from him on this point, about which it is vitally important to learn more. . . .

From Tocqueville | To Theodore Sedgwick

Bonn, Aug. 14, [18]54

Dear Mr. Sedgwick,

Three days ago I received your letter of last July 20. It came as a great relief. I had been quite worried about the state of commercial affairs in America and, in particular, about the panic that seemed to have befallen transactions in railway securities. Thanks to you, I now clearly see the causes of this situation and the extent of the damage. On the basis of what you tell me, I don't think I have anything to fear, because I have no need of my capital for now and can wait until the crisis passes and prices go back up again. I cannot tell you how grate-

25. Anthony's Nose was a well-known peak along the Hudson River, which Tocqueville and Beaumont viewed from Mount Pleasant, New York.

ful we are to you for regularly supplying information that you think might be useful or agreeable. Your attitude is that of a true friend, and it is impossible not to reciprocate. So that is what I will do, I assure you, with the greatest of pleasure. I hope that you will count on me if ever there is anything I can do for you in France.

I wrote you from Bonn on the 17th of last month, and today I am once again writing from there, but on the eve of leaving this small city, where I have spent two very profitable and indeed very pleasant months. I am clever enough to take great pleasure in discovering new mores and adapting readily to them. Here I have fallen in with a group of German professors and been welcomed by their families, and it did not take long before I felt like one of them. I have learned a great deal, met good minds, and in nearly all cases discovered people of genuinely simple habits and truly good nature. What I have seen of private mores in Germany strikes me as quite interesting and even likable. Public mores are best left unmentioned, however. They are what two centuries of absolute government, sixty years of centralization, and a very lengthy period of administrative dependence on the part of both officials and citizens have made them. In short, they can lead to only two things: either servitude or revolution. What can you make of such people when they arrive in America? And yet they are coming to you in steadily increasing numbers, already at the rate of 140,000 per year, according to what I have been told. However great your powers of assimilation, it is quite difficult to *digest* so many foreign bodies quickly enough to incorporate them into your substance, or to make them sufficiently enough *yourselves* that they will not disrupt your economy and the health of your society. I wish that you could grow less quickly. But an inevitable destiny hastens you toward greatness and peril. . . .

From Tocqueville | To Gustave de Beaumont

Compiègne, February 21, 1855

. . . The sight of these huge trees in the snow reminds me of the Tennessee woods we traveled through almost twenty-five years ago in even worse weather. What was most different about the picture then was me. Twenty-five years in the life of a man is a veritable revolution. I had this melancholy thought as I made my way through the snow. But after turning these many years over in my mind, I consoled myself with the thought that if I had this quarter of a century to do over again, I would not, all things considered, choose very differently. I would try to eliminate many minor errors and some outright blunders, but as for the bulk of my ideas, my feelings, and even my actions, I wouldn't change a thing. I realized how little my thinking about men in general had changed over that long stretch of time. People talk a great deal about the illusions of youth and the disillusionments of maturity. I haven't noticed this in my personal experience. The vices and weaknesses of human beings were plain to me from the first, and as for the good qualities that I found in people in my youth, I cannot say that I haven't found them virtually unchanged since. This brief backward glance

restored my good spirits, and to top off my rejuvenation, I remembered that I
have retained to this day the friend with whom I hunted parrots in Memphis,
to whom time has only tightened the bonds of trust and friendship that existed
between us then. . . .

From Tocqueville | To Francisque de Corcelle

September 5 [1855]

. . . It is certain that not just since independence but for more than a century the
population of the United States has roughly doubled every 22 years. I see no
reason why this population [growth] should not continue for another century,
and I believe that you could base your calculations on this observation with a
fair degree of certainty, since the present population is known. I do not know
the exact figure. For the Catholic population, any American almanac would give
it to you, and it should be very easy for you to obtain one from Galignani in
Paris or any other bookseller who handles English-language books. As for the
probable increase of American Catholics, it is impossible to offer anything other
than conjectures, since the growth of that part of the American population is
subject to different laws than the total growth. Nevertheless, I see no reason
why the Catholics ought not to grow in number as rapidly over the next twenty
years as they have done for the past twenty. Anyone who knows the latter figure
should therefore have a fairly precise idea of the former. . . .

From Tocqueville | To Theodore Sedgwick

Tocqueville, September 19, [18]55

. . . Tell us about your country after telling us about yourself. Tell us whether
the Know-Nothing Party is as much a threat to the domestic tranquility of the
Union as it seems from afar.[26] The recent popular uprisings in the West have
done nothing to lift the flagging cause of liberty in Europe.[27] The weakness and
incompetence of the English government also harm the cause, as does the penchant for violence, intolerance, and hostility to law that seems to be overtaking

26. The Know-Nothing Party, also known as the American Party, was organized in
the 1840s by nativists who sought to oppose the rising tide of Catholic immigrants and the
Democratic Party that courted them. Thanks to the decline of the Whig Party, the Know-
Nothings had their greatest success in the 1855 New England elections. However, the party
split over the issue of slavery the following year; many northern members fell into the ranks
of the nascent Republican Party, while some Southerners tried to cohere under the banner of
the South American Party.

27. In 1854, Congress had passed a bill stating that the question of slavery in the Kansas
and Nebraska territories would be decided by the popular sovereignty of the settlers. Americans with strong and opposing opinions about the expansion of slavery rushed to the territory to cast their votes, and voter fraud and violence broke out. At one point, rival governments both claimed authority over the territory. The violence died down by 1856, but Kansas
was not admitted to the Union until 1861, when proslavery Americans left the territory to cast
their support with the Confederacy.

parts of the Union. Yet for me the cause of liberty is the good old cause and will remain so as long as I live. . . .

From Tocqueville | To Theodore Sedgwick

Tocqueville, by St.-Pierre-Église (Manche)
August 29, 1856

. . . The success in France of the book that interests you has surpassed my wildest dreams. In seven weeks, the first edition has sold out. Yet this edition appeared at the least favorable time of the year, and the print run was as large as for the first three editions of *Democracy*.[28] If any important American newspapers or journals publish articles on this work that might be of interest to me, I would be very grateful if you could send me copies. I also hope that someone will be good enough to send me the American translation.

Here in Europe we are beginning to believe that you are not far from breaking apart.[29] I hope that that moment is still farther off than is commonly believed. I think that your reserves of practical common sense will for some time yet continue to prevent you from taking such a risk. Unfortunately, so many foreigners land on your shores with each passing day that before long you will cease to be as you were, and arguments based on your "nature" will become increasingly dubious. Now that your population is a mixture of so many different races, who can say exactly what your nature is these days? There is no doubt that in the past few years you have inexplicably abused the privilege that the Good Lord granted you to make great mistakes with impunity, and that you have managed to inspire everywhere in Europe doubts as to your wisdom and fear as to your strength. On this side of the Atlantic you have become Hobbes's *puer robustus*.[30] You dismay the friends of democratic liberty and gladden the hearts of its adversaries. You are much indulged as an unpredictable and dangerous force. Yet at bottom people are becoming increasingly hostile toward you, and the number of those who would be happy to see you stumble into serious trouble and deep disgrace is growing daily. . . .

28. Tocqueville is referring to his book *The Old Regime and the Revolution;* the first and second French edition and first English edition were published in 1856. Publishers printed about two thousand copies of the book, even though June was the month when wealthy residents of Paris left the city for the summer.

29. In his letter of July 29, 1856, Sedgwick had written that American politics were in a chaotic state and that it was impossible to predict the winner of the 1856 presidential election, which unfolded around the explosive topic of the expansion of slavery. The Democrats nominated James Buchanan (1791–1868), the electoral victor, because of his distance from territorial disputes, while the young Republican Party nominated John Fremont (1813–1890) as a proponent of the movement known as Free Soil, which opposed the expansion of slavery. Millard Fillmore ran as the Know-Nothing candidate.

30. Thomas Hobbes (1588–1679), in his book *De Cive* (1642; published in English in 1651), described the danger of "boys with strength," meaning men. Tocqueville had made this allusion in the first volume of *Democracy in America,* part 2, chapter 6.

From Tocqueville | To Francis Lieber

Tocqueville near St.-Pierre-Église (Manche)
September 1, 1856

My dear Lieber,

I received your letter of July 19 and was distressed to see that you had left Columbia, where it seems to me you spent a fairly happy period.[31] I would be very glad to learn what consequences this event will have for you and what new direction you plan to take with your life. You live in a country where life has more ups and downs than it has here. You are subject, even as a private individual, to more vicissitudes than in Europe. But you also have far more means than Europeans do to take advantage of the new situations that events create for you.

Thank you very much for your early expression of interest in the book I have just published. I am most eager to know what you will think after you have read it. I beg you to read it in French. You know our language well enough that I am very keen to show you my ideas in their national costume. The best translation is never more than a wretched copy. This book has thus far enjoyed considerable success in France. The first edition, which was quite large, sold out in seven weeks, and I am right now occupied with the second. There is no doubt that you should be able to find a French copy in New York.

At the time the book appeared, I suffered the great misfortune of losing my father, who, despite his very advanced age, remained for all his children the surest support and guide. We were deeply affected, and every day something happens that reminds us anew of the magnitude of our irreparable loss. Immediately after that sad event, which is to say toward the end of June, we left Paris and came here in search of solitude. We will remain here until spring. You should send your letters here for now. Now that I have no public duties, I spend only a few months in Paris each year. I spend the rest of my time in retirement. I am living in an old family home in a beautiful setting near the sea. I have many books, which my predecessors and I have collected over the years. Here I live a very healthy and agreeable existence, and though not wealthy my situation is one of secure comfort, so that I ask nothing of God except health for me and my dear wife so that we may enjoy the rest of our days here in pleasant retirement. Time marches on. I have just turned 51. Hence I have passed the peak of the mountain and can only descend from here. Along the way I console myself with the thought of how seldom the world works out according to my taste. I passionately hoped to see a free Europe, yet I find that the cause of true liberty is more compromised than it was at the time of my birth. All around me I see nations whose souls seem to falter as they gain in prosperity and physical strength and which remain, to borrow a phrase from Hobbes, "robust children" who deserve to be punished with the rod and given toys to play with. Even your America, once the object of the dreams of all who lacked the reality of liberty,

---

31. Lieber left the University of South Carolina in Columbia to take a teaching appointment as professor of history and political science at Columbia University in New York City.

has in my opinion given very little satisfaction to friends of liberty for some time now. It is as though the despots of the Old World have assigned you to play for their subjects the role that the Spartans assigned the Helots to play for their children,[32] so that the follies and blunders to which liberty may lead can be held up as examples to cure them of the desire of ever wishing to be free. Yet still, the world today presents a strange and utterly novel spectacle, and it would be worth living if only to satisfy one's curiosity.

Farewell. Know that I remain your sincere friend. My wife wants particularly to be remembered to you.

A. de Tocqueville

From Tocqueville | To Theodore Sedgwick

Tocqueville, by St.-Pierre-Église (Manche)
October 14, [18]56

... Like you, I am inclined to believe that however inauspicious the political situation in your country may be, you will not allow yourselves to be drawn into secession and civil war. For the sake of all humanity, I hope so. My hope would be even greater if you were still the same people you were sixty years ago, or even the people I saw twenty-five years ago, although I was already aware of worrisome changes. What frightens me, however, is on the one hand the prodigious number of foreigners, who are turning you into a different people, and on the other hand the race of desperate gamblers to which prosperity in the midst of a still half-empty country has given rise, a race that combines any number of the passions and instincts of the savage with the tastes, needs, vitality, and vices of civilized men. I do not believe that the world has ever seen anything like it. Who can say where this race will lead you if it ever takes control of your politics? What is certain is that in Europe the idea that you are rapidly drawing closer to revolutionary times has taken hold more and more and is spreading very quickly. I do not yet share these fears, or at any rate I do not believe that the event is yet at hand. That is why I am staying with the investment in railway bonds that I mentioned to you. I am counting on you to let me know when you deem it wise to withdraw these funds. To tell the truth, I do not yet see any serious danger. ...

From Tocqueville | To Henry Reeve

Tocqueville, November 21, 1856

... I cannot believe that I haven't yet spoken to you about the pleasure I felt on reading Mr. Gregg's [sic] article.[33] I thanked him more than a month ago, and I was under the impression that I had done the same with you. That is why I

32. Helots were the serfs in ancient Sparta.

33. William Rathbone Greg (1809–1881) was a prolific British essayist for leading periodicals who often espoused free-trade ideals in his essays on society and politics. By 1850, he had given up his business of running a family mill to devote himself fully to writing. In 1856,

didn't mention it in my last letter, even though I discussed the October issue. The truth is that the article about my book that you published in your journal is one of those with which I have most reason to be pleased and perhaps the best of them all, and I am infinitely grateful to both the author and the editor.

Since I imagine that my letter of the 15th reached you with some delay, I will not again go over the subjects with which I dealt there. In any case, I have nothing new to tell you. The election of Mr. Buchanan, which, like you, I expected, has now taken place. Also like you, I believe that it will start the Union down a slippery slope that will end in civil war and that southern secessionists are threatening to do such great harm not only to their country but to all of humanity that true friends of America (and I count myself among them) are reduced to hoping that someone will stop them, even if it means once again bringing war to a vast region that has lived without it for so many years. . . .

I still plan to go to England in the spring. Lewis,[34] who knows everything and more, assured me that the largest archive of revolutionary documents in the world is to be found in London. For me, that is an additional reason for the journey. I hope that when I am able to travel, you will help me rent a small apartment, which would allow me to combine the pleasure of seeing my friends with the delight of not putting myself into bankruptcy. You know that I am determined to have a *place of my own,* and you promised to help make this possible. . . .

From Tocqueville | To Edward Vernon Childe[35]

Tocqueville, December 12, 1856
By St.-Pierre-Église (Manche).

. . . During my brief stay in the United States, more than twenty years ago, Boston seemed to me the most pleasant city to live in. I found there a large number of educated and friendly people, and if I had had to settle somewhere in America, I believe I would have chosen Boston. . . .

What is happening right now in America should be of interest to all civilized men and is of interest to me particularly, since I am half Yankee. It would be very valuable for me to know what a man as sensible as you and who, though American at heart, has long lived outside the orbit of the parties, thinks of the

---

Sir George Cornewall Lewis made him commissioner of customs. Greg's unsigned review of Henry Reeve's English translation of Tocqueville's *The Old Regime and the Revolution* appeared in the October 1856 edition of the *Edinburgh Review* (vol. 212, pp. 273–88).

34. Sir George Cornewall Lewis (1806–1863) was a poor-law commissioner in England from 1835 to 1847. He was editor of the *Edinburgh Review* from 1852 to 1855 and later served as chancellor of the exchequer (1855–58), minister of the interior (1859–61), and secretary of war (1861–63).

35. Edward Vernon Childe (1804–1861), a graduate of Harvard College, was an American newspaper correspondent in Paris for the *New York Times* and the *Courier and Enquirer.* His wife, Catherine Mildred Lee, who was Robert E. Lee's sister, had died in 1856, and Childe had just moved his family back to the United States.

political situation in which the Union finds itself, and what course he imagines the new president will take. I therefore do not excuse you from talking politics when you write. . . .

From Tocqueville | To Theodore Sedgwick

Tocqueville, by St.-Pierre-Église (Manche)
January 10, 1857.

. . . Your country's affairs continue to distress friends of America and of liberty. On this side of the ocean, the election of the new president was taken to signify the triumph of the cause of slavery, perhaps more than is actually the case.[36] Speaking for myself, as one who has never been an abolitionist in the common sense of the term, which is to say that I never believed it possible to eliminate slavery from the older states, I confess that I am vehemently opposed to the extension of this dreadful ill beyond the already too broad confines to which it has been limited until now. To do so would seem to me one of the greatest crimes that men could commit against the general cause of humanity, and on this issue I feel violent political passions—as if a Frenchman aged fifty who has seen four or five revolutions were still allowed to have passions of any sort and to take human affairs very seriously. You can imagine the interest with which I would listen to you if, as I hope, I have the opportunity to converse with you next summer. I think I may be able to tell you a thing or two about France that you don't already know, and I'm sure that you will have volumes to teach me about America of which I am unaware.

I have at last received, rather belatedly, the American translation of my book. I think the translation is very good, and I would like to write to its author.[37] . . .

From Tocqueville | To Arthur de Gobineau[38]

Tocqueville, January 24, 1857

. . . I confess that it was impossible for me to believe that you did not recognize the difficulty of reconciling your scientific theories with the letter and even the spirit of Christianity.[39] As for the letter, what in Genesis is clearer than the unity of the human race and the descent of all men from the same man? And as for the spirit of Christianity, isn't its distinctive trait to have desired the abolition of

36. Only five free states voted for James Buchanan.

37. John Bonner (1828–1899) translated *The Old Regime and the Revolution* (New York: Harper and Brothers, 1856).

38. Arthur de Gobineau (1816–1882) was a struggling poet and writer when Tocqueville took him under his wing. Gobineau founded a newspaper with Kergorlay in 1848, and in 1849, he served as Tocqueville's secretary while Tocqueville was minister of foreign affairs. His most notable work was *Essai sur l'inégalité des races humaines* (1853), which Tocqueville criticized as a tract that wrongly supported genetic predetermination instead of free will.

39. As he stated in *Essai sur l'inégalité des races humaines,* Gobineau believed that three separate and unequal races existed: white, yellow, and black.

all the distinctions of race that the Jewish religion had allowed to subsist, and to create but one human species, all of whose members were equally capable of perfecting themselves and of coming to resemble one another? How can this spirit be reconciled—in a natural way comprehensible to the crude common sense of the multitude—with a historical doctrine that posits distinct and unequal races, some of which are more capable than others of understanding, judging, and acting, and this on account of a certain original disposition, which cannot change and which peremptorily limits the perfection of certain among them? Christianity has clearly tended to make all men brothers and equals. Your doctrine makes them at best cousins, whose common father exists only in heaven. Here below there are only victors and vanquished, masters and slaves by birthright. And this is true to such an extent that your doctrines are approved, quoted, and commented on by whom? By the owners of Negroes and in behalf of eternal servitude based on radical racial difference. I know that there are in the southern United States at the present time Christian priests, and perhaps good priests (though slave owners), who preach from the pulpit doctrines that are no doubt similar to yours. But rest assured that most Christians whose interests do not unwittingly warp their thinking to resemble yours cannot feel the slightest sympathy for your doctrines. I am not speaking of the materialists, whose views, you say, are not contained therein. Even supposing that to be true, it is impossible that many will not derive such views from yours. I confess that reading your book left me in doubt as to the solidity of your faith, and I have disrespectfully placed you among those whose doubts do not prevent them from treating Christianity with true and profound respect, and who do not believe that they are committing an act of hypocrisy in seeking to make their ideas as compatible as possible with Christian teachings. . . .

From Tocqueville | To Edward Vernon Childe

April 2, 1857

. . . You have supplied me with very interesting details about your internal affairs, and I've read them with the greatest pleasure. I have tremendous confidence in your judgment, and everything you write about a country that has played such an important role in my life and that should have so much influence on the destiny of the human race in general will always be extremely precious to me. The greatest blemish on America, after slavery, is indeed as you say the government of the country by the less respectable and perhaps the less capable segment of the population.[40] I cannot help but think that this evil is partly the result of a major good, namely, the fact that the country has been prosperous at home and at peace abroad. I believe that in more difficult circumstances, the people would soon be inclined to choose more respectable leaders. At the moment they give in to their penchants, because they see no danger in doing so.

40. In a letter of February 22, 1857, Childe expressed his lack of confidence in President James Buchanan and his secretary of state, Lewis Cass (1782–1866) of Michigan.

Like all sovereigns, they naturally love courtiers and flatterers. But I have enough confidence in their practical good sense to believe that in a time of crisis they would bestow their trust more carefully. At least I hope so, because I ardently wish that America's great experiment in self-government will not fail. If it were to fail, that would be the end of political liberty on this earth. What is going on with respect to slavery plunges me into despair. I have always strongly opposed the abolitionist party because of its desire to bring a premature and dangerous abolition of slavery to regions in which that abominable institution has always existed. But to introduce slavery into new states, to spread that horrible plague over a vast territory hitherto exempt from it, and to subject millions of people (masters as well as slaves) who might otherwise escape to the crimes and miseries that invariably accompany it would be a crime against the human race, and this strikes me as horrifying and inexcusable.

I am familiar with your American winters, although I never spent one in Boston. I remember that the day I arrived in Washington, in January 1832, it was extremely hot. That night, the Potomac froze. As you might imagine, having witnessed this, I can understand everything. . . .

From Tocqueville | To Theodore Sedgwick

Paris, April 13, 1857

Dear Mr. Sedgwick,

On arriving here I found your letter of February 5 waiting for me. I regret having taken eight days to reply, but you will forgive me, I hope, when you think of all the worries that beset a man who returns to Paris after an absence of nine months.

Of course I would have preferred better news about the sales of the book. Perhaps the success the work has enjoyed in England will eventually influence your public. In France, we are about to publish a new edition. This will be the third in less than ten months, and each print run has been so large that the first three editions of the *Ancien Régime* comprise nearly as many copies as the first six editions of *Democracy in America*. What you tell me about Mr. Bancroft's opinion touches me very deeply.[41] Your mother's letter was of even greater interest to me.[42] Do you know that in learned Europe, which still prides itself on being the center of intellectual activity, and especially in France, which used to have a literary life, one meets precious few women with the admirable curiosity and liveliness of mind that your mother displays in the fragment of a letter that you sent me? I would add that one meets few women capable of reading a work like

41. Sedgwick had reported that, among other scholars in New England, George Bancroft (1800–1891), the noted American historian and member of a prominent Boston family, had complimented Tocqueville's work.

42. With his letter, Sedgwick had sent a note from his mother, Susan Livingston Ridley Sedgwick (1788–1867), who had read Tocqueville's *The Old Regime and the Revolution*. Susan Sedgwick had written several popular works of fiction in her middle years.

Grote's and formulating such a true and accurate judgment.[43] You are proud of your mother, you say, and you surely have reason to be.

I was extremely interested to read what you had to say about your public affairs. How could you apologize for the length of your letter? It seemed too short to me. You made me understand better than I had before why a very respectable part of the population of the North voted for Mr. Buchanan.[44] May it please God that Buchanan live up to the hopes you have placed in him. He is a very distinguished man, I know, but his task is truly difficult. I agree with you that the greatest domestic danger that the northern states face today is not slavery but the corruption of democratic institutions—corruption whose seeds were quite easy to see twenty-five years ago when I was in the United States, and which I think I did anticipate rather well, but which, if I am to believe what I've been told, have spread more rapidly than I feared. As for the policy that is allowing slavery to spread to parts of the territory in which it was hitherto unknown, I am willing to grant, as you do, that in the interest of the Union as it stands today one cannot help but allow it to spread. But as a foreigner, I confess that the sight of it horrifies me and plunges me into despair. I cannot be converted on this point. I cannot accept that in the face of such a terrible calamity, the majority of a great nation does not have the right to an opinion and the right to act, and I cannot accept the idea that any contract can nullify the right and duty of the present generation to prevent the most horrible of all social evils from afflicting millions and millions of people in generations still unborn; I thank God for not putting me in a position where it would be my duty as a citizen to jeopardize a present good as great as the Union, or my duty as a man to allow such an awful plague to spread over such a large portion of the habitable earth and perhaps for as long as the world shall live. I have the feeling that I might write for two hours on this subject, but I will soon be out of paper, and my fear of boring you leads me to change the subject and to take up a far more pleasant one, which is your first trip to Europe.[45] We would be delighted to have you as a guest. You know this already. My wife will receive your daughters as old friends, and we will do our best to make their stay as pleasant as possible. Only we would rather that you bring them to Tocqueville instead of Paris. We don't see people here, as much as we would like to. A few days in the country

43. Tocqueville refers to George Grote's *History of Greece,* whose final volume Susan Sedgwick had just read.

44. Sedgwick had written on February 5 that Buchanan was a more appealing choice than the other potential Democratic candidate, Stephen A. Douglas (1813–1861). He explained that Buchanan appealed to Northerners more than Douglas did because Buchanan had been in Britain during the territorial disputes over slavery and because Buchanan was from a free state. As a result, voters were able to distance him from the issue of slavery more than Douglas, who had been responsible for the 1854 Kansas-Nebraska Act, which provoked intense debate and violence in response to its declaration that settlers of western territories should decide whether to allow slavery by popular sovereignty.

45. Tocqueville means Sedgwick's first trip to Europe since his wife's death in 1856.

would do more to further acquaintance than two months in Paris. We will be in Normandy from July 15 on and won't budge until next spring. If you come this year, you should look for us there. The journey is a bit long, but the region is beautiful and full of remembrances of old Europe that I'm sure will interest the Misses Sedgwick. . . .

From Tocqueville | To Theodore Sedgwick

Paris, June 13, 1857

Dear Sedgwick,

I am a little worried about the fate of a letter that I wrote you some three months ago. Not only have you not answered, but this letter contained another addressed to the translator of my work, who has not answered me either. The coincidence of these two facts makes me fear that the letter did not arrive, yet this is unlikely, because the postal service to America is most exact. In any case, if this brief note cannot take the place of the lost letter, I hope that it will at least shake you from your laziness and encourage you to send me your news.

You had also spoken of a book of yours that still has not reached me.[46] I was most eager to receive it before leaving Paris, so that I might offer it in your name to the Académie des sciences morales et politiques, along with a short comment of my own, which would have been printed in the proceedings of the academy. But I have reached the end of my stay in this city. I leave today and now must wait until the winter is over, sometime around February, before I can have the pleasure of introducing you to my colleagues. Perhaps you would prefer not to wait that long. In any case, send me your instructions. If I cannot introduce the book, I will see to it that you lose nothing in the exchange, which will not be difficult.

I am leaving not for home but for England, where I have many friends whom I have not seen for a long time, and which in any case I want to visit in order to do some research on documents pertaining to the French Revolution. The British Museum owns the most complete collection of sources of this kind that exists anywhere in the world, or so I am told. This might seem surprising if one did not know the English habit of using their great wealth to purchase rare objects, including some to which they attach little value and which scarcely interest them. I am therefore leaving for London and will not return to Tocqueville until the end of July. I sincerely hope that the year there will not end without a visit from you and yours. But I have almost abandoned hope of persuading you for this year.

I beg your pardon for the insignificance of this letter. But the frequent violation of the secrecy of the post makes it very difficult to send abroad anything

---

46. Sedgwick's book was entitled *A Treatise on the Rules Which Govern the Interpretation and the Application of Statutory and Constitutional Law.* Tocqueville wrote a report on it in July of 1858 in which he used Sedgwick's work to emphasize his belief that, as exemplified in America, judges were the most important check to legislative power.

interesting about what is happening in France. I want to be sure that this letter reaches you. That is why I do not want even to allude to politics.

You are not, thank God, in the same situation, and I hope that when you write, you will not forget to tell me a little about public affairs in your country, in which you know I share a concern which is no less keen for being disinterested. Is the government of the new president of a nature to calm the almost revolutionary agitation provoked by his election? I devoutly hope so. Passions in the most recent elections seem to me to have reached a degree of vehemence that in Europe would be a sure sign of impending civil war and may fairly rapidly lead to such an outcome in America if they cannot be calmed. May God forbid such a great misfortune! When I think of the immense gifts that Providence has bestowed on you, of the almost superhuman prosperity that you enjoy, and of the prodigious future that awaits you if you remain united; and when I see so many goods on the verge of being diminished or squandered by the wicked passions of men, I am tempted to exclaim with Molière:

L'homme est, je l'avouerai, un méchant animal.[47]

It would be even more just, however, to say that he is a limited and imperfect animal more deserving of pity than of wrath. I still count on the practical common sense of the American people to give me a better opinion of our species.

Farewell, dear Sedgwick. My wife asks to be remembered to you, and I beg you to believe, as always, in my sincere friendship.

A. de Tocqueville

P.S. You must write to me now at *Tocqueville,* by *St.-Pierre-Église* (Manche).

From Tocqueville | To the Massachusetts Historical Society[48]

[June 1857]

Sir

I have received the letter you wrote to me announcing that I had been unanimously elected an honorary member of the Massachusetts Historical Society.[49]

I pray you to tell in my name to your colleagues that I accept with the deepest feeling of gratitude the title they have conferred to me.

I know that your society (which is already an ancient and celebrated institution) has produced excellent works and contains many very distinguished members and I consider as highly honourable for me to be nearly connected with it.

All the links which bind me with the American people are very dear in my

---

47. "Man, I admit, is a nasty animal." Tocqueville paraphrases this line from act 5 of *Tartuffe,* a play by Molière (1622–1673) first performed in 1664 at the court of Louis XIV.

48. Tocqueville wrote this letter in English.

49. The Massachusetts Historical Society was founded in 1791 and was one of the premier intellectual societies in America. Throughout the nineteenth century, American and French intellectuals conferred memberships on one another as a way of sustaining intellectual exchange across the Atlantic.

estimation and I feel very proud and happy when I know that my name is not unknown in your grand and glorious country.

Believe me, Sir, your very humble servant.

From Tocqueville | To Francis Lieber

Tocqueville near Saint Pierre Église (Manche)
October 9, 1857

My dear Lieber,

I was indeed beginning to believe that you had forgotten me when I received your letter of May 30. When I say that I received it, I mean when I read it, which was a fairly short time ago. When your letter arrived at my house, I was in England, where I had gone for both business and pleasure. I wanted to see friends whom I had not seen in quite some time, and I also hoped to profit from their position in the government to obtain from the Queen's archives information that I need for the continuation of my work and that might have been impossible to get if I hadn't had friends in the cabinet. I was wholly successful in achieving my goal, and my trip was as fruitful as it was agreeable.

Your letter was a source of great pleasure to us because of the news of your new position. It is a quite honorable one, and you obtained it as one should, by unanimous election. Please accept our sincere congratulations. Although it is true that in American society the ground (though fundamentally solid) is always shifting beneath one's feet, I hope that this time you will have found a firm footing. They say that this is always difficult for a foreigner, especially when he does not belong to the English race. As for that great and singular country, in which I take such a sincere and even passionate interest, tell me, then, what you think of the current situation. I am speaking not of the situation of the parties, exactly, but rather of what is more permanent than the contest between the parties, namely, the ground of political mores and habits themselves. I hear distressing things from most Europeans, even well-intentioned ones, who return from the United States, and sometimes even from Americans. They assure me that the portion of the population whose mores are still violent and whose habits remain coarse is increasingly setting the tone for the rest, and that acts of personal violence and of self-enforced justice are increasingly justified as mores, so much so that many peaceful men carry weapons in case they need to invoke the right of legitimate self-defense. Some add that this evil is compounded by the growing flaws of the justice system, which, in becoming more and more unstable and dependent on the multitude or the parties (because judges are elected by universal suffrage and their tenure is short), in many cases fails to offer sufficient guarantees to individuals to prevent them from defending themselves. How much of this is true? I beg you to answer frankly. I have no intention of making any use *whatsoever* of your response, other than to enlighten myself and make up my mind about an issue in which I take the utmost interest.

I am very flattered by your good opinion of my latest work and by what you tell me of the approval it has garnered from the competent judges you mention. In France I have already published three *large* editions in 11 months, and the third is rapidly selling out. I am deeply absorbed right now in the work I need to do in order to complete my œuvre.

Farewell, dear Lieber. Be well, and from time to time think of us and our sincere friendship for you.

A. de Tocqueville

P.S. Since I never know when I will be here and when in Paris, I ask you to address all your letters to the Institut in care of M. Pingard, the head of the secretariat.

From Tocqueville | To Charles Sumner

Tocqueville, by St. Pierre-Église (Manche).
November 14, 1857

. . . Now that you are back in America, I hope that you will supply me with information that I am very eager to obtain. I am counting on your clarity of mind and good judgment to supply this information in a useful form. I have some funds invested in America. I am going to tell you the names of the firms in which I have invested in order of the size of my holdings.

Michigan Central Railway. I have BONDS of this company. According to information already supplied to me by Mr. Baring, who advised me to buy these bonds, this company, though in difficulty, should recover. The railroad is excellent. Its profits have risen steadily for several years, and the *bearers of bonds* need not fear a serious loss. The bulk of my funds are here.[50]

Chicago and Galena Railway. I also have bonds of this company, but in a smaller amount than for Michigan Central.

Marietta and Cincinnati Railway.[51] I have only two bonds of this company.

Finally, I own a very small number of *shares* of *Lacrosse and Milwaukee Railroad.*[52]

You will have gathered how important it is for me to be up-to-date concerning everything that affects these railroads, especially the Michigan and Galena. You would be doing me a valuable service *as a friend* to keep me informed, for as long as this terrible crisis lasts, about the situation of these companies and anything important concerning them. I ask you to do me this favor, and I hope,

50. Bonds had fallen 50 percent in value during an economic downturn later called the depression of 1857. New York financiers had taken over the Michigan Central Railroad, but Sedgwick continued to reassure Tocqueville that the railroad bonds would recover their value.

51. Originally founded as the Belpre and Cincinnati Railroad in 1845, this railroad eventually connected Wheeling, Virginia, to Cincinnati, Ohio, by running through the town of Marietta, Ohio. Work stalled in 1857 when the company went bankrupt, but construction resumed in the 1860s.

52. Completed in 1858, the Lacrosse and Milwaukee Railroad connected Milwaukee on Lake Michigan with Lacrosse to the west.

dear Mr. Sumner, that you will not refuse, given the critical situation in which we find ourselves. Funds such as those I have invested in Michigan and Galena would be safe in Europe from any crisis, but the financial convulsion that has gripped your country is so violent that it is impossible to say what might happen in a situation as unprecedented as this. All of this must of course remain strictly between ourselves. What I have said about my affairs is for *you alone.*

I have not forgotten my promise to keep you abreast of affairs in Europe, but since you have just left our continent, there is nothing yet to tell you. I am convinced that the financial crisis in America will affect us all, and for a time money matters will become the most important issue for governments everywhere.

I was pleased to see that the people of Kansas have voted to move in the direction of freedom![53] May it please God that slavery shall disappear from the contested territory! Be sure to let me know in your reply (*which I beg you to send as soon as possible*) how you found the state of the slavery question, in which you take such a great interest, upon your return.

Please convey my warmest greetings to your brother. And don't forget to mention me to the Ticknor family should you run into them in Boston. My wife asks particularly to be remembered to you. Rest assured of my deepest esteem and friendship.

From Tocqueville | To Gustave de Beaumont

Tocqueville, November 16, 1857

. . . I have no need to tell you that, all this time, I've been deeply concerned and often quite agitated about our American investments. I don't know if my wife told yours about our reasons for hoping that we might escape this cataclysm without drowning entirely. According to figures provided to us by an American friend, whose opinion has been corroborated by Mr. Baring (the head of England's leading banking house, as you know), it seems quite certain that the major railroad in which we have invested is one of the best in America and that its revenue has been growing steadily for several years, so that even if its income were suddenly cut in half instead of continuing to grow, the company would still have more than enough to pay the interest on its bonds (the bond debt being senior to all others). Despite these figures and assurances, I confess that I am experiencing great anxiety, from which I fear I will not escape anytime soon. What is more, we in France will have a hard time surviving a crisis that is by no

---

53. In 1857, Kansans defeated the proslavery Lecompton Constitution by a large margin in a referendum vote. Though President Buchanan tried to push the defeated state constitution through Congress for approval, Kansans drafted a new constitution that outlawed slavery in the territory. Debate over the issue continued until Kansas was admitted to the Union as a free state in 1861.

In a letter of November 3, 1857, Sumner had written to Tocqueville that it was becoming increasingly important that the United States rid itself of the corrupt politicians who sought to advance the interests of slaveholders.

means identical but still grave. The contraction of the money supply has already caused prices to fall. Everyone is afraid to buy. That may be the reason why you were unable to sell your woods. There, at least, capital cannot escape, and over time it cannot fail to increase a good deal. . . .

From Beaumont | To Alexis de Tocqueville

November 19, 1857, Beaumont-la-Chartre

No matter how closely we follow what people refer to as the financial and commercial crisis in America, we are not fully aware, my dear friend, of its nature and consequences. . . . How much do you stand to lose if the still-uncertain disaster were to come to pass? That is what we would like to know. I cannot understand how American or other railway bonds can become worthless, because with bonds in general, the collateral for the investment is worth twenty times as much as the face value. . . .

From Tocqueville | To Gustave de Beaumont

Tocqueville, December 6, 1857

. . . I did not respond to the pressing questions that you as a friend put to me in your penultimate letter regarding our American investments, because I thought I had said everything in the letter that crossed yours in the mail. Nearly all of the considerable sum we have invested in America is in bonds of two railroads: (1) Central Michigan Railway; (2) Galena-Chicago. Most of the money is in the Central Michigan Railway. Everything we heard about these railroads before as well as after we lent them our money convinced us that they were reputed to be the best on the continent and were doing very well indeed when the crisis began. You know that in America as in Europe, lenders have collateral in the railroad. They must be paid before anything is given to the stockholders, and interest on the loan will go unpaid only if the railroad is not earning any money. That is all I know. I see in the *Times* that the Michigan Railway is still listed on the stock exchange and that its bonds are at 75. This leads me to believe that people think it will recover from the crisis, which has caused the suspension of all [interest] payments in America. But until this semester's interest payments come due, we cannot be certain whether or not they will continue to pay. My impression is that the capital is not in serious danger, but a suspension of interest payments would cause us real pain at the moment and raise concerns about the future. In short, although business is improving in America and I am no longer as *stunned* as I was at first, my anxiety remains high and hard to bear. What worries me in the current situation is not so much the magnitude of the danger as the amount I have at risk. Hence I am extremely impatient for direct news from America. Unfortunately I have few regular correspondents there. Sedgwick, who was the best, is either dying or dead. Others are absent from the country. I wrote to Sumner (the senator), who came to see me this summer. He is a celebrated New York lawyer. I have no doubt that he is in a position to know what is going on and more than willing to share with me the benefit of what he knows. Yet even with steam it takes a very long time to receive a response from the United States, and I do not expect one in less than three weeks at the earliest. That is all I can tell you for now. The improvement in the business climate, the quality of the railroad itself, and the opinion of Baring bring us some measure of reassurance. But it is not so easy to feel reassured when a large part of one's fortune is at stake. . . .

From Tocqueville | To Edward Vernon Childe

Tocqueville, January 23, 1858

. . . You said nothing about your commercial crisis or the current state of affairs in America, which would have been of great interest to me. I hope that the abolitionist cause will win in Kansas. I hope so with all my heart, for the sake of the human race. The Mormons may well give you a good deal of trouble.[54] Isn't it strange to find polygamy, an institution characteristic of nascent or half-barbarous societies, emerging from the heart of an old civilized society? . . .

From Tocqueville | To Pierre Freslon[55]

Tocqueville, March 5, 1858

. . . How right you were to admire Washington and to place him at the head of our species! This proves what I knew already: that you recognize and love true grandeur and true glory. Of how few of our compatriots and even our contemporaries could I say as much? Washington is the product of the society from which he sprang and of the time in which he lived. In France he would have been thought lackluster, for we require theatrical virtues, big words, and impressive vices. Indeed, audacious words and vices are enough. . . .

From Tocqueville | To Charles Sumner

Tocqueville, by St. Pierre-Église (Manche)
March 28, [18]58

. . . It is becoming increasingly dangerous for anyone in France to write about the state of public affairs. So do not expect me to talk politics with you, unless it is American politics. In any case, I am much concerned with American politics too, yet even though I read what the newspapers have to say, I have a hard

---

54. In 1857, President Buchanan sent federal troops to Utah to bring the Mormons under government control. Buchanan perceived their practice of polygamy and theocracy as a threat to federal authority. Though violence occurred during the episode, Mormon leader Brigham Young avoided outright war and eventually reached an agreement with the U.S. government that allowed the Mormons to build a community in Salt Lake City.

55. Alexandre Pierre Freslon (1808–1867) was a lawyer who shared many of Tocqueville's views about republican government. He worked with Tocqueville in the administration of the Second Republic, as minister of public instruction, and founded a republican newspaper, *Le Précurseur de l'Ouest.*

time understanding anything. Will Kansas be condemned to endure the horrors of slavery? Will it ultimately escape that fate? As a friend of America and of humanity, I eagerly await any answer you might have to this question.

Many in Europe have begun to accuse you of trading in slaves. I do not know whether this allegation has any basis in fact. The charge is that you are trading in slaves not only on behalf of countries where slavery is still established but also for yourselves. Our newspapers occasionally carry stories about cargoes of blacks being unloaded in the southern states along the Gulf of Mexico. Is there any basis for this accusation?[56]

But what is even more harmful to you in European public opinion, which, as you know, is not much concerned with slavery, is the behavior that has lately been ascribed to many in America who are involved in public affairs and who are leaders either in individual states or of the Union.[57] We constantly hear anecdotes that may well be false or exaggerated but which invariably tend to suggest that most American public figures lack moderation, in some cases honesty, and above all education, and that they belong to a breed of political adventurers—an energetic and intelligent breed but also violent, crude, and unprincipled. Please note that I am far from asserting that this is in fact the case. I speak only of the public impression and of the harm this does to America and its institutions. Since I take a most lively interest in your nation, I am often chagrined by what I hear said about it in France and even in England. Without going so far as to believe everything I hear, I am nevertheless inclined to believe that the development of unlimited democracy often attracts to government men more fit to obey than to command and that *on the whole* the governors are inferior to the governed. Am I wrong? . . .

From Tocqueville | To Sir George Cornewall Lewis

Tocqueville, September 5, 1858

. . . The ultrademocratic system has triumphed among the Americans to such a degree that it would be almost impossible to take it any further, and it is favored by a majority so overwhelming and so well defended by laws that it would be madness to attempt to combat it. There are infinitely more proponents of aristocracy and even monarchy in the United States than people imagine. I believe that at bottom most wealthy people lean nowadays in this direction. But the battle would be totally unwinnable, so they resign themselves and keep quiet. In many cases they even join in with the applause of the multitude. Democrats

56. Regardless of the ban on the importation of slaves, passed in 1808, a number of cargo ships had been found trying to bring slaves into the United States.

57. The Thirty-fifth Congress investigated a number of scandals in 1857 and 1858. In one instance, Massachusetts manufacturers had paid Congress to pass tariffs that favored their businesses. In another, associates of Secretary of War John Floyd were involved with speculative purchases of military lands, which put Floyd under suspicion of corruption. Sumner blamed slavery for what he saw as growing corruption in the United States.

have the stage to themselves, and it is very difficult for them to find a subject of legislation on which they disagree profoundly. But England, fortunately for it, is still a level-headed country. The classes balance one another; the democratic element subsists and remains powerful, even though the government belongs to the aristocracy, though I concede that the sharp conflict between these major components of society is for the time being in abeyance. But the *substance* of the great parties continues to exist, while it would be difficult today to find it in America apart from the slavery question. . . .

From Tocqueville | To Nassau William Senior

Tocqueville,
August 21, 1858

. . . I continue to lament the fact that you were forced to give up your grand tour of America. I expected most interesting things to come of it. I thought that by reading you I would at least begin anew to understand a country that has changed so much since my journey there that it has become more and more obscure to me. . . .

Tocqueville's Political and Occasional Writings on America

ON ANDREW JACKSON AND REPARATIONS, FROM "NOTE ON THE POWERS OF THE PRESIDENT OF THE UNITED STATES," 1835

I first examine what the *Constitution* says and then turn to *commentaries* and *customs.*

Article II, section 2, of the Constitution states:

[The president] *shall have power, by and with the advice and consent of the Senate, to make treaties, provided two-thirds of the senators present concur; and he shall nominate and, by and with the advice and consent of the Senate, shall appoint ambassadors. . . .*

Section 3 of the same article reads:

He shall receive ambassadors and other public ministers.

Commentaries

I consulted the three most respected commentaries: *The Federalist,* a work published by three of the principal drafters of the federal Constitution; the *Commentaries* of Chancellor Kent; and those of Judge Story.[58]

58. The *Federalist* essays, written by Alexander Hamilton, James Madison, and John Jay (1788); *Commentaries on American Law,* by James Kent (4 vols., 1826–30); and *Commentaries on the Constitution of the United States,* by Joseph Story (1833).

Here are the doctrines that emerge from these commentaries (I list my authorities in the margin).

The Senate of the United States is a body with a dual character: it is at once a legislative body and an administrative body. In the former case its deliberations are public; in the latter they are secret.

The Senate, in its character as an administrative body, is jointly responsible with the president for making treaties. That being the case, it would strictly speaking be entitled to take part in negotiations, but in practice it is wisely agreed that the Senate must allow the president, as *sole representative of the nation in dealing with foreign ministers,* to initiate, direct, and provisionally conclude treaty agreements. Treaties are subsequently submitted to the Senate, which may approve, reject, or amend them as it chooses.

The question of whether the treaty thus concluded had to be submitted to Congress or whether it committed the nation *ipso facto* was a contentious one in the United States.

In 1796 the House of Representatives declared that if the execution of treaty clauses required passage of a law, Congress had the right in connection with said law to deliberate on the treaty itself. In the same year Washington issued a message denying that the Congress had any such right.

According to Kent, Washington's view seems to have prevailed in America. In 1816 the House of Representatives had the opportunity to demonstrate that it shared Washington's view. This opinion to some extent explains General Jackson's attitude; he used it in support of his statement that France would fail to meet its *commitments* if the Chamber of Deputies rejected the treaty.[59]

It is clear to me on the basis of the texts and commentaries I have just cited, as well as what I learned myself in America, that both under the Constitution and by custom the president is the regular and sole representative of the nation in dealing with foreign powers. Ministers communicate with him alone, and it is through him that all verbal and documentary undertakings must pass to reach the Senate.

59. During the reign of Napoleon (from 1799 to 1815), the French navy had seized a number of American ships, and the United States had asked France to pay reparations for these seizures, to no avail. After President Andrew Jackson (1767–1845) was inaugurated in 1829, he revived the issue by sending minister William Cabell Rives (1793–1868) to France to collect reparations. Though Rives negotiated a treaty supported by King Louis-Philippe to this effect in 1831, the French Chamber of Deputies did not appropriate funds to make the payments to the United States. In 1833, Jackson appointed Secretary of State Edward Livingston as a minister to France to retrieve the payments outlined in the 1831 treaty. When Livingston also proved unable to secure French funds, Jackson condemned the French government for not fulfilling its agreement and threatened to seize French property as compensation; his approach deeply insulted French officials.

Diplomatic tensions between France and the United States reached such a height that many officials feared war would erupt; negotiations between the two countries came to a halt, and Livingston returned to the United States in 1835. In 1836, Jackson tempered his bellicose language, and the French chamber sent the agreed-upon funds to the United States.

Now, if President Jackson (who is after all only a functionary) did not commit the American nation to a dispute with the French nation by issuing his message, there can be no doubt that he did insult France as an individual. Can France maintain its honor while continuing to treat this man as the *sole and necessary intermediary* between it and the American nation? Until this man has at least explained himself in a way that we can accept, I do not think so as either an individual or a citizen of France.

For three months now, President Jackson has shown no inclination whatsoever to retract his outrageous insinuations, and in fact his conduct has become more and more arrogant. His letter to Mr. Livingston indicates that he would have been pleased if the ambassador of the United States had left France the moment his passports were delivered to him.

In sum, I think that by accepting the principle of the law and agreeing to distinguish between the American nation and its president (which is already to act differently from Louis XIV),[60] the chamber can do no less than declare that it acted as it did in the conviction that its ministers will not accredit any diplomatic agent to the president of the United States unless said president offers a satisfactory explanation for his words.

Such a course will impede affairs only temporarily, since the president's term expires in two years.

ON THE MISSISSIPPI VALLEY, FROM "THE EMANCIPATION OF SLAVES," OCTOBER 1843

... The Gulf of Mexico and the Sea of the Antilles[61] join to form an interior sea that is already a major artery of trade and is surely destined to become even more important in the future.

I will say nothing about things that are merely likely to happen, rather than certain: the construction of a canal across the Isthmus of Panama, which would make the Sea of the Antilles the regular route to the Pacific Ocean; the development of civilization in the vast regions, now half empty and barbarous, that border the Sea of the Antilles in the southern portion of America; the pacification of Mexico, a vast empire that already boasts a population almost as large as that of Spain; and the commercial progress of the Antilles themselves. If all these fine territories, which though they differ in customs, tastes, and needs are nevertheless geographical neighbors, were eventually to be filled with civilized, industrious peoples, the sea that links them would surely become one of

60. Louis XIV (1638–1715), the Bourbon king who sat on the French throne for all but the first five years of his life, once famously declared, *"L'état, c'est moi"* (I am the state). Known as the Sun King, he believed in the divine right of monarchs and worked to centralize the French government to bring the country more tightly under the control of what he believed was the king's God-ordained authority.

61. Today, the Sea of the Antilles is more commonly called the Caribbean Sea.

the world's major trading areas. Some say that all these things are problematic and may never occur at all. Some have already occurred. But let us concentrate on what is certain. It is into these seas that the waters of the Mississippi flow, and with those waters come the fruits of the incomparable valley on which the river draws. No one can doubt that the Mississippi will soon become the world's most important trade route. The Mississippi Valley is the heartland of North America. It is a thousand leagues in length and nearly as many in breadth. It is watered by fifty-seven major navigable rivers, several of which are a thousand leagues long, as is the river into which they empty. Much of the valley comprises the richest soil in the New World. Empty forty years ago, this valley is today home to ten million people. New waves of immigrants arrive every day, and new states are formed each year.[62]

To communicate with the rest of the world from almost anyplace in this vast valley one must follow the Mississippi downstream. The mouth of the river, where it joins the Gulf of Mexico, is virtually the only exit from the valley.[63] Thus the wealth of the entire North American continent, which the Anglo-American race is exploiting with such amazing success and rare energy, will increasingly be carried by the Mississippi. Without a doubt, the sea that supports not only the trade of the Antilles themselves but also that of Colombia, Mexico, and perhaps China, and which also serves as the most convenient outlet for nearly all the products of North America, must be regarded as one of the most strategic places on earth. To put it simply, this sea is already *the Mediterranean* of the New World, and it will become more so with each passing year. Like the Mediterranean, it will be a center of trade and maritime influence.

It is here that control of the Atlantic will be disputed and won. The United States is already the world's third naval power. In the near future it will vie with England for superiority. There is no doubt that this contest will be centered primarily in the Gulf of Mexico and the Sea of the Antilles, because naval warfare always follows trade. Its primary purpose is either to protect or interdict trade routes. . . .

62. While Americans moved west to populate new territory, new states were admitted to the Union less frequently than Tocqueville claims. Most of the states in the lower Mississippi River valley had been admitted in the 1810s. Arkansas, admitted to the Union in 1836, was the first state to be added since Missouri in 1821.

63. By 1843, several railroad lines had established east–west transportation across the Mississippi Valley. Tocqueville was most likely relying on observations made during his travels down the Mississippi in the winter of 1831–32.

M. Guizot's speech has put a new face on the America question.[64] It is no longer the past that is at issue but rather the future. It is about Oregon, not Texas. France has spoken. She has made an important statement to the world.

I will not dwell on the major balance-of-power issues, which have already been dealt with so prudently. I will simply say a word about three nations whose power is growing while we stand pat in a position of *modesty* and *moderation,* which I recognize but do not approve.

Which of these powers is likely to offend us least? America. And which do we offend more? America. I call upon each of you to consult your conscience.

Others have shown the degree to which your *actions* and your language were contrary to the interests of France. I want to show how useless they were, and in doing so, I shall lay bare your policy's hidden purpose. . . .

You wanted to prevent the United States from taking control of Texas.[65] This was pointless. In the wake of these actions, and contrary to all diplomatic custom, you have formulated theories about the need to halt the territorial expansion of the United States. This was pointless. . . .

I do not accuse you of sharing the error implicit in your actions and words. You know America too well to have made such crude mistakes. If your intention was not that implicit in your actions and words, what was it?

It was this:

The outcome of the Oregon dispute hung in the balance; the two nations were negotiating. And do you know what one of America's main advantages in this negotiation was? *Uncertainty* as to the attitude of France.

The English were afraid that we would favor the Americans. The Americans hoped for the same thing. And what was the basis of their hope? Our interests, *their interests,* and old ties of friendship.

You wanted to deprive them of this advantage. And to that end you first sought an occasion to demonstrate your disfavor, an occasion that might show the world that you stood with the English against the Americans. In the end,

64. In June of 1845, during debates over the annexation of Texas to the United States, the French foreign minister François Guizot (1787–1874) had argued that France's best interest depended on a balance of power among nations. France should ensure that this balance of power remained in place. The United States, Britain, and Spain all battled for power and territory in North America throughout the 1840s, and though Guizot advised French leaders to support whichever power could best help France at a particular moment, he had a close working relationship with several British ministers. Guizot articulated this position with regard to Texas. Tocqueville applied it to the Oregon boundary dispute between the United States and England.

65. The United States annexed the independent Republic of Texas in 1845, with the consent of its leading inhabitants. The annexation led to the Mexican-American War (1846–48).

when no such occasion presented itself, you were quick to let the Americans know that they could expect nothing in the way of support from you.

That was the secret goal of all your conduct. . . .

But to proclaim this neutrality in advance was so harmful to American interests that the question arises, was it in our own interest? Why tie our hands in advance? Why withdraw so openly from this business, when it may well become a matter of considerable interest in the future? Be that as it may, how do you understand this neutrality? The main purpose of this speech is to raise this question, because we need to know the answer. Do you envision something like the armed neutrality of the northern powers in 1800?[66]

It is not we of the opposition who need to know the answer to this question; it is France.

Significance of actions and words.

Actions: official documents.

Three things follow from this:

1. French policy is not just aligning itself with English policy but merging with it entirely.

Not only are we doing things *in concert* and sharing documents; we have also given our agents general orders to reach an agreement.

Yet even if we grant that we have an interest—a remote interest—in the question, it is clear to everyone that the interest of the English is vastly superior to ours.

2. How far might we have gone according to the documents?

There is no evidence that we would not have gone so far as to *break off* relations or even declare *war* if the United States had tried to seize Texas.

If the treaty of annexation had been ratified by the Senate, France would have opposed it (dispatch of August 1, 1844) and more: the Senate's resistance eliminated the need for France and England to take a public stand against the treaty.

France's actions committed the country to a course that might have ended in war with the United States or in something no less absurd, namely, a pledge to guarantee the existence of both Texas and Mexico. In other words, we might have been formally implicated in any disputes that might arise between those two states.

3. The documents and, even more, M. Guizot's speeches show that commitments were made. That is a serious matter. It is not simply a matter of poor policy in the past; a menace hangs over the future.

One must never lose sight of the fact that immediately behind the Texas question looms the question of Oregon. And all the reasons that M. Guizot gave for intervening in Texas pertain directly to Oregon.

France did not intervene in Texas for *narrow* or *temporary* reasons but for *general* and *permanent* ones. The doctrine according to which France has an interest

66. The Northern League, established by the Russian tsar Paul I in 1800, included Russia, Sweden, Denmark, and Prussia. The league and France shared an enmity against England.

in confining the United States within its present boundaries and establishing a balance of power in America is just as applicable to the Oregon question as to the Texas question.

When I think of the philosophical and historical rather than diplomatic tenor of M. Guizot's contribution to this debate, I cannot help but recall that he is a proponent of general ideas who, in this case, did not give in to the general tendency of his thinking. He followed instead a preconceived plan, which went as follows:

1. Help the English in their pending negotiations by raising the specter of a French threat.

2. Lay the groundwork for still more effective aid to the English if war came. . . .

In other words, the plan was to form a defensive alliance with England against America. Compare Guizot's language to Lord John Russell's.[67]

Is the policy described by these actions and these words consistent with our interests?

This policy is *new,* a first step in a direction that is not only *different from* but *absolutely contrary* to the course that France has followed for the past eighty years.

On this one point, Louis XVI, the Republic, Napoleon—who went so far as to surrender France's finest colony for the sole purpose of achieving what you are trying to prevent, namely, an expansion of the maritime power of the United States—and the July Revolution were all in agreement. Only the Restoration, it seems, chose not to pursue a different course but to pursue the existing one with diminished zeal.

The rhetoric has remained unchanged over the years. If I could not easily persuade the minister of foreign affairs of this, I would call upon the minister of the interior to repeat to his colleague what he said in 1834. Here are his words:[68] . . .

But, says M. Guizot, the United States itself does not want such a close alliance. Its basic policy is not to enter into alliances of this sort.

While this is true, it is also open to question.

America was not our ally in 1793. It did not throw itself into battle at our side, but it came close to doing so. It is fair to say that the majority of the American people wanted to do so. Washington *expended* some of his immense popularity to prevent it.

But suppose that we cannot hope for a true alliance.

The point is that *America* serves our interests not through alliance but through its *importance.* It will share the seas and restore a *balance* of maritime power.

67. Lord John Russell (1792–1878) had given a speech on Anglo-American relations in January of 1846, but it is unclear to which specific points Tocqueville is referring. Russell would become prime minister of England later that year.

68. In 1834, Charles Marie Tanneguy Duchâtel delivered a speech arguing that a close French-American alliance would bring many advantages to France, particularly free trade.

It serves us without wishing to, without entering into an agreement with us. A recent example: the right of inspection. . . .

I believe that in matters of *well-defined and limited common interest,* we can easily conclude a narrow alliance. . . .

The very presidential message that has been invoked as proof of the *selfishness* of American policy proves it: ". . . France, which had been our ancient ally, the country which has a common interest with us in maintaining the freedom of the seas. . . ."[69]

ON FEDERALISM, FROM A LETTER PUBLISHED IN *Le Commerce,* 21 APRIL 1845

. . . The Swiss government is said to be powerless because Switzerland is not a unitary republic but a federal regime. Yet other nations of the world live under federal constitutions in which the central government knows how to command obedience. The example of America stands as proof. To be sure, it is more difficult for a single power to govern twenty-eight distinct nations, several of which are as large as all of Switzerland, and which together cover a territory almost as vast as Europe, than it is to govern the twenty-two small societies contained within the narrow confines of the Swiss state. Nevertheless, the American government is strong, recognized as legitimate, and respected, while the Swiss government has seen its legitimacy contested and exists in name only.

Thus the problem lies not with federal institutions in general but with the particular federal institutions that Switzerland has adopted, or, rather, that were imposed on it in 1815.[70]

What accounts for the peculiar weakness of Swiss federal institutions? To give a full answer to this question would require more ample space than a newspaper article allows. Nevertheless, I shall try to offer a brief overview.

To begin with, it is easy to see that what makes the Swiss government so weak is not that its powers under the federal pact are unduly limited. The Diet possesses nearly all sovereign powers. It can make peace and war, sign treaties, raise troops and money, and lest it find itself unduly confined by this precise delimitation of its powers, the federal pact allows it to take *all other measures* that it may deem necessary to ensure the internal and external security of Switzerland,

69. Polk delivered this message on December 2, 1845. He continued as follows: "most unexpectedly, and to our unfeigned regret, took part in an effort to prevent annexation and to impose on Texas, as a condition of the recognition of her independence from Mexico, that she would never join herself to the United States."

70. From 1798 to 1803, Switzerland was under the influence of Napoleonic France and was known as the Helvetic Republic, which was more egalitarian and centralized than the previous Swiss Confederation. In 1803, the Act of Mediation restored the Swiss Confederation and declared equality among all of its peoples. The Congress of Vienna reestablished Swiss neutrality in 1815 and gave more independence to the cantons. The renewed independence of the cantons and free cities within the confederation instigated a conservative backlash and renewed tension between city dwellers and country residents.

a provision that would provide an enterprising government with a pretext to do anything it wanted to do.

The extreme weakness of the Swiss government is therefore not a consequence of imprudent limitation of its powers. What, then, is its cause? Simply this: that while the government was granted great powers, it was not accorded the means to make regular and easy use of them. What was the reason for this?

The Swiss federal government does not exert direct command over its citizens. It acts on them only through the cantonal governments. That is the principal reason for the weakness of the federal government. Now, experience shows that this weakness could be eliminated without violating the federal constitution. Compare the Constitution of the United States of America with that of Switzerland: Congress has no more powers than the Diet, so why can Congress do what the Diet cannot? Because it wields instruments of its own. Because when it comes to implementing its will, it does not need to borrow its means of action from another power, as the Diet does. Its sphere of action is limited, as is the Diet's, by the sovereignty of the several states, but in its sphere, at least, it is equipped with everything it needs to act quickly and efficiently. When the American government orders money to be raised, it has its own tax collectors, who require each citizen to pay his proper share. When it recruits an army, it has its own agents to levy troops. When it establishes a customs barrier, it has its own customs agents. And finally, when a taxpayer refuses to pay or a soldier refuses to march or a customs agent refuses to obey orders, it has courts that represent it alone and compel citizens to respect its laws. What can the Swiss government do to achieve the same ends? It cannot directly address its citizens but must rely instead on the cantonal governments exclusively. Should it wish to use its power under the constitution to levy a tax, for example, it has no way to reach the taxpayers; instead, it must ask the cantons to deliver a certain amount. It has no administrative apparatus of its own, no courts to enforce respect for its orders, and almost no contact with citizens. In fact, it cannot even claim Switzerland's two million residents as its subjects. Its only true subjects are the twenty-two governors of the cantons that make up the Helvetic Republic. It cannot govern its citizens without the help of the governors, and if the governors refuse to obey or simply take no action, the central government is reduced to what? To a choice between impotence and war. . . .

ON CHERBULIEZ'S *Democracy in Switzerland,* FROM *Séances et travaux de l'Académie des sciences morales and politiques,* 15 JANUARY 1848[71]

Gentlemen,

The importance of the subject that M. Cherbuliez addresses in this book seemed to me worthy of detailed examination, and believing that such examination might prove useful, I have decided to give the work my attention.

---

71. Tocqueville delivered this speech on January 15, 1848, at the Académie des sciences morales et politiques in Paris; it was subsequently published in the journal of that institu-

My intention is to set aside all preoccupations of the moment, as is only fitting within these walls. I will say nothing about current events, which are none of our concern, and deal not with the behavior of political society in Switzerland but rather with Swiss society itself: the laws that constitute it and their origin, tendencies, and character. I hope that, circumscribed in this way, the portrait will still be worthy of interest. What is happening in Switzerland is not an isolated fact. It is a particular aspect of a more general movement that is hastening the whole ancient institutional edifice of Europe toward ruin. While the theater may be small, the play does not therefore lack for grandeur. Indeed, it has one striking characteristic. Nowhere else has the democratic revolution that is turning today's world upside down been attended by such bizarre and complicated circumstances. A single people composed of several races, speaking several languages, professing several faiths, with various dissident sects and two equally established and privileged churches, where all political issues quickly turn into religious issues and all issues of religion culminate in politics, and finally, two societies, one very old, the other very young, married despite the difference in their ages—that is the image of Switzerland today. To paint its portrait adequately, in my opinion, one would have had to adopt a loftier vantage than does the author of this work. In his preface, M. Cherbuliez states that he subjected himself to the law of impartiality, and I take this assertion to be perfectly sincere. Indeed, he expresses fear that, because his work is so impartial, it might make the subject seem somewhat monotonous. Any such fear is assuredly unjustified. The author does indeed wish to be impartial, but he is unsuccessful at it. His book gives evidence of knowledge, perspicacity, real talent, and a sincerity that is manifest even amid expressions of passionate approbation, but what one does not find in it is, precisely, impartiality. There is much intelligence in the work but little independence of mind.

Toward what forms of political society does the author lean? At first sight this seems rather difficult to say. Although he approves to some extent the political conduct of Switzerland's most ardent Catholics, he is a staunch adversary of Catholicism, so much so that he is not far from favoring legislative measures to prevent the Catholic religion from spreading to places where it is not yet dominant. He is, moreover, a staunch enemy of dissident Protestant sects. Opposed to government by the people, he is also opposed to government by the nobility. In religion, a Protestant church controlled by the state; in politics, a state controlled by a bourgeois aristocracy: such is apparently the author's ideal. It is Geneva, before the most recent revolutions.

Although it is not always easy to make out clearly what the author likes,

---

tion and also as an appendix to the twelfth edition of *Democracy in America*. Tocqueville commented on *Democracy in Switzerland* (Paris, 1843), a two-volume work by Antoine-Élysée Cherbuliez (1797–1869), a Swiss professor of political economy who was also active in Swiss government. Tocqueville's remarks on Cherbuliez, who disliked democracy and warned that it would spread throughout Europe, came just before the start of the revolutions that swept across Europe in 1848.

there is no difficulty at all in seeing what he hates. What he hates is democracy. With his opinions, his friendships, and perhaps his interests under attack by the democratic revolution he describes, he never speaks of it except as an enemy. He attacks not only certain consequences of democracy but its very essence. He fails to recognize its qualities while arraigning its flaws. Among the ills to which it may give rise he does not distinguish between those which are fundamental and permanent and those which are accidental and fleeting, those which must be endured as inevitable and those which one must seek to correct. Perhaps the subject could not have been treated in that way by a man as deeply involved in his country's turmoil as M. Cherbuliez. This is regrettable. In the course of the analysis we shall see that Swiss democracy is greatly in need of someone capable of explaining the imperfections of its laws. But to do so effectively, the first condition that must be met is that the analyst not hate what he is analyzing.

M. Cherbuliez's work is entitled *Democracy in Switzerland,* which might suggest that, in the eyes of the author, Switzerland is a country about which one can write a doctrinal treatise on democracy and form legitimate judgments about democratic institutions as such. In my view, this is the principal source of nearly all the book's errors. Its title should actually have been *On Democratic Revolution in Switzerland.* Indeed, for the past fifteen years, Switzerland has been a country in revolution.[72] Democracy there is not so much a regular form of government as an arm that has been used regularly to destroy, but at times to defend, the old society. One can indeed use the Swiss case to study phenomena associated with revolutionary conditions in the present democratic era but not to portray democracy in its permanent and tranquil condition. Anyone who fails to keep this point of departure constantly in mind will find it difficult to understand the picture that emerges from the present study of Swiss institutions. For my part, moreover, I would find it impossibly difficult to explain how I judge what is without saying how I understand what was.

Many people mistake what the situation in Switzerland was when the French Revolution broke out. Since the Swiss had long lived under a republican government, it was easy to believe that they were much more familiar than other Europeans with modern liberal institutions and the spirit that animates them. In fact, the opposite was true.

Although the Swiss gained their independence through an insurrection against the aristocracy, most of the governments established at that time were quick to borrow the customs and laws and even the opinions and penchants of aristocracy. They viewed liberty solely as a privilege, and the idea of a general,

72. After the fall of Napoleon, the Swiss Diet reestablished a federation of cantons, guided by a constitution organized at the Congress of Vienna in 1814–15. This act restored the power imbalance between city and country populations, and residents of the countryside, along with radical democratic leaders, organized a number of revolts to challenge the urban aristocratic leaders who had regained control of the cantonal and federal governments. The radicals had some success in the 1830s, which included placing restrictions on the powers of the Catholic Church, but conflict and revolts continued throughout the 1840s.

preexisting right of all men to be free remained as alien to them as it was to the princes of the house of Austria whom they vanquished. All powers were soon claimed and jealously guarded by small aristocracies, which were either closed or self-recruiting. In the north, these aristocracies took on an industrial character; in the south, a military constitution. In both regions they were equally restrictive and exclusive, however. In most cantons, three-quarters of the population was excluded from participation in government of any kind, direct or even indirect. In addition, each canton had subject populations.

These small aristocratic groups, which formed in the midst of such great turmoil, soon became so stable that they ceased to be affected by change altogether. Because the aristocracy was neither challenged by the people nor guided by a king, it draped the body of society in old medieval trappings and resisted all change.

With the passage of time, the new spirit had long since infiltrated Europe's most monarchical societies, but Switzerland continued to shut it out.

All political writers accepted the division of powers, but Switzerland refused it. Freedom of the press, which existed *de facto* at any rate in any number of absolute monarchies on the Continent, did not exist in Switzerland in either fact or law. Political association was neither practiced nor tolerated. Freedom of speech was very narrowly restricted. Equal taxation, toward which most enlightened governments were already moving, was no more to be found in Switzerland than equal rights. Industry was hobbled in a myriad of ways. Individual liberty had no legal guarantee. Religious liberty, which had begun to penetrate even the most orthodox states, had yet to appear in Switzerland. Dissident sects were entirely prohibited in several cantons and repressed in all. Religious differences gave rise to political disqualifications throughout much of the country.

Switzerland was still in this condition in 1798, when the French Revolution invaded its territory by force of arms. It briefly overthrew the old institutions but established nothing solid or stable in their place. Napoleon, who a few years later rescued the Swiss from anarchy through the Act of Mediation, gave them equality but not liberty. The political laws that he imposed were combined in such a way as to paralyze public life. Power, exercised in the name of the people but kept far beyond its reach, was placed entirely in the hands of the executive.

When the Act of Mediation collapsed along with its author a few years later, the Swiss gained nothing in the way of liberty; they merely lost what they had of equality. The old aristocracies regained the reins of government everywhere and restored the exclusive and superannuated principles that had reigned before the Revolution. As M. Cherbuliez rightly asserts, things returned almost to the state in which they had been in 1798. The coalition of monarchs was wrongly accused of having imposed this restoration on Switzerland by force. In fact, they agreed to the restoration but were not responsible for it. The truth is that the Swiss, along with the other peoples of the Continent, became caught up in a brief but universal reaction, which abruptly revived the old society across Europe. And since in Switzerland the restoration was carried out not by monarchs, whose interests after all differed from those of the formerly privileged classes, but by the formerly privileged themselves, it was more complete, more blind, and more obstinate than in the rest of Europe. It proved to be not tyrannical but quite exclusive. A legislative power entirely subordinate to the executive; an executive entirely in the hands of the hereditary aristocracy; a middle class excluded from public affairs; and an entire people deprived of political existence: such was the state of nearly all of Switzerland until 1830.

It was then that the new democratic era began for the country.

The purpose of this brief survey was to clarify two points.

First, Switzerland was one of the countries in Europe in which the revolution was least profound and the restoration that followed most complete. As a result, institutions alien or hostile to the new spirit either maintained or regained a great deal of influence there, and the revolutionary impulse was bound to remain more powerful.

Second, to this day, throughout most of Switzerland, the people have never played the slightest role in government. The legal forms that guarantee civil liberty, freedom of association, freedom of speech, freedom of the press, and religious freedom were as unknown to the vast majority of citizens of these republics as they were to the subjects of most monarchies in this period, and I might even say more unknown.

These are facts of which M. Cherbuliez often loses sight but which we must keep constantly in mind as we carefully examine the institutions with which Switzerland has endowed itself.

As is well-known, sovereignty in Switzerland is divided into two parts: federal power on the one hand and cantonal governments on the other.[73]

M. Cherbuliez begins by discussing what happens in the cantons, and he is right to do so, because that is where the real government of society takes place. I shall follow him down this path and concern myself, as he does, with cantonal constitutions.

All cantonal constitutions are today democratic, but the characteristic features of democracy are not the same in all of them.

In the majority of cantons, the people have delegated the exercise of their powers to representative bodies, while in a few they have retained those powers for themselves. The people themselves assemble as a body and govern. M. Cherbuliez calls the first type of government *representative democracies* and the second, *pure democracies*.

I shall ask the Academy's permission not to follow the author in his very interesting study of pure democracy. I have several reasons for doing so. Although the cantons that live under pure democracy have played a great role in history and may yet play a considerable one in politics, to study them would be more diverting than useful.

---

73. The Diet rotated its meetings among three Swiss cities to avoid choosing a single federal capital.

Pure democracy is highly unusual in the modern world and quite exceptional even in Switzerland, since only one-thirteenth of the population is governed in this way. Moreover, pure democracy is only temporary. It is not sufficiently widely known that in those Swiss cantons where the people have retained most of their powers, there are nevertheless representative bodies that bear some of the burden of government. Now, it is easy to see, in studying the recent history of Switzerland, that the portion of public affairs dealt with by the people has gradually decreased, while the portion dealt with by representatives has grown steadily in both importance and variety. Thus the principle of pure democracy has been losing ground, while the opposite principle has been gaining. The former has little by little become the exception, the latter the rule.

In any case, Switzerland's pure democracies belong to another era. Although one is obliged to refer to them using a term borrowed from modern political science, they live only in the past. Every century has a dominant spirit, which nothing can resist. If alien or contrary principles are introduced, as sometimes happens, the spirit of the age quickly permeates them, and if it cannot annihilate them, then it appropriates or assimilates them. The Middle Ages imposed an aristocratic shape even on democratic liberty. Amid the most republican laws, and even alongside universal suffrage itself, the religious beliefs, opinions, feelings, habits, and associations of families that held themselves aloof from the people took hold, and real power rested with them. The little Swiss cantons should be seen as analogs of the democratic governments of the Middle Ages. They are the honored relics of a world that is no more.

By contrast, the representative democracies of Switzerland are descended from the spirit of modernity. All are built on the ruins of an ancient aristocratic society. All embody the principle of popular sovereignty and none other. All have made virtually identical application of that principle in their laws.

As we shall see, those laws are far from perfect, and if history were silent, they alone would suffice to show that in Switzerland democracy and even liberty are new forces with which the Swiss have had little experience.

Note first that even in Switzerland's representative democracies, the people have retained the direct exercise of some of their powers. In some cantons, the most important laws, once approved by the legislature, are still subject to popular veto. Hence in these specific instances, representative democracy degenerates into pure democracy.

In nearly all cantons, the people must be consulted from time to time, usually at frequent intervals, to ascertain whether they wish to modify or maintain the constitution. Hence all laws regularly become subject to simultaneous modification.

All legislative powers that the people have not retained for themselves are entrusted to a single assembly, which acts in the name of the people and under their watchful eye. In no canton is the legislature divided into two branches. Everywhere it consists of a single body. Not only are its actions not slowed by the need to reach agreement with another body; its will is not even impeded by the need for prolonged deliberation. Debate on general laws is subject to certain formalities that extend the time of discussion, but the most important resolutions can be proposed, debated, and expeditiously approved by designating them "decrees." Decrees turn lesser laws into something as powerful, impetuous, and irresistible as the passions of a multitude.

Outside the legislature, there is no possibility of resistance. There is in fact no such thing as the separation or even relative independence of legislative, administrative, and judicial powers.

In no canton are the representatives of the executive power elected directly by the people. The legislature chooses them. Hence the executive has no power of its own. It is merely the creation of another power and can never be anything but its servile agent. This source of weakness is combined with several others. Nowhere is executive power wielded by a single individual. It is entrusted to a small group, which is alone empowered to act and among whose members responsibility is divided. It is deprived of several of the inherent prerogatives of the executive. It has no veto power over the laws, or only an insignificant one. It has no power to pardon and cannot appoint or dismiss its own agents. Indeed, one might say that it has no agents, since it is usually required to rely on ordinary magistrates.

But the flaws of Swiss democracy are most apparent in the poor constitution and composition of the judicial power. M. Cherbuliez is aware of this, but not sufficiently, in my opinion. He does not seem to understand that in a democracy the judicial power is intended to be both the primary barrier against the people and the primary safeguard of the people.

The idea of an independent judicial power is a modern concept. The Middle Ages had no such notion, or at best only a confused version of it. It is fair to say that in all the nations of Europe, the executive power and judicial power were initially mingled. Even in France, where, in a welcome exception, justice developed a strong individual identity early on, it is still permissible to say that the division of the two powers remained quite incomplete. To be sure, it was not the government that retained the powers of the judiciary, but the judiciary that assumed some of the powers of government.

Of all the countries of Europe, however, Switzerland was perhaps the one in which the judiciary was the most completely identified with political power and in which it became so completely an attribute of government. Our idea of justice as a free, impartial power that stands between all other interests and powers in order to enforce respect for the law has always been absent from the mind of the Swiss, and they have no firm grasp of it even today.

The new constitutions have undoubtedly given the courts a more separate place than they occupied among the old powers but not a more independent position. The lower courts are elected by the people and subject to reelection. The supreme court of each canton is chosen not by the executive power but by the legislative, and nothing protects its members from the daily whims of the majority.

Not only do the people or the assembly that represents them choose the judges; what is more, their choice is not constrained in any way. Generally speaking, no particular competence is required. Furthermore, the judge, as a simple executor of the law, does not have the right to investigate whether that law conforms to the constitution. In truth, it is the majority itself that judges, using magistrates as its agents.

In Switzerland, moreover, even if the law had granted the judicial power the necessary independence and prerogatives, judges would still find it difficult to play their role, because justice is based on traditions and opinions that require the support of judicial concepts and mores.

I could easily point out the defects of the institutions I have just described and show that they all tend to make the government of the people unpredictable in its procedures, precipitous in its decisions, and tyrannical in its acts. But to do so would take me too far afield. I will instead limit myself to a comparison with the laws adopted by an older, more peaceful, and more prosperous democratic society. M. Cherbuliez thinks that the imperfect institutions of the Swiss cantons are the only ones that democracy can foster or tolerate. The comparison that I am about to make will prove the contrary and show how, with greater experience, art, and wisdom, it has been possible elsewhere to draw different consequences from the principle of popular sovereignty. I shall take as my example the state of New York, whose population is equal to that of all of Switzerland.

In the state of New York, as in the Swiss cantons, government is based on the principle of popular sovereignty, which is enacted through universal suffrage. But the people exercise their sovereignty only on election day, through the choice of their delegates. They normally retain no part of the legislative, executive, or judicial power for themselves. They choose those who are to govern in their name and then abdicate until the next election.

Although the laws change, their foundation is stable. No one imagined subjecting the constitution to regular revision, as in Switzerland, where society remains in suspense at the mere approach of the date when such changes may be envisioned. When a new need is felt, the legislature determines that a modification of the constitution has become necessary, and the next legislature takes care of it.

Although the legislative power can no more ignore public opinion in New York than it can in Switzerland, it is organized in such a way as to resist the caprices of that opinion. No bill can become law until it has been examined by two assemblies.[74] These two parts of the legislature are elected in the same way and composed of the same elements. Both therefore emanate from the people, but they do not represent the people in the same way: one is responsible primar-

74. Tocqueville is describing the bicameral New York State legislature. Most of Tocqueville's information about the New York State government came from John C. Spencer; Edward Everett also communicated his views on American bicameralism to Tocqueville.

ily for reproducing the people's day-to-day impressions, while the other represents their habitual instincts and permanent propensities.

In New York, the division of powers exists not only in appearance but also in reality.

The executive power is exercised not by a body but by a man who bears sole responsibility for it and decisively and forcefully wields its rights and prerogatives.[75] Elected by the people, he is not, as in Switzerland, the creature and agent of the legislature. He stands as its equal and represents as it does, although in a different sphere, the sovereign in whose name both act. He draws his strength from the same source from which it draws its strength. He not only bears the name of the executive power but exercises its natural and legitimate prerogatives. He is the commander of the state's armed force, whose principal officers he appoints. He chooses several of the most important officials in the state. He has the right to pardon. He has the power of veto over acts of the legislature, a power which, though not absolute, is nevertheless effective. Although the governor of the state of New York is no doubt much less powerful than a constitutional monarch in Europe, he is infinitely more powerful than a small Swiss executive council.

The most striking difference, however, has to do with the way in which the judicial power is organized.

The judge, although he is an emanation of and responsible to the people, is a power to which the people themselves submit.

The judicial power owes this exceptional position to its origins, permanence, competence, and, above all, to public mores and opinion.

The members of the higher courts are chosen not, as in Switzerland, by the legislature, a collective power that is often passionate, sometimes blind, and always irresponsible, but by the governor of the state. Once established on the bench, a magistrate is considered to hold his position for life. No case escapes him, and no one else can impose punishment. Not only does he interpret the law, he also judges it. When the legislature, impelled by hasty changes in the positions of the parties, departs from the spirit or letter of the constitution, the courts recall it to order by refusing to enforce its decisions, so that while the judge cannot compel the people to keep their constitution, he can at least force them to respect it as long as it exists. He does not direct the people, but he does constrain and limit them. The judicial power, which barely exists in Switzerland, is the true moderator of American democracy.

When we examine the constitution of New York in minute detail, we find in it not the slightest trace of aristocracy. Nothing that resembles a class or a privilege, and everywhere the same rights, with all powers emanating from the people and returning to them, and with a single spirit animating all institutions and no warring tendencies: the principle of democracy suffuses and dominates everything. Yet this government, though so completely democratic, stands on a

---

75. Tocqueville refers to the office of governor of the state of New York.

far more stable footing and seems far more tranquil and smooth in its operation than the democratic governments of Switzerland.

It is reasonable to say that this stems in part from a difference in laws.

The laws of the state of New York, which I have just described, are contrived so as to counter the natural defects of democracy. By contrast, the Swiss institutions that I portrayed earlier seem intended to foster them. Here they restrain the people; there they spur the people on. In America, there was fear that the power of the people might turn tyrannical, whereas in Switzerland it seems that the only desire was to make that power irresistible.

I have no wish to exaggerate the influence of laws on the fate of nations. I know that the chief causes of the great events of this world are more general and more profound. Yet there is no denying that institutions have certain virtues of their own and contribute to making societies prosperous or miserable.

If, instead of absolutely dismissing nearly all the laws of his country, M. Cherbuliez had pointed out their defects and explained how they could have been improved without altering their principle, he would have written a book more worthy of posterity and more useful to his contemporaries.

After showing how democracy operates in the cantons, the author examines its influence on the confederation itself.

Before following M. Cherbuliez down this path, I must first do what he did not do himself and explain what the central government is, how it is organized in law and in fact, and how it functions.

It is legitimate to ask first whether the lawgivers of the Swiss Confederation wanted to draft a federal constitution or simply establish a league. In other words, did they intend to sacrifice a portion of each canton's sovereignty or alienate none of it? Since the cantons gave up several of the inherent rights of sovereignty and permanently conceded them to the federal government, and since they wanted the majority to rule on the matters thus conceded, there can be no doubt that the legislators of the Swiss Confederation sought to establish a true federal constitution and not just a league. It must be granted, however, that they went about it very badly.

I have no hesitation in saying that, in my view, the Swiss federal constitution is the most imperfect of all constitutions of this type that the world has yet known. Reading it, one would think that it came straight from the Middle Ages, and it is impossible to overstate one's astonishment that such a confused and incomplete work is the product of a century as enlightened and experienced as our own.

It is often said, not without reason, that the pact unduly limited the rights of the confederation and that it excluded from the sphere of the federal government certain actions essentially national in nature that should have fallen within the competence of the Diet: for example, the administration of the post office, the regulation of weights and measures, and the minting of money. The weakness of the federal government has been attributed, moreover, to the limited number of powers attributed to it.

It is indeed true that the pact omitted from the constitution of the government of the confederation any number of rights that it ought by nature and even necessity to have. But that is not the real cause of its weakness, for the rights that the pact did grant to it would have sufficed had it been able to use them to acquire, or at any rate to conquer, those that it lacked.

The Diet can assemble troops, raise money, make war, grant peace, conclude commercial treaties, and appoint ambassadors. The cantonal constitutions and even the principle of equality before the law are placed in its safekeeping. And these powers should allow it, if need be, to involve itself in all local affairs.

Tolls and powers over the roads are regulated by the Diet, which is thus authorized to direct and supervise major public works.

Finally, the Diet, according to article 4 of the pact, *takes all necessary measures to safeguard the internal and external security of Switzerland,* which provision grants it the prerogative to do anything.

Not even the strongest federal governments have had greater prerogatives, and, far from believing that the competence of the Swiss central government is too limited, I am inclined to think that its limits have not been delineated with sufficient care.

Why is it, then, that despite such handsome privileges, the government of the confederation ordinarily has so little power? The answer is simple: it was not given the means to use the right that was granted to it, namely, the right to speak its will.

Never was a government more irrevocably condemned to inertia and impotence by the imperfection of its organs.

It is of the essence of federal governments to act not in the name of the people but in the name of the states of which the federation is composed. If it were otherwise, the constitution would immediately cease to be federal.

Among other necessary and inevitable consequences, it follows that federal governments are usually less bold in their decisions and slower in their actions than other governments.

Most drafters of federal constitutions have sought, through more or less ingenious means that I do not wish to delve into here, to correct this inherent flaw of the federal system. The Swiss, however, adopted specific provisions that made this flaw more apparent than anywhere else. In Switzerland, not only do members of the Diet act only in the name of the various cantons that they represent; broadly speaking, they make no decision that has not been cleared or approved by the cantons. Almost nothing is left to their free choice. Each representative believes himself to be bound by an imperative mandate, set forth in advance. Hence the Diet is a deliberative body where in fact no one has any interest in deliberating, and where members speak not to those who must take the decision but only to those who have no power except to carry out a decision already made elsewhere. The Diet is a government that has no will of its own and merely puts into practice what twenty-two other governments have willed separately. It is a government which, regardless of the nature of events, can decide nothing, anticipate nothing, and provide nothing. It is difficult to imagine an arrangement more apt to increase the natural inertia of a federal government or to transform its weakness into a sort of senile debility.

There are, moreover, in addition to the flaws inherent in all federal constitutions, many other factors responsible for the habitual impotence of the government of the Swiss Confederation.

Not only does the confederation have a feeble government; it barely has a government of its own at all. Its constitution is the only one of its kind in the world. The heads of the confederation do not represent it. The directory, which constitutes the executive power of Switzerland, is chosen not by the Diet and still less by the Helvetic people. It is a temporary government, which the confederation borrows every two years from Berne, Zurich, or Lucerne. This power, elected by the residents of a canton to direct that canton's affairs, thus becomes, in addition, the head and arms of the entire country. This is surely one of the greatest political oddities in the history of human lawmaking. For instance, there is nothing in history more bizarre than what happened in 1839. In that year, the Diet met in Zurich, and the government of the confederation was the directory of the state of Zurich. A revolution occurred in the canton of Zurich. A popular revolution overthrew the recognized authorities. The Diet immediately found itself without a president, and federal activity ground to a halt until it pleased the canton to adopt other laws and elect other leaders. The people of Zurich, in changing their local administration, had unintentionally decapitated Switzerland.

Had the confederation had an executive power of its own, the government would still have been incapable of winning obedience for want of any direct and immediate means of acting on its citizens. This in itself is a greater source of weakness than all the others put together, but in order to understand it properly, one must do more than merely point this out.

A federal government can have a fairly limited sphere of action and still be strong if, within its narrow sphere, it can act on its own, without intermediaries, as ordinary governments do within the unlimited sphere in which they act. If it has officials who deal directly with individual citizens and courts that compel each citizen to submit to its laws, it can easily induce obedience, because the only resistance it has to fear is that of individuals, and all the difficulties that are put in its way end in court.

By contrast, a federal government can have a very vast sphere of action and still enjoy only very limited and tenuous authority if, instead of dealing with citizens individually, it is obliged to proceed by way of cantonal governments, for if these resist, the federal government is immediately confronted not with a subject so much as a rival, which it can vanquish only by going to war.

The power of a federal government therefore lies not so much in the extent of the prerogatives it is granted as in the degree to which it is allowed to exercise those prerogatives by itself. It is always strong when it can issue orders to citizens. It is always weak when it is reduced to issuing orders solely to local governments.

Examples of both systems can be found in the history of confederations, but in no confederation that I know of was the central power as completely deprived of the means to act directly on its citizens as in Switzerland, where it enjoyed none of the prerogatives that a federal government can exercise on its own. It had no officials responsible solely to it and no courts that represented its sovereign power exclusively. It resembled a creature endowed with life but deprived of organs.

Such is the federal constitution defined by the pact. Let us now briefly join the author whose book we are analyzing to see what influence democracy has had on it.

There is no denying that the democratic revolutions that have altered nearly all the cantonal constitutions over the past fifteen years have had a great influence on the federal government, but that influence has worked in two diametrically opposed directions. It is essential to attend carefully to both aspects of the phenomenon.

The democratic revolutions in the cantons intensified local political activity and increased its influence. The new governments created by the revolutions and supported and spurred on by the people discovered that they were stronger than the governments they had overthrown, and they also took a loftier view of their power. Furthermore, since no such renewal occurred in the federal government in this period, it was bound to follow, and did in fact follow, that the federal government found itself weaker relative to the local governments than it had been before. Cantonal pride, instinctive local independence, impatience with any outside control over the internal affairs of each canton, and jealousy of any central and supreme authority were all sentiments that increased after democracy was established. In this sense, it is fair to say that democracy weakened the already weak government of the confederation and made its usual daily tasks more arduous and difficult.

In other respects, however, democracy bestowed upon the federal government an energy and, in a sense, an existence that it did not have before.

The establishment of democratic institutions in Switzerland introduced two entirely new things.

Previously, each canton had its own separate interests and its own distinctive spirit. The advent of democracy divided the Swiss of all cantons into two parties, one favorable to democratic principles, the other opposed. It created common interests, ideas, and passions, which, for their own fulfillment, created the need for a common general power extending over the entire country. For the first time the federal government therefore possessed a great power that it had always previously lacked. It was able to draw upon the support of a party—a dangerous but indispensable force in free countries, where governments can do almost nothing without it.

As democracy divided the Swiss into two parties, it made Switzerland a member of one of the great parties that divided the world between them. It created a foreign policy. Although it provided the country with natural allies, it also created necessary enemies. To cultivate and reassure the former while keeping an eye on and fending off the latter, democracy made the Swiss aware of their irresistible need for a government. It replaced a local public spirit with a national public spirit.

These direct effects of democracy fortified the federal government. Its indirect influence was no less important and will be even more important over the long run.

The resistance and difficulties that a federal government must face are greater and more varied when the confederated populations are more dissimilar in their institutions, feelings, customs, and ideas. It is less the similarity of interests than the perfect congruence of laws, opinions, and social conditions that makes the task of the government of the United States so easy. Similarly, it can be argued that the peculiar weakness of the old federal government in Switzerland was due primarily to the prodigious difference and striking contrast among the various populations that it had to govern with respect to spirit, views, and laws. To subject men so remote and so dissimilar from one another to a single government and a single policy was quite an arduous task. Even a government with a far better constitution and a far cleverer organization would not have succeeded at it. The effect of the democratic revolution in Switzerland was to ensure the dominance in all cantons of certain similar institutions, maxims of government, and ideas. If the democratic revolution made the cantons more independent of the central power, it also made it easier for that power to act. It eliminated many of the causes of resistance, and though it did not make the cantonal governments more eager to obey the federal government, it did make it far easier to obtain their obedience to its will.

The two contrary effects that I have just described must be studied with great care if we wish to understand the present state of the country and anticipate its future.

If one attends to only one of these two tendencies, one is led to believe that the immediate effect of the advent of democracy at the cantonal level will be to extend the legislative reach of the federal government and concentrate power over local affairs in its hands. In short, it will modify the whole structure of the pact in the direction of greater centralization. Nevertheless, I, for one, am convinced that this revolution will continue to face more obstacles than one might imagine for quite some time to come. Today's cantonal governments will no more want this sort of revolution than their predecessors did, and they will do everything they can to avoid it.

Despite these resistances, I believe that the federal government is bound to claim steadily increasing power. Circumstances will do more to bring this about than laws. It may be that the federal government will not increase its prerogatives in any very obvious way, but it will use them differently and more frequently. It will grow a great deal in fact, even though it remains the same in law. It will develop more by interpreting the pact than by changing it, and it will dominate Switzerland before it is prepared to govern it.

One can also anticipate that the very people who have thus far been most opposed to the steady expansion of the federal government will soon desire it, either to escape the intermittent pressure of a power so poorly constituted or to protect themselves from the more immediate and oppressive tyranny of local governments.

What is certain is that, regardless of what modifications are made to the letter of the pact, the federal constitution of Switzerland has already been profoundly and irrevocably altered. The nature of the confederation has changed. It has become something never before seen in Europe. A politics of action has supplanted a politics of inertia and neutrality. An existence that was purely municipal has become national, and therefore more arduous, more troubled, more precarious, and more grand.

ON THE ALLIANCE OF THE FRENCH AND AMERICAN REPUBLICS, FROM AN ADDRESS AT THE PEOPLE'S BANQUET IN CHERBOURG, 19 MARCH 1848[76]

M. Alexis de Tocqueville gave the following toast to the union of the two great republics. He said:

I did not intend to speak, and despite the kind mention of my name earlier, I would not have spoken had I not in a sense been driven toward this podium by the emotion I felt at the homage that has just been paid to the memory of a man whom I held in the highest esteem and for whom I felt the deepest affection. I am speaking of the courageous Colonel Briqueville.[77] Yes, I was moved to hear his name resound once more before so many who were so dear to him. I was moved to hear his name greeted with cheers. I was moved to see so noble a memory honored in such a public and formal setting, and I felt the need to add my feeble voice to the louder voice of my country. Would that Briqueville were here in my place! Would that he could enjoy the sight of this assembly, in which the entire society is represented, since he never looked upon himself as the deputy of a class but rather as the deputy of all classes, and all the people were dear to his heart. May the name Briqueville never be forgotten. Since we cannot bring the man back to life, let us try at least to keep alive the great qualities for which he was so beloved. Let us all honor his memory by seeking to follow his example. Never was there a spirit more generous, a heart more noble, or a soul more intrepid.

76. Although a number of the nearly two thousand attendees at this banquet had hoped for Tocqueville to attend, the leaders of the event gave him a cold reception and did not invite him to sit at the head table of dignitaries. During a series of toasts that followed formal speeches, Tocqueville improvised this address in response to a toast to Colonel de Briqueville.

77. Colonel Armand de Briqueville (1785–1844), descended from an old Norman family, had distinguished himself in military service in Napoleon's imperial army. Briqueville was an opponent of the Bourbons and was elected as a deputy from Cherbourg several times. Tocqueville omits "de" from Briqueville's name in this year of political revolution.

Since I am at this podium, let me not return to my seat without offering another toast of my own:

In everything that has been said here today, two words have recurred again and again, two words that I was very pleased to hear, namely, UNION and HARMONY. Never before have union and harmony been so essential if we are to preserve the fatherland. Let the word "union" therefore be always on our lips and in our hearts. Why shouldn't it be? What reason have we to reproach one another? Although a great revolution has just taken place, property remained untouched, and individual life and liberty remained safe.[78] Union is therefore not only necessary but should also be easy to achieve. But union among citizens is not enough. Union among nations is no less important, and especially union among nations with similar institutions. I therefore propose this toast: To CLOSER UNION AMONG REPUBLICS! And I add in particular: To THE UNION OF THE TWO GREATEST REPUBLICS THAT EXIST ON EARTH TODAY: THE FRENCH REPUBLIC AND THE REPUBLIC OF THE UNITED STATES OF AMERICA!

The word "republic" still frightens many among us who, still preoccupied with the glorious but melancholy memory of our own history, have not expanded their horizons to consider what has taken place elsewhere in the world. Let them cast their eyes across the Atlantic and look beyond its other shore, and they will discover a great nation occupying a territory far larger than that of France, a nation that has had democratic and republican institutions for sixty years now. I once lived in this vast republic and attempted to describe its laws, and I think of it whenever I feel the need to reassure myself about the future of our own institutions. No other country in the world is so rich in useful examples for us, nor a source of so many legitimate aspirations. In America, the Republic is not a dictatorship imposed in the name of liberty; it is liberty itself—real, true liberty, liberty for all citizens. It is sincere government of the country by the country; it is the uncontested rule of the majority, the rule of law. Under the protection of America's laws, property is safe, order is strictly maintained, industry is free, the burden of taxation is light, and the tyranny of a single individual or a few individuals is unknown, and it has been this way for sixty years. During those sixty years, while Europe was torn apart by an endless series of disputes, wars, and revolutions, republican and democratic America has not experienced so much as a riot. I was therefore right to tell you that you should look to America as a source of impressive examples and lofty hopes. But that is not all we should ask of America. We should also join with it to demand freedom of the oceans.

78. At the beginning of the year, King Louis-Philippe abdicated and named his nine-year-old grandson his successor. Tocqueville initially supported this proposed succession, but Alphonse de Lamartine, a speaker in the Chamber of Deputies, successfully encouraged the declaration of the Second Republic of France on February 24, 1848. Tocqueville and Beaumont both were elected to serve on the committee that wrote the new constitution. Though the Second Republic lasted only until 1852, the new government instituted a number of liberal reforms, including universal male suffrage and public work programs for the poor.

The land is free, but the sea remains enslaved. It is ruled by a single nation, which is not merely a hegemon but a tyrant. And why is it not free? Because the two major powers that have the most obvious interest in breaking its fetters as well as the most extensive means to do so have not yet managed to reach an agreement and join forces, separated as they are not so much by distance as by the differences of their institutions. What was impossible a month ago is possible today. Let the French Republic and the American Republic reach out across the sea that separates them, let them join hands, and that sea will be free. No war would be needed: God forbid that I should call for war. The mere sight of their close union would make their common will all-powerful.

Is there any place in the world where it would be more natural or proper to express such a wish than here in Cherbourg? What is Cherbourg if not a living protest against the enslavement of the seas? What is the meaning of the admirable public works that I can almost see from where I speak? What are these jetties and channels carved into the rock? What is this new city of shipyards and arsenals? What is this marvelous island that man has brought forth from the waves to hold back the sea and defend the coast? What is all this if not France's most ambitious and energetic effort to emancipate the ocean?

Cherbourg is therefore the proper place to propose this toast: To the close union of two great republics and, through that union, the freedom of the seas!

GENERAL PRINCIPLES: ON BICAMERALISM, FROM THE PROCEEDINGS OF THE CONSTITUTIONAL COMMISSION OF 1848, 24 MAY 1848

M. Tocqueville: . . .

There has in any case been only one democratic republic in the history of the world, the United States, where there are two houses of Congress.

I am not here to praise the Constitution of the United States, a true work of art from which it is scarcely possible to borrow. But there are thirty other republics in North America that are in a position similar to ours. All have two chambers, and not a single American believes that any other arrangement is feasible.

Let it not be said that the bicameral arrangement is an English tradition, because the Union began with only one chamber but later reverted to two.

In Massachusetts and Pennsylvania, a single chamber was initially chosen. After a trial of thirteen years and extensive debate, the public recognized the need for two chambers. This example is worth noting.

I believe that the widespread support for a single chamber in France stems from a misunderstanding.

People think that the bicameral system is an aristocratic institution, because it gives voice to two different segments of the population. This is a mistake.

I do not favor aristocracy. I recognize that our society is deeply democratic and that any attempt to introduce the merest trace, the least atom, of aristocracy would be disastrous.

As in America, however, both chambers can and should represent the same interests and classes of people in the same manner and by similar means.

Some say that if the second chamber does not represent some kind of aristocracy, it is useless. This is a mistake.

The utility of the second chamber, though of a secondary order, is nevertheless quite substantial. It may be broken down under three heads:

1. The executive power must be strong, but to prevent abuse of that power one can set alongside it a small, secret body whose members are drawn from the second chamber and made responsible for overseeing certain important actions, such as appointments to very high posts, negotiation of treaties, etc.

One might turn to a state council to perform this function, but there are other advantages that can be obtained only with two chambers.

2. The executive power is in a dangerous situation if it faces a single chamber. There will be constant conflict, and eventually either the executive power will destroy the legislative, or the legislative will absorb and engulf the executive after a short period of struggle.

3. Even the soundest of bodies is subject to a variety of ills. The chronic disease that kills the lawmaking power is legislative intemperance. This is the form of tyranny assumed by a body that is driven to legislate incessantly.

To be sure, two chambers will not prevent revolutions, but they will prevent bad government, which leads to revolution.

Wherever a single body exists, it brushes aside any obstacle that stands in its way. The body that represents all shades of opinion and all varieties of interest makes its own way and rides roughshod over everything; it is irresistible.

To seek for halfway measures to slow it down may succeed temporarily, but not for long.

If the power of the legislature is to be limited and tamed, it must be divided between two chambers composed of similar elements, and if you do not seek in the name of one class to impose sovereignty over all classes, you will end up with two bodies that represent the same interests but do not always think alike.

Everyone profits from this diversity of views. Different minds examine the facts twice, and do so in different ways.

Another advantage is that a faction cannot fortify its position in the assembly and thereby seize sovereignty over the nation as a whole.

One proposal is to require a single chamber to submit every bill to a second reading, but this remedy is useless, for to read a bill twice to the same deputies is no more likely to prove fruitful than to appeal a judgment to the same judges who rendered it in the first place.

Impetuosity, or what one might call legislative light-headedness, is the leprosy of democracy, and impetuosity leads to oppression.

I am convinced that unless the bicameral system is adopted, the Republic will be lost.

ON PRESIDENTIAL POWERS, FROM THE PROCEEDINGS OF THE
CONSTITUTIONAL COMMISSION OF 1848, 27 MAY 1848

... M. Tocqueville. The two difficulties—the question of the reelection of the president and the question of whether the mandates of the legislative and executive powers should be equal in length or different—reinforce each other. Nevertheless, my first thought is that the principle of immediate reelection is unacceptable.

M. de Beaumont has already said, quite rightly, that if the president is eligible for reelection, his primary concern will be to see to it that he is reelected, and in order to ensure his reelection he will govern in the interest of a party.

This drawback is glaringly apparent in America, and it is becoming a greater and greater problem with the passage of time, with increasingly troublesome consequences. In France, however, the evil would be even greater.

Because in America the president has little power. He appoints only a small number of officials. In France, however, where the executive controls a very large number of posts and can appoint many people, the excessive influence of the president may constitute an enormous danger.

It is true, moreover, that if the president is not eligible for reelection, it may be an enormous source of discontent for an eminent man who finds himself unable to continue in power and complete whatever grand designs he may have in mind. One thereby reduces him to the ambition of desperation and tempts him to violate the Constitution.

This is an evil, but I would rather see the Constitution exposed to accidental and temporary danger than have society constantly subjected to the corrupting influence of a president who uses the force at his disposal to prolong his hold on power.

I also believe that a legislative mandate of four years is too long, and despite the drawbacks indicated by M. Dufaure,[79] I think that the legislature should remain for only three years, while the executive should be allowed four or five years.

ON DEMOCRACY AND SOCIALISM, FROM THE MEETING OF THE
CONSTITUTIONAL ASSEMBLY, 12 SEPTEMBER 1848

Citizen de Tocqueville:

I said earlier that socialism claimed to be the legitimate continuation of democracy. Unlike several of my colleagues, I will not try to ascertain the true etymology of the word *democracy*. I will not explore the garden of Greek roots, as was done yesterday, to find out where the word came from. (Laughter.) I will

---

79. In the 1840s, Jules-Armand-Stanislas Dufaure (1798–1881), a lawyer who promoted liberal causes, was an associate of Tocqueville's who belonged to the younger generation of liberals in the French government.

look for democracy where I have seen it alive, dynamic, and triumphant, in the only country in the world where it exists, the only country in which it has been able to establish anything great and lasting, namely, America. (Murmurs.)

There you will find a nation in which all conditions are more equal than they are among us; in which the social state, mores, and laws are all democratic; in which everything emanates from and returns to the people; yet in which each individual enjoys a more complete independence and greater freedom than at any other time and in any other country on earth—an essentially democratic country, I repeat, the only democracy that exists in the world today, as well as the only truly democratic republics that history has ever known. And in these republics, you would search in vain for socialism. Not only have socialist theories failed to take hold of the public spirit, but they have played so small a role in the debates and affairs of this great nation that one cannot even say that they are feared.

America is today the country in which the exercise of democracy is most sovereign, and it is also the country in which the socialist doctrines that you contend are so well attuned to democracy are least widely discussed, as well as the country in which proponents of those doctrines would surely fare least well at the polls. I confess that I would not be loath to see them go to America, but in their own interest I would advise them not to do so. (Loud laughter.)

FOREWORD TO THE TWELFTH EDITION OF *Democracy in America,* 1848

As great and sudden as were the events that have just unfolded in an instant before our eyes, the author of the present work is entitled to say that they did not surprise him. This book was written fifteen years ago with but a single thought as the author's constant preoccupation: the impending, irresistible, universal advent of democracy in the world. Reread this book: on every page you will find a solemn warning to all men that the form of society and the condition of humanity are changing and that new destinies are at hand.

At the beginning these words were inscribed:

The gradual development of equality[80] *is therefore a providential fact. It has the essential characteristics of one: it is universal, durable, and daily proves itself to be beyond the reach of man's powers. Not a single event, not a single individual, fails to contribute to its development. Is it wise to believe that a social movement that originated so far in the past can be halted by the efforts of a single generation? Does anyone think that democracy, having destroyed feudalism and vanquished kings, will be daunted by the bourgeois and the rich? Will it stop now that it has become so strong and its adversaries so weak?*

The man who, in the face of a monarchy strengthened rather than shaken by the Revolution of July, wrote these lines, which events have made prophetic, may today, without fear, once again draw the public's attention to his work.

80. The actual text reads "equality of conditions," but in this foreword Tocqueville, quoting himself, wrote simply *"égalité."*

He should also be permitted to add that current circumstances give his book a topical interest and practical utility that it did not have when it first appeared.

Monarchy existed then. Today, it is destroyed. The institutions of America, which were merely a subject of curiosity for monarchical France, should be a subject of study for republican France. It is not force alone that provides the seat of a new government; it is good laws. After the combatant, the lawmaker. One has destroyed, the other lays a foundation. To each his work. If the question in France is no longer whether we shall have a monarchy or a republic, it remains to be seen whether we shall have an agitated republic or a tranquil one, a regular republic or an irregular one, a peaceful republic or a belligerent one, a liberal republic or an oppressive one, a republic that threatens the sacred rights of property and family or one that recognizes and consecrates them. An awesome problem, the solution to which matters not just to France but to the entire civilized world. If we save ourselves, we also save all the peoples who surround us. If we go down, they all go down with us. Depending on whether we have democratic liberty or democratic tyranny, the destiny of the world will be different, and it can be said that today it is up to us whether in the end the republic is established everywhere or abolished everywhere.

Now, this problem, which we have only just begun to face, was resolved in America sixty years ago. There, for sixty years, the principle of popular sovereignty that we have just now enthroned among us has reigned unchallenged. There it has been put into practice in the most direct, the most unlimited, the most absolute manner. For sixty years, the people that has made this principle the common source of all its laws has grown steadily in population, territory, and wealth, and—note this well—throughout that period it has been not only the most prosperous but the most stable of all the peoples of the earth. While all the nations of Europe were ravaged by war or torn by civil discord, the American nation has remained, alone in the civilized world, at peace. Nearly all of Europe has been turned upside down by revolutions; America has not even had riots. There, the republic has not disrupted all rights but preserved them. There, individual property has enjoyed more guarantees than in any other country in the world, and anarchy has remained as unheard-of as despotism.

Where else can we look for greater hopes or greater lessons? Let us look to America not to copy servilely the institutions it has adopted but to better understand those that suit us, not so much to extract examples as to draw lessons, to borrow the principles of its laws rather than the details. The laws of the French Republic can and should be different in many cases from the laws that govern the United States, but the principles on which American constitutions rest—principles of order, balance of powers, true liberty, and sincere and profound respect for what is right—are indispensable in any republic and should be common to all. And one can say in advance that where such principles are not found, the republic will soon have ceased to exist.

Examine the mode of presidential election established by the Constitution itself, and you will see that it facilitates, as much as the law possibly can, this unfortunate revolutionary result. A large nation spread over a vast territory, a nation in which the sphere of executive power is virtually unlimited and in which the sole representative of that power is directly elected by universal suffrage, with each citizen voting separately and with no way of clarifying the issues, gathering information, or deliberating in common—I do not shrink from saying that no such thing has ever been seen anywhere on this earth. The only country in the world in any way comparable is America. Yet how prodigious the difference! In America, direct and universal suffrage is the general rule; only one exception to this great principle was introduced into the law, and that exception pertains to none other than the election of the president. The president of the United States of America also emanates from a universal vote, but not directly. And yet, gentlemen, the role of the executive in the Union, compared to what it is now and will always be, come what may, in France, is small. Despite that, in this country where a republic has existed from the beginning, as it were, even under the monarchy, in habits, ideas, and mores, and in which it had only to appear rather than come into being—in this country no one dared to entrust the election of the representative of executive power to the hazards of a direct and universal vote. The power of the presidency was seen as too great and, more importantly, too remote from the voter to permit an enlightened and mature choice. The American nation therefore chooses only delegates, who in turn choose the president. These delegates no doubt represent the general spirit of the country, its tendencies and tastes and often its passions and prejudices, but they are at least equipped with knowledge that the people do not have. They can form a precise idea of the nation's general needs and true perils; they can know the candidates and compare one to another, weigh and choose, whereas the average citizen, tethered to his home and often to his ignorance, absorbed by his work and by the concerns of private life, cannot. Thus have we seen that over the past sixty years Americans have frequently eliminated well-known and in some cases quite illustrious citizens from the highest office, choosing instead relatively obscure men who were more responsive to the political needs of the moment.

TOCQUEVILLE TO THE *Liberty Bell,* "TESTIMONY AGAINST SLAVERY," 1856[81]

I do not think it is for me, a foreigner, to indicate to the United States the time, the measures, or the men by whom slavery shall be abolished.

Still, as the persevering enemy of despotism everywhere, and under all its forms, I am pained and astonished by the fact that the freest country in the world is, at the present time, virtually the only civilized Christian nation that still permits personal servitude; and this while serfdom itself is about to disappear, if it has not already done so, from the most degraded nations of Europe.

An old and sincere friend of America, I am uneasy at seeing slavery retard her progress, tarnish her glory, furnish arms to her detractors, compromise the future of the Union that guarantees her security and greatness, and designate to all her enemies the spot where she is most vulnerable. As a human being, moreover, I am moved by the sight of man's degradation by his fellow men, and I hope to see the day when the law will grant equal civil liberty to all who live under one government, as God grants freedom of the will, without distinction, to all who dwell upon this earth.

REPORT ON A BOOK BY MR. THEODORE SEDGWICK, FROM *Séances et travaux de l'Académie des sciences morales and politiques,* JULY—SEPTEMBER 1858

I am honored to lay before the Academy on behalf of the author a book entitled *A Treatise on the Rules Which Govern the Interpretation and the Application of Statutory and Constitutional Law.*[82] This is the work of Mr. Theodore Sedgwick, one of the most distinguished lawyers in the city of New York, where he also serves as a high judicial officer of the federal government.

I take the liberty of commending this book to the special attention of the Academy. It is worthy of such a recommendation on several grounds. As a treatise on jurisprudence, it has great merit. The author demonstrates a profound knowledge of his subject. His perspicacious, vigorous, and sober mind has enabled him to discern the central argument and crucial authority touching each point, so that he is able to enlighten the reader without overburdening him. His invariably clear and straightforward style leads easily from the word to the idea.

Mr. Sedgwick's treatise cannot fail, therefore, to facilitate the study of American law, yet it is even more essential to readers concerned with the general science of law and with the relation between justice and the government of so-

81. The *Liberty Bell* was an annual publication produced by the Female Anti-Slavery Society of Boston between 1839 and 1858. Tocqueville gave his testimony at the request of Maria Weston Chapman (1806–1885), a founder of the society.

82. This book was first published in New York in 1857. In 1858, Sedgwick was named district attorney for southern New York.

ciety. On this point [it is worth pausing] to recall certain facts that will facilitate the explanation that is to follow.

In a modern society the proper functions of justice are two: to apply the law when it is clear and to interpret it when it is obscure. When a judge finds that the language of the law admits of two meanings, he has the right to choose the one that seems most probable to him. But when the legislature's meaning is unambiguous, the judge has no choice but to respect its will scrupulously.

That is the way things are everywhere in Europe. They are different in America, where the judicial power enjoys the uncontested exercise of prerogatives that, unless I am mistaken, are not yet *granted* to it anywhere else.

The American judge not only applies and interprets the law but also has the power in certain cases to judge the law itself and, after determining that its meaning is clear, nevertheless to declare that it is null and void.

This singular legislation has existed in the United States for more than sixty years. It is not based on a legal text but is rather a product of custom. No constitution formally granted the courts such great power. They attributed it to themselves; no one called for it. Public opinion approved what judges did, and lawmakers, though themselves representatives of popular sovereignty and duly elected under universal suffrage and in full liberty, gave in without a murmur. No principle seems to me less openly admitted in America today and yet more frequently applied than this one.

Mr. Sedgwick shows very clearly the sources from which American courts drew this exceptional power and explains how they exercise it.

The Academy knows that each of the states that make up the American Union has a constitution of its own, a constitution freely debated and voted on by the people of that state and therefore undeniably a product of the people's will.

The American Union also has a special constitution that the American people as a whole adopted when their revolution ended as ours was beginning.

Each of these constitutions imposes obligations not only on ordinary citizens but also on all who govern in the people's name, officials as well as legislators.

It was on this principle that judges drew in claiming the power to set limits to the law itself.

The people, they said, stand above the legislature, just as they do here. Although legislators may claim to speak in the people's name, it is not lawful for them to violate the general rules that the people themselves have laid down in the Constitution. Consequently, a judge need not hesitate to invalidate a law that he deems unconstitutional.

A few examples will help to clarify the way in which this extraordinary jurisprudence works. The constitution of the state of New York (which I choose at random, for all American constitutions contain similar provisions)—to repeat, the constitution of the state of New York states that no accused can be deprived of the right to trial by jury or the guarantees of standard criminal procedure.

Suppose the legislature of the state of New York passed a law that denied the right to be judged by a jury to a certain class of criminals or subjected that class to a special procedure or placed the accused in the custody of authorities other than the courts. Defendants who stood to suffer from the enforcement of such a law could petition the state tribunal, which would have not only the right but also the duty to hear their case.

Another example: the Constitution of the United States prohibits the states from enacting retroactive punishments. Suppose once again that the legislature of the state of New York decided to change the status of certain prisoners, to draw from their prior conviction certain consequences not anticipated by their judges, and to subject them to penalties that did not exist when the original crime or misdemeanor was committed. The unfortunate victims of these tyrannical measures could petition one of the courts of the Union, and that court would not fail to declare the exceptional law contrary to the Constitution of the United States and therefore null and void.

I beg the members of the Academy to observe that what is *new* is not the principle invoked by American judges but rather the use they make of it.

The idea that the constitution of a country imposes a *legal* obligation on the legislature itself is accepted in Europe as well as the United States, but in Europe there is seldom anything but the occasional revolution to indicate to high state authorities that they have violated the constitution or neglected its spirit, whereas in America, it is the judge who, whenever the executive or legislature strays from the Constitution, stops them in their tracks by refusing to grant judicial sanction to their will.

Even in England this counterweight was never used. The author wonders why the English, so nobly amorous of their liberty that they are unable to put up with arbitrariness in government even when exercised by the authorities they most love and respect, did not make use of the means on which Americans have so often relied to protect themselves from the vehemence of lawmakers. He offers an ingenious answer, which is worth mentioning: in England, he says, the nation has for centuries devoted all its efforts to combating the despotism of the prince. All the precautions that were put in place were directed against him and not against Parliament. The English were too afraid of the arbitrariness of the king to think of protecting themselves against the tyranny of the legislature. In America, where the executive is weak and the legislature is constantly cloaked in all the prestige of popular sovereignty, the law itself might often become oppressive if the courts did not have the power to purge it of any provisions that might exceed the bounds of the Constitution.

The explanation lacks neither forcefulness nor depth, but it seems to me insufficient to explain everything that the author finds surprising. Unless I am mistaken, one needs to add something else: namely, the fact that the English have no constitution in the strict sense of the word. To be sure, they accept the idea that certain general principles are beyond the reach of the legislature and no statute may violate them. But those principles are seldom set forth in a precise way in a text that can be cited when it becomes necessary to invoke the letter of the constitution against the letter of the law. Since the limits of the constitution are not well-known, it may often be as difficult for the courts to spell them out clearly for the legislature as it is for the legislature to respect them. This explains how the English courts, which have so frequently availed themselves of interpretation to evade laws that seemed unfair or contrary to the general law of nature, have never formally refused to enforce such laws.

The avowed aim of Mr. Sedgwick's book is to show how American judges have exercised and should exercise the awesome tutelary power that their fellow citizens have vested in them. His objective is to show his country's magistrates what rules might guide them in the exercise of their power and what limits they ought to observe in a realm that might seem entirely subject to their discretion. To that end, he treats all the various subjects on which the courts have ruled to date as well as those that might arise in the future. In investigating these specific issues, as well as in setting forth the principles of the subject, he demonstrates profound knowledge of precedent, rare skill in interpretation, and, to my mind, great common sense. By delving into details with him as a guide, one can achieve a full and complete picture of this vast judicial power, which only in America dares to look democracy in the face from time to time and lay down its limits.

I have said enough to accomplish my purpose, which was to indicate the general utility of a book that might seem to deal only with certain specific points of foreign legislation. The author did not intend to write a work of political science; he confined himself to writing an excellent law book. This is the work of a lawyer, but I will allow myself to recommend it to anyone interested in public affairs.

NOTE ON SOURCES

Of the many texts presented here, Tocqueville published only a few in his lifetime (the foreword to the twelfth edition of *Democracy in America,* the penitentiary report co-authored with Beaumont, and some political speeches and academic texts). All of his letters, notebooks, and travel narratives were published posthumously, in several installments, with each edition adding new material and correcting errors. In preparing this translation, we have relied on the most recent French editions, but only after comparing them to the previous ones and occasionally returning to the original manuscripts for additional textual checking when in doubt. The exact archival location of each original document is given in the modern French edition of Tocqueville's complete works (see *Œuvres complètes,* below).

The two main repositories for Tocqueville manuscripts are the Château de Tocqueville (with duplicate microfilm of the entire family-owned archival collection at the nearby public Archives de la Manche in Saint-Lô) and the Beinecke Rare Book and Manuscript Library at Yale University. The latter owns a vast collection of both Tocqueville and Beaumont papers.

Gustave de Beaumont published a two-volume selection of his friend's works as *Œuvres et correspondance inédites d'Alexis de Tocqueville* (Paris, 1861), followed by a larger, nine-volume selection entitled *Œuvres complètes d'Alexis de Tocqueville publiées par Madame de Tocqueville* (Paris, 1865–67). The two-volume set became tomes V and VI of the nine-volume edition:

> Tome I–III, *De la démocratie en Amérique* (1866).
> Tome IV, *L'ancien régime et la Révolution* (1866).
> Tome V, *Correspondance et œuvres posthumes* (1866).
> Tome VI, *Correspondance* (1867).
> Tome VII, *Nouvelle correspondance entièrement inédite* (1866).
> Tome VIII, *Mélanges, fragments historiques et notes sur l'ancien régime, la Révolution et l'empire, voyages, pensées, entièrement inédits* (1865).
> Tome IX, *Études économiques, politiques et littéraires* (1866).

From tome VII of Beaumont's edition, we have selected a letter to Blosseville (October 10, 1831) and one to Molé (August 1835) that are to be reissued in the forthcoming tome XVII of the modern *Œuvres complètes* (see below).

Since 1951, a French national commission (Commission nationale pour la publication des œuvres d'Alexis de Tocqueville) has undertaken to publish Tocqueville's complete works under the Gallimard imprint (*Œuvres complètes;* hereafter cited as O.C.), as follows:

> Tome I, *De la démocratie en Amérique,* 2 vols., ed. J.-P. Mayer (1951).
> Tome II, *L'ancien régime et la Révolution,* 2 vols., ed. J.-P. Mayer (vol. 1) and André Jardin (vol. 2) (1952–53).

Tome III, *Écrits et discours politiques,* 3 vols., ed. André Jardin (1962, 1985, 1990).

Tome IV, *Écrits sur le système pénitentiaire en France et à l'étranger,* 2 vols., ed. Michelle Perrot (1984).

Tome V, *Voyages,* 2 vols., ed. J.-P. Mayer (vol. 1, *Voyages en Sicile et aux États-Unis*) and J.-P. Mayer and André Jardin (vol. 2, *Voyages en Angleterre, Irlande, Suisse et Algérie*) (1957–58).

Tome VI, *Correspondance anglaise,* 3 vols., ed. J.-P. Mayer and Gustave Rudler (vol. 1, *Correspondance d'Alexis de Tocqueville avec Henry Reeve et John Stuart Mill*); Hugh Brogan, A. P. Kerr, and Lola Mayer (vol. 2, *Correspondance et conversations d'Alexis de Tocqueville et de Nassau William Senior*); and A. P. Kerr (vol. 3) (1954, 1991, 2003).

Tome VII, *Correspondance étrangère, Amérique-Europe continentale,* 1 vol., ed. Françoise Mélonio, Lise Queffélec, and Anthony Pleasance (1986).

Tome VIII, *Correspondance d'Alexis de Tocqueville et de Gustave de Beaumont,* 3 vols., ed. André Jardin (1967).

Tome IX, *Correspondance d'Alexis de Tocqueville et d'Arthur de Gobineau,* 1 vol., ed. M. Degros (1959).

Tome X, *Correspondance et écrits locaux,* 1 vol., ed. Lise Queffélec-Dumasy (1995).

Tome XI, *Correspondance d'Alexis de Tocqueville avec P.-P. Royer-Collard et avec J.-J. Ampère,* 1 vol., ed. André Jardin (1970).

Tome XII, *Souvenirs,* 1 vol., ed. Luc Monnier (1964).

Tome XIII, *Correspondance d'Alexis de Tocqueville et de Louis de Kergorlay,* 2 vols., ed. André Jardin (1977).

Tome XIV, *Correspondance familiale,* 1 vol., ed. Jean-Louis Benoît and André Jardin (1998).

Tome XV, *Correspondance d'Alexis de Tocqueville et de Francisque de Corcelle; Correspondance d'Alexis de Tocqueville et de Madame Swetchine,* 2 vols., ed. Pierre Gibert (1983).

Tome XVI, *Mélanges,* 1 vol., ed. Françoise Mélonio (1989).

Tome XVII, *Correspondance à divers,* ed. Françoise Mélonio (forthcoming).

Tome XVIII, *Correspondance d'Alexis de Tocqueville avec Adolphe de Circourt et avec Madame de Circourt,* 1 vol., ed. A. P. Kerr (1983).

For this edition, we have translated texts from tomes I, III, IV, VI, VII, VIII, IX, XI, XIII, XIV, XV, and XVI of O.C. From the forthcoming tome XVII, we have included letters to Ernest de Chabrol dated May 18, October 7 and 18, November 19 and 26, and December 6, 1831, and January 16 and 24, 1832; to Eugène Stöffels of June 28, 1831; to Dalmassy at the end of August 1831; and to an unknown recipient dated November 8, 1831, courtesy of Françoise Mélonio and the Commission nationale.

The Bibliothèque de la Pléiade (Paris: Gallimard) has published three volumes of Tocqueville's *Œuvres:*

Tome I, *Voyages* and *Écrits académiques et politiques,* ed. André Jardin, Françoise Mélonio, and Lise Queffélec (1991).

Tome II, *De la démocratie en Amérique,* ed. André Jardin, Jean-Claude Lamberti, and James T. Schleifer (1992).

Tome III, *État social et politique de la France avant et depuis 1789; L'ancien régime et la Révolution; Esquisses de "L'ancien régime et la Révolution"; [Considérations sur la Révolution];* *Souvenirs,* ed. François Furet and Françoise Mélonio (2004).

We have based our translations of the travel notebooks and excursions on tome I.

Françoise Mélonio and Laurence Guellec have edited a vast selection of Tocqueville's letters in *Lettres choisies, Souvenirs* (Paris: Gallimard [Quarto], 2003). From this edition, we have included some letters to Tocqueville's friends, especially Stöffels and Chabrol, that will appear in tome XVII of O.C.

Beaumont published *Marie* in 1835 with the Parisian house Charles Gosselin. We have selected our excerpts from the fourth edition, printed in 1840. The reader may wish to consult a fuller (yet still abridged) translation: *Marie; or, Slavery in the United States,* trans. Barbara Chapman, with an introduction by Gerard Fergerson (Stanford, CA: Stanford University Press, 1958).

André Jardin and G. W. Pierson carefully edited *Gustave de Beaumont: Lettres d'Amérique* (Paris: Presses Universitaires de France, 1973).

To supplement our volume, the reader should naturally turn to Tocqueville's classic *Democracy in America,* trans. Arthur Goldhammer, ed. Olivier Zunz (New York: Library of America, 2004). In this translation of *De la démocratie en Amérique,* the reader will find the original English texts that Tocqueville had translated into French, reprinted from the editions Tocqueville used.

Eduardo Nolla has published a historical-critical edition of *Democracy in America* in which he augments Tocqueville's text with the author's surviving drafts and manuscript notes. The reader may now consult this expanded edition in English, translated by James T. Schleifer (4 vols.; Indianapolis: Liberty Fund, 2010).

Finally, Aurelian Craiutu and Jeremy Jennings in *Tocqueville on America after 1840: Letters and Other Writings* (New York: Cambridge University Press, 2009) have published all surviving letters between Tocqueville and his American correspondents after 1840. Their volume includes not only the letters Tocqueville wrote to his American friends and acquaintances but also the surviving letters he received from them.

Beaumont left two sketchbooks of his American travels. The Beaumont family presented one to George Pierson, who, in turn, gave it to the Beinecke Library, where it is available for consultation. We reproduce most of it here, except for plates too pale to print. The other sketchbook, in private hands, was on display at the Library of Congress during the 1989 exhibit "A Passion for Liberty: Alexis de Tocqueville on Democracy and Revolution." We reproduce here photographic glass plates of this sketchbook that George Pierson deposited in the collections of the Beinecke Library.

Beaumont's portrait and the plan of the Cherry Hill penitentiary also come from the Beinecke holdings. Tocqueville's portrait is printed courtesy of The Image Works, Inc., his drawing of Indians courtesy of the Archives de la Manche.

BIBLIOGRAPHICAL REFERENCES

"Alexis de Tocqueville (1805–1859): A Special Bicentennial Issue." *The Tocqueville Review/La Revue Tocqueville* 27, no. 2 (2006).

Antoine, Agnès. *L'impensé de la démocratie: Tocqueville, la citoyenneté et la religion.* Paris: Fayard, 2003.

Aron, Raymond. "Tocqueville." In *Main Currents in Sociological Thought,* trans. Richard Howard and Helen Weaver. New York: Basic Books, 1965.

Benoît, Jean-Louis. *Tocqueville moraliste.* Paris: Honoré Champion, 2004.

Boesche, Roger. *The Strange Liberalism of Alexis de Tocqueville.* Ithaca, NY: Cornell University Press, 1987.

Boudon, Raymond. *Tocqueville aujourd'hui.* Paris: Odile Jacob, 2005.

Brogan, Hugh. *Alexis de Tocqueville: A Life.* New Haven, CT: Yale University Press, 2007.

Damrosch, Leo. *Tocqueville's Discovery of America.* New York: Farrar, Straus and Giroux, 2010.

Drescher, Seymour. *Dilemmas of Democracy: Tocqueville and Modernization.* Pittsburgh, PA: University of Pittsburgh Press, 1968.

———. *Tocqueville and England.* Cambridge, MA: Harvard University Press, 1964.

Eisenstadt, Abraham S., ed. *Reconsidering Tocqueville's "Democracy in America."* New Brunswick, NJ: Rutgers University Press, 1988.

Elster, Jon. *Alexis de Tocqueville: The First Social Scientist.* New York: Cambridge University Press, 2009.

Furet, François. "The Conceptual System of *Democracy in America*." In *In the Workshop of History,* trans. Jonathan Mandelbaum. Chicago: University of Chicago Press, 1984.

Gannett, Robert T., Jr. *Tocqueville Unveiled: The Historian and His Sources for "The Old Regime and the Revolution."* Chicago: University of Chicago Press, 2003.

Guellec, Laurence. *Tocqueville et les langages de la démocratie.* Paris: Honoré Champion, 2004.

———, ed. *Tocqueville et l'esprit de la démocratie.* Paris: Sciences Po les Presses and *The Tocqueville Review/La Revue Tocqueville,* 2005.

Howe, Daniel Walker. *What Hath God Wrought: The Transformation of America, 1815–1848.* New York: Oxford University Press, 2007.

Jardin, André. *Tocqueville: A Biography.* Trans. Lydia Davis with Robert Hemenway. New York: Farrar, Straus and Giroux, 1988.

Jaume, Lucien. *Tocqueville: Les sources aristocratiques de la liberté.* Paris: Fayard, 2008.

Kahan, Alan S. *Aristocratic Liberalism: The Social and Political Thought of Jacob Burckhardt, John Stuart Mill, and Alexis de Tocqueville.* New York: Oxford University Press, 1992.

Kelly, George Armstrong. *The Humane Comedy: Constant, Tocqueville, and French Liberalism.* With a foreword by Stephen R. Graubard. New York: Cambridge University Press, 1992.

Lamberti, Jean-Claude. *Tocqueville and the Two Democracies.* Trans. Arthur Goldhammer. Cambridge, MA: Harvard University Press, 1989.

Manent, Pierre. *Tocqueville and the Nature of Democracy.* Trans. John Waggoner. With a foreword by Harvey C. Mansfield. Lanham, MD: Rowman & Littlefield, 1996.

Mansfield, Harvey C. *Tocqueville: A Very Short Introduction.* New York: Oxford University Press, 2010.

Manzini, Charlotte. *Qui êtes-vous Monsieur de Tocqueville?* Saint-Lô: Archives de la Manche, 2005.

Mélonio, Françoise. *Tocqueville and the French.* Trans. Beth G. Raps. Charlottesville: University Press of Virginia, 1998.

Pierson, George Wilson. *Tocqueville and Beaumont in America.* New York: Oxford University Press, 1938. Reprinted as *Tocqueville in America.* Baltimore: Johns Hopkins University Press, 1996.

Schleifer, James T. *The Making of Tocqueville's "Democracy in America."* Chapel Hill: University of North Carolina Press, 1980.

Welch, Cheryl B., ed. *The Cambridge Companion to Tocqueville.* New York: Cambridge University Press, 2006.

————. *De Tocqueville.* New York: Oxford University Press, 2001.

Wolin, Sheldon S. *Tocqueville between Two Worlds: The Making of a Political and Theoretical Life.* Princeton, NJ: Princeton University Press, 2001.

INDEX

Italicized page numbers indicate illustrations; **bold page numbers** indicate biographical notes. The abbreviations AT and GB are used for Alexis de Tocqueville and Gustave de Beaumont, respectively.

Abbot, Samuel, **107n129, 305n132**

abolition of slavery: AT's report advocating (French colonies), 581, 582–83, 593; AT's testimony for, 655; comparison of states with and without, 181–82, 191–92, 272–73, 274, 288, 358, 530, 532; GB's *Marie* on, 530–42; gradual approach to, 153n197, 530, 538; implementation challenges of, 534–38; in Kansas, 620; objections to, refuted, 531–36; rationale for, 530–31; unlikely in South, 539–42. *See also* colonization; free blacks; slaves and slavery

absolutism, 572, 627n60. *See also* monarchies

Académie des sciences morales et politiques: AT's speech on democracy for, 633–34n71 (*see also* "On Cherbuliez's *Democracy in Switzerland*" [AT]); AT's speech on Sedgwick's book for, 617, 655–58; Lieber's position proposed in, 595–96, 599

Académie française, 503, 569–70, 602n16

Achaean League, 349–50, 350n189

Act of Mediation, 636

Adams, Herbert Baxter, 134n168

Adams, John, 258, 575–76

Adams, John Quincy, **204n239;** ambassadorship of, 241n39;

interviews of, 204, 242–44, 291; literary ability of, 558; on political patronage, 575n22

Adlard, George, 580, **580n29**

Aesop's fables, 31

African Americans. *See* blacks; free blacks; slaves and slavery

agricultural crops: corn as, 413; in Kentucky, 275; labor required for, 255–56, 532–34; in Michigan, 331; South's interests in, 270; in tropical climate, 276–77

Alabama: family scene in, 312; Mobile Bay, GB's sketch of, *200;* steamboat travel in, 284; temperance societies of, 481; various attitudes in, 282–83; violence in, 282

Albany (N.Y.): arrival at, 62–63; description of, 68; founding and population of, 62n75; Fourth of July celebrations in, xxx, 67, 72–73, 78–79, 80–81; plans to visit, 49, 58; return to, 122

Albany and Schenectady Railroad, 62n78

alcohol, 307; effects on American Indians, 84, 327, 346, 403–4; electioneering and, 270, 352; laws on, 546–47

Algeria, French conquest and colonization of, 600–601n13

Ali, Mehemet, 581n31

almshouses and poorhouses, 220–21, 261. *See also* debt

Alphabetic Notebooks A and B (AT), 314–38; associations, 333–34; blacks, 338; Canada, 315–23; convention, right to hold, 334–36; dueling, 336; Indians, 325–28; individual vs. common good, 332–33; land and cultivation, 331–32; Massachusetts, 328–29; mores, 336–37; national character of Americans, 314–15; pardons, 324; penitentiaries, 329–31; prostitution, 337; public education, 324

America. *See* American character; Americans; United States

American and Commercial Daily Advertiser (newspaper), 309n139, 500

American character: French and English compared with, 323; habits instilled in, 310; influences on, 243; northern vs. southern, 243–44, 252, 254–55, 265, 282, 287, 310; notebooks on, 314–15; as perfect specimen of Englishman, 313; pioneers as exemplars, 408–12; remarkable nature of, 150–51; social state linked to, 311. *See also* society in America

—specific traits: common sense, 513; enlightenment, 349, 354; happiness, 29; hospitality, 9, 14–15, 18, 39–40, 43, 48, 62–63, 120–21, 128–31, 443, 552; industriousness, 30,

American character (*continued*) 39, 63–64, 93, 366, 513–14, 515–16; love of praise, 34–35; money-making focus, 77 (*see also* commerce); multiple skills and occupations, 283; pride, 18, 25, 79, 176–77, 365, 517, 548, 555–56; restlessness, 39, 49, 165–66, 314–15; self-control, 175, 557, 576; sociability, 551–53

American Colonization Society, 287n98, 536n10

American Fur Company, 89n110, 107n129, 300, 300n120, 305

American Indians: alcohol's effects on, 84, 91–92, 293, 327, 346, 403–4; American attitudes toward, 112, 288, 327–28, 331–32, 402, 517; attitudes toward European immigrants, 433; beliefs of, 92, 194–95, 325–26, 343, 435; burial practices of, 108; canoes of, 106, 111; chiefs and justice among, 222, 224, 225–26, 305, 344; Christian conversion of, 222–23, 224, 232, 305, 343–45; clothing and accoutrements of, 75, 105, 108–9, 297, 298, 302, 306, 327, 403–4, 417–18, 422; —, GB's sketch of, *418;* as common race, 233; conditions of, 75, 80, 91–92, 293, 302; conversation with, 306; daily lives of, 224; description of, 142–43; desire to see, 49, 296, 402; destruction of, 84–85, 195, 224, 288, 292–93, 328, 402; diet of, 420, 427; differences among, 104; encountered on trail to Saginaw, 90–91, 417–20; face painting of, 108–9; first encounter with, xxv–xxvi, 75, 326–28; freedom of, 344–45; GB's views on, xxxiv, 550–51; as guides, 94–96, 298–300, 422–24, 425, 427–30; —, GB's sketches of, *426;* Houston's views on, 343–47; mar-

riage among, 550–51; morals of, 213, 344; mounds of, 345n180; notebooks on, 325–28; others' anecdotes about, 325–26; perceived fondness for French, 224, 232–33, 303, 305; rifles of, 419–20, 560; steamboat's arrival and, 104–5; suicide rate among, 550–51; trade with, 300–301; trustworthiness of, 297, 300, 416–17, 435; uprising of, 109; villages of, 95; warfare among, 222, 223, 303, 305. *See also* Indian removal *and specific tribes by name*

American Museum (Scudder's Museum), 66

American Party (Know-Nothing Party), 608, 608n26, 609n29

American Philosophical Society, 146

American Revolution: aftermath of, 164, 263; causes of, 250; English-American attitudes after (1830s), 544–45; inheritance laws changed by, 53–54; Iroquois alliances in, 223n18; Lafayette's role in, 4n2; Luzerne's role in, 5n4; political and social aspects of, xxvii–xxviii; veterans of, 78. *See also* Articles of Confederation (U.S.); Declaration of Independence

Americans: as all emigrants, 92–93, 180; beliefs (opinions) of, 49–50; English as underlying influence on, 555–56; English attitudes toward, 544–45; knowledge about French affairs, 234; mutual awareness among, 364. *See also* American character

American Temperance Society, 333n172

Amiens (France), Albany compared with, 62

Ampère, Jean-Jacques, 602–3, **602n17**

Amphictyonic League, 349–50, 349–50n189

Anglican ministers, prison work of, 330–31

Anthony's Nose (Hudson River area), 61, 61n74, 606

Anti-Masonic Party, 545–46

antiquity: fascination with objects of, 345n180; heroic times in, 515; republic in, 38n44; slavery in, 528–29, 530

Arbre-Croche (Cross Village, Mich.), 221, 222–23

Argence, Madame d', 77

aristocracy: advocates in U.S., 624–25; in Maryland, 252–53, 254–56, 263; personal view of, 573; in Switzerland, 635–36; translating *Democracy* parts on, 582; of wealth, 18, 212

Arkansas: Indian territory of, 346; statehood of, 628n62

Arnold, Benedict, 80n102

Aron, Raymond, xxi

Articles of Confederation (U.S.), xxiv, 347–48

associations and associational movement: AT's approach to, xxix, xxxi; debates about, xxx–xxxi; in Fourth of July celebrations, xxx, 72–73, 78; New England town as original, xxxii; power of, 333–34; Protestant sectarianism and, xxxiii; structure of (book excerpt), 480–81. *See also* public opinion

Astor, John Jacob, 305n129. *See also* American Fur Company

Atala (Chateaubriand): AT and GB influenced by, xxv; AT's description of, 125–26; Chactas (character) in, 94n115, 194n230; on Niagara Falls, 114n135; questions about, 94–95; recommendation to read, 143; summary of, 94n115

Atlantic Ocean: call for freedom of, 648–49; virgin forest compared with, 424–25. See *also Havre, Le* (ship); voyage to America

Auber, Daniel François Esprit, 104, **104n126**

Auburn (N.Y.), hotel of, 82

Auburn Prison: administrator of (*see* Lynds, Elam); chaplain at, 331; discipline of, 459; GB's sketch of, *449;* plans to visit, 11, 43, 58, 68; recidivism rate of, 446, 470; research and visit at, 76, 82, 83, 87, 448–49; revenues from, 451–52; Sing Sing Prison compared with, 448–54. *See also* Auburn system

Auburn system: in Auburn vs. Sing Sing, 449–54; basics of, 11n16, 31–32, 77–78, 215–16, 329–30, 455, 492; beginnings of, 215n8; cell size in, 464; conclusions about, 463; European debates on, 500–501; labor of prisoners in, 215, 216–17; Philadelphia method compared with, 458, 464, 493n19, 494–99; possibility of transfer to France, 215, 444, 453–55; purpose of, 460; reflections on, 32, 83, 330; reservations about, 454; solitary confinement in, 444; work and silence in, 444–46. *See also* penitentiary systems

Australian penal system, 139n175

Austria, GB as ambassador to, xxxviii

balance of power concept, 629n64

Baltimore (Md.): Catholicism in, 242, 256–57, 258; growth of, 254; Maryland State Penitentiary in, 464; newspaper in, 309; plans to visit, 153, 464; slavery in, 163, 533; social activities and people in, 161–63; witnesses imprisoned in, 480

Baltimore and Ohio Railroad, 489

Bancroft, George, 602n17, 615n41

Bank of the United States. *See* Second Bank of the United States

bankruptcies: attitudes toward individual, 288–89; of Biddle's bank, 264n66; causes of, 269, 347; falsely declared, 491; GB's *Marie* on, 548–49; law on, 249, 368; number and tolerance of, 548–49; in Panic of 1837, 575n21

banks and banking: bankruptcies of, 264n66, 269; in Cincinnati, 359; usefulness of, 288. *See also* bankruptcies; economy; Second Bank of the United States

Baptists, 516

Baraudière, Rose Préau de la (GB's mother), **11n17;** GB's letters to, 11–15, 31–36, 187–89, 201–4

Barclay, James J., 387–88, **387n213**

Baring (banker), 620, 621, 623

Barnum, P. T., 66n84

Barrot, Odilon, 595, **595n5,** 601n15

Bates, Edward, 601–2n16

battles: Alamo, 352n193; Lake Erie, 295n111, 406; New Orleans, 201, 203n237, 308; Québec (Battle of the Plains of Abraham; 1759), 170, **170n214**

Bauer, Bruno, xxxv

Bayard, seigneur de (Pierre Terrail, the "Good Knight"), 514

bears, 89, 422, 439

Beaufort (Quebec), 319

Beaumanoir, Philippe de, 366, **366n202**

Beaumont, Achille Bonnin de La Bonninière de (GB's brother), 19, **19n27,** 145; cajeput oil sent to, 154; GB's letters to, 40–43, 98–110, 161–63; marriage of, 131n161; sketches for use of, 35

Beaumont, André Bonnin de La Bonninière de (GB's uncle), 162

Beaumont, Armand Bonnin

de La Bonninière de (GB's uncle), 162

Beaumont, Charles Bonnin de La Bonninière de (GB's uncle), 162

Beaumont, Eugène Bonnin de La Bonninière de (GB's uncle), 147

Beaumont, Eugénie Bonnin de La Bonninière de (GB's sister). *See* Sarcé, Eugénie de (GB's sister)

Beaumont, Félicie de Bonnet de Bellou (GB's sister-in-law; Achille's wife), 131, **131n161;** GB's letter to, 151–55

Beaumont, François de (GB's nephew), 68

Beaumont, Gustave Bonnin de La Bonninière de (GB): age at time of voyage, xvii; analytical tools of, xxiv; AT's friendship with, xvii–xix, xxxiii, xxxvi; AT's letters to, 4–5, 492–93, 493n19, 572, 606, 607–8, 621–23; AT's papers published by, xx; diary fragments of, 132–34, 175–78; family history and prospects of, xvii–xviii; Germany visited by, 605–6; home of, 6n6; homesickness of, 207; *Ireland,* xix, xxxvi, 575; Lieber's position and, 596, 597, 598; marriage of, 574–75; political career of, xix–xx, xxxviii, 42; post-1840 interests of, xxxviii–xxxix; on presidential election, 651; self-portrait of, *416;* as social reformer, xxxvi–xxxvii; swimming lessons for, xxvii, 33, 61; topics of focus on voyage, xxxiii–xxxvi; tutor of, 23n32; virtuous determination of, xxvi–xxvii, 19, 65, 80. *See also* letters; *Marie; or, Slavery in the United States* (GB); *On the Penitentiary System of the United States and Its Application in France* (GB and AT); sketches (GB)

Beaumont, Jules Bonnin de La Bonninière de (GB's brother), **13n19,** 31, 74, 145, 188; GB's letters to, 59–68, 126–31, 178–82; letter received from, 59; sending map for, 153–54; sketches for use of, 35

Beaumont, Jules Bonnin de La Bonninière de (GB's father), **6n6;** GB's letters to, 6, 15–20, 57–58, 113–14, 118–23, 145–47; marriage of, 11n17; on United States, 127

Beaumont, Léonce Bonnin de La Bonninière de (GB's nephew), 68

Beaumont (parish in Quebec), 120–21

Beaver and Erie Canal, 294n109

Belisle, Bon Georges Charles Evrard de, 10, **10n13**

Bellou, Marie-Louise-Gabrielle Bonnet de, 155, **155n199**

Belpre and Cincinnati Railroad, 620n51. *See also* Galena and Chicago Union Railroad

Benjamin (American publisher), 580

Benoist, Pierre-Vincent, 147, **147n188**

"Bible tree," 299

bicameralism: concept of, xxviii, 649–50; in New York vs. Switzerland, 640–42

Biddle, John, 296, **296n115,** 407–8

Biddle, Nicholas, 264–65, **264n66**

birds, description of, 60–61, 92, 97, 301. *See also* hunting

blacks: advocates of, 517–19; colonization in Liberia for, 252n52, 287n98, 517, 536–37; education of, 153, 338, 511, 532; equality challenged by, 556–57; Indians compared with, 91; intelligence of, 344–45; in prisons, 484, 486, 487; rights (and realities) of, 338, 509–10, 511, 540–42. *See also* free blacks; slaves and slavery

Blosseville, vicomte de (Ernest Poret), 139, **139n175,** 144, 207

Blouet, Abel, **492n16**

Bois-Brûlé (mixed Indian and European blood): appearance of, 303; assistance crossing Saginaw River, 96, 299–300, 429–30

Bois-le-Comte, André-Ernest Olivier Sain de, 600–601, **601n14**

Bonner, John, **613n37**

Bossuet, Jacques-Bénigne, 58, **58n71**

Boston (Mass.): education for black children in, 532; flag consecration ceremony in, 130–31; intellectual and religious milieu of, 57, 129, 328–29, 612; layout and population of, 128, 328n165; number of Catholics in, 157; plans to visit, 24, 43, 58, 123, 447; prostitution in, 337; recidivism rate in, 470; reform school in, 471, 472, 473–76; street organ-playing prohibited in, 558; theater in, 559; travel to, 127; Unitarianism in, 233, 244; urban reform in, 236n34; wealth in, 234–35; welcome and social activities in, 128–31

Bouchitté, Louis Firmin Hervé, 155, **155n200,** 157–60

Bourbon Restoration: AT's father's role in, 27n38; "Marseillaise" forbidden during, 103n124; North American policy of, 631; parliament in, 578n24; reflections on, 68; support for, 57n69, 162n210

Briqueville, Armand de, 647, **647n77**

British Museum, 617

Brooks, Preston, 500n24

Brown, James, 251–52, **251n51**

Browne, Walter, 25, **25n35**

Buchanan, James: concerns about, 614n40, 618; conflict with Mormons, 623n54; election of, 609n29, 612, 613n36; Lecompton Consti-

tution supported by, 621n53; support for, 616

Buffalo (N.Y.): description of, 83; growth of, 293n108; Indians in, 84, 293, 402–4

Bulfinch, Charles, **128n152,** 240n38

Buller, Charles, **596n8**

Burns (Scottish physician), 301, 331

Cadillac, Antoine de la Mothe, 295n113

cajeput oil, 154, 155, 156, 160–61

Calhoun, John C., 286–87, **287n97**

Cambreleng, Churchill C., 62–63, **62n79**

Campe, Joachim-Heinrich, *Voyage d'un Allemand au Lac Onéida,* 86n106, 398–99

Canada: attitudes toward French visitors and old France, 96, 120–21, 124, 126; British control of, 119–20, 124, 170, 224, 226–27, 229–30, 250, 576–77; Catholics and Catholicism in, 119, 122, 124, 157, 228, 317, 320–21, 323; citizenship rights in, 232; civil tribunal of, 318–19; curiosity about, 44; education in, 227, 231–32; elections and voting in, 231; external appearance of, 315–17; feudal remnants in, 226, 231; French Canadian rebellion in, 576–77; French people in, 124n147, 169–70; general remarks about, 322–23; laughter and good cheer in, 121–22; marriage in, 317–18; newspapers in, 227–28, 317, 320, 321, 322; people and ways of, 124–25, 230–31, 319–22; plans to visit, 49, 58; population of, 119n140, 124, 227, 232n28; purity of morals in, 119; Upper and Lower divisions of, 148n191, 226–27n23, 318n148, 322–23, 339. *See also* French Canadians; Montreal (Quebec); Quebec and Quebec City area

Canadian House of Commons, 231, 232

Canadien, Le (newspaper), 317

canals and canal development: importance in Ohio, 359; Panama, predicted, 627; plans for, 309, 406; public prosperity linked to, 363–65. *See also* Erie Canal

Canandaigua (N.Y.), visit to, 83, 87–88, 293

canoe travel: crossing Saginaw River, 95–96, 299–300, 429–30; Lake Superior explored via, 105–7; in Sault St. Marie area, 106, 110–11, 303–4

capital punishment: argument for, 387; for free backs, 524, 525; for fugitive slaves and collaborators of escape, 522–23, 524–25; for master who killed slave, 277; sheriffs as executioners in, 239–40, 554; for slaves, 527

Caribbean Sea, importance to development, 627–28

Carné, Louis de, 156–57, **157n204,** 174

Carroll, Charles, **162n209;** on American Revolution, 164; Catholicism of, 242; characteristics of, 162; death of, 533n8; inheritance of, 253; interview of, 262–63; on slavery, 533–34

Carroll, James (Charles's nephew), 260n61

Carroll, James (unknown), 260–61, 263–64

Cartwright, George W., 35, **35n41**

Cass, Lewis, 614n40

Catholic Church: appointments in, 258–59; authority in, 71; bishoprics of, 100, 223; Canadian examples of, 120, 123; contributions to, 260; governance of, 258; government support and, 221–22; hermits of, 71–72; Louisiana attitudes toward, 279; nunneries of, 226. Specific orders: Cister-

cians, 71n90; Jesuits, 222–23, 232, 259; Sulpician Fathers, 258n59; Trappists, 71, 444

Catholicism: AT's focus on, xxxiii; in Baltimore, 242, 256–57, 258; in Canada, 119, 122, 124, 157, 228, 317, 320–21, 323; conversions to, 51–52, 222–23, 224, 232, 259, 344; democracy and, 242; education and, 256–57; familiarity of rituals, 10; growth of, 11, 17, 51, 100, 157, 223, 244, 256, 259, 296, 608; as ill-suited to idea of liberty, 220; notebook on, 220, 221–23, 226, 228; questions about, 157–59; in Saginaw area, 434–35; sources on, 44; in Switzerland, 634; turn from, 245; Unitarianism vs., 57–58

Catholics: attitudes toward pope and councils, 259–60; European priests for, 223; as fellow travelers, 100–101; intolerance among, 51; nativist opposition to, 608n26; number of, 11, 51n62, 608; opposition to British government in Canada, 120; political situation of, 157–58; Protestants' conflict with, 100, 222, 305; as religious society, dependent on pope, 158–59; zealousness of, 260

central government: American vs. French, 446–47; explanation of, 642–43; Louis XIV's role in French, 627n60; notebook on, 347–50; questions about, 134–37, 138, 139, 144. *See also* federal government

centralization: of prison governance, 79–80; questions about meaning of, 137–38, 139

Cessac, Gérard de, 601, **601–2n16**

Cessac, Jean-Gérard Lacuée de, **602n16**

Chabrol-Chaméane, Ernest de, **21n29,** 118; AT's bond with,

207; AT's concerns about, 21–22; AT's letters to, 21–24, 38–40, 45–46, 77–80, 111–13, 138–40, 149–50, 155–61, 167–68, 170–74, 186–87, 197–99, 200–201, 206–8; cajeput oil sent to, 154, 156, 160–61; GB's letters to, 83–85, 88–98

—topics of discussion with: American traits and character, 38–40; cholera, 156–57, 160–61, 167, 200; conditions in France, 21–22, 207; daily activities, 23–24, 46, 80; Fourth of July celebrations, 78–79; government administration in France vs. U.S., 138–40; Green Bay trip, 111–12; judicial system, criminal and civil levels, 46, 149–50, 155–56; judicial system, federal and state courts, 170–73; land sales, 112–13; Marie, 22, 173; political questions, 22–23; possible book about America, 207–8; prison study, 45, 77–78, 79, 150, 167–68; public education, 198–99; religious sects, 157–60; travel difficulties, 173, 186–87, 197–98, 200–201, 207

Chamber of Deputies, 501n27; AT in, xix–xx, xxxviii, 580; AT on colonization in Algeria, 600–601n13; AT on Eastern Question in, 581; AT's campaign for, 591; AT's causes in, 580n28; AT's report on abolition of slavery, 581, 582–83, 593; GB in, xix–xx, xxxviii; mail delivery to, 599; news about, 179; prison reform debates and, 501; reparations and treaty issues for, 626–27

Chamber of Peers, 501, 501n26

Champlain, Samuel de, 120n144

Champlain, Lake: steamboat crossing of, 122

Channing, William Ellery, xxiv, **52n63,** 516; French knowl-

tural work in tropical, 276–77; changes in, 315; fall colors, 150; Irving on, 548; morals and behavior linked to, 188, 337; public discourse on, 131; summer heat, 40, 44, 397, 427, 437, 438; winter cold, 169, 175–78, 184, 186, 187, 188–89, 190–91, 193, 615

clothing and accoutrements: French influences on, 64–65, 89, 130, 153, 406; gloves, request for, 27; of Indians, 75, 105, 108–9, 297, 298, 302, 306, 327, 403–4, 417–18, 422; —, GB's sketch of, *418;* moccasins, purchase of, 143; of pioneers, 410; of Quakers, 251; of Shakers, 70, 81. *See also* women: appearance

colonization: of blacks to Liberia, 252n52, 287n98, 517, 536–37; by French of Algeria, 600–601n13

Colwells (N.Y.), 50, 61

Commentaries. See Kent, James; Story, Joseph, *Commentaries on the Constitution of the United States*

commerce: American passion for, 16, 17, 38–39, 63–64, 66, 101, 513; energy devoted to, 515–16; French-U.S. relations in, 278–79, 594, 600; GB's *Marie* on, 548–49; with Indians, 223; industriousness evidenced in, 513–14; maritime, 283–85, 341; markets for prison-made goods, 452; men's focus on, 542–43; northern focus on, 254; sociability based on interests in, 551–53. *See also* manufacturing interests; slaves and slavery; taxation and tariffs; wealth

Commerce, Le (newspaper): AT's interest in, 596; AT's "On Federalism" in, 632–33; circulation of, 596n7; editor of, 599; foreign correspondent for, 596–98, 599–600

Commission nationale pour l'édition des œuvres d'Alexis de Tocqueville, xxin13

communication, public prosperity linked to, 363–65. *See also* internal improvements; mail delivery

concubines, notes on, 251–52. *See also* prostitution

Connecticut: crime statistics in, 466, 470; democracy in, 132–33; education in, 353, 467; judicial system of, 382, 386; plays prohibited in, 558; temperance societies of, 481; westward movement from, 247. *See also* Hartford (Conn.); Wethersfield Prison (Conn.)

Constitution, U.S. See United States Constitution

Constitutional Assembly (France, 1848), 651–52

Constitutional Commission (France, 1848), 651

Constitutional Revision Commission (France, 1851), 654

conventions, power and example of, 334–36

Coolidge, Ellen Wayles Randolph, 242n40

Coolidge, Joseph, Jr., 242, **242n40**

Cooper, James Fenimore: AT's and GB's reading of, xxiv, 326, 402–3; French knowledge and translations of, 568; *The Last of the Mohicans,* 67; letters on travels of, 5; literary ability of, 557; *Notions of the Americans,* 5n5

Corcelle, Francisque de, 574, **574n19,** 599n10, 608

Corneille, Pierre, 517

corporal punishment: disallowed in Philadelphia system, 456; discipline based on, 445, 449–54; general principles vs. individual recipients of, 458; Metz's rejection of, 492; in reform schools, 473–76; reservations about, 454; of slaves,

244, 524–26, 527; solitary confinement compared with, 462; support for, 77–78, 216. *See also* Auburn system

Corsaire, Le (periodical), 493

Coster, Gerard, 41n52

Coster, Mathilda Prime, 41–42, 44n58

Costilla, Miguel, 290n101

Cottu, Charles, 391, **391n216**

Council of State (France), 144

Courcy, Adalbert Roussel d'Epourlon de, 41n51

Courcy, Léon Roussel d'Epourlon de, 41n51

courtship and engagement: freedoms in, 16, 37, 64, 174, 213; GB's *Marie* on, 505–6. *See also* marriage

Coxe, Charles Sydney, 248, **248n48,** 387, 388

Cranche, John Mary Joseph, 258–60, **258n58**

Crawford, William, 492, **492n17,** 498

Creek Indians (Muscogees): beliefs of, 343; civilization and legal code of, 346; forced removal of, 345n181; laws of, 344

Creek War, 343n179

Creoles, 276

crimes and criminals: causes of, 467–68, 495; costs to society, 496; difficulty with statistics of, 453–54, 466–68; habituation to, 478; joint crimes and associations of, 460–61; public response to, 333–34; questions about, 465; slavery laws in context of, 521–28; states with most, 247; types noted in interviews of inmates, 481–92. *See also* penitentiary systems; prison inmates; recidivism

Crockett, David "Davy," xxviii, 351–52, **352n193**

Cruse, Peter Hoffman, 309, **309n139**

Crusoe, Robinson (character), 31

Cuba, Spanish-U.S. negotiations on, 603

currency and expenses: cost of land vs. labor, 332, 412–14; cost of living in New York, 27; money vs. goods for Indians, 423, 435; of penitentiary systems, 137, 458, 463–64, 496; provisions and establishment of settlers, 97; of reform schools, 473; steamboat travel, 353. *See also* economy; wealth

Curtis, Charles Pelham, 375–77, **375n205**, 378

Cuvier, Georges, 572, **572n15**

Dallas, George M., 383, **383n210**

Dalmassy (magistrate, Versailles tribunal), 117–18

Dannery, Jean Germain Samuel Adam, 147, **147n187**

debt: causes of, 347; civil suits concerning, 375; imprisonment for, 241, 479

Declaration of Independence: Fourth of July celebrations of, xxx, 63, 67, 72–73, 78–79, 80–81; reading aloud of, 78–79; surviving signer of, 162, 164, 262–63, 533–34

Delaware, temperance societies of, 481

Delaware River, 147

delegation vs. representation, 567

democracy: antidote to, xxviii–xxix; approach to, 585–86; common law linked to, 381; in England and France, 565; equality as interchangeable with, xxxi; exemplars of, 180–81, 185, 186, 269–70, 273, 357, 359; foreign policy and, 262; hopes for, 263–64; key challenge in, 567; legal habits and ideas as counterweight to, 55–56; leveling effects in Jacksonian, xxvii–xxviii; limits and problems of, 250, 507, 510, 540–42, 556–57, 577–78, 582, 614; as "mob," 263; New England as cradle of, 132–34; paternal

power antithetical to, 352–53; personal view of, 573; possibility for French adoption of, 54–55; Poussin's view of, 601n15; public debates in, 260–61; recommended French study of, 652–53; religion and, 242, 246–47; socialism absent in, 651–52; Swiss cantonal governments and, 637–39, 642–45; tolerated by wealthy, 211; triumph of, 624–25. See also *Democracy in America* (AT); elections; equality; liberty/ freedom; majority rule; "On Cherbuliez's *Democracy in Switzerland*" (AT); suffrage

Democracy in America (AT): American views of, xxviii, xxix; AT's reflections on, 652–53; blindspots in, xxxii–xxxiii; copy sent to Mill, 584–85; corrections noted, 570, 576; defense of, 578n24; French context of writing, 582, 583, 587; GB's *Marie* juxtaposed to, xxxv; GB's reference to, 548; Livingston thanked in, 155n201; notes and introduction to (English translation), 578n26; opinions expressed in, 563–64; as political science textbook, xxix; reviews of, 566–68, 572, 573, 574n19, 575n22, 576, 585; Sedgwick's assistance with, xix, 126n150; Spencer's influence on, 83n104; success of, 585–86; working notes of, xx. *See also* letters; notebooks; voyage to America

—letters related to, 563–89; editor's note on, 561; Adams (John Quincy), 575–76; GB, 572; Hall, 570–71; Kergorlay, 577–78, 586–89; Mill, 564–65, 566–68, 582–83, 584–86; Molé, 566; d'Orglandes, 563–64; Reeve, 569–70, 571–72, 573–74, 576–77, 581–82, 583–84; Royer-

Collard, 578; Sparks, 574–75; Spencer, 578–81; U.S. correspondent, 568–69

—publication concerns: completion of, 581–82; delay in writing and publishing, 571–72, 574, 579–80; details, 563n3; editions of, 579, 580, 581, 615; foreword to twelfth edition, 652–53; length of, 569; printing, 583, 584; profits, 580; timing of publication, 574; translations, xvii, 569–70, 574, 578n26, 579 (*see also* Reeve, Henry); writing and, xix, xxxvi

—topics: American Indians, xv–xvi; associations, xxxi; Hobbes referenced, 609n30; plans for, 576; women and marriage, xxvi–xxvii

Democracy in Switzerland (Cherbuliez). *See* "On Cherbuliez's *Democracy in Switzerland*" (AT)

Democratic Party: 1856 presidential candidate of, 609n29; goals of, 253; immigrants welcomed by, 608n26; leadership of, 133n165; state constitution influenced by, 269–70

Denisart, Jean Baptiste, 318

Dens, Mr. (judge), 247

Descorches, Marie-François, 155n199

Detroit (Mich.): desire to see, 83–84; founding and population of, 295n113; visit to, 88–89, 98, 295–96, 301, 406–7

diaries: fragments of GB's, 132–34, 175–78. *See also* notebooks

diet and beverages, 10, 25–26, 40, 64. *See also* alcohol

disease. *See* health and illness: specific diseases

disestablishment, xxxii–xxxiii

District of Columbia: slavery in, 540; temperance societies of, 481. *See also* Washington, D.C.

documents gathered: amount of, 167; difficulties in obtain-

bated in, 581n31, 586; economic difficulties in, 622; equality's meaning in, 354–56; government administration in, 137–38, 139, 144; immorality in garrison towns of, 17; imperial conquests of, 600–601n13; inheritance laws of, 129, 235; issue of Oregon and Pacific control for, 629–32; judicial system of, 172, 371, 372, 639; juries eliminated in, 377–78; land and labor costs in, 413; legislative and executive powers debated in, 651; maritime commerce of, 285; newspapers of, 219–20, 596; oaths required in, 312–13; political upheavals of, xvii–xviii, xxvii, 3–4, 47, 601–2, 623–24; prosecutor's office in, 382, 388; religion in, 245; revolution of 1848 in, 587n39, 652–53; scientific theories in, 516; Tocqueville readers in, xx–xxi. *See also* Bourbon Restoration; Chamber of Deputies; French language; French prisons; French Revolution; French society; French-U.S. alliance; July Monarchy; July Revolution (1830); Paris (France); Second Republic (1848–52)

Franklin, Benjamin, 248, 258, 569

free blacks: colonization in Liberia for, 252n52, 287n98, 517, 536–37; crime statistics and, 467; education of, 153, 338, 511, 532; expected extermination of, 250; as factory workers, 274; Ohio laws on, 272–73; rights and realities of, xxxiv–xxxv, 256; transition from slave to, 537; treatment in New Orleans, 279–80; white fear of, 254, 288, 538–42; whites' expectations of, 508, 509. *See also* blacks
—GB's *Marie* on: excluded from public education, 511;

legal punishments for, 524–25; race relations, 506–10; rights, 510, 511, 517–19

freedoms: of the press, 133, 219, 226, 636 (*see also* newspapers and periodicals); of speech (Switzerland), 636; of trade, 334–36. *See also* liberty/freedom; suffrage

Freemasonry, xxx, 219, 545n13, 545–46

Free Soil movement, 609n29

Fremont, John, 609n29

French Canadians: attitudes of, 322–23; education and religion of, 227, 319–21; English as overtaking, 316, 319–21; English coexistence with, 229–30, 322; English numbers compared with, 227–28; French people compared with, 323; as guides, 105–7, 305; habits maintained by, 310; happiness of, 226; interviewee's contempt for, 228; interviews of, 223–24; leader of, 229; Louisiana French compared with, 278; radical segment of, 227n23; rebellion of (1837), 576–77; in Sault St. Marie area, 303; speech of, 299–300. *See also* Canada; French language

French language: in Canadian villages, 316–17; clergy's preservation of, 230, 320–21, 323; Indians who speak, 108; Mill's use of, 564; opportunities to speak, 40–41, 44

Frenchman's Island: GB's sketch of view from, *399;* legend of, 75–76, 85–86; narrative of excursion to, 395, 397–401; visit to, 86–87. *See also* Oneida Lake

French prisons: contractual system of, 451; debates on laws concerning, 499, 500–501; economics of U.S. vs., 137, 446, 451, 454–55; inmate labor in, 217, 452; mortality rate (post-1835) in, 497; possibility of transfer of U.S.

system to, 215, 444, 453–55, 463, 494; recidivism rate in, 494; solitary confinement opposed for, 458; U.S. prisons compared, generally, 26, 450; U.S. reform schools and, 443–44

French Revolution: American attitudes toward, 244; AT's research on, 612, 617, 619; causes of, xxxviii; Lafayette's role in, 4n2; Switzerland at time of, 635, 636–37; Terror in, xxvii; Tocqueville family in, xvii. See also *Old Regime and the Revolution, The* (AT)

French society: country dances of, 71; flirting in, 505; frivolity amid politics in, 515; funerals of great men in, 79; importance of religious beliefs in, 50–51; married women in, 506; middle vs. upper classes in, 354; public celebrations in, 73; social state of, 341; women's morals in, 549

French-U.S. alliance: AT's improvised toast on, 647–49; reparations and treaty issues in, 626–27; right of inspection proposed, 632; steadfastness of, 594; tariff and commerce issues in, 278–79, 594, 600

Freslon, Alexandre Pierre, 623, **623n55**

fugitive slave laws, 522–23

Fulchiron (conservative deputy), 493

Fulton, Julia, 41–42, **42n53**

Fulton, Robert, 42

fur traders, 233. *See also* American Fur Company

Galena and Chicago Union Railroad, 604–5, 604–5n21, 620–21, 622

Gallatin, Albert, **40–41n47,** 334; interview of, 212–13; introduction to, 40–41; literary ability of, 558; on settlements in America, 412 gambling, 546–47, 558

game. *See* hunting

Gazette de Québec, La (newspaper), 317, 320

gender roles: among Indians, 344; race and, xxvii, xxxv; of Shakers, 69–71, 81. *See also* courtship and engagement; marriage; women

genealogy, pride in, 555–56

Geneva (N.Y.), 83

Georgia: forced removal of Cherokees from, 511–12; temperance societies of, 481

Germanic Corps, 349–50, 350n189

German people in America: customs and mores of, 152–53, 310, 607; number of, 152, 180, 606

Germany: America compared with, 605–6; AT's visit to (Bonn), 607; divisions among peoples of, 240; GB's visit to, 605–6; plans to visit, 572; political liberal banned from, 238; request for newspaper correspondent in, 596–97, 599, 600; revolutionary forces in, 586–87, 587n39; scientific theories in, 516. *See also* Prussia

Gilpin, Henry D., 366, **366n201**

Gisles, Madame, 126

Gobineau, Arthur de, 613–14, **613n38**

Goodwin, Isaac, *The Town Officer,* xxxii, 182, 183

Gosselin, Charles, 574, **574n18**

government: comparative approach to, xxv, 447–48; definition of, 340; enlightened leadership for, 55–56; fear of meddling by, 242; lack of, xxix, 29, 38, 45, 68; land sales of, 332n171; middle classes capable of, 353–54; by one vs. all, 307; politically appointed jobs in, 271, 575n22; role in public prosperity, 364–65; self-reliance as replacing, 56; state reli-

gion and, 221–22. *See also* central government; federal government; political institutions; presidency; republican government; United States Congress

governors: election of, 76–77; power of, 241, 641

Grancey, Eugénie de Cordoue de, xxv, 140–43, **140n176**

Gratiot, Charles, 102n123

Gray, Francis Calley, 131, **131n159,** 237–38, 240–41

Great Britain: AT's visits to, xix, 564–65, 619; AT's writing about France in journal of, 567–68; attitudes toward America, 544–45, 552; Canada controlled by, 119–20, 124, 170, 224, 226–27, 229–30, 250, 576–77; cholera in, 200; democratic ideas in, 565; documents on French Revolution in, 612, 617, 619; Eastern Question and, 581n31, 586; GB's sketch of coast, *206;* GB's visit to, xix; imperialism of, 594, 649; issue of Oregon and Pacific control for, 629–32; lack of racial mixing by, 311; maritime commerce of, 284–85, 341; morals in, 239, 286; newspaper correspondents in, 596, 598; parliamentary history of, 595; political balance in, 625; prisons and prison reform in, 497, 498, 500; Protestantism in, 245; reflections on dispute with, 263; revolutions in, 588; social state of, 341, 543; Sundays observed in, 547; as underlying influence on U.S., 555–56; U.S. prison study of, 492, 498; U.S. relationship with, 285n95, 295n111, 544–45; virtuous women of, 571. *See also* English language; English legal concerns and law

Great Lakes: beauty of, 98; clear waters of, 103. *See also* Erie, Lake; Huron, Lake;

Michigan, Lake; Ontario, Lake; Superior, Lake

Green Bay, 108n130; GB's sketches of, *304;* Indians of, 223–24; steamboat travel to, 98–109; visit at, 108–9, 111, 305–6

Greg, William Rathbone, 611, **611–12n33**

Grote, George, *History of Greece,* 616

Guillemin, J. N. François, 277–80, **277n88**

Guizot, François, **23n32,** 585; appointed foreign minister, 581n31; AT and GB as students of, xvii; on French policy in North America, 629, 630–31; request for lectures of, 23; Washington's letters translated by, 604

Gulf of Mexico, 627–28; GB's sketch of, *200*

Hall, Basil, 570–71, **570n12**

Hamilton, Alexander: circle of, 41n49; *Federalist* essays by, 347n186, 349n188, 350nn190–91; on taxation, 350

Hamilton, Thomas, 556, **556n20**

Harrison, William Henry, 270, **270n77**

Hart, Nathaniel C., 40n46, 213n6, 471, 476

Hartford (Conn.), 137. *See also* Wethersfield Prison (Conn.)

Harvard University (Cambridge): AT's honorary degree from, 603n19, 603–4; president of, 182, 236; Unitarian influence at, 57

Haviland, John, GB's sketch of prison design by, *457*

Havre, Le (ship): daily routine of, 6, 47; difficulties aboard, 7, 21; GB's sketch on return voyage, *206;* landing at Newport, 7, 12–13, 21, 48; other passengers on, 9n12

health and illness: of AT, 40, 177–78, 187–88; of children

in reform schools, 473; fragility of, 128, 543; of pioneers, 413–14; of prison inmates, 454, 456, 458, 462, 481, 482, 483, 484, 485–88, 489–91, 492; in prison vs. society, 497–98

—specific diseases: cholera, 154, 155, 156, 160–61, 167, 200; mental difficulties in prison, 490; pulmonary phthisis, 490; tertiary fever, 44; venereal, 337; yellow fever, 277, 509

Henri-IV (ship), 147

Henry VII, **367n203**

Hobbes, Thomas, 609, **609n30**, 610

Horace, 517

horseback riding: as common diversion, 65; Detroit to Saginaw trip, 89–97, 408, 415–21, 423–30, 439–40; —, GB's sketches of, *426;* GB's self-portrait, *416;* Mexican horses for, 343

horse races, 161–62, 307, 558

housing: boardinghouses, 9, 14, 33–34; — GB's sketch of, *34;* cottages, 8, 14, 36–37; European immigrant, Indian, and half-breed, compared, 432–34; French in Canada, 124; inadequacies of, 275; inns, 93; Kentucky and Tennessee, 177–78, 187–88, 360, 361; log cabins and houses, 74, 406, 409–10; —, GB's sketch of, *431;* Shakers, 69

Houston, Sam, **343n179;** on American Indians, 343–47; on elections, 352

Howard, George, 162–63, **163n211**, 260, 308

Howard, John Eager, 260n62

Howard, William, 309, **309n138**

Hubscher, Catherine (Madame Sans-Gêne), **140n178**

Hudson River: beauty of, 26–27; GB's sketch of, *60;* Mount Pleasant area of, 27–

29; navigation of, 48; plans to travel up, 24; Rhine River compared with, 605–6; steamboat race on, 61–62; Yonkers area of, 60–61

humanity: belief in wisdom and perfectibility of, 49; education's importance to, 199; improvability of, 165; miseries of, 306–7; similarity across peoples, 432

Humboldt, Alexander von, 599, **599n11**

Hume, David, 244

hummingbirds, 97, 301

hunting, 76; Green Bay area, 305–6; Memphis area, 178, 193; past abundance for, 82; rifles for, 435; Saginaw area, 95, 300–301, 435–36, 437–38; Saint Clair River area, 302; Sandy Bridge area, 188; success of whites and Indians, 433; Yonkers area, 60–61. *See also* horseback riding

Huron, Lake: GB's sketches of, *101, 102, 103, 106;* steamboat travel on, 98, 102–3, 109–10, 149, 301–2

Huron Indians, 223, 232, 233, 305

Illinois: slavery prohibited in, 530n6; temperance societies of, 481

Illinois River, 309

I&M (Illinois and Michigan) Canal, 309

immigrants: Americans as all, 92–93, 180; conditions in U.S. vs. Europe, 414; effects on U.S. population, 609, 611; housing of, 432–34; political parties and, 608n26; prejudices faced by, 619. *See also* English settlers in North America; German people in America

Indiana: slavery prohibited in, 530n6; temperance societies of, 481

Indian removal: AT and GB's encounter with, 194–95, 197; —, GB's sketches of, *196;*

GB's *Marie* on, 511–12, 519–20; Houston's view of, 345–46; Jackson's role in, 84n105, 194n231, 345n181, 511n1

Indian Removal Act (1830), 84n105, 293n108, 345n181

Ingersoll, Charles Jared, 324, **324n160**, 335–36

inheritance laws: fortunes destroyed by, 64, 234–35, 253, 255; in France vs. U.S., 129, 235; initial perceptions of, 36, 53–54; intellectual decline due to, 211; practices concerning, 555; slavery and, 256; westward movement and, 247; wills and civil suits concerning, 375

Institut de France, 596n6, 620. *See also* Académie des sciences morales et politiques; Académie française

intellectual spirit: of blacks and whites, 531–32; in Boston society, 57, 129, 328–29, 612; common vs. codified law and, 379–80; decline of, 211; European home of, 595–96; of French Canadians, 319; membership exchanges in, 618n49

internal improvements: funding for, 359; industriousness evidenced in, 513–14; public prosperity linked to, 363–65. *See also* canals and canal development; railroads and railroad development; roads and road development

Ireland: AT's and GB's travel to, xix; GB's book on, xix, xxxvi, 575

Iroquois Confederacy, 85; demise of, 80, 82, 402; remnants of, 305, 403; tribes listed, 80n101; village of, GB's sketch of, *304;* warfare of, 223. *See also* Mohawk Indians; Oneida Indians; Seneca Indians

Irving, Washington, 548, **548n15**, 557, 568

Italy: prison reform in, 500n25; religion in, 516

Jackson, Andrew, **133n165**; appointments by, 269n73, 271, 575n22; Clay's opposition to, 133, 133n165; criticism of, xxviii; economic policy of, 264n66, 575n21; election of, 545n14; foreign policy and, 626–27; as Freemason, 545; Indian removal under, 84n105, 194n231, 345n181, 511n1; military ventures of, 308, 343n179; political circle of, 62n79, 63n80, 366n201; political parties and, 265; presidency of, 204n239, 242, 260–61; public opinion of, 235, 260–61; visit with, 201–2

James, Edwin, 551n18

Jardin, André, xxii

Jefferson, Thomas: AT's reading of, xix; deism of, 258; on lands for freed blacks, 536; *Notes on the State of Virginia,* xix, 529n5, 536n9; on slavery, 528–29

Jesuits, 222–23, 232, 259

John Malone (steamboat), 120

Johnston, Josiah Stoddard, 281, **281n92**

"Journey to Oneida Lake, The" (AT): editor's note on, 395; narrative of, 397–401

Judaism, 81

judges and magistrates: appointments of, 266, 268; election of, 306, 352; incompetency of, 281; power and responsibilities of, 237–38, 369–73, 374–75, 376, 379, 388–89, 656–58; precedents as constraints on, 218–19; questions about, 385; removal of, 372, 388; role of, generally, 171–72, 212–13; status of, 212–13; in Switzerland, 640, 641

judicial system: appeals and writs of error in, 171, 172, 369, 371–72, 392; bail for witness and accused in, 479–80; cases of fact vs. law in, 369; chancery courts, 376;

civil courts in Canada, 318–19; common pleas court in, 369–70, 376–77, 384; criminal and civil components, 149–50; equality in, 554; execution of judgments in, 391–92; federal vs. state courts in, 170–71; filing lawsuit in, 375–76; independence of, as modern idea, 639; instability reported in, 619; key informant on, 83n104; political influence on, 266; power of, 237–38, 656–57; presumption of innocence in, 527; procedures in France vs. U.S., 46, 172, 371, 372, 382, 388; questions about, 389–93; structure of, 468; of Switzerland, 639–40. *See also* Chabrol-Chaméane, Ernest de; judges and magistrates; juries; justices of the peace; law; lawyers; legal system; prosecutor's office; Travel Notebook F (AT); trials; *and specific states by name*

Julius, Niclaus Heinrich, 492, **492n17**, 498

July Monarchy: Molé's role in, 142n180; parliament in, 578n24; political life in, xxxviii

July Revolution (1830): aftermath of, xvii–xviii; Lafayette's role in, 4n2; North American policy and, 631; remembered, 149, 440; summary of, 21–22n30

juries: advantages of, 373; cases assigned to, 238; in civil trials, 369–72, 376; composition of, 282, 283, 374, 392–93; in criminal trials, 374–75; decisions of grand, 388–89; eliminated in advanced states, 377–78; in Masonic case, 219; power of, 390; public support for, 378; questions about, 385, 390–91; reluctance to return death penalty, 387; requirement of, 313; right to trial by, 387, 390,

526; role of, generally, 171–72; state's payment for service, 374

justices of the peace, 375, 386, 490–91

juvenile delinquents. *See* reform schools (*maisons de refuge*)

Kansas: AT's hopes for, 623, 624; proslavery elements defeated in, 621

Kansas-Nebraska Act (1854), 608n27, 616n44

Keane, John, 308n135

Keating, William Hypolitus, 550n16

Kent, James, **41n48**; AT's reading of, xix, 209; *Commentaries on American Law,* 41, 209, 351, 352, 353, 379, 625, 626; on education, 353; on intolerance, 353; introduction to, 41; on judges, 352; on presidential power, 625, 626

Kentucky: imprisonment for debt abolished in, 241, 479; Ohio compared with, 181–82, 191–92, 272–73, 274, 358; population of, 192n229, 274n80, 358n195; reflections on, 360–63; slavery in, 181, 274–75, 361–63; southern character evidenced in, 265; temperance societies of, 481; training for black children in, 532. *See also* Louisville (Ky.); Westport (Ky.)

Kergorlay, Blanche de la Luzerne de, 156, **156n203**

Kergorlay, Louis de, **20n28**; AT's concerns about, 56–57; AT's letters to, 20–21, 49–57, 577–78, 586–89; family of, 156; on German government, 587n39; newspaper of, 613n38

—topics of discussion with: American growth, 20–21; conditions in France, 56–57; democracy and equality, 55–56, 577–78; politics and political institutions, 53–55; Prussian affairs, 586–87; religious beliefs, 49–51, 587–89; religious sects, 51–53

King, James Gore, 41, **41n50**

Know-Nothing Party (American Party), 608, 608n26, 609n29

Lacretelle, Jean Charles Dominique de, 570

Lacrosse and Milwaukee Railroad, 620, 620n52

Lafayette, Marie Joseph Paul Yves Roch Gilbert Motier de, **4n2;** American friend of, 162; avoiding discussion about, 42; family of, 574–75; politics of, 4n2, 22n30, 59n72, 239; U.S. attitudes toward, 18, 59, 234

La Fontaine, Jean de, xxiv, 31n39, 65, 111, 194, 423n7

Lamard, Major, 224–25

Lamartine, Alphonse de, 570, 574, 648n78

Lancaster, Joseph, 472, **472n11**

land and land use: clearing techniques, 82, 113; considerations of labor and cost of, 332, 407–8, 412–14; cultivation, 331–32; English control of Canadian, 322; proposed for freed blacks, 536; U.S. attitudes toward, 92, 194–95, 288, 402. *See also* Indian removal; Michigan; westward movement

Land Ordinance (1785), 113n134, 267n70

Langley, G. H., 580n29

Langlois, Honoré, **493n19,** 493–99

language. *See* English language; French language

Lantivy, count of, 146

La Roche, Sophie von, 85–86n106

Latrobe, John Hazlehurst Bonval, **252n52;** education of, 256n56; interviews of, 252–57, 262

law: basis for, 238; changeability of, 315; English law underlying, 366–68, 378–

82; generative principles of, 311–12; obedience to, 215; people as barrier to some, 350; piecemeal nature of, 377; precedents in, 218–19, 381; Puritanism evidenced in, 546–47; respect for, 554; Sedgwick's treatise on, 617, 655–58; state-federal relationship in, 348–49, 537; in Switzerland, 639–40. *See also* bicameralism; Chabrol-Chaméane, Ernest de; Indian removal; inheritance laws; judicial system; juries; lawyers; legal system; Kent, James; slaves and slavery; Travel Notebook F (AT)

—specific types: adultery, 384, 546; bankruptcy, 249, 368; common law (English), 366–68, 378–82; contract, 367, 369; imprisonment for debt, 241, 479; maritime commerce, 284–85; minors, 368; paupers and almshouses, 220–21; plays and theater, 558; slave imports, 288n100; slavery, 521–28, 537, 540–41; theft, 344; trust states, 367–68

Lawrence, James, 295n111

lawyers: advantages of common law for, 380, 381; attitudes of, 218–19; civil suits and, 375; as prosecutors, 382–85, 388; questions about, 384–85; status and role of, 212–13, 253

League of Augsburg, 594, 594n3

Lecompton Constitution, 621n53

Lee, Ann, 69n88

Lee, Catherine Mildred, 612n35

Lee, Robert E., 612n35

Lefebvre, François Joseph, 140n178

legal system: Indian vs. European need for, 92; oaths in, 312–13; obligation of, 657–58; particular books on, 41n48; penalties in, 387;

questions about, 386, 390–91; reflections on, 377–78; self-governing aspect of, 56; state-level codes in, 155–56, 198. *See also* bicameralism; judges and magistrates; judicial system; juries; law; lawyers; prosecutor's office; recidivism; Travel Notebook F (AT); trials; *and specific states by name*

Le Peletier d'Aunay, Félix, 443–48, **443n1**

Lesueur, Abbé Christian (Bébé), **10n14;** AT's letters to, 25–27, 58–59, 98, 123–25; death of, 140n177; remembered, 140; students of, xxiv, 10n14, 27n38

letters, contents summarized, xxv–xxvii, xxxviii. See also *Democracy in America:* letters related to; letters on America post-1840; letters on travels (1830–32); mail delivery; penitentiary-related letters

letters on America post-1840, 593–625; editor's note on, 591

—Beaumont's recipients: AT, 605–6, 622

—Tocqueville's recipients: Barrot, 595; Childe, 612–13, 614–15, 623; Corcelle, 608; Everett, 600–602; Freslon, 623; GB, 606, 607–8, 621–23; Gobineau, 613–14; Lewis, 624–25; Lieber, 595–600, 610–11, 619–20; Massachusetts Historical Society, 618–19; Reeve, 611–12; Sedgwick, 602–3, 604–5, 606–7, 608–9, 611, 613, 615–18; Senior, 625; Sparks, 593, 603–4; Spencer, 594; Sumner, 620–21, 623–24

letters on travels (1830–32), 1–208; cajeput oil included with, 156–57; correspondents asked to save, xviii, 80; delays in sending/receiving, 59, 77, 155, 179–80; dispatch of, 15; editor's note on, 1–2;

ascension of, xvii–xviii, 22n30; AT's concerns about, 57; circle of, 599n11; foreign ministers of, 581n31; opposition to, 20n28; reparations and treaty issues for, 626n59; supporters of, 4n2, 22n30, 141–42n180, 595n5

Louisville (Ky.): Cincinnati compared with, 360; growth of, 274–75; population of, 360n199; travel to, 176, 188–89, 190–91; winter cold in, 184, 186

Louisville (steamboat), 178, 353

Lucas, Charles, **77n98**, 167, 469; AT's opinion of, 77n99, 150; on Auburn system, 500n25; on recidivism, 446; whip use advocated by, 77

Lutherans, 435

Luzerne, César-Anne de La, 5, **5n4**

Lynds, Elam, **75n93;** on gubernatorial elections, 76–77; interviews of, 75, 214–18; on outside contractors (prison), 451

MacCulloch, J. H., 91

Mac Heidge, Mrs., 33, 35

MacIlvaine, Bowes Reed, 274–75, 373–75, **373n204**

MacKenney, Thomas, 91

Mackenzie, William Lyon, 577n23

Mackinac Island, 304–5, 306. *See also* Michilimackinac (Mackinaw City)

Macomb, Alexander, Jr., 102, **102n122**

Macomb, Mathilda, 102, 105

Madison, James, 350n190, 536n10

magistrates. *See* judges and magistrates

Mahon, Lord, 604n20

mail delivery: delays in, 59, 77, 155, 179–80; maintaining secrecy in, 599; public prosperity linked to, 363; reliability of, 617–18; suspended, then relaxed on Sundays, 547

Mailly, Adrien-Auguste-Amalric de, 77, **77n97**

Maine, temperance societies of, 481

majority rule: anxieties about, xxvii–xxviii; associations as antidote to, xxix–xxxi; implementation of, 133; mediocrity's triumph in, 514–15; problems with, 242, 249; Protestant sectarianism and, xxxiii; right to hold convention and, 334–36. *See also* democracy; elections; suffrage; tyranny of the majority

Malesherbes, Chrétien-Guillaume de Lamoignon de, **7n8**

manufacturing interests: black workers in, 274; energy devoted to, 515–16; feudalism compared with, 515; hobbled in Switzerland, 636; as key in North, 270; slavery as detrimental to, 509; southern expansion of, 534; wartime as impetus to, 285

Marcel, R. Pierre, xix*n*7

Marie; or, Slavery in the United States (GB), xix; background of, xxvi; *Democracy* juxtaposed to, xxxv; editor's note on, 503–4; Marx's reading of, xxxv–xxxvi; model for priest in, 295n114; Montyon prize for, 503; summary of, xxxiv

—excerpts: chapter 2, 505–6; chapter 8, 506–10; chapter 9, 510–11; chapter 10, 511–12; chapter 11, 512–14; chapter 12, 514–17; chapter 13, 517–19; chapter 14, 519–20; appendix on slaves and freed people, 520–42; note on American women, 542–43; note on English-American relationship, 544–45; note on Freemasonry, 545–46; note on mores, 546–47; note on political parties, 548; note on national pride, 548; note on bankruptcies, 548–49; note on French morals, 549; note

on Indians, 550–51; note on American sociability, 551–53; note on equality, 553–57; note on self-control, 557; note on literature, 557–59; note on American army, 559–60; miscellaneous notes, 560

—topics: advocates for blacks, 517–19; American army, 559–60; American sociability, 551–53; American women, 542–43; bankruptcies, 548–49; courtship and marriage, 505–6; English-American relationship, 544–45; equality, 553–57; Freemasonry, 545–46; French morals, 549; gender and race, xxvii, xxxv; Indians and Indian removal, 511–12, 519–20, 550–51; literature, 557–59; mores, 546–47; national pride, 548; political parties, 548; race relations, 506–10; self-control, 557; slavery, character of, 528–30; slaves, conditions of, 520–28; slaves, emancipation possibilities, 530–42

Marquette, Jacques, 302n126

marriage: age for, 337; of blacks and whites, 251–52, 279–80, 351, 509–10, 517–18, 541; Catholic-Protestant, 259; fidelity in, 213, 286, 571; GB's *Marie* on, 505–6; happiness of, 16; of Indians and Europeans, 105, 300, 433–34; Oneida practice of, 550–51; of pioneers, 411; polygamy in, 623; sanctity of, 48; unlikely between French and English, 317, 321; women's lives after, 37, 174–75, 506, 542–43, 571. *See also* courtship and engagement; mixed-race peoples

Marseillaise, La (French national anthem), 73, 102

Marx, Karl, xxxv–xxxvi

Maryland: aristocratic class in, 252–53, 254–56, 263; constitution and universal suffrage in, 252, 260–61; crime sta-

Maryland (*continued*)
tistics in, 466–67, 470; dual
jurisdiction in, 262; family
names in, 555; free blacks in,
338; imprisonment for debt
in, 479; inheritance laws of,
253, 254–55; judicial system
of, 389; penal code of, 256;
public debates in, 260–61;
public education in, 256–57;
slavery in, 254–56, 533, 540;
temperance societies of, 481.
See also Baltimore (Md.)
Maryland State Penitentiary,
464, 464n7
Masons (Freemasonry), xxx,
219, 545–46
Massachusetts: bicameralism of,
649; blacks in, 338; church
requirement in, 183; crime
statistics in, 466, 467, 468;
democracy in, 132–33, 268;
elections in, 270; interracial
marriage in, 351, 541; judicial system of, 237–38, 376–
77, 382; New York com-
pared with, 328; notebooks
on, 328–29; plans to visit, 35;
political structure and governance of, 133–34, 236–37,
241, 242; Puritanism in laws
of, 546; scandal concerning
(1857–58), 624n57; state-
house of, 128; Sunday laws
of, 547; temperance societies
of, 481; wealth and prosperity in, 127. *See also* Boston
(Mass.); Stockbridge (Mass.)
Massachusetts Historical Society, 618n49, 618–19
Massachusetts State Prison
(Charlestown), 470, 470n9
materialist positivism, 514–15
Maxwell, Hugh, 213–14, **213n5**
Mazureau, Étienne, 276–77,
276n84
McLane, Louis, 203–4,
204n238
McLean, John, 268–69, **268–
69n73**
Mediterranean Sea, Caribbean
compared with, 627–28
Memphis (Tenn.): Choctaws

crossing river at, 194–95, 197
(*see also* Indian removal); —,
GB's sketch of, *196;* forced
stay in, 191–92, 197–98;
steamboat's arrival in, 193–
94; travel to, 176–78, 187,
189, 190–91
Menou, Jules de, 162, **162n210**
Methodists, 271–72, 282, 414,
516
métis (half-breeds). *See* mixed-
race peoples
Metternich, Klemens Wenzel
von, 605
Metz, Frédéric de, 492–93,
492n16, 498
Mexican-American War (1846–
48), 603n18, 629n65
Mexico: adoption of republic
form, 289–90, 339; future
predicted for, 627
Michaud, Joseph, 570
Michigan: innkeepers of, 93;
land and labor costs in, 332,
407–8, 412–14; new settlers
and land in, 92, 112–13, 331–
32; pioneers in, described,
408–12; population of,
112n133; religion in, 295–96;
slavery prohibited in, 530n6;
temperance societies of, 481.
See also Detroit (Mich.); Flint
River; Pontiac (Mich.); Saginaw (Mich.); "Two Weeks in
the Wilderness" (AT)
Michigan, Lake: Illinois River
and, 309; steamboat travel
on, 108–9, 148–49. *See also*
Green Bay
Michigan Central Railroad,
604–5, 605n21, 620–21, 622
Michilimackinac (Mackinaw
City), 221n14: British transfer
to U.S., 302n124; colonization of Indians around, 296;
debate on religion at, 100,
109; GB's sketches of, *101,
102, 103, 106;* rock forma-
tions near, 108; travel to, 106;
visit at, 107–8, 111
Mignet, François, 596, **596n6**
militia, 309, 519. *See also* United
States Army

Mill, John Stuart, **564n4;** AT's
letters to, 564–65, 566–68,
582–83, 584–86; circle of,
596n8; on delegation vs. representation, 567n7; *Democracy
in America* reviewed by, 561,
566–68
Milton, John, 178, 417, 584
Minnesota, slavery prohibited
in, 530n6
Mississippi: slavery in, 540;
temperance societies of, 481
Mississippi River: Choctaws'
crossing of, 194–95, 197; —,
GB's sketches of, *196;* frozen
and unnavigable, 178, 189,
191, 197–99; GB's sketch of,
198; as key transport route,
627–28; plans to visit, 149;
plantation along, 342; steamboat travel on, 176, 178,
193–94
Mississippi Valley: early civilizations of, 345; transportation development in, 627–28
Missouri: slavery in, 275; statehood of, 628n62; temperance
societies of, 481
Missouri Compromise (1820),
275n81
mixed-race peoples: attitudes
toward blacks, 288; in Canada, 232n28; English at-
titudes toward, 311; GB's
Marie on, 506, 512, 517–18;
homes of, 433–34; in Mackinac Island area, 305; in New
Orleans area, 251–52, 276,
279–80, 509–10; in pris-
ons, 486; in Saginaw area,
96, 299–300, 429–34; in
Sault St. Marie, 303. See also
Bois-Brûlé (mixed Indian and
European blood)
Mobile Bay, GB's sketch of,
200
Mohawk and Hudson Railroad,
62n78
Mohawk Indians, 325–26
Mohawk River, 67, 75
Molé, Louis Matthieu, 141, **141–
42n180,** 566
Molière, 77, 618

Molson, John, 120n143

monarchies: advantages of common law for, 380; advocates in U.S., 624–25; demise of, 653; freedom of the press under, 636; individual liberties in, 578n24; Protestantism as, 51, 157; republics compared with, 307; translated terms for, 570. *See also* Bourbon Restoration; July Monarchy; *and specific rulers by name*

Mondelet, Dominique, 227–28, **227n24**

Mondelet, Joseph-Elzéar, 227–28, **227n24**

money. *See* currency and expenses

Moniteur, Le (periodical), 150, 155

Montaigne, Michel Eyquem de, xxiv

Montalivet, comte de, 493n19

Montcalm, Louis-Joseph de, 170; monument to, GB's sketch of, *123*

Montebello, Napoléon-Auguste Lannes de, 5, **5n3**

Montesquieu, Charles de Secondat Baron de La Brède et de, xxiv, 38n44, 164

Montesquiou, Gonsalve de, 601–2n16

Montesquiou, Raymond de, 601–2n16

Montmorency River and Falls, 121; GB's sketch of, *121*

Montreal (Quebec): countryside around, 316–17; departure from, 120; founding of, 315–16n141; French Canadian rebellion in, 576–77n23; French cities compared with, 315; population of, 118n138, 316; visit to, 118–19

Montulé, Édouard de, 98

moral character: absent among volunteer troops, 559; discipline in, 166; GB's *Marie* on French, 549; independence and dignity in, 56; of Indians, 213, 344; influence of prisons limited on, 468–69; of people of color, 251–52,

279–80; prison inmates instructed in, 32–33, 216, 450, 452–53, 495–96; purity of American, 16–17, 39, 48, 213, 252, 286, 336–37; purity of Canadian, 119, 124, 228, 231; reform school inmates inculcated with, 471, 474–75, 477; self-control needed to support, 576; testimonial evidence and, 392; U.S. beliefs about French, 549; in U.S. vs. Europe, 239. *See also* American character; mores; virtue

mores: GB's *Marie* on, 546–47, 555–57; of German professors, 607; informal in courtrooms, 46; of men vs. women, 66; Puritan origins of, 546, 558, 559, 560; violence and coarseness in, 619. *See also* moral character; social state; society in America

Morgan, William, 219, 546

Mormons, 623

Morris, Gouverneur, 557, 574

mosquitoes: bites of, 430; buzz of, 421, 429; defenses against, 89, 299–300; impossibility of sleeping around, 97, 438; swarms of, 95, 97, 427, 437

Mottley, Mary "Marie" (married to AT in 1835), **22n31;** AT's concerns about, 22, 160–61; AT's feelings for, xxvi, 168; AT's references to, 22, 24, 173, 198, 593, 595, 597, 600, 611, 616, 618, 621; on Chabrol, 160; letters sent via Chabrol for, 22; marriage of, 571n13; travels of, 598–99

Mount Pleasant (N.Y.), 606; GB's sketch of, *28. See also* Anthony's Nose (Hudson River area)

Mount Pleasant Penitentiary. *See* Sing Sing Prison

Mullon, James Ignatius, **100n120;** career of, 221n13; in debate on religion, 100, 109; interview of, 221–23; sermon of, 306; travels of, 100, 107, 303, 305

municipalities. *See* New England: town system; towns

Muscogees. *See* Creek Indians (Muscogees)

music: criticism of, xxvi, 45, 64, 66, 203; decent performance of, 146; lack of feeling for, 130; of Shakers, 73; women's lack of ability in, 34, 45, 155

Napoleon: Act of Mediation under, 636; Council of State under, 144n181; Louisiana territory sold by, 276n85, 631; Mazereau's opposition to, 276n84; Molé's support for, 141–42n180; North American policy of, 631; U.S. ships seized by, 626n59

Napoleon III (Louis-Napoleon), xx, xxxviii, 595n5, 601n15

Napoléon à Schönbrunn et à Sainte-Hélène (play), 146

Napoleonic Codes, 144n181

Narrative of an Expedition to the Source of St. Peter's River, Lake Winnepeek, Lake of the Woods, Etc. (Keating), 550–51

Narrative of the Captivity and Adventures of John Tanner . . . during Thirty Years Residence among the Indians of North America, A (Tanner), 550–51

Nashville (Tenn.), 176, 187n228

national character: basis for, 124–25; concept of, xxiv; maintenance of French and English, 322–23; similarity across peoples despite, 432. *See also* American character

natural religion, fear and predictions of, 89, 157, 244, 245

natural rights, slaves excluded from, 522–23, 527–28

Neilson, John, **120n145;** on Indians, 328; interview of, 229–33; Quebec area tour with, 319; respect for, 320; welcome and assistance of, 120–21

Netherlands, United Provinces period, 349–50, 350n189

neutrality, 629–30

Old Regime and the Revolution, The (AT): editions and number of copies printed, 609, 615, 620; request for Lieber to read in French, xvi, 610; reviews of, 611, 612n33, 615n41, 619–20; title of, xxxviii–xxxix; translation of, 569n9, 613

"On Cherbuliez's *Democracy in Switzerland*" (AT), 633–47; appropriate title for, 635; AT's approach to text, 633–34; author's approach to subject, 634–35; bicameralism explained, 640–42; central government explained, 642–43; democracy's effects on foreign policy, 645–46; federal and cantonal governments explained, 637–39, 642–45; future of federalism, 646–47; publication of, 633–34n71; revolution and restoration in, 635–37

Oneida Castle (N.Y.), 75, 326–28

Oneida Indians, 550–51

Oneida Lake: description of, 75–76, 85–87, 86; narrative of excursion to, 395, 397–401. *See also* Frenchman's Island

Ontario, Lake, 58–59

On the Penitentiary System of Europe and the United States (Lucas), 77n98

On the Penitentiary System of the United States and Its Application in France (GB and AT): American recipients of, 575n22; editor's note on, 441; GB as primary author, xxxvii; Montyon prize for, 503, 569–70; publication of, xix; success of, xxxviii; translation of, xxxvii. *See also* penitentiary-related letters; penitentiary systems; prison study
—excerpts: "Imprisonment, Witnesses" (Appendix 5), 479–80; "Imprisonment for Debt" (Appendix 4),

479; "Philadelphia Penitentiary" (Appendix 7), 481–92; "Public Education" (Appendix 2), 478–79; "Reform," 466–70; "Reform Schools," 470–78; "Temperance Societies" (Appendix 6), 480–81

opinions of others, 563

Oregon Territory: control of Pacific and, 629–32; sovereignty over, 600, 603n18

Orglandes, Camille d', 563–64, **563n1**

Osage Indians, 343, 345, 346

Otis, Harrison Gray, 240, **240n38**

Ottoman Empire, Egypt's dispute with, 581n31

Pacific Ocean: access to, 627; control of, 629–32

Pageot, Estelle (née Sérurier), **203n236**

Palmer, Charles, 9, **9n12**, 15

Panama Canal, 627

Papineau, Louis-Joseph, 227n23, 576–77n23

pardons, 217, 324, 389

Paris (France): American newspaper correspondent in, 612n35; anticlerical mob in, 279n89; cholera in, 154, 155, 156, 160–61, 167, 200; dangers of holding convention in, 336; fashion influenced by, 64–65, 89, 130, 153, 406; as influence on rest of country, 220

paroles, hopes for, 457. *See also* pardons

Parris, Alexander, 129n155

Pascagoula (Miss.), 551

Pascal, Blaise, xxiv

paternal power, 352–53, 543

Patriotes, in Canada, 227n23, 576–77n23

patriotism, 361

Patterson, Daniel Todd, 203, **203n237**

Peel, Robert, 573, **573n17**

penitentiary-related letters, 443–65, 492–501; editor's note on, 441. See also *On the*

Penitentiary System of the United States and Its Application in France (GB and AT); prison study
—Tocqueville and Beaumont joint letters recipients: Périer (Minister of the Interior), 448–65; Riker, 465
—Tocqueville's recipients: GB, 492–93; Langlois, 493–99; Le Peletier d'Aunay, 443–48; Niles, 499; Sumner, 500–501

penitentiary systems: absence of centralized governance of, 79–80; abuse and disorder in, 214; commitment of convict to, 389; comparative approach to, 454–55; danger perceived in, 445–46; direct management vs. outside contractual systems for, 450–51; economics of U.S. vs. French, 137, 446, 454–55; father of U.S., 214; first state prison of, 248n47; French and American compared, generally, 26; French expert on, 77n98; initial impressions of, 443–48; mortality rate (post-1835), 497–98; notebooks on, 329–31; pardons in, 217, 324, 389; politically appointed jobs in, 148, 248; possibility of transfer to France, 215, 444, 453–55, 494; purpose of, 468; reform schools distinguished from, 213–14; social economy influenced by, 463; truths about, 167–68; two types of, xxxvii, 493n19, 494–99. *See also* Auburn system; French prisons; Philadelphia system; prison buildings; prison inmates; prison inmates: labor; prison reform; prison study; reform schools (*maisons de refuge*); *and specific facilities by name*

Penn, William, 145n182, **151–52n194**, 152

Pennsylvania: bicameralism of, 649; constitutions of (1776 and 1790), 218n11; crime statistics in, 466, 469, 479; first state penitentiary of, 248n47; German population of, 152–53, 310; imprisonment for debt in, 479; judicial system of, 368–75, 384, 386, 387–88; political structure and governance of, 218, 241, 268; public education in, 267; religious freedom in, 151–52n194; right to trial by jury in, 387; slavery, gradual emancipation and abolition in, 153n197, 530, 538; state codes of, 170–73; temperance societies of, 481; winter weather in, 169. *See also* Cherry Hill Prison (Eastern State Penitentiary, Philadelphia); Philadelphia (Pa.); Pittsburgh (Pa.); Walnut Street Prison (Philadelphia)

People's Banquet (Cherbourg), AT's improvised toast at, 647–49

Périer, Casimir Pierre, **179n218, 448n3;** AT and GB's letters to, 448–65; force used against rioters by, 179n218

Perry, Oliver Hazard, 295n111, 406

Philadelphia (Pa.): arrival at, 145, 148–49; bankruptcies in, 347; blacks in, 153n197, 338, 532; convention on freedom of trade held in, 334–36; education for black children in, 532; fall weather in, 150; imprisonment for debt in, 479; layout of city, 145n182, 147–48, 166; length of visit, 147, 149; murder and arrests in, 387–88; plans to visit, 123, 447; population of, 145, 147n190, 151; reform school in, 470, 472, 473–74, 476, 478, 510–11; social activities in, 145–47, 154–55; story of eloping couple in, 166–67; theaters of, 558–59; witnesses imprisoned in, 480; women of, 153. *See also* Cherry Hill Prison (East-

ern State Penitentiary, Philadelphia); Walnut Street Prison (Philadelphia)

Philadelphia system: approval of, 495–96; Auburn method compared with, 493n19, 494–99; basics of, 11n16, 455–58; costs of, 458, 463–64, 496; discipline of, 458–60; drawbacks of, 496–97; European debates and support for, 500–501; opposition to, 233n31, 456; possibility of transfer to France, 463; purposes of, 460–63; reservations about, 462; typical inmate in, 457–58. *See also* Cherry Hill Prison (Eastern State Penitentiary, Philadelphia); penitentiary systems; solitary confinement

Phoenix (steamboat), 122

physicians: in prison, 486–87, 490; scarcity of, 87, 414; status of, 257–58

Pierce, Franklin, 603n18

Pierson, George Wilson, xx–xxi, xxii

Pingard (head of secretariat of Institut de France), 620

pioneers: characteristics of, 432–33; costs and provisions of establishing, 97; description of daily life and home, 408–12; encountered on trail to Saginaw, 419–20; greed of, 422–23; land and labor considerations of, 412–15; New England origins of, 560; outpost of (*see* Saginaw [Mich.]). *See also* land and land use; westward movement

Pittsburgh (Pa.), 169, 464

Pittsburgh system, 464

plantations: characteristics of owners of, 178, 187–88, 191–92, 275–76, 358, 362–63, 509; as industrial enterprise, 529–30; revenues of, 342; type of laborers needed for, 532–34. *See also* slaves and slavery

Poinsett, Joel Roberts, **202n235;** on codification of law, 381; GB's opinion of, 202; interviews of, 265, 283–90; on nullification, 265n67

Poland, consecration of flags sent to, 130–31

police force, perceived lack of, 79. *See also* militia; United States Army

political institutions: commercial freedom from, 279; conventions vs. representative, 243; decline of leadership of, 55; delegation vs. representation, 567; energy devoted to, 515; games of, in reform school, 474–75; impossibility of transferring to France, 30–31, 36, 73–74, 127, 234, 239; initial impressions of, 30–31; jury system in, 378; logical relation among, 313; opposition's role in, 595; perfect balance in, 29–30; racial separation in, 541–42; types of instability in, 311–12. *See also* democracy; elections; judicial system; legal system; political parties; public office

political parties: absence of, 16, 133, 548; changes in, 264–65, 608n26; demise of, xxx, 342; GB's *Marie* on, 548; great and minor, 342; opportunity for emergence of, 312. Specific: American (Know-Nothing), 608, 608n26, 609n29; Anti-Masonic, 545–46; Democratic, 133n165, 253, 269–70, 608n26, 609n29; Federalist, xxx, 253, 264–65; Republican (1850s), 608n26, 609n29; Republican (Jeffersonian), xxx, 253, 260–61, 264; Whig, 132n163, 133n165, 608n26. *See also specific political leaders by name*

political patronage: civil servant jobs and dismissals, 271, 575n22; penitentiary jobs, 148, 248

Shakers (Shaking Quakers); Unitarianism

Protestant Reformation, 50–51, 71

Prussia: immigrants to U.S. from, 606; newspaper correspondents in, 596–97; prisons and prison reform in, 500n25, 598n9. *See also* Germany

public education: beliefs in, 49; for black children, 532; blacks excluded from, 511; clergy's role in, 199, 220, 256–57; crime statistics as unrelated to, 467–68; general principles of, 198–99; pros and cons of, 324; public opinion and funding of, 256, 267; racial separation in, 541; state and local funding of, 221; structure of (book excerpt), 478–79. *See also* education

public libraries, 66

public office: lack of interest in, 35–36, 38, 76–77, 280; landed family members elected to, 253, 255; oaths of, 312–13; type of men holding, 212, 250. *See also* elections; political institutions; politics

public opinion: on Andrew Jackson, 235, 260–61; on corporal punishment, 454; influence of press on, 219–20; on liberty, 234; power of, 258; on prison reform, 214–15, 453; senators' vs. legislators' status in, 134; on slavery, 274–75, 277, 530, 531, 533. *See also* associations and associational movement

public prosperity: communication and internal improvements key to, 363–65; democracy and, 186; in slave vs. non-slave states, 181–82, 191–92, 272–73, 274, 358, 531. *See also* banks and banking; commerce; internal improvements; mail delivery

Puritanism, 546, 558, 559, 588

Quakers: abolitionism of, 539; beliefs of, 159n206, 251; characteristics of, 152, 159–60, 516; equality of, 553; GB's *Marie* on, 512; Shakers compared with, 81; theater prohibited by, 559; Walnut Street Prison under, 248, 469. *See also* Shakers (Shaking Quakers)

Quebec Act (1774), 318n148

Quebec and Quebec City area: civil tribunal of, 318–19; description of, 120, 316–17; French cities compared with, 316; GB's sketches of, *121, 122, 123;* plans to visit, 43–44, 58; population of, 316n143; tour of area around, 319–22. *See also* Montreal (Quebec)

questions and questionnaires: for AT's father, 137–38; on Auburn vs. Philadelphia systems, with AT's response, 493n19, 493–99; for Chabrol, 139; on government administration in France, 134–39, 144; on judges, 385; on judicial procedures generally, 386, 389–93; on juries, 385; on justices of the peace, 386; on lawyers and prosecutor's office, 384–85; for Sparks, 134–37

Quiblier, Joseph-Vincent, 118–19, **118n139,** 226–27

Quincy, Josiah, III, 182, **182n224,** 236–37

race and race relations: GB's focus on, xxxiii–xxxv; GB's *Marie* on, 506–10; Gobineau's view of, 613n39; of Indians vs. Negroes, 91; as key question in U.S., 540–42; in New Orleans, 251–52, 279–80, 509–10; separation of races, 509–10, 511, 512, 536, 541–42; superiority question about, 531–32. *See also* American Indians; blacks; mixed-race peoples

Racine, Jean, 317, 517

railroads and railroad development: AT's investments in, xxxviii, 604–5, 606–7, 611, 620–23; east–west expansion of, 628n63; GB's investments in, xxxviii, 621–23; plans for, 62; workers for, 489

Randolph, Ellen Wayles (née Coolidge), 242n40

Randolph, Mary, 161

Randolph, Virginia Jefferson (née Trist), 291n105

rape, Ohio law on, 384

realists, political tendency of, 583–84

recidivism: cost of, 496; evaluating prisons based on, 469–70; failure to punish, 384; in France, 494; inadequate statistics on, 453–54, 469; of prison interviewees, 483, 484, 486, 487; questions about, 446; of reform school inmates, 478

Redier, Antoine, xx

Red Jacket (chief), 325–26, **325n161**

Reeve (judge), 353

Reeve, Henry, **569n9;** "anti-aquatic instincts of," 582; AT's letters to, 569–70, 571–72, 573–74, 576–77, 581–82, 583–84, 611–12; AT's works translated by, xvii, 561, 569n9, 612n33; circle of, 596n8; Milton's *Paradise* and, 584; reference to translation, 578n26, 579; on slave trade, 581n32

reform schools (*maisons de refuge*): applicability to French situation, 443–44; costs of, 473; disciplinary measures of, 473–76; education and work in, 471–72, 473; GB's *Marie* on, 510–11; goals of, 213–14; health concerns in, 473; isolation and classification in, 476; moral and religious instruction in, 50; release from, 476–77; structure of, 470–71; success of, 477–78; visit to, 40 religion: of American Indians, 92; avid discourse on, 100, 109, 157; confusion about, xxxiii, 53, 234, 257–58; democracy and, 242, 246–47; denominational differences tolerated, 33, 50, 51, 88–89, 100–101, 220, 296, 353; human nature and belief in, 245–46; as key to society, 58, 242, 257, 337, 365; Massachusetts requirement concerning, 183; natural, fear of, 89, 157, 244, 245; New York law on, 353; northern vs. southern differences, 279–80, 282, 295–96; Ohio vs. New England differences, 271–72; political influence of, 286, 331, 587–89; prison inmates instructed in, 32–33, 216, 330–31, 452, 482–84, 486, 487, 490, 495–96; reform school inmates inculcated with, 471, 472, 474, 477; respect for, 17–18, 48, 53, 251; in Saginaw area, 434–35; slavery in context of, 530, 614, 655; slave's right to practice, 527–28; as source of order, 516; state's coexistence with, xxxv; state support for, 221–22; in Switzerland, 634, 636. *See also* Catholicism; Channing, William Ellery; Christianity; Protestantism; Quakers; Unitarianism

Report on the Penitentiaries of the United States (Crawford), 492n17

representation: in cantonal governments, 637–39, 642–45; delegation distinguished from, 567; in Protestant context, 51

republic: characteristics needed in, 234; dangers of, 306; fascination with nobility and, 26; individual vs. common good in, 332–33; military influence in, 308; monarchy compared with, 307; Montesquieu on ancient, 38n44;

praise for, 648–49; society underlying, 238–39, 242; toasts to, 42

republican government: beliefs in, 49; causes of, 314; dangers facing, 340, 352; factors in maintaining, 339; French correspondents questioned about, 19, 23; future of, 38, 340; "image of life" in, 307; impossibility of transferring to France, 30–31, 36, 73–74, 127, 234, 239; religion's influence on, 286; state-federal system underlying, 268–69, 347–50; study of, 127–28; universal satisfaction with, 56

Republican Party (1850s), 608n26, 609n29. *See also* elections: divisions in 1856

Republican Party (Jeffersonian), xxx, 253, 260–61, 264

Rhine River, Hudson (North) River compared with, 605–6

Rhode Island, temperance societies of, 481. *See also* Newport (R.I.)

rich, use of term, 63–64. *See also* wealth

Richard (unknown), *Natural and Physical History of Man,* 531

Richard, Gabriel, 88–89, **88n109**, 295–96

Richards, Benjamin W., 248–49, **248n50**

Richelieu (steamboat), 122

rights: aristocratic understanding of, 635–36; political, civil, and natural types of, 521–22, 527–28. Specific: to hold convention, 334–36; presumption of innocence, 527; religious practice, 527–28; to trial by jury, 387, 390, 526. *See also* freedoms; liberty/freedom

Riker, Richard, 386, **386n212,** 465

Rives, William Cabell, 601n15, 626n59

roads and road development: as access for settlers in wild

places, 92, 165, 408, 560; funding and maintenance of, 289; public prosperity linked to, 363–65; rivers as, 436

Rochefoucauld-Liancourt, duc de La, 469

Roman, André Bienvenu, **281n91**

Roman law, 391. *See also* English legal concerns and law

Romanticism: AT influenced by, 395, 398–99, 402–3; AT's and GB's narratives as, xxv–xxvi; in description of pioneers, 408–12

Rossini, Gioachino, 104, 104n25

Royer-Collard, Pierre-Paul, 570, 578, **578n24**

Russell, John, 631, **631n67**

Sagan-Kuisko (Indian guide), 425, 427–30; GB's sketches of, *426*

Saginaw (Mich.), 300n119; daily lives in, 430–34; description of, 96–97, 300–301, 430–31; future envisioned for, 437, 438; hunting in area of, 95, 300–301, 435–36, 437–38; population of, 432; religion in, 434–35; return from, 439–40; trading post of, 89n110, 300, 435; travel to, 89–96, 296–300. *See also* "Two Weeks in the Wilderness" (AT)

Saginaw River: crossing of, 95–96, 299–300, 429–30; hunting along, 435–36

Saint Clair River: hunting along, 302; steamboat travel on, 99–102, 110

Saint-Domingue, revolution in, 254

Sainte-Marie River, 110–11

Saint Joseph Island, 302

Saint Lawrence River: description of, 120, 123; English interests in, 229; GB's sketch of, *122;* lands and villages along, 321–22; steamboat travel on, 120n143, 122, 148

Saint Mary's College (Balti-

sketches (GB) (*continued*)
Eastern State Penitentiary,"
457; "A mill, a cow, and a
bull," *30;* "Mount Pleasant,"
28; "Mrs. Smith's house, near
Sing Sing," *34;* "Newport,"
12, 13; "Peter Schermerhorn's
Greek billiard house," *42;*
"Stockbridge," *335;* "View of
Auburn prison," *449;* "View
of the Hudson at 'Younker,'"
60
—Ohio area and Ohio River:
"Burlington Bar on the
Ohio," *176;* "Ohio," *272, 273;*
"View from Wheeling," *177*
—Old Northwest locations:
"Beaumont, self-portrait on
his horse," *416;* "Fort Howard, Green Bay," *304;* Indian accoutrements, *418;*
"Log House," *431;* "Michilimackinac, Lake Huron," *102,
103;* —, Giant's Arch, *106;*
"Montmorency Falls, two
leagues from Quebec," *121;*
"Monument to Montcalm
and Wolfe," *123;* "Niagara
Falls," *115, 116;* "Saginaw forest . . . with Indian guide,"
426; "South Bay village . . .
from Frenchman's Island,"
399; "Steamboat . . . Buffalo to Detroit," *294;* "View
of Fort at Sault St Marie,"
96, 97; "Steamboat on Lake
Huron at Michilimackinac,"
101; "View of Lake Superior,"
99; "View of the St. Lawrence," *122*
—southern locations: "Aground
in the Mississippi," *198;* "Gulf
of Mexico," *200;* "Memphis,
departure of the Indians," *196;*
"View through cedars," *190*
slaves and slavery: AT's testimony against, 655; as basis
for southern wealth, 537;
characteristics of owners,
178, 187–88, 191–92, 275–
76, 358, 362–63, 509; characteristics of slaves, 529;
Christianity and, 614, 655;

comparison of states with
and without, 181–82, 191–92,
272–73, 274, 288, 358, 530,
532; English treatment of Irish
compared with, xxxvi; future
predicted for, 235, 250, 274–
75, 287–88, 467, 535–36,
539–42, 593, 613; history of,
508, 528–29, 530; inheritance
laws and, 256; Kansas referendum on, 621n53; in Kentucky
and Tennessee, 181, 274–76,
361–63; legislation concerning, 351, 520–28; in Maryland, 163, 254–56; mid-1850s
uprisings over, 608n27; in
New Orleans, 251–52, 279–
80; northern and southern
differences in, 538–42; number in U.S., 535; opposition to,
243–44; peasants and feudalism compared with, 338, 508–
9; in religious context, 530,
614, 655; revolts of, 254, 287–
88; spread of, as crime against
humanity, 615, 616; trade in,
288n100, 581n32, 624. *See also*
abolition of slavery; colonization; plantations
—GB's *Marie* on: abolition
and emancipation, 530–42;
character of slavery, 528–30;
dehumanization, 507; legal
condition of slaves, 520–28;
peasants and feudalism compared with, 508–9
Smith (historian), 353
Smith, B. C., 331, **331n168**
Smith, George Washington,
307, **307n134**
Smith, John Jay, 338, **338n176**
snakes, 89–92, 97, 301, 438
sociability, 551–53
social activities, generally:
amusements in, 65–66; ceremonial dinners, 25–26;
comical predicaments, 36;
dancing, 41–42; fee-for-
subscription ball, 161, 308;
overview of, xxvii; post-
wedding visits, 44–45; social
calls, 15, 18; typical day of,
64–65. *See also* music

social class: absence of theoretical spectators in, 30;
commerce and industry as
creating single, 17, 63–64;
democracy as eliminating,
54–55; differences in U.S.,
248–49; education and, 240;
of Maryland's aristocratic
families, 252–53, 254–56,
263; money as distinguishing, 308, 355, 554–56; terms
of address and, 17; in U.S. vs.
France, 140–41. *See also* inheritance laws; wealth
socialism, 651–52
social sciences, xxi, xxxvi–
xxxvii. *See also* prison study
social state: absence of ambition in, 577–78; of Cana-
dian peasants, 230–31; causes
of, 314; in democracy left to
own devices, 354; equality
in, 212, 354–56; jury trials
eliminated in advanced, 377–
78; national character linked
to, 311; of Ohio, 356–57;
parts vs. whole of, 583–84;
types of, 340–41, 543; U.S. as
single, egalitarian, 405–6. *See
also* civilization; moral character; mores; virtue
society in America: British
travel accounts of, 573n17;
coarseness of, 512–13; common sense in, 513–14; energy
devoted to, 515; equality in,
554–57; GB's *Marie* on, 551–
57; Hall's critique of, 570n12;
imagination in, 165; intrigue
and agitation in, 249–50;
lawyers' position in, 46, 212–
13; middle class in, 353–54,
365–66; order and tranquility in, generally, 570–71;
political education in, 339;
questions about, 29, 134–37;
self-interest as unifier in, 38,
333; separation of men and
women in public gatherings,
130; slave's role in, 523–24;
study of, 138–39; Trollope's
critique of, 552–53; unique
qualities of, 15; vicissitudes

and opportunities of, 610. *See also* American character

solitary confinement: in Auburn system, 444; changing opinion of, 498–99; in Cherry Hill Prison, 455–58, 460–63, 481–92; corporal punishment compared with, 462; drawbacks of, 496–97; key to Philadelphia system, 455–58, 460–63; objections to, 497–98; as only path to reform, 495–96; in Prussian penitentiary system, 598n9

Somme River (France), Hudson River compared with, 62

South, the: abolition of slavery unlikely in, 539–42; agricultural interests of, 270; character of field labor in, 532–34; crime statistics in, 467; dueling in, 336; leisure possible in, 552; northern character compared with, 243–44, 252, 254–55, 265, 282, 287, 310; nullification crisis in, 265n67, 286–87; questions about, 310; slavery-based wealth of, 537; slavery laws in, 521–28, 530; tariff debates in, 66, 132n162, 243n42, 334; westward movement and power of, 287. *See also* abolition of slavery; slaves and slavery; *and specific states by name*

South America: impossibility of republic in, 339; maritime commerce of, 284–85; morals of, 290; Spanish in, 290

South Bay village, GB's sketch of, *399*

South Carolina: nullification crisis in, 265n67, 286–87; population of, 286n96; slavery and number of blacks in, 539, 540; slavery laws in, 521, 522, 524, 527–28, 530; tariff debates in, 132n162, 243n42; temperance societies of, 481. *See also* Charleston (S.C.)

sovereignty. *See* popular sovereignty

Sparks, Jared, **132n164**; AT's and GB's questions for, 134–37; AT's letters to, xxviii, xxxviii, xxxix, 182–84, 574–75, 593, 603–4; Channing's speech at ordination of, 52n63; edition of Washington's letters, 604; interviews of, 235, 241–42, 247; *The Life of Gouverneur Morris,* 557, 574; literary ability of, 557; on New England town, xxix, xxxii; "Observations on the Town Governments of Massachusetts," 134n168; on tariffs, 132; translation of *Democracy* and, 574; on tyranny of the majority, xxviii

Sparks, Mary Crowninshield, 593n1

Spencer, John Canfield, **83n104**; advice of, 227n24; AT's letters to, 578–81, 594; on bicameralism, xxviii, 640n74; cabinet positions of, 594; interview of, 83, 88, 218–21; legal case of, 219; notes and introduction to English translation of *Democracy,* 578n26

stagecoach (and carriage) travel: Albany to Auburn, 74, 82; description of, 82; halt in, due to AT's illness, 177–78; Louisville to Nashville to Memphis, 176–78, 188, 189, 191; sociability of passengers, 551; steamboats compared with, 80

states (U.S.): bicameral systems of, 649–50; constitutions of, 656; dangers posed by emerging Southwest and West, 340, 352; development of, 349; differences among, 198, 270–71; executive power absent in, 281; federal relationship with, 268–69, 347–50; governors of, 76–77, 241, 641; legislative structure and elections in, 133–34, 218, 236–37, 241, 242, 352; power of, 537; rights of, and

nullification crisis, 265n67, 286–87; schools founded by, 199, 324; slave and free, compared, 181–82, 191–92, 272–73, 274, 288, 358, 530, 532; slavery issues and admission to Union, 275, 608n27, 616n44, 621, 623, 624; as sovereign entities, 170–71. *See also* North, the; South, the; *and specific states by name*

steamboat travel: costs of, 353; Detroit to Cleveland, 293–95; —, GB's sketch of, *294;* Detroit to Green Bay, 98–109, 110–12, 148–49, 301–6; Memphis to New Orleans, 178, 193–94; Montreal to Quebec City, 120, 122; near-sinking in, xxvii, 173, 175, 557; Newport to New York, 8–9, 14, 21, 48; Pittsburgh to Cincinnati and west, 169, 175–79, 186, 188–89; pleasures of, 178–79; race and fireworks on, 61–62; self-control of passengers, 175, 557; shipbuilding for, 284; speed of, 58–59; Trollope's view of, 552–53; Yonkers to Albany, 61–62, 68, 80

Stewart, Richard Spring, 257–58, **257n57**

Stockbridge (Mass.): GB's sketch of, *335;* location of, 126n150; visit at, 126, 334

Stöffels, Charles, 3–4, **3n1**

Stöffels, Eugène, **3n1**, 47–49, 148–49

Storer, Bellamy, 266, **266n68**

Story, Joseph, *Commentaries on the Constitution of the United States,* xix, xxx, 625, 626

suffrage: in Canada, 231; in Ohio, 181, 267–68, 269; property qualifications abolished, 221; vagabonds excluded, 54. *See also* elections; universal suffrage

Sulpician Fathers, 258n59

Sumner, Charles, **500n24**; AT's letters to, 500–501, 620–21, 623–24; confidence in

Sumner, Charles (*continued*)
knowledge of, 622–23; on political corruption and slaveholders, 621n53, 624n57

Sundays: laws on, 546–47; mass on, 17; services at prisons, 452; strict observance of, 48, 50, 183, 482; Unitarian services on, 52

Superior (steamboat), 98n117; capacity of, 301n122; Detroit to Green Bay trip on, 98–109, 110–12, 148–49, 301–6; size of, 99

Superior, Lake: explored via canoe, 106–7; forests of, 125; GB's sketch of, *99;* Indian people along shores, 142–43; steamboat travel on, 103–8, 148–49; views of, 111

Swiss Diet, 635n72, 637n73

Switzerland: AT's visit to, 571; effects of democracy in, 645–46; federal and cantonal governments in, 349–50, 632–33, 637, 642–45; future of federalism in, 646–47; Helvetic Republic period of, 632n70; judicial system of, 639–40, 641; newspapers of, 317; New York bicameral system compared with, 640–42; as "pure" democracy, 638–39; revolution and restoration in, 635–37, 644. *See also* "On Cherbuliez's *Democracy in Switzerland*" (AT)

Syracuse (N.Y.), 67, 75–76

Tacitus, *Germania,* 377n206
Taney, Roger, **158n205**
Tanner, John, 550–51
Tariff of 1841, 594n4
Taschereau, Jean-Thomas, 121, **121n146**

taxation and tariffs: Alabama attitudes toward, 282–83; debates on, 66, 132, 243n42, 334–36; enforcement of, 633; inequalities in Switzerland, 636; opposition to, 285, 350–51; perceived lack of, 38; scandal concerning (1857–

58), 624n57; state-federal relationship in, 348; town's right to impose, 237

Taylor, Zachary, 601n15
Tellkampf, Johann, 598n9
temperance societies, 333, 480–81

Tennessee: Houston as governor of, 343, 352; Ohio compared with, 191–92; people and housing of, 360–61; population of, 192n229, 276n83; reflections on, 360–63; reminders of, 607–8; slavery in, 275–76, 361–63; slavery laws in, 521, 524, 526; southern character evidenced in, 265; temperance societies of, 481. *See also* Memphis (Tenn.); Nashville (Tenn.); Sandy Bridge (Tenn.)

Tennessee River, 192, 193, 198
terms of address, 17

Texas: annexation and statehood of, 600, 603n18, 629n65; French policy on, 629n64, 630–31

theater, 66, 146, 317, 558–59
Thiers, Adolphe, 581n31, 596n7
Thomson, Miss, 102, 105
Throop, Enos T., 76, **76n95**

Tocqueville, Alexandrine Ollivier de (AT's sister-in-law), **44n57**, 150; AT's letters to, 44–45, 147–48

Tocqueville, Alexis de (AT): in Académie française, 602n16; age at time of voyage, xvii; analytical tools of, xxiv; blind spots of, xxxii–xxxiii; dispiritedness of, 168; fire in château of (1954), xxi–xxii; GB's friendship with, xvii–xix, xxxiii, xxxvi; GB's letters to, 605–6, 622; GB's sketches of, *60, 426;* Harvard's honorary degree for, 603n19, 603–4; health and illness of, 40, 177–78, 187–88; homesickness of, 29, 56–57, 207; in July Revolution events, 22n30; marriage of, 22n31, 571n13; nearsight-

edness of, 109; political career of, xix–xx, xxxviii, 42, 580, 591, 601 (*see also* Chamber of Deputies); post-1840 interests of, xxxviii–xxxix; prospects at time of voyage, xvii–xviii, 3–4; as *rapporteur* on prison-related commission, 499; retirement of, 603, 610; as social reformer, xxxvi–xxxvii; tutors of, 10n14, 23n32; twenty-sixth birthday, 440n11; virtuous determination of, xxvi–xxvii, 19, 80

—works: editor's note on, 591; "Note on the Powers of the President of the United States," 625–27; "On Bicameralism," 649–50; "On Democracy and Socialism," 651–52; "On Federalism," 632–33; "On Oregon and Control of the Pacific," 629–32; "On Presidential Powers," 651; "On the Alliance of the French and American Republics," 647–49; "On the Mississippi Valley," 627–28; "On Universal Suffrage," 654; "Political and Social Condition of France," 565n5; report on colonization in Algeria, 600–601n13; report on Sedgwick's book, 617, 655–58; "Report . . . on the Abolition of Slavery in French Colonies," 581, 582–83, 593; "Testimony against Slavery," 655. See also *Democracy in America* (AT); letters; notebooks; *Old Regime and the Revolution, The* (AT); "On Cherbuliez's *Democracy in Switzerland*" (AT); *On the Penitentiary System of the United States and Its Application in France* (GB and AT)

Tocqueville, Édouard de (AT's brother), **24n34;** AT's letters to, 24–25, 169–70, 204–5

Tocqueville, Émilie de Belisle de (AT's sister-in-law), **8–**

United States (*continued*)
journey in, *xxiii;* as nation
of joiners, xxix; as nation of
merchants, 16, 17, 20, 24;
navy and coast guard of, 213,
284; newspaper correspon-
dent in, 596–98, 599–600;
recommended French study
of, 652–53; Tocqueville readers in, xx–xxi
United States Army: challenges
of conscription for, 351; disbanded, as source of crime,
468; perceived lack of, 38,
79; self-policing as replacing, 56; shortcomings of,
559–60; size of, 109. *See also*
militia
United States Congress: bicameral system of, 649–50;
conventions juxtaposed to,
334–36; number of law-
yers in, 290; power of Senate and House of Repre-
sentatives, 626; presidential
power in relation to, 241–42,
265; scandals investigated by
(1857–58), 624n57; Sumner
attacked in, 500n24; Swiss
Diet compared with, 633;
visit to, 202–3, 204, 205;
westward movement evi-
denced in, 247
United States Constitution:
Articles of Confederation
compared with, 347–48;
AT's notes on, xxiv, 349; AT's
praise for, 649; limits on
states in, 656–57; Mexican
adoption of, 290; oath of
obedience to, 312; on presidential power, 625, 626; ratification of, 347n187; on right
to assemble (Bill of Rights),
xxx, 334–36; on states' rights,
537; Story's treatise on, xxx,
625, 626; Swiss structure
compared with, 633
United States Supreme Court:
on Georgia law and Chero-
kee lands, 511–12; justice
interviewed, 268–69; questions about, 389–90

universal suffrage: in France,
648n78; poor choices due to,
267–68, 270, 282, 351–52,
359; pros and cons of, 340–
41, 654; questions about,
249, 252, 261, 267–68, 282.
See also elections; suffrage
University of Maryland Medical
School (Baltimore), 257n57
Utah, conflict with Mormons
in, 623n54
Utica (N.Y.), 66–67, 74–75

Van Buren, Martin, 42n54,
62n79, 63n80, 76n95,
366n201
Van Matre, Daniel, 383,
383n209
Van Schaik, John B., 73n91
Vaughn, John, 248, **248n47**
Vaux, Robert, **152n195,** 469;
assistance of, 152; circle of,
173–74; interview of, 249
Vermont, judicial elections in,
268
Viennet, Jean Pons Guillaume,
570
Viger, Denis Benjamin, **321n154**
Viger, Jacques, **321n154**
Viger, Louis Michel, **321n154**
Vigne, Godfrey Thomas,
100n119, 305n133; painting
by, 107; travels of, 99, 113–14
villages. *See* New England: town
system; towns
Villemain, Abel François, 570
Vindicator, The (Montreal newspaper), 322
violence, 281–82, 283. *See also*
crimes and criminals
Virgil, 517
Virginia: arrival in, 200; decline
of, 291; slavery in, 181, 540;
temperance societies of, 481;
voting changes in, 268
virtue: absence of, 314; of Englishwomen, 571; enlightenment juxtaposed to, 349, 354;
morals distinguished from,
286; self-interest compared
with, xxxi
Volney, C. F., 5, **5n5**
Voltaire, 244, 317

voluntary associations. *See* associations and associational
movement
voting rights. *See* suffrage; universal suffrage
*Voyage d'un Allemand au Lac
Onéida* (Campe), 86n106,
398–99
voyage to America: age of AT
and GB, xvii; AT's rationale
for, 3–4; common experi-
ences as reformers in, xxxvi–
xxxvii; details summarized,
xxii, xxiv–xxvii; finances
on, 19, 27; GB's focus on,
xxxiii–xxxvi; length of, xix,
566; map of, *xxiii;* particular
concerns in, xxvii–xxxiii;
plans for return to France,
167, 200, 204, 205, 207; reminders of, 605–6, 607–8;
as series of magic lantern
images, 36–37; social reform
underlying, xxxvi–xxxvii. *See
also* canoe travel; documents
gathered; *Havre, Le* (ship);
horseback riding; stagecoach
(and carriage) travel; steamboat travel
Voyageur (steamboat), 122

Wainwright, Jonathan Mayhew,
330–31, **330n167**
Walker, Timothy, **266n69;** interviews of, 266–67, 269–73
Walnut Street Prison (Philadelphia): blacks in, 338;
Cherry Hill compared with,
482, 484, 485, 486–89; decreased crime and, 469; oversight and operations of, 248;
recidivism rate of, 470
Walsh, Robert, 146, **146n184,**
557
wardens (or agents): of Auburn
and Sing Sing, compared,
449; full power needed by,
215–16, 217, 445; inmate
labor overseen by, 450–51;
interviews allowed by, 461;
of reform schools, 40n46,
213n6, 471, 472, 474, 476,
477

CABRINI COLLEGE

610 KING OF PRUSSIA ROAD

RADNOR, pa 19087-3699

DEMCO